Living Birds of the World

Photographs by

ELIOT PORTER

JOHN MARKHAM

PAUL SCHWARTZ

ERIC J. HOSKING

LOKE WAN THO

HEINZ RUHE & TED ROTH

ALLAN CRUICKSHANK

and others

Living Birds of the World

by E. Thomas Gilliard

Associate Curator of Birds, American Museum of Natural History

A CHANTICLEER PRESS EDITION

DOUBLEDAY & COMPANY, Inc., *Garden City, New York*

PLANNED AND PRODUCED BY CHANTICLEER PRESS, INC., NEW YORK

Library of Congress Catalog Card No. 58–10729

PREFACE

This book presents a general survey of the birds of the world. Extinct forms, fossil and subfossil, are treated briefly in an introductory chapter, but the bulk of the work is devoted to living birds. All orders and families are described, as are many sub-families and many of the more important and interesting species. But no attempt has been made to treat all of the existing species of birds, about 8600 in number, for that would be beyond the scope of any single volume.

The orders and families are presented in a sequence customary in books of this character: the most primitive groups first, the most highly developed last, and the rest fitted in between. The position assigned to each is the result of careful study; but a number of birds remain little known, and their placement in the series must be provisional. In general, the sequence is based on Alexander Wetmore's *A Revised Classification of the Birds of the World* (1951), correlated with Ernst Mayr's and Dean Amadon's *A Classification of Recent Birds* (1951) (from which were taken the species counts) and with subsequent studies by those authorities and by W. J. Beecher, W. B. Stallcup, H. B. Tordoff, Jean Delacour, C. G. Sibley and the author himself. The songbirds have been largely arranged in accordance with Dr. Amadon's revision of 1957.

The reader will appreciate that such a lowest-to-highest arrangement is intended to represent the tree of avian evolution, as nearly as that can be done in a two-dimensional list rather than a three-dimensional figure. But the evolutionary history of birds is especially hard to unravel, because their light, fragile bones do not fossilize readily, and hence there are comparatively few paleontological specimens to build on. Much of our understanding of the evolution of birds is inference from living forms rather than evidence from fossils. But, fortunately, among the fossils are two that seem to belong at the bottom of the avian tree, and these show us that the root stock consisted of birdlike relatives of the dinosaurs—in short, that birds are glorified reptiles.

Written descriptions are confined to essentials, for the splendid color and black-and-white illustrations convey the form and character of the main groups better than any words could do. Both scientific and vernacular names of the species are used, and technical language has been held to a minimum.

For each family, the author has tried to give the chief characters, structure, relationship, characteristic species, courtship and breeding behavior, number of species, range throughout the world and any specially interesting items of information. Thus the treatment varies somewhat from family to family, in accordance with the amount and importance of available material.

It was neither possible nor desirable to list, in footnotes or otherwise, the sources of the many thousands of facts that form the foundation of this work. But the reader will find that the most important of these are mentioned in the text itself, and a bibliography is included in the volume. In an effort to go beyond such sources as often as possible, the author has examined a vast amount of life-history material. He has worked into the text as much fresh information as he could, and to the best of his knowledge no scientific revisions of families and no major discoveries or re-discoveries up to February, 1958, have been overlooked. If he learned anything by this survey, it was the almost incredible lack of popular works on the birds of South America, the "bird continent." This great area, which has the largest number of families and of species of any continent—including many that are highly colorful and interesting—cries out for an illustrated handbook, so that visitors and residents alike can identify the birds and study their habits. For this reason the writer, who has been in South America many times, has paid particular attention to the species of that continent.

Of course a book like this one, although it bears only one signature, is not the work of a single unaided hand. The writer's primary debt is to the people who taught him ornithology, chiefly to Frank M. Chapman, with whom he worked in the field in Central America, to Ernst Mayr, with whom he was associated at the American Museum of Natural History, and to Thérèse Waelchli, who instilled in him a love of nature.

His secondary indebtedness is to the authors of several score standard reference books (most of which are listed in the bibliography) and to the many authors of works mentioned in the text. Those to whom the writer is especially indebted are: Salim Ali, Dean Amadon, Edward A. Armstrong, Emmet Blake, Neville Cayley, Norman Chaffer, James P. Chapin, Frank M. Chapman, Philip J. Darlington, Jean Delacour, Eugene Eisenmann, Herbert Friedmann, G. M. Henry, Charles Kendeigh, Loke Wan Tho, Ernst Mayr, R. Meinertzhagen, Robert Cushman Murphy, Roger Tory Peterson, William H. Phelps, A. L. Rand, D. L. Serventy, Charles Sibley, Alexander Skutch, B. E. Smythies, George M. Sutton, V. G. L. van Someren, Charles Vaurie, Alexander Wetmore, Hugh Whistler and H. M. Whittell.

Paul Schwartz had the great kindness to provide the writer with his unpublished notes on South American birds, as well as many splendid photographs, thus filling an important gap.

Kenneth C. Parkes, Associate Curator of Birds at the Carnegie Museum in Pittsburgh, carefully checked all of the manuscript and added many important facts from his exceptionally wide store of knowledge. His thorough research and constant encouragement have been of inestimable help.

To his editors, Milton Rugoff, Miss Jean Tennant, and J. R. de la Torre Bueno, the writer is particularly grateful for their editorial assistance and willingness to explore seemingly endless sources for the wealth of illustrations brought together here.

Miss Constance D. Sherman typed most of this work from a difficult original draft, doing much preliminary editing. Miss Mary Elizabeth Brock did the same for the first quarter of the book. To both, the writer extends his sincere thanks.

To Melville Grosvenor of the National Geographic Society, who assisted in the obtaining of certain rare pictures for prior publication in this volume—for example, *Steatornis* on its nest—and to Miss Helen Hays, who helped in captioning many photographs, the author is very grateful.

To his wife, Margaret Gilliard, he can only say that without her help at home and in the field this book would not have been written.

E. THOMAS GILLIARD

Spuyten Duyvil, New York
February 20, 1958

CONTENTS

INTRODUCTION

Feathers are known only in birds. Because of them birds cannot be confused with any other creatures in the animal kingdom—a vast assortment of life that has been estimated at over one million species. The feathered creatures called birds are warm-blooded animals. They are the only warm-blooded animals other than a small group of 3500 species of mammals; but the blood of a bird is about ten degrees warmer than that of a mammal. Other characters the birds share more widely. For example, the bony vertebrae (backbone) running through the body occur in the fishes (18,000 species), the reptiles and amphibians (5500 species) and the mammals. But, as there are about 8600 species of birds in the world and there is little likelihood of discovering many more, it is safe to say that there are about as many birds in the world as there are all other backboned animals, excluding only the fishes.

Often man seems unaware of the fact that birds are vital to his survival. Of the multitudinous species of animals known, the vast majority are insects, and the primary agents of insect control throughout the world are birds. In fact, there is agreement among economic biologists that without birds the earth would become virtually uninhabitable to man. Ornithologists know that every surface from the ground to the highest limbs and cliffs is relentlessly scoured by birds for insects, their larvae and their eggs, and that for each feeding niche there are specially equipped small, medium-sized and large birds to prey on small, medium-sized and large insects. They know that when man transfers a bird or an insect to a new environment, these feeding zones are challenged and often a native species of bird is driven to starvation amid feeding niches that it cannot retain. When man destroys large numbers of insect species with mass spraying he is flirting with disaster. The intricate web of nature that holds in check those species harmful to man can be broken by such means; and once it is broken, it is possible—even likely—that native species of noxious insects will break loose with the devastating force of such immigrants as the gypsy moth. The resulting imbalance could mean extinction for many animals and plants and economic disaster for man.

The destruction of even a single species of bird is a loss not only from a practical point of view but also in terms of beauty of form, melody of voice, color, grace of flight—those things that have made birds the most studied and among the most cherished and admired of all animals. Birds seem to have aroused interest in man since his most primitive beginnings. An important reason for this is the extraordinary hardiness and mobility that have permitted them to conquer every portion of the world, including the most remote oceans, the wastes of the Antarctic, the depths of deep caves, the top slopes of the Himalayas, the mud bottom 200 feet below the surface of the sea, and the darkest recesses of the jungle. Their ability to navigate still confounds man, although he himself already finds his way through space and will soon travel to the moon. But even as some men are finally mastering the problems of interplanetary navigation, others are solving the mystery of bird migration; witness the experiments of Dr. Franz Sauer with birds that "migrate" under the synthetic stars of a German planetarium (see shearwaters).

Birds provide a "window" through which both laymen and scientists can learn of their kinship to the rest of the animal kingdom. Birds, like man, are "eye" animals, as against the "nose" animals that prevail in much of the animal kingdom. As such, their patterns of behavior, particularly those involving courtship, dress and motion, are largely of such design as appeal to the eye of man. This appeal is very old. The first known pictures of birds are those by Neolithic men who painted in Spanish caves some 8000 years ago. From the time of Aristotle onward, this interest has helped man decipher some of the basic principles of evolution contributing to his own emergence. Darwin, Wallace and the great scientists of today have used this "window" to peer deeply into the mists of evolutionary change. By studying birds from many parts of the world, they have found ways of discerning some of the most revealing clues to speciation—the ever-changing lines in the stream of life. In birds these changes are very clear, because birds are extremely sensitive to their surroundings and their evolution is thus often relatively accelerated. This may be easily understood from a simple comparison of a feather with a reptile scale. The feathers of some birds reach five feet in length and even twenty feet in some domesticated chickens. Even ordinary feathers consist of thousands of barbs and barbules all hooked together like microscopic zippers, yet they are really only a form of reptilian scales, such as birds still wear on their legs and toes. In fact, it is difficult to distinguish an embryonic feather from a young reptile scale, whereas a hair grows very differently.

The illustrations in this volume may help to open that "window" for the reader. The great majority show birds that were photographed in the wild at their nests. Whenever possible, illustrations that reveal habits and habitat have been favored over those showing the bird alone, and thus they contain a wealth of ecological information. Of course, a number of species have never been adequately photographed in the wild. For many of these, the best available shots of living birds in captivity have been reproduced. And for some families it was not possible to obtain suitable pictures of living birds, because no satisfactory photographs have ever been made of them.

Many of the color and black-and-white photographs brought together in these pages represent countless hours of dedicated work by amateur photographers who use cameras as instruments for the study of birds. Some employ special rigs that make a photograph each time the bird visits the nest, others use spotting strobe lights, and others arrange electric devices so that the birds photograph themselves in flight. The speeds at which photographs can be made have reached the point where even the hummingbird can be "stopped cold." Other advances include the elimination of the need for daylight by the use of strobe lights that are operated by electronic "eyes." Even with these, there are "amateur" photographers who will make as many as fifty exposures of a single species in flight in order to obtain the perfection of form desired. It is this sort of dedication that has enabled the publisher to present what is probably the finest collection of bird reproductions ever brought together in one volume.

Interest in birds has long since spread from a small circle of professionals and dedicated amateurs to a great audience throughout the world. For such a wide audience a popular book on all groups of the birds of the world, incorporating detailed accounts of key species, their range, habits and relationships, has long been needed. Such a book can right the unbalanced picture of bird life that one may get from specialized treatises on families or even on individual species, or on birds of a particular region or niche: it is thus the primary object of this work to give a general, over-all view of each group of birds and its place in the hierarchy of the birds of the world. The last attempt of this sort in English, Knowlton and Ridgway's *Birds of the World,* was admirable, but it was issued nearly half a century ago, and much has been learned since then.

There is information still to be gathered on little-known birds, and the young ornithologist-photographer-explorer can find hundreds of projects that will help shed needed light on such birds. To be most useful, observations of a species should include ecological information, annual and daily cycles, abundance, acoustical abilities, methods of food-getting, the use of tools, nest structure and camouflage, defense of the nest territory, participation of the sexes in building the nest and in incubation, brooding and feeding the young, the presence of social parasites, the duration of pair bonds, the number of mates and the possible reversal of roles in parental care, the patterns of resting and sleeping, nesting singly or in flocks, methods of display, reactions to predators, the return to nesting sites, and so forth.

The importance of the observation of seemingly trivial actions cannot be overemphasized. Behavior is becoming a new and important tool of classification as a result of such observations. In fact, taxonomists are coming to attach more weight to behavior than to many "morphological characters," such as the shape of the bill, legs and feet, which have long served as major keys to classification. They find more and more that the latter change easily, whereas the former, stemming from deep within the nervous system, are more stable and often persist long after the stock has split into deceptively different-looking lines of species. The method of drinking in the pigeons and the sand grouse is a notable example of this phenomenon. Both families of birds drink water by sucking it up in a long draught like a horse, whereas all other birds take it by mouthfuls and then lift the head and let the water run down the throat. The sand grouse were first taken for aberrant grouse, but when their peculiar drinking behavior was noted, they were carefully studied, and it was found that they were aberrant pigeons that had taken to living on the ground and on sand in treeless deserts. Once the importance of behavior as a vital clue to relationships of superficially different birds is understood, it will make clear the significance of our attempt in these pages to cover patterns of behavior in popular form for the first time.

Testimony to the outstanding importance of behavior in classifying birds is the fact that in revising the waterfowl of the World, Jean Delacour and Ernst Mayr recently used as their chief key the instinctive movements made during courtship displays. Similarly, in recent reclassification of the bowerbirds, other students have used the design of the birds' courtship houses as an index to their relationships. Nothing could be more revealing of underlying relationships than finding that differently dressed birds living hundreds of miles apart build complicated dance pavilions that are architecturally similar and are used for similar dances. The approach through behavior is of course not restricted to birds; thus, for example, Alfred E. Emerson has found the nest built by termites a morphological expression of relationship.

Such are some of the clues to behavior, of great importance to the science of ornithology, that can be gathered by the dedicated amateur. Anyone who doubts that this discipline is heavily dependent upon behavior for a true knowledge of relationships should consider the modern definition of a species of bird (or of any animal) as a group of freely interbreeding populations that are *"reproductively isolated"* from all other such groups. Thus the very definition of a species calls for observation of behavior: it asks whether one group of animals can mate with another and produce fertile, viable offspring. To reach reasonably accurate answers to this vital question, the systematist usually does not attempt to breed wild birds but does the next-best thing—which is to inspect the total picture as represented by the behavior of the species in question. If two species look alike but one builds a domed nest and lays white eggs and the other builds a cup-shaped nest and lays green eggs, he is justified in considering that they are reproductively isolated and hence are different species. The same holds if one group incubates its eggs for 15 days and the other for 11. Moreover, it should be noted that in the definition cited above no reference is made to the shape and the structure of the bird, for it is known that through the phenomenon of convergent evolution very different species can become so deceptively similar in pattern and shape that they can hardly be told apart.

In addition to discoveries of such scientific significance, the observations of the watcher can uncover remarkable and sometimes almost incredible characteristics of birds. Among the many reported in this book are: The discovery of a bird that uses sonar to fly in the total darkness of South American caves (see *Steatornis*); the owl that attacks living prey in absolute darkness (see barn owls); the rediscovery of a petrel long thought to be extinct (see Cahow); the rediscovery of a famous New Zealand "fossil" (see *Notornis*); the bird that weighed a thousand pounds and laid a two-gallon egg (see Madagascar Elephant bird); the coot that carries half a ton of rocks to build an island on which to lay its eggs; the extraordinary fasting of penguins; the terns that have breeding seasons not related to the calendar; the skimmer that marks the water with a "chalk" line of glowing animal life to lure its prey; the frog-

mouth that mimics a colorful flower and then feeds on the insects that come to it; the fresh evidence concerning hibernation among birds; the bizarre social parasitism of cuckoos, cowbirds, and others; the associations between birds and other animals and the one bird that consistently hunts in partnership with African tribesmen (see honey-guides); the records of tool-using among birds; the storing of food and the dispersal of new generations. There are, in addition, the records of birds that live in groups with migratory locusts; there is the little bird that, like the locust, can bring famine and is being fought with flame throwers, poison gas and fire (see weaver birds); there is the phenomenon of the millions of birds that sometimes "explode" over the countryside, appearing out of nowhere (see bramblings); and there is the evidence that some birds can smell (see both kiwis and the New World vultures). Beyond these there are accounts of such unique phenomena as the communal habits of some birds (see anis), the function of "cock nests" and bowers, the colonization of new lands by windblown stragglers (see Cattle Heron), the shedding of feathers as an escape mechanism (see trogons and pigeons), the use of the heat of the sun in nesting (see megapodes), the technique of impaling prey (see the shrikes), mass fainting as a defense (see stilts), the transfer of courtship signals from colorful feathers to colorful objects and the construction of bachelor houses in which the male displays to the female (see bowerbirds), and, finally, the "painting" of the plumage with a pink pigment during the nuptial season (see tropic-birds).

These are a few of the many facts that bird-watchers have discovered for science and that it is the writer's great pleasure to report in this book.

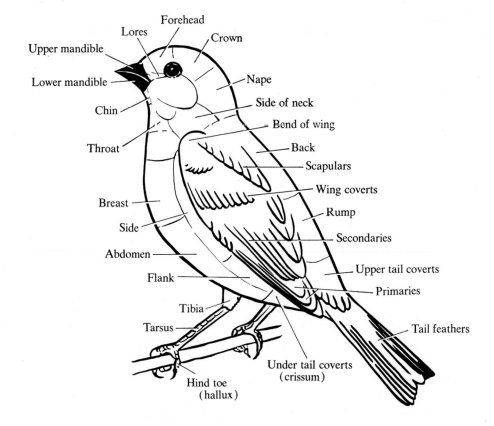

FOSSIL BIRDS

Although birds are widely known vertebrates, their evolutionary history is extremely hard to unravel because they disperse rapidly over barriers that block other land vertebrates and sometimes, after evolving into new species, reverse the direction of their dispersal. This tendency has largely obscured the origin of many bird families, and, together with fragile bones that tend to disintegrate quickly and leave few traces, has made their evolution difficult to chart. With regard to such fossils as have been found, Philip J. Darlington, in his recent *Zoogeography,* suggests there is little to be learned from them because they may reflect the geographical distribution of paleontologists much more than that of primitive birds.

This is particularly exasperating because we know that hundreds of thousands of species—perhaps a million—have come and gone. Our estimate of the abundance of fossil species is reinforced by finds showing that while most of the birds that lived only several million years ago are already extinct, 150 million years ago, there were birds flying about in what is now Germany. These, Archaeopteryx and Archaeornis, constitute the greatest fossil discoveries of birds ever made. They indicate a history of bird life with perhaps 50 or more different horizons, each horizon falling away into extinction as a new one appeared, bringing a new "generation" of species. And they thus provide a good picture of the bird life that has come and gone between the time of Archaeopteryx and that of the sparrow.

A great many of these numerous extinct species of birds have disappeared without a trace—without descendants. But some have contributed to stems of bird life that are still with us today and form the twigs and buds of the avian tree, i.e. the species described in this book. Of all extinct species only 786 are known to science, according to the list made in 1951 by Alexander Wetmore, authority on fossil birds.

Next to the German finds, the most interesting fossils are the primitive divers (Hesperornis) of Cretaceous times (60 to 125 million years ago). These birds had teeth like those of the reptiles, and it was only late in this epoch that species without teeth began to appear. As far as is known, birds of the Eocene epoch (40 to 50 million years ago) were all toothless; and some belonged to gradually forming lines of descent that are clearly recognizable today. Some authorities believe that many families of existing birds had their beginnings as far back as the opening of the Tertiary epoch (about 60 million years ago), but others believe the majority of living birds arose as genera or species in the Miocene epoch, which began some 30 million years ago, or in the Pliocene, about 15 million years later.

With regard to the geographical origin of birds, the fossil record is thickly clouded, but one thing is known—that there has been more movement of bird species from the Old World to the New than the other way around. This is much the same situation that George Gaylord Simpson noted in mammals and that Dr. Darlington found in cold-blooded vertebrates. It is therefore likely that birds developed from Old World reptiles some 200 million years ago, but we cannot say where. We know only that two creatures resembling reptiles but dressed in feathers once lived in what is now Solenhofen, Bavaria. These two represent the most eloquent testimony that birds are, so to speak, glorified reptiles. They are known from two skeletons and a feather impression discovered in the 1870's in a quarry among slates laid down as boggy sands during the upper Jurassic period of about 150 million years ago. Bavaria at that distant time was a land of swamps overgrown with ancient palms and teeming with animal life, and in some fashion these lizard-tailed birds met their death in a bog and were preserved.

These Jurassic birds had the forelimbs and tail modified for flight. Engraved in their tomb are impressions of feathers that are virtually indistinguishable from those of living birds (see cast of fossil). The flight feathers of Archaeopteryx were attached to the arm and hand, but the latter was equipped with distinct, long fingers and tipped with claws. In modern birds the fingers are fused. The feathers of the tail of Archaeopteryx were attached in pairs (two to a vertebra) to a lizard-like appendage consisting of 23 separate vertebrae, an arrangement that is completely different from anything known in living birds. Its legs, which began in falcon-like feather "pants," were already much like those of modern birds and were equipped with four toes, one of which was turned backward. Excluding the tail, Archaeopteryx looked something like a large pigeon—in other words, an arboreal land bird. But in its mouth were conical teeth, each set in an individual socket, and in its skull were large eyes like those of a reptile. It had an open pelvis, which was similar to that of the small, jumping dinosaurs and completely different from that of all other known birds. Thus it was a reptile-like bird or a birdlike reptile, and the consensus is that it was the former. Whether Archaeopteryx was warm-blooded or not we can only guess. Biologists have long thought that other flying reptiles, such as the Pterodactyls, may have been warm-blooded, and it has often been noted that certain of the so-called cold-blooded reptiles of today maintain temperatures that are higher than that of their surroundings.

Hesperornis lived in the inland sea covering part of the state of Kansas some 85 million years ago. It was a flightless, loonlike bird that could probably dive and swim faster than any of our present-day birds and most fishes. This remarkable creature had sharp teeth set in deep continuous grooves, a small, reptile-like brain case, rudimentary wings, and powerful legs and feet set far to the back and side of the body. Its tail was beaver-like in that it could be moved up and down as an aid to swimming. Another curious adaptation was the long, slender jaw that was united in front with a flexible cartilage, rather like that of present-day snakes, and that must have permitted Hesperornis to swallow large prey. This "western bird" was a resident of Cretaceous seas and was fitted for aquatic life more completely than any other bird, living or fossil. So modified for swimming were its legs that Hesperornis probably could not walk on land. *Hesperornis regalis,* one of the eight known species, had a length of nearly six feet, and if it could stand would have been fully three feet tall, or larger than our largest pelican. Hesperornis spent its entire life in water except for brief periods ashore for breeding.

Contrasting with this flightless diver was another sea bird that lived during Cretaceous times in the same general areas of North America. This strong-winged, gull-sized bird, today known as the "fish-bird," *Ichthyornis,* had a keeled sternum and was first reported to have teeth, but it is now believed that the jaw found near the bird's skeleton was that of a reptile—a mosasaur.

From the Eocene onward bird fossils are less scarce, but some are quite extraordinary. In the North America and Europe of 50 million years ago there were many long-legged, wading birds resembling cranes and shorebirds, and, perhaps 40 million years ago, in North America some of these developed into huge, flightless creatures with heads and thick necks shaped something like that of a horse seven feet tall. If a modern bird-watcher could be thrust back to a Eocene lake edge, he would see ducklike birds, heron-like birds, grouselike birds, rail-like birds as well as owl-like birds. All would be recognizable as to types, but none would represent species alive in the twentieth century. Some would be hawklike, and some of these would be rather like the Secretary Bird, only much more so! Such great terrestrial "eagles" as Phororhacos and Andrewsornis were fabulous creatures of an era when birds were probably among the largest flesh-eaters.

Coming down to only a couple of million years ago, we find relatively numerous bird fossils. These have turned up chiefly in tar pits like that at La Brea in California. In such areas animals coming to drink water became trapped in soft tar, were entombed and thus preserved for science, along with the predators—the saber-toothed tigers and even the vultures. Other recent remains are from old lake sites in Oregon and Florida, from a number of places in Europe, and from bogs in New Zealand and Madagascar. Most are of non-passerine birds, but about forty Pleistocene fossils are thought to be of perching birds.

The egg of one species, the colossal Madagascar Elephant bird (*Aepyornis maximus*), is the largest single cell known. It had a volume six times that of an ostrich egg or more than that of twelve dozen chicken eggs, and it weighed about eighteen pounds. Madagascar natives used these eggs as two-gallon containers, and, according to Leonhard Stejneger, science first learned of their existence on Mauritius Island, to which Madagascar seafarers had carried them in order to fill them with rum. Discovery in 1851 of this egg fired anew the speculation based on the wondrous tales told by Marco Polo of a giant Madagascar bird. Its plumes, he had reported, had long since been carried to the Great Khan of the Tartars, and the Arabians had told him it could fly off with an elephant. They called it the Roc. E. Geoffroy Saint-Hilaire's name for the bird, *Aepyornis maximus* (mountain-sized bird), reflected his amazement, and for a time members of the French Academy of Science believed they had found the bird the great Venetian traveler had reported. We now know that the Roc actually was flightless and that it weighed about 1000 pounds—far more than any other bird, living or fossil.

Aepyornis was a massive ratite—a relative of the ostriches—with huge legs. It reached a height of about nine feet, almost that of the largest moa. Its remains have been found in considerable numbers, and its eggs, amazingly enough, are still being discovered in Madagascar swamps, where the natives hunt them by probing the muck with slender rods. Some of the eggs are so well preserved that they appear to belong to living rather than to extinct birds. Many other species of elephant birds have been found. Some are about the size of an ostrich, and some are as small as a large heron or bustard. In all, the hindquarters are disproportionately large and have greatly thickened leg and thigh bones.

The excellent state of preservation of some of the eggs and skeletal remains, and the tales of giant birds in Arabian fables, suggest most forcefully that elephant birds lived on Madagascar until historic times and that the last of them met their death at the hands of primitive man, as is almost certainly the case with the last of the moas.

Gigantism is a common result of the chains of evolutionary events that affect animals on remote, underpopulated islands, particularly those lacking a normal complement of predaceous mammals. It is a

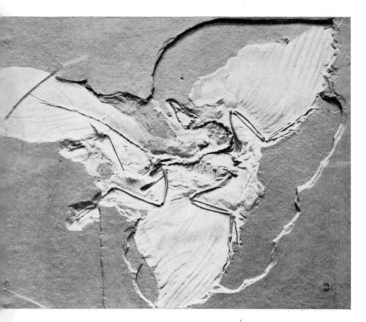

Restoration (right), from skeleton impression (left) of *Archaeornis*, made for American Museum of Natural History exhibit under the direction of Dr. Ernst Mayr and Dr. William King Gregory.

condition leading to helplessness in the face of change. The Dodo, the moas, and the elephant birds are examples of this paralyzing evolutionary phenomenon.

The story of the moas (family Dinornithidae) is one of the most interesting among fossil birds. Lost in remote seas, New Zealand was never reached by mammalian predators, and birds descended from tree tops to browse like giraffes, feed like sheep, and burrow into the ground like woodchucks, filling the roles of the absent mammals. Until the coming of man on these islands, the weirdest of birds, the four-toed moas, lived in a kind of sanctuary.

All of the known moas were large, and some were huge. The largest species, *Dinornis maximus,* with a wide breastbone, relatively slender legs and a broad skull, was about 13 feet and almost 500 pounds. The smallest, *Anomalopteryx parva,* was about the size of a turkey. Legends of modern Maoris suggest that their forefathers hunted these birds, but some experts believe that these tribal stories stem from bone implements and egg-shell water bottles made by ancient men from the subfossil remains of long-dead birds.

The mystery of the disappearance of the 20 species is heightened by the fact that moas were numerous until several thousand years ago, and that they had probably occupied New Zealand for millions of years. Great beds of moa remains have recently been discovered in boglike traps bordering the edges of ancient lakes of Pyramid Valley, South Island. There Robert Falla, Robert Cushman Murphy and others have excavated a number of complete skeletons—some 140 in all—representing most of the known genera and species.

By using a system of dating involving the fluctuations of plant pollen at known periods of the earth's history, it was established that these skeletons represented birds that died, in a kind of quicksand, some time after 600 B.C. Later, using the famous radiocarbon dating technique—based on the rate of decay of radioactive carbon—it was found that the maximum age of the bog in which the Pyramid Valley moas died was 3700 years. More interesting still, Edward S. Deevey, Jr. found, by means of radiocarbon tests, that food remains from the stomach of one of the large trapped moas was only about 670 years old. These discoveries suggest that moas survived until very recently and that primitive man played a part in their extinction (apparently borne out by recent press reports of a pre-Maori village site excavated on North Island). In this light, Maori reports pertaining to the life history of the moas, as obtained by early naturalists, should be considered carefully. The Maoris said that moas were large, sluggish, and dangerous birds that traveled in pairs and made a nest of grass and leaves.

Muscles, ligaments, bits of skin, feathers and parts of greenish eggshells, as well as skeletons of the birds, have been found—some suspiciously close to the cooking places of early man. A number of the feathers were black with reddish brown bases and white tips; others were blackish brown or yellowish. Some clearly showed an aftershaft.

A number of species of birds known from very recently extinct species represent families that still survive. Such species must not be considered sub-fossils. In a slightly different category is a family of extinct terrestrial pigeons, some of which man actually took to Europe as living curios before they became extinct. As such, one might argue that, like the Passenger Pigeon and the Great Auk that were killed off by man, these extinct pigeons are not subfossils but merely extinct birds. However, these too were flightless giants and, as in the moas and elephant birds, it is probable that man merely nudged doomed birds over the threshold of extinction. These birds, the dodos and the Solitaire (family Raphidae) were ponderous, clumsy and flightless. The most famous species, the Dodo, disappeared several centuries ago. The common use of its name as a synonym for blundering stupidity apparently does no injustice to these huge, poodle-tailed birds with their fat, wobbling gait, disproportionately large heads, and huge, hooked bills—or, at least so reported the early seafarers, the men who saw them alive on the Mascarene Islands of the Indian Ocean.

The dodos were pigeons that reached the Mascarene Islands as flying birds and then, like the moas, lost their powers of flight on the predator-free islands. There were three species, the most famous being the Dodo (*Raphus cucullatus*) of the Island of Mauritius, which was discovered by Portuguese sailors in 1507 and became extinct by about 1681. Another was the Reunion Dodo (*R. borbonicus*), which became extinct at an unknown date on Reunion Island, some 100 miles from the home of the true dodo. The third species was the Solitaire (*Pezophaps solitaria*) of nearby Rodriguez Island, which was harassed to extinction about the year 1730. The Dodo, which weighed between 40 and 50 pounds, was abundant when first discovered in the forest of Mauritius. Mariners easily captured the defenseless, flightless birds, and several were shown alive in Europe during the early part of the seventeenth century. Today some skeletal remains in various museums and a head and a foot in the Oxford University Museum are all that remain to show that the Dodo ever lived.

Less famous is the Solitaire, which was taller but more slender than the Dodo. This species had a ball-like growth of bone on the bend of the wing, which probably was used to club animals that menaced it.

The Dodo is said to have laid a single egg on a mat of leaves in deep forest. Incubation was apparently shared by both sexes. The Solitaire fluttered its rudimentary wings when it called, and it engaged in a whirling courtship dance which it advertised by means of loud wing-rattling. These things we learn from the quaint diaries of such travelers as Brontius, who wrote: "The Dronte or Dodaers is for bigness and mean size between an ostrich and a turkey . . . [but] it was like a pygmy among them if you regard the shortness of its legs. It hath a great ill-favored head, covered with a kind of membrane resembling a hood; great black eyes; a bending prominent fat neck, an extraordinary long, strong, bluish-white bill, only the ends of each mandible are of a different color, that of the upper black, that of the nether yellowish, both sharp pointed and crooked. Its gape, huge wide, as being naturally very voracious. Its body is fat and round, covered with soft grey feathers after the manner of the ostrich; in each side, instead of hard wing feathers or quills, it is furnished with small soft-feathered wings of yellowish-ash colour. It hath yellow legs, thick, but very short; four toes on each foot; solid, long, as it were scaly, armed with strong black claws. It is a slow paced and stupid bird, and which easily becomes a prey to the fowlers. The flesh, especially of the breast, is fat, esculent, and so copious that three or four dodoes will sometimes suffice to fill one hundred seamen's bellies."

Those interested in reading of other strange creatures that once lived on the Mascarene Islands are referred to *The Dodo and Kindred Birds* by the famous Japanese ornithologist, the Marquess Hachisuka. Some of them, such as a parrot that is now extinct, and a water hen (*Leguatia gigantea*) that stood six feet tall, may well convince the reader that many birds in the Dodo's world were just as fantastic as the Dodo itself.

Living Birds of the World

SPHENISCIFORMES

Penguins (*Spheniscidae*)

The dumpy, tuxedo-clad penguin with its clownishly human demeanor has charmed us and become very familiar in spite of the fact that its home in southern seas and along the coasts of the bleak Antarctic Continent is so remote.

Penguins come by their name through a mistake, for "penguin" was first applied to the largest of the auks, the recently exterminated Great Auk, which belonged to a very different family but bore superficial resemblances to it that confused early mariners. With the passing of the Great Auk of northern seas the name was transferred to the 16 species of penguins comprising the primitive Sphenisciformes.

All penguins are flightless. They are robust birds of medium and large size—a New Zealand fossil penguin stood about six feet high and must have weighed nearly 200 pounds. The neck is short, the bill strong and often deeply grooved. The tail is short, the feet are webbed and flat, and the legs are short and set far back on the body so that on land the bird must assume a nearly erect stance. Although penguins are undoubtedly descendants of flying birds, their wings are very short, flipper-like and devoid of quills except in the embryo. The component bones are strongly fused. The body is covered with scale-like barbless feathers peculiar to the family, not set in patches as in other birds but distributed over the entire surface.

Penguins are the most completely aquatic of living birds—even their eyes are adapted for underwater vision—and the most proficient of avian swimmers. Power for propulsion is derived from a kind of underwater flight, the feet playing no part in swimming. Observers have reported that penguins seem to enjoy the wildest surf and are strong enough to outride raging seas. When the going is particularly rough they submerge to take advantage of calmer water, but they must, of course, come up frequently to breathe. The larger species achieve considerable speed underwater and have developed the habit of plunging in and out of the waves like porpoises. At times great shoals of penguins remain at sea for months, coming ashore only to breed. In landing, a number of species catapult themselves in salmon style from the water, sometimes leaping to the tops of otherwise inaccessible rocks and shelf ice.

Some idea of the confusion in their rookeries is gained from an observer's account of his stroll through a Rock-hopper Penguin colony: "The nests are placed so thickly that you cannot help treading on eggs and young birds at almost every step. A parent bird sits on each nest, with its sharp beak erect and open, ready to bite, yelling savagely, *caa caa, urr urr,* its red eye gleaming and its plumage at half cock, and quivering with rage. No sooner are your legs within reach than they are furiously bitten, often by two or three birds at once. . . . At first you try to avoid the nests, but soon find that impossible; then maddened . . . by the pain, stench and noise, you . . . resort to the expedient of stampeding."

Despite the very effective mobbing actions of penguins, they appear to be unable to hold their own in areas inhabited by man and his lethal accompaniment of predaceous animals, or to breed inland on any of the larger land areas except the Antarctic Continent. They abound around the edges of Antarctica and sometimes breed hundreds of miles inland, performing prodigious marches to and from the sea, their only source of food fish and mollusks. Their ability to fast—there are records of penguins going without food for nearly four months—makes it possible for them to occupy icy wastes far beyond the reach of other nonflying vertebrates. Elsewhere penguins follow cold water such as the Humboldt Current, which flows northward along the western coast of South America to equatorial latitudes, and the

Adelie Penguin (*Pygoscelis adeliae*)

Benguella Current, off the West African shores. One species is purely tropical (see Galapagos Penguin, page 20). The family is best represented on islands in the Southern Seas such as those of the southern part of South America, the Falkland Islands, those off the coast of New Zealand and Australia, those in the southern part of the Indian Ocean and others off the southern part of Africa. Although penguins are virtually symbols of Antarctica, only two species actually inhabit that continent.

One of the most amusing habits of penguins is their tobogganing on snow banks. Large species habitually fall on their stomachs and slide downhill, using the wings to paddle in the snow. When hotly pursued this is their method of escape. Hunters have reported that even on flat ground among grass tussocks it is extremely difficult to capture a penguin because it "bellywhops" about with great speed, using the wings almost like forelegs and sliding powerfully forward with piston-like thrusts of the strong legs.

Penguin courtship rites are diverse and complicated. Some of their activities would seem to rank them close to the intellectual giants of the bird world, the crows and the parrots. Indeed, it may be that the aquatic niche occupied by penguins demands special abilities for survival such as are found in higher animals—for example, the seals—that have succeeded in penetrating the sea. Among these peculiarly advanced habits in certain species are the social organization and the long, sometimes lifelong, bond between pairs. A great deal has been learned of these habits in recent years, and especially from Dr. L. E. Richdale's studies of the Yellow-eyed Penguin (*Megadyptes antipodes*) of southern New Zealand. His observations are based on 973 visits over a period of ten years to breeding grounds where he watched 88 males and 96 females which he had both banded and "foot-marked." Among other things he found that 50 per cent of the young disappeared during the first year, that one pair remained together for 11 years, that 82 per cent of returning migrants remated, and that there was an average "divorce" rate of 18 per cent. The species he studied nested in holes under rocks and in the ground, and families kept together.

Other species such as the Emperor and the King are surface-nesters and are apt to be more social in their activities. For example, Dr. Robert Cushman Murphy observed that many of them engage in communal care of the young and the adult nurses often feed any offspring that pleads strongly enough. Another investigator, Mr. B. Stonehouse, recently found that almost immediately after the egg of an Emperor Penguin is laid the male takes full charge and the female goes off to sea for two months. The incubating male then huddles in a cluster with others and fasts for about two months. Shortly after hatching time the female returns, but it no longer remembers its long-suffering mate, and solicits various males for chicks. The chicks are first fed with a special crop secretion produced by the male, although it

has not taken food for many weeks. Dr. W. J. L. Sladen reports (see below) that the fasting period of the Emperor is about twice that of the Adelie, although its weight is seven times as great. He further notes that these two species fast longest among birds, with the Emperor holding the record.

Perhaps one of the most remarkable aspects of the breeding of the Emperor Penguin is the fact that pair formation takes place during the blackness of the Antarctic night. The French ornithologist, J. Prevost, has shown that the male and female recognize each other by differences in voice. The egg is laid before the arrival of Antarctic daylight and the young mature sufficiently to care for themselves before it is over.

When the down-covered young are able to hobble about they join a crèche or kindergarten and huddle together, sometimes by the hundreds. A few adults seem to have the task of looking after the crèche and providing a windbreak by standing close together, but sometimes thin sheets of snow cover the young as they snuggle together. The chicks sleep standing up with the bill tucked under a flipper, the long "heels" flat on the ground but the toes and feet often elevated.

Important information on the Adelie Penguin (*Pygoscelis adeliae;* Plate 5) has come from Dr. William J. L. Sladen, British Medical Officer and Antarctic explorer, who while at Hope Bay, Antarctica, lived beside a colony of 100,000 birds. At times deep snow completely covered the colony, and in one area during his 1948–1949 expedition more than 80 per cent of the eggs were lost in bad weather.

During his 1950–1951 expedition Sladen marked some 1300 Adelies with paint and another 338 with aluminum wing bands. One result of this was the discovery that, in this species at least, the adults find and feed their own young in the crèches. Earlier observers had believed that the adults fed any young bird that dunned them sufficiently, as do the Emperor and King Penguins. Sladen believes the adults recognized their young by their facial characteristics.

When spring comes, the Adelie, which stands about 1½ feet tall, marches slowly over the broken ice to its ancestral nesting areas. At times it falls on its chest and toboggans along. The route changes with every storm, yet it finds its way to the very same nest, and often pairs again with its former mate. Upon arrival, the male establishes a small territory and builds or rebuilds a nest some six inches high, using small stones; this serves to protect the eggs from the water of melting ice.

About a month after the arrival of the Adelies the first eggs appear, usually with two in a set. The male does most of the incubating because, soon after laying, the female leaves the nest and marches to the sea to break her long fast. By the time of her return after about 17 days, the male has fasted for about six weeks and lost almost half of his weight. He then departs for the sea, leaving eggs that are about to hatch or chicks just hatched. The latter are fed with

Adelie Penguin (*Pygoscelis adeliae*) at stone nest

of the Humboldt Current. This grayish bird, which has the throat and chin white with narrow white bands emarginating the crown and neck, is the only penguin that lives entirely in the tropics.

The largest and most southerly of penguins, the Emperor (*Aptenodytes forsteri*), reaches four feet in length and 75 pounds in weight. Above, it is bluish gray with much black on the head and throat; below, it is white. Distinctive sulphur-orange areas occur on the upper neck. Somewhat smaller but rather similarly dressed is the King Penguin (*A. patagonica*), which breeds at the southern tip of South America and on various islands such as South Georgia and Kerguelen, and wanders north to the shores of New Zealand and Tasmania. Like the Emperor, the King runs nimbly and never hops. In incubation the egg is

Emperor Penguin (*Aptenodytes forsteri*)

semidigested, regurgitated food. Incubation requires about 35 days. The male, when he returns, helps to feed and guard the young, and parental care continues for about 5½ weeks. After this the young gather in crèches of 100 to 200.

Among the predators are the Sheath-bill (*Chionia alba*), which breaks open unguarded eggs and devours them on the spot, and the Antarctic Skua (*Catharacta skua*), which carries the egg off or drags weak nestlings from the crèches. Others are the Leopard Seal (*Hydrurga leptonyx*) and the Elephant Seal (*Mirounga leonina*), the latter causing damage by crawling and rolling on the eggs and chicks.

The Rock-hopper Penguin (*Eudyptes crestatus*) is one of the smaller members of the group, reaching two feet in length and inhabiting islands of the southern oceans, occasionally north to Argentina, South Africa, New Zealand and Australia. This species is bluish above and white below, with distinctive, stringy, pale yellow plumes springing from the forehead and eyes in a disheveled mass. The Galapagos Penguin (*Spheniscus mendiculus*), a 20-inch bird, inhabits equatorial waters at the northern terminus

held in a pocket-like, feather-lined fold of the lower abdomen close to the tops of the feet. No nest is built, and in transferring the single large egg the parents juggle it from one to the other so that it does not touch the ice.

The Macaroni Penguin (*Eudyptes chrysolophus*) of the southern Atlantic and Indian Oceans owes its name to its peculiar head feathers. A relative in the Pacific is the Snares Crested Penguin (*E. robustus;* Plate 4) which breeds in large numbers on the Snares Islands south of New Zealand.

The Jackass Penguin (*Spheniscus demersus*), so called because of its donkey-like bray, inhabits the southern coast of Africa, sometimes reaching equatorial waters near Angola and Natal. It produces commercially significant quantities of guano on its breeding islands. It is a black-and-white species that reaches some 30 inches in length. The Little Blue Penguin (*Eudyptula minor*) is hardly larger than a duck. It is the only species that occurs commonly in Australian waters. It is a bluish gray above and largely grayish white below.

STRUTHIONIFORMES

Ostriches (*Struthionidae*)

The African Ostrich (*Struthio camelus*) is peculiar in that it has only two toes, whereas all other birds, including even the other ratites, have three or four. Ostriches formerly occurred over much of Asia and until recently lived in Arabia and Syria. Today they are found only in the sandy grasslands of Africa, where they compete successfully with a wide variety of animal life. Their alertness, keenness of vision and fleetness of foot enable them to hold their own in a country filled with predators.

Ostriches avoid forests, keeping to open regions where they can observe the distant landscape. Often they travel in company with large mammals such as wildebeests and zebras in a kind of mutually beneficial association. The four-footed animals probably flush food for the ostrich, which, though virtually omnivorous and deriving much of its nourishment from fruit, seeds and plants, also feeds on small mammals, reptiles and insects. In turn, the mammals depend on the seven-foot stretch of the ostrich and on its keen vision to alert them to danger.

A large male ostrich stands nearly five feet high at the back and may weigh over 300 pounds; the female is considerably smaller. It can run at speeds of about 40 miles per hour, with strides sometimes 15 feet long, and men on horseback would rarely get a shot at it if it did not have the habit of running in great circles. There is no truth in the tale that the ostrich hides its head in sand in time of danger.

The African Ostrich has a long, virtually naked

AL BLOOM: MONKMEYER

African Ostrich, male (*Struthio camelus*)

neck and a relatively tiny head that is flattish and equipped with a broad, shallow bill. Its most prominent features are powerful, nearly naked thighs and strong, long legs tipped with short, nailed toes that seem on their way to becoming hoofs. Of the two toes—osteologically speaking, the third and fourth—the third is much longer—about seven inches in length.

Male ostriches have the body plumage black and the short plumes of the wing and tail pure white. Females are generally grayish. In this connection it is interesting to note that, unlike the other ratites, the female participates in incubation, but only by day and only during cold spells. Otherwise, by day the eggs are left alone under a partial covering of sand. The male does all of the nocturnal incubation. The presence of cryptic coloration in only one sex, the female, is probably correlated with its need for camouflage while incubating in daylight.

In both sexes the neck has a covering of down and, like the thighs, is in some races sheathed in reddish skin and in others in bluish skin. The call is a penetrating, grunting roar most frequently heard during the early hours of the day. During the nonbreeding season ostriches travel in parties of as many as 20. They can go without water for days, but relish fre-

RHEIFORMES

Rheas (*Rheidae*)

The American ostriches, or rheas, of southern South America, although several feet shorter than their nearest relative, the true Ostrich of Africa, are the largest birds found in the New World. Like the Ostrich they are flightless, although the wing is proportionately longer and is tipped with a horny process that probably is used in fighting. Like the emu and cassowary of Australia and New Guinea, rheas have three toes. The lores (that is, the space between eye and bill), the eye ring and the ears are not feathered, although the ears are sheathed in fine bristles. Thin hairy feathers cover the head and neck. The body plumage is soft and virtually lacking in barbules, and the aftershaft, which is so prominent in emus and cassowaries, is apparently lacking, as in the Ostrich.

The rheas, like the Ostrich, practice harem polygamy. The male is distinctly the larger and acquires half a dozen or more females for his harem; in doing so he fights with other males, fencing with the long neck and bill and delivering deep, booming notes. All the females lay their eggs, up to five dozen, in a single nest on the ground, which the male alone attends, performing all the incubation. In one species the eggs are yellowish, in the other dark greenish. Later the male devotes his energies to rearing the young during a period of at least six weeks. When threatened with danger he at times displays great courage and may even attack a man on horseback. After the breeding season rheas gather in large parties.

For generations the rhea was hunted en masse by Indians, who encircled large areas and killed everything in the enclosure, and is still hunted by gauchos on horseback, who pitch bolas at the bird as it flees with neck extended and wings open. The gaucho tries to wrap the bola, a three-stoned weapon, around the neck, legs and body of the rhea; and since the bird is extremely fleet of foot and keen of eye and when closely pressed often doubles back and falls flat on the ground, this form of hunting is considered a great test of sportsmanship. All this, combined with its protective colors, also makes it a difficult bird to trap. Indeed, the famous naturalist-novelist, W. H. Hudson, remarked that their pale bluish gray plumage enabled them to melt mysteriously into the haze.

Rheas feed on vegetable matter of many kinds, as well as on land mollusks, lizards and worms. They do well in zoos and young ones are frequently kept as pets in South America; they are ideal except that they are apt to gobble up any shiny small object. Like cassowaries and emus, they swim strongly, frequently taking to the water and swimming with the body nearly submerged.

The pampas and highland savannas of Brazil and Argentina are the home of the Common Rhea (*Rhea americana*), the larger and more abundant of

HERBERT LANKS: MONKMEYER

Common Rhea, young (*Rhea americana*)

quent drinking and bathing; they sometimes submerge all but the neck and head.

As breeding time approaches males frequently square off to fence with their beaks and necks, often within sight of a group of hens. At other times they fight with powerful kicks and are dangerous adversaries when cornered. Like the rheas, they practice harem polygamy, each vigorous male usually mating with three or four females. He selects a nest territory and scrapes a shallow cavity, and in this the females deposit their eggs—sometimes as many as 20—each weighing about three pounds, straw-yellow or buff in color, very hard and shiny and of porelike texture. In about six weeks the eggs hatch, and soon the precocious chicks, covered with spiny down, are able to travel in coveys with the adults.

Ostriches thrive in captivity and have a life span about equal to that of humans. Captive breeding populations are kept in a number of places in both Old and New Worlds to satisfy an age-old demand for ostrich plumage. The feathers are plucked from the adults without harming them. In Africa ostriches still are numerous in many desert regions such as the Kalahari, and in many national parks they enjoy a protection that guarantees that these, the largest of living birds, will not be exterminated. The populations that formerly lived in the deserts of Egypt and Nubia as well as those of South Africa have been virtually extirpated.

the two known species. In coloration it is brownish gray above and dull white below, with a black crown and nape and scattered areas of black on the neck and upper chest. Its sides are bluish gray, its iris and its long naked legs gray. The female is slightly paler.

In the mountains of Peru, Bolivia, Chile and Argentina is found the Long-billed Rhea (*Pterocnemia pennata*). It is smaller, has slim legs and a relatively long bill, and is generally darker, with a brown cast to the dark plumage of the body.

CASUARIIFORMES

Cassowaries (*Casuariidae*)

Cassowaries are extremely powerful birds and among the very few that can easily kill a full-grown man. They are huge flightless ratites occurring only in the New Guinea region, on a few nearby islands including the Arus, Ceram, New Britain and Jobi Island, and along the northernmost fringes of Aus-

Australian Cassowary (*Casuarius casuarius*)

tralia. Unlike their nearest relatives, the grassland-loving emus of Australia and the other ostrich-like birds, cassowaries dwell in thick forest and along jungle rivers.

The primary character of the six known species is a bony helmet or casque worn like a crown and used in fending off obstructions as the huge bird rushes through thick underbrush. Other special modifications for warding off thorns, vines and saw-edged leaves are found in the rudimentary wings and hard, bristle-like body plumage. The wing quills, which show no trace of feather vaning, are modified to bare black spines, some like knitting needles and others like the tines of a large pitchfork. They curve slightly to conform to the body but in action are extended to thrust aside such dangerous vegetation as barbed rattan. The body is wedge-shaped. When the bird runs, its naked head is directed forward and, like the rail, it slithers between obstructions.

Despite their size, cassowaries are wary, skulking, and hard to detect in the wild. They are abroad chiefly in the early morning and late afternoon, and when frightened can run at speeds of 30 miles an hour through all sorts of obstructions, leaping prodigiously, plunging, and even swimming with a facility that must be seen to be believed. With its helmet and its naked, often wattled neck painted garishly in reds, greens, blues, purples and sickening yellows, a swimming cassowary presents a frightening spectacle to the uninitiated.

Female cassowaries, like female hawks and a few other birds, are larger than their mates. Another curious modification is an aftershaft—the little twin feather that sprouts from the lower shaft in many birds—so long that each feather appears to be double.

When cornered, cassowaries attack by leaping feet first, striking with the powerful, heavily muscled legs. The inner or second of the three toes is fitted with a long, straight, murderous nail, which can sever an arm or eviscerate an abdomen with ease. There are many records of natives being killed by this bird.

Young cassowaries are brown and have buffy stripes. They are often kept as pets in native villages, where they are permitted to roam like barnyard fowl. Often they are kept until they become nearly grown and someone gets hurt. Mature cassowaries are placed beside native houses in cribs hardly larger than the birds themselves. Garbage and other vegetable food is fed them, and they live for years in such enclosures; for in some areas their plumage is still as valuable as shell money. Caged birds are regularly bereft of their fresh plumes.

These primitive birds feed almost entirely on fruit, but insects and plants are also eaten. The favorite food of the *muruk,* as the bird is called, is a plum-sized blue fruit that abounds in the forest.

As with all ratites, it is the male cassowary that attends to domestic chores. After the female deposits from three to six granular-surfaced, huge, pear-green eggs on a mat of leaves near the foot of a

[23

PAUL STEINEMANN: PIX

Common Emu, male (*Dromiceius novaehollandiae*)

forest tree, the male assumes the responsibility of incubating, brooding and feeding the young for some seven weeks. Males discovered at the nest sit tight until the last moment, then sprint off, leaving the young—a flight that appears to be a form of distraction display. The adult is conspicuous, whereas the young are colored cryptically and thus are easily overlooked among the debris of the forest floor. The calls of grown cassowaries include deceptive little squeaks, resonant honkings or windy grunts. These can be heard in all of the less populated areas of New Guinea despite the fact that the birds have been hunted since ancient times for their tasty flesh, particularly their livers.

Perhaps the most abundant species is the Two-wattled Cassowary (*Casuarius bicarunculatus*) of the coastal swamplands. It stands four feet high, and has the neck brilliant cobalt blue washed with scarlet and two pendulous wattles of a yellowish hue. A hard, bladelike casque crowns the head. Like all cassowaries, it gathers in small flocks when not in the nesting season.

The Single-wattled Cassowary (*C. unappendiculatus*) of New Guinea and the islands to the west has a single naked pendant wattle hanging from the lower neck. Bennett's Cassowary (*C. bennetti;*

Plate 6) of the lowlands and hill forests of New Guinea and New Britain lacks the wattles, wearing great splashes of cobalt blue on the naked neck. The Australian Cassowary (*C. casuarius*), which reaches a height of more than five feet, has the largest helmet in the family and grotesque, deeply cleft, red-tipped wattles below a cobalt-blue throat.

Emus (*Dromiceiidae*)

Sadly enough, the second largest of living birds, the emu of Australia—a close relative of the cassowary—is rapidly being extirpated in many areas. This is particularly regrettable because it is a friendly bird which sometimes stalks men for the sole purpose of examining them. Until recently two species inhabited the Australian region and others occurred on islands in Bass Strait and in Tasmania. Now all but one are extinct, and of some of the extinct species no specimen exists or, as in the Kangaroo Island species, only a single one is known.

The surviving species, the Common Emu (*Dromiceius novaehollandiae*) of eastern Australia, stands fully five feet tall despite a stooped posture in which the backbone is carried nearly parallel to the ground. This huge bird competes with grazing cattle in its chosen habitat, grasslands; because it is very harmful to agriculture and destroys fences with its powerful body and legs, it is much disliked by farmers and cattlemen. In South Australia an emu-proof fence nearly 500 miles in length is maintained in an attempt to restrict the birds, and wardens police the barrier in vehicles. Nevertheless emus continually attempt to break through to the greener fields beyond. When chased along a road bordering the fence, the birds, sometimes accompanied by their remarkably fleet-footed young, flee straight down the road at speeds of nearly 40 miles per hour.

Emus differ from cassowaries in having the head and neck feathered and in lacking the helmet. Also, they lack the stiletto-like inner nail on the second of the three toes, and have much more rudimentary wings without long, wirelike quills.

The bill, unlike the narrow one of the cassowary, is broad and compressed. This difference is doubtless correlated with a difference in feeding habits. In color emus are earth-brown and gray. The sexes are similar and the young are sooty with buff stripes. They resemble the cassowaries in nesting habits, the male doing most of the incubation, brooding and rearing of the young. After laying, the female sometimes attempts to incubate the eggs and does so until driven off the nest by the male. Up to 12 dark greenish eggs are laid, each nearly five inches in length.

Like the cassowary, emus are expert swimmers. In the nonbreeding season they congregate in small flocks but at other times associate in pairs. They

24]

breed readily in captivity and make excellent zoo animals. When cornered, they strike out to the side or backward with their powerful feet. They have a deep, booming call that seems to be amplified in a tracheal chamber connected with the windpipe.

APTERYGIFORMES

Kiwis (*Apterygidae*)

Kiwis are the least birdlike of all birds. They are shy, flightless, surviving relatives of the extinct moas of New Zealand. Fortunately, despite their highly specialized structure, they possess traits that enable them to hold their own in the face of man and his predaceous camp followers and pets.

Kiwis differ from all living birds in having the openings of the nostrils near the tip of the bill and in possessing a well-developed sense of smell. They are probably "living fossils," and a study of their characteristics may shed light on their cousins, the extraordinary moas. The bill is long and slender, the wings so rudimentary that they cannot be seen on the outside of the body. In grown birds there are no distinct wing quills or tail feathers, but embryo studies have revealed that three to four primaries and nine secondaries appear for a short while on the tiny wing; tail feathers apparently never develop. The body is covered with an almost continuous mat of hairlike feathers, but two bare spots occur along the sides. Kiwis, like a few other species of birds, have a penis which protrudes from the body. They also have abdominal air sacs such as are found in much enlarged form in all flying birds, but the skeleton is solid and mammal-like and without any evidence of the air spaces that lighten flying birds.

Further suggesting that the kiwi is a specialized "dwarf" moa are the relatively enormous eggs laid by the three surviving species. These sometimes reach a length of more than five inches and a width of more than three, and weigh as much as 18 ounces. They are reported to reach a maximum weight equal to one-quarter that of the adult female and are thus relatively the largest eggs known. (It should be noted, however, that judged by such standards the ostrich egg is the smallest in birds.) Ordinarily, only one egg is laid at a time, but sometimes the set is three. Recent experiments in the rearing of kiwis in captivity indicate that the male does all the incubation; he also

Common Kiwi (*Apteryx australis*)

NEW ZEALAND INFORMATION OFFICE

does the nest-building, but the female helps burrow the nest hole. Males have been observed to incubate for a week without leaving the egg to get food and drink. After some 80 days of this, and the successful hatching of a chick, the female often presents him with another egg and he starts all over again. Birds usually travel in couples and may remain paired for life.

Kiwis range over all of the main islands of New Zealand. The Common Kiwi (*Apteryx australis*) has the widest range, occurring on North, South and Stewart Islands. Two other species, the Great Spotted Kiwi (*A. haastii*) and the Little Spotted Kiwi (*A. owenii*), have limited ranges on South Island. The largest species is the Common Kiwi of Stewart Island, which has a bill slightly more than eight inches long. All species are very similar in form, but the Common Kiwi is generally brownish or brownish gray with blackish streaks, while the others have bars instead of streaks.

Kiwis dwell in dense forests up to altitudes of 2000 feet. They sleep in protected burrows by day and hunt by night. Their wanderings are sometimes punctuated by rushes, and it is reported that they can outrun a man and sometimes even a dog. The walk is a waddle, each foot being placed directly in front of the other. Frequently the bill appears to be used as a crutch, but actually the bird touches the ground with it in order to smell worms, insects and their larvae, which comprise the chief items of food. When a worm is found, the bill is used rather like a small crowbar, and the worm is pulled out. In drinking, the bill is inserted to its base in water and then tipped nearly straight up.

The call is a shrill whistle; that of the male is high-pitched and that of the female is guttural. The name "kiwi," which the Maoris were the first to apply to the bird, was in fact derived from its cry.

There has been much difference of opinion as to what the kiwi really is. Some have thought it a relative of the penguins; others in the past have even refused to believe such a bird exists. Some students have thought that it and the other ratite birds represented primitive stages in the evolution of true birds; but evolutionists today believe that the kiwi and all ratites, including the moas, have modified, partly as a result of changes in predator pressures, becoming unwary, cumbersome and vulnerable as they fitted niches normally occupied by terrestrial mammals.

For long years the kiwi was hunted and killed in large numbers to supply trout-fly feathers. It also suffered greatly from the introduction of stoats and ferrets by settlers to control rabbits; finally it has had to fight off cats and dogs. Fortunately, it is nocturnal, living by day in deep, many-chambered burrows under tree roots and similar objects. It is apparently able to protect itself in such situations despite its very poor daytime eyesight. The kiwi defends itself by kicking forward like a cassowary, and men's hands have been cut to the bone and dogs' legs slashed open by such kicks. These qualities have enabled it to hold

out in many areas until conservationists came to its rescue, first in 1908 and then with almost airtight legislation in 1921. In the latter year certain populations of kiwis that were barely holding out were shifted to island sanctuaries and are now prospering.

New Zealanders dote on the kiwi. It is the national emblem, its name is used for all New Zealand soldiers and airmen, representations of it ornament their coins, stamps and paper money, and the government has decreed that no kiwi shall ever again be exported. With this kind of protection we can be sure that it will not soon join its unfortunate cousin, the moa.

TINAMIFORMES

Tinamous (*Tinamidae*)

Tinamous are game birds of uncertain ancestry. Ranging from quails to chickens in size, they inhabit the grasslands and jungles of the New World, some as far north as Mexico and others as far south as Patagonia. In the language of science the 33 species are terrestrial, volant birds bearing skeletal resemblances to ratite, or ostrich-like, birds on the one hand and to gallinaceous, or chicken-like, birds on the other. Anyone who has had the experience of having a tinamou fly up from underfoot in a tropical jungle will never forget it. Relying on its camouflage—for its plumage perfectly matches the debris of the forest floor—the tinamou sits tight until an intruder is almost upon it. Then, with a roar of wings, it rockets off with such speed that sometimes it kills itself against a tree. Such flights are rarely more than a thousand yards long, and if the tinamou is flushed several times it becomes exhausted and cannot fly.

Tinamous have relatively heavy bodies and small skulls, with slender, slightly curved bills so deeply cleft they seem to split the bird's head to its eye. The neck is slender, the wings small, rounded and equipped with relatively weak muscles. The legs are slightly elongated and nearly naked. Most species have four toes, others only three, and the hind toe, when present, is elevated and very small. Most species also have powder downs, and all have very short tails, the latter in some species being hidden under the feathers of the rump.

Because of these characters and a number of similarities in the skeletons, it is probable that the nearest surviving relative of the tinamou is the rhea. In tinamous, as in rheas and other ratites, the role of the sexes in parental care is reversed. The male clears a shallow nest area on the ground, usually at the foot of a tree, and then incubates the eggs that his mate or mates deposit on a thin mat of dead leaves. The eggs, which vary from pale blue to rich vinaceous depending on the species, have a glossy, almost porcelain-like texture.

Incubation requires some 21 days, the chicks emerging and leaving the nest within a day thereafter. They are covered with thick buffy to reddish or rust-colored down shot through with black lines and blotches. The male shepherds the chicks about, his brood ranging from two to twelve, and does all the rearing of the precocial young. The chicks soon learn to fly and to care for themselves.

In some species, the female soon returns to deposit more eggs in the nest for the male to incubate. Female tinamous are larger and more aggressive than their mates, and, while one male is busy incubating, the female is apt to solicit another. Many years ago the famous naturalist, Dr. William Beebe, found that the males of the Variegated Tinamou (*Crypturellus variegatus*) of British Guiana outnumbered the females four to one. More recently it was found that in Bonaparte's Tinamou (*Nothocercus bonapartei*) of Venezuela the sex ratio was about equal. In this species the old males have several mates, and all females belonging to one male lay their eggs in a communal nest. This unusual form of breeding behavior has also been observed in the Ornate Tinamou (*Nothoprocta ornata*) more than 13,000 feet up in the Andes of Peru.

Tinamous keep in touch with each other by means of lovely plaintive deep whistles emitted most frequently in the morning and late afternoon. They feed chiefly on vegetable matter, especially fallen berries, but also devour some insects and their larvae.

Tinamous are so distinct from all other birds that they are placed in an order of their own, the Tinamiformes. One of the largest, the Great Tinamou (*Tinamus major*), is 15 inches in total length, or about the size of a large fowl, and occurs from tropical Mexico to Brazil. Its home is in deep forest. Above, it is brownish olive with black markings; below, it has a whitish throat, a cinnamon neck and a grayish abdomen with fine blackish bars and speckling. Its eggs are china blue.

Ranging from Southern Mexico to Brazil, the Little Tinamou (*Crypturellus soui*) is quail-sized and relatively heavy for its nine-inch length. Above, it is brown with a rufous lower back; below, it is paler, more grayish olive and with tints of cinnamon and rufous. Its head and cheeks are a slaty blue.

GAVIIFORMES

Loons (*Gaviidae*)

Loons, or divers, as they are more aptly known in the Old World, are the most gifted of all diving birds, being able to penetrate deeper and stay underwater longer than any other bird.

Four species comprise the family—the only one in the order Gaviiformes. Two are duck-sized and two are as large as small geese. They live in colder regions of the Northern Hemisphere, where they move with the seasons, usually keeping to frigid waters, including even those of the Arctic that thaw for only a few months each year.

All loons live almost continuously in water—usually oceanic waters in winter and fresh waters in summer. Unlike their remote relatives, the petrels and albatrosses, they are at home in high surf. They live largely on fish, which they outswim and capture in chases that sometimes take them to depths of 160 to 180 feet. These underwater fishing expeditions may last as long as a quarter of an hour, during which the birds may swim, completely submerged, for two or more miles, often in bursts of high speed. It is believed that supplemental oxygen stored in the muscles makes such underwater marathons possible.

The propelling force is the rapid sculling motion of the webbed feet. Steep turns are executed with the aid of the wings. To such a degree have the legs been developed for swimming—they are set so far back on the body that they appear to be affixed almost at the end, like a ship's propeller—that the birds can hardly stand on land. The birds often swim or rest with only the head above water; when trying to avoid detection, they at times slowly settle beneath the surface, leaving hardly a ripple, and then swim off so rapidly that they cannot be successfully pursued by even an expert canoeist.

Usually loons are found singly or in pairs that keep far apart, but sometimes in winter they form little flocks off shore. Also, in late summer the pairs are apt to keep fairly close together with their young. At such times an adult often keeps to the surface even in the face of an approaching canoe or raises its body in mock attack.

At other times the larger loons rise cumbersomely from the water, flapping their powerful, narrow wings and running on the surface with their webbed feet. When take-off speed has been achieved, they rise into the air in straight-line flight like that of ducks. Although they can reach speeds of 60 miles per hour, they fly only as far as safety dictates before alighting. In the air the feet extend backward beyond the tail, and the thick neck and heavy body present a rather hunchbacked silhouette. In landing, the birds hit the water with the chest rather than with the feet as in ducks, and send up a high splash. In short, loons are much more at home in and under water than in air, and on land they are nearly helpless. When weather conditions are bad and they are forced down on dry land, they cannot take off again.

However, in migration some species execute surprisingly long overland flights from their habitual nesting areas in and around small ponds and inland rivers. For example, Old World populations of the Black-throated Diver (*Gavia arctica*), according to banding studies reported in 1954, winter mainly in the Black Sea. In spring they move northward on a roundabout route via the Baltic Sea and Scandinavia to breeding grounds in northern Siberia. In fall they do not retrace their spring flight but strike out overland to their wintering waters, thus executing a clockwise migration involving long overland flights where landings would prove fatal.

City-bred folk, hearing the nocturnal cries of loons for the first time, are apt to feel stabs of fear. Coming out of the darkness of a remote northern lake, the demoniacal laughter and screams—often taken up far and wide and relayed like distress signals—can chill the soul of a listener until he identifies the source. Thereafter, the camper may come to look forward to this wilderness crescendo. Loons are at their most vocal and eerie at night, but they also emit harsh grating cries during flight.

Annually, in spring and summer, loons emerge from their watery element to nest. Grass and reeds are gathered in a mound close to water, the birds often sliding about on their abdomens and breasts as they build. The nest may be a large, bulky affair; almost always it is located on a little island or on a shore where a good view of the surroundings is available, and is placed so close to the edge that the attending bird can slip unobtrusively into the water. The nest is built on exclusive territory, small lakes and large ponds usually supporting only a single pair of loons, whereas large waterways and lakes are divided into sectors.

Two eggs are laid. These are generally olive to olive-green with blackish mottling. Incubation, a matter of some 28 to 30 days, is performed alternately by the sexes, and when the young emerge they are clad in thick down that is dark above and paler below. The young are very active and take to the water almost as soon as they are hatched. There they keep together with the adults and often ride pickaback on the bodies of their parents, who, in taking them aboard, may partially submerge and then lift them from the water like an elevator. Loons settle and rise in water by compressing the body feathers and the air in the air sacs of the body; their bones are not penetrated by air-filled cavities—that is, are not pneumatic.

Loons sometimes rise on the water by treading with the feet, and in a nearly vertical position flap the wings, then slide back into the water and swim off. An aquatic diving dance, during part of which both birds run on the water and flail it with the wings, is one of the chief ceremonies of the courtship display. This dance, much like that of some of the grebes, is regarded as one of the most remarkable sights in the bird world.

In America, the best known of the loons is the Common Loon or Great Northern Diver (*Gavia immer*), a black-headed bird that reaches 36 inches in length. Although chiefly a Canadian breeder, it nests in the United States in such places as the mountain lakes of New York, Pennsylvania, Michigan and California, and winters south to the Gulfs of Mexico and California. In Eurasia it winters as far south as the Mediterranean. The sexes are similar, but the upper plumage of both changes through a double molt. In summer it is boldly and evenly checked with white spots on black, and wears a checked collar and throat spots; in winter the contrasting plumage changes to dull dark gray. As in many other aquatic birds, the flight feathers of the wing and tail are lost more or less simultaneously, with the result that loons are completely flightless for a few weeks each year.

The Black-throated Diver or Arctic Loon (*Gavia arctica;* Plate 3) is representative of the two smaller loons, both of which have generally grayish heads instead of blackish as in the large species. It is a 27-inch bird that breeds in the northern British Isles, Scandinavia, the shores of the Baltic Sea and westward through Asia to Alaska and the Canadian Arctic. In winter it reaches the Mediterranean and the shores of China and Mexico. In summer this species has the head gray, the throat black with narrow white stripes bordering it as well as the sides of the breast. In winter it is dark gray above, with white underparts.

Two other wide-ranging species have names that indicate their distinguishing characters. One, the Red-throated Loon (*Gavia stellata*), which reaches a length of more than two feet, is unlike the other loons in that it sometimes nests in colonies or on shores near salt water, such as are found in Newfoundland. It also takes off easily and prefers flying to diving when fleeing from intruders. The other, the Yellow-billed Loon (*Gavia adamsii*), is very similar to the Common Loon except for the color and shape of its bill. It breeds in western Canada, Alaska and eastern Asia. It winters farther north than the other three species, seldom going south of Scandinavia and southern Alaska.

PODICEPEDIFORMES

Grebes (*Podicepedidae*)

Many years ago an American ornithologist, Leonhard Stejneger, wrote of these peculiar waterbirds: "The grebes look extremely old-fashioned; that is, they impress us as if their grotesque figures were only survivors of bygone periods." Largely responsible for this impression is the fact that their legs are not only set far back under the tail but are compressed and bladelike for cutting through water and that the tail is rudimentary and almost gone.

Grebes are the most perfectly aquatic of all flying birds. Unlike the penguins and auks, they rely solely on their lobed feet for locomotion; they use them like propellers to progress through water like the loon and probably much like the famous Hesperornis, a powerful swimmer that 85 million years ago lived in the Cretaceous seas covering what we now know as Kansas.

Grebes, of which 18 species are known, are virtually cosmopolitan in their distribution. At first glance they resemble small ducks; however, the moderately lengthened, pointed bill, which is very much more slender than that of the duck, and the habit of turning the head constantly when floating, make them easy to distinguish. They have a number of unique characteristics that serve to set them off sharply, even from their familiar relatives, the loons. The most picturesque of these is the way in which they protect their young. Grebes not only feed, sleep, court and mate in water, but are the only birds known that carry the young pickaback under the surface. When pursued, grebes habitually dive and swim away underwater and often perform such escapes with their downy young clinging to their backs. Unlike loons, mergansers and swans, which carry their young on their backs above water and turn to defend them when threatened, grebes depend on their ability to carry the young underwater to safety, and do not turn to defend them if they happen to be left behind.

Another ability of grebes is one they share with loons: when alarmed they compress the plumage and the air in internal reservoirs. This effects changes in their buoyancy so efficiently that a grebe floating high on water can make itself settle and disappear beneath the surface almost magically. Usually, however, they merely submerge the body and neck and use the head as a periscope.

Grebes are covered with very soft, silky feathers which, during the era of plume collecting, were much in demand for feminine adornment. These grow in great profusion. According to recent feather counts of some 94 different species of birds, the grebe has more feathers than any other; a Pied-billed Grebe was found to have 15,016 feathers, whereas a hummingbird had only 1518.

The grebe appears to use its feathers in a unique way. The American ornithologist, Dr. Alexander Wetmore, has suggested that the large mats of feathers usually found in its stomach, but apparently not in any other bird, may serve as a strainer to detain the sharp bones of fish prey from entering the intestines until they are sufficiently decomposed for digestion.

The majority of grebes are ornamented with crests, ruffs and patches of color about the head and neck during the nuptial season. This period is invariably passed in fresh-water regions: rivers, ponds, lakes, all with areas of grass and reeds. There the grebes indulge in aquatic dances, which are among the most spectacular sights in nature. Of the two kinds of dances employed, one is a toe dance in which the partners run side by side over the water, moving so lightly that they resemble penguins running on ice and so rapidly that long "fish-tails" of water appear in their wake. At the end of these runs they fall forward in a plunge, creating large cascades of water. The second dance involves inanimate objects and, because the male and the female closely approach each other as in a formal human dance, is particularly interesting. First, both participants disappear underwater on long submarine swims. When they emerge,

each carries a strand of aquatic vegetation in the bill. Very quickly their bodies are forced upward so that the birds appear to be standing almost stationary and upright. With the feet sculling strongly to hold them aloft, the two birds now move toward and away from one another, sometimes almost touching chests and appearing very much like human dancers.

The Western Grebe of North America and the Great Crested Grebe of Eurasia, which are among the largest species (each is about 28 inches long), are the most renowned dancers.

Grebes winter in fresh water or along the edges of continental shelves in places free of ice. Often they congregate in large flocks and with the coming of spring move northward to their fresh-water breeding areas. Such movements are of two kinds. By night they indulge in long flights. By day they settle: if on lakes to feed, or if on oceanic waters they swim, fishing as they move, in the direction of their destination at a rate of about 1¼ miles per hour.

Grebes are difficult to see, and usually their arrival on their breeding grounds is first noticed when their calls are heard. They bark, wail, trumpet and moan, and the sound is weird, especially when heard at night.

Following the courtship dances, the pairs select a reedy area usually in knee-deep water where, according to Dr. J. S. Huxley, who studied the Great Crested Grebe, both sexes participate in building the nest. This they accomplish in a few hours, swimming rapidly underwater and returning with pieces of aquatic vegetation about every thirty seconds for periods of up to an hour at a time. From three to seven eggs are laid, originally pale grayish white or tinted with green but soon stained brownish. When leaving the nest the parents cover the eggs with damp vegetation like that used in the construction of the nest. One observer found that the warm eggs of completed clutches were invariably covered but that incomplete sets of cool eggs were often left exposed; he therefore suggested that covering the eggs was a mechanism for preserving heat rather than protection by camouflage. Both sexes incubate, and the female continues adding material to the nest while doing so. Although disorderly in appearance, the nest is a marvel of engineering. Composed of buoyant aquatic vegetation, it forms a floating island and thus can adjust itself to the rises and falls in water level. The shallow nest cup usually is located just above water level; in some instances, however, the eggs become partially submerged when the adult rides atop the floating raft. These rafts are tethered to adjacent vegetation by floating guy shafts or slide up and down among vertical shafts.

The incubation period, variously reported at from 18 to 29 days, may be of irregular length. Upon hatching, the chicks are covered with pale down and a striping of dark colors. They soon leave the nest to swim and dive and be carried about by their parents, both of whom care for them. The family probably

KLEMENS SÖDING

Great Crested Grebe (*Podiceps cristatus*)

grebes is the Eared or Black-necked Grebe (*Podiceps caspicus*) of Europe, Asia, Africa and the New World. In the latter area it breeds in colonies in company with Franklin's Gull and winters in Middle America. The commonest grebe of Central and South America is the Least Grebe (*Podiceps dominicus*; Plate 2).

A few grebes have a very limited range, and in the New World, where 12 of the 18 species are found, two are restricted each to single lakes, one being the Atitlan Grebe (*Podilymbus gigas*) of Atitlan Lake, Guatemala, the other the Flightless Grebe (*Centropelma micropterum*) of Lake Titicaca in the high Andes of South America.

The Great Crested Grebe (*Podiceps cristatus;* Plate 1) is found widely in the Old World, with breeding populations occurring from Scandinavia to Australia. It has long, blackish horns extending backward along the sides of the crown and prominent reddish brown and black fans springing from the back of the head and encircling its sides like little skirts. As in other grebes, these ornaments disappear during the nonbreeding season.

Among the smaller grebes is the Little Grebe (*Podiceps ruficollis*), sometimes known as the Red-throated Dabchick, an 11-inch bird that lives throughout the Old World. It is distinguished by its chestnut throat and its small size. The slightly larger, wide-ranging Pied-billed Grebe (*Podilymbus podiceps*) of the New World chiefly frequents small inland lakes, often as high as 6000 feet above sea level. It is one of the best of all bird swimmers. Its name is based on a vertical black mark on its small whitish bill. Before the invention of smokeless powder, this species escaped the hunter by diving as soon as it saw the flash of his gun and thus reaching safety before the arrival of the bullet—or so the story goes.

returns nightly to the nest or its immediate vicinity until the young are fledged. This seems a difficult process in grebes because the young cling to the adults until they are driven off. When parting comes, the parents break the bond by pecking their young, sometimes even pecking a persistent chick to death.

Grebes fly strongly in straight lines but have difficulty in rising from the water, their take-offs involving much running on the surface. But they can barely manage to get about on the ground, and as a result never resort to land when in danger. Their food consists of fish, insect larvae, crustaceans, an occasional frog and vegetable matter, most of it gathered underwater.

The largest grebe in North America is the Western Grebe (*Aechmophorus occidentalis*), which ranges in western North America south to Mexico. It reaches a length of more than two feet and has a long, slender neck and vividly contrasting black and white plumage. It is unique among grebes in having unstriped young. Probably the widest-ranging of the

PROCELLARIIFORMES

Albatrosses (*Diomedeidae*)

Of the few birds that have learned to live in the remote ocean wastes, none is more nomadic or self-sufficient than the albatross. It can go to sea for weeks or months, sleeping on the ocean's surface, drinking sea water and returning to land only to breed. Recent observations show that albatrosses rarely follow ships for more than a few days, but have traditionally been reported as making prodigious ship-following flights because the ones that follow a ship often give way to others at night.

Banding records confirm that albatrosses wander great distances. Thus, an albatross banded at Kerguelen Island in the southern Indian Ocean was captured about three years later near Cape Horn, some 6000 miles away; and Dr. Oliver Austin, Jr. has made observations indicating that some albatrosses may

Laysan Albatross (*Diomedea immutabilis*)

make one or more trips around the world between breeding seasons.

Albatrosses are essentially birds of the cold oceans of the Southern Hemisphere, where they range northward to the tropics from the borders of the Antarctic Continent. One of the 13 known species, the Waved Albatross (*Diomedea irrorata*), breeds in the Galapagos Islands, and three others breed on small islands in the central Pacific. Tropical hurricanes infrequently carry albatrosses far into the Northern Hemisphere. For example, the Yellow-nosed Albatross (*D. chlororhynchos*) has been carried as far north as the Gulf of St. Lawrence, Canada.

One of the most distinctive features of the albatross is the tubular nostrils protruding from the base of the upper maxilla along the top of the bill. The bill is strong, plated with horny segments, and tipped with a powerful hook. Albatrosses feed to a large extent at night on small marine animals such as cuttlefish. These are also taken from the surface of the ocean by day. A favorite pastime of sailors is catch-ing albatrosses with a baited hook dragged in the ship's wake, but the birds are almost invariably released because of the superstition that killing an albatross brings bad luck.

In landing, the albatross descends on a wave and furls the wings high on its back. When taking off it sprints laterally along a wave top, beating the water with its webbed feet and becoming airborne over a trough. Their legs are so short that they must run with great vigor in order to launch themselves.

The Wandering Albatross (*Diomedea exulans*) has the largest wing span of any living bird—nearly 12 feet! Its wings are long and very narrow and, despite their size, seem perfect instruments of flight. The bird may soar hour after hour on fixed wings, tacking across the wind, descending rapidly to the waves, ascending steeply and tacking again. In recent years man has solved the mystery of the albatross' effortless flight and sailplane pilots can now duplicate some of it. The bird soars high in flowing air and then derives speed and inertia by diving

[31

Wandering Albatross (*Diomedea exulans*)

Petrels, Fulmars and Shearwaters (*Procellariidae*)

Like their relatives, the albatrosses and the diving petrels, the 53 species comprising this interesting family of somberly colored oceanic birds are so much at home on the high seas that they come ashore only to breed. Some are as large as small geese; others are smaller than pigeons. Nearly all are excellent fliers and certain—especially the shearwaters—are among the finest of aerialists. They also excel as avian navigators, and several, such as the Manx and Greater Shearwaters, can execute homing migrations with an accuracy that cannot be explained in the light of present knowledge.

A few species have developed mechanisms of nest defense involving the projecting of highly offensive stomach oils for distances of up to five feet. Some have overcome their predators by nesting on sheer cliffs; others—the great majority—dig into the turf or slip into crevices on isolated islands to hide by day and travel to and fro by night. Some build nests in their subterranean lairs, but the majority lay on the bare rock or ground or add only a bit of grass to the nesting cavity.

All of the Procellariidae are widely pelagic, seeming to disperse over vast areas of the ocean almost at random, yet all adhere to set patterns of travel, somehow finding "landmarks" even on the bleakest ocean. They regularly visit every open ocean of the world. Some species land on the surface of the sea to feed on squid, fish and all manner of floating animal life, alive, dead, and decomposed—not excluding the waste scattered by man. Others execute shallow dives in quest of minute animal life; and still others prey on smaller sea birds. All of this matter may be converted into the musky liquid that is regurgitated to feed the young.

Like albatrosses and diving petrels, all Procellariidae have the maxilla sharply hooked and the tip of the mandible equipped with a short but sharp downward hook. And, as in those other families, the air for the lungs is carried back in paired tubes along the ridge of the bill to the nostrils; hence the name Tubinares, often used for this group of birds. All have the feet webbed and the legs short and relatively weak. In many species the wings are pointed and comparatively long, the very name, shearwater, indicating the sense of power conveyed by these birds in flight, especially as they sail through oceanic troughs. When steady winds blow, the wings may remain fixed in the glide position for as much as a

[continued on page 49]

steeply, penetrating the semistatic cushion of air near the water with outstretched wings and, like a bouncing ball, shooting up into the air again. Besides the long wings, albatrosses have massive heads and small, rudder-like tails.

Albatrosses are amusing and quite photogenic. During World War II, service men saw and, one might say, lived with albatrosses. On Midway Island the Laysan Albatross (*Diomedea immutabilis;* Plate 7) nested all around the barracks buildings. They were a constant menace to aircraft but soldiers and sailors alike disdained to kill them and special details had to be assigned to carrying the eggs and escorting the birds away from runways.

During courtship, albatrosses grunt and cry and lumber about, preening clumsily, bowing to each other and lifting the bills skyward. They are highly gregarious. In former years plume collectors plundered their rookeries, reducing many species and nearly bringing extinction to the Short-tailed Albatross (*Diomedea albatrus*), which nests on islands just southeast of Japan. However, the Japanese are now offering this rare species complete protection.

Albatrosses lay a single chalky egg in a bare area of ground or sand or on a simple grass nest. Both sexes share the incubation which, in the Royal Albatross (*Diomedea epomophora*), lasts 70 to 80 days. The young are fed by regurgitation, becoming very fat on a diet of predigested fish. The chick may be brooded some 42 days and Dr. L. E. Richdale found that the young of the Royal Albatross stays aground until its wings are very long—a matter of 229 to 251 days!

1. Great Crested Grebe
   (*Podiceps cristatus*)
   Range: Old World

2. Least Grebe
(*Podiceps
dominicus*)
Range:
Central and
South America

[PAUL SCHWARTZ]

3. Pacific Loon (*Colymbus arcticus*)
Range: Colder areas of Northern Hemisphere [WALTER E. HIGHAM]

4. Macaroni Penguin
(*Eudyptes
chrysolophus*)
Range:
Southern Hemisphere

[ROBERT CUSHMAN MURPHY]

5. Adelie Penguin
(*Pygoscelis adeliae*)
Range: Antarctic waters

[FRITZ GORO: LIFE MAGAZINE]

6. Bennett's Cassowary
and young
(*Casuarius bennetti*)
Range: Mountains
of New Guinea

[ALLEN KEAST]

7. Laysan Albatross
   and young
   (*Diomedea
   immutabilis*)

   Range: Western
   Hawaiian Islands

   [KARL W. KENYON]

8. Bonin Island Petrel
   (*Pterodroma
   hypoleuca*)

   Range: Bonin Islands
   and Western Hawaiian
   Islands

   [KARL W. KENYON]

9. Fulmar (*Fulmarus
   glacialis*)

   Range: Northern
   Hemisphere

   [ROGER TORY PETERSON:
   NATIONAL AUDUBON]

10. Northern Gannet and young (*Morus bassanus*)
Range: North Atlantic Ocean [JOHN MARKHAM]

11. Shags in center (*Phalacrocorax aristotelis*) and Kittiwakes (*Rissa tridactyla*)
    Range: Northern Hemisphere [ERIC J. HOSKING]

12. Brown Pelican
    (*Pelecanus occidentalis*)
    Range: Coasts of America

    [ALLAN CRUICKSHANK: NATIONAL
    AUDUBON]

13. Magnificent
Frigate-bird
(*Fregata
magnificens*)

Range:
Warm waters
of Atlantic
and eastern
Pacific Oceans

[KARL W. KENYON]

14. Magnificent Frigate-bird (close-up)

[KARL W. KENYON]

15. Cattle Heron in nest
(*Ardeola ibis*)

Range: Cosmopolitan
in warmer land areas

and Little Egret
(*Egretta garzetta*)

Range: Old World

[ERIC J. HOSKING]

16. Great Blue Heron
(*Ardea herodias*)

Range: Alaska to
Galapagos Islands
and West Indies

[L. W. WALKER]

17. Common Egret (*Casmerodius albus*)
Range: Cosmopolitan in warmer areas of world [ELIOT PORTER]

18. **Black-crowned Night Heron**
(*Nycticorax nycticorax*)

Range: Cosmopolitan in warmer
areas of world

[WALTER E. HIGHAM]

19. **Old World Bittern**
(*Botaurus stellaris*)
Range: Eurasia

[JOHN MARKHAM]

20. Common Egret and young
(*Casmerodius albus*)

Range: Cosmopolitan in
warmer areas of world

21. Little Blue Heron
and young
(*Florida caerulea*)

Range: Warmer parts
of the Americas

22. Black-necked Stork
(*Xenorhynchus asiaticus*)
Range: India to Australia

23. White Stork (*Ciconia ciconia*)
Range: Eurasia and Africa

24. Lesser Adjutant Stork (*Leptoptilus
javanicus*)
Range: Southern Asia and Malaysia

25. Whale-head or Shoebill (*Balaeniceps rex*) Range: Africa [YLLA: RAPHO-GUILLUMETTE]

26. European Flamingo (*Phoenicopterus ruber*) Range: Southern France and southern Spain

27. American
Flamingo
(*Phoenicopterus
ruber*)

Range: Caribbean
region and
Galapagos
Islands

[RUSS KINNE: NATIONAL
AUDUBON]

28. Common Eider, male (*Somateria mollissima*)
Range: Cold parts of Northern Hemisphere

29. Common Eider, female

30. Wood Duck (*Aix sponsa*)
Range: Temperate North America
[RUSS KINNE: NATIONAL AUDUBON]

31. Black-necked Swan
(*Cygnus melanocoriphus*)
Range: Southern South
America
[H. RUHE AND T. ROTH]

32. Greylag Goose (*Anser anser*)
Range: Eurasia
[SVANTE LUNDGREN]

[continued from page 32]

mile and a half as the bird shears through the air, often within inches of the sea.

When breeding time approaches, the far-wandering birds converge in small flocks, or sometimes in huge concentrations, on an ancestral breeding island with unerring accuracy, some from thousands of miles. After a few days of mass courtship in rafts at sea and over the island at night, the pairs split up and begin the nest. The typical nest, usually one of many close together, is a cavity drilled in turf and resembles a rat hole. The incubating bird remains on the single white egg both day and night until replaced by the mate. The latter remains at sea by day but often returns to the nest by night to feed its partner or to exchange duties.

After some seven weeks of incubation the young hatch; and ten to twelve weeks later they finally leave the nest, looking like the adults. During the last week or two the young are usually not fed at all or only rarely. Once out of the nest mouth they shuffle to the cliff edge and then waveringly plummet into the sea. In many species this fateful jump occurs after the parents are already several thousand miles on the way to their winter homes, often in another hemisphere.

The mystery of uninitiated, abandoned offspring

striking out over the open ocean, eventually to join their kind in a given wintering area, and then to return on schedule to breed on a minute speck of land in a vast ocean is one of the wonders of nature. It may be that we shall soon have an explanation of this as a result of experiments by the British ornithologist, G. V. T. Matthews, on the migratory abilities of the Manx Shearwater (*Puffinus puffinus*). His experiments reveal that this more or less typical species, when released in unfamiliar waters, immediately strikes out in the general direction of its home, even though it be thousands of miles away.

The Manx, which is blackish above and whitish below, is a small shearwater about 14 inches in length and with narrow, eight-inch wings. Its primary breeding grounds are on islets off Iceland, the Faroes, Britain, the Azores and the islands of the Mediterranean. It is not at home in oceanic waters bordering North America; nevertheless, in one of Matthews' experiments, a Manx Shearwater captured off the Welsh coast and released at Boston was recaptured on its nest in Wales 12½ days later. Dr. Matthews suggests that it covered the 3200 miles with such amazing accuracy by extrapolating the sun's arc across the sky and thus estimating the sun's position. This ability, together with a time "memory" based on the

Wedge-tailed Shearwaters (*Puffinus pacificus*)

JOHN WARHAM

Little Shearwater (*Puffinus assimilis*) feeding young underground

time zone of its nesting grounds, Matthews believes, permitted it to determine direction. In other experiments birds released when the sun was overcast took much longer to return to their nests.

The existence of this seeming ability to migrate more efficiently when celestial bodies are visible—and it has been found in both day- and night-flying birds—may be borne out by astonishing experiments being conducted at Hamburg, Germany, by Dr. Franz Sauer, a researcher of the highest integrity and ability. At the 1957 meeting of the American Ornithologists' Union, its president, Dr. Ernst Mayr, told of experiments, part of which he had witnessed. Dr. Sauer, Mayr stated, was working with Old World warblers, a group of highly migratory, night-traveling birds, which he had hand-raised. Dr. Sauer was using the Hamburg Planetarium for his experiments, and when the warblers were liberated under a synthetic night sky with star-settings indicating Siberia, the birds flew without hesitation toward synthetic Hamburg! But when the mechanical spotlights of the planetarium were set to simulate the night stars of the northern United States, these Old World warblers again flew, without hesitation, toward synthetic Ham-

burg. Dr. Mayr agreed that what he had just seen in Hamburg seemed quite incredible.

For these reasons the experiment with the Manx Shearwater is a notable one and, along with hundreds of other experiments, seems to have set us on the threshold of a scientific discovery perhaps as important in the realm of animal behavior as Darwin's studies of the Galapagos finches in the realm of evolution. Other examples of these remarkable birds include the Little Shearwater (*Puffinus assimilis;* shown in the accompanying photograph feeding its young) and the Wedge-tailed Shearwater (*Puffinus pacificus*). Both were photographed in the Australian region.

Of circumpolar distribution is the Fulmar (*Fulmarus glacialis;* Plate 9), a large, smoke-gray, gull-like bird that reaches 20 inches in length. It is unusual in that it also has a light color phase in which the head and upperparts are nearly white. The breeding grounds of this bird are on small arctic islands and southward as far as England; in winter it reaches the latitude of Japan, Mexico, New York and Spain.

Unlike most other species of the Procellariiformes, it nests on cliff-ledges in the open, depositing its chalky white egg in a slight depression, usually lined with grass, and being chiefly diurnal in its nest activities. Sometimes hundreds of thousands nest together in colonies, but after the nesting season, they scatter in small groups over the ocean from the edge of the ice down to the beginning of warm seas. They feed on living and dead organic matter of all kinds. Most of the members of this family, even the nestlings, are able to expel an obnoxious liquid, the product of certain digestive glands, when they are attacked on the nest by gulls or four-footed predators. This mechanism is most highly developed in the Fulmar, which can spit a distance of more than four feet.

In one of the most exhaustive works ever devoted to a single bird, Dr. James Fisher has shown that the Atlantic Fulmar has increased prodigiously in numbers and range in areas traversed and fouled by man's activities, especially his whaling and fishing. One cannot help thinking of the plight of these millions of birds when man begins saving such waste matter for the production of fertilizer.

The Bermuda Petrel, or Cahow (*Pterodroma cahow*), which is a near relative of the Jamaica Petrel (*P. hasitata*), is a 16-inch bird. It resembles the Greater Shearwater (*Puffinus gravis*) in coloration and is a sooty grayish brown above with whitish lores and underparts. The Cahow formerly bred on Bermuda abundantly but, with the coming of human settlers, who killed the birds for food, its numbers rapidly decreased. As early as 1621 it had virtually disappeared, and for almost three centuries was considered extinct. Then, in the early twentieth century, four specimens were discovered, and in 1951 the American ornithologist Dr. Robert Cushman Murphy and the Bermuda naturalist Mr. L. S. Mowbray discovered colonies numbering perhaps 100 birds on satellite islets fringing Bermuda. It is now making a slow recovery. The Cahow, which is named for the odd sounds it makes during courtship, differs from most of its known relatives in that it builds a fairly large nest of sticks and leaves in the burrows it drills in the turf of islets. Another rare species is the Bonin Island Petrel (*Pterodroma hypoleuca*; Plate 8).

The largest member of the family, the Giant Petrel (*Macronectes giganteus*), sometimes reaches three feet in length and resembles a small albatross but is stouter and has shorter wings. This species, which lives in the southern seas from Antarctica to the temperate zone, is the well-known "stinker" of sailor lore. It comes in a white phase, most often found near the Antarctic, and a dark brownish one, most often found in warmer seas.

Another well-known bird of the literature of the seas, the Mutton-bird, or Sooty Shearwater (*Puffinus griseus*), is sooty except for grayish brown underparts and a dark bill and feet. It reaches a length of 20 inches, breeds on bleak cold islands of the Southern Hemisphere and winters in the Northern Hemisphere as far as the Aleutians, Greenland and the Faeroe Islands, thus covering virtually all of the Atlantic and Pacific Oceans.

Four species of Prions (*Pachyptila*) occur around the world, chiefly in the southern oceans. All are nearly alike, being less than a foot in length and having pale gray upperparts and white underparts. Two medium-sized, whitish petrels occur on and around Antarctica. An example is the Snow Petrel (*Pagodroma nivea*), which is nearly pure white except for a black spot in front of the eye. In his *Birds of the Ocean* W. B. Alexander credits the Snow Petrel of Antarctica with having the most southerly range of any bird in the world.

Storm Petrels (*Hydrobatidae*)

Famous in fable, the 23 swallow-sized species comprising this family are the smallest of web-footed birds. They are also the tiniest of all sea birds, although they are close relatives of the mighty albatross. Superstitions concerning petrels have long circulated among sailors because of their almost magical appearance at the onset of storms, even in the remote reaches of the broadest oceans. Long ago seafarers named them "Mater Cara" (whence the popular name "Mother Carey's Chickens") after the Virgin Mary, and others, noting how their feet pattered on the water, as though they were walking on it, called them "petrels" after Saint Peter.

Petrels are chiefly birds of the dark and they often seem to vanish somewhat weirdly into the troughs of a stormy sea. They need not come to land except to breed, and it is probable that they remain at sea for months at a stretch. Indeed, their legs are so weak that on land they cannot be used without support from the wings. In getting about in burrows and on rocks, petrels slide along on the tarsus, using the back of the "leg" as a broad support somewhat in the manner of the penguins and the mousebirds.

Petrels feed on minute marine organisms called plankton, picking these with their small bills from the restless surface of the sea. They seem as much at home on the wing as small mammals are on foot, and there is reason to believe that they can fly continuously for exceptional lengths of time. When they do land on water, they float high like corks. In times of great storms they seem to prefer to ride them out on the wing, flying in the wave troughs for shelter. When conditions become too severe, "wrecks" occur in which thousands of birds are dashed ashore to die. Thus it is that even a resident of waters far inland, for example along the Mississippi or the Rhine, occasionally comes on a starving petrel.

Storm Petrels are small, generally sooty birds with usually white rumps, narrow, sharp wings and long, thin legs. Their bills are hooked and their talons flattish and dull. The characteristic nostrils are tubular and joined in a single, forward-directed orifice opening midway along the top edge of the bill. A few species such as the White-faced Storm Petrel (*Pelaga-*

White-faced Storm Petrel (*Pelagadroma marina*) entering burrow

droma marina) of the southern oceans (shown at its nest burrow in the accompanying photograph) are largely white below.

All Storm Petrels breed in burrows which they excavate themselves, or in rock crevices. The breeding sites are oceanic islands and rocky coastlands, and burrows of certain species are scattered over a vast area of the globe. For example, the Band-rumped Petrel (*Oceanodroma castro*) breeds in the Atlantic on the Madeira Islands, the Azores, Ascension Island and St. Helena Island, and in the Pacific from the Galapagos to the Hawaiian Islands. Other species breed in very limited areas, but between breeding seasons range far and wide over the world's oceans. Such is the Wilson's Petrel (*Oceanites oceanicus*), which breeds on subantarctic islands and on Antarctica but ranges into the North Atlantic and North Pacific. The most widely known species is Leach's Petrel (*Oceanodroma leucorhoa*), which breeds on islands in the Bering Sea, the North Pacific and the North Atlantic, including those off of the coasts of Maine, Nova Scotia, Greenland, the Faroes, Iceland and the British Isles. This eight-inch bird has a deeply forked tail and whitish upper tail coverts. During the nonbreeding season it wanders to waters along the southern coasts of Asia, South America and Africa.

The author once spent many days in June and July in a breeding colony on Bonaventure Island, Canada. At first he was unaware of the presence of hundreds of birds in the sod underfoot, although little tunnel mouths showed here and there in the grass. But at night the colony seemed to come to life as some birds worked at excavating their tunnels and others came to the tunnel mouths to cry out shrilly to their homecoming mates. Overhead in the darkness their mates, pouring in from far oceanic wanderings, circled about, screaming as though for landing directions.

Observers report that each pair digs its nest burrow, a wrist-sized hole one or more feet deep and requiring about three "days" to excavate. The pair proceeds to spend a number of days in the nest cavity in a kind of prolonged honeymoon. After the single white egg is laid on bare earth deep in the tunnel, one bird incubates and the other goes to sea to find food. Incubation is conducted in relays, with each bird remaining on the egg continuously for from one to five days and occasionally as long as nine days. The incubation period extends up to seven weeks, and the newly hatched nestling, thickly covered with down, remains in the cavity yet another eight weeks. There is a short brooding period during which the adults sometimes resort to diurnal feeding, but toward the end of the eight weeks the chick becomes very fat and the feeding periods slack off sharply and sometimes cease. How the adults feed the young after they leave the nest is not known. Recent studies by an American ornithologist, Janet Hawksley, on an island off the coast of New Brunswick indicate that the young go to sea for months and then return with uncanny accuracy to the same colonies where they were reared, and that their parents often occupy the same nest holes year after year.

Diving Petrels (*Pelecanoididae*)

Diving Petrels live in the cold oceanic areas of the Southern Hemisphere. They form a family in the tube-nosed assemblage, which includes albatrosses, true petrels and fulmars. But, unlike all of these strong-winged birds, the Diving Petrels fly only haltingly and dive continually. They closely, but only superficially, resemble the smallest of the arctic auks, the dovekies; they are nondescript sea birds, blackish above and whitish below, with small bills and webbed feet. They often gather in immense flocks on the surface of the sea, and although they can fly rapidly, they usually flutter close over the water for short distances, then land on the surface or dive directly under the water. They swim with the wings, employing what may be called underwater flying, and they have been seen to emerge from one wave and plunge out of sight into another with no interruption in the movement of the wings.

Each of the Diving Petrels occupies a separate range in the cold waters ringing Antarctica and radiating northward. Cold currents such as the Humboldt carry them as far north as Peru, New Zealand, Australia and other southern land areas of the Indian, Atlantic and Pacific Oceans. They breed on small oceanic islands, occasionally as much as a mile inland. The nest is a burrow or a tunnel drilled in soft earth under a rock. Both parents dig the nest and, after the single white egg is laid, both incubate (for a period of eight weeks) and feed the young, which remains in the burrow seven weeks. Like the building of the nest, the feeding of young goes on mostly at night, with small fishes and other small marine animals constituting the food.

The Peruvian Diving Petrel (*Pelecanoides garnoti*), the largest of the five species, reaches a length of about nine inches. It is blackish above and whitish below and has bright bluish feet and a black bill. This species reaches the western coast of South America, where it seems to breed throughout the year. The Common Diving Petrel (*P. urinatrix*), 6½ inches in length, is the smallest of the family and the most widespread, with breeding populations in the Falkland Islands, Tristan da Cunha, Tasmania, Snares and even Bounty Island.

PELECANIFORMES

Tropic-birds (*Phaëthontidae*)

Tropic-birds are found in all the warm oceans of the world. The three species are pigeon-sized, with two very long, narrow, central tail feathers that distinguish them from all other sea birds. Like the pigeon, they fly rapidly and directly, but unlike it, they are adept at hovering, which they do most frequently over shallow fishing grounds around oceanic islands. Such shoal waters are usually radiant with fluorescent greens and blues, and, not infrequently, the white plumage of these birds is enhanced by the reflected luminescence of these vivid aquatic hues.

White is the predominant color in all tropic-birds. Often, however, observers have seen a pink tinge, which because of its irregularity has been something of a mystery. This was only recently found to be caused by an orange-red oil secreted by a gland at the base of the tail and used by the bird to waterproof its plumage.

In the air tropic-birds are marvels of grace, but on land they are clumsy, the toes being fully webbed and the legs disproportionately small. On the ledges and crevices where they usually breed once a year they often use the wings to steady themselves as they waddle about. Take-offs are made by stepping off the cliffs into space, with the powerful ternlike wings strongly plowing the air. Tropic-birds often make long flights out over the high seas—frequently alone. When food, chiefly small fish and squid, is sighted, the tropic-bird hovers, marks its prey, then plunges

White-tailed Tropic-bird (*Phaëthon lepturus*)

FRED LA TOUR

like a gannet, head first, the wings trailing back and the long tail giving the bird the appearance of a falling lance. Such dives often carry the bird some distance underwater. The prey is captured in the bill. Upon emerging the bird floats buoyantly with the neck held high and the tail angled jauntily upward.

No nest is made. The single oval egg is pale gray or pale brownish, usually spotted with violet, purple and black. It is generally laid in a protected niche or hole in rock, but on remote coral islands it is sometimes placed on a flat open area. Both sexes assist in incubation for some 28 days, but it is possible that the female performs more of these duties since the male is known to feed her on the nest.

Both parents feed the young bird, which hatches with a heavy covering of down. Feedings are frequent during the first ten days but thereafter are usually limited to mornings. This regimen persists until the youngster has grown heavier than its parents and has acquired plumage much like that of the adults. The wings of the nestling, although large, are only barely able to support it when, after some two months on the nest, it plunges clumsily into the ocean and desperately swims away from the deadly waves crashing into the nesting cliff. Despite the concentration of nests, tropic-birds are not particularly inclined to community nesting.

Once safely down on the surface, the young swim for many days, unable to fly or dive until they become strong and lean. It is probable that the parents do not feed them after they fledge and that during this critical period they live on fat stored beneath the skin.

Although tropic-birds rarely stray from tropical waters, the Yellow-billed, or White-tailed Tropic-bird (*Phaëthon lepturus*) breeds as far north as Bermuda. This species reaches a length of 32 inches. It is a white bird with large black shoulder patches and a black line through the eye. Despite its name, its bill is bright orange-red when adult and yellow only when immature. It sometimes visits our shores on the heels of hurricanes. It breeds in the Caribbean and far and wide in the Atlantic and Pacific.

The Red-tailed Tropic-bird (*P. rubricauda*) roves over vast distances and is found throughout warmer regions of the Indian and Pacific Oceans. It is one of the most colorful and beautiful of water birds and is probably the species most frequently called the Boatswain Bird—a name that has long been applied to all tropic-birds. It has the white body plumage strongly tinted with pink, and has some black over the eye, on the feather shafts of the wings and on the flanks. It reaches a length of nearly three feet and nests on the flat surfaces of remote islets.

Pelicans (*Pelecanidae*)

The pelican's enormous pouched bill, crested head and grossly proportioned, short-legged body make it seem more a caricature than a living bird. It has been celebrated so often in story and limerick that it hardly warrants detailed description here.

The eight known species, six of which occur in the Old World and two in the New, are chiefly inhabitants of tropical and warm areas. In all species the sexes are dressed alike, and the young require several years to acquire the adult plumage. All are highly communal in most of their activities.

These ponderous, malproportioned, waddling birds are aerial acrobats par excellence. Their feet are equipped with four toes, joined together by large webs. The birds have difficulty in rising from the water and to do so must run vigorously, the short legs pounding the surface. Despite their size, these birds float buoyantly and fly nimbly, partly because their skeletons are very pneumatic, and also because they have large air reservoirs in the body. On the wing they go in groups, sometimes flying in V formations but usually moving in regular lines or in single column; they are probably the only birds that often fly one behind the other with wing beats synchronized as regularly as though they were in a chorus line. This conformity in flight, high aloft if running with the wind and low to the water if against it, is such that, when the leader extends his wings to glide, his troop does likewise. At times pelicans circle high and soar like vultures. Some hunt by circling and diving, often going out of sight underwater; others, and they are in the majority, land on the water and submerge only the forepart of the body.

The white pelicans (five species) have developed a form of group hunting that is hard to believe. Teams of birds gather on the water with their wings partly open to cast large shadows. They range themselves in a line to drive shoals of fish into shallow waters, or they form large circles around the fish and gradually close in on them. As in flight, the movements of the birds are synchronized. This is most striking when the fish have been concentrated and all the members of the team suddenly tip their bodies and submerge their heads simultaneously. This results in the near annihilation of the trapped fish.

The pelican moves the bill from side to side underwater, with the massive bag open and deep. The top of the pouch is attached to the sides of the lower mandible over its entire length, which in some species is more than 15 inches. The capacity of the bag may exceed twelve quarts, and on land it sometimes sags almost to the ground. In flight the pelican normally carries its fish prey in the gullet, and the flexible sac is then retracted.

In addition to its primary function in catching food, the sac is believed to assist these birds, which nest in excessively hot places, in keeping cool; in such places it sags and may provide an extensive surface for evaporation.

The Brown Pelican (*Pelecanus occidentalis*; Plate 12), which in summer ranges from the southern coasts of western Canada to southern South America, and does all its fishing in salt water (its relatives, the team hunters, nearly always hunt in fresh water), has developed a totally different method of hunting. It dives into the sea rather like a gannet and often from a considerable height, striking the water with wings partly folded and trailing far back from the shoulders. In the dive the head and neck are retracted, with the neck crooked in a loop from the chest to the upper back; thus the head rides close over the body and the bird strikes the water with the forward part of the body, throwing up so much spray that it is often completely hidden. The shock may stun fish as much as six feet below the surface. Since the Brown Pelican does not use the bill as a spear, this bombing technique may play an important part in its fishing, and may also account for the loudness of the impact, which can sometimes be heard as much as half a mile away. Under the skin of its breast it has a layer of pockets of air enclosed in membranes, and this undoubtedly serves to protect it from the force of its dives.

The Brown Pelican abounds along the southern coasts of the U.S.A., particularly when sharks and large fish drive smaller fish inshore. When it emerges from the water with fish, small gulls often pilfer some of its catch by landing on its head or stealing from

American White Pelican, nestling (*Pelecanus erythrorhynchos*)

CAROLA GREGOR

its pouch. The pelican must first empty the water from its pouch by tilting its bill steeply downward before it can raise its head to drive off the gulls.

The five species of white pelicans make their homes on large inland lakes, where they breed on isolated islands sometimes by the tens of thousands. In Africa such breeding colonies may be measured in miles; many large concentrations also occur in the western part of the United States. Sometimes, as in America's Great Salt Lake, they are found on isolated islands in waters altogether devoid of fish. In one colony at this lake the nesting birds must fly 30 to 100 miles to obtain sustenance for themselves and their offspring. Such food is carried in the gullet, or swallowed and regurgitated.

The great hooked bill with its flabby pouch seems a cumbersome tool for feeding tiny offspring. But the American White Pelican (*Pelecanus erythrorhynchos*) of North and Central America, a huge bird with a wingspread of ten feet and a bill five times as long as its newly hatched young, nevertheless regurgitates a watery food during the first days of feeding, and, keeping its bill shut, manages to dribble this into the mouths of the nestlings. Later, when the chicks are stronger, the parent opens its huge mouth for them, folding the lower jaw tightly against the breast and lifting the maxilla to expose the gullet; each youngster then roots around in the throat, sometimes burying its bill and head as it devours the offering of partially digested fish.

Pelicans display great adaptability in nesting. Certain species nest on the bare ground, on ledges and even in trees. The nest may be a mound of pebbles and sand several inches high and about a foot and a half across with a slightly saucered top, or it may be a structure of sticks in a tree. From two to four eggs are laid, depending on the species. These are fairly shiny and pale bluish when laid but quickly become encased in whitish lime (see Gannets). Incubation is performed by both sexes and requires up to six weeks, after which the young remain another five weeks on the nest and in its vicinity. Tree nesters remain in the nest, but ground-bred chicks leave it about a week or more before they are truly fledged and then wander in groups with other young. These squads or crèches are very aggressive, and when the adults return with food they are sometimes mobbed by the youngsters. However, the adult refuses to feed any but its own young and sometimes does so with considerable belligerence.

Perhaps unique in the white pelicans is the seasonal "horn" on the upper side of the bill. In many species this horn begins to grow on both sexes as soon as the pairs form in the spring and reaches its full development about the time the young hatch. Then it may be three inches wide and about as tall, and is roughly similar in shape to the centerboard of an inverted sailboat. As the breeding season wanes the horn weathers and becomes jagged, and before the nesting grounds are deserted it falls off like a discarded antler. Bushels of these have been found in large nesting areas.

During the breeding season, the coloration of the naked areas of the legs and face of many species changes in a most spectacular way from grayish buff to flame oranges and reds. This change may be correlated with the beautiful fugitive pink tint that invades the white plumage during the breeding season. The color is produced by a bright orange-red secretion of the oil gland, distributed through the plumage by the bird as it preens. That extracted artificially from the Eurasian and African White Pelican (*Pelecanus onocrotalus*) has been used experimentally to obtain exactly the same pinkish tint in white fowl feathers.

Gannets and Boobies (*Sulidae*)

Nine species of gannets and boobies occur in the tropical and temperate seas of the world. All resemble each other in both habit and structure, but vary in size from about that of a duck to that of a small goose. Their bills are long, pointed and roughly conical, not hooked as in their relatives, the cormorants and pelicans. In adult boobies and gannets the nostril is hidden. Beneath the bill is a small gular pouch, which is partly naked, as is part of the face. The body is streamlined and ends in a wedge-shaped tail.

In flight, the legs, which are short and sturdy, and the four toes, which are long and are joined to-

Eurasian and **African Pelican** (*Pelecanus onocrotalus*)

gether with large webs, are extended backward and concealed beneath the under-tail coverts. The bill, head, neck, body and tail form a straight projectile-like shape, and the long wings are extended laterally like those of an airplane. The birds propel themselves by alternate flapping and long glides. Gannets wheel and dip into wave troughs with an exhilarating abandon that often seems to carry them close to destruction against cliffs or breaking waves. Frequently they fly in lines like pelicans, and they live in tight-knit groups both at sea and on the breeding grounds.

Flocks are often seen in the neighborhood of oceanic islands or headlands, and usually indicate the presence of schools of fish. To obtain this quarry they perform twisting dives of great velocity, sometimes folding their wings as much as 100 feet over the sea and screaming down with the partly closed wings trailing back at the moment of impact. These plunges carry them far below the surface, where they capture fish with the bill. Once underwater they swim with both the wings and the feet. Before returning to the surface they swallow the fish, which are sometimes of considerable size but which the flexible throat accommodates quite readily.

Gannets and boobies dive with such speed that it is believed that the impact stuns fish as far as six feet below the surface and sometimes sends splashes a dozen feet into the air. A feature of these birds is a system of subcutaneous air sacs that resembles a spongy cushion and protects the bird as it strikes the water.

Gannets and boobies inhabit outer coastal waters and islands and usually do not wander far out over the ocean. However, they need not visit the land except to breed, and indeed rarely do so unless driven by violent storms. They habitually sleep on the surface of the water.

As the breeding season approaches, they return to favored cliffs and islets to court in large groups, each pair fencing with the bill and assuming strange breast-to-breast postures. The nest is a shallow cavity scraped in the ground, or it may be constructed of seaweed and sometimes sticks. The Northern Gannet (*Morus bassanus;* Plate 10) usually lays one egg, which is initially pale bluish but becomes heavily stained by the development of a chalky substance soon after it is exposed to the air. In all gannets and boobies both sexes share in the incubation and rearing of the young, and often the mate of an incubating or brooding bird spends the night beside the nest. Both sexes defend the nesting territory, which extends a little more than a foot around the nest. Gannets are so gregarious in their nesting habits that their rookeries appear to be solidly sheathed with their white bodies. They cry and scream in and around their nesting cliffs and long served to warn sailing ships in foggy weather of the proximity of dangerous reefs.

The Northern Gannet, which when adult cannot be mistaken for any other bird in its breeding range, nests on many islets fringing the British Isles, the

Northern Gannet (*Morus bassanus*)

Faroes and Iceland. In the New World it breeds only in six gannetries, one of which it was the author's good fortune to discover in 1936 on Funk Island, northern Newfoundland. The largest breeding colony in the New World is that on Bonaventure Island near the mouth of the St. Lawrence River, where in 1940 an estimated 7200 pairs bred.

After an incubation of approximately six weeks, a nearly naked chick emerges from the egg. The adults feed it with partially digested, regurgitated fish, the young obtaining this by inserting the bill and sometimes the whole head into the parent's throat. Feeding continues for another six weeks and is then followed by a parentally enforced period of starvation of up to 20 days. For the first half of this period the young remains on and about the nest. Finally, driven by hunger, it glides into the sea and swims off. It is believed that it spends the last ten days swimming about and drawing energy from stored fat. At last it takes to the air, where it adopts the diving technique used by the adult gannets to obtain fish. Its dress is chiefly mottled brown, the colors it wears until after two or three years it assumes the handsome white body plumage, yellow-washed head and black primaries of the fully adult male and female. Adults reach a length of some 40 inches.

Similar patterns occur in two other species: the Cape Gannet (*M. capensis*), which breeds off the extreme southern coast of Africa, and the Australian Gannet (*M. serrator*), which breeds on islets off the coast of South Australia, Tasmania and New Zealand. The Cape Gannet, however, has the tail blackish brown, whereas the North Atlantic Gannet has the tail white. The Australian Gannet has the outer tail white and the central tail blackish.

The remaining species of this family are all tropical and are known as boobies because of the ease with which they are caught. One is the Red-footed Booby (*Sula sula*), which breeds on islands in the Caribbean and the tropical Atlantic as well as in the Indian and Pacific Oceans. In addition to red

Blue-footed Booby (*Sula nebouxii*) and young

feet this species has a blue face, and unlike other members of the family it always nests in bushes rather than on the ground. Another tropical species, the Blue-footed Booby (*S. nebouxii*), which breeds in tropical waters of the Pacific from western Mexico to Peru, is also small and is chiefly cinnamon-brown mottled with white. Finally, there is the Brown Booby (*S. leucogaster*), which breeds on tropical islands encircling the globe. Probably the most widespread and numerous species, it reaches a length of 30 inches and is distinguished by its solid brown upperparts and white underparts. The clutch in all boobies is usually two eggs, but sometimes one or three are laid.

Cormorants (*Phalacrocoracidae*)

Cormorants, or shags as they are commonly called in the Old World, are almost cosmopolitan in the lakes and littoral regions of the world. They are much maligned birds over vast reaches of their range, John Milton reflecting the attitude of many sportsmen and professional fishermen when he characterized Satan as a cormorant. Curiously, however, in the Orient this "Satan" has been taught to work for man and is highly valued.

In India, China and Japan two species of cormorants are trained by means of food rewards and whistles to capture fish for their owners. Some perform long underwater chases while attached to a leash; others hunt with only a hemp collar, which is so tight around the neck that the birds cannot swallow their prey but must return with it to their owners.

Although cormorants hunt in fresh water, they do most of their fishing in salt water and rarely beyond sight of land. Much of their catch consists of "waste" fish and eels which, as fishermen well know, they are adept at stealing from fish nets. In 1952 W. H. van Dobbin reported that each bird in a colony of Common Cormorants (*Phalacrocorax carbo*) in Holland ate a little less than a pound (about 400 grams) of fish per day. He estimated that the colony required a total of 1½ million pounds of food during the breeding season, and that the eels and pike-perch in this catch represented one-tenth of the total quantity of these species caught in the same fishing grounds by commercial fishermen.

For the most part adult cormorants are black, or black and white, often with deep bronze and greenish reflections in the dark plumage. They range in length from about 1½ to 3 feet and resemble long-necked ducks. The bill, which is rather like that of a frigate bird, is sharply hooked, slender and compressed, with the nostrils almost completely obliterated in the adults. The short, strong legs are located far back on the body so that the birds appear extremely clumsy and unsure when walking; the four toes are joined by broad webs. The gular pouch, as well as part of the face, are usually quite naked, and often these areas are brightly tinted with yellows, blues and reds. The predominant eye color is green.

The 30 species of cormorants are all very similar in structure, although the stiff wedge-shaped tail and the neck vary considerably in length, the tail being relatively longer in the small-bodied species. Aside from the snakebirds, to which they are closely related, their nearest kin appear to be the gannets, boobies and pelicans.

Cormorants are highly gregarious, both in the water and on the breeding and roosting grounds. In hunting they usually fly low over the water in small groups or in large skeins and lines or even in sharp V's. Their wing movements are steady, with the head extended forward and slightly upward. When a school of fish is spotted, they land on the water and swim low, with the bill pointed forward and upward. To submerge they lunge forward with little splash and then plunge headfirst out of sight. Beneath the water they swim with both the wings and the webbed feet. Sometimes the dives are very deep, and fish are flushed to the surface, where they are more readily caught. At other times they swim with great rapidity into caves, along the bottom and along ledges, pursuing prawns as well as fish.

Unlike the gannets, cormorants cannot or do not swallow their prey underwater. However, they successfully fish in river water so muddy it is almost opaque, and this ability has led some to believe that, when sight does not avail, they employ acoustics in tracking their prey. This theory seems to be supported by the capture of a blind cormorant that appeared well fed. Like pelicans, some species of cormorants seem to hunt in packs, forming lines across rivers or partially encircling schools of fish.

Unlike many swimming and diving birds, cormorants presumably cannot remain long in water or sleep afloat because their plumage is not water-repellent and soon becomes sodden. Even after short submersions they must therefore dry their plumage, and often sit in the sun with wings outspread.

Cormorants, like pelicans, display a wide tolerance for nesting sites and nest in colonies with other water birds. The majority build on the tops of flattish sea-washed rocks or on ledges, but when the occasion demands they build nests of sticks in bushes and even trees. The terrestrial nests are usually placed very close together and are, in the main, constructed of seaweed and guano. Nesting colonies may include from a dozen nests to tens of thousands.

Large breeding colonies located in arid areas are economically important to man. For example, the Peruvian or Guanay Cormorant (*Phalacrocorax bougainvillii*), which ranges along the western coast of Central and South America to Chile and nests on islands in the Humboldt Current south of the equator, has been called the most valuable wild bird in the world. Dr. Robert Cushman Murphy, the ranking authority on oceanic birds, reached this conclusion after a study of the immense tonnage of valuable guano which for almost a century the Peruvian government has been harvesting for use as fertilizer. The Guanay Cormorant is chiefly dark greenish black above and white below, and has a naked red face and a green eye ring.

Another guano-producing species, found off the southern coasts of Africa, is the Cape Cormorant (*P. capensis*), a smaller, entirely black bird with a yellow gular pouch. Since 1927 commercial companies in South Africa have constructed and maintained special breeding platforms to increase the size of the colonies and the yield in guano.

Cormorants are relatively silent birds except during the mating season, when they utter harsh cries and croaking noises. In some species the male gathers the nesting material and the female forms the nest. Both parents share the duties of incubation, brooding and feeding the young. At daily intervals, from two to four (and sometimes up to seven) long oval eggs are laid; these are at first pale bluish or greenish but soon acquire a covering of lime. Incubation takes about 25 days, brooding somewhat less than 3 weeks, and the young are fed with fish food for a total of about 5½ weeks. The newborn chicks are fed by food inserted into their mouths. Later, the nestlings feed by plunging their bills into the parents' gullets.

When hatched the chicks are naked, but they are soon covered with a dark mat of down. The immature plumage is generally brownish, and in some species the adult garb is not completely acquired until the fourth year. In adult cormorants the sexes are always dressed alike. At the onset of the breeding season both the male and the female acquire nuptial plumage. Varying with the species, this consists of elongated crests and even double crests growing from the forehead and crown, of tufts and fanlike horns and elongated ornamental plumage interspersed among the feathers of the neck and the sides. Before the young are fledged the adults begin to lose this nuptial plumage.

In New Guinea the Sepik River head-hunters believe that the Common Cormorant is the harbinger of ill omen. One reason for this is that on foggy evenings great flocks going to roost not infrequently become lost and for some unknown reason are attracted to firelight; at such times they are apt to become confused and, as the author himself has reason to recall, they "home" on campfires and lanterns, flying through doorways, crashing into the flames and scattering burning embers through the thatched houses.

Fourteen species of cormorants are large, with black plumage above and below. These occur in both the Northern and the Southern Hemispheres. About 11 species of large, medium and small cormorants are black above but white below. These occur only in the Southern Hemisphere.

Included in the first group is the Common Cormorant (*P. carbo*), which has the most extensive range and is the largest cormorant known, reaching a total length of 40 inches. This is the species used for fishing in India and China. It is essentially glossy, greenish black and is distinguished by its white flanks and large size. It breeds at many points around the globe between the latitudes of Norway and New Zealand, except for the more remote Pacific islands, the only large area of the world, exclusive of Antarctica, not visited by cormorants. Very similar to it in appearance, the Japanese Cormorant (*P. capillatus*) breeds in northeastern Asia, Japan and Korea, and is also used for fishing. A smaller Old World species is the Shag (*Phalacrocorax aristotelis*; Plate 11) of Europe and North Africa. The unique Flightless Cormorant (*Nannopterum harrisi*) is found in the Galapagos Islands. Its wings are scarcely larger than those of a small penguin and it walks on land with an upright, penguin-like waddle.

In North America the most widely distributed species is the Double-crested Cormorant (*P. auritus*), which often breeds in large colonies scattered from Alaska through Canada to the islands of the North Atlantic as far south as the Bahamas and Central America. During the breeding season this orange-and-yellow-faced black bird sports ragged tufts of curly black and white feathers on either side of the crown. Its habitat includes rivers and lakes far in the interior as well as oceanic littoral.

Typical of the smaller white-breasted cormorants

Spotted Cormorant (*Phalacrocorax punctatus*)

is the Blue-eyed Cormorant (*P. atriceps*), which has the naked areas of the face bright blue. This species breeds in the subantarctic region and on islands off southern South America.

Many other white-breasted cormorants occur in the Southern Hemisphere. Among them is the Pied Cormorant (*P. varius*) of Australia, Tasmania and New Zealand, which is the commonest species of that portion of the world. Another, the smallest of the family, is the Little Pied Cormorant (*Haliëtor melanoleucus*), which ranges from Malaysia to New Guinea, Australia, New Zealand and other islands. And finally there is the Spotted Cormorant (*Phalacrocorax punctatus*) of New Zealand coasts, which is shown in the accompanying photograph.

Snakebirds or Anhingas

(*Anhingidae*)

Reaching nearly a yard in length, snakebirds derive their name from their necks, which comprise one-third of their total body length. They resemble cormorants but seem more slender because of their long necks and tails. They often swim with the bill, head and serpentine neck completely or slightly above water level and with the remainder of the body sub-

merged. Like grebes, they can shift internally stored air to change their buoyancy. Thus one minute they may float high, and the next sink with hardly a ripple. This mechanism is useful in stalking prey and in escaping from danger.

Underwater, snakebirds hunt like skin divers armed with spears. The straight bill is needle-sharp and slightly upcurved, and is attached to a head so small and slender that it looks hardly larger than the neck. The latter is abruptly crooked in the middle. By a peculiar arrangement, the cervical vertebrae form a Z-shaped kink with the foreneck, head and bill. Together these parts become a "triggered spear," to quote Dr. Alexander Wetmore, when the kink springs open. Fish taken from the stomachs of snakebirds almost invariably are found to be punctured as though shot with a miniature speargun.

After impaling their quarry underwater, snakebirds swim to the surface and free the bill with violent retracting motions of the head, and then with the serrated bill recover and swallow their prey. A curious feature of the stomach is an intestinal lobe that is lined with hairlike filaments and probably plays a part in separating out the sharp bones of fish. Although fish comprise most of their food, Madagascar snakebirds sometimes devour many water lily seeds.

The homes of snakebirds are usually in swamps, ponds, lakes and rivers with bushy and wooded edges and much floating vegetation. They are rarely if ever found in brackish or salt water. In the tropics snakebirds sometimes occur as high as 3500 feet above the sea, where they live at temperatures about equal to the warm temperate regions in which they are generally found.

Although very similar in size, structure and habits, the various populations of snakebirds differ greatly in coloration. Many authorities recognize four distinct species, while others believe the color variation represents well-marked races of a single world-wide species. For the sake of convenience, the four species are recognized in the present volume. One, the Anhinga (*Anhinga anhinga*), occurs in the Americas from the southern borders of the United States to Argentina. Another, the African Darter or Snake-necked Bird (*A. rufa*), is widely distributed in Mesopotamia, Africa and Madagascar. The Indian Darter (*A. melanogaster*) occurs in the Indo-Malayan region. The Australian Darter (*A. novaehollandiae*), inhabits New Guinea and Australia.

Snakebirds have long tails composed of twelve broad, stiff plumes. The central pair of tail feathers and the tertial wing feathers are uniquely rippled or corrugated. The plumage is peculiarly specialized in that the contour feathers of the body are small, coarse and rather evenly distributed over a layer of down, somewhat in the manner of penguins. The feathers of the back and scapulars are long and lance-shaped, and each has a central stripe of silvery gray. Otherwise the plumage is generally dark with a metallic luster. Unlike the cormorants, the male and female

Indian Darter or **Snakebird** (*Anhinga melanogaster*)

snakebirds differ in their plumage: usually the female is paler below, and in the Australian Darter the male is almost solid black and the female has white underparts.

The plumage absorbs water and must be dried in much the same manner employed by cormorants. All are relatively unwary and generally permit boats to approach closely. They are usually encountered singly or in pairs, sitting on floating logs or in trees and bushes growing in water. If approached too closely, those perched in trees usually fly off rapidly, like cormorants. Their flight is ordinarily direct, but they often soar like vultures, when their long necks, wings and tails give them a uniquely cross-shaped silhouette. Those perched low to the water usually dart beneath, and so derive the name of "darters."

Underwater, snakebirds swim with the wings slightly expanded and with the head moving forward in lightning jerks. The head freezes after each thrust, and the neck and body coil under it. It is characteristic of birds in general thus to freeze the head in relation to the ground when walking, but curiously enough, none does this while flying.

As in cormorants, pelicans, gannets and boobies, all four toes of the snakebird are webbed together with broad membranes. The rear toe is turned inward and joined to the inner front toe (that is, the second digit), whereas in all other web-footed birds

Indian Darter or **Snakebird** (*Anhinga melanogaster*)

(except those just mentioned) only the three front toes are joined.

The nesting of the four species follows a common pattern. They build shallow, cupped nests of sticks in forks of trees and bushes, usually growing in water. The nests, which are often lined with green leaves, may be placed from three to 20 feet above the ground, or even higher. Three to five eggs, resembling the eggs of cormorants but more pointed, are laid at irregular intervals so that the clutch may be laid over a period of four to ten days. Though the eggs are pale blue when laid, they soon become coated with chalk and soiled.

Frigate-birds *(Fregatidae)*

Frigate-, or Man-o'-War, birds are peerless marauders of the tropical oceans. Long ago John James Audubon compared their aerial prowess with that of the hunting falcon and concluded that the Frigate-bird "is possessed of a power of flight which I consider superior to that of perhaps any other bird." With its seven-foot wing spread, this bird can soar effortlessly for hours on end. It generally stays out over the ocean, usually within sight of land, wheeling high one minute, furling the wings and gliding steeply the next, or diving to within inches of the waves to snatch objects from the water's surface and then lightly swinging up and away, the wings set like those of a sailplane.

This flight, which is more rapid than that of any other sea bird, is employed to harass and steal food from many other birds, including boobies, pelicans, cormorants, terns and gulls—and it is for these parasitic activities that the Man-o'-War or Frigate-bird has been named. These robbers frequently follow flocks of terns or gulls in order to obtain a continuing supply of food. Often several of them will gang up on any victim spied carrying a fish. Once they have badgered the bird into dropping its prey, the Men-o'-War dive down and overtake it in the air. They may then flip the fish in flight in order to catch it headfirst for swallowing. In chasing the swift and obstinate booby, they sometimes slash at its tail with their long, hooked bills. In addition to what they pilfer in the air, Frigate-birds obtain many kinds of food on the surface of the sea, including jellyfish, mollusks, fishes, surface-swimming crustaceans and carrion. Normally the bill, which is rather like that of the cormorant, is dipped into the sea in full flight to snatch up the food. At times, however, the Man-o'-War hunts by hovering just above the water.

Although it has such complete mastery of flight, the Man-o'-War is land-bound. It is a remarkable fact that its tremendous wings are so sail-like, its body so small and its legs so short and fragile that, once down on water, it can never gain the air again by itself and will die. The Frigate-bird lands only on rock promontories, snags and treetops—places from which it can lunge into the air. Evidence that it is a descendant of birds that once swam strongly is the vestigial webbing that links its four toes.

Despite its unique structural modifications, which include legs feathered almost to the toes and an exceptionally light skeleton, the Frigate-bird shares some anatomical characters with the primitive Tubinares and many with the pelicans, cormorants, anhingas and gannets, and thus is clearly an offshoot of these primitive birds. The gular pouch is one of these. In the Man-o'-War, during the courtship season, a relatively huge ornament formed of gular skin, inflated, red and balloon-like, develops under the chin on the front of the neck (Plate 14). Another unique character is the long, scissor-shaped tail, normally folded to resemble a sharp sword but often opened like giant shears. A character shared with tropic-birds and cormorants is a comblike process that grows on the inner edge of the middle toe. Unlike its relatives, the male is much smaller than its mate.

Frigate-birds are quite gregarious, roosting and nesting together in colonies, usually in company with other water birds. They are silent except on the breeding grounds, where they grunt and make a clatter with their bills. Favored nesting areas are in the tops of bushes, mangroves and small trees growing on uninhabited oceanic islands, but nests are sometimes placed on rock tops. Usually close together, they are formed of sticks arranged in fragile platforms; during the construction of these there is much pilfering of nest material. A single chalky white oval egg is laid. Incubation requires about 41 days, and although both parents share in the duties of incubating, brooding and feeding the young, the male seems to shoulder the bulk of the work. If approached by a man during this period, the birds sit tight and bite at his hands. Young Frigate-birds are hatched naked but later become covered with white down. They call for food by clattering and during this period must be guarded constantly against other members of the colony lest they be carried away and eaten. The young acquire adult plumage at about two years of age.

All Frigate-birds are predominantly blackish above with varying amounts of white below. The females are lighter in color than their mates. The male Great Frigate-bird (*Fregata minor*), which reaches 40 inches in length, is mostly black with a greenish hue. This species is found in the Indian, Pacific and Atlantic Oceans. It is distinguished from the Magnificent Frigate-bird (*F. magnificens;* Plate 13) of both tropical coasts of the New World by its prominent brown wing band. The Magnificent, a solid black bird, is reported to fly from the Atlantic to the Pacific across the Isthmus at Panama and, on occasion, to visit Bermuda, Florida and Southern California. In another Atlantic species, the Ascension Frigate-bird (*F. aquila*), which breeds only on Ascension Island, both sexes are black. Although breeding in the Atlantic, Pacific and Indian Oceans, the Lesser Frigate-bird (*F. ariel*) is common only in Australian waters. In the fifth species, the Christmas Island Frigatebird (*F. andrewsi*), which breeds only on a few islands in the Indian Ocean, both sexes are white below.

CICONIIFORMES

Herons and Bitterns (*Ardeidae*)

In 1956 Walter J. Bock of the Biological Laboratories at Harvard University published an important revision of this very old, nearly cosmopolitan assortment of water birds. He recognized 64 species in 15 genera in place of the 70 species in 32 genera formerly admitted. Bock noted that only one new species had been discovered in the last half-century, and concluded that none remained undiscovered. He noted also that very little was known about the breeding biology of the Ardeidae.

Herons, egrets and bitterns are wading birds that depend chiefly on fish, aquatic animals and insects for food. Structurally speaking, all of them are very similar. All have very long legs and a long neck kinked in the middle so as to form a tight S when retracted, as in flight. Another function of the highly versatile neck vertebrae is to enable the slender, sharp bill to act as a hunting instrument—a kind of spear. When prey is spotted, the bill is quickly projected forward, often spearing the victim but sometimes pinching with the mandibles. Most species have naked areas in the region of the eyes and generally soft plumage. Powder downs on the sides of the chest and rump and a comblike serration on the inner side of the middle claw are other characteristics of all herons and bitterns. Powder downs are small feathers that grow continuously and crumble into a kind of talc, which is used in preening the feathers. The bill serves as a tool to crumble the powder downs, the dust then being rubbed on the plumage in areas soiled by the slime of fish. It is then permitted to soak up the oil, and at length the pectinated claw is used to comb out the oil-soaked powder.

Powder downs are relatively rare in birds. In herons they vary from two to four pairs and serve as the major feature distinguishing the various groups. During the breeding season, both sexes generally have specialized ornamental plumage on some part of the body. These nuptial plumes were long hunted for human adornment, and it was only a few years ago that the taking of aigrette plumes was largely halted. In the taking of the plumes, the breeding birds were stripped of their hides and left to perish together with their young.

Herons are gregarious and resort to group nesting, usually three, four or more species breeding in the same rookery. A colony on San Sebastian Island, Spain, where birds have lately been rigorously protected, in 1953 contained 2250 nests of Cattle Herons or Cattle Egrets (*Ardeola ibis*), 2060 of Snowy Egrets (*Egretta garzetta*), 550 of Black-crowned Night Herons (*Nycticorax nycticorax*), and a few of the Squacco Heron (*A. ralloides*) and the Gray Heron (*A. cinerea*). These birds generally converge on this island to court and breed in the safety of a massive rookery. They come from wintering homes perhaps thousands of miles apart; for example, some Cattle Egrets (Plate 15) come from Saint Helena and the Canary Islands, both far out in the Atlantic, others from winter quarters in South Africa.

One of the notable ornithological events of recent history was the crossing of the South Atlantic by the Cattle Herons. These emigrants which arrived shortly before the turn of the century have increased so rapidly that their New World range today extends deep into South America and north to Canada. In reaching the New World (their probable point of arrival was British Guiana), these birds followed a pattern of dispersal that had earlier enabled them to reach Australia, New Guinea and many of the larger islands of the Australian region.

The Ardeidae are split into three subfamilies, the most primitive of which consists of the bitterns, a group of 12 species that differ from the herons in having the legs generally shorter and the body usually shorter and stockier. Most bitterns are inhabitants of marshes of the cattail type, where concealment is possible, whereas herons usually keep to the more open edges of streams and swamps. This has led to another important distinction between herons and bitterns, namely the tendency of the former to take flight when alarmed and of the latter to use their cryptic plumage and poses to duplicate the color and shape of swamp vegetation. So adept are bitterns at this that they can seem to disappear before one's very eyes by stretching the head and neck straight up like a stalk of marsh grass.

A superb account of this camouflage by a slightly wounded Variegated or Streaked Bittern (*Ixobrychus involucris*) is given by the famous W. H. Hudson. The bittern, which stood on a rush no more than eight inches from his knees, faced him with its body extended vertically and its head and bill held straight up like a reed. The underparts resembled faded rushes, and as Hudson moved around, the bittern turned so that the thin leading edge of its body always faced him. Other observers have noted that a bittern among wind-blown rushes will simulate the motion of the rushes. These remarkable displays are known to last as much as fifteen minutes. Other distinctions include the fact that bitterns tend to nest alone in grassy marshes, have only two pairs of powder-down patches and have ten soft tail feathers.

The large bitterns, of which there are four nearly similar species, are generally streaked and reed-brown in color. They occur throughout the world, even in New Zealand. The most famous are the Old World

Bittern (*Botaurus stellaris;* Plate 19) and the American Bittern (*B. lentiginosus*). All have the voice box specially modified in the breeding season. One of the most unmusical of avian love songs issues from the partially inflated gullet and voice box of the American Bittern. Drifting out from sloughs and bogs in spring, it is a mysterious, resonant, pumping noise that has been compared to the sound of stake-driving and bog-pumping. These notes are accompanied by strange contortions of the body, including the displaying of tufts of white scapular feathers uncovered on the back near the base of the wings.

The American Bittern stands about 28 inches high. It breeds in North America and winters south to Panama. Its nest is a platform of bent-over grasses placed on the ground in dense reeds, and from three to five pale greenish eggs are laid in it. The incubation period is 25 to 26 days, with both parents incubating. The nestlings are fed on regurgitated liquids for the first few days and then on partially digested food.

Some of the large species such as the Brown Bittern of Australia (*B. poiciloptilus*), and perhaps all species, have their own very small feeding territories in dense reed beds, where they spend much of their time waiting for frog and insect prey.

The small bitterns, of which the Least Bittern (*Ixobrychus exilis*) of temperate and tropical America south to Brazil is fairly typical, are extremely secretive inhabitants of the floor and low reeds of grassy swamps. They are rarely seen, and even their soft hollow calls usually go unnoticed. There are eight species in three general color patterns. In this group are found the only members of the family in which the females are differently colored from the males; generally they are lighter and more boldly streaked. Different color phases, some blackish, some reddish, also are found in these species. One, the black or melanistic phase of the Least Bittern, was long known as Cory's Least Bittern.

Although little bitterns sometimes nest in low trees and bushes, like some of the herons, the nest is usually terrestrial. The structure is built of grass, loosely canopied, and is held in place by reeds. From three to six eggs of a greenish or bluish white are laid.

The second subfamily of the Ardeidae contains the true herons. Bock has divided these into three tribes: the Tiger Herons, the Night Herons and the typical or day herons. The most primitive species, the Tiger Herons (formerly called Tiger Bitterns), have three or more pairs of powder downs and are generally dark brownish with streaked or barred plumage rather like that of the large bitterns. These birds are found in many parts of the world and presumably represent a group that once was widely dispersed but is now disappearing. Like the large bitterns, they have a deep booming voice, are chiefly solitary, protectively colored, and resort to cryptic camouflage when in danger. In this group is found the Banded Tiger Heron (*Tigrisoma lineatum*), which occurs widely through tropical America.

Next above it on the evolutionary scale come the night-feeding Night Herons, consisting of nine species, all of which have well-developed head plumes. Stocky of body, with relatively short legs and a broadened bill, these birds occur throughout the world and may be either solitary or gregarious. The call is also variable, ranging from booming to harsh and even to high-pitched notes. A primitive example of the group is the Japanese Heron (*Gorsachius goisagi*), one of four related species that have the crest only slightly elongated and are always solitary.

More advanced are the better-known Night Herons of the genus *Nycticorax,* of which there are five species ranging widely over the world. They are handsome, generally black-headed birds, with long, usually whitish, lanceolate nuptial plumes springing jauntily from the crown. The plumes range in number from three to about fifteen. A good example of this group is the Black-crowned Night Heron (*N. nycticorax;* Plate 18), which is virtually world-wide in distribution, being absent only in Australia and the

Old World Bittern (*Botaurus stellaris*)

Least Bittern (*Ixobrychus exilis*) young mimicking reeds

MASLOWSKI AND GOODPASTER

adjacent Pacific. It is some 28 inches long with crest plumes like slender wires reaching to the lower back, but usually carried drooped over one or both shoulders. This heron is a tree nester, but in prairie regions it builds in low bushes. The nests are made of sticks usually placed over or near water and are generally found in large groups. From two to five pale bluish green eggs are laid. By day Night Herons roost in groups, usually in forested areas near water, but they have been seen to roost beside highways and to wander en masse over surburban lawns. Wild colonies frequently take up residence on the grounds of zoological parks, sharing the food of penned relatives.

The third and most highly evolved tribe of the heron subfamily contains the typical or day herons. Well over half of the Ardeidae (36 of the 63 recognized species) belong in this category, which is typified by the Pond and Cattle Herons (*Ardeola*), the Green Herons (*Butorides*), the Small Blue Herons (*Hydranassa*), the Reef, Snowy and Little Egrets (*Egretta*), the Purple, Great Blue, Goliath and Imperial Herons (*Ardea*), and the aberrant Chestnut-bellied Heron (*Agamia*).

These are medium-sized to large herons with slim bodies, long, slender bills, and ornamental plumage generally highly developed. Included are the largest of the herons, the most colorful and the most highly ornamented. Most of the species are highly gregarious, feeding and nesting together.

The Squacco Heron and Cattle Egret (Plate 15) represent the most primitive birds of this tribe. They are stocky, short-legged herons with light-colored bodies. All acquire dark breeding plumage on the head, chest and particularly on the back, and all are solitary hunters except the Cattle Egret, which has struck up a profitable association with grazing animals, both wild and domesticated. As mentioned earlier, this heron is moving into new areas all over the world; wherever it goes, it immediately joins grazing animals, feeding mostly on the ground on insects disturbed by the stamping and grass-tearing of the animals. It even rides on the backs of water buffalo and cattle, feeding on insects that presumably disturb the beasts, so that the association is one of mutual benefit. This presumption is reinforced by the fact that African herdsmen do not kill this heron but encourage it to feed with cattle.

The Green Herons (three species) are missing only from Europe and the colder parts of Asia. Two of the three species enjoy broad geographical ranges. The third, the Galapagos Green Heron (*Butorides sundevalli*), is restricted to the Galapagos Islands. This bird seems black in contrast to the predominantly green variegated upperparts and striped underparts of the other green herons.

A good example of this group is the Little Green Heron (*Butorides virescens*) of tropical and temperate North America, which breeds as far north as Nova Scotia and Manitoba and winters south to northern South America. Although the second smallest North American heron (it stands 12 inches high), this is probably the best-known American species of the family. Its purplish black crown, greenish back and deep chestnut neck and chest, as well as its squawking alarm call, are easily distinguished. The call is uttered whenever the bird, which is usually solitary, is startled along the edge of a woodland lake or stream, which is its typical habitat.

Next in order of evolutionary development are the five herons of the genus *Hydranassa*, formerly *Florida* (Plate 21), a group which includes the Louisiana Heron (*H. tricolor*) and the Little Blue Heron (*H. caerulea*), both inhabiting the warmer parts of America. These regions, along with the warmer parts of Africa and the Australian region, complete the range of the group. All are variable, colorful birds, and range from small to medium in size.

Essentially of the tropical to subtemperate region, the Little Blue Heron reaches a length of 22 inches and is slaty blue with a vivid maroon neck and head. In 1955, M. B. Meanley, an American ornithologist, reporting the results of his study of this bird in Arkansas, found that courtship occurs only at and near the nest, and actual pairing only at the nest. This structure, a loose platform, is built of sticks gathered by the male and installed by the female. The average clutch is slightly over four eggs, and incubation lasts 23 to 24 days. Both parents incubate and care for the young, but nevertheless the birds are extraordinarily promiscuous, the females associating more frequently with strange males than with their own mates. This is a peculiar characteristic in a colonial-nesting bird, and with four or more species nesting in a rookery, it may have led to the development of the highly elaborate, ornamental plumage worn like an identifying uniform during the breeding season.

Nearly cosmopolitan in warmer parts of the world is a large white heron known as the Common Egret (*Casmerodius albus;* Plates 17 and 20), which is one of the most graceful of all herons.

Banded Tiger Heron (*Tigrisoma lineatum*)

HARALD SCHULTZ

The most famous herons are the aigrette-wearers. These medium-sized birds are world-wide in distribution and, in season, gorgeously plumed; they include, among others, the Little Egret (*Egretta garzetta;* Plate 15), the Snowy Egret (*E. thula*), the African Reef Heron (*E. gularis*) and the Madagascar Egret (*E. dimorpha*). Typical of the group is the Snowy

Reddish Egret (*Dichromanassa rubescens*) of North America

LEWIS W. WALKER: NATIONAL AUDUBON

Egret of the warmer parts of America. This egret is white with black legs and yellow feet and stands about 18 inches high. During the breeding season, when it acquires about fifty upswept filamentous, white, lacelike plumes on the back between the wings and a long lacelike crown, it becomes one of the most beautiful of birds. To obtain these feathers this bird was nearly wiped out in North America. And the "curse of beauty," as Dr. Frank M. Chapman called it, still leads men to hunt it to satisfy women's demands for adornment. For example, recent reports indicate that aigrette-collecting continues in Argentina, and the International Committee for Bird Preservation recently reported a revival of egret-hunting in Venezuela. At the height of the demand, the slaughter was almost unbelievable. For example, in Venezuela alone consular records show that in 1898 the plumes of 1,538,000 "white herons" were shipped out of the country. There can be little doubt that in North America the doom of the White Egret would have been sealed if conservationists had not stopped the slaughter a quarter of a century ago.

The Great Blue Heron (*Ardea herodias;* Plate 16) breeds from the edge of the American Arctic and winters south to northern South America. This stately bird, often wrongly called "blue crane," is mainly bluish and grayish. It reaches a length of more than 50 inches and is one of twelve herons of similar type and medium to very large size that range around the world in the temperate and tropical regions. These birds are colonial nesters. They hunt both by day and by night, stalking game with great

Squacco Heron (*Ardeola ralloides*) displaying

patience in shallow waters. Frogs and fish are taken regularly, as well as insects and sometimes even mice. The voice of the large blue herons is generally an unattractive rasping croak. Considered to be near the top of the heron evolutionary tree, this group includes the largest of all species, the Goliath Heron (*A. goliath*) of Africa, and the Gray Heron (*A. cinerea*), which is very similar to the Great Blue of North America.

Placed in a group by itself is a heron whose relationships are a mystery, the Chestnut-bellied Heron (*Agamia agami*) of tropical America. This species has legs disproportionately short, a neck disproportionately long, an extremely slender bill and long, blue ornamental plumes springing from the crown. Its chief distinguishing character, however, is sickle-shaped neck feathers; these, together with its glossy green upperparts, bright chestnut underparts and creamy white throat and abdomen, render this the brightest, most colorful member of the family.

Boat-billed Heron

(*Cochleariinae*)

An aberrant heron living in tropical fresh-water mangrove swamps from Mexico to southern Brazil, the Boat-billed Heron (*Cochlearius cochlearius*) is the solitary occupant of this subfamily. This odd bird stands some 20 inches tall and in all respects save the bill resembles the Night Herons, being mostly gray above and on the flanks, with much black on

Common Egret (*Casmerodius albus*)

the head and neck and with long, ribbon-like ornamental feathers springing from the back of the head. Although its bill, shaped like an inverted boat, is extraordinarily different from that of the Night Herons, Walter J. Bock has placed this bird in the same tribe with the Night Herons because it is similar to them in structure and known behavior. Until its feeding behavior has been observed and evaluated, however, we feel that it should be assigned a subfamily of its own.

The bill of the Boat-bill is three inches long by two inches wide, much flattened and tipped with a small hook. Because of the broadness of the bill, the fleshy tissue extending between the arms of the mandible is very wide and flexible, and it, together with the skin of the gape and the skin of the upper throat, can be stretched to form a deep pouch that hangs down to the middle throat. Little is known of the eating habits of Boat-bills or how they use their strange bill. Some observers believe they eat small fish and shrimps. Others report that they feed chiefly on worms and aquatic animal life, which, it is believed, they obtain by groveling with the massive bill in the muddy edges of swamps. It is almost certain that they cannot catch fish.

As might be expected because of their very large eyes, they are chiefly nocturnal, like Night Herons, and therefore difficult to observe. By day they are relatively inactive and appear stupid and sluggish. If alarmed they fly only a short distance, always keeping close to their aquatic haunts, which are usually fringed with dense jungle vegetation. They cry harshly and emit croaking noises, and are usually found singly or in pairs. Their eggs are said to be white, but otherwise nothing is known of their breeding habits.

Hammerhead (*Scopidae*)

For many primitive peoples the Hammerhead (*Scopus umbretta*) of tropical Africa, Arabia and Madagascar is a creature of wisdom and power—a sort of avian witch with almost human capabilities. So feared is it in places that houses are abandoned if it flies over them.

This heron-like bird is also disturbing to naturalists concerned with classification. Although resembling the herons and bitterns, the Hammerhead lacks the characteristic powder-down feathers and seems structurally about intermediate between herons and storks. It is a dark brown bird with a crested head and has a large bill which is laterally compressed, and thus more bladelike than those of the herons. Its legs are strong and its toes are of medium length and, as in storks, narrowly webbed, but the middle toe has a pectinated comb as in herons.

The most striking thing about it is its nest, as the following description by Richard Lydekker indicates: "This is a huge, domelike structure of sticks, so firmly built that it will bear the weight of a man, and fre-

Boat-billed Heron (*Cochlearius cochlearius*)

quently from a yard and a half to two yards or more in diameter. Generally placed in a fork of a tree near the ground, although sometimes in a rocky cleft, the nest has a single entrance situated on its most concealed side. Internally it contains three chambers—a hall, a drawing room, and a sleeping compartment, with entrances so small that the bird can only creep in. The sleeping-chamber occupies the highest portion of the nest, in order to be safe from floods, and in it, upon a bed of water plants, are laid the white eggs, which are from three to five in number and are incubated by each parent in turn. The middle chamber serves for the young when they are too big for the inner one, while the hall is used as a 'lookout station.' "

Occasionally six or eight nests are located within a fifty-yard area, and not uncommonly two or three old nests are found near a new one in a single tree. Built by a single pair of birds, each is made up of a vast quantity of sticks and is so fortress-like that it is difficult even for a man to break into it. The birds also add curious decorations of bright objects—stones, bleached bones, buttons—to the dwelling.

Many kinds of animals are understandably attracted by these nests. Barn Owls use them, and there are a number of records of Gray Kestrels (*Falco ardosiaceus*) having taken them over. In addition, insects, particularly bees, appropriate the empty nests for hives. All in all, the nest must require vigorous defense. Actually the entrance is a

[69

form of defense since it is relatively very small. To get in, the Hammerhead flies straight at the little doorway, folds its wings at the last moment and plummets into the hole. In flight the Hammerhead carries the head and neck extended in a slight curve and the feet trailing straight back.

Hammerheads keep close to swamps and slow-moving streams, feeding on small crayfish, grasshoppers, water insects and frogs. Sluggish by day, they become active at twilight. Although often found alone, they also go about in small groups or pairs and remain mated for years, perhaps for life. At times they perform a dance that involves bowing toward each other and flapping the wings. At night they roost in trees or in the fortified sleeping chamber of the huge nest. From three to five white eggs are laid, and these are incubated by both parents for about 21 days. The young remain in the nest for seven weeks.

Whale-headed Stork

(Balaenicipitidae)

The Whale-headed Stork, Bog-bird or Shoebill (*Balaeniceps rex;* Plate 25) of the papyrus marshes of the White Nile and its affluents is one of the most grotesque of birds. It stands 40 inches high on crane-like legs and carries atop a stubby neck an enormous swollen bill shaped like an inverted wooden shoe. This maxilla is equipped with a ridge that terminates in a strong nail-like hook. In coloration the Shoebill is dull gray with a powdery bloom pervading a faint greenish sheen. Apparently intermediate between storks and herons, the Shoebill developed unique feeding habits during the course of its evolution, and for long ages, with little competition from other birds, has exploited a nearly exclusive feeding niche and grown increasingly different from its relatives—so different, at least in its modifications for feeding, that a separate family has had to be established for it. Yet, like the heron, it has powder downs. In the Shoebill these grow only on the back, and how it manages to dress the plumage without a pectinated claw on the third toe is unknown.

The Shoebill no longer occurs north of the Sudan region, but from sketches of the bird on the walls of the Tomb of Ti, it appears that some 5000 years ago this now rare bird, as well as the hippopotamus, occurred in northern Egypt. Shoebills today are in great demand because, like cranes, they make interesting, tame and hardy zoo birds.

The Shoebill breeds in tall grass, usually in a swampy area, assembling a nest mound of water plants sometimes a yard high. The eggs are blunt oval in shape and chalky white, although when first laid they have a blue tint. The nest is something like that of the stork, and equally storklike is the fact that adults as well as young make clapping noises with the bill. Shoebills are reported to roost on the ground, but they land in trees when threatened. In flight they draw the massive bill back to the chest, normally flying close to the ground, and going only short distances. They are usually found in pairs or small groups, and keep to the shallow waters of river swamps remote from man. Unless disturbed they remain on foot, standing motionless for long periods, sometimes with the abdomen touching the water and the head close to the surface, like a heron. They feed on fishes, baby crocodiles, frogs, and on occasion small turtles. Indeed, the specialized bill may be used to dig out lungfish and turtles from the mud of river bottoms. This seems confirmed by the fact that one autopsied specimen had five lungfish in its stomach.

Shoebills also engage in cooperative fishing, two or three birds striding side by side with partly opened wings, thus driving their aquatic prey to shallow water. Another source of food is floating carrion.

Storks and Jabirus

(Ciconiidae)

Seventeen species of storks and storklike birds occur widely throughout the tropical and temperate regions of the world. Those of the colder areas are migratory. They range in size from medium to very large and have robust bodies and strong, long legs. The neck is usually relatively short, and the bill straight and sharp. They have short, stubby toes, partly webbed except for the first toe, and claws that are blunt and like nails rather than talons.

The storks resemble the herons except that they do not have a comb on the middle toe or powder-down feathers, and, having no syrinx or voice box, are mute. To overcome this last shortcoming they resort to a loud clattering of the bill. In flight the neck and legs are stretched out to the maximum, and the wing-flapping is interspersed with soaring.

Storks feed chiefly on small animals caught in water and in swamps and marshes, including frogs, eels, lizards, rodents, birds and insects. Some species, however, live on carrion. They are completely diurnal in their hunting and are usually found in flocks, but split into pairs during the breeding season.

The nest is a solidly constructed platform of sticks, which may be built on trees or ledges or, in one species, on top of human habitations. Both sexes help to build the nests, with the male generally gathering most of the material and the female arranging it. Storks usually lay from three to five chalky white eggs, which are soon covered with stains. These are laid at two-day intervals and are incubated by both parents for a period of 30 to 38 days.

The White Stork (*Ciconia ciconia;* Plate 23) of Europe and Asia is probably the most famous member of the family, and in Europe it is protected by common sentiment and the widely held belief that it brings good luck. This stately bird, which reaches a length of almost four feet, is also protected in Africa, where it winters south to the Cape Province. So much is it cherished that, when bad nesting years occur and few birds breed on the rooftops, the newspapers refer to stork disasters. One such year was 1949, when for unknown reasons all parts of Europe were affected. In every country, moreover, accurate counts of the breeding pairs are maintained. Thus, a recent survey showed a population in Spain of about 26,000 pairs.

The White Stork is white, with black in the wings, and has a dark red bill and pinkish red legs. As the northern spring approaches, it begins to make high, spiral flights in its wintering grounds, thus calling together large flocks, and as though at a predetermined time they start northward, often flying at great heights and in huge masses. They reach Europe and Asia by following flight lines along the coast of the Eastern Mediterranean and by crossing the sea to the Italian "boot" and in the region of Gibraltar. In late March or early April they reach their nesting sites all over Europe and much of Asia. Often the same birds return to nest on the same chimney as before, and, as an indication of the esteem in which they are held, they frequently find a special wicker-basket platform welcoming them.

Although one of a pair soon accepts a new mate if the other is late in returning, many instances of pairs breeding over a period of years are known. In one case a female that had injured a wing and remained in Europe each winter was rejoined for many years by the same male when he returned from his long migration.

Storks have a vivid language of postures. For example, when a White Stork returns to his incubating mate, he immediately throws back his massive head so that it is completely upside down, with the crown pressed to his back, clatters the bill and angles it toward his tail. The female answers by making precisely the same movements, so that at times the pair look as if their necks were broken.

The Woolly-necked or White-necked Stork (*Dissoura episcopus*) of Africa and southern Asia is about the size of the largest herons, but is heavier and has a forked tail. The sexes are alike in color, but the female is slightly smaller. This species has the neck, abdomen and under-tail coverts white, the crown and remainder of the body blackish.

The Black Stork (*Ciconia nigra*) of Eurasia is glossy blackish brown above and largely white below, with red spots on the sides of the forehead, throat, bill and legs. It breeds in Europe and Asia—and occasionally in the mountains of southern Africa, its normal wintering home—building its nest either in tall trees or on cliffs. A close relative living from southern Asia to Australia is the Black-necked Stork (*Xenorhynchus asiaticus;* Plate 22).

One of the largest and most colorful species is the Saddle-billed Stork (*Ephippiorhynchus senegalensis*) of tropical Africa, which reaches a length of 52 inches. It has a white body, with some white in the wings and the lower neck; elsewhere it is dark brownish black with greenish reflections. Most of the neck and the basal half of its exceptionally long bill are black. The outer half of the bill is coral red, as are the sides of the forehead. The legs are sooty colored, splashed with scarlet on the knees and feet. This stork hunts in the shallows of large rivers and breeds in tall trees bordering such waters.

A handsome South American bird—especially common in Argentina—is the Maguari Stork (*Euxenura galeata*). It reaches a length of some 40 inches and is white but has much black in the wings and upper tail coverts, red feet and naked areas on the sides of the head. Its tail is somewhat forked. It hunts its prey in the shallows of streams and rivers, on pampas and plains and in cultivated fields, feeding on snakes, small rodents, toads and insects. As W. H. Hudson said, "To rise they give three long jumps before committing themselves to the air."

Another New World stork is the Jabiru (*Jabiru mycteria*), which ranges from Argentina to Mexico. Chiefly white, it has the head and upper half of the neck naked and blue-black, becoming bright orange and scarlet at the base of the naked area. The Jabiru is one of the largest flying birds in the New World, attaining a length of 55 inches. Its nest is usually placed in tall palm trees, and its eggs are tinted blue-green. Although usually found in pairs or families,

White Stork (*Ciconia ciconia*)

Jabirus sometimes gather in large flocks to plow for food in shallow mud with their large bills, and they often converge on grass fires to prey on animals flushed from hiding by the flames.

The largest and least attractive of all storks is the Marabou or Adjutant Stork, of which there are three species in Asia, India (Plate 24) and Africa. Despite a short, thick neck, the African Adjutant or Marabou Stork (*Leptoptilus crumeniferus*) attains a length of some 60 inches. It is generally whitish, with dark grayish back, wings and tail. Its neck is largely naked and dull pinkish to brown, as is the bill, and a naked skin-covered pouch hangs down a foot or more from the throat. This unattractive appendage is not a part of the throat, nor a secondary sexual character, but appears to belong to the respiratory system. The legs are dark gray. These birds have a military gait, which together with their pompous bearing reminded British Colonial troops of their adjutants.

The Adjutant is fairly common in tropical Africa and from Zululand northward is found in lion country far from water, its favorite food being the carcasses of animals—mostly those killed by lions and hunters. The hunters do not molest the Adjutant any more than they do the vultures with which it associates. The latter birds always defer to the Adjutant, which has the advantage of an enormous, sharp bill capable of dealing a lethal blow. At a concentration of carrion or garbage, Adjutants stride

majestically through the massed vultures, jabbing this way and that to clear a path, and then, like a lion, eat the best morsels undisturbed.

These unkempt birds nest in colonies like many other storks. In Africa they sometimes nest over native villages, but in Burma they frequently prefer rocky ledges. Being scavengers, they are widely protected, and in Asia sometimes become tame and numerous.

The Open-bills, or Shell Storks, are small storks of Asia and Africa. They get their name from the fact that the maxilla and mandible are so bowed that, when closed, a gap remains in the middle. The Indian Open-bill (*Anastomus oscitans*) is the size of a large heron and is the smallest of the Asiatic storks. It is white, with greenish black in the wings and tail, and has a dull greenish bill. This stork is common over much of southern Asia eastward to southern China and Thailand. Its oddly shaped bill is designed for feeding on fresh-water snails and mussels, but it also takes fishes and invertebrates. The Open-bill nests in colonies in bushes and trees close to or in water. The African Open-bill (*A. lamelligerus*) is said to carry mussels ashore and to deposit them in the sun, where the heat causes the mussels to open, allowing the bird easily to extract the soft flesh. The Painted Stork (*Ibis leucocephalus*), found in southern Asia, has a yellow bill and orange face.

Another member of the stork family, despite its misleading name, is the African Wood Ibis (*Ibis ibis*) of Madagascar and Africa. Like so many storks, it is chiefly white, with black in the wings and tail, bare red head, yellow bill and relatively undersized legs. It nests in trees over native villages, sometimes in company with pelicans and Adjutant Storks.

The American Wood Ibis (*Mycteria americana*), also a stork, is chiefly white with glossy black wings and tail. Its head and upper neck are featherless and scaly, suggesting the local names "flinthead" and "gourdhead." These birds sometimes hunt in packs in shallow lakes. When they come upon game they jump about, stirring up the mud, so that fishes, snakes, small alligators and invertebrates are flushed to the surface, struck with the bill and killed.

Ibises and Spoonbills
(*Threskiornithidae*)

The Sacred Ibis (*Threskiornis aethiopica*), one of these heron-like, water-loving birds, was once held in the greatest veneration by man—so much so, indeed, that in ancient Egypt no self-respecting Pharaoh would permit himself to be mummified without a Sacred Ibis by his side.

Ibises and spoonbills, of which 28 species are known, occur in most of the tropical regions of the world. They have the tail short and the forward toes partially webbed, and are divisible into two groups: the ibises, with curved, slender bills and often naked

Indian Open-billed Stork (*Anastomus oscitans*)

heads; and the spoonbills, with spatula-shaped bills.

Both groups lack the powder downs that are so typical of their relatives, the herons. Both fly with the neck extended, and both are gregarious, roosting and nesting usually in trees, although in many species, chiefly among the spoonbills, the nests are also built on the ground or on rocky ledges. The ibises are especially gregarious, often nesting together in the thousands, whereas the spoonbills are more inclined to nest alone or in small clusters scattered among colonies of herons and other water birds.

Both groups lay eggs that are light in ground color and often rather vividly marked with browns and grays. The set ranges from about three to five, and the incubation period in several genera (*Plegadis* and *Threskiornis*) has been found to be about 21 days. The flight of ibises is particularly interesting in that they indulge in group gliding; that is, they fly in measured cadence, gliding or sailing together and then flapping their wings in unison. It has been described as a gliding which begins at the front of a column and is carried back in ripples, like that of pelicans. The spoonbills, on the other hand, form skeins and wide V formations when flying en masse and do not resort to intermittent gliding.

Perhaps the most beautiful of these birds is the Scarlet Ibis (*Eudocimus ruber*) of tropical South America. This bird reaches two feet in length and is scarlet with black primaries. It is identical in size and form with the White Ibis (*E. albus*) of Mexico south to northern South America, the only difference being that one bird is white and the other scarlet.

An American ornithologist, Dr. Paul Zahl, who studied these birds on their breeding grounds in Venezuela, informed the author that, of some 10,000 ibises comprising an Orinoco River colony, about 95 per cent were scarlet and less than 5 per cent white. In the nests that he found, only one was attended by a white bird and its mate proved to be white also. This record is of much interest to ornithologists, who have long wondered whether these ibises might be color varieties of one species.

The Sacred Ibis (*Threskiornis aethiopica*) is one of three species representing a group that ranges almost throughout the Old World. It favors the wetter parts of Africa and Asia, where it feeds on frogs and other small aquatic animals. However, in South Africa it is called the Chimney Sweep because there it eats carrion and rakes or "sweeps" out the insides of dead birds, probably in quest of insect feed. It also congregates to hunt in close flocks.

The Sacred Ibis reaches a length of 2½ feet and has a rather large body and fairly short legs. The head and neck are naked and sooty black, but it is otherwise largely white with black in the wings and some buff shading. Closely related species are found in Madagascar and in the Asian and Australian regions. The Indian White Ibis (*T. melanocephalus*) reaches 30 inches in length, and has the naked head areas bluish black. As in all members of the family,

Painted Stork (*Ibis leucocephalus*)

the sexes are virtually alike. It keeps chiefly to inland waters where it breeds in colonies of a dozen birds or so.

Other characteristic ibises are the Glossy Ibises, of which there are two species ranging around the world in the tropics and, seasonally, migrating into the temperate zones. One, the Glossy Ibis (*Plegadis falcinellus*), a heron-sized blackish brown bird glossed with green and purple, lives in the warm parts of eastern North America and has recently extended its breeding range as far north as southern New Jersey; it is also widespread in the Old World Tropics. It is some two feet in length. In Africa the Hagedash Ibis (*Hagedashia hagedash*) somewhat resembles the Glossy Ibises in having the face naked and the plumage dark, but has much green in the wings and gray in the forepart of the body.

In India is found the Black Ibis (*Pseudibis papillosa*), which is sometimes called the Warty-

Wood Ibis or **Wood Stork** (*Mycteria americana*)

headed Ibis because part of the naked crown is covered with a patch of red wartlike papillae. This species, which grows to a length of 27 inches, is generally dark brown with glossy reflections and with prominent white patches above the wings. It builds its nest alone or in groups of two or three in tall trees, but also uses old nests of birds of prey. It has a screaming cry, like that of a bird of prey. These ibises often fly in wedge formations like water birds.

The four Old World species of spoonbills are largely white and very closely related, whereas the Roseate Spoonbill (*Ajaia ajaja*), the lone spoonbill occurring in the New World, is quite distinct. For one thing, it is rose-colored with carmine wing coverts, and in the adult has a bare head. Otherwise it has the neck, back and breast largely white and the feet pale pink. This splendid bird reaches 30 inches in length. In his autobiography Dr. Frank M. Chapman published an extraordinary photograph of a young Roseate Spoonbill which, although about as large as its parent, was feeding by forcing its massive spoon-shaped bill deep into the throat of the parent. This clearly follows an ancient feeding pattern.

One of the two members of this family found in Europe is the European Spoonbill (*Platalea leucorodia*), which breeds north to Denmark, is often seen in Britain and even occasionally wanders as far north as Finland. It is some 34 inches long and almost pure white. It differs from the New World

spoonbill in that it often breeds in bushy marshes, with nests raised a foot or so above the mud and usually surrounded by water. Of similar size is the African Spoonbill (*P. alba*), which is generally a group nester but often resorts to solitary habits. It also nests in marshes, making a shallow nest of aquatic plants. On the other hand, the Asiatic Spoonbill, currently believed to belong to the same species as the European Spoonbill, which also has a distinct white crest in the breeding season, nests in tall trees. This species occurs from Egypt to Japan. It is fond of dozing in groups along the edges of swamps and streams by day, after which, at dusk, it becomes very active. It hunts in the characteristic spoonbill manner by sweeping the flat bill back and forth like a scythe to filter minute crustaceans from water.

PHOENICOPTERIFORMES

Flamingos (*Phoenicopteridae*)

Flamingos are among the most beautiful and graceful of all birds. Highly gregarious, when they assemble together in a nesting area or ascend to fly in skeins or V's, they look like a bold splash of crimson across the landscape. Four species of flamingos are known, two in the high Andes of southern South America and one or more species in all of the large land areas of the world where warm weather prevails, including Madagascar, Ceylon and the Galapagos Islands, but excluding the Australian region.

Despite the long legs and neck that give the flamingo its deceptively heron-like appearance, it is an ancient offshoot of the ducks, geese and swans. Besides the anatomical evidence, indications of relationship are found in the flamingo's habit of honking on the wing and gabbling at other times, and in its highly gregarious breeding habits, and also in the fact that the freshly hatched young are perfectly at home when swimming. Furthermore their parisites resemble those of ducks rather than of herons.

Some of the flamingos reach a length of 6½ feet and stand more than 5 feet in height. All have the legs and neck tremendously elongated. In flight the neck is extended forward and the legs trail backward, and both are allowed to sag slightly. On the ground the flamingo is found chiefly in muddy water, preferably brackish or fresh water two or three inches in depth. This preference for shallow water may seem odd considering the great length of the naked legs. At times, however, the flamingo shows its ancestry by wading in water almost up to its abdomen or even swimming with the aid of its webbed feet. Two of the species have four toes and two have three. Some are richly colored with crimson and deep rose, others are white with crimson on the wing coverts or scapulars, but all have strong flashes of crimson somewhere in the plumage and all have prominent black flight feathers.

In resting or sleeping, the flamingo frequently stands on one leg with the other drawn up and pressed into the feathers of the flank. This posture looks odd in a flamingo because the bend of the long, gangling leg projects far behind the tail. As for the neck, the long, snakelike convolutions are draped over the chest and back and the head is snuggled under the scapulars of the back.

The most unusual character of this unusual bird is its bill, which bears vague resemblances to that of a goose but is actually different from that of any other bird. The flamingo's lower mandible resembles an expanded box and the upper mandible a thin, profusely laminated lid that just fits into it. Both are sharply bent just in front of the nostrils, apparently so that the bill in the inverted position may be raked backward and forward like a scoop, each sweep sieving small invertebrates and vegetable matter from the mud. As it does this, the flamingo makes a sputtering noise which, if anything, adds to the incongruous way the long neck hangs down like a kind of anchor between the stiltlike legs. In addition, the neck and partially submerged head sway to the cadence of passing waves.

It has long been known that flamingos are "filter feeders," but only recently was it found that there are two kinds of filter bills, one a shallow-keeled bill of the type found in the Common Flamingo (*Phoenicopterus ruber*), and the other a deep-keeled

BAVARIA VERLAG
Sacred Ibis (*Threskiornis aethiopica*)

Indian White Ibis (*Threskiornis melanocephalus*)

LOKE WAN THO

type, such as that of the Lesser Flamingo (*Phoeniconaias minor*). These two forms are so different that flamingos of the two types can hunt side by side without competing.

The world around, flamingos nest in very specialized and very similar ways. A flock of several hundred to many thousand gathers, and each pair builds a nest in a muddy area. The mud is scooped from the bottom and piled in a mound that is about 15 inches in diameter and may be from several inches to 1½ feet high. This mound becomes very hard and potterylike, resembling a plate on a pedestal. One or two chalky white eggs are laid on its concave top. These are incubated by both parents for from 30 to 32 days, after which the downy, precocial chicks emerge. The chicks are brooded on the nest for several days longer, and then they take to the water and swim easily, somewhat like young goslings. The young are fed with regurgitated food by the parents for yet another fortnight, after which they join in bands to wander about more or less independently. In incubating, the parent draws its legs up under its body and extends the bend of the legs—the heel—far back of the body.

The Common Flamingo (*Phoenicopterus ruber*) has the plumage white with a rosy cast except for the flight feathers, which are deep black, and the scapulars, which are scarlet (Plate 26). This bird breeds in huge numbers in the brackish marshes of southern Europe and the warmer parts of Asia. Large breeding colonies are located in the south of France and Spain. Recent banding records in the heavily protected colonies of the Camargue—some 1600 birds were marked between 1946 and 1954—revealed that the young left the rookeries very soon after the breeding season and flew westward to Corsica and then across the Mediterranean to wintering areas in Africa. More than a million flamingos were observed by Roger Tory Peterson on one African lake in 1957.

The European Flamingo is a vagrant to Britain and other countries of middle Europe and Asia, just as the American Flamingo (*P. ruber*) is a vagrant to the United States. However, in Audubon's time the brighter American Flamingo (Plate 27) with its rosy plumage was a resident of Florida. A colony of semidomesticated birds at the Hialeah race track is all that remains today, and even such famous breeding areas as Andros Island in the Bahamas are no longer visited by flamingos. These birds seem to have gone out as the airplane came in, and indeed the practice of flying low over breeding colonies to see the colorful birds rise in a rosy cloud may have played a major part in the depletion of the American Flamingo.

Today the American Flamingo ranges from the Bahamas to Southern South America and the Galapagos Islands. Farther southward are two nearly white species of flamingos whose wing coverts are scarlet red. These species, the Andean Flamingo (*Phoenicoparrus andinus*)—the largest of all—and the James' Flamingo (*P. jamesi*), both of which lack the hind toe (hallux), dwell on high Andean lakes and presumably are relict species. The Andean Flamingo, which is very uncommon, was recently "rediscovered" in Chile. That these widely distributed but very local birds of the New and Old World are ancient is indicated by the fact that fossil flamingos have turned up as far back as the Cenozoic Era.

ANSERIFORMES

Geese, Swans and Ducks
(*Anatidae*)

Since prehistoric times waterfowl and men have lived in close association, and references to such birds in literature go back more than 2500 years. The waterfowl, of which there are about 140 surviving species with representatives in virtually every part of the world, chiefly in the Northern Hemisphere, are descendants of a very old family, fossil finds indicating that they flourished in Miocene times. The major types—the geese, swans, and ducks—although superficially distinct, are much alike in structure and behavior. Most modern classifiers therefore lump them in the family Anatidae, with two subfamilies: the geese, swans and whistling ducks; and the rest of the ducks. These are grouped in seven tribes: 1) Sheldrakes, 2) River Ducks, 3) Pochards, 4) Perching Ducks, 5) Sea Ducks, 6) Stiff-tailed Ducks, and 7) Torrent Ducks. In his recent revision of *The Waterfowl of the World*, Delacour recognizes still another subfamily for the Semipalmated Goose (*Anseranas semipalmatus*) of Australia, the most primitive of waterfowl.

All waterfowl have the legs very short, much shorter than the wing; and all have the bill quite short, straight, and bordered by laminations along

European Spoonbills (*Platalea leucordia*)

European Spoonbill and young

BAVARIA VERLAG

the edges. The most aberrant bills are those of the fish-hunters, the mergansers, which have the laminations developed to toothlike edges. Most food is taken underwater by this family, the water and mud in the bill being sieved out through the laminations when the head is raised. A number of geese have the laminations modified to assist in shearing grass.

All of the Anatidae have the plumage very dense and heavily underlaid with down. In many the down is plucked for lining the nest, and in some it is used to conceal the eggs when they are left unattended. So pronounced is this habit that men have made a business of taking eider down for human use.

Waterfowl have ten primaries and a variable number of tail feathers. During the primary molts, which usually occur after the breeding season, the wing quills are simultaneously shed and, like many waterfowl, the birds become flightless for several weeks. All lay eggs which, like those of their nearest relatives, the flamingos and screamers, are uniform in coloration. Incubation requires as long as 40 days in some species. The clutch is large, usually numbering not less than 10 and sometimes as many as 20 eggs. The young are down-covered and readily swim within a day of hatching. Another general characteristic is pronounced gregariousness, the Anatidae almost always being found in flocks, sometimes of great size. So concentrated are these in some species

that it has proved possible to picture the total inhabitants of a continent in a single aerial photograph. Such, for example, was a photograph of Pacific Black Brant (*Branta nigricans*) showing 174,740 birds and another showing most of the 42,000 Greater Snow Geese still surviving.

This flocking is most pronounced during spring and fall migrations of northern-nesting species, many of these moving in tight bands from the arctic and temperate zones along well-established routes to wintering grounds in the southern temperate and subtropical zones of the Northern Hemisphere, although some winter to or beyond the equator. In the north the majority nest on marshy and rolling tundra near fresh water—sometimes more than a dozen species together—and in immense concentrated groups on islands surrounded by pack ice. In some—the Snow Geese, for example—adults and young gather in knots which, from the air, resemble flocks of grazing cattle; and, curiously, because immaturity and molting render them flightless, such flocks can be driven like sheep. A few groups nest in tree holes, but nearly all breed on the ground.

After the breeding season the geese and swans move in family clans to the wintering grounds. In both, the pair bond is very strong, possibly lasting for life—which may in swans, for example, mean nearly a century. In the majority of ducks, pairing takes place on the wintering grounds before the northward migration. The bond may last for several years or only a few days, and a few species are promiscuous, the males accepting as many females as they can attract. In almost all species the female does the incubating. The males generally assist in the care and feeding of the young.

To achieve flight, many kinds, particularly among the geese and swans, run on the water, pounding the surface with their webbed feet and often striking it with their wing tips. An example is the Mute Swan (*Cygnus olor*) of Eurasia, which has been introduced into North America and Australia. Others, such as teals and mallards, rise directly from a sitting position in a kind of helicopter take-off. Maximum normal flight speeds are 45 to 50 miles per hour, but when frightened by aircraft several species can reach 75 miles per hour. In the air various species adopt the patterns known as "V" flight, "chevron" flight, and "frontal" flight, the last resembling an irregular isothermic line. Leaders are changed in flight, and it is believed that some forms of group flying lead to more rapid speeds in proportion to the energy expended.

Several species have taken to nesting with gulls and terns, the Tufted Duck (*Aythya fuligula*), for example, nesting alongside the Black-headed Gull (*Larus ridibundus*), apparently profiting from the attacks that the gull directs at any predatory intruder. This would seem to be substantiated by the fact that when the gulls shift to a new nesting area the ducks follow. One species of duck, the Black-head (*Heteronetta atricapilla*) of South America, has developed parasitic habits, having learned to deposit its eggs in the nests of other ducks and thus avoid the problem of raising its own young. This parasitism is occasionally practiced by the Redhead (*Aythya americana*) and is well developed in four other families of completely unrelated birds.

Two of the three species of South American steamer ducks (*Tachyeres*) have become flightless and have taken to the sea much like penguins. Ducks, swans and geese are generally omnivorous, but certain species, such as the mergansers, feed almost exclusively on fish. Others eat shellfish and crustaceans gathered from as much as 180 feet beneath the sea, often swallowing them whole. Others have feeding habits rather like those of grazing animals, consuming tender plants in tundra fields and prairies far away from water. Still others feed in fresh and salt water, both on the surface and by "dabbling," with the feet and the rump up and the head and neck directed straight down underwater. Many hunt in the

Mute Swan (*Cygnus olor*), adult male

Canada Goose (*Branta canadensis*)

mud of the water's bottom for small vegetable and animal foods. One curious fact about ducks is that thousands of them perish annually from lead poisoning induced by shotgun pellets sieved from the mud bottom under waters where much shooting is done. To counter this, special underwater harrows have been devised to force the pellets downward to a safe depth in the mud. But there are other kinds of lead poisoning that are even harder to cope with: a recent X-ray and fluoroscopic analysis of large numbers of migrating waterfowl showed that nearly 50 per cent carried lead pellets in their bodies!

The Anatidae dress the plumage with oil from a gland located near the base of the tail. This oil, transferred to the feathers with the bill, serves to waterproof the body covering and is vital in other ways. It has recently been shown that surgical removal of the gland in Mallard and Redhead ducklings results in deterioration of the plumage and actually impairs growth.

The dumping of oil and sludge by tankers has resulted in massive losses of waterfowl all over the world. Often thousands of birds are attracted by the calm, oiled waters, which in effect represent a vast death-trap. Virtually all birds that land on these slicks soon have hopelessly oil-soaked feathers and are doomed to flightlessness and slow starvation. Other examples of man's intrusion are less frightful but more mysterious. One involves radar: somehow migrating ducks become confused when they encounter a radar beam—even at a distance of a mile or more from the sending station—lose all sense of direction and often give up the flight. But in another way radar has become a valuable instrument: in Canada biologists use it to force migrating ducks to land in specific banding and study areas.

In olden days waterfowl abounded in fantastic numbers; then came the era of market hunting with outsized weapons and brutally efficient traps. This and the great ecological shifts wrought by changes in terrain following the settlement of the country—the pollution of rivers and bays, the draining of swamps and the introduction of foreign predators—brought about a rapid decline of waterfowl. Today, with the establishment of breeding and wintering reserves, carefully timed hunting seasons and moderate bag

G. K. YEATES

Pink-footed Goose (*Anser brachyrhynchus*)

limits, virtually all New World species are holding their own. Thus the valuable wildfowl we know will probably not suffer the fate of the Labrador Duck (*Camptorhynchus labradorium*), the last definite record of which was a bird shot on Long Island, New York, in 1875. An example of successful recovery through conservation is the Trumpeter Swan, a large and lumbering bird that made an easy target and was seemingly destined for early extinction. At present authorities estimate that approximately 2000 survive.

Fourteen species of geese (Plate 32), five of swans (Plate 31) and eight of Whistling or Tree

Néné or **Hawaiian Goose** (*Branta sandvicensis*)

J. R. WOODWORTH: HONOLULU ZOO

Ducks are recognized as comprising the subfamily Anserinae. Among the better-known examples are the Canada Goose (*Branta canadensis*) of North America, the White-fronted Goose (*Anser albifrons*) of Eurasia and western North America, the Whooper Swan (*Olor cygnus*) of Eurasia and the Spotted Tree Duck (*Dendrocygna guttata*) of the islands of the southwest Pacific. All have the characteristically gooselike posture with the neck elongated, and the same plumage and similar display calls in both sexes; all molt feathers only once a year. One of the rarest is the Néné or Hawaiian Goose (*Branta sandvicensis*) of which less than 70 wild birds are thought to survive of an estimated 25,000 in the eighteenth century. The Pink-footed Goose (*Anser brachyrhynchus*) of Eurasia is a close relative of the Bean and Greylag Geese.

In dealing with these birds we follow the recent revision of the Anatidae by Jean Delacour and Ernst Mayr in which behavior is one of the primary guides to relationships. In nearly all the aforementioned birds the display is simple, involving the dipping of the head by both birds until the female flattens her body and partially sinks down with the neck outstretched. There are some variations: in the Australian Black Swan the sexes face each other and raise their bodies part way out of the water, and—as in the Mute Swan and some of the mergansers—the

[continued on page 97]

33. Red-tailed Hawk, young
(*Buteo jamaicensis*)
Range: North America

[RUSS KINNE: NATIONAL AUDUBON]

34. Red Kite (*Milvus milvus*)
Range: Widespread in Old World

[ERIC J. HOSKING]

35. Golden Eagle
(*Aquila chrysaëtos*)
Range: Northern Hemisphere

[WALTER E. HIGHAM]

36. Red-shouldered Hawk
(*Buteo lineatus*)
Range: North America from
southern Canada to Gulf Coast

[AUSTING AND KOEHLER: NATIONAL AUDUBON]

37. Sharp-shinned Hawk
(*Accipiter striatus*)
Range: Northwestern Alaska,
Canada and south to Panama
and West Indies

[HEINZ MENG]

38. Red-legged Partridge (*Alectoris rufa*)
Range: Western Europe, Corsica and Canary Islands

39. Capercaillie (*Tetrao urogallus*)
Range: Cold and cooler parts of Eurasia

40. Peacock (*Pavo cristatus*)
Range: Southern Asia

[H. RUHE AND T. ROTH]

41. European Quail
(*Coturnix coturnix*)
Range: Warmer areas
of Old World

[JOHN MARKHAM]

42. Sarus Crane (*Grus antigone*)

Range: Southern Asia from
India to Malaya

[CY LA TOUR AND DETROIT ZOOLOGICAL PARK]

**43. Crowned Crane
(*Balearica pavonina*)**

Range: Africa

[GATTI EXPEDITIONS]

44. Stanley Crane
(*Anthropoïdes
paradisea*)
Range: South Africa

[H. RUHE AND T. ROTH]

45. Black Crake
(*Limnocorax flavi-
rostra*)

Range: Africa
south of Sahara

[H. RUHE AND T. ROTH]

46. European Coot (*Fulica atra*)

Range: Nearly cosmopolitan in Old World

[JOHN MARKHAM]

47. Purple Gallinule
(*Porphyrula martinica*)

Range: Warmer parts of North and South America

[ELIOT PORTER]

48. Corn Crake (*Crex crex*)

Range: Eurasia

[JOHN MARKHAM]

49. Water Rail
(*Rallus aquaticus*)
Range: Old World

[JOHN MARKHAM]

50. Clapper Rail
(*Rallus longirostris*)
Range: Warmer coastal
marshes of North and
South America

[JACK DERMID]

→

53. European Oystercatcher
(*Haematopus ostralegus*)
and European Curlew
(*Numenius arquata*)
Range: Eurasia

[G. K. YEATES]

51. Banded Plover (*Zonifer tricolor*)
Range: Australia

[H. RUHE AND T. ROTH]

52. Killdeer (*Charadrius vociferus*)
Range: Canada to Mexico, West Indies and coastal Peru and Chile [ALLAN CRUICKSHANK: NATIONAL AUDUBON]

54. Ruffs displaying
(*Philomachus pugnax*)
Range: Cooler parts of Eurasia

[ARTHUR CHRISTIANSEN]

55. European Oystercatcher
(*Haematopus ostralegus*)
Range: Eurasia and
North Africa

[P. O. SWANBERG]

56. Black-tailed Godwit
(*Limosa limosa*)

Range: Cosmopolitan
in Old World

[G. K. YEATES]

57. European Woodcock
(*Scolopax rusticola*)

Range: Old World

[JOHN MARKHAM]

58. Common Snipe
(*Gallinago gallinago*)
Range: World-wide

[AUSTING AND KOEHLER]

60. Dunlins (*Erolia alpin*

59. Ibis-bill (*Ibidorhyncha struthersii*)
Range: High plateaus of Middle Asia

[LOKE WAN THO]

61. American
Avocet
(*Recurvirostra
americana*)
Range: Western
North America

[CY LA TOUR]

...ge: Cosmopolitan in Northern Hemisphere, and nests mostly in Arctic [ERIC J. HOSKING]

62. Black-winged Stilt
(*Himantopus himantopus*)

Range: Southern Eurasia
and Africa

[WALTER E. HIGHAM]

63. Black-necked Stilt
(*Himantopus himantopus*)

Range: Southern and
northern South America
and southern U.S.A.

[ALLAN CRUICKSHANK: NATIONAL
AUDUBON]

[continued from page 80]

young are ferried on the backs of the parents when they become tired and cold. In this subfamily is found one of the closest and most enduring of family associations among birds: the geese, which mate for life, migrate southward in family groups, spend the winter together and then return to the breeding grounds. Only then do the young go their own way.

There may be a kind of goose language, or at least it would seem so from the so-called "triumph ceremony" whenever a gander drives off an intruder. At such a time he invariably utters a "triumph note" and almost invariably the female repeats the note and stretches out her head and neck close to the ground. The young, including even down-covered babies, perform in the same approving way. A very similar performance occurs in both geese and swans during courtship; such a specialized "language" is taken as indicating a close relationship.

The eight species of Whistling or Tree Ducks, among the least known of ducks, comprise a tribe of their own. Their courtship displays are rather like those of some of the swans in that the pairs face each other in the water, lift the breast and raise the wings. Unlike the other members of the family, except the Black Swan, the males assist in incubation. Most of the species nest on the ground but some nest occasionally in trees. These ducks walk with ease on land. The Fulvous Tree Duck (*Dendrocygna bicolor*) of both the New and Old World tropics, which is typical of the group, is 22 inches long, mostly rust brown, and has white upper tail coverts and relatively long legs.

The various tribes of the remainder of the world's ducks, Sheldrakes, River Ducks, Pochards, Perching Ducks, Sea Ducks, Stiff-tailed Ducks and Torrent Ducks, have been placed by Delacour and Mayr in the second subfamily, the Anatinae. These wide-ranging and often very different-looking birds are linked by the fact that all have a double annual molt, a similar pattern in the scalelike scutellations of the tarsus, audible and visual displays that differ greatly between the sexes, and usually a different plumage in the male. The sheldrake tribe includes such species as the Crested Duck (*Lophonetta specularioides*) of South America, the Korean, African, Australian and Ruddy Sheldrakes, the Egyptian, Orinoco, Andean, Magellan and Kelp "Geese," and the very large gray Magellanic and Falkland Island Flightless Steamer Ducks. Many of the species resemble geese, but the patterns of the downy young, the spurlike wing knobs and the general conformation distinguish them from the true geese. Also, the smooth rather than rough eggs and the differences between the courtship displays add much weight to this division. In the Ruddy Sheldrake (*Tadorna ferruginea*) of Eurasia a different pattern occurs: the male, which seems to have no initiatory courtship performance, is solicited by a female, who incites many different males to fight and then mates with the most aggressive.

ARTHUR W. AMBLER: NATIONAL AUDUBON

Egyptian Goose (*Alopochen aegyptiacus*) of Africa and Palestine

Nearly cosmopolitan is the second tribe of the Anatinae, consisting of some 36 species of surface-feeding ducks. Most are smaller than the sheldrakes, and in about half the males are brightly dressed. In the other half the sexes are similar. In most species the wing has a bright patch or speculum.

The Mallard is typical of these high-floating, swift-flying "river ducks." Most of these live on fresh water or along the coasts in shallow water, where they feed on aquatic plants, insects and mollusks, usually securing these by dabbling in the up-ended position described earlier. These "river ducks" differ from the "bay ducks" and "sea ducks" in lacking a well-developed flap of skin on the hind toe. In all surface-feeding ducks the display is roughly similar to that of the Mallard, which begins with the male swimming around the female with its head partially sunken and its feathers puffed. There is much raising and shaking of the head and tail, followed by stretching of the neck, erratic swimming, dipping of the bill and caressing of the breast feathers, accompanied by the ejecting of water as the bill is jerked upward. As he performs, the male whistles, and the female responds by quacking and following the male with her head turned away. Finally there is much bobbing of heads and then the female flattens over the water to accept the male.

In the galaxy of species—many of them aberrant in form—that follow this pattern of courtship are such river ducks as the Bronze-winged Duck (*Anas specularis*) of South America; Salvadori's Duck (*A. waigiuensis*) of New Guinea; the Cape Teal (*A. capensis*) of Africa; the Common Pintail (*A. acuta*) of the Northern Hemisphere, a grayish 28-inch bird with sharply pointed black tail feathers; the Blue-winged Teal (*A. discors*) of North America, only 15 inches long, the speediest flyer and one of the strongest migrants (one of these, banded in Alberta, Canada, was recaptured in Venezuela 3800

[97

miles away one month later); the little, brownish Laysan Teal (*A. laysanensis*) which, like species on the Hawaiian and Mariana Islands, has largely replaced the bright male garb with the costume of the female in both sexes; and the Gadwalls, Widgeons, Shovellers, the Pink-eared Duck (*Malacorhynchus membranaceus*) of Australia, and even the rare Pink-headed Duck (*Rhodonessa caryophyllacea*). It might be added that in 1956 the Laysan Teal, which lives only on the small island of Laysan, far west of Hawaii, was studied, and it was estimated that more than 500 still survive; eight were taken to the Hawaiian Zoo "as a buffer against extinction."

Fourteen fresh-water ducks, some of which are famous in sporting circles, comprise the pochards. All have the legs far back on the body and lack metallic colors on the wing. All are good divers, and in display the males pursue the females with what is termed "mock brutality." Among this group is found the Red-crested Pochard (*Netta rufina*) of Europe and Asia; and the 20-inch Canvasback (*Aythya valisineria*) of North America. The last, the most prized "sporting" duck in America, has the back finely barred with black and white and the head and neck reddish brown.

The perching ducks, which include 13 species from many regions of the world, spend much time perching in forest trees, and most of them nest in holes well above the ground. All but two species are inhabitants of the tropics and subtropics. Some have metallic colors in the plumage and most have a spur-like knob on the bend of the wing. In many the male is much larger than the female, and there seems to be no pair formation. Among this group are found the Mandarin (*Aix galericulata*) of Asia; the North American Wood Duck (*A. sponsa; Plate 30*), a beautiful 18-inch bird with a long, green, purple and white crest; the African Spur-winged Goose (*Plectropterus gambensis*); the Brazilian Teal (*Amazonetta brasiliensis*); the Pygmy Goose (*Nettapus coromandelianus*) of the Indian, Malay and Australian regions, which is the smallest member of the family; and the aberrant, heavily wattled Muscovy Duck (*Cairina moschata*) of tropical America, which has been taken around the world as a domestic bird.

Sea ducks comprise a tribe of 21 species, among which are the eiders (Plates 28 and 29), the scoters, the golden-eyes, the Bufflehead and the mergansers. Included also are the now extinct Labrador Duck and the colorful Harlequin and Old Squaw. With few exceptions these are truly sea-loving birds that walk with difficulty on land. All are expert divers, and many species fold the wings underwater and swim solely with the feet. Excepting the scoters and eiders, most species nest in hollow trees or rock crevices and feed on mussels and fish, the eiders and scoters swallowing such food whole. With two exceptions, the Auckland Island Merganser (*M. australis*) and the Brazilian Merganser (*Mergus octosetaceus*), most species live in the cold parts of the temperate zones.

Pink-eared Duck (*Malacorhynchus membranaceus*)

The former is probably extinct and the latter was thought to be extremely rare until its recent rediscovery in the province of Misiones, Argentina. Señor William H. Partridge, who found the nest of this great rarity, published observations in 1956 indicating that the bird probably lives all its life in one small area of a stream. Its food consists chiefly of fish secured in shallow dives but also of insects and snails. The nest Partridge found was 75 feet over the water and about 9 feet inside a hollow limb in a tree growing at the edge of a stream. The female incubated and brooded while the male remained on the river. Four black and white downy young managed to get to the water from the high nest, but it is not known if they jumped or were carried out. Earlier Partridge had found that the female left the nest once each day to feed. He also noted that the courtship ceremony consisted of noisy chasing and circling, and that the downy young were very agile, being able to run on the water when pursued, but never diving as one would expect of mergansers. The Goosander of the Northern Hemisphere, shown at its nest hole in the photograph, is known in the New World as the American Merganser (*Mergus merganser*).

Stiff-tailed Ducks form a tribe very different from the others. They have the legs so far back that walking is very difficult, and they lay relatively the largest of duck eggs in elaborate nests. The male assists in caring for the young, which often number eight. They are expert divers. Some strange species are placed in this group, as, for example, the Black-headed Duck of South America (*Heteronetta atricapilla*); the Australian Musk Duck (*Biziura lobata*), which has a decided odor, apparently a mechanism of defense; and the 15-inch North American Ruddy Duck (*Oxyura jamaicensis*), which is characterized by long, stiff tail feathers that it usually holds up at a jaunty angle while swimming.

The final tribe contains one bird, the Torrent Duck (*Merganetta armata*), which lives on rushing streams in the Andes. It has wing spurs and a stiff tail resembling that of the Ruddy Duck.

Screamers (*Anhimidae*)

In the tropical and subtemperate environs of South America are found three species of highly unusual swan-sized birds called screamers. They lack the uncinate process—the little rib projections strengthening the thorax or rib-case—that occurs in all living birds and many reptiles, but not in Archaeopteryx, the oldest known fossil bird. Despite this skeletal difference, screamers are believed to be distant relatives of waterfowl and flamingos. Like waterfowl they are aquatic and highly gregarious.

In screamers the sexes are similar and the pairs probably remain together, like swans, for life. Their

Black-necked Screamer (*Chauna chavaria*)

ARTHUR W. AMBLER: NATIONAL AUDUBON

G. B. KEAREY

Goosander (*Mergus merganser*), female, at nesting hole

eggs resemble those of swans and their young, as in the Anatidae, are thickly covered with down at hatching. But they have disproportionately massive legs (which are nude far above the ankle joint), chicken-like bills and large, unwebbed toes.

Perhaps their most unusual characteristic is a skin filled with small bubbles of air. This covers the body and legs to the toes and is about a quarter of an inch in thickness. When pressed with the finger, it produces crackling noises as though tiny balloons were being broken. Nothing quite like it is known in other birds. Among its other unusual characters are excessively long intestines and pairs of spurs up to an inch in length on the bend of the wing. With blows from these weapons, which are present even in new chicks, a screamer can cripple a man.

Screamers are named for their harsh resounding calls, which can carry for as much as two miles. They live in pairs and call back and forth in a kind of fiendish duet, both by day and by night. When the pairs congregate in the nonbreeding season—sometimes by the thousands—the whole assemblage takes up the concert.

Screamers walk and wade through flooded forests and marshes or swim like large gray swans. In taking off from water they rise heavily, but, once airborne,

[99

fly strongly and even soar in groups high above the jungle. Screamers eat vegetable food gathered while on foot or afloat. In the breeding seasons in June and in September and October, the pairs split away from the large flocks to take up an aquatic life in lagoons. The nest is an island-like pile of rushes that rises several feet from a watery base, usually in thick reeds. Up to six buffy white oval eggs are laid and incubation takes about 44 days. The buff-colored downy young desert the nest a few days after hatching and follow the parents like ducklings.

Screamers have been tamed for use in guarding barnyard fowl and have been bred in captivity. In one pair of the Crested Screamer (*Chauna torquata*), bred in England, both members incubated, and when they changed places the approaching bird cast herbage backward with its feet in a kind of ceremony of nest relief.

The Horned Screamer (*Anhima cornuta*) of tropical South America has a spine up to six inches in length growing forward in a curve on the head between the eyes. The Crested Screamer (*C. torquata*) of southern South America is slate-colored with a black neck-ring and red around the eyes and legs. A third species, the Black-necked Screamer (*C. chavaria*), found in a limited area of northern Colombia and Venezuela, is a much darker bird, with a jet-black neck and a white cheek-patch. Although so dissimilar in color, the two species of *Chauna* are otherwise much alike, and a hybrid between them has been raised at the San Diego Zoo.

FALCONIFORMES

New World Vultures
(*Cathartidae*)

The American vultures include the largest flying birds alive today as well as the largest ever known to have lived. The former, the Andean Condor (*Vultur gryphus*) of South America, has attained a wing-spread of 12 feet, and the latter, the Teratornis (*Teratornis incredibilis*) of California—in Pleistocene times—had a wingspread of 18 feet or more. Only six surviving species of New World vultures are known. All are superficially quite similar in structure and habit to the vultures of the Old World. Internally, however, they differ in many ways, including the structure of the skull and the arrangement and proportions of the toes.

American vultures range from the giants described above to birds the size of large hawks. All are recognizable by their naked heads and perforated nostrils, which have no partition and give the impression of a hole drilled through the bill. Another unique character is their complete lack of voice, due to the absence of a syrinx. Then too there is their

marvelous soaring flight, which is probably more highly developed than that of any other New World land bird. And finally there is their almost incredible ability to find carrion.

The species most widely distributed is the Turkey Vulture (*Cathartes aura*), which occurs commonly throughout much of temperate and all of tropical America and is distinguished by its naked red head and neck. In the last quarter-century this species has become increasingly familiar in New England and southern Canada. The northern populations are migratory, but where they go is a mystery; their wintering grounds may be south of the equator. Although weighing less than three pounds, this brownish black bird attains a length of 2½ feet and has a wing span of up to six feet. One well-marked race of this species has succeeded in populating the Falkland Islands. In Central and South America is found a closely similar species whose primary difference is indicated by its name, Yellow-headed Vulture (*C. burrovianus*). Another aptly named species is the Black Vulture (*Coragyps atratus*), which ranges from the southern United States through South America. This square-tailed bird with a naked black head is the poorest flyer of the group. It scavenges for food in villages, towns and cities throughout the warmer parts of America and is thus truly useful to man.

In Middle and South America occurs the great black and white King Vulture (*Sarcorhamphus papa*). Its habitat is pure forest and semiforested plains, where sometimes groups of 25 or more can be seen flying with almost as much grace as albatrosses. Its head and foreneck are naked and covered with bright, many-colored but oddly unattractive warts and wattles. It is white-eyed and has white above and below with much black in the wings, tail and rump; a mufflike collar of grayish feathers encircles the neck.

King Vulture (*Sarcorhamphus papa*)

they seem to be jutting through a soft muff collar of pure white cottony feathers. Ugly wattles rise from the forehead and the naked neck of the male; otherwise the adult is blackish with much gray in the wings. Despite its great size and seeming ungainliness, this bird takes living game, particularly fawns and lambs. It is reputed to have marvelous powers of sight and to dive out of the sun like a fighter plane. Its home is primarily in mountains between 7000 and 16,000 feet, but in the far south it visits cliffs bordering the sea.

The Black and Turkey Vultures nest on the ground, placing their two (rarely three or four) eggs under rocks, in rock crevices, or under and in the trunks of fallen trees. The California and Andean Condors nest on remote mountain ledges like falcons and eagles. Their one or two eggs are up to four inches in length and are largely white, with dark brownish smudges. Incubation varies from about six weeks in the Black Vulture to about seven in the condors. The young develop very slowly, remaining on and close to the nest for eight to ten weeks. Both parents assist in the incubation of the eggs and the care of the young.

The food-finding abilities of American vultures are extraordinary. Waterton, Darwin and Humboldt believed they smelled decomposing matter. Audubon, disagreeing, attracted vultures with artifacts shaped like animals and even caused them to bite. A few later observers, including Dr. Frank M. Chapman and the author, have studied this phenomenon. Their sense of smell may have something to do with food-finding, but their eyesight, which is extremely keen, is probably the key factor.

Another enigmatic character of the vultures is their method of communication. When one of them finds a dead animal, others come flying in from 20 and even 40 miles away. How do they all find the one point? Here again it is believed that eyesight is the key. Soaring birds, hunting for food, probably watch each other carefully even when miles apart.

Andean Condor (*Vultur gryphus*)

In the mountains of far western North America the California Condor (*Gymnogyps californianus*) still survives, but this magnificent creature stands on the verge of extinction. In 1953 Dr. C. B. Koford estimated that only about 60 condors survived in the half-dozen California counties where it lived, but they did seem to be holding their own. With wings spanning more than ten feet, this orange-headed bird is the largest flying creature in North America.

In the coastal Andes of Venezuela and south along the great mountain chain to Patagonia occurs the largest flying bird in the world, the Andean Condor (*Vultur gryphus*). The naked head and neck of this great bird are dark gray and wrinkled, and

Andean Condor, young

When one makes a find, the others rush toward it, each bird drawing others as though they were strung together in an invisible network.

Secretary Bird (*Sagittariidae*)

The Secretary Bird (*Sagittarius serpentarius*) is the most adroit of avian snake-hunters. This famous bird, found from Senegambia and the Egyptian Sudan southward over the whole of Africa to Cape Province, makes its home chiefly on the ground in sparsely wooded grasslands or veldts. Only one species is known and its ancestry is somewhat in doubt; it probably is most nearly related to the diurnal birds of prey, but some experts think it is distantly related to the long-legged Cariamas of South America.

The Secretary Bird is an imposing creature, reaching four feet in height, with most of this height due to its gangling, cranelike legs. Another peculiar character is the elongation of the paired central tail feathers, which are nearly two feet long and extend far behind the others. But it is most famous for the spray of spectacular quills worn jauntily on the back of the head; these are gray and black and remind one of old-fashioned quill pens stuck over the ear.

Secretary Birds usually wander in scattered pairs or families, communicating by means of deep hoots. They cruise through large tracts of land, but the pairs usually travel the same way year after year. Dr. V. G. L. van Someren believes that they may remain paired for life.

If chased, they keep to the ground, where they can walk faster than a man can run. When pursued on a horse, they are apt to run on the ground un-til exhausted, and not attempt to fly to safety. Yet they are expert aerialists. In flight the neck protrudes ahead and the long legs trail behind.

Many years ago Dr. Jules Verreaux reported that Secretary Birds killed snakes up to six feet in length. Later observers found certain populations that fed primarily on rodents, lizards and insects, and certain ones were observed to subsist primarily on tortoises; therefore some doubt was expressed as to the earlier observations. Recently, however, Dr. Van Someren has confirmed that these great ground-loving birds do kill snakes, as well as vermin of all kinds, and that they even exact a heavy toll in young birds. In his *Days with Birds* he describes in detail their methods of stalking, killing and swallowing large snakes. On one occasion he saw a Secretary Bird kill a cobra measuring more than four feet in length. The stalking bird walked erratically, frequently raising its wings in an apparent effort to confuse its prey; then it pinned down the snake with its foot, parried the strikes with its wings, and seized the reptile behind the head with its strong bill. The bird then battered the cobra on the ground. Dr. Van Someren adds that when a snake is too large to be stunned or killed in this manner, the bird wings heavily into the air with it, flies high, and kills the snake by dropping it on hard earth.

Except for Van Someren's studies, very little information is available on parental care among these birds. Courtship may begin in the wet season, but the young do not hatch until the veldt is dry and subject to raging grass fires. Such fires are closely watched by the Secretary Bird for fleeing and dying game of all sorts.

The pairs cooperate in nest building, incubation and the care of the young. The nest may be a platform-like structure of sticks a foot or so thick and several feet wide, or it may be a huge object large enough to support a man. It is placed from 10 to 25 feet up in the flattish top of a thorn, mimosa or acacia tree. Large nests are the product of many years' use by the same birds. Two white, red-smudged eggs comprise the normal set, but occasionally three are laid. Incubation requires about 46 days, and the young remain on the nest for about three months. The nestlings are fed by means of regurgitation. Several weeks after hatching, the young develop flaglike head quills. On leaving the nest the fledglings are about as large as the adults and similarly dressed.

Hawks, Old World Vultures and Harriers (*Accipitridae*)

We come now to the diurnal birds of prey, a highly varied group of flesh-eaters, many of them famous in fable and heraldry. Two hundred five species are

Secretary Bird (*Sagittarius serpentarius*)

found in the land and coastal regions of the world, exclusive of Antarctica and large areas of Oceania. Hunters of birds, mammals, reptiles, amphibians, fishes and many kinds of invertebrates, they range from the size of a small dove to nearly that of the largest of flying birds, the Andean Condor, but all are closely similar in structure and habit. The bill is always strongly hooked, and the nostrils are located in an area of soft, leathery skin, called a cere, at the base of the maxilla. The feet are strong, with three toes directed forward and one backward, all armed with long, sharp nails. The eyes are among the most highly developed in the vertebrates; indeed, many hawks, eagles and vultures seem to see as well as a man aided by binoculars. One reason for this is that these birds have two foveas or focusing points in each eye, instead of one as in man, and therefore can use monocular vision for objects near-by or binocular vision for those far away. The eyes are laterally situated and capable of much movement.

Pursuit flights and stealthiness have been developed to a remarkable degree in these birds. All have the wings strong and relatively large, and in all forms flight is used in hunting. Many types swoop to the ground or to the water while in full flight or from a hovering position, or even from an arboreal perch; others dive or "stoop" from above and kill their prey in the air. In virtually every case the long claws serve in dispatching prey, while the feet hold down the kill and the sharp bill dismembers it.

In almost all species the female is considerably larger than the male—sometimes so much so that they seem to belong to different species. In the Cooper's Hawk (*Accipiter cooperii*) of North America, for example, the female is about one-third larger than the male. In other birds this usually indicates a polyandrous relationship but here the pairs are monogamous, and in many species seem to remain paired for life. Both sexes generally take part in the building of the nest, the incubating of the eggs and the brooding, feeding and protection of the young.

A platform of sticks in a tree is the usual form of the nest, but many species build on ledges or in caves, and some even nest on the ground. The set may range from one egg to seven, and the incubation period from one to two months. In all species the young are hatched blind, quite helpless—some can hardly stand until they are three weeks old—and covered with fine whitish or dusky down. They may remain on the nest from one to four months, as in the Hooded Vulture (*Necrosyrtes monachus*) of East Africa. In many species they are nearly as large as the adults when they finally depart from the nest, although strikingly different in plumage; in others, particularly those in which the sexes differ in color, the young wear a plumage somewhat like that of the female. The general coloration of this family is brownish or grayish, and many of the species are virtually identical in color. But some have white in the body plumage, and many have the legs and bill

yellow. Some are dressed in colorful reddish browns and blues. And in many there is much polymorphism, so that birds of a single species are often highly variable in color and pattern.

The most primitive of the eight groups or subfamilies of diurnal birds of prey are the kites, which occur in most of the warmer regions of the world. They are long-winged and mostly long-tailed birds that are particularly adept at soaring, circling and gliding. They habitually work their way languidly over semi-open country, often in groups, their wings cocked at a slight dihedral angle.

The White-tailed Kite (*Elanus leucurus*), about 16 inches in length, ranges from the southern borders of the United States through much of South America. Both sexes participate in nest construction, and four eggs are normally laid. Incubation requires up to 32 days, with both parents taking part. The young remain on the nest for about a month and then return to it for some time thereafter to obtain food.

Typical of the next subfamily, the Perninae, is the two-foot-long Honey Buzzard (*Pernis apivorus*), which ranges over much of Eurasia and usually usurps an old crow nest for its eggs. This long-tailed, soaring hawk digs into the ground for honeycombs and the larvae of wasps and bees, its favorite source of food; however, it also captures small insects, frogs, rodents and birds. In summer it follows its insect prey quite far north, but in winter it retreats to the tropical climes of Africa and the Middle East. Probably the most beautiful is the Swallow-tailed Kite (*Elanoïdes forficatus*), which is found from southern United States to southern South America. This two-foot hawk has slender wings of grayish black with greenish reflections, contrasting with a body and head that are largely white. Its graceful black forked tail is normally carried like a pair of opened shears.

The third subfamily consists of the true kites (*Milvinae*). One is the Black or Pariah Kite (*Milvus migrans*), about 20 inches long and generally dark brown with the tail forked. One of the most abundant and easily observed of all hawks, it is encountered almost everywhere throughout the warmer parts of the Old World, where it often congregates about villages and along waterways and beaches. Unlike most of the diurnal birds of prey, it is largely a scavenger, snatching food from watery or terrestrial surfaces while in full flight. The food is carried in the feet and devoured in flight with deft, tearing motions of the bill. From the Mediterranean region eastward to the Southwestern Pacific these birds may be seen in flocks, haunting the wakes of coastal ships and the harbors and docks for carrion. In Australia and India hundreds are frequently seen in the middle of towns and cities, and large gull-like flocks may suddenly appear in the wake of grass fires or when grasshoppers and mouse plagues are rampant. The Black Kite often nests in old crow nests. Two eggs are the usual set, and the female does most of the incubating and brooding, with the male bringing food. Another closely related species is the Red Kite (*Milvus milvus;* Plate 34).

The Brahminy Kite or Red-backed Sea Eagle (*Haliastur indus*) of the Indo-Malayan and Australian region is another common, spectacular species. It is 18 inches in length and bright chestnut brown and has a white head and underparts. Its food is carrion, crabs, lizards, grasshoppers and the like, all of which are taken and devoured in flight.

The Lizard Hawks, or Bazas, are characterized by a long, thin crest which, except in flight, stands up at a jaunty angle from the hind crown and is constantly moved. An example is the Crested Lizard Hawk (*Aviceda jerdoni*) of the Indo-Malayan region, which is brown and heavily barred, with a rufous breast and abdomen. It is a forest bird that travels in small flocks and hunts in twilight. Its bill is serrated or toothed, somewhat like that of the Double-

toothed Kite (*Harpagus bidentatus*) of Central and South America. Other relatives are the Plumbeous Kite (*Ictinia plumbea*), of similar range, and the Everglade or Snail Kite (*Rostrhamus sociabilis*), of the warm parts of America from Florida south.

The last mentioned feeds on snails in a way that has generally been misunderstood but was (as Dr. Robert Cushman Murphy points out) accurately described by the American explorer Herbert Lang, who observed it in British Guiana. The hawk, after perching, holds the snail until it crawls part way out of the shell. The bird then spears the animal with the maxilla, waits about two minutes for the snail to become limp, then shakes it from the shell and swallows it whole, including the operculum.

The bird-catching Accipiters, or true hawks, are an assemblage of 46 species of long-legged, long-toed goshawks, sparrow hawks and harriers. They

Red-shouldered Hawk (*Buteo lineatus*) of North Ameria, about to strike

are swift, fierce killers, ranging throughout the non-polar land areas of the world. In the Old World they were long used for hunting, sometimes with more success than with a true falcon. There are records of as many as 70 quail killed in a day by a single trained Accipiter (Plate 37).

Some of the best-known members of the family are among the ninety species of the subfamily Buteoninae, which is virtually world-wide in its distribution. The large hawks of the genus *Buteo* are known in England as "buzzards." The early English-speaking settlers in North America unaccountably attached this name to the American vultures of the family Cathartidae, merely using the general name "hawk" for the New World representatives of the true buzzards. Of the latter, the best known and most widely distributed is the Red-tailed Hawk (*B. jamaicensis;* Plate 33), a heavy-bodied bird found from Alaska south to Panama and the West Indies. As suggested by the name, the adult has a conspicuously reddish-brown tail; the upperparts are dark brown, and the underparts whitish with varying amounts of black streaking. Although primarily rodent-feeders, the Red-tail and its relatives, such as the Red-shouldered Hawk (*B. lineatus*) of North America, are all too frequently shot for "chicken-hawks," since their relatively slow flight and large size make them tempting targets for hunters, farm boys, and game-keepers.

The best-known member of the genus *Buteo* in Europe is the Common Buzzard (*B. buteo*), which is found from Scandinavia south to the islands of the Mediterranean. There is a definite tendency toward variability in color in many species of this genus, and particularly toward the development of an excessively pigmented, or melanistic, color phase. In the Common Buzzard this variability is carried to an extreme. E. L. Schiøler's great work on the birds of Denmark illustrates no less than eight different color types of adult plumage, varying from a white bird with a few brown spots and bars to an almost solidly-colored dark chocolate-brown bird. Like many other members of the genus, the Common Buzzard spends hours on end in graceful soaring flight, hardly seeming to move its wings at all. When hunting for its prey of small mammals, reptiles, insects, carrion and occasional birds, however, it flies over the countryside in low sweeps. The related Rough-legged Hawk or Rough-legged Buzzard (*B. lagopus*) is an arctic species that feeds almost entirely on small rodents. It nests at high latitudes in both Eastern and Western Hemispheres, wandering south in winter as far as the shores of the Adriatic Sea in Europe and southern United States in North America.

Several groups of large diurnal birds of prey, not particularly closely related to one another, have been given the general name "eagle." The original bearer of the name, the "aquila" of the ancient Romans, is the magnificent Golden Eagle (*Aquila chrysaëtos*). Originally found in the wild mountain-

Ferruginous Hawk (*Buteo regalis*) of North America

ous areas of most of the Northern Hemisphere, the Golden Eagle (Plate 35) has been exterminated in several portions of its range, including most of eastern North America and the British Isles (except Scotland, where a remnant population still exists). The nest, made of branches lined with ferns, grasses or rushes, is usually placed on an inaccessible cliff. The normal clutch is two eggs, white with spots of brown and gray. Incubation, chiefly or entirely by the female, lasts about 40 to 45 days, and the young remain in the nest for at least 11 weeks after hatching.

Best known of the eagles in North America is the Bald Eagle (*Haliaeetus leucocephalus*), national emblem of the United States of America (against the protests of Benjamin Franklin, who preferred the wild turkey). The familiar plumage of the adult, with its brown body and snow-white head and tail, is not attained until the bird is seven years of age. Yearling Bald Eagles are completely brown, and are sometimes mistaken for Golden Eagles. The white head and tail develop gradually, becoming purer in color at each succeeding molt. The Bald Eagle is a member of the group known as sea-eagles; its Old World counterpart is the White-tailed Eagle or Gray Sea-eagle (*H. albicilla*), in which the tail but not the head is white. This species is the "ern" or "erne" which appears so often in crossword puzzles. Another in this group is the powerful Steller's Sea Eagle (*H. pelagicus*) of the Pacific coast of Asia.

Tropical forests around the world are the home of a small group of huge, crested, immensely powerful eagles, of which the Monkey-eating eagle (*Pithecophaga jefferyi*) of the Philippines is an example. This rare and spectacular species has a shaggy crest, an exceptionally heavy, sharply hooked bill, powerful feet, and bright blue eyes. As indicated by its name,

Bald Eagle, young (*Haliaeetus leucocephalus*)

the Monkey-eating Eagle apparently subsists largely on the Philippine Macaque, but its habits are actually little known.

The fourteen species of fierce, handsome eagles in the subfamily Circaetinae are found only in Eurasia, Africa and Madagascar. All have disproportionately large heads crowned with fanlike expandable crests. All feed primarily on reptiles.

The best known is the Short-toed Harrier Eagle (*Circaëtus gallicus*) of Eurasia and Africa, about two feet in length, grayish brown above and whitish below. It has a relatively long barred tail and blackish flight feathers. It hunts by quartering open forest and bushy grasslands rather like a harrier, flying slowly and hovering before it falls steeply on its reptile prey. This it clasps in its talons and kills with its bill before carrying it off to a tree to be devoured. The female does most of the 35 days of incubating the single egg and brooding. The young remain in the nest—sometimes for more than eleven weeks.

The Brown Harrier Eagle (*C. cinereus*) of Africa builds a huge stick nest in thorny trees. A specimen raised by Dr. Van Someren did not acquire the adult plumage until it was two years old. This bird is one of the most fearless of the snakehunters; Van Someren saw it kill and eat a threefoot Puff Adder.

Most majestic of all is the Bateleur Eagle (*Terathopius ecaudatus*), which ranges widely through the grasslands and open forests of Africa. Besides having a splendid rufflike crest, this imposing bird has most of the underparts and head black and most of the upperparts, including the very short tail, reddish brown; the wings are broadly slashed with gray above and whitish below. Because of the short tail the total length of the female is only about two feet. The male is some four inches shorter. Bateleurs hunt from on high, soaring effortlessly for hours, sometimes in groups. At the onset of the breeding season they engage in aerial displays, gliding,

Gray Sea Eagle (*Haliaeetus albicilla*)

flailing the wings with a sharp woodpecker-like tapping and uttering their well-known barking "caw." They prey on reptiles—chiefly snakes—but also take young antelopes and sheep. The nest is a large stick structure far above ground; from two to four white eggs are laid.

The Serpent Eagles of the Indo-Malayan region, including the Philippines, have the crest feathers more rounded, less pointed and shorter; and the brownish plumage is heavily spotted with round white marks. One of the five species, the Serpent Eagle (*Spilornis cheela*), occurs widely through India, China and the

Philippines. The author found it usually the most prominent large hawk in the forests of Luzon. This bird is almost two feet in length and has the legs naked and yellow and the tail heavily barred. It feeds on frogs, lizards, rodents and chiefly snakes. Its acrobatics in the mating season involve rolling, drumming the wings and moving the tail. The nest is built of sticks in a forest tree. The usual set is one white egg with brownish markings.

Excluding the carrion eaters, the birds most unlike the hawks among the Accipitridae are the harriers or marsh hawks (subfamily Circinae), found in all of the major land areas of the world except Antarctica. The 17 species are remarkably similar in structure and habits. All are graceful birds that almost always hunt over wet, swampy ground and prey on marsh life—frogs, lizards, snakes, small birds, small mammals. Like almost all other members of the family, the young are different in dress from the adults, but unlike most hawks, the sexes in their adult plumage are colored very differently from each other. Harriers are sizable birds, with a wing span that reaches four feet, but they are extremely light, some weighing less than two pounds. All have the tarsus nude and the legs long and slender and fitted with thin, sharp claws. The female is larger, as in most

Gray Sea Eagle, young

SVANTE LUNDGREN

hawks. Both sexes wear facial disks of feathers something like that of the owl. Another owl-like trait is the marked crepuscular habits, marsh hawks being adept at hunting side by side with bats and owls in the late dusk. In hunting they quarter the ground, usually flying just over the reed tops, wheeling, circling, gliding and soaring, shifting direction abruptly, and ever and again hovering momentarily, or dropping sharply to capture their terrestrial prey. In flight the long, slender wings are usually carried dihedraled like those of a gull. When the bird attacks, the long tail is expanded and the long yellow legs dangle with talons open. The kill is often eaten on the ground.

Harriers usually nest on the ground, constructing a nest of reeds, grasses and sticks. It often resembles a broad, saucer-like island in water surrounded by a screen of tall rushes. The nests are scattered far apart in marshes. Each is near the center of a hunting territory that may have a radius of five miles. The three to seven eggs are nearly white. Unlike most of the hawks, the female does nearly all the incubating and brooding, while the male hunts and carries food to her and to the young. Incubation requires about four weeks and the young leave the nest in another five weeks. Thereafter the birds of the year tend to disperse over wide areas—sometimes wandering hundreds of miles off.

Harriers always roost on the ground. The difference in coloration between the sexes seems to be correlated with the separate roles played by them in parental care. The female wears darker plumage, which probably provides a better camouflage for her duties on and about the nest. The more ashy gray plumage of the male may enable it to hunt more effectively in the half-light of dawn and dusk.

The Marsh Hawk or Hen Harrier (*Circus cyaneus*) ranges around the world in the Northern Hemisphere. The North American race is about 20 inches long, with pale gray upperparts and a prominent white area on the rump. Below it is chiefly white. The female is dark brown above and cinnamon brown below. This species is found in marshy and savanna areas from Canada to Mexico, and wintering birds have been taken in northern South America. Known as the Hen Harrier in Eurasia, where it is more pallidly colored and less spotted on the underparts, this species is occasionally found as far north as the Faroe Islands and Scandinavia. The largest of the group is the Marsh Harrier (*C. aeruginosus*), which occurs in Eurasia, the Philippines, Africa and even Malaya and New Guinea. This bird is dark reddish brown above with a grayish tail. It is the most aggressive of the group and in Madagascar occasionally kills ducks and chickens. Two Australian harriers have also developed aberrancies of behavior: The Spotted Harrier (*C. assimilis*), which is a bird of sandy inland areas rather than swamps, erects a nest of sticks in a tree instead of on the ground like other harriers. Rabbits are included in the fare of this unusual bird. The Swamp Harrier (*C. approximans*) of Australia reuses the same nest.

In middle and northern South America the Crane-Hawk or Frog Hawk (*Geranospiza nigra*)—a black harrier with two vivid white bars in the tail—deviates from the typical mannerisms of the harriers. A more solidly built bird, it keeps pretty much to swampy woodlands near water.

The "jackals" and "hyenas" among Old World birds are the 14 species of eagle-like, carrion-feeding Raptores known as Old World Vultures (subfamily Aegypiinae). These birds range widely through Europe, Africa and Asia, but are absent from Malaya and Australia. Although called "Old World" vultures, they were found in the New World during the Pleistocene epoch, when the fauna of western North America was not unlike that of the Africa of today. Some are among the largest of all flying birds, with wings spreading ten feet and bodies reaching a length of four feet, but one species is no larger than a chicken. All but one species have the head partially naked or clothed in soft downlike feathers. This nakedness is reminiscent of New World Vultures, which seem similar but are anatomically distinct.

The Old World Vultures are generally considered to be eagles that have become modified for carrion-eating and are usually included as a subfamily of the hawks and buzzards, as is done here. However, unlike the hawks and eagles, the sexes are fairly similar in size. There are other differences—such as the social nesting of some of the vultures—that indicate that the two groups have long been separated.

Steller's Sea Eagle (*Haliaeetus pelagicus*)

ARTHUR W. AMBLER: NATIONAL AUDUBON

Old World Vultures have the legs relatively short and equipped with weak, blunt toes. One carefully studied species, the Hooded Vulture (*Necrosyrtes monachus*) of Africa, lays but a single egg in a nest like that of an eagle. The female does most of the incubating and is fed at the nest by the male, who regurgitates food for it. According to Dr. Van Someren, the naked head of the female is normally grayish, but when the male appears the color changes in a kind of blush to a bright pinkish red. Incubation requires 46 days, the female taking almost complete charge of the young for the first week or so, and the male devoting its time to bringing food. As do many birds of prey, the Hooded Vulture adds green leaves to the nest, apparently to protect the young.

The most abundant and easily observed of the Old World Vultures is the Neophron, Egyptian Vulture, or Pharaoh's Chicken (*Neophron percnopterus*), which ranges to all of the countries bordering the Mediterranean and eastward to southern Asia. Once the author saw this ghostly vulture sitting on a limb at dusk at 6000 feet in the Vale of Kashmir. It was hawk-sized, and seemingly impertinent in its tameness. It had an immaculate white body with a ruff around the neck and naked yellow skin on the head and throat. At other places these birds live in and around Indian villages and feed like farmers' pets on offal. For ages this vulture has been closely associated with human life in parts of Eurasia.

Another species not always pleasant to behold is the Griffon Vulture (*Gyps fulvus*), one of the largest of the carrion-eating birds of prey. In Nepal and India it haunts the rivers, preying on the human bodies that often fall from funeral pyres before being reduced to ashes. One that the author observed at Katmandu, Nepal, stood with water swirling around its belly as it wrestled with a large piece of carrion. The Griffon Vulture nests on cliffs and in caves. Sometimes when groups of 10 or 15 pairs breed close together on a cliff it becomes so stained that it can be seen for miles. A single egg is laid. The young, which are clothed in buffy down at first, gradually assume the dress of the adult before they leave the protection of their eyries three or more months after hatching. A close relative, the Long-billed Vulture (*Gyps indicus*), builds a large nest of sticks in a tree.

Another of the large Eurasian vultures is the Black Vulture (*Aegypius monachus*), which reaches more than 40 inches in length. It also habitually nests in groups, but the nests are usually in a tall tree rather than on a cliff. Its tail is slightly wedge-shaped, whereas the Griffon has a square tail.

The most dramatic member of the family is the magnificent Bearded Vulture (*Gypaetus barbatus*), or Lammergeyer, which wears tassels of spiny black feathers hanging from its nostrils like an Oriental mustache. Adding to the unusual appearance of this bird is a black mask across the eyes. Once at 12,000 feet in the Himalayas the author was able to observe this great bird as it flew back and forth along a steep-walled mountain, its masked

Long-billed Vulture (*Gyps indicus*) of India

Osprey or Fish-hawk

(*Pandionidae*)

The sole representative of this family, the Osprey or Fish-hawk (*Pandion haliaetus*), is an eagle-sized, sharp-billed hawk occurring throughout almost all temperate and tropical regions of the world. The species consists of five geographical races. Although chiefly a habitant of continental coastal waters, this majestic bird is also found along the edges of inland rivers and lakes, and in Oceania, where few hawks ever wander, it has succeeded in settling on some of the more remote islands. For example, in Micronesia, on Palau and Guam, it is the only member of the Falconiformes that is permanently established.

The Osprey feeds on fish. Only rarely does it prey on other marine life such as the flat-tailed sea snakes of the Pacific and Indian Oceans. When fishing, it usually flies 50 to 150 feet over the sea. It may hover when the target is sighted, then partly furl the wings and rocket down on or into the water, its needle-sharp talons and legs extended to impale the fish. Sometimes only the feet enter the water; at other times the entire bird goes below the surface for a few moments. Shortly after the attack, the Osprey, using its strong wings, rises quickly from the water and flies off to a perch, commonly a tree or a cliff, to devour its catch. Its flight is very graceful, with extensive soaring and wheeling on wings that are slightly crooked.

The Osprey differs from other hunting hawks in having the outer toe reversible, as in the owls, and all the talons approximately the same length and strongly curved. The pads lining the underside of the toes are modified with sharp scales to assist in gripping slippery prey, and the leg tendons are of a different pattern from those of hawks, being actually more like those of the New World Vultures.

In America the Osprey normally nests in trees, often dead ones, whereas in Europe it usually finds a place on cliff edges. Nest-building is performed by both sexes, and the same nest may be used year after year until it becomes as much as six feet deep and five to six feet wide. Two to three, rarely four, eggs splotched with deep brown are laid. For the required five weeks the female does most of the incubating, and for several weeks after the young are hatched she does most of the brooding and feeding. During these periods the chief role of the male is to fish and to carry food to its mate and the young. The nestlings remain on the flat-topped nest for as long as seven weeks.

The male and female Ospreys are dressed very much alike; the lower parts, neck and head are chiefly white, and the back and long, pointed wings chiefly dark brown. The chest is collared with brown spots, and the head is usually ornamented with a short blackish crest and a dark eye streak; however, the latter markings are reduced or absent in the Carib-

head twisting and turning as it scanned the moraine and snowfield for food. The long spike of its central tail, which extended backward like a wedge, the massive wings, set like those of a sailplane, and the dark buffy gray head and back as well as the buff underparts were clearly visible. Northern Lammergeyers have the legs feathered almost to the toes. They live only in the most remote mountains from eastern Europe to China. In the high mountains of Africa is found a subspecies in which the legs are largely unfeathered. Only in the last several years have they again wandered occasionally to Switzerland and the mountains bordering the Black Sea. The food of the Lammergeyer is derived from the bones of animals—usually bones that have already been picked clean by vultures. To get further nourishment from this source the Lammergeyer carries the bones to great heights and drops them on certain rocks to fracture them.

Although the Lammergeyer feeds almost exclusively on bone marrow and probably cannot kill game of any kind, nevertheless, on account of its uncommon size, the folklore in many countries credits it with carrying off human beings. If nothing else, the weak structure of the toes and nails confirms the fact that it is not a killer but rather a "bone-breaker." These wonderful birds nest on remote mountain cliffs, laying only a single egg.

bean population. As in other hawks, the female is larger, being two feet long, with the male some four inches shorter.

Laughing Falcons, Caracaras, Falconets and Falcons (*Falconidae*)

Among this group of 58 diurnal birds of prey are the magnificent long-winged hunting hawks that have fascinated sportsmen since Egyptian times. In England where for 800 years a Keeper of the Falcons was attached to the royal household, the Gyrfalcon (*Falco rusticolus*) was reserved for royal use, the Peregrine (*F. peregrinus*) was used by earls, and sporting priests were given the Kestrel (*F. tinnunculus*) to hunt with. However, many less glamorous relatives occur in the family.

Primitive species are the Laughing Falcon (*Herpetotheres cachinnans*) and the medium-large Collared Forest Falcon (*Micrastur semitorquatus*) of Central and South America. The first is the only white-headed, black-masked hawk in the region, and the second has an exceptionally long tail and is blackish above with a white collar.

The caracaras of Middle and South America form an aberrant subfamily. Typical is the Red-throated Caracara (*Daptrius americanus*) of tropical forests and forest edges. It reaches 22 inches in length, is chiefly black above with much white below and has a naked red area on the face and throat. A more northern-ranging, slightly larger species is the Crested Caracara (*Caracara cheriway*), which feeds largely on carrion. It has long, naked legs and a black cap and crest surmounting a partially naked face. Its neck and upper chest are white with blackish bars across the lower chest. It occurs from southern United States to the Amazon. Both sexes assist in building the nest and incubating the eggs. The young hatch in 28 days. Caracaras run rapidly on the ground and often associate with vultures.

The third subfamily, the Falconets (five species), occurs in South America and Africa, but its stronghold is in the Indo-Malayan region. Smallest of the diurnal birds of prey is the Philippine Falconet (*Microhierax erythrogonys*), six inches long and shaped like a swallow. Black above and across the eyes and shiny white below, it hunts like a flycatcher from the tops of trees, and nests in old woodpecker holes.

The true falcons, of which there are 37 species ranging to all the continents and large islands except Antarctica, are among the most aggressive of all birds. The Peregrine is generally credited with being the most wide-ranging diurnal land bird known. This single species reaches virtually every portion of the world, from the cold regions of the Arctic to the

SVANTE LUNDGREN

Fish-hawk (*Pandion haliaetus*) at nest

southern tips of Africa, India, Ceylon, Australia, Tasmania and South America, and throughout this vast range it varies very little. The female of the American race, also known as the Duck Hawk, reaches 20 inches in length: the male is about 5 inches shorter. Except for size, the sexes are very much alike. The upperparts are dark slate with the head and flight feathers more blackish. Below the coloration is generally whitish with black barring.

All members of this subfamily have the wings sharply pointed, the neck short and the legs covered with well-developed "pants" or "flags." Some, for example the Peregrine, keep mostly to coastal areas, while others, such as the American Prairie Falcon (*Falco mexicanus*)—smaller and somewhat pallid —inhabit drier inland areas. A well-known small species of the Northern Hemisphere, the Pigeon Hawk or Merlin (*F. columbarius*), is very similar to the Peregrine in general shape and color but has no ventral barring and is only a foot long. It frequents coastal bogs and wet fields.

The Gyrfalcon inhabits the Arctic around the world, and in winter it occasionally flies as far south as the northern United States, England and middle Asia. The species divides into many races, some of which are nearly pure white except for black flight

Peregrine Falcon (*Falco peregrinus*) and young on ledge

prey in the Americas. It generally lays four to six eggs in old woodpecker holes.

The members of this varied family hunt in dozens of unusual and specialized ways. Some prey entirely on insects which they seize in the air, whereas others hover over and then pounce on lizards, frogs, beetles, grasshoppers, etc. Many feed largely on small rodents and birds, seized either on the ground or by swift chases executed from hunting perches. The most aggressive hunters dive on flying game. But falconers recognize only two types of hunting hawks: first, the yellow-eyed, roundish-winged chasers and pouncers, which are the Accipiter type; and second, the brown-eyed, sharp-winged, short-necked divers, which are the falcons. The latter are the most gifted of hunting birds and have been trained to hunt many sorts of game birds for man, even those much larger than themselves. Some have even been taught to attack other birds of prey, chiefly kites, and such contests once ranked as a sport for kings. Great speed (up to 120 m.p.h.) and impact are their chief weapons.

On occasion these hunting hawks seem to exact an unusually heavy toll. For example, Dr. William Beebe concluded that a breeding pair of the 11-inch-long Bat Falcon (*F. albigularis*) caught not less than 600 birds and mammals during the 5½ months he studied them in Venezuela. But, because they take their toll chiefly of the weak, sick and aged, such predators as falcons are now believed to be vital to the general health of animal populations.

GALLIFORMES

Grouse (*Tetraonidae*)

Of the 18 species of this interesting family, ranging in size from hen to turkey, many are considered the finest of game birds. All but a few dwell in the northern portions of the Northern Hemisphere, some living most of their lives in the snows of the Arctic region. Grouse appear to have split off a long time ago from the stock that produced the curassows, the pheasants and the turkeys, all of which are presumed to be of tropical origin.

Structurally, the Tetraonidae are fowl-like, but have the tarsus mostly or entirely feathered and the toes either edged laterally with comblike filaments or covered with feathers, which in snow serve rather like snowshoes. All have the nostrils cloaked in feathers, and most have bare skin over the eye. Many have peculiar, distensible, naked or nearly naked air sacs on the neck. In all, the male is considerably larger than the female.

Many species of grouse have developed fascinating modes of behavior. One of these is a form of harem polygamy that enables the population to recover quickly from the severe attrition imposed by adverse weather, predation, disease and starvation.

feathers, which can be concealed. Gyrfalcons often nest in tundra on snow-covered hillocks, where their white plumage is a splendid camouflage. This two-foot-long bird is a fierce hunter, preying on waterfowl and ptarmigan.

Gyrfalcons differ from most other hawks in building their nests on the ground. They lay three or four whitish eggs heavily blotched with rich brown. Duck Hawks generally nest on cliffs. Other members of the genus *Falco* generally use nests of their own construction built in trees, or even old crow or magpie nests. On occasion isolated populations living on islands develop localized habits. In Eurasia the Kestrel nests chiefly in old crow nests but in the Orkney Islands it nests on the ground. This small falcon hovers when searching for prey, feeds on insects and small birds, and takes quickly to life in cities. Its incubation requires about 28 days, and the young remain on the nest for from four to five weeks. The very similar Sparrow Hawk (*F. sparverius*) is about ten inches long and is perhaps the commonest bird of

An unsolved mystery affecting all of the species is the periodic fluctuations in abundance, which seem to be related to external factors of cyclic occurrence. As a result, the populations wax and wane in number, the birds being relatively abundant in some years and scarce in others. Even in areas reasonably distant from hard winters—England, for instance—the populations of grouse fluctuate greatly. Another phenomenon is a kind of "insanity" that affects various populations from time to time. When it strikes, large numbers of grouse "explode" into areas far removed from their usual habitat.

Two very different types of breeding behavior are found in the Tetraonidae: (1) a primitive one in which the pairs are seasonally monogamous and the male assists in the rearing of the young by remaining on guard and plays a vigorous part in defending the offspring; and (2) an advanced type in which the male may be said to be polygamous if not promiscuous. In this type the male maintains a kind of fluctuating harem, competing with many other males for the females but playing no part in the rearing of the family.

The ptarmigan, of which four species are known, are marked by the primitive, monogamous type of mating behavior. All have the tarsus and toes very heavily feathered. All lay large clutches of eggs which the female incubates and the male defends with much bravery, often using its body as a lure to distract attention from the incubating or brooding female.

The Rock Ptarmigan (*Lagopus mutus*), or Ptarmigan as it is known in Europe, is about 14 inches long, with permanently white wings and abdomen. This species lives in the rocky barren grounds of the Far North around the world and in the mountains of Eurasia, nesting on the ground. This bird has developed three distinct plumages to cope with the changes in the coloration of its habitat: during the breeding season, when the ground is usually exposed, it wears a brown body plumage; in autumn, when the vegetation is dry and grayish, its dorsal plumage is gray; in winter, when the ground is snow-covered, it dons a nearly pure white body dress. The ptarmigan are almost unique among birds in having this triple annual plumage sequence.

By summer, Rock Ptarmigan scatter in pairs and press northward to occupy rocky tundra close to the limits of vegetation. There they feed on berries and tender shoots of plants. By winter, when the barren Far North becomes too dangerous, the birds gather in large flocks in protected woody valleys. At this season they feed on buds and tender tree twigs, and excavate little igloo-like burrows in the snow as shelter from the wintry blasts.

In the New World the White-tailed Ptarmigan (*L. leucurus*) occurs in the mountains of Alaska and Canada and, at high elevations, southward to the Rocky Mountains in the United States. This species, which is about a foot long, never loses the white tail. Another species, called the Red Grouse (*L. scoticus*), is several inches longer and occurs only in England and Ireland. It is notable as the only ptarmigan that does not wear the white protective coloration at any season. Its winter habitat, in islands warmed by the Gulf Stream, is chiefly brown and free of snow, and brown is therefore its winter color. This lack of a

Sparrow Hawk or **American Kestrel** (*Falco sparverius*)

G. RONALD AUSTING AND DONALD KOEHLER

ELSA AND HENRY POTTER: NATIONAL AUDUBON

Ruffed Grouse (*Bonasa umbellus*) drumming

white winter plumage is its chief difference from the Willow Ptarmigan (*L. lagopus*) of the New and Old World arctic, and some authors believe the two are geographic races of a single species.

Among the monogamous relatives of ptarmigans living in North America are the Ruffed Grouse and the Spruce Grouse. The Ruffed Grouse (*Bonasa umbellus*), which occupies deciduous woodlands throughout the northern two-thirds of America from Alaska to Newfoundland, is the best-known and one of the most popular of game birds. The male is chiefly rich brown, with a vividly barred tail and flaglike, erectile, blackish tufts on the neck, which it elevates in display.

This fine bird reaches a length of 1⅓ feet. It habitually dances on dead logs in the forest. A primary part of the dance is the beating of the wings, first spasmodically, then rapidly, producing a thumping, drumming sound that carries long distances through the forest and is accompanied by low, ventriloquial noises. When the female has been attracted by these sounds and has arrived within visual range, the male elevates the tail and neck tufts, slowly struts and, with neck twisting about, often bends the bill sharply toward the ground or toward the seemingly inattentive, casual female.

As in the ptarmigan, the Ruffed Grouse male assists in the defense of the 11 or so eggs or young. The eggs hatch in about 24 days. The female does the nest-building, incubating and even all of the feeding and brooding of the precocial young. The Ruffed Grouse nests on the ground in woods and thickets.

Spruce Grouse (*Canachites canadensis*) occupy a wide but generally more northern range and are largely restricted to little-settled regions heavily overgrown with conifers. Slightly smaller than the Ruffed Grouse and darker in coloration, the Spruce Grouse, like the porcupine, has long been known to the woodsman as an easy source of food. They often come into a bush camp, apparently out of pure curiosity, and the oft heard story that they can be killed with a club is well founded.

In display the male Spruce Grouse dances on a low limb or partially fallen trunk, fluttering the wings, elevating the tail and vibrating the wings stiffly at the sides. The female performs all of the nesting duties. Only four to seven eggs are laid.

Another in this monogamous group is the Blue Grouse (*Dendragapus obscurus*), a species living mainly at higher altitudes in the western part of North America. The Rocky Mountain population, often called "Dusky Grouse," employs an orthodox terrestrial wing display, accompanied by low bubbling hoots. On the other hand, the "Sooty Grouse" of the coastal ranges displays on high pine limbs and has a vocal range so loud that the notes carry more than a mile through the forest. These differences in behavior, together with certain plumage differences, have led some ornithologists to consider the two populations as separate species.

The polygamous species of America and the Old World are generally larger than the monogamous, and are marked by greater differences in size between the sexes. The most beautiful is the Black Grouse (*Lyrurus tetrix*) of the wetlands and forests of England, Europe and Asia. In both sexes the area above the eyes is festooned with elaborate scarlet carunculated wattles. The male is a burnished black, with some white in the wings and white under-tail coverts, and has a lyre-shaped tail. Approximately five inches longer than the female, it is roughly the size of a large chicken.

This species performs communal dances with other males. These begin at dawn on the floor of the wet forest and on exposed hills and rocks, the males fighting and tumbling, all the while emitting slurred, wheezing, gobbler-like notes that boom over the countryside and serve to draw females to the dance arena. The stronger, more attractive males then mate with the females.

The female, known as the Gray Hen, fashions a simple nest on the ground and lays seven to ten eggs and performs all of the nest duties, while the male continues disporting before an ever-changing harem.

The communal dances of the Black Grouse are performed on ground used for generations. Curiously enough, these performances are attractive to female grouse of different species, and as a result there are some well-known intergeneric hybrids between this species, the Red Grouse and the Capercaillie (*Tetrao urogallus;* Plate 39).

The Capercaillie, largest of the grouse, formerly occurred in the original pine forests covering the British Isles and the northern portions of Europe and Asia. By 1785 it had become extinct in Britain but it was successfully reintroduced from Scandinavian stock in 1837. The male reaches nearly a yard in length and is almost a foot longer than its mate. The massive body proportions and tail, plus the red wattles over the eye and a rough beard of dark feathers, serve to distinguish this dusky bird from all other grouse. At most times it is notoriously wary and hard to approach or detect, even when in the canopy of pine forest where it feeds on pine needles and buds.

In display the male goes into a trancelike dance that so carries him away that hunters can steal up to him as he performs. At the height of the act he rears the head over the back and flexes the long, rounded tail. If on a limb, he prances sideways; if on the ground, he struts about, intimidating other males, hissing, gobbling and fighting vigorously with them.

After the ceremony, which usually begins slightly before dawn, the males mate with the females, who shoulder all the duties of nest-building and rearing the young. Twelve eggs form the average set. The precocial young follow the female soon after hatching and can flutter a little in two weeks.

In the New World three groups of grouse, namely the Prairie Chickens, the Sharp-tailed Grouse and the Sage Grouse, are polygamous. All have colorful air sacs on the sides of the neck, which during the breeding season are swelled with air to the size of golf balls or slightly larger. The dances or group courtship displays of these birds are among the most colorful and spectacular in the animal kingdom.

Best known of this group is the Prairie Chicken (*Tympanuchus cupido*) of the American West from Canada to Texas. In olden times it reached New England, but the last of the eastern populations, known as the Heath Hen, died on Martha's Vineyard in 1932. This chicken-sized, pale brown species with a short tail wears neck epaulettes composed of stiffly pointed black and brown feathers, which ride nearly straight up when the large, orange-colored air sacs are inflated during display. This occurs when males converge in the early dawn to dance on the community courting stage, which may be in flat grassland or on a little knoll. Standing about two yards apart, each actor shuffles its feet, scurries back and forth with the wings dropped, the neck held erect, and the bill pointed nearly straight down. Deep pumping noises reverberate over the fields from the cluster of eager males. Soon the females gather to watch and then indicate the male of their choice.

After breeding, the female makes a simple nest —hardly more than a small cleared area—on the ground and deposits about a dozen eggs in it. She incubates the eggs for about 21 days and broods the young for the first week after hatching; thereafter they follow her in a covey.

Sharp-tailed Grouse (*Pedioecetes phasianellus*) courtship dance

Sharp-tailed Grouse (*Pedioecetes phasianellus*) follow a similar pattern of polygamous behavior in and around the pine forests of western North America. Like the Prairie Chicken in size but with smaller gular sacs, this species has the tail much more pointed and the plumage more spotted, less regularly barred.

The Sage Grouse or Sage Hen (*Centrocercus urophasianus*) is the largest of the North American grouse. Males weigh six to eight pounds (females are

Sage Grouse (*Centrocercus urophasianus*) courtship dance

several pounds lighter) and reach a total length of nearly 2½ feet, the long, slender tail accounting for much of this length. During full display this ornament is erected like an extended fan and forms a beautifully animated background for the head and the pair of grossly inflated gular sacs—which at times resemble oranges—worn high on the sides of the neck.

An integral part of the display is deep bowing, accompanied by resonant booming and groaning and by the vibrations of stiffened wings held partly open. This splendid show is put on in competition with other males on dance stages generally used for generations. Like the Prairie Chicken, the female Sage Grouse assumes all the duties of nest-building, incubation and care of the young. The clutch is usually seven eggs, and incubation requires about 21 days.

Pheasants, Quails and Peacocks (*Phasianidae*)

The family Phasianidae contains the most valuable birds in the world, as well as a galaxy of species virtually unrivaled in beauty except by the birds of paradise. They number about 57 genera and 170 species and range from about the dimensions of a small sparrow (see Chinese Quail) to those of that universally known species, the peacock. The majority have chicken-like bodies with long, naked legs and toes; and in nearly all species the males are more highly colored and often wear spurs.

This highly variable and interesting family is split into a New World subfamily and an Old World one. The Odontophorinae, or New World Quails, is an assemblage of 34 medium-sized species that occur over most of the New World and are thought to be the descendants of an ancient invasion from the Old World, where the family still predominates. These species are best known through the wide-ranging, friendly Bob White (*Colinus virginianus*).

In the wild state in the Old World, but cosmopolitan as a result of domestication and introduction as game, is the other subfamily, the Phasianinae, which consists of 48 genera and about 136 species. One of this assortment is the most valuable bird in the world. It is, of course, the chicken. Also included are the peacocks of the Indo-Malayan region and the famous Congo Peacock, which lives so secretively that it remained unknown to science until a few years ago. Then too there are the beautiful pheasants. Also among the group are found the tiny true quails, the francolins and the true partridges, which most nearly resemble New World quails.

The only native member of the family in the eastern United States is the Bob White. This excellent game bird ranges west to Colorado and south to Mexico. Three other species of *Colinus* are found in Middle and South America, most of which are more chestnut, less buff below, and usually with black throats. One, the Black-throated Bob White (*C. nigrogularis*), an eight-inch bird, lives in Yucatan and Central America. The Bob White itself is a stocky brownish bird some nine inches long. This well-known species has habits much like those of other New World quails. It is nonmigratory; in fact, the only migrations that occur in this subfamily are shifts in altitude to avoid freezing weather.

The Bob White is confiding and gentle, even nesting in city parks. The male selects a territory, announces his occupancy and eligibility by singing from a rock and selects a mate. Then, after several weeks, the female constructs a simple nest in thick grass, usually under a tussock formed into a protective dome to conceal from twelve to eighteen pure white, sharply pyriform eggs. Both parents share in the incubation, which requires some 23 days. As soon as they crawl free of the eggshells, the young leave the nest in company with the parents, who continue to brood them, usually in different locations each night, for about three weeks. After about one week the young can make short jumping flights because their wings develop much more rapidly than the rest of their plumage, resembling in this respect most other gallinaceous birds.

An interesting mechanism of defense in quail is their habit of gathering together in circles on the ground. The individuals of such a circle are usually the members of a family. All sit with tails in and heads out. When a predator comes too close, the birds leap into flight, going in all directions and probably confusing the predator. This mechanism also provides warmth: when the occupants of such a cluster are flushed from snow, the marks left behind resemble those from a small explosion.

New World Quail generally resort to "freezing" for security, and to sudden flight when too closely pressed, but some species try to escape by running. Bob Whites flush like rockets, the covey keeping more or less together and close over the ground—usually grassy ground with bushes and a few trees. The fleeing birds intermittently beat their wings and then glide, flying and sailing with the curved wings cupped downward; then suddenly they drop into the grass and, if flushed again, may fly in different directions, dispersing across the countryside.

Typical of the three species of the genus *Lophortyx* in the southwestern United States south to Mexico is the California Quail (*L. californicus*). In this species the male differs from the female in having an erect recurved plume growing from the crown, olive-brown upperparts and a bright chestnut abdomen. Also known as the Valley Quail, this bird can dwell almost anywhere. For example, it can live for months and even years without drinking water, if provided with succulent vegetation. It is chiefly an inhabitant of bushy grasslands and semideserts, and where formerly it was found in flocks of as many as 500, today it is sorely depleted as a result of gunning.

At the onset of breeding time the males fight and call from specific territories which they select and in which the nest is made. The female usually does the incubating of from 12 to 16 buffy, spotted eggs, with the male aggressively guarding the territory. Later, both parents take charge of the young.

Closely related is the Desert or Gambel's Quail (*L. gambelii*) of the southern United States and Mexico, which also has a black plume on the crown, a black throat, but has a black abdominal patch and a reddish instead of a blackish head. Mearns' Quail (*Cyrtonyx montezumae*), also known as the Harlequin Quail, is an eight-inch, clown-faced bird, which inhabits the open, rugged mountain grasslands from southwestern United States to Mexico, where it is also called the Montezuma Quail. Just as in a related species, the Ocellated Quail (*C. ocellatus*), both sexes of Mearns' Quail incubate and care for the young. In winter they join in large flocks to execute a kind of walking migration down to valleys from the high slopes. The food of this quail is chiefly seeds and tender grasses, but some insects are eaten.

Another bird of the high mountain slopes is the very distinctive Mountain Quail (*Oreortyx pictus*), which has a long, blackish plume projecting from the mid-crown. This vivid chestnut-throated, 11-inch bird of the California–Nevada mountains goes up to the snow line. Like all quails it roosts on the ground.

In the deep woodlands of Central and South America the 16 species of relatively very little known Spotted Wood-quails (*Odontophorus*) are found. These birds are generally brown and are so cryptically colored that they melt into the floor of the jungle which is their home. All have the head crested, and the females are not sharply differentiated from the males as in the other quails. Their calls are liquid, rapidly delivered whistles. The Spotted Wood-quails are very shy birds and are rarely seen in their forest habitat. Usually one gets only a flashing glimpse of them as they rocket off from underfoot.

Dr. Frank M. Chapman's reports on the Marbled Wood-quail (*O. gujanensis*) on Barro Colorado acquaints us with one of the most remarkable bird duets. Dr. Chapman observed it delivered by two birds standing head to head about a foot apart. The call is a rapid and repeated *corcorovado,* one bird singing the *corcoro,* and the second the *vado.*

A very large proportion of the world's most beautiful game birds are members of the Old World subfamily Phasianinae—an assemblage that includes the pheasants and the true partridge. Among the pheasants the male is usually much more ornately dressed, and in many his ornamental plumage rivals that of the birds of paradise and the small but very colorful hummingbirds. The plumes were probably developed from behavior involving polygamy.

In the pheasants, each male has a harem of many females, and he takes no part whatever in any phase of nest-building or parental care. All are relatively large birds that live on the ground and roost in trees; and all nest on the ground with the exception of one group of highly colorful, tree-nesting species called tragopans. Members of the Phasianinae can run almost from the moment they crawl from the shell.

Most of the species are fairly sedentary, and almost the only especially migratory member of this purely Old World assemblage is the European Quail (*Coturnix coturnix;* Plate 41), which has a very wide range in Eurasia and Africa. Slightly smaller than the average American Quail, it has a white throat and is cryptically marked with brown and black in a way suggesting the New World species to which it is distantly related. A close relative is the Australian Quail (*Synoicus ypsilophorus*), a typically stocky little brown quail, which has successfully invaded New Guinea and Australia from Asia. Only two other members of this family have been able to cross the restless seas from the Indo-Malayan region to New Guinea and Australia successfully; one is the Chinese Painted Quail (see below), and the other is the Stubble Quail (*C. novae-zealandiae*), which was formerly found in both Australia and New Zealand but has been extinct in the latter country since 1870.

The European Gray Partridge (*Perdix perdix*), also called the Hungarian Partridge, is a swift-flying, medium-sized bird easily recognized by its transversely barred sides, black horseshoe-shaped abdominal patch and generally grayish plumage. This bird, which is a resident of the middle portions of Europe and Asia between sea level and 15,000 feet, was long ago introduced into America. It is reported that a quarter of a million living birds have been brought in and that the species has now become established in virtually all of the western states and in many parts of Canada. The Hungarian Partridge is highly regarded as a gunning target because of its fast take-off and erratic flight. Relatives are the francolins (*Francolinus*), of which there are 35 species extending over Eurasia and Africa. Most of these have the legs sharply spurred, sometimes even the females having such armor, and in some the males are equipped with twin sets of spikes. They are all rather similar in appearance and in their general selection of habitat. Most of them are found in bushy grasslands. They are larger than the American Bob White, ranging from about 12 to 18 inches in length. The nest is a scrape on the ground in grass and from three to seven buffy to brown eggs are laid in it. Another famous species is the Red-legged Partridge (*Alectoris rufa;* Plate 38) of Europe, Corsica and the Canary Islands.

Francolins have many smaller relatives, all highly gregarious, quail-like birds. The smallest, the Chinese Painted Quail (*Excalfactoria chinensis*) of Eastern Asia, the Indo-Malayan region and Australia, are no larger than sparrows. The coveys run about like rodents in the grass of the high interior valleys of New Guinea, particularly in the vicinity of native gardens. The male is blue-gray with vivid white markings on the head and neck; the female is earth-brown with buffy markings.

The Short-tailed Pheasants, or monals, are quite partridge-like in the shape of their wings and are among the most glitteringly beautiful of the pheasants. One, the rooster-sized Impeyan Pheasant (*Lophophorus impejanus*), is colored like a Morpho butterfly, its iridescent blues, greens and bronzes giving the impression of a bird of burnished metal.

Blood-pheasants are splashed with patches of the brightest yellowish green and crimson. Some range to the snow line in the Himalayas, their stronghold; one, the Blood Pheasant (*Ithaginis cruentus*) of the mountains of Asia, is gray and green with crimson on the head, throat and tail.

Tragopans differ from all other members of the Phasianidae in their habit of building a bulky nest of leaves and twigs in a tree. They are similar to pheasants in body size but differ in having "horns" on the head. Their habitat is more or less the same as that of the Blood Pheasant, and they breed near the snow line in the Himalayas. All are quite wonderfully colored and marked, their brilliance being surpassed only by a handful of birds in the world. The Crimson or Satyr Tragopan (*Tragopan satyra*) of Nepal and Bhutan is largely orange-scarlet with a black head and white spots. The cock has two large hornlike wattles, blue ornaments that stand up from their concealment under the crown feathers when the male displays to the female. He does this a foot or so in front of her, the head being rapidly shaken and the wings opened to show crimson linings.

Other splendid species include the Fire-backed Pheasants of Malaysia, which are smaller. One example is the Crested Fireback (*Lophura ignita*) of Borneo and Sumatra, in which the male of most species is considerably larger than the female, being 29 inches to the 24 of the female. Both sexes have a brushlike crest and bright blue facial wattles. The species is named for the glowing crimson back and rump of the male. Curiously, in two of the three species the males have the back bright red and in this respect differ greatly from their blackish mates, whereas in the third species, an inhabitant of Sumatra, the male and the female are both blackish.

The true pheasants are known to virtually everyone because of the wide use of the plumes for millinery purposes, because many of them are familiar zoo birds, and, finally, because in many parts over the world some are famous game birds. These pheasants have the tail generally long and pointed and the sides of the head usually highly colored and naked. There may, in addition, be wattles or saw-tooth combs of bare, colorful skin on the head, and in the male there is always at least one pair of sharp spurs. As in most of the Phasianinae, the female is drab and small, whereas the males are much more colorful and highly pugnacious. They strut and exhibit their plumage, which often includes "horns" growing over the ears.

The most cosmopolitan of the pheasants is the Ring-neck (*Phasianus colchicus*), a handsome bird that grows to a length of three feet. The first to be taken to America were introduced by Benjamin Franklin's son-in-law and liberated in New Jersey, but the earliest really successful introduction took place in Oregon in 1882. The Ring-neck that is now America's most popular game bird is actually a mixture of several Old World races of the species, some of which lack the white collar. In Eurasia the species ranges widely and varies greatly. The western birds lack the collar and are darker and more greenish, while the eastern birds are more amber and copper, with prominent white collars and greenish rumps. Both kinds are now found in the New World but the latter predominates.

Ring-necks are hardy birds. They eat seeds and tender plants as well as many injurious insects. Their preferred habitat is in and about farmlands. The male defends a breeding territory. During display he circles the female with one wing extended and the tail partially expanded and slanted so his prospective mate can see its splendid coloration. The females—there is usually a harem—do all the work of rearing the young. The nest is a hollow, sparsely lined scrape in grass. From 8 to 15 eggs are laid. Soon after hatching, the young give up roosting on the ground and join their parents to sleep in trees.

Game birds too beautiful to shoot, it would seem, are the Lady Amherst (*Chrysolophus amherstiae*), the Golden (*C. pictus*) and the Reeves Pheasant (*Syrmaticus reevesi*), all of which live in the mountainous regions of eastern Asia. The Lady Amherst—a delicately colored white, green and black bird—has central tail feathers that reach a length of 46 inches. This species wears a delicate capelike fan that opens to cover the neck and sides of the face in display, a "shyness" that belies its polygamous habits.

The Golden Pheasant is a fabulous creature of gold, scarlet, green and black. Because of its color and beauty, plus its readiness to live and breed in captivity, it has become a very common zoo bird, although in the wild areas of Tibet and China, its original home, it is now quite uncommon. The Reeves, a relative of the Ring-neck, one of the longest birds in the world, is a wondrous gold and black bird of China that reaches a length of eight feet, counting its immense train of tail.

Some of the most beautiful of the pheasants are found in the most inhospitable regions. For example, the Lady Amherst has been observed at 15,000 feet in the Himalayas and the Silver Pheasant (*Lophura nycthemera*) at 9000 feet, in the dripping mountain forest of Burma. The latter, a well-known aviary bird, is silvery white above with a black crown and black underparts. Its face is decorated with naked red areas of skin. Its female is drab, being generally olive-brown, as is customary in true pheasants. The Brown Eared-Pheasant (*Crossoptilon mantchuricum*) is one of three unusual species of the bleak mountains of northeastern China. The sexes are alike in color.

The Red Jungle Fowl (*Gallus gallus*), which ranges in the wild state throughout the Oriental region

Brown Eared-Pheasant (*Crossoptilon mantchuricum*)

from sea level to altitudes of 5000 feet, is a member of the pheasant family and the ancestor of all domestic poultry. It closely resembles a domestic chicken both in its calls and adornments. It has the characteristic long, high-arched tail, twin-wattled throat and saw-toothed frontal comb. Wild populations in the Philippines and on other islands are evidence of man's ancient travels.

In the wild, the chicken is a typical bird of the woodlands, living in the deep woods, along the forest edges and in bushy fields. It goes in flocks and in the air has the typical pheasant flight consisting of bursts of wing beats followed by glides. Dr. Kenneth C. Parkes has pointed out that the presence of a roost of Jungle Fowl along a trail may often be detected through the familiar chicken-yard odor. When flushed, the wild birds, just like their domestic relatives, call noisily.

The Red Jungle Fowl has been associated with man at least as long as has the dog. Asiatic records of it go back more than 3000 years, and the Greeks and Romans knew of it. Domesticated fowl were kept by the Polynesians but, although these people traveled to almost every land mass in the Pacific before recorded history, there is no record of the chicken reaching the New World prior to the time of the Spaniards.

This long period of domestication has produced three major types of chickens—food birds, show birds and fighting birds. A splendid example of the first is the White Leghorn, which is one of the most prolific egg-layers known, laying an average of nearly an egg a day. Others are the Plymouth Rock and Rhode Island Red, both of which are large and yet are prolific layers too. A spectacular example of the second group is the Long-tailed Yokohama, which the Japanese have bred for long graceful plumage. It develops an arched tail that reaches 20 feet in length. The third type, the fighting bird, has been bred for bravery and an instinct to kill, the result being a fighter of such ferocity that those who see it in action often react with mixed feelings of shock, horror and fascination.

A bird almost too beautiful for words is the Great Argus Pheasant (*Argusianus argus*) of Malaya and Borneo. It has the inner wing feathers greatly broadened and elongated, and is painted with round, colorful markings which, because of their similarity to huge eyes, caused the bird to be named after the Greek monster with the hundred eyes. Argus Pheasants are very large, and in display the enormously elongated secondary feathers are elevated to form two partitions of eye-spotted feathers and are angled upward like reflectors, the bird's back forming the base.

The Great Argus reaches six feet in length. It displays on a site in the forest, which it clears and keeps clean of fallen debris. The male owner remains in and around this bower during much of the day, sitting quietly or displaying, and fighting any intruders. There is a record of a courtship combat between an Argus and a Fire-back on such a bower. So intent on keeping the area clean is the Argus that the natives of Borneo trap it by inserting razor-sharp slivers of bamboo in the cleared ground of the dance stage. In trying to remove these, the Argus becomes so angry that it often cuts its own throat.

Another pheasant with eyelike markings in its plumage is the Ocellated Pheasant or Crested Argus (*Reinardia ocellata*) of Indochina and Malaya. It is very shy and secretive, and it was hardly known until Captain Jean Delacour succeeded in capturing and bringing live birds to Europe. The rectrices, or tail feathers, of this species are the largest wild feathers known, the central pair being almost six feet long and six inches wide. This fantastic bird appears to have been the inspiration for the legendary Chinese Fenghuang, or Phoenix.

The peacocks of India (Plate 40) and Africa comprise the last group of the family Phasianidae. Those of the Indian region, including Ceylon, rival the glittering splendor and jewel-like quality of Oriental treasure troves. Because they take easily to domestication and are so beautiful, almost every zoo has them on display. Since ancient times the Hindus have protected the peafowl with a religious zeal.

In the wild, peafowl live in parties, usually in dry open forest. They habitually go to roost early in tall trees, calling and bugling loudly as they move upward in short stages in the afternoon and as they come down in the early morning. The males usually display solitarily, and in full display outdo even the Argus in sheer shimmering splendor (Plate 40). The huge tail coverts are elevated to form a massive, lacy fan, supported from behind by the unadorned tail feathers. The train extends from ground to ground over the back and is angled over the head like a tilted umbrella thickly hung with glittering ornaments. This lovely sight is attended by rasping noises from the fluttered wings and prancing movements of the feet. The casual reaction of the females to this display is hard to credit. The harem ranges usually from two to five females. Each generally lays from three to five brownish buff eggs.

Some years ago Dr. J. P. Chapin discovered a peacock in the forests of Central Africa, an area far removed from the previously known haunts in the

Long-tailed Yokohama Chicken
(strain of *Gallus gallus*)

120]

Indian and Malayan regions. While clearly a peacock, this bird was so different that a new genus had to be erected for it. Thus we have the Congo Peacock (*Afropavo congensis*), an important discovery to ornithologists.

Dr. Chapin's first clue that there might be such a bird in the Ituri forest came in 1913 when he collected a single secondary quill from a native's hat. He next discovered similar feathers in two old mounted and incorrectly identified birds in a Belgian museum. He finally discovered the new species in 1937. Since then live specimens have been carried to American and European zoos. The male Congo Peacock is glossy blackish with a tuft of white ornamental plumes in the crown, somewhat as in the Oriental peacocks. The females are brown and green and show the peafowl ancestry of this species even more clearly than the males.

Guinea Fowls (*Numididae*)

The widely distributed Guinea Fowl, which has become an important domesticated bird throughout the civilized world, is descended from the Common Guinea Hen (*Numida meleagris*), one of seven known species of a family restricted to Africa and Madagascar. These birds generally occur in flocks in bushy grasslands and open forest.

Guinea hens are related to pheasants and other fowl-like birds, except that in the guinea fowl the sexes are dressed almost alike, all having the plumage usually blackish or deep bluish, with profuse white or gray spotting. The guinea fowl's head is partially bare and the crown usually bears an ornament. In addition, some of the species wear bulging gape wattles.

Two primitive guinea fowl wear spurs somewhat similar to those in pheasants and chickens. One is the Black Guinea Fowl (*Phasidus niger*) of western Africa, which is the size of a small chicken and has the naked portions of the head and neck washed with yellow and orange. The five species comprising the true guinea fowls lack spurs. The most wide-ranging is the widely domesticated Common Guinea Hen, which has red on the naked portions of the head and helmet and on the wattles on either side of the mouth. The neck is washed with red and blue. Three species of Crested Guinea Hens (*Guttera*) wear hairy, inky black feather tufts above their naked faces. The most aberrant species is the Long-tailed or Vulturine Guinea Fowl (*Acryllium vulturinum*) of eastern Africa, in which the head is shaped like that of a small vulture and the naked areas are bright blue in color. Another unusual character is a pair of long central tail feathers like those of a pheasant.

Guinea fowls occur between sea level and about 9000 feet. They move warily over the ground, running rather than flying when escaping from enemies. When fleeing, they make no attempt at concealment, apparently being confident that they can outdistance their enemies. When closely pressed by horsemen, they will burst into the air, fly a short distance and then settle in a tree. Their call is a rasping, stuttering, metallic click.

The Common Guinea Fowl travels in flocks which may, according to Colonel Meinertzhagen, number as many as 2000 birds. They move many miles per day, but at night they roost in trees. They feed on vegetable matter such as seeds, berries and tender shoots, and on invertebrates such as slugs.

Nests are built in shallow hollows in grass and are sparsely lined with grass. From 6 to 15 very hard-shelled eggs, generally yellowish buff and deeply pitted, are laid. Incubation takes more than a mouth.

Turkeys (*Meleagrididae*)

The Common Turkey (*Meleagris gallopavo*) of North America and the tableland of Mexico and the Ocellated Turkey (*Agriocharis ocellata*) of the lowlands of the Yucatan peninsula and adjacent Guatemala and British Honduras are the sole representatives of this family. Both are so similar to pheasants that it is probable that they are descendants of a pheasant stock that long ago invaded the New World from Asia.

The Turkey was once so characteristic of North America and seemingly so indelibly identified with the pilgrims that Benjamin Franklin thought it should replace the Bald Eagle as the emblem of the United

Vulturine Guinea Fowl (*Acryllium vulturinum*)

States of America. The most spectacular, largest and most valuable native American game bird, it is today nearly world-wide in distribution as a domestic bird. It was once abundant in most of the great forests of North America from Mexico to Canada, early travelers writing of hundreds congregating in the fall and winter to feed on acorns, tender shoots and buds on the floor of deciduous forests. Such flocks, which usually consisted of females and their offspring, moved over the ground by day and took to the trees by night. The fully adult males went about in smaller groups, gobbling, chattering and fearing nothing.

These wild birds, like the curassows in the virgin forests of Amazonia today, were fearless and inquisitive when first encountered by settlers, and this apparently encouraged a wanton slaughter, which, together with the destruction of much of the original forest, extirpated them on a large part of their former range. Thanks to wise management practices, the birds are now increasing in some areas, and have spread into parts of Pennsylvania and New York where they have been absent for generations. Also, they have become very wary and hard to kill.

Year after year at Thanksgiving time a very large percentage of the population of the United States eat the meat of the domestic Turkey. Back of this custom lies the story of how the early colonists brought the bird back to America from the barnyards of Europe, whither it had been carried decades earlier by Spanish explorers. This was the Mexican race, which has a white-tipped tail and upper tail coverts, whereas the native Wild Turkeys were of a race with a brown-tipped tail. Today the bird of the Conquistador lives in the New England forests and the native bird has largely vanished. And all through this area and to the south and west one finds turkey farms, making this bird, first domesticated by the Aztecs, the source of an American industry.

But it is doubtful that an Aztec warrior would recognize many of the birds that are called "turkeys" today. Some of these are: the Broad-breasted Bronze, developed on Rhode Island; the Bourbon Red, which first was developed in Bourbon County, Kentucky; the Black Norfolk, a turkey still remarkably like the bird the Pilgrims brought from Europe; the White Holland, an albino or mutant strain first developed in Holland. Another albino is the popular Beltsville Small White, which has been selectively bred for smallness. This Maryland breed is now in great demand because, in the language of the breeders, it is an apartment-sized bird.

The derivation of the name "turkey" as applied to this bird is shrouded in confusion. The name was originally applied to the bird we know as Guinea Fowl, but writers of the sixteenth and seventeenth centuries confused the two species, and Linnaeus applied the generic name *Meleagris* to our turkey, although this was the classical word for Guinea Fowl. The ultimate fixing of the name on the bird brought from Mexico may have been hastened by resemblance to the "turk-turk-turk" call notes of the gobbler. There appears to be no known connection with the name of the country, Turkey.

An illustration of the way these birds are dispersed in domestication occurred in 1952 in the high mountains of New Guinea. Catching sight of a native with a "new" species of bird-of-paradise plume in his headdress, the author plunged into a crowd of dancing men only to find that the feather came from the Mexican race of the Common Turkey. Later he learned that settlers had flown turkeys from the coast to a remote farm in the central part of the island some years earlier.

Common Turkey gobblers reach 50 inches in length, or about a foot more than the female. They are polygamous and, like the grouse and pheasants, keep a harem. Initially the females of such a harem are defended as a group from other males and are escorted closely. The male spends much time displaying his splendid feathers to the group and to individual birds. This display hardly requires describing, except to say that the performing male looks very much like the cartoons, drawings and trade marks so often made of him. But it is important to note that, in addition to the feather show, there is a rolling accompaniment of grunts and gobbles and a sound like that of fingernails scratching on parchment, which is produced by the shaking of wing feathers.

After copulation the male pays no further attention to the female. She hides her nest very carefully on the ground under a bush and lays from 12 to 20 buffy, spotted eggs. Incubation requires some 28 days. The young are precocial and soon after hatching leave the nest. In a few weeks they can fly well enough to flutter into the arboreal roosts.

In Yucatan, Guatemala and British Honduras occurs the Ocellated Turkey (*Agriocharis ocellata*). It is much like the Common Turkey in size, form and behavior; however, unlike the Common Turkey, which in Mexico lives in the high mountain pine and oak forests, the Ocellated inhabits bushy, semiforested lowlands. This splendid bird lacks the kind of beard sported by the Common Turkey gobbler, is generally more metallic in appearance and has brighter coppery colors. The chief character of this well-marked species is a neck and head that are bare, blue and profusely covered with coral-colored pimples. It also has a yellow-tipped protuberance growing on the crown between the eyes.

Megapodes (*Megapodiidae*)

Brush Turkeys, Scrub Fowl, Mallee Fowl, Mound Builders, Thermometer Birds, Incubator Birds, or Megapodes, as they are variously called, are great-footed gallinaceous birds that occur in Australia, New Guinea, Malaya and the islands of Micronesia east to Samoa and north to the Philippines. Except for Palawan Island in the Philippines, they completely supplant the pheasants throughout this vast range. Their nearest relatives are the New World guans and curassows and the Old World chickens and pheasants. Like those, they are largely terrestrial birds that roost on limbs by night.

Megapodes (from the Greek words for large feet) are the only known birds—and indeed the only vertebrates above the level of reptiles—that utilize heat other than that of the parent's body for the incubation of their eggs. Thus, like the young of turtles, alligators, crocodiles and snakes, their young are hatched beneath earth, sand, forest litter and volcanic ash. Their use of three different sources of natural heat with many curious variations is one of the most interesting stories in nature.

The first of the major divisions of this family consists of hen-sized fowl with brown- and gray-crested heads. Of these the Scrub Fowl (*Megapodius*), with three species, is the most wide-ranging. The second division consists of blackish, turkey-sized birds with naked or partially naked bright-colored heads, helmets or wattles.

In all megapodes the wings are short and rounded, the tail fairly large, and the legs and feet very strong and tipped with powerful claws. The sexes are much alike, although the males are generally a little larger and darker. They eat fallen fruit, seeds, berries, insects, crabs and snails.

Of all the strange birds that were encountered by the armed forces during World War II, none was more interesting than the Scrub Fowl (*M. freycinet*). In many Pacific jungles its peculiar mounds provided the only dry spots to stand on, and—in New Guinea at least—nearly every bivouac area was ringed with their nests. Some idea of the immense range of this bird can be gained by noting a few of the more famous areas where it occurred: Port Moresby, Buna and Hollandia, all on New Guinea; Townsville, Guadalcanal, Saipan, Guam, all overseas from New Guinea, the presumed point of origin of the family; and Leyte and Bataan.

In Micronesia soldiers trapped the resident species of Scrub Fowl (*M. lapérouse*) and traded live birds to natives for souvenirs. To the surprise and gratification of naturalists, on tiny war-torn Peleliu the Scrub Fowl survives in the brush and vines that have overgrown the bomb craters and flame-scorched battlefields. On other islands starving Japanese garrisons nearly or completely wiped out the birds. Such may be the fate on Saipan, Tinian, Rota and Guam of the Brush Fowl, which were apparently already very rare on those islands before the war.

Like its near relative, the Chicken, the overwater dispersal of the Brush Fowl was assisted by mariners in dugout canoes traveling unbelievable distances long before the dawn of recorded history. But in general the bird managed to cross those water barriers to remote ocean islands long before the coming of man.

The bond between man and this bird is very old. The aborigines in Australia, New Guinea and many

G. E. KIRKPATRICK: NATIONAL AUDUBON

Ocellated Turkey (*Agriocharis ocellata*) displaying

of the Micronesian islands protect their bizarre nesting sites and as a rule do not kill the birds although the flesh is quite palatable. Instead, they "farm" the nesting sites for eggs. Sometimes the sites are "owned" for generations without a bird being killed for food. For example, the dangerous Sepiks in the interior of New Guinea know each owner of the 30 to 50 nest mounds located within a radius of five miles of the village of Kanganaman; they do not rob nests owned by other members of the tribe. The nest mounds are often within a hundred yards of villages, and, like omnipresent barnyard fowl, Scrub Fowl can be heard at all hours, particularly at night.

Of the three basic methods by which megapodes harness natural heat for incubation—warmth generated by decomposing vegetation, warmth captured from the sun and warmth thrown off by subterranean volcanism—the first system as used by the Scrub Fowl is the most remarkable, if only because of the extraordinary work involved.

Pairs or groups of birds rake together the debris that lies under tangled brush, usually near the seashore but also in tall dark riverine forests hundreds of miles inland. Each bird moves slowly backward, raking with its huge nails and feeding on grubs, small animals and fruits thus exposed. It stands on one foot and rakes powerfully with the other, sending dead leaves, sticks and all manner of litter cascading backward toward an ever accumulating heap. Sometimes the mound reaches a height of 15 feet, and one nearly 50 feet in diameter was reported from Australia. But usually they are 5 to 7 feet high, about 20 feet in diameter and roughly conical. The largest mounds are almost certainly the product of many generations of birds and are very durable.

After completion and maturation, the compost-like mound warms to about 95 degrees or 96 degrees F. It is then that the heat-sensitive female excavates high on the side of the heap a hole several feet deep and slanted steeply inward. In this she lays her large, white, oval, thin-shelled eggs, drilling a new hole for each egg. A full clutch probably is from five to eight eggs, yet dozens are sometimes taken from a mound during the course of the year, indicating that some mounds are communal. After the eggs have been in the mound for a few weeks, the shells become thickened and coffee-colored. Each pair of Scrub Fowl remains for many months attending the mound, which must be aerated and have its temperature regulated!

Once the writer camped within forty yards of a mound of *M. freycinet,* and all through the day and night could hear the bugle-like calls of the birds. Apparently they never wandered more than half a mile away, and the solitary pair in attendance remained together in their travels. The calls were almost always delivered in a duet. The second or answering call, possibly that of the female, was superimposed on the end of the initial call, but sometimes after a slight delay. The period of incubation, up to 63 days, is the longest known in birds and contrasts strikingly with 11 to 12 days for a Cowbird and 21 days for a domestic fowl.

Sepik head-hunters of the Iatmul tribe claim that the Scrub Fowl returns often to listen for the peeps of newly hatched birds and eventually to assist them from the mound. There are unconfirmed reports from Australia that the adults rebury the young for protection at night. In partial support of these stories is the fact that chicks that appear to have discarded the shells days before have frequently been found in the mounds. How the chicks live in their dark, warm prisons for days after hatching is not known. Perhaps they eat the ants that often abound in such places. Certainly many species of worms, insects, spiders, small lizards and snails are drawn to the warm mounds. Even large reptiles are attracted, and the eggs of lizards have been found side by side with those of the megapode.

Some megapodes bury their eggs to a depth of many feet, others only a foot or so. When the young megapode finally emerges from its incubator, its feathers are free of their waxy sheathing and the plumage is so well developed that, if necessary, it can spring into the air and fly, though it is still relatively small and rather quail-like in appearance. It is fully able to and frequently does take care of itself from the moment of hatching.

A near relative, the Ocellated Megapode (*Leipoa ocellata*) of Australia, constructs an incubator that functions like that of the Scrub Fowl, but is much more orderly in form. First the bird digs a shallow hole and fills it with debris. Next a doughnut-shaped heap of leaves and rotted debris is raked around the freshly filled pit, leaving a mound with an open core. Then this formation is covered with sand and grass heaped on so generously that the hollow center is covered and the pile assumes the shape of an inverted flattish cone. This fireless cooker draws its heat from the impounded and decomposing debris.

The bird deposits her eggs in this mound in an amazing way. For each she digs a hole in the warm, sandy core, where she deposits the large conical egg with the small end down. Days apart, she deposits her eggs on the same plane and in an almost perfect pattern, with each of the first four eggs laid as if at the corners of a square. Next the gaps are filled so as to form an orderly circle. The way in which the female (or females) accomplishes this feat is unknown and hard to imagine, considering the fact that as each egg is laid it vanishes under a thick covering of sand. The young of this species dig their own way out.

Garishly colored large megapodes, approaching a small turkey in size, are *Alectura* of Australia, *Talegalla* and *Aepypodius* of New Guinea, and *Macrocephalon* of the Celebes Islands.

Although first reported from the Philippines in 1521, it was not until the eminent naturalist, John Gould, visited Australia in 1839 that the world began to hear something of the wonders of megapodes. Among the birds that he saw was the Wattled Talegallus (*Alectura lathami*), usually known as the Brush Turkey—a close relative of *Talegalla* and *Macrocephalon*. All have colorful naked or partially naked heads and neck wattles. The Brush Turkey of Australia is a shy bird of hill forests. It builds a structure that is roughly pyramidal and may be ten feet tall and normally uses it year after year. The female lays from 7 to 12 eggs, placing them in a circle about two feet down and always with the large end up. The three species of New Guinea *Talegalla*—all forest birds—are blackish brown with naked pink heads and necks showing through a sparse covering of tiny black feathers. They construct their mounds on steep slopes above the coastal lowlands, which are occupied by the Scrub Fowl. Often several families make a communal nest. Again the eggs are laid with the smaller end down.

Another large relative is the New Guinea *Aepypodius,* of which two mountain-loving species are known. One, *A. bruijnii,* a brownish black, chestnut-rumped bird with three spectacular reddish wattles, was first discovered by native plume collectors about the year 1878 somewhere in the islands fringing the western end of New Guinea. It remained one of the world's "lost" species for over 50 years—this despite the fact that some ten expeditions looked for it. Finally in 1939 a native collector rediscovered it on Waigeu Island and collected a specimen, now at the Academy of Natural Sciences in Philadelphia.

The second species, *A. arfakianus,* lives above 3000 feet on all the great ranges of New Guinea. Very little is known of its breeding habits, although a laying female has been found in October. This species has a naked face that is a bluish gray washed with apple-green. It has a wine-colored comb, a pale blue throat, a gray neck wattle and honey-yellow eyes.

The last member of the turkey-like Megapodes on our list is the Maleo of the North Celebes and Sanghir Islands, the only Megapode with short toes. It is a handsome bird with blackish, glossy upper plumage and reddish and pinkish white underparts. Surmounting its naked neck and head is a grayish black helmet of cellular tissue that rides like a cap turned backward. This species is famous for the migrations it makes between its normal habitat and the very specialized areas in which it builds its incubators. At breeding time the Maleo swarms out of the hill forests to the relatively few areas of beach that are black and composed of coarse, pebble-like sand. Here, in August and September, the pairs dig holes four to five feet in diameter, each hole serving as a communal incubator, with many females joining to lay their eggs one or two feet down in the same excavation. The much greater capacity of black sand

—which appears where old lava enters the sea—to store heat is the reason for the choice of these areas. The natives sometimes pilfer up to eight eggs from a single hole. The Maleo egg is huge, being more than 4 inches long and nearly 2½ inches wide. It has been estimated that it nearly fills the lower abdomen of the female. The time between layings is about 13 days.

At hatching, the young of this species are perhaps the most highly developed of all birds. Upon digging their way out of the mound, they flee from the beach to the adjoining forest. How they find their way back to the mountains is an unsolved riddle.

Many populations of Maleos resort to still another source of heat that is almost unbelievable. These birds excavate holes in the earth of cool mountain forests, lay their eggs in the ground and cover them up. The first naturalists to discover their egg pits were greatly puzzled as to how the eggs survived. Soon they found that the holes were always in the vicinity of hot springs and that the Maleo, with the ease of a housewife switching from gas to electricity, uses two sources of inorganic heat: sun-warmed sand and earth heated by volcanic action. Later, Maleos were found that dug egg pits in ground heated by volcanic steam on the side of Lokon Volcano in the Celebes.

Wattled Talegallus (*Alectura lathami*)

Curassows, Guans and Chachalacas (*Cracidae*)

Scattered fairly widely through the wooded grasslands and jungles of the New World from the southern borders of the United States to Argentina are some 38 species of game birds closely related to grouse, pheasant, quail, Guinea fowl, turkeys and megapodes, and known collectively as curassows.

Many of their relatives, the chicken for example, have been domesticated for ages and are very valuable to man, and although the curassows remain undomesticated, they readily associate with barnyard fowl and breed in capitivity in zoos. Indeed, these endemic New World game birds represent a potentially valuable, nearly untapped source of food.

Curassows are moderately gregarious, long-tailed birds. Some live in forests as much as 8000 feet above sea level, and some have taken to bushes and small trees growing in warm grasslands, but the greatest concentration occurs in lowland tropical forests. In the jungles the largest species, the true curassows, roost in trees and spend a large portion of their time scratching for food—much of it animal—among fallen leaves. Guans are medium-sized species, chiefly fruit eaters that live in the crown of the jungle. The smallest species, the chachalacas, are birds of the forest edge and bushy grasslands.

In all curassows the skeleton is very light and the voice is developed for the production of harsh cries, chicklike peeps, and deep, windy, hooting sounds such as come from blowing across the mouth of a bottle. In forests unspoiled by man, these birds sometimes abound in incredible numbers, suggesting the vast population that an undisturbed forest will support. For example, in the untouched jungles of the Macarena region of southeastern Colombia they were still so numerous in 1941 that it was not uncommon near our camp to see dozens of chicken-sized guans in a single tree, and everywhere the large black-and-white turkey-sized curassows walked on the ground in pairs in seeming fearlessness.

During the nonbreeding season curassows and guans are often highly gregarious, and all of them roost in trees by night. The large curassows feed on the floor of the deepest forests, the flocks or pairs keeping in contact by means of deep hoots that have a ventriloquial quality. The small brownish chachalacas are denizens of drier, better lighted feeding grounds, usually on the floor of bushy fields. They are very noisy, emitting chattering cries that suggest their name. Often several chachalacas will call together, one setting off the other, with the result a scramble of sound.

The guans habitually congregate to feed in the upper tiers of fruiting trees in all kinds of forest. As they stream through the forest in bands from feeding tree to feeding tree, they follow one another, crying weakly. In the air they alternately flutter and glide.

Of the large species of *Crax,* one, the Great Curassow (*C. rubra*), occurs in tropical forests from Middle America to Ecuador and seven others from Mexico to Argentina. All wear a shaggy, permanently erected, forward-curling crest, and all the males have contrasting black upperparts and partially white underparts. In some the base of the bill is bulbous, and generally the females are differently colored with bars and patterns of brown. The male is more than three feet long, with a bright yellow knob on the forehead. The female is considerably smaller, has no knob and has a curled crest vividly slashed with white and underparts more brownish. In another species widespread in Amazonia, the Crested Curassow (*C. alector*), the female is rather similar to the male in color but the male has a pendant wattle at the base of the bill. The Razor-billed Curassows of the genus *Mitu* are very much like *Crax* except that they have the crest shorter and not curled and wear a bladelike casque on the forehead. An equally large black-and-white relative is the Helmeted Curassow (*Pauxi*)— a purely local inhabitant of the forest floor—of the Andes from Venezuela to Peru, which wears on the forehead a large upward-projecting casque that resembles a partially shriveled fig or a cashew nut. Odd kinds of head ornaments appear often in these birds. Thus the Horned Guan (*Oreophasis derbianus*) of the mountain forests from southern Mexico to Guatemala, which is nearly as large as the largest black-and-white curassows and, like them, is semiterrestrial, differs from them in having a long spike, completely nude and bright orange-red, growing straight up between the eyes.

Occupying a feeding niche in the crown of the forest above that of the true curassows are some twelve species of guans belonging to the genus *Penelope.* Not only are these birds smaller and more graceful than the others, but they generally have the plumage dark grayish or greenish with coppery reflections and the face and throat partially naked. One of the most wide-ranging (Mexico to Argentina) is the Crested Guan (*Penelope purpurascens*), which, with its long tail, is about three feet in length and slender in appearance. The dorsal plumage of this bird is generally dark greenish olive with dull bronzy reflections. Below there is much light streaking. The naked parts of the face are a slaty blue and those of the throat apricot-colored.

The Wattled Guan (*Aburria aburri*), which the author has collected in the thick mountain forest of the eastern Andes of northern South America, is the sole representative of its genus. It is about 2½ feet long and dark olive green in color. The sexes are similar, both wearing long pendant wattles on the upper neck and having the outer primaries narrow and switchlike. Another bird with similar wings is the Sickle-winged Guan (*Chamaepetes goudotii*) of Colombia, Ecuador and Peru.

The largest group in the family, the chachalacas,

falls in the genus *Ortalis*. They have the proportions of a small slender female pheasant and the tail long and expansive. These birds have the throat mostly naked and brick reddish in color with a midline of small feathers; also their ocular areas are naked and generally slaty in color. The Plain Chachalaca (*Ortalis vetula*), which ranges up to two feet in length, is fairly typical. It is rather plain brownish olive with a long dull greenish tail washed with metallic green and tipped with pale gray.

The members of the Cracidae build nests of sticks, vines and leaves in bushes and trees and place them close to the ground, as in *Ortalis,* or 30 or more feet high, as in *Penelope*. The eggs are white, and in the Plain Chachalaca (*O. vetula*), which occasionally nests within the borders of the United States, are incubated chiefly by the female for 22 to 24 days. Like the young of all of the Galliformes, or chicken-like birds, young curassows are covered with down and extremely precocial. Their wings develop quickly, and they can soon flutter to ground and follow parents like barnyard chicks.

Hoatzin (*Opisthocomidae*)

The Hoatzin (*Opisthocomus hoazin*) of the hot river valleys of northern South America is one of the most perplexing and remarkable of all birds. Although pheasant- or Galliformes-like in many ways, it bears resemblances to cuckoos. But it also has so many unique characters that a distinct suborder has to be provided for it.

The Hoatzin is somewhat longer than a crow but more slender in body, with large rounded wings and a long tail composed of ten loosely fitting feathers. It wears a shaggy longitudinal crest atop an abnormally small head, which is partially naked and bright blue. Its general coloration is brown, dark on the upperparts with much pale streaking, and more of a tan color on the lower parts with a large patch of rufous on the lower abdomen.

Two characters serve to distinguish the Hoatzin from all other birds. First, the young are hatched nearly naked but with functional claws on the second and third digits of the fore limb, but the parents show no trace of these claws. Thus, as E. A. Brigham, who announced this in 1884, said: "From an egg laid by a two-footed, two-winged bird hatches a quadruped animal." He and others confirmed that the quadrupedal nature of the young bird disappears after a few days, and the wings thereafter develop as wings and the legs as legs. But during the period of immaturity, the young Hoatzin gets about remarkably well as a quadruped. It soon learns to crawl about on the limbs and even to shuffle up and down sloping trunks, moving rather freely in the middle portions of the riverine trees that are its permanent home. When accidentally dropped into the water the nestling

Sickle-winged Guan (*Chamaepetes goudotii*)

swims and even dives easily and then crawls out, using the bill, legs and fore claws in returning to its nest.

A second character totally different from that of any known bird is the enormous size of the crop. This organ for food storage extends over most of the upper third of the body and penetrates deeply into a huge pocket of the chest made possible by skeletal and musculature modifications not found in any other bird. Hoatzins apparently store in this crop the tender tree leaves and shoots on which they feed.

Hoatzins live close to sluggish rivers in scraggly trees of small or medium size, keeping together in loose flocks. The nest, a collection of sticks fitted crudely together in a tree crotch from 6 to 20 feet above the river, is constructed by both parents. The bird deposits in it two, but sometimes up to five, oval eggs that are whitish, with brownish and purplish spots, and resemble those of a rail. The length of incubation is not known.

GRUIFORMES

Mesites, Roatelos and Monias (*Mesoenatidae*)

The three species comprising this small family live on Madagascar and rank high among the many odd forms of life found on that remote island. For one thing, they have functional wings but do not fly.

Among the Mesites the White-breasted Mesite (*Mesoenas variegata*), a bird of the deep forest, is thrush-sized with reddish brown upperparts, a gray collar, much white on the sides of the face and chest, and the chest heavily spotted with black. But the most striking character is a white line over the eye. The Brown Mesite or Roatelo (*M. unicolor*), a rare bird inhabiting the humid forest floor, is somewhat smaller and stockier. Above it is solid reddish brown, and below it is inclined to chestnut. The Monias, or Bensch's Rail (*Monias benschi*), the size of a large slender thrush, is locally common on the forest floor and on brush-covered sandy plains. Above it is gray; below the male is white on the throat and chest and the female is dull brick red. Both sexes have a white line over the eye and spotting on the chest.

For years experts have pondered the origin of these three birds. It was variously thought they showed similarities to pigeons, rails, gallinaceous birds and perching birds, and some even thought they should be placed in an order of their own. The problem arises from the fact that Mesites have five sets of powder downs—which are relatively rare—and that males assume some functions normally belonging to the female. Dr. A. L. Rand reported that the male Monias seems to perform all the duties of incubation and care of the young and that the Mesites may practice polyandry. He observed groups of males each accompanying a single aggressive female; such groups were inquisitive and, led by the female, would walk up to Rand in the forest to examine him. The female bobbed the head, depressed the tail and frequently called *nak, nak*. Rand records that the Bensch's Rail or Monias has well-developed wings but seems never to use them to fly. Even a tethered bird that he frightened did not try to fly, and when he tossed it into the air, it opened the wings only as it fell to the ground. Recent investigators have shown that the clavicles in the three species of Mesoenatidae are reduced to small rudimentary bones, a condition closely correlated with the loss of flight.

On the ground the Monias run rapidly and nervously, seeking always to escape on foot, even when fleeing from gunfire. According to reliable native testimony, the Monias male, working alone, constructs a thin nest of sticks four to six feet up in a bush usually in sandy grasslands. It is reached by way of an inclined trunk, so that there is no need for the bird to fly at any time. A single white ellipsoid egg, irregularly marked with brown, is deposited on the platform-like nest. This bird apparently is the only tree-nester in which the male takes full responsibility for the nest and eggs. The young are covered with brown and white down and are precocial.

Recently an American collector, Harry Hoogstraal, found two nests of the Brown Mesite (*Mesoenas unicolor*) in the Madagascar rain forest. They were thin platforms of sticks with scant lining placed in sloping trees a yard or so from the ground. In both were found single eggs with females in attendance at the nests. The Mesite chicks are covered with a blackish, rail-like down. Like most of the birds of Madagascar, these birds breed during the wet season, the last three months of the year.

The Mesites with their peculiar behavior are thought by recent authorities to be aberrant members of the ancient order of Gruiformes. This order, Drs. Mayr and Amadon believe, has no obvious ties with any of the more primitive orders. It is composed of many kinds of relict birds, such as cranes, limpkins, trumpeters, Sun-grebes, Kagus, Caniamas and bustards. Some of the more primitive families of the Gruiformes also have the roles of parental care reversed. To this writer, the general body shape, color pattern and fullness of the tail of the females of the Mesoenatidae suggest the African Finfoot.

Button Quail (*Turnicidae*)

Also known as bustard-quail and hemipodes, the 13 species of the button-quail family are found in the temperate and tropical portions of the Old World. Although related to the cranes and the bustards and differing from true quails in many ways, these secretive, elusive birds live in brushy grassland and act very much like miniature quail. They sit tight, flush with a whirr of wings, fly close over the grass, land quickly and run on the ground like quail. Unlike true quails and hemipodes, however, the bustard-quails lack the hind toe (hallux). Also unlike quail, the female bustard-quail, much larger than the male and more richly dressed, plays the aggressive role in courtship, displaying to the male and fighting with other females for attention, as well as building the nest and laying the eggs. Then, while the male incubates the eggs and tends the young, the female polyandrously embarks on other conquests, with the result that it customarily breeds with several males each season.

An even dozen species of the genus *Turnix* occur in Africa, Eurasia, Indo-Malaya, New Guinea and Australia. All are very much alike, and a good example of all of them is the Painted Bustard-quail (*T. varia*) of Australia and New Caledonia. As in all bustard-quail, the sexes are very different from each other in appearance. They are much alike below, being dull whitish with broad gray areas on the chest and upper abdomen, and both have crimson eyes. But above the male is dark brown with blackish markings, whereas the female is broadly painted with bright chestnut on the upper back, lower neck and

[continued on page 145]

64. Stone Curlew (*Burhinus oedicnemu*
Range: Eurasia, Northern Africa
and Canary Islands

[ERIC J. HOSKING]

65. Long-tailed Jaeger (*Stercorarius longicaudus*) Range: Cold seas of Northern Hemisphere [FRITZ GORO: LIFE MAGAZINE]

66. Ring-billed Gull (*Larus delawarensis*) Range: Seas of North America [RUSS KINNE: NATIONAL AUDUBON]

67. Kittiwake
(*Rissa tridactyla*)
Range:
Northern seas;
in winter south
to Mexico

[JOHN MARKHAM]

68. Black-headed Gull (*Larus ridibundus*) Range: Chiefly seas of northern Europe and Asia [ERIC J. HOSKING]

69. Sooty Tern (*Sterna fuscata*)
Range: Southern seas

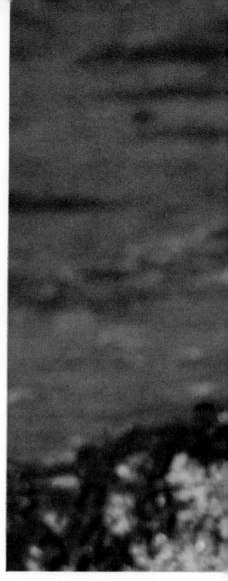

70. Herring Gull (*Larus argentatus*)
Range:
Seacoasts of Northern Hemisphere

71. Lesser Black-backed
Gull (*Larus fuscus*)

Range:
Chiefly eastern Atlantic
from Scandinavia
to France

[WALTER E. HIGHAM]

72.
Fairy Tern
(*Gygis alba*)
Range: Warm
southern seas

73.
Inca Tern
(*Larosterna
inca*)
Range:
Off west coast
of South America

74.
Tufted Puffin
(*Lunda cirrhata*)
Range: North Pacific

[KARL W. KENYON]

75.
Black Skimmer
(*Rynchops nigra*)

Range: Chiefly coasts
of the New World

[ALLAN CRUICKSHANK:
NATIONAL AUDUBON]

76.
Atlantic Puffin
(*Fratercula arctica*)

Range: North Atlantic
coasts

[HELEN CRUICKSHANK:
NATIONAL AUDUBON]

77. Crowned Pigeon (*Goura victoria*)

Range: New Guinea

78. Common Ground Dove (*Columbigallina passerina*)

Range: Warmer parts of the Western Hemisphere

79. White-fronted Dove (*Leptotila verreauxi*)

Range: Texas to Argentina; also Caribbean islands

80. Red-sided Eclectus Parrot, female
(*Larius roratus*)
Range: Southwest Pacific

[AUSTRALIAN INFORMATION BUREAU]

81. Red-sided Eclectus Parrot,
male

[AUSTRALIAN INFORMATION BUREAU]

82. Budgerigar, male feeding female
(*Melopsittacus undulatus*)
Range: Australia

[JOHN MARKHAM]

83. Masked Lovebird (*Agapornis personata*)
Range: Eastern Africa

[CY LA TOUR]

84. Green Leek Parrot (*Polytelis swainsonii*)
Range: Southeast Australia

[J. FITZPATRICK: AUSTRALIAN INFORMATION BUREAU]

85. Mutant of the genus *Aratinga*
Range of the genus: Mexico to Argentina

[CY LA TOUR]

86. Galah (*Cacatua roseicapilla*)
Range: Australia

[NORMAN CHAFFER]

87. Pink Cockatoo (*Cacatua leadbeateri*)
Range: Australia

[J. FITZPATRICK: AUSTRALIAN INFORMATION BUREAU]

**88.
Black Cockatoo
(*Calyptorhyn-
chus magnificus*)**

Range: Australia

[J. FITZPATRICK:
AUSTRALIAN INFOR-
MATION BUREAU]

89. Cuckoo-tailed Parrot (*Alisterus chloropterus*)
Range: New Guinea

[E. THOMAS GILLIARD]

90. Sulphur-crested Cockatoo (*Cacatua galerita*)
Range: Australia, New Guinea and nearby islands

[RUSS KINNE: NATIONAL AUDUBON]

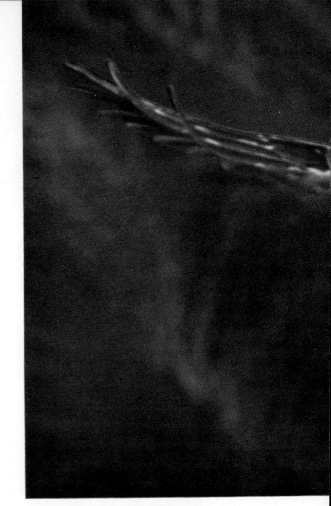

91. Screech Owl (*Otus asio*)
Range: North America south to central Mexico

92. Little Owl (*Athene noctua*)
Range: Eurasia and parts of East Africa

93. Saw-whet Owl (*Aegolius acadicus*) Range: Alaska to Mexico [AUSTING AND KOEHLER: NATIONAL AUDUBON]

94.
Burrowing
Owl
(*Speotyto
cunicularia*)

Range:
Canada to
Tierra del
Fuego; also
Caribbean
islands

[ELIOT PORTER]

95. Barn Owl (*Tyto alba*)
Range: Nearly cosmopolitan

[JOHN MARKHAM]

96. Tawny Owl (*Strix aluco*)
Range: Eurasia and North Africa

[JOHN MARKHAM]

[continued from page 128]

shoulders. The male is about 6½ inches long and weighs about 2¾ ounces, while the female is more than 8 inches in length and weighs about 4½ ounces.

Both by day and by night the female Painted Bustard-quail delivers resonant booming notes during the breeding season. In display it frequently runs around the male with the tail spread and the body plumage puffed out like a ball, stamping and scratching on the ground and fighting with other females. Later it makes a small depression in the ground, using its breast as a form, and rakes together a nest of rootlets and grasses, usually well concealed under a bit of vegetation in grassy, sandy areas.

Four or so whitish oval eggs are laid; they are spotted and blotched with brown and gray, much like the eggs of rails. Immediately after they are laid, the male takes over all the duties of incubation. In 12 to 14 days the down-covered, brownish young emerge. These youngsters resemble gallinaceous chicks, are very precocial and soon follow the male, who solicitously shepherds and feeds them.

In Thailand the author was surprised to find the tiny eggs of these birds (they are somewhat smaller than those of a starling) commonly offered for sale in the markets of Bangkok. Like chicken eggs in America, they were done up in paper containers and sold by the dozen. In Australia, females kept in captivity have been known to lay as many as 17 eggs, or about four normal sets, per season.

Painted Bustard-quail are fond of seeds and insects. They scour the ground in grasslands between sea level and 8000 feet, scurrying haltingly about, frequently stopping stock still, then picking up termites, beetles and other insect or vegetable food.

In the many parts of the Indo-Malayan and Australian regions that the author has encountered these birds he has always found them wary and elusive. In the Philippines he found the five-inch, mottled Barred Bustard-quail (*T. suscitator*) common in the tropical grasslands of Luzon. The female of this bird has a chestnut collar across the hind neck and a black throat; the male lacks the collar and has a whitish throat. This species occurs also in India, Malaysia, China and Japan.

Unlike true quails, the bustard-quails do not travel in large coveys but move about singly or in pairs. The birds can be trapped fairly readily by native woodsmen but are extremely difficult to shoot because they rarely flush, and then go only a short distance and rarely take wing a second time.

The six-inch Striped Button Quail (*T. sylvatica*) is a very wide-ranging species and is the only representative of this family occurring in Europe. An inhabitant of grasslands and plains, it is easily distinguished by its vivid orange-reddish breast.

The most aberrant bustard-quail, the Lark Quail (*Ortyxelos meiffrenii*), is found in Africa. It lives in arid grassy regions and is said to flush without the wing-whirring of a quail. Structurally, this little cinnamon-backed, white-breasted bird looks more like a tiny lark than a quail. The male and female are much alike in coloration and size, each about 4 inches in length, with whitish feet.

Plains-wanderer or Collared Hemipode

(*Pedionominae*)

The pattern of parental care in the Plains-wanderer or Collared Hemipode (*Pedionomus torquatus*) of the arid parts of Australia is much like that of the Button Quails, the male incubating the eggs and feeding and protecting the precocial young. In fact, judging from behavior, this lone bird seems certainly to be a Button Quail. Judging from structure, however, one must conclude otherwise, for it has a well-developed hind toe or hallux, whereas in Button Quails this toe is missing; also its eggs are pyriform, whereas those of the Button Quails are oval; and it possesses paired carotid arteries, whereas in the Button Quails only the left carotid artery is present. Despite these differences, the Plains-wanderer is most probably a primitive But-

Whooping Crane (*Grus americana*) at nest

CHARLES A. KEEFER: FISH AND WILDLIFE

ton Quail that has retained characters discarded by the Button Quails.

The single species of this family is shaped like a small quail and has orange-yellow legs. The female is about five inches long, an inch or more longer than the male. It is grayish brown with a vivid chestnut chest patch and a broad collar of black and white. This coloration is missing in the male.

Plains-wanderers rarely fly, preferring to hide by squatting in the grass. Their chief foods are seeds and insects. The nest is a grass-lined scrape in which three to four dull grayish, blotched eggs are laid.

Cranes (*Gruidae*)

Cranes are tall, stately birds occurring throughout the tropical and temperate regions of the world, with the exception of large areas of Oceania and South America. Despite this wide range only 14 species are known, and some of these are on the verge of extinction. Their wide range and distribution is believed to indicate that they are remnants of a group of birds formerly much more numerous and widespread.

A good example of this family is the Whooping Crane (*Grus americana*) of North America, the more spectacular of the two species found in the New World. The tallest of American birds, it stands nearly 5 feet in height and has a wingspread of 7½ feet. It is immaculate white, with black flight feathers and red, naked areas on the sides of the head and neck. As in most cranes, the legs and neck are very long, and the hind toe is small and elevated above the other toes. The bill is long and powerful, and serves as a sharp hammer for killing snakes, small alligators, frogs and many other animals.

The Whooping Crane is named for its call. Other species are named for their ornamental plumage, coloration, wattles or geographical ranges—as, for example, the European or Common Crane (*Grus grus*) of Eurasia and (in winter) south to Africa; the Black-necked Crane (*G. nigricollis*) of Asia; the White-headed Crane (*G. monacha*) of eastern Asia and Japan; the Sandhill Crane (*G. canadensis*) of eastern Siberia and North America south to Mexico, the Isle of Pines and Cuba; the Japanese Crane (*G. japonensis*) of eastern Asia and Japan; the White-naped Crane (*G. vipio*) of eastern Asia; the Sarus Crane (*G. antigone;* Plate 43) of Indo-Malaya and the Philippines; the Native Companion or Brolga (*G. rubicunda*) of New Guinea and Australia; the Asiatic White Crane (*G. leucogeranus*) of eastern Asia; the Wattled Crane (*Bugeranus carunculatus*) of Africa; the Demoiselle Crane (*Anthropoïdes virgo*) of Eurasia and Africa; the Paradise or Stanley Crane (*A. paradisea;* Plate 44) of southern Africa; and the Crowned Crane (*Balearica pavonia;* Plate 43) of Africa. Many of these are well-known zoo birds since cranes do well in captivity, becoming very tame and breeding readily.

European or **Common Crane** (*Grus grus*)

All cranes have exceptionally powerful voices, with some of them among the mightiest found in birds. This stentorian sound is produced in a specially modified windpipe or trachea that has been likened to a French horn. The convolutions of the windpipe enlarge and lengthen as the crane ages and eventually, in old birds, resemble serpentine coils and penetrate the walls of the breastbone, particularly the keel, in a most unusual manner. In the Whooping Crane the trachea reaches five feet in length. Nearly 30 inches of this length winds its way through breast muscles and bone, and it is this part of the anatomy that produces the notes reputed to carry a full two miles.

In migration the voice is used constantly, presumably to keep the birds together, and frequently a flock leader does most of the calling. Migration is carried out both by day and night, and often the flights are of long duration. In many species large concentrations of birds migrate together, moving in chevron and multiple skein formations, flying low or high depending on the direction of the wind, always with the neck and head extended at full length ahead and the legs trailing straight back. Often in migration cranes fly at considerable heights, as, for example, a group of 80 birds observed from an airplane 13,000 feet above the English Channel.

After wintering in the southern parts of their ranges, many of the species move northward to breed in parts of the Northern Hemisphere. Upon arrival, the flock splits into pairs which engage in colorful dances that are particularly dramatic because of the huge size of the performers. In these performances the male bows and walks with the neck bent forward, the head projected far in front of the body and the wings half unfurled. In this posture he periodically leaps high into the air above the female while trumpeting and whooping. Unlike many other birds the female crane joins exuberantly in the dance, jumping high in the air nearly as often as does the male. She also bows to the male and splashes through the shallow sheets of water where the dance is often performed. After mating, the birds live in pairs.

Cranes lay only two eggs and rear only one family per year. The eggs are deposited in a nest of grasses and reeds that both the male and the female build on marshy ground. Often the nest platform, which may be several inches thick and several feet wide, is surrounded by water and reeds. No attempt is made to hide the nest, the birds apparently relying on their alertness and the sentinel position of the nest for security. Both sexes participate in incubation, which lasts some 32 days, but the female is reported to do all of the nocturnal incubating. A remarkable feature of young cranes is their ability to leave the nest on the day they are hatched, despite the fact that they are only about $\frac{1}{100}$ the size of the adult.

Limpkin (*Aramus guarauna*)

REX GARY SCHMIDT: FISH AND WILDLIFE

Such precocity is hard to credit in birds that must acquire so much of their growth after hatching. Although the young run about so soon, they must be fed and protected by the parents for periods up to six months, and they do not acquire the adult plumage for two years. They cannot fly until they are about four months old.

Because of the vast amount of publicity that the Whooping Crane has received, people everywhere have come to think of it as a symbol of conservation. For the record, this is its history to date:

Near Louisville, Kentucky, in March, 1810, John James Audubon showed Alexander Wilson the first Whooping Crane the latter had seen. These birds were then common. By 1923 Whooping Cranes were thought to be extinct, but year after year a few birds continued to appear. The last survivors wintered in one small area of Texas, and in 1937 this area, comprising 47,000 acres of coastal swamplands, was set aside as the Aransas National Wildlife Refuge. Since then the birds have wintered there in the following numbers: 1940, 32; 1949, 35; 1954, 24; 1955, 28; and 1957, 24.

The progressive reduction in numbers caused the authorities to make every effort to find and protect the birds on their undiscovered breeding grounds. In 1945 the United States Fish and Wildlife Service, the Canadian Wildlife Service and the National Audubon Society undertook this task. The search was headed by Robert Allen of the Society, who sought the breeding grounds of the birds for four years, enlisting the aid of thousands of observers. Finally, in 1954 adults and a young bird were spotted from a helicopter near Great Slave Lake in Canada, and in May, 1955, Allen, along with the United States and Canadian Wildlife officers, went in on foot and discovered the elusive breeding grounds. Thus at last it was learned that Whooping Cranes build their nests in rolling marshlands in the heart of a vast wilderness in western Canada, 2400 miles north of the Texas swamplands where they winter.

Cranes are most abundant in Eurasia, in both species and number of birds. One reason for this seems to be that Asians believe harming cranes brings bad luck. An example of the species found in this region is the Sarus Crane, a huge gray bird reaching five feet in height and splashed with red on the head and upper neck. It is a feature of the landscape in southern Asia and is never killed. It occurs commonly in pairs wherever there are ponds and rice fields, the pairs keeping so regularly to given areas and being so constantly together that the inhabitants believe they mate for life. They also believe that if one of a pair is killed the other dies of a broken heart. The birds take readily to captivity and soon become very tame. They are efficient at killing snakes, insects and small rodents, and oft-times in India their young are captured and used as "watchdogs."

Africa is the home of some of the most beautiful cranes. One, the Crowned Crane, ranges from the middle Nile to the Cape. Standing only three feet tall, it wears on its head a fan of strawlike bristles. In front of this ornament is a velvety spray of blackish feathers. Otherwise, the Crowned Crane is generally dark, with white in the wings. Another small but beautiful species is the Demoiselle Crane, a bird of dry, grassy regions. It is smoky gray and has a white spray of feathers behind each eye and black lanceolate feathers extending over the chest from the base of the neck.

Only two species of cranes visit Europe. One is the Demoiselle, which reaches Denmark and the British Isles as a vagrant, and probably still breeds in Rumania and southern Spain. The other is the Common Crane, which stands some 45 inches tall and is generally gray and has a small red spot on the head. Until the middle of the nineteenth century this species bred as far north as Denmark, and then presumably was wiped out. However, in 1952 it was again found breeding in Denmark.

Australia and New Guinea are the home of the Native Companion, or Brolga, a silvery gray crane that stands four feet tall and has a seven-foot wingspread. This species, like all of the members of the genus *Grus*, has naked red skin on the face and neck. But unlike the other cranes, it is said to lay its two eggs on the bare ground without benefit of a nest.

Limpkins (*Aramidae*)

The heron-sized Limpkin (*Aramus guarauna*) of tropical America is the lone survivor of an ancient line of long-legged birds related to both the cranes and the rails. In its skeleton and its flight the Limpkin resembles a crane, but in general form and plumage texture and in the fact that the young are hatched covered with blackish down it is like a rail.

Limpkins, of which there is a single species with five races ranging from Argentina to the Caribbean islands and the southern United States, are large-headed birds that reach a length of some 26 inches and have a long, straight bill twice the length of the head. They are generally dark brown. Some races have prominent streaks and spots of dull white in the plumage; others show dull bronze reflections on the upperparts.

Along the edges of marshes and shaded waterways—often on well-established paths—this bird skulks jerkily and with much tail-switching, lifting its feet high between steps and frequently snapping its head up to look around. Its posture is normally somewhat hunched over, like that of a rail, and often the bill is driven into mud in quest of fresh-water snails and mussels. Other food, such as small reptiles, frogs and invertebrates, is also taken, but less commonly. Limpkins usually hunt alone, but sometimes go about in small groups, and, on rare occasions in South America, bands of as many as twenty.

Within the borders of the United States, except for local concentrations in Florida and Georgia, Limpkins are quite uncommon. Unfortunately, they are rather tame in the vicinity of man and when stalked by boat permit the hunter to approach very closely. Nevertheless, in recent years they have been increasing in numbers in such places as Everglades National Park, and they are abundant in the large swamps of Lake Okeechobee.

Limpkins build large, platform-like nests of rushes, grass and sometimes moss in marsh vegetation, bushes and trees. They are usually placed a few feet above water, but some have been found as high up as 17 feet. The usual clutch is six or seven pale olive eggs spotted with brown. The role of the sexes in the incubation and care of the young is not known. At hatching time the young can take to the water immediately and swim, but they usually do not leave the nest for a day or so. During incubation the adults resort to distraction displays when danger threatens.

The melancholy quality of the Limpkin's calls, which are heard most frequently by night, is suggested by some of its local names: in Florida and the Okefenokee region it is known as the "Crying Bird," and its Spanish name means "Mad Widow." The notes have been described as shrieks, wails and piercing cries.

In flight Limpkins employ a steady but labored flapping motion that sometimes brings the wings almost into contact over the back. They never fly far, and in the air the head is extended forward like a crane's and the legs are angled steeply backward like those of a rail.

Trumpeters (*Psophiidae*)

Trumpeters, of which there are three species in a single genus, dwell in the humid tropical jungles of South America. All are pheasant-sized but with necks of medium length and legs that make them resemble small cranes.

These interesting, generally dark-colored birds are virtually restricted to the floor and the lowest tier of the forest, where they travel in tight flocks of six to about twenty, feeding chiefly under trees frequented by coatis, howling monkeys, parrots and toucans. Trumpeters are rather like the megapodes of the Australian region in that they follow large, arboreal, fruit- and nut-eating animals to pick up food that such species drop.

Trumpeters fly poorly. In fact, they hardly use the wings except when startled, and then merely fly to low limbs and stare at the intruder. Normally they seek safety by running, but when fired upon they may flush from the cover of the jungle and fly across a river if it is not too wide. Their flight, however, is so weak that some of the flock fall into the water and complete the crossing by swimming—which they do well. Trumpeters have their center of abundance in the vast Amazon region, which is cut by many rivers, and in several areas these waterways seem to limit the range of species (three) and of races (eight).

Trumpeters are believed to be related to the cranes on the one hand and the rails on the other, and to bridge the gap between the two. Their dancing habits reinforce this supposition. They are highly gregarious, feeding, sleeping and dancing in groups. When dancing they are very noisy, strutting and executing acrobatic leaps and even somersaults. After pairing, they build nests on the ground in deep forest. Up to ten green eggs are laid.

Trumpeters roost in trees, apparently some 30 feet up, where they are sometimes loud and quarrelsome by night. On one occasion a trumpeter was trapped by the author and tethered to a tree, and when in a few days it appeared rather tame, its curious calls could be studied. These were exceedingly deep, ventriloquial and of uncertain source. The notes were delivered with the bill closed and motionless, and the sound reverberated from deep within the body, as though from a drum.

The three species of trumpeters are rather similar. They are the White-winged Trumpeter (*Psophia leucoptera*), the Common Trumpeter (*P. crepitans*) of northern South America, and the Green-winged Trumpeter (*P. viridis*) of Brazil. The

White-winged Trumpeter (*Psophia leucoptera*)

D. SETH-SMITH

last named is the largest, being some 20 inches in length, with a blackish body, long, bright-green legs, and a short green bill shaped something like that of a chicken. The feathers of the neck and head are so soft and short that they feel furry to the touch. They are black and glossy with purplish reflections. The lower back and wings are brightly washed with rusty brown and the wings are mostly light gray.

Trumpeters do well in zoos. In South America the young are captured and raised with domestic fowl; they are said to perform very well as "watchdogs" and to become affectionate pets. Unfortunately their unwary nature, their habit of keeping together, and the fact that their flesh is tasty, quickly lead to their extirpation in areas invaded by man.

Rails, Gallinules and Coots (*Rallidae*)

Rails, gallinules and coots (132 species) occur through the nonpolar regions of the world. Among the varied species are tiny, drab, flightless birds no larger than small sparrows and, at the opposite extreme, bright greenish purple birds of some bulk.

All have compressed bodies and are able to thread their way through thick and sometimes seemingly impenetrable labyrinths of swamp vegetation. The most generalized species dwell in marshlands in deeply shaded areas; some live on the floor of thick tropical and mountain forests, sometimes to heights of 10,000 feet above sea level; others live as quietly as mice in grassy fields and on sandy surfaces far from fresh water, relying on rainwater puddles forming in the shells of land snails. The second group of rails, called gallinules, are equipped with long toes to walk on floating vegetation. The third kind has taken to the water much like the ducks. Some of the last mentioned live at altitudes of 16,000 feet in Andean lakes so cold that hardly any vegetation grows about them.

In general, rails tend to be brownish with dark mottling, but some of the forest rails are highly tinted in reddish browns and some of the grass rails are yellowish. The gallinules are vividly colored in purples, greens and violets, and the coots are sooty. With the exception of the coot and the gallinule, the species are generally secretive—so secretive that one may hear rails calling many times for years on end and yet rarely see one. Most rails are active at night, walking on marsh reeds like oversize wrens and clinging to the vertical shafts with their long toes. The majority can be forced to fly if they are closely pressed, but some continue to hide by lying quiet until picked up. The rail hunter—and in many areas the birds are hunted for sport—waits until the reed beds are flooded, prohibiting a running escape. He then shoots the birds as they flush straight up from the reeds and fly weakly off, with the neck extended forward and the legs trailed; even the gallinules and coots fly in this manner.

While the flight seems weak and is usually of short duration, many rails nevertheless execute long migratory flights, traveling mostly at night. Many strike the buildings of large cities and others become lost in terrain unfit for rails. This instinct for migration has led to the establishment of rails in many odd corners of the world. There is hardly an oceanic island without its rail, and a population of the Old World Water Rail (*Rallus aquaticus;* Plate 49) lives in the warm vegetation rimming a few hot springs in Iceland. There are endemic species, mostly flightless, on such remote islands as Wake, Guam, Tahiti, Viti Levu, Laysan, Hawaii, Henderson and Kusai in the middle of the vast Pacific. Several of these island species have become extinct. Some species live in areas relatively or completely free of predators, where they seem to lose their powers of flight rather quickly; they are thus at the mercy of rats, cats and other predators introduced by man.

Rails are fairly gregarious, keeping together in parties in the nonbreeding season and in families at other times. Some species build special nests in which to sleep. Most of these have been found in marshes, but the writer once found three Forbes Rails (*Rallicula forbesi*) sleeping in a nest of leaves and bark 11 feet up in a pandanus tree 9500 feet above sea level in New Guinea. Most rails are monogamous, but some have several mates. The nest is usually built of marsh vegetation—reeds and grass—by both members of the pair, and both share in the incubation of the eggs. The normal set ranges from 8 to 15 eggs and they are usually blotched, speckled and whitish or buffy in color. Incubation varies from 16 to 25 days depending on the species.

The Clapper Rail or Marsh Hen (*Rallus longirostris;* Plate 50)—a grayish brown, long-billed rail nearly 15 inches in length, with a pale cinnamon breast and barred flanks—is a good example of the type of rail favoring salt marshes. Although still common, it long ago ceased being the abundant bird it was in Audubon's time; then a good egg collector could find in a day a hundred dozen of its eggs in the New Jersey marshes.

Another true rail is the tiny Black Rail (*Laterallus jamaicensis*), a five-inch bird that is largely black, with a reddish nape and white barring on the back. This species, which ranges over much of temperate North America, is so secretive that it is rarely seen, yet its sharp *kik-kik-kik, queeah* calls are not uncommon to trained ears.

The Sora Rail (*Porzana carolina*) and its close relative in the Old World, the Corn Crake (*Crex crex;* Plate 48), breed in the Northern Hemisphere and winter south to northern South America in the New World, and to Africa in the Old. Both are eight-inch rails, and are the easiest to see and the best known, with the exception of the coots. This is

Ypecaha Wood Rail (*Aramides ypecaha*)

because they venture out on floating vegetation more than most rails.

One of the very common African species is the Black Crake (*Limnocorax flavirostra;* Plate 45), which congregates in swampy grasslands around the lakes of Central Africa.

One of the largest of New World rails is the Ypecaha Wood Rail (*Aramides ypecaha*) of Middle America, which is the size of a small hen.

As mentioned earlier, many island rails have lost their powers of flight. Most are small, but in New Zealand the chicken-sized Weka (*Gallirallus australis*) is flightless, although it has the wing well developed. This large, brown, chiefly nocturnal bird has relatively short legs, is omnivorous, and in former times was so abundant that it was hunted for its oil. There are records of as many as 2000 birds being killed in a day of good hunting. The Weka is chiefly a bird of the forest, sleeping in burrows under roots and calling shrilly at night. It is very adaptable and has taken to entering houses and to stealing trinkets. This rail runs down, kills and eats mice and rats, as well as taking nestling birds and the eggs of ground-nesting birds up to the size of a duck. The usual nest is a small cluster of grass under a tussock or log or in a burrow. Four whitish blotched eggs are laid. These are incubated for about 20 days. The precocious young leave the nest at three or four days and follow the parents for about three months. Wekas perform a kind of duet, their whistles being delivered one after the other, the male's coming first.

The rails that have taken to the water and walk on floating vegetation apparently have fewer enemies to face and as a result are less wary and secretive than those of swamp and forest. The best known of these are the gallinules, which range around the world and are found wherever there are extensive bodies of semistagnant water. They are cryptically colored, not in the drab mud and shadow tones of true rails, but in hues that match green vegetation, bright flowers and sparkling blue waters. These colors are protective as the birds walk out among the flowers on floating water lilies (see Plate 47), moving along the surface on agile feet that are often deeply submerged, or swimming between rafts of plants, hunting for insects, frogs, lizards, and grain, even eating buds and flowers.

The gallinules nest in clumps of grass over water. They are very inquisitive birds; they go in pairs and often climb up out of the rushes to peer at a river boat, the two gleaming purplish blue bodies offering inviting targets to crocodile hunters. In walking they lower the head and elevate the tail straight up parallel to the back, displaying the usually white undertail feathers. The head is constantly bobbed and the comically small tail is constantly flicked. Gallinules, like rails, are highly migratory. Both groups

Takahe (*Notornis hochstetteri*)

H. J. OLLERENSHAW

C. A. FLEMING

Weka (*Gallirallus australis*)

wandered to New Zealand ages ago. Some became flightless and then were wiped out. One "fossil" turned up alive in 1949. It was the giant flightless Takahe (*Notornis hochstetteri*), which had not been seen for half a century. Today it is estimated that 30 to 35 birds comprise the total population, living 2000 or more feet above the sea.

One of the best-known gallinules is an exception among this generally brightly colored group. This is the Moorhen (*Gallinula chloropus*), known in North America as the Florida Gallinule, a dark gray bird with a brownish back, its only spot of bright color being its red bill. It is found virtually throughout the world except for the Australian region, where its place is taken by a related species. A shy bird over much of its range, it has become a tame bird of city park ponds in England.

The writer, working twenty years ago in the region of Angels Falls in southern Venezuela, spent weeks in a futile search for one of the rarest of rails, the Schomburgk Rail (*Micropygia schomburgkii*). Learning of our quest, some Arecuna Indians casually started a field fire and, to our amazement, captured 20 of these "rare" birds. This will give some idea of the rail's ability to hide and the reason Notornis may have remained undetected for so long. Also it will indicate why the author feels that, contrary to the general belief, there remain many undiscovered species of birds.

Coots are intensely interesting birds. They are rails that are as aquatic as ducks. They dive even more abruptly, some species staying down as long as 16 seconds and feeding as far as 25 feet below the surface. All coots have the toes broadly lobed, and in the water they swim with the feet acting like the rubber fins of a skin diver. All living coots belong to one genus: *Fulica*. Signs of extinct coots are fairly common, attesting to the age of the group. One, the Mauritius Coot (*Leguatia gigantea*), stood more than

[151

four feet tall. Coots generally build nests of floating vegetation in flooded fresh-water reed beds. The American Coot (*Fulica americana*), which ranges from Alaska to South America, is sooty blue-black and smoky gray, like all the coots, with the head and neck almost solid black. It has the bill usually strong, whitish, and rather fowl-like. Nearly cosmopolitan in the Old World is the European Coot (*Fulica atra;* Plate 46). Coots in winter go in huge flocks. In India these may number many thousands. Each flock somehow manages to keep apart from the others so that a lake covered with wintering coots is a mosaic of separate flocks.

Because of their number and their supposedly poor-tasting flesh, coots are generally disliked by hunters, who think they deplete duck food and kill too many young ducklings. Although they occasionally eat small birds, the food of coots is primarily vegetable matter and aquatic invertebrates.

The African Knob-billed Coot (*Fulica cristata*) lays four to six eggs in a sodden, floating nest. These are incubated by both parents from 21 to 22 days. The newly hatched chicks are covered with black, hairlike down. This is the dress worn by all young born to this large family, although some wear brightly colored facial adornments in the downy stage.

Bonaparte's Horned Coot (*Fulica cornuta*) of the highlands of southern Bolivia, Chile and northwestern Argentina is not only one of the largest

European Coot (*Fulica atra*)

coots but is a great ornithological rarity and is above all unique in its manner of nesting. Because it nests in frigid lakes in the Andes, so high (usually above 13,000 feet) that the surrounding terrain is nearly devoid of vegetation, it has taken to building with stones. We know of these structures from recent observations made by the Chilean scientists W. R. Millie and Luis G. Pena, who found this bird constructing islands of stone for the foundation of its nest, sometimes more than 100 feet from shore. Señor Millie wrote to Dr. S. D. Ripley of Yale University: "I watched a pair constructing their nest for about three hours. They, too, had selected a sheltered place with comparatively shallow water. They were just finishing the stone structure made of stones of the size of small potatoes, carried there by them in their beaks. On this mound, which I later measured and found to be about one meter in diameter and sixty centimeters high . . . they proceeded to place algae [later identified as a flowering plant] carried to and fro in rapid journeys."

Other unique features of this Coot are its horns or frontal wattles and its caruncle, which replace the frontal shield found in other coots. These become enlarged in the courtship season but are apparently of equal size in both sexes.

Also in the Andes, but farther north in Peru, occurs the largest species, the Giant Coot (*F. gigantea*), which reaches a length of 20 inches. Although this coot also nests in high-altitude lakes, it builds normal floating nests of water weeds.

Finfeet or Sun-grebes
(*Heliornithidae*)

This family consists of three grebelike birds living in widely separated regions of the world—one in South America, one in Africa and one in Asia. But the similarities between these highly aquatic birds and grebes are purely superficial, and modern students of bird evolution believe that the finfeet are of gruiform (cranelike) ancestry—a line that includes few if any water birds other than the coots.

The finfeet are all very much alike in general conformation and habits, despite their geographical isolation. All have the bill grebelike with perforate nostrils; all have lobed toes like grebes and coots; and the nails are similar to those of the coots. They have the neck elongated, the legs short, the tail rounded and stiffened and the plumage fairly soft and not dense as in the grebes.

Before the reports of the American ornithologist, Dr. J. P. Chapin, little was known about these seemingly highly developed water birds. He found that they did not dive to escape danger but fled ashore into the forest, like rails. He also noted that the African Finfoot (*Podica senegalensis*) keeps close to the surface when it flies, soon dropping back into it.

African Finfoot (*Podica senegalensis*)

Sun-grebes, or finfeet, live in small tropical and subtropical fresh-water streams, usually surrounded by lush vegetation. The birds are usually found alone or in pairs and are very secretive. They swim very low in the water and hunt from low and even partially submerged perches, often standing still for long periods. They eat beetles, dragonfly larvae, grasshoppers, snails, shrimps, millipedes, prawns, and even small frogs.

Chapin identifies the call of the African species as a "low, reiterated booming sound." He describes platform-like nests built of reeds and grass in debris as much as five feet above water in deep forest. Courtship booming was heard when the water was rising, and presumably the eggs were laid when the flood was near its peak. The set of three to five white eggs had rufous and buff streaks and smudges. The chicks were covered with varying colors of brown natal down and much blackish striping. Best studied of the three species is the African Finfoot of tropical Africa, the male of which is about 16 inches long. Above it is dark brown, with vivid black and white spotting on the upper back. Below it is whitish, with a sooty gray throat and a vivid white line extending from the eye along the neck to the body. The female is smaller, with a white throat. Both sexes have barred flanks.

In Bengal, Malaysia and Sumatra is found the Asian Finfoot (*Heliopais personata*), which is some 20 inches in length. This shy, uncommon bird is generally brown above with a black face and throat in the male, and with a yellow bill and green legs. It, too, has a white stripe along the side of the head and neck. Unlike the African and American species, it is said to dive well.

The smallest of the three species is the 12-inch American Finfoot (*Heliornis fulica*), which ranges from Mexico through South America. This scarlet-billed bird has the feet vividly banded with black and golden yellow. It is quite rare and probably never strays away from sluggish, heavily wooded streams. Its color is olivaceous brown; below it is whitish, with a light streak extending backward over the eye and a white stripe on the neck. As in all three species, its tail is composed of 18 long, rounded rectrices.

Kagu (*Rhynochetidae*)

This family was established for a single heron-sized bird found only on the island of New Caledonia and known to the natives as the Kagu. This rail-like relict teeters on the verge of extinction. When discovered about 1860, it was thought to be a heron, but observation of its behavior has established it as a probable relative of the colorful South American Sun Bittern, which in turn is thought to be an aberrant relative of cranes, limpkins, trumpeters and

Kagu (*Rhinochetus jubatus*)

rails. Like many of the last, the Kagu (*Rhinochetus jubatus*) is chiefly nocturnal, sleeping by day in rocky niches and under the roots of trees. Its habitat today is in the remote interior mountains, but formerly it ranged throughout the forests of New Caledonia.

For many years men hunted the Kagu with dogs and sold it in the markets like a domesticated fowl. The miracle is that any survive, especially since it is a relatively large, virtually flightless ground bird, and dogs, cats and wild pigs—all introduced by man—are its mortal enemies.

In conformation the Kagu resembles an outsized heron. It has a rather large head and a big, shaggy crest projecting some five inches backward to a point when folded and an equal distance straight upward when extended fanlike in display or in anger. Its color is dark gull gray above and pale gray below and its fairly large wings are barred with vivid markings in black and white. In display, the wings are opened laterally, much like the Sun-bittern.

The Kagu has orange-red legs and a strong, slightly curved bill with nostrils shielded by a membrane that apparently serves as a protection when the bird is digging. When hunting for food, the bird is reported to run very rapidly and to halt abruptly, freezing for long periods while awaiting its prey—chiefly worms, insects and mollusks. The Kagu has powder downs, but these occur as scattered groups of feathers, not regular patches as in the herons, bitterns and other birds.

Years ago the superintendent of the London Zoological Gardens wrote of the Kagus he had observed in captivity: "With its crest erect and wings spread out, the Kagu runs or skips about, sometimes pursuing and driving before him all the birds that are confined with him. At other times he will seize the end of his wing or tail, and run around, holding it in his bill. From a piece of paper or dry leaf he derives much amusement, by tossing it about and running after it. During his frolic he will thrust his bill into the ground, spread out his wings, kick his legs into the air, and then tumble about as if in a fit."

The male is said to be very aggressive and fond of attacking the feet of his prospective mate, moving in with crest extended, tail dropped and wings spread. During courtship the pairs sometimes face each other, standing very erect with the crests peaked and the wings open. In captivity, the males may pick up sticks and stones during display. Both the male and the female participate in building a nest of twigs and leaves. Both take turns incubating the single egg, which is a bright rust color with large dark-brownish blotches. The incubation takes 36 days; the chick is cloaked with dark brown down at hatching and has a relatively huge head and pale brown wings.

In the wild the Kagu begins calling in the late evening and is most vociferous about dawn, its sharp, rattling notes carrying for as much as a mile.

Sun-bittern   (*Eurypygidae*)

Another relict cranelike bird is the Sun-bittern (*Eurypyga helias*) of the New World tropics which occurs from Guatemala to southern Brazil. This 20-

Sun-bittern (*Eurypyga helias*): warning display

inch bird is not related to the bitterns, although there are certain superficial resemblances. The Sun-bittern, like the Kagu of New Caledonia—which appears to be one of its nearest relatives—is the last survivor of its family. Sun-bitterns fly very little and habitually walk with the snakelike neck extended forward, often parallel to the ground. They have the legs rather heron-like in shape and orange in color; and the wings rather full and round, with concealed bright chestnut patches. The tail is long and fan-shaped and has prominent black banding. The crown is black, and much white occurs on the face and throat. Numerous powder downs grow on the body.

Sun-bitterns inhabit the floor of dense tropical forest and swamps and are secretive, occurring singly or in pairs and feeding on insects and small fishes. Semi-aquatic in habits, the single species (three races) is often found in dark places close to water, but, as the name implies, seems to revel in sunlight. It is a rare and beautiful sight when it displays its golden brown wing and tail plumage next to a tropical stream. In display the bird lowers the body nearly to the ground and suddenly opens the wings, tipping the leading edges downward and trailing edges upward. At the same time the tail is fanned and brought upward to the wings. The very colorful wing and tail feathers than make a splendid backdrop for the head and bill. This climax display is often maintained rigidly for a minute or more.

Sun-bitterns are very quiet, apparently uttering only plaintive, whistling notes. Their prey is captured by spearing with the bill much in the manner of herons and bitterns. After pairing, the male and female assist each other in building the nest, incubating the eggs, brooding and feeding the young. The nest, composed of sticks, grass and mud, may be placed on the ground or in bushes or low trees. The normal set is two eggs, bright rusty to brown in color and with vivid dark blotchings and marks.

Although normally quite shy, Sun-bitterns become quickly acclimated to captivity and can be bred in zoos. Eggs hatched in England were incubated for 27 days. The chicks are precocial and covered with brown down.

Cariamas or Seriemas

(Cariamidae)

In South America there occur two species forming a family of large, cranelike land birds, the Cariamas, that somewhat resemble the well-known Secretary Bird of Africa. Anatomical studies have shown these to be related to extinct flightless gruiform birds, such as the extraordinary South American Phororhacos, a flightless bird that was five feet tall and had a head as large as that of a pony.

Others of their close relatives, most of which are fossils, consist of two groups of flightless predaceous giants from the Eocene of North America and Europe. The most unusual of these, *Diatryma steini* (family Diatrymidae), was a cranelike bird that stood seven feet tall and had a bill shaped like a meat cleaver.

The two surviving species, while closely related, are generically distinct. One, the Crested Cariama (*Cariama cristata*) is found in pampas and grass-lands, and the other, the Burmeister's Cariama (*Chunga burmeisteri*), is found in forests and wooded savannas. Both are restricted to the southern half of

Crested Cariama (*Cariama cristata*)

South America. The grassland species is about 32 inches long and stands some four inches taller than its woodland cousin. It is more generally brownish, while the forest species is more grayish, and it has a crest some five inches long, whereas the forest species has a crest that is only an inch or so in length.

The Crested species nests generally on the ground, whereas Burmeister's Cariama usually nests in bushes or trees. Both species roost off the ground at night, with Burmeister's preferring very high places in forest trees. Both are noisy, screaming at an intruder while he is far away and then settling into complete silence when he draws near. In both, the set of eggs is two and the eggs are rail-like, with a pale base color heavily splotched or dotted with rufous brown. In the Crested the eggs are generally more of a buff color, while in the Burmeister's Cariama they are often nearly white. Cariama eggs exhibit the extreme example of what is apparently a tendency among birds' eggs to differ from each other. As reported by Dr. F. W. Preston of Butler, Pennsylvania, the first egg of a clutch in many species of birds tends to differ slightly in shape, color and texture of shell from later eggs. In the two-egg clutch of the Cariama there is a decided difference between the two in shell surface, one being glossier, somewhat more pyriform in shape and usually more heavily pigmented than the other. It is not yet known whether, as in other birds, the glossy egg is laid first.

The incubation period is 25 to 26 days. The young are heavily covered with down and marked with blackish lineations at hatching. The food of these birds consist of snails, worms, insects and reptiles of many sorts, including snakes. Fruit is also eaten.

Both Cariamas enjoy the protection of man because of their friendly natures and the fact that, as snake-killers, they perform a valuable service. Their young are frequently taken from the nest and raised in company with fowls, which they quickly learn to protect like watchdogs. The cariama soon becomes attached to man and breeds readily in captivity.

Cariamas have very long legs and long necks, and they wear erectile crests above a short, broad bill They have the tail long and graduated rather like that of the bustard, and are bustard-like in many of their habits, including their courtship displays. They keep in pairs or small groups and seek to escape by running with the head down; they fly when closely chased.

Bustards (*Otididae*)

The heaviest flying birds in the world are found in this primarily terrestrial Old World family of superficially ostrich-like birds. Although chiefly centered in Africa, the bustards, of which there are 23 species, send a few offshoots to Europe and Asia, and one species to Australia. They are probably

D. SETH-SMITH

Great Bustard (*Otis tarda*) displaying

related to the New World Cariamas. All are exceptionally shy birds, living in grassy savannas and semideserts. They are three-toed and have long, naked, ostrich-like legs, and well-developed wings which they are very reluctant to use, preferring to walk with cranelike stateliness or, when in danger, to run with great speed. If running does not serve, they fly strongly in a straight line, the wings beating steadily, the neck stretched straight forward and the long legs trailing straight backward in the typical gruiform manner. Several species carry out fairly extensive migrations.

Bustards never perch in trees. The nest is a natural depression in an open grassy field or perhaps a slight hollow scraped and then lined with a little grass by the female. From one to four eggs are incubated by the female for 20 to 28 days, depending on the species. The precocial young are cared for solely by the female, while the male continues to display for many weeks in certain areas, sometimes alone, sometimes in company with other males. The young leave the nest very soon and are able to fly in about five or six weeks; like many other gruiform birds, they master flight before they reach full size.

The Great Bustard (*Otis tarda*) is one of the largest flying birds in the world. It reaches a weight of about 30 pounds and a length of about 45 inches and stands nearly four feet tall. As in most bustards, the sexes are different from each other in color and the male is heavier and larger, being about a foot longer than his mate. He wears a long whitish beard, is generally rufous above and black and white below and has a bright chestnut breast. The female lacks the chestnut markings as well as the beard.

This species ranges from Poland and Greece to Siberia, China and Japan, and winters in India, Persia and northern Africa. Unfortunately, this great bird has long been hunted for its flesh and in many regions it has now been extirpated—in the British Isles as early as 1838. One reason for its demise is that, instead of flying off, it tries to hide on the ground; but long ago the hunter learned that, to get within range, he need only go toward it in circles.

The Great Bustard performs a bizarre group courtship dance, the males hissing and barking and inflating huge air pouches and often displaying together well in advance of the true mating period. Messrs. Knowlton and Ridgway in their old but excellent *Birds of the World* describe the dance thus: "The male has the curious habit known as showing off, which consists in inflating the throat pouch until the ends nearly touch the ground, and at the same time spreading and raising the tail until it almost touches the neck and elevating the wings and erecting the individual feathers until the bird looks like a huge ball of rumpled up feathers. In this attitude it totters and struts about before the female in an exceedingly grotesque manner. It is also very pugnacious at this season, attacking others of its kind and even, it is said, human beings."

The Australian Bustard (*Choriotis australis*), also a four-foot bird with an immense inflatable "bib," is probably the heaviest of all flying birds, with males weighing 32 pounds having been taken. This great weight is borne aloft on wings that span about seven feet. It is brown with light brown markings; the crown, an elongated crest and the tail are blackish brown. Below it is white with a broad blackish chest band. In display the male inflates the neck pouch to form an almost incredible air chamber that hangs from the white-feathered foreneck like a giant apron; in full distention it brushes the ground and is swayed as the crest is raised and the tail elevated over the back until its tips brush the back of the crown with the under-tail coverts spread out in a bright open fan. The female seems to remain aloof.

The Australian Bustard usually lays one egg near a bush on the bare ground. It is pale brownish olive with large dark brown splotches and smudges. The chick is heavily covered with brown and black down. The mother has a habit very like that of the Cariamas; when approached, she slinks away on foot with her head and neck lowered, leaving the young to the security of their cryptic plumage and instinctive habit of freezing in the face of danger.

The Australian Bustard feeds on grasshoppers, beetles and even mice and young birds; it is also very fond of berries and fruits. The Australian aborigine traps the hapless birds by digging narrow, deep slit trenches beside certain species of berry bushes. The birds used to walk about in bands of hundreds but these were sorely depleted by hunters until in 1935 complete protection was afforded them. Today, once again, they are common except in heavily populated districts.

The story of the Great and the Australian Bustard is pretty much the story of the other bustards, with minor variations. The Little Bustard (*Tetrax tetrax*) of Northern Africa and Eurasia nests in northern Eurasia and then migrates south in large numbers. This species is reported to dance either solitarily or in groups, the performances being given on little hillocks. When a female comes within range of a performer, he leaps into the air in odd, contorted positions. Another variation is that of the Lesser Indian Bustard (*Sypheotides indica*), which is confined to India, Nepal and Baluchistan. This bird is reported to stake out a territory and to defend it. Dr. S. Dillon Ripley reported recently that the adult male leaps some five feet into the air when performing on its solitary display ground; his act is accompanied by the clapping of wings and by deep, resounding rattles. This species is a relatively long-legged smallish bird in which, unlike other bustards, the males are smaller than the females. In breeding plumage they are chiefly black and white, with long, black ornamental feathers on the head.

In Africa, the stronghold of the bustards, Dr. J. P. Chapin found that the small, wide-ranging Black-bellied Bustard (*Lissotis melanogaster*), likes burned areas but will tolerate grass a yard high. The voice is a whistle followed by a kind of pop. Dr. Chapin reports that this bird probably breeds in the rainy season and that it generally lays but a single dull greenish egg on the bare ground. Its food is normally insect, but occasionally flower buds are eaten. His autopsies of stomach contents showed grasshoppers, caterpillars, crickets, termites, mantises (of which one bird had eaten 20), centipedes, cicadas, ant-lions, wasps and ants.

CHARADRIIFORMES

Lily-trotters or Jacanas
(*Jacanidae*)

Seven species comprise this well-marked family of plover-sized, slender, long-necked marsh birds. They occur in warm fresh-water marshes of most continents and many islands. Their chief distinction is nails that sometimes reach four inches in length. It is rare to find the jacana walking anywhere except on rafts of floating lilies and buoyant water plants in sluggish streams and swamps, where their long toes and immense nails distribute their weight over a large area of floating vegetation. In such locations the birds are not shy but seemingly confident of the protection afforded by this special footgear. They also have a spectacular ability to melt out of sight, even when standing in prominent places.

Another character of most jacanas, and of many plovers, which are probably their closest relatives, is the metacarpal spur, which grows like a sharp thorn from the bend of the wing. In some species it is dull and knoblike, in others sharp, but in either case it is a highly effective weapon. Most species have naked wattles and lappets growing on the head, such as are found in some plovers.

In jacanas—known also as lily-trotters and lotus birds—the sexes are similarly colored except during the breeding season, when the female assumes an elaborate plumage complete with long plumes and bright accessory adornments. She is somewhat larger than the male, and the American ornithologist, Dr. Alden H. Miller, discovered that the roles of the sexes are largely reversed in this family, as they are in a few other birds. Thus the female displays aggressively to the male, and her mate does most of the incubating and cares for the young.

Jacanas perform a kind of winged dance, with the flocks frequently flying up, circling and landing more or less like some shorebirds. The American Jacana (*Jacana spinosa*), ranging from southern Texas to Argentina, performs such maneuvers. These are usually preceded by wing-waving—an action that consists of raising, holding open and fluttering the prominent, lemon-yellow, concealed portions of the wings. This jacana is reddish maroon with a blackish head and neck and with yellowish leaflike frontal wattles. Some populations are entirely black; in others both black and maroon color phases occur.

Following this the pack becomes very noisy, and then off it goes, providing a very pretty spectacle. The apple-green and yellow wings flash in the air and the head and longish legs extend in a line to front and rear. Frequently the pack wheels about close to the water and then glides and flutters down to land en masse on the flotsam, where all wave the wings in unison and emit catlike cries.

Jacanas feed on soft vegetable matter and small invertebrates. These "aquatic plovers" build small nests of buoyant swamp plants among thick concealing vegetation such as floating water lilies. In the Indo-Malayan area the eggs are often half-submerged in tepid swamp water, and it is believed that "stored sun" in such waters contributes materially to their incubation. The eggs are four in number, pear-shaped and glossy, usually buff or brown but sometimes tinted with green, and generally scrawled or spotted rather like plover eggs. They are arranged in the nest with the small ends together. Incubation requires 22 to 24 days. The young at hatching have the toes

Pheasant-tailed Jacana (*Hydrophasianus chirurgus*)

and nails well developed and soon can follow the male over the rafts of floating vegetation. A young jacana that the author once photographed on Gatun Lake in the Panama Canal Zone ran nimbly, but when hard pressed took to the water and swam.

The largest of the seven species is the Pheasant-tailed Jacana (*Hydrophasianus chirurgus*) of the Indo-Malayan region, including Ceylon, the Philippines and Java. This beautiful 12-inch bird is found from sea level to the high lakes of Kashmir and occasionally the Himalayas. In its nuptial plumage the female with its long tail is unmistakable, reaching 20 inches in length. In common with many water birds, it nests during the rainy season. Its call is a catlike mewing. Its wing spurs are very sharp, and a number of the primaries have lance-shaped tips, the purpose of which is unknown.

Another Indo-Malayan species is the Bronze-winged Jacana (*Metopodius indicus*), some ten inches long, very dark and with a chestnut tail. It has a white line over the eye and a red, green and yellow bill. Its eggs are extraordinarily glossy in texture. Its note is a piping squeal, and Mr. E. H. N. Lowther has observed that it destroys its eggs and nest when disturbed.

In Eastern Asia, the Philippines, Malaya, New Guinea and Australia is found a smaller species, the Comb-crested Jacana (*Irediparra gallinacea*), which wears an orange to scarlet comb on the crown. It is black and brown with straw-yellow on the sides of the head. Its four eggs are so glossy they appear to be varnished.

An aberrant species is the African Jacana (*Actophilornis africanus*), which is about a foot long with a bright brown body and a blue forehead. It occurs as high as 6700 feet. It has been observed walking on mossy rocks and along the grassy shores of swamps, which is very unusual for a jacana. A chick taken from an egg had the bill red and the body covered with velvety black down, apparently very much like that of a young rail.

A small species is the 6½-inch Lesser Jacana (*Microparra capensis*), found over most of tropical Africa. It is whitish below and brownish above and is dressed much like the immature of other jacanas.

Painted Snipe (*Rostratulidae*)

Painted Snipe, aberrant relatives of the shorebirds, are named for their bright colors and snipelike bodies, but their breeding behavior is very different. Two species are known, one found in southern South America; the other in Africa, Madagascar, the Indo-Malayan region and the Australian region. Despite the wide water barriers that have long isolated these species, they are quite similar in structure and remarkably so in aberrant habits.

Structurally the Painted Snipes differ from true snipes in having a hard and inflexible bill and wings shaped so that their flight is sluggish, not swift. The most striking difference, however, is in the trachea of the female, which executes several loops before entering the lungs. This adaptation is most developed in the Australian population, with four loops of the windpipe common in mature females. In the male the windpipe is straight, as in true snipes, and the voice is a mere chirp, whereas the female's is deep and resonant, like the noise made by blowing over the neck of a bottle. As in a few other birds, notably the phalaropes, the female Painted Snipe is more colorfully dressed and larger than its mate and takes the initiative in courtship, fighting other females for the males and defending the nest site. The male builds the nest, incubates the eggs and cares for the young. Female Painted Snipe appear to be polyandrous and to lay many sets of eggs in nests provided by their various mates during each breeding year.

The female American Painted Snipe (*Nycticryphes semi-collaris*) is about ten inches long with a greenish and flesh-colored, red-tipped bill. It appears sluggish by day but is active at twilight and probably at night, at which time it goes about alone or in small numbers, keeping usually to swampy areas. The male American Painted Snipe builds a slight nest of rushes on wet ground. The three eggs that comprise the usual set are oblong, rather blunt and white but almost covered with a dark scrawl.

The Old World Painted Snipe (*Rostratula benghalensis*) is distinguished from all shorebirds and rails by the brightness of its plumage. It is a stocky bird with much chestnut, gray, buff and white marking and a broad buff crown stripe. Its eggs are greenish. In flight it looks like a rail but is more sluggish. This bird is said to travel in small parties in marshy areas and to flush sparingly, taking to the air only when in danger of being trod upon. It then flies a short distance like a button quail, drops into the grass and runs to a new position, sometimes back at the point of take-off. In Madagascar Dr. A. L. Rand noted that when first alighting it tends, like many sandpipers, to bob its hind parts, presumably drawing attention away from the head and more vulnerable portions of the body.

In displaying to males and in threat displays the female spreads the wings to beyond the tip of the bill, meanwhile elevating the tail to form a large tilted disc of plumage. Since its wings are spangled with chestnut spots and black bars, it may virtually disappear into its own bright markings. Hissing accompanies this performance, which is surprisingly like that of the Sun-bittern.

This bird lays four moderately oval, somewhat glossy yellowish eggs, densely streaked and blotched with dark brown. The nest may be a depression in the ground lined, if the ground is very wet, with some grass or a small pile of rushes. If the nesting area is dry, the nest may be dispensed with. In Australia grasses growing over the nest may be intertwined to form a rooflike canopy.

Oystercatchers (*Haematopodidae*)

Oystercatchers are large and spectacular shore-birds occurring along most of the warmer coasts of the world. The family consists of six species ranging in length from about 16 to 21 inches. All are predominantly black and white, or pure blackish, have brightly colored legs and bills, stocky bodies, and legs to which are attached three toes; the hallux is missing. The most distinctive feature of these birds is a bill about 2½ times as long as the head. It is laterally compressed, knifelike and has a tip like a chisel. Its chief function is to spear mussels, clams and oysters, but it is also used in capturing and killing crabs, marine worms and an occasional cuttlefish.

When the tide recedes and shellfish begin to appear from under the water, oystercatchers converge on food-bearing shoals, arriving singly, in pairs or small flocks. Their feeding techniques are probably unique, at least among birds. During the brief period of ebbtide, when shellfish hold their lips open as they normally do underwater, the oystercatcher drives his strong, specially formed bill deep into the open shell, severing and paralyzing the animal within. Sometimes, as in Arabia, oystercatchers frequent the muddy shores of inland waters for small crabs.

The European Oystercatcher (*Haematopus ostralegus;* Plates 53 and 55) has long been studied because of its unusual breeding behavior. As a result, we know that individual pairs tend to keep together for several years and that wild oystercatchers sometimes live to the age of 27. We know too that they have a form of partially promiscuous, partially monogamous courtship. The males compete vigorously for the females but, instead of fighting, engage in a dance (usually involving three birds but sometimes more) in which when one male displays to a female, another male is apt to push his way in and try to occupy the spot on which the first is standing. To counter this, the first dancer begins a kind of mimicry of the interloper and apparently this works as well as fighting, the transgressor usually being forced to leave. Sometimes the female accepts a number of temporary mates during the preliminary "engagement" stages of the courtship period but later she becomes permanently bonded to a single male.

Oystercatchers usually nest along oceanic beaches. The eggs, which number from two to four, are deposited on the bare sand in a mere scraped depression, sometimes with a meager lining of bits of vegetation and chips of shell and stone. The eggs, the color of dull sand and with prominent black and brown markings, are laid at intervals of one to three days. Incubation is shared by the male and female for a period of 26 or 27 days. The young leave the nest a few hours after hatching. Precocial and covered with down, they are brooded and fed by both parents.

Oystercatchers are among the few birds that will remove their eggs to a safer location when trespassers cause them to feel unsafe. Both sexes are very noisy when danger threatens and both use the broken-wing display to lure predators away from the nest. In addition, both sexes distract predators by performing "false brooding" movements, the performer running ahead of a predator and then settling on the ground as though incubating eggs or covering young. So successful is this that even human beings sometimes get an erroneous impression of the nest location.

The American Oystercatcher (*H. palliatus*) is found along most of the temperate and tropical coasts of the New World. It is 17 inches in length, with the female slightly the larger of the sexes. Both are similarly colored, as in all oystercatchers. Above and on the neck and upper chest the bird is black; below it is white. The bill and eye are red and the large, longish legs pinkish.

The Black Oystercatcher (*H. bachmani*) of the western coasts of North America and the Sooty Oystercatcher (*H. fuliginosus*) of Australia are sooty black with flesh-colored legs. Both are chiefly inhabitants of rocky coasts.

The European Oystercatcher (*H. ostralegus;* Plates 53 and 55) is 17 inches in length with an orange bill. It is generally black above and has a black head and neck and white underparts. More than any other oystercatcher, this bird is inclined to wander far from salt water along estuaries and rivers and to breed along the grassy edges of interior lakes, even in fields far from water.

Plovers, Turnstones and Surf Birds (*Charadriidae*)

The plovers, turnstones and surf birds range from small to medium size and are found throughout the world. The family is divided into three segments: the plover-like birds (Vanellinae) known as lapwings, of which there are 11 species, mostly in the Old World; the true plovers (Charadriinae), of which there are some 36 species; and the turnstones and surf birds (Arenariinae), three aberrant species of the ocean edge which have often in the past been accorded family rank. The majority are shore-loving birds, but many plovers frequent the uplands.

The most interesting of the lapwings is the Crocodile Bird or Spur-winged Lapwing (*Hoplopterus spinosus*) of southwestern Asia, the Mediterranean Region and much of Africa. It is particularly common in Egypt, where typically it frequents the shores of fresh-water swamps and streams, and since ancient times has been credited with entering the mouths of crocodiles to feed on leeches, but this remains to be confirmed. This species has well-developed spurs on the wings. It is about ten inches long and is essentially black and white with a short crest.

A near relative, the Masked Plover (*Lobibyx miles*) of the Indo-Malayan and Australian regions, is nearly 15 inches long. Brownish gray above, with a black head and white underparts, it is immediately recognizable by naked, bright yellow wattles that hang like drapes, one set over the eyes and one between eyes and bill. Its chief food is insects, worms and mollusks. Like plovers in general, the Masked Plover lays its eggs—usually four, pear-shaped and heavily blotched—in a slight depression near water.

Most plovers are partially nocturnal, and this species often has been caught in fine nets set by the author for bats. One that he took near New Guinea's Sepik River was put in a box with food and water. The next day, when the author put his hand into the box, the plover delivered a series of rapid-fire hammer blows with its wings, sending into the author's flesh the thornlike spurs at the bend of each wing; the punctures were deep and blood flowed freely. Such blows directed to the head of a lizard, snake or bird could easily cause blindness or death.

In India the pigeon-sized Red-wattled Lapwing (*Lobivanellus indicus*) also has fleshy wattles hanging between the eyes and the red bill. This common species of the paddy fields travels in pairs or small parties. Like others of the lapwing group, it is roundly damned by hunters because of its vigilance in alerting other animals to impending danger by means of screams. The pairs usually circle the hunter if he is near their nest or young, and the latter lie flat on the ground with necks outstretched until danger passes. A relative is the Banded Plover (*Zonifer tricolor;* Plate 51).

Lapwings have three or four toes, depending on species; their name alludes to the slow motion of the wings. The most widespread species is the very striking Common Lapwing (*Vanellus vanellus*) of Eurasia, which has a long, graceful, glossy black crest and squarish wings. In common with the four-toed groups, it lacks a wing spur. It is about a foot long, blackish above and white below with a broad black chest band, and its dark plumage is enriched with iridescent green and bronze. It winters in the warm parts of Asia and Africa, often migrating southward in huge flocks. In many areas of Europe, particularly in Holland, vast numbers nest. Each pair generally lays four eggs. Commercial egg-taking is legal in Holland until April 20; virtually all pairs losing their eggs before that date successfully replace them. Incubation by both parents requires 24 days.

Three lapwings live in South America, one of which is the Southern Lapwing (*Belonopterus chilensis*), which ranges from Chile to Panama. This large, crested, black-and-white bird keeps in pairs and favors rocky islands in swift streams.

In North America, where no lapwings occur, other shorebirds fill their place. Chief among these is the ten-inch Killdeer (*Charadrius vociferus;* Plate 52), which breeds widely in meadows, pastures and similar locations. Its black breast rings are double, and they contrast unmistakably with the white of the body and the bright chestnut brown of the lower rump and tail coverts. This species winters south to Peru, where there is also a resident, nonmigratory population. Like other members of the family, the Killdeer is extremely noisy, calling its

Killdeer (*Charadrius vociferus*): distraction display

alarm note, *kill-dee kill-dee*, at the least sign of danger. A habit of plovers in general and this bird in particular is falling seemingly exhausted and crippled at one's feet when the nest or young are in danger, and then flying off as soon as the threat is gone.

Most of the ringed plovers keep close to salt-water beaches and mud flats, where they feed on small aquatic animals. The Ringed Plover (*Charadrius hiaticula*), a plump species measuring seven inches, is canvas-brown above and white below with a black chest band and orange legs. It breeds in northern climes around the world and winters along equatorial shores. The Semipalmated Plover (*C. semipalmatus*), which breeds in the New World arctic and winters in Middle and South America, also has a single black chest ring. It is just short of seven inches long and is named for a small web between the bases of the middle and inner toes. One of the smallest of the group is the Piping Plover (*C. melodus*), which is about five inches long. It breeds from Virginia northward and winters south to Mexico and the West Indies. Its upperparts are amazingly similar in color to the sandy beaches it usually inhabits.

The best-known and most widespread plovers are the two species of Golden Plover, which breed in the arctic around the world and winter in the tropics, often far south of the equator. In migration these birds make long overwater passages and transequatorial flights that frequently follow circuitous routes. The American Golden Plover (*Pluvialis dominica*) winters south to Patagonia, and the Old World species (*P. apricaria*) in South Africa, Tasmania and New Zealand. Golden Plovers are about ten inches in length. They are blackish below and brownish above, with conspicuous golden-yellow spots, and the sexes are, as in all plovers, virtually alike. The vivid blackish underparts are replaced by pale grayish plumage in winter. Although the Golden Plovers visit coastal lagoons, they are chiefly inhabitants of interior meadows, some of which may be 5000 feet or more above sea level. Golden Plovers migrate and winter in flocks. Their hunting run is rather typical of all plovers: first they run in short springs, then halt abruptly and freeze, next bend over to pick up a grasshopper or other insect, and finally dart off in a new direction to repeat the process. Flying in tight formation, the flock gives off a rattling sound as it whips and dives in unison.

The Dotterel (*Eudromias morinellus*) of Eurasia is a medium-sized plover with a bright russet belly. Recently in Swedish Lapland it was found that only the male incubated and that he fed on mosquitoes caught from the nest while incubating.

Perhaps the most unusual and geographically restricted member of the group is the Crook-billed or Wrybill Plover (*Anarhynchus frontalis*) of New Zealand, which breeds on South Island and winters on North Island. It is unique in having the outer quarter of its bill bent to the right. It feeds on rocky beaches and pursues small insects, which attempt to seek

refuge under water-worn stones. The angled bill is thought to be an adaptation that assists this plover in capturing its prey in such situations. Like most plovers, Wrybills are highly gregarious during the nonbreeding season. As many as 700 have been seen together. Unlike plovers in general, which lay four eggs, the Wrybill usually lays only two. This bird is gray above with a white forehead, and white below with a black chest band.

The third group of related species, the Turnstones and Surf Birds, constitutes the subfamily Arenariinae. There is only one Surf Bird (*Aphriza virgata*). It has a short, hard bill as in the plovers and turnstones, which it approximates in size, being about ten inches long. It is mottled with gray and white, its tail is black with a broad white base and it is stocky in build. Surf birds range along the coasts of the New World from Alaska to Chile and prefer rocks wet by the surf. They perform long migrations between their winter and summer ranges, deserting the coast to nest among rocks on Alaskan mountains. There they lay four eggs in the plover manner, the small ends of the extremely conical eggs being fitted together in a terrestrial depression so as to form a buffy cross with concealing brown spots. As in their relatives, the Dotterels and the turnstones, the male apparently does all the incubating.

One of the two species of turnstones is the Ruddy Turnstone (*Arenaria interpres*), which breeds on islands and coasts ringing the Arctic and winters south to Chile, South Africa, Australia and New Zealand. One of the most vividly marked of all shorebirds, it is dark brown above with large bright areas of chestnut and black, and with a white lower back and a white zone on the upper tail coverts. Below it has a black chest band, a white abdomen and rich orange legs. The Ruddy Turnstone frequents marine beaches

Dotterel (*Eudromias morinellus*)

where it turns over small stones and beach debris in quest of food. It has a habit rare among shorebirds, namely, occasionally feeding on the eggs of sea birds. The closely related but less colorful Black Turnstone (*A. melanocephala*), is much more restricted in distribution, breeding along the coast of Alaska and wintering to Lower California.

Sandpipers, Snipe and Woodcock (*Scolopacidae*)

Seventy-seven species of snipelike birds ranging in size from a small sparrow to a hen and reaching every coast of the world are collected in this highly varied family. Correlated with the extremes of size are extremes of habitat preference and feeding specializations; these are accompanied by highly developed capacities for migration and direction-finding. Compared with the nearly related plovers, the typical sandpiper is slender, with a smaller head and a longer bill. Also it has the legs more elongated, and it retains the hind toe, which is above the level of the frontal toes.

Almost all these birds breed in cold northern regions and winter far to the south, many of them in the Southern Hemisphere. In general, four eggs are laid in a depression made in ground, sand or among pebbles and lined with a meager amount of grass; they are incubated for from 19½ to 24 days depending on the species. Usually both parents incubate, and within a few hours after hatching, the downy, cryptically colored young can follow the adults. They may be cared for by either or both of the parents. Variations of this pattern are notable in the Ruff (*Philomachus pugnax*) of Eurasia, the Solitary Sandpiper (*Tringa solitaria*) of North America and the Green Sandpiper (*Tringa ochropus*) and Wood Sandpiper (*T. glareola*) of the Old World. The latter three have nesting habits that seem quite out of character for sandpipers; they deposit their eggs in the abandoned nests of arboreal birds, such as thrushes, pigeons and blackbirds. At such times these sandpipers perch in trees.

Sandpipers, snipe, woodcock and their allies feed on small invertebrates, chiefly insects, but certain species take berries during the breeding season, and others catch small fish. Still others capture insects in flight, and some of the aberrant species feed almost entirely on worms. Examples of this family are the Black-tailed Godwit (*Limosa limosa;* Plate 56) and the Dunlin (*Erolia alpina;* Plate 60). Some others are the Greenshank (*Tringa nebularia*), the Sanderling (*Crocethia alba*) and the Redshank (*Totanus totanus*), all of which breed in the Northern Hemisphere.

Swarms of sandpipers congregate along the shores of all of the warmer continents, particularly during the southward migration of late summer and fall, and scour the water's edge for food. Many gather

Greenshank (*Tringa nebularia*) with young

in loose flocks and sweep like a moving carpet back and forth with the waves. When they flush, they fly as a closely-knit group in complicated maneuvers requiring remarkable leadership and coordination. In flight the legs are trailed under the tail and in a few species they protrude behind it. The wings are pointed and swallow-shaped, and the tail is generally short and square. In some species, particularly of woodcock and snipe, the flight feathers are used to make audible notes during courtship flights.

Although very swift of wing and capable of long, sustained flights, they move slowly southward in fall migration and can best be studied at such a time. In spring the species make their way rapidly northward, often flying over the interior or following river valleys, such as the Mississippi, if they offer a direct route.

Some species are not highly migratory. The European Woodcock (*Scolopax rusticola;* Plate 57) is, for example, migratory only in the northern part of its range and sedentary elsewhere. This 13-inch bird has the reddish coloring of dead leaves. In New Guinea at altitudes of more than 9000 feet the author has found the darkest of all woodcocks, *Scolopax saturata rosenbergii,* living on the floor of deep wet moss forest where black and dark gray prevail.

All woodcock are equipped with long sensitive bills that are flexible over the outer third of their length. In probing the ground—usually damp swampy terrain—the bill is inserted straight down like an awl, and it has been shown that in this position the tip can be opened to clasp a worm. Woodcocks are crepuscular. They are remarkable for their courtship flights, which are executed over grassland at the edge of forest. In courtship the male climbs high in the air at dawn and at dusk, and sometimes at night, to conduct his maneuvers. The whistling notes heard as the bird mounts upward are thought to be made with the flight quills. Other notes accompany his dives back to earth.

Found in swampy grassland far from the shore is another group of aberrant shorebirds that have their eyes set far back in the head like the woodcock. These are the snipe (*Gallinago*), 13 species of long-billed birds found in all major land areas. They are mottled and striped with grass-brown, blackish and buff, are adept at evasive flying and are therefore highly regarded as sporting birds. Snipe travel in flocks, feeding mostly by night, and most are highly migratory. A typical species is the Common Snipe (*Gallinago gallinago;* Plate 58).

Eight species of curlews are known. They are tall, stately birds with long, slender, downcurved bills. The largest of the family is the Madagascar Curlew (*Numenius madagascariensis*), which reaches a length of 24 inches and attains a wingspread of 42 inches. Much like the Common Curlew (*N. arquata*), which is only about an inch shorter, it frequents mud flats and estuaries. In flight it generally moves in groups with a measured, rather gull-like cadence. The Whimbrel (*N. phaeopus*) of both the New and Old World reaches a length of 18 inches and has a bill four inches long. Above it is dark brown and gray with a barred tail, and its white underparts are heavily streaked both on the breast and on the flanks. Several inches shorter is the famed Eskimo Curlew (*N. bore-* *alis*), which is almost extinct due to wanton market hunting before the era of enlightened game management. Both species breed in northern portions of the New World and winter on the pampas of southern South America. Another famous species is the Bristle-thighed Curlew (*N. tahitiensis*), which in 1948 was for the first time discovered breeding far inland in the mountains of Alaska. It migrates across the Pacific to winter on the islands of Polynesia south to New Caledonia, fully 6000 miles from its place of breeding in the New World. During its long overseas migrations it has the unusual habit of feeding on bird's eggs on islands such as Laysan.

A relative of the curlews that also left the shore to breed in pastures and meadows is the short-billed, sweet-voiced bird known as the Upland Plover or Bartramian Sandpiper (*Bartramia longicauda*). Found from the latitude of Virginia northward, this species stands about 11 inches high and often perches on fence posts. Together with the killdeer it fills the ecological niche occupied by the lapwings in the Old World. Still another species that frequents the interior is the Spotted Sandpiper (*Actitis macularia*), which has been called the best-known American shorebird. This seven-inch species is brownish gray above with a burnishing of faint green. In summer it

Sanderlings (*Crocethia alba*)

Redshanks (*Totanus totanus*)

is white below with profuse small black spots, and plain white in winter. It breeds almost throughout its wide range in North America, from the edge of the sea to the shores of mountain lakes. Its teeter-tail movements and short flights along the shores of lakes and streams are familiar to millions of people. Almost identical except for its plain rather than spotted underparts is the Common Sandpiper (*A. hypoleucos*) of Eurasia.

Another inland species is the rather similar Solitary Sandpiper (*Tringa solitaria*), one of a closely related group of nine species ranging around the world. It is eight inches long and has a brownish gray, white-spotted back with faint greenish reflections. Its head and neck are streaked, and its underparts are white with dark markings on the chest and flanks. This species is a lone traveler and in fall visits bogs in the midst of pine barrens. It catches insects in flight but takes most of its food on the ground. A close relative, the Green Sandpiper (*T. ochropus*), which breeds in Eurasia, is dark greenish brown with light underparts and olive-green legs. This species feeds in swampy woodlands. Another species, the Wood Sandpiper (*T. glareola*), is quite similar but

has the legs longer; it has the upperparts largely bronzed brown and the underparts mostly smoke gray. It is very common, usually nesting on the tundra of northern Europe and Asia, but, curiously, it occasionally lays its eggs in abandoned tree nests of some of the aberrant-nesting sandpipers.

A variety of shorebirds belong in this family. Some, like the Yellow-legs, the Tattler and the Willet, are large, while many are small and confusingly similar. The smallest member of the family is the Least Sandpiper (*Erolia minutilla*), a six-inch bird which above is blackish with buffy brown edging, and below is whitish and has mud-dark streaking. Thirteen species belong in this group of world-wide, diminutive and exceedingly abundant shorebirds, collectively known as stints, or, to the birdwatcher, "peeps." Six occur regularly in the New World and four more reach it occasionally. One, the Spoon-billed Sandpiper (*Eurynorhynchus pygmeus*) of Siberia, is unique in its spoon-shaped bill tip.

Other snipelike shorebirds are the dowitchers (*Limnodromus*), of which two species are known. The Short-billed Dowitcher (*L. griseus*), which breeds in middle and northern Canada and winters

[165

from Florida to Middle America, is 10½ inches long and has prominent, reddish brown underparts. This bird is peculiar in that only the female incubates the eggs and only the male cares for the young. The dowitchers keep to mud flats and in feeding plunge the bill deep into the mud, rather like a woodcock.

In Eurasia a relative of the dowitcher and the snipe, the Ruff (*Philomachus pugnax;* Plate 54), has developed traits extraordinarily different from those of other members of the family, especially in its courtship ceremony. Ruffs breed on tundra in the far north of Eurasia and in damp meadows farther south. They winter in Africa and southern Asia. The males are about 11 inches in length, considerably larger than the females. In the breeding season the Ruff grows a massive erectile ruff, ear tufts of feathers, and facial warts. These ornaments are lost at the end of the breeding season, and for the rest of the year both sexes are dull brown and inconspicuous.

Dr. C. R. Stonor has called the courtship of these birds "as strange a phenomenon as is to be found in birds." The first extraordinary thing about it is that males and females live apart for all but a few minutes of the year, remaining in distinct flocks even in winter. In spring the male returns thousands of miles to ancestral courtship areas consisting of slightly raised ground in a field and stakes out a "run" that may be only a foot in diameter. From two to twenty males stand on a display mound, several yards in diameter, each defending his territory against wandering males, mostly young ones, that try to invade the dance area. At such times many males join in with much charging and bravado but very little actual combat. When excited, males display to other males and to other species of birds. The display consists of a charge in which the ornamental ruffs are expanded and the wings opened and drooped, and then a trancelike collapse in which the Ruff slowly sinks to his abdomen with his bill driven into the ground and for a few seconds remains thus, quivering the wings. He then recovers and after a short flight returns to his territory to sleep or doze.

The spectacle of many males standing around, fighting and dozing in their varied plumage is an amazing one. The color variation among ruffs is so pronounced that its function has been the subject of much discussion. Some males wear immense white collars; others have the collars black or brown; still others are variegated. When the female Ruff, called a reeve, is attracted to the scene, she strolls rather aloofly into the display area and, in a few minutes at most, selects her mate by biting one. As she strolls along, the males fall into veritable trances and shiver at her feet. Pairing takes place immediately.

Ruffs have no loud calls, their antics on the communal display ground being punctuated by deep guttural notes that carry only a short distance. The female does all the nest-building and rears the young while the male continues to stand by at the service mound. Observers have noted every kind of pairing from monogamy to polygyny and polyandry in these extraordinary birds.

Phalaropes *(Phalaropodidae)*

One of the riddles of avian parental care is how and why the usual roles of the sexes came to be reversed in the three species of aquatic shorebirds known as phalaropes. Phalaropes, along with sandpipers and plovers, belong to that very large assemblage of birds comprising the order Charadriiformes. Unlike most of these relatives, however, it is the female phalarope that does the wooing! Once she has secured a partner she selects the nesting site, which is usually a slight depression in grass. There the male builds a nest of grasses and moss and the female lays three to four eggs that are pear-shaped, light in color, and have irregular blotches. Thereafter he shoulders all the work of incubating and rearing the young. Shortly after hatching, the young are able to run and swim. For protection their down is mottled and striped.

The "henpecked" male is smaller in stature and much less colorful in dress than the female in summer, when the females of all three species wear bright nuptial plumage. In winter both sexes change their dress to one consisting chiefly of drab grays and whites. Reversal of the roles involving parental care is rare in birds.

Phalaropes are rather silent smallish birds with long necks. They range from 6 to 8 inches in total length. The name "phalarope," meaning "cootfooted," alludes to the development of the feet, which are somewhat like those of the much larger coots and grebes in that lobes and scalloped membranes extend from the toes. These form flexible paddles that provide propulsion in water.

Another specialization for swimming is the flattening of the tarsi, which permits the legs to cut through water more easily. Phalaropes spend most of their lives on or over water. Their plumage is thick and dense. Bubbles of air become trapped in the feathers and provide an unusual degree of buoyancy, which enables the bird, like a little gull, to ride high on the water's surface. This buoyancy and the characteristic near-vertical position of the phalarope's longish neck are primary marks of identification.

In autumn, phalaropes leave their northern breeding grounds around the globe and move southward in large flocks. These seasonal flights take them over broad ocean wastes and outer coastal waters fringing most of the New and Old Worlds. Favorite wintering areas are in the vicinity of cold currents off the western coasts of both Africa and South America, but large concentrations, sometimes composed of all three species, collect far out in the equatorial waters of the Atlantic and the Pacific. Despite their pelagic habits these masses of "swimming plovers" are peculiarly sandpiper-like in their group movements. Often they rise in unison, fly rapidly in tight formations, wheeling and whipping about, and then land as one bird on the water. These water-hopping rafts of birds pass along outer coastal waters every year, but unless hurricanes or severe storms blow them landward, they go unnoticed.

The phalarope's food consists of tiny marine animals—invertebrates such as insects, mollusks, and crustaceans—obtained on or beneath the surface of the water. A kind of dancing movement is employed by the bird to flush the small animals from their sanctuaries in mud and sand underlying shallow water. The feet and legs are used to stomp and tread in a circular path, stirring up the bottom and flushing out quarry, which is then picked up with rapid bobbings of the bill. Phalaropes also capture flying insects in somewhat the manner of flycatchers.

Another method of feeding involves associations with large marine mammals. Phalaropes land on the backs of whales in order to feed on small invertebrates clinging there, and at other times they eat minute animals flushed up in the wake of these large oceanic mammals.

Wilson's Phalarope (*Steganopus tricolor*), which has the head striped with black and brown, is the most sandpiper-like of the three species. It is one of the best-known phalaropes in the New World because of its unusually southerly breeding range and its habit of feeding close to shore. In summer this species frequents inland lakes in western North America south to central United States. In winter it occurs chiefly along the western coasts of North and South America to Chile.

The Northern Phalarope (*Lobipes lobatus*), which is gray-headed, is known in Europe as the Red-necked Phalarope, a name that adequately describes the female in nuptial plumage. This species sometimes visits inland lakes in the United States while in transit from its breeding grounds in lakes and ponds throughout the Arctic to the waters where it winters off the coasts of South America and Africa, and even in the southwest Pacific.

In nuptial dress the female Red Phalarope (*Phalaropus fulicarius*), known as the Gray Phalarope in Europe, is largely reddish maroon below and has much white on the head. This is the northernmost breeder of the family. It nests in the Arctic around the world and winters off the coasts of Chile and South Africa.

Avocets and Stilts

(*Recurvirostridae*)

The seven beautiful species of this nearly cosmopolitan group of long-legged shorebirds indulge in strange activities to protect their homes. Thus the Pied Stilt (*Himantopus himantopus*) of New Zealand, a colony nester, will defend the colony by feigning illness and lameness and may even play dead, whereas the New World race of the same species, the Black-necked Stilt (Plate 63) distracts by flying close to the ground like a wounded bird. Another race found in southern Eurasia and Africa is the Black-winged Stilt (Plate 62).

Notwithstanding the scientific name of the family—Recurvirostridae—only the avocets have the bill recurved or bent upward; but in all species it is long and awl-like. Variations in its shape are correlated with such feeding habits as that of the avocet, which sweeps the bill from side to side in shallow water, and of the stilt, which generally probes the underlying mud. Crustaceans, insects and other small animals constitute the prey of both groups. Except for the bill, these birds are very similar in structure and habits. Both have the hind toe absent or rudimentary and the three frontal toes webbed—fully in the avocets, partially in the stilts. The ventral plumage is very dense, presumably because only the underside of the body comes into contact with water. They are long-legged waders that occur chiefly in fresh-water marshes but also frequent similar salt-water habitats.

The two different species of stilts that are known are considered to be more primitive (that is, more like the archetype) than the avocets. One is the Pied Stilt, already mentioned, and the other the Banded Stilt (*Cladorhynchus leucocephala*). The only country in which both occur is Australia. The Australian race of the Pied Stilt is a white bird about 14 inches in length with very long, spectacular pink legs, a long, slender, black beak, black wings and a red iris. Its nest is a simple cluster of grasses piled up in shallow water or a slight grass-lined scrape. Its eggs, usually four in number, are pear-shaped and olivaceous with brownish markings, and are placed in the nest so that the small ends are centered. The Australian ornithologists, Serventy and Whittell, describe its call as resembling the yapping of a small dog.

The relatively rare Banded Stilt, which occurs in the interior of Australia, is nearly 18 inches in length, generally whitish with dark brown wings, and has a

Red Phalarope (*Phalaropus fulicarius*) adult in winter plumage

KARL W. KENYON

Old World Avocet (*Recurvirostra avosetta*)

bright chestnut chest band and a brown iris. This splendid bird's breeding grounds, along the edges of inland salt lakes, were not discovered until 1930, apparently because the small colonies shift position, nesting seemingly being correlated with rainfall and the appearance of lakes. These lakes quickly become filled with inland shrimp, which constitute the bird's major source of food and apparently a breeding stimulus. The eggs of this species are chalky and lusterless, and the young are said to be covered with pure white down.

The Black-necked Stilt (*Himantopus h. mexicanus*), ranging in America from the United States to Brazil, Peru and the Galapagos Islands, is a pink-legged shorebird standing almost 16 inches tall on disproportionately long legs. It is black above and white below and, although now rare in large areas of its range, is still locally abundant in many regions. It feeds among grassy vegetation bordering freshwater and brackish marshes and streams. Normally it wades about, taking very high steps, but it can swim and dive, and the neck with its very small head is hunched back so far that it appears stubby.

The male performs the distraction displays, but because of the great length of its legs, it cannot drag its body along the ground as do many other birds. It therefore performs in the air as much as forty yards away, mimicking a wounded bird by fluttering just above the ground with its long, highly colorful legs dangling.

Avocets are the most graceful of shorebirds. Four species, all much alike in structure and behavior, are recognized: the Old World Avocet (*Recurvirostra avosetta*) of Eurasia and Africa, the Australian Avocet (*R. novae-hollandiae*) of Australia, New Guinea and, formerly, Tasmania, the American Avocet (*R. americana*) of North America, and the Chilean Avocet (*R. andina*) of the high Andes north to Peru.

Some of the courtship performances of avocets are hard to credit. For one thing, they have specific head movements which they use to communicate with the other members of the flock, and it is believed they are able to perform their large group movements, with as many as a dozen in a circle around a flat stone, in almost perfect cadence because of this "language." Both sexes participate in these extraordinary performances, which represent a courtship stage prior to mate selection. We still do not understand why certain disturbances cause whole flocks of these courting birds to engage suddenly in mass mating.

The Old World Avocet has the bill slender and upcurved and the legs dark gray. Its head is larger than that of the stilt. Its habitat seems much the same as that of the stilt but, as earlier indicated, it occupies a different feeding niche. Apparently quite vulnerable to rats and to man, this avocet has been extirpated or greatly diminished in numbers over much of its former range. But after a lapse of nearly a hundred years it has once more begun to breed in England.

The American Avocet (Plate 61), a slightly larger species, reaches 18 inches in length. This very graceful creature breeds north to southern Canada and winters south to Guatemala, and in migration ordinarily keeps west of the Mississippi River. Its hunting areas may be in such marshes far inland as Great Salt Lake. Dr. Frank M. Chapman has described how the birds feed there: "They wade into the water and drop the bill below the surface until the convexity of the maxilla probably touches the bottom. In this position they move forward at a half run and with every step the bill is swung from side to side, sweeping through an arc of about 50 degrees in search of shells and other aquatic animals. The mandibles are slightly opened, and at times the birds pause to devour their prey."

The nest of this avocet, a slight scrape with a few rootlets for a lining, is usually placed on the ground in low vegetation near water. The four pyriform eggs usually laid are stony olive in color with heavy dark spots. Incubation requires about 23 days and like the nest-building is performed by both sexes. The young leave the nest almost as soon as they are hatched but are brooded for another 11 days.

The Chilean Avocet is much like the American Avocet but is generally darker above, with white appearing only on the rump, head and neck. The Australian or Red-necked Avocet has the lead-colored legs and the bill black and upcurved in the unmistakably avocet manner. Some 18 inches in length, this bird is white with a reddish brown head and neck. This species has invaded New Zealand on several occasions but has never managed to establish itself there.

At very high elevations from Kashmir to Burma is found the most aberrant species of this group, the Ibis-bill (*Ibidorhynchus struthersii*; Plate 59). This 15-inch, avocet-like bird with its red, sharply curved bill is one of the most difficult to photograph on the nest because it breeds ten or more thousand feet above sea level along the edges of stony mountain creeks.

Crab-plover (*Dromadidae*)

The family Dromadidae was erected for a single species—the Crab-plover (*Dromas ardeola*), which inhabits the northern and western shores of the Indian Ocean. It is a black and white, long-legged wading bird with characteristics of habit and structure that suggest affinities with shorebirds, terns, and petrels.

Specifically, the Crab-plover is about 16 inches in length and has a black bill shaped something like that of a tern. Attached to dull, greenish blue legs are three webbed toes in front and a well-developed hind toe. The sexes are similar in color. In its habits this bird is unique in that it finds its food like a shorebird on exposed coral reefs and mud flats, yet it nests in colonial groups in long tunnels in sand banks bordering the sea. These burrows are often drilled downward at an angle from relatively flat surfaces, like some of the burrows of petrels and puffins and even certain bee-eaters. Just inside the entrance the tunnel curves upward so that the egg cavity may be placed four or even five feet from the opening in inky blackness, but sometimes—mole-like—only a few inches below the surface of the ground and with the lowest part of the tunnel well below the nest. In this way the eggs and young are rather well protected in the event of heavy rains. The eggs of this strange bird are large and pure white, and only one is laid per clutch. They are almost the only white eggs among the Charadriiformes—a large group noted for its heavily spotted eggs. The chick emerges covered with gray and white down as in the shorebirds. It soon runs about, but nevertheless remains on the nest for a long time.

Crab-plovers are highly gregarious. Colonel Meinertzhagen in his *Birds of Arabia* wrote of his experience in collecting birds out of a flock. "I wanted two specimens and had the greatest difficulty in securing them without injuring others. My shot killed four birds at about thirty yards on the fringe of the flock. Instead of flying away, the pack crowded round the dead birds and advanced towards me, chattering in the wildest concern for their dead comrades, which they tried to assist and rescue, pushing them along in the water and refusing to leave them until I was scarcely ten yards from them." Meinertzhagen observed Crab-plovers perched on the backs of hippopotami sleeping in sea water on a coral reef.

In feeding, the Crab-plover walks, runs and swims well. Its chief fare is crabs, but it also feeds on other marine life. As the tide ebbs, it frequents shoals in search of freshly exposed crabs, grasping them in the bill and battering them to death or insensibility before swallowing them. Tiny crabs are swallowed whole, large ones are ripped apart. In flight, which is somewhat ternlike, the long legs trail. An unusual habit of the Crab-Plover is that while airborne it often utters loud, semimusical notes.

Thick-knees or Stone Curlews (*Burhinidae*)

Thick-knees are shorebirds that resemble small bustards and like them have deserted the shore to live in dry savannas, often hundreds of miles from the ocean. They are particularly fond of stony semidesert country and are sometimes called Stone Curlews or Stone Plovers, but, unlike curlews and most plovers, have only three toes. The seven species range from a foot to some 20 inches in height, and are colored in somber grays and browns, with the sexes wearing similar dress. They have large yellow eyes and relatively large heads, and, as implied by their name, they have bulging "knees."

Thick-knees have learned to exploit a nocturnal niche that seems to be largely unoccupied in most of the warmer parts of the world. By day they sit on their legs, using the leg almost like a long foot and the "knee" like a heel. So well do they hide that they are rarely seen by day, and in several places they manage to survive even near large cities. In hiding, they obliterate the silhouette by stretching out on the ground, apparently having unbelievable confidence in their cryptic coloration. In Australia they have been known to hold their prone position even when picked up and replaced on the ground again.

Thick-knees feed on insects, worms, mollusks and occasionally lizards and small rodents. They travel in pairs and small parties, calling back and forth with whistles and owl-like notes. On migration they may gather into flocks of as many as 200.

The pair builds no nest but deposits two or three eggs in a slight ground depression. The long, oval eggs are pale brownish in color with a heavy spattering of gray and brown. Both sexes incubate, but the female takes the major part and apparently does the nocturnal incubating. Thick-knees are among the few birds known to move the eggs to a new location when the nest is threatened. In some 27 days the young emerge, heavily covered with brownish down and within a day they leave the nest to follow their parents. During early stages of incubation the adult slinks away from the nest if it is approached in daylight, but in later stages it hides on the nest by sprawling flat, thus covering the eggs. In some species the nonincubating parent remains on guard and warns of danger by whistling.

The thick-knee of Europe, called the Stone Curlew (*Burhinus oedicnemus;* Plate 64), is 16 inches long, ranges through Asia and North Africa and still breeds in populous England. Of the three species in Africa, one, the Cape Thick-knee (*Burhinus capensis*), which is found over most of the continent, often ventures close to farm homes by night and causes alarm among the superstitious with its eerie calls. Like all thick-knees, it squats by day in the shade and, if flushed, runs rapidly with the head held low.

In India, Burma and Ceylon is found the Great Stone Curlew (*Esacus recurvirostris*). This species stands 1½ feet high, alternately jerks the head and tail if alarmed, and when hiding in daylight, lays its head and bill flat on the ground. The Australian Stone Curlew (*B. magnirostris*) stands 22 inches tall and has a wing span of more than three feet. In the New World there are two thick-knees, the Double-striped Thick-knee (*B. bistriatus*), ranging from Mexico to Brazil, and the South American Thick-knee (*B. superciliaris*), ranging from Ecuador to Peru. The former is 20 inches tall and has green legs.

Pratincoles and Coursers
(*Glareolidae*)

This is an unusual group of 16 species of somewhat plover-like birds ranging from small to medium in size. As they feed on the wing, some vaguely resemble giant swallows; others sleep by day and hunt at night like the thick-knees. The family is centered in the warm parts of Africa and Asia, but a few species have found their way to Europe (two species breed there) and to Australia. They frequent dry, stony places, deserts, burned areas, plowed lands, etc. They are fleet of foot, most species being able to run faster than a man; in the air they fly strongly.

The family is divided into two sections, the more primitive containing the coursers, which feed on the ground and have only three toes (the hallux is missing), whereas the pratincoles feed on the wing and have four toes. The coursers also have the middle toe and the legs much longer and the tail square, not deeply forked.

The two groups are, nevertheless, anatomically very similar. They all nest in very simple ways with the exception of the Crocodile Bird or Black-backed Courser (*Pluvianus aegyptius*), a species common along the sandy banks of the Nile and one of the very few birds that depend largely on the sun's heat to incubate their eggs. Normally three are laid, and these are buried in the sand, which then serves as an incubating oven (see Megapodes). The Crocodile Bird is black above with white-banded wings.

The Cream-colored Courser (*Cursorius cursor*) of Africa ranges occasionally to Europe and southwestern Asia. As is typical of this family, both sexes are similarly dressed. It is some ten inches in length and generally tawny buff with a gray nape and with black on the wings and side of the head. This species lays two eggs densely streaked and spotted with dark colors on bare sand. Incubation, which requires 17 to 18 days, is performed by the female. The young hatch covered with brown down and rather heavily streaked. In Arabia, according to Colonel Meinertzhagen, this species feeds on lizards, beetles, small snails and grasshoppers; but, generally speaking, insects are the primary fare of this family.

Other species are the Double-banded Courser (*Rhinoptilus africanus*), a nine-inch bird confined to the driest parts of eastern and southern Africa, such as the Kalahari Desert. It lays a single egg which exactly matches the ground. A relative, the Bronze-wing Courser (*R. chalcopterus*), usually lays two eggs. The Bronze-wing hunts by night and sleeps by day, normally in a squatting position with the head and neck stretched out on the ground. Coursers habitually follow field fires to prey on small animals flushed by the heat and smoke.

At first glance the pratincoles with their swallow-like wings and long, forked tails seem very different from the coursers. But they are the only members of the family that employ their wings instead of their legs in searching for food. So often are they found preying on swarms of grasshoppers and locusts that one of their African names is Locust Bird. In the air pratincoles employ a graceful, swallow-like flight, but they can get about on the ground very well, running on long slender legs like plovers. Their feet are peculiar in that the middle toe is equipped with a comb (see Herons) and a short web joins the outer and middle toes.

Typical of the group is the Collared Pratincole (*Glareola pratincola*), a starling-sized bird. Above it is brownish, below buffy white washed with chestnut, and with the throat white edged with black. This pratincole hunts with the deftness of a swallow, especially in the early morning and late evening over low-lying pastures near water. It is gregarious and highly migratory, ranging from the Mediterranean region and northern Africa to Asia and the Philippines, and thence south to the Malay Archipelago.

The nesting behavior of pratincoles is usually colonial. The males engage in courtship flights accompanied by singing. Each pair lays two to three eggs on the surface of a dry plain and both parents incubate for 17 to 18 days. In defending their nesting areas they resort to mass distraction displays rather like those of some stilts. This phenomenon is well documented by the British ornithologist Douglas Dewar, who, while he was inspecting the eggs of a pratincole in India on one occasion, suddenly found himself surrounded by about twenty "swallow plovers" nearly all of which were striking odd attitudes. He wrote: "Some were lying on the sand as though they had been wounded and fallen to the ground; others foundered in the sand . . . some were fluttering along with one wing stretched out limply, looking as though it were broken; while others appeared to have both wings broken."

Seed-snipe (*Thinocoridae*)

The seed-snipe, a short-legged relative of the shorebirds, looks somewhat like a cross between a plover and a small quail. The family is confined to South

America, and consists of four species of plump birds with pointed wings, short bills and four-toed legs.

Seed-snipe favor stony, desolate wastelands scantily clad with vegetation, although they feed chiefly on seeds and buds. In tundra areas of Patagonia and the Falkland Islands, they live near sea level; toward the equator they keep to similar habitats in the Andes up to 14,000 feet above the sea.

Seed-snipe usually nest on bare ground in a simple depression. The Patagonian Seed-snipe (*Thinocorus rumicivorus*), a bird six inches in length, buries its grayish, brown-spotted eggs in dry earth when it leaves the nest. The length of incubation and the roles played by the sexes in rearing the young apparently remain unknown. It is highly migratory, moving from breeding areas near the southern tip of South America to wintering areas in the sparsely covered pampas of Argentina as well as the desolate valleys of the high Andes. This bird is chiefly brown above and white below with black markings, particularly on the front and sides of the neck. In flight it moves in flocks; on the ground it is hard to flush, preferring to freeze under vegetation, and uttering scratching staccato notes when taking flight.

A large species of high mountains—sometimes up to 14,000 feet—is D'Orbigny's Seed-snipe (*Thinocorus orbignyianus*), which is found from Peru to Tierra del Fuego.

Sheath-bills (*Chionididae*)

The home of the sheath-bill is in bleak lands of snow, ice and rock rarely visited by man—islands lost in the cold southern oceans and along the perimeter of the antarctic continent. Nevertheless this little family—it consists of two species—of pigeon-sized birds is interesting because of its peculiar affinities to both the shorebirds—chiefly the plovers—and the gulls.

On their home grounds sheath-bills display a considerable curiosity, flying up to greet a visitor and perching on rocks around him. One observer reported that they came so close he was able to catch one with his hand.

Despite their superficially pigeon-like appearance, sheath-bills display plover-like characteristics. They have peculiar growths on the forepart of the head, and the carpal spurs, which are thornlike and distributed one on the bend of each wing, resemble those found in many plovers. The name "Sheath-bill" is derived from a horny saddle-like casing that covers the base of the bill and partially conceals the nostrils.

Two very similar species comprise the family. At present little is known of their life history. Their food is seaweeds, mussels and small crustaceans, but the length of the incubation period and the roles played by the sexes in parental care are not known.

White Sheath-bill (*Chionia alba*)

The White Sheath-bill (*Chionia alba*) is snowy white, has black legs and a black bill with a yellow base and is about 15 inches in height. It breeds on the islands of South Georgia, in the South Orkneys, on Booth Island and probably on small islands off the tip of South America. Dr. Robert C. Murphy states that this species lays from two to three eggs and that usually only one young survives. The nest is composed of grasses and is hidden in rock crevices or under tufts of grass.

Similar in size despite its name, the Lesser Sheath-bill (*C. minor*) is less well-known. It breeds on the far southern islands of Prince Edward, Marion, Crozet, Possession, Kerguelen and Heard.

Skuas and Jaegers

(*Stercorariidae*)

The skuas and jaegers are gull-sized birds of prey inhabiting the seas and seacoasts of the world. They are extremely rapacious and assume the same roles in their oceanic habitat that the diurnal birds of prey —the hawks, falcons and vultures—fill over land. But some of the species of these gull-like "sea falcons" are much more pugnacious and courageous than even the most daring falcon. Indeed it may not be an exaggeration to say they are the most "courageous" of all birds in the defense of their nests. This comes as a surprise in view of their piratical habits, calling for the killing of young and stealing not only the eggs of other birds but also their catches of fish. In terms of human behavior these activities might lead one to think they would be cowardly. That this is not true

[171

is indicated by the experience of a collector who visited Kerguelen Island to study the Great Skua (*Catharacta skua antarctica*). Discovering a nest with two eggs, he attempted to collect them, but before he could do so the parents, each the size of a large hawk and equipped with a sharp-hooked bill and strong claws, attacked him so fiercely that he was forced to kill one of the birds with his pistol. He then emptied his weapon at the other and finally, taking cover, he threw stones at it as it swooped at his head until he at last disabled it.

The skuas and jaegers are found along all of the coasts of the world, even those within the Arctic and Antarctic. In fact, Dr. Carl R. Eklund on May 16, 1957, reported that his biologists had caught, weighed, banded and liberated 324 skuas and 15 Giant Fulmars near the Wilkes Station of the American Geophysical Year team, Antarctica. This catch was made with a net 1800 feet square, towed through a flock of birds by projectiles from three cannons. It is clear that penguins are not the only abundant birds on the Antarctic continent.

Skuas and jaegers have the wings long and pointed, the legs short and strong, the talons strong and sharply curved. In flight they resemble hawks, and close at hand they are deceptively hawklike because of the presence of a cere at the base of the bill and a sharp aquiline bill. These characters are all the result of convergent evolution, for skuas and jaegers are closely allied to gulls. In fact, they are aberrant gulls that have become modified for food-getting of a sort requiring swift flight and aggressiveness. During their early stages young skuas hunt and fish like gulls.

The Great Skua is nearly two feet long and very sturdy. Unlike the jaegers, it has the tail short and blunt and in flight resembles a bulky gull rather than a falcon. Despite its clumsy appearance, it can fly with great speed, and obtain much of its food by chasing gulls and forcing them to disgorge their catch in the air. Very rapacious, the Great Skua kills birds up to the size of a small chicken and is the terror of colonially breeding birds, especially the penguins, in the Antarctic region. It breeds in the colder regions of both the northern and southern parts of the globe, but its main stronghold is the Southern Hemisphere.

The jaegers are smaller and more falcon-like. They breed chiefly in the Arctic but wander southward to warmer seas during the nonbreeding season. The size of small gulls, they all have the central tail feathers characteristically elongated and protruding from two to eight inches beyond the other tail feathers. Three species comprise the group, which occurs over most of the waters of the world. All of the species have two color phases, a grayish white one and a dark sooty brown one. The Pomarine Jaeger (*Stercorarius pomarinus*), which is some 20 inches long and has twisted, blunt-ended central tail feathers, is chiefly an offshore bird. It breeds in the Arctic, often close to fresh water, and feeds to a large extent

Great Skua (*Catharacta skua*)

on lemmings and other land animals. The Parasitic Jaeger (*S. parasiticus*) is smaller—18 inches long—but has the central tail feathers protruding several inches and ending in points. The Long-tailed Jaeger (*S. longicaudus;* Plate 65) has the central feathers much lengthened in an unmistakable wedge shape.

In winter jaegers wander widely over the oceans of the world, reaching Australia and Tasmania, as well as more remote land areas in the southern seas. Both the skuas and the jaegers nest on the ground, laying the eggs—usually two—in a depression. The eggs of the skua are earth-colored and marked with dark blotches and spots. Those of the jaeger are stone-colored and sometimes dull greenish buff with dark spots. Apparently both sexes share the duties of incubation and the care of the young. Incubation in the skuas requires from about 23 to 26 days and the young leave the nest fairly soon after hatching, being "tardily nidifugous."

All skuas and jaegers breed colonially on isolated islands and tundra-covered wastelands of the Far North and Far South. The nests may be built in swampy areas or in high, dry grasslands, depending on the species.

Gulls and Terns (*Laridae*)

Gulls and terns are graceful, long-winged "sea birds" that are nearly world-wide in distribution. The gulls are larger and heavier than the terns and differ from them in having the bill hooked, not pointed; the tail generally rounded, not forked; the wings more rounded and less pointed. In flight, gulls direct the bill straight forward, not downward as do the terns. Also, gulls normally alight on water or land to feed, and their food consists largely of carrion, whereas the terns usually dive for live prey. Despite these seemingly considerable differences, there are terns that look and act like some of the smaller gulls, and vice versa.

The gulls (subfamily Larinae), comprising 43 species, are found chiefly along the oceanic coasts of the world. They are essentially white and gray, with some black appearing in the wings and tail, and often on the head. The black may be seasonal, with gray replacing the black of the head in the nonbreeding season. Gulls range from about 11 to about 32 inches in length. They are closely related to the skuas and jaegers, and in their bloodthirsty robbing of eggs and young of other sea birds some gulls seem to resemble them closely in habits.

Gulls are highly gregarious scavengers of the sea and coastal rivers, feeding on all kinds of rubbish and to a lesser extent on fish. They have a way of mass hunting resembling that of the New World vulture; namely, the birds spread out to scan a strip of sea many miles in width, and when one sights food his actions notify the others, who then join the hunt. In this way large numbers of birds sometimes seem almost mysteriously to converge on a source of food.

A large concentration of feeding gulls is indeed a splendid sight. The birds are extraordinary flyers, soaring and gliding seemingly without effort. In hunting they wheel and alight on rough seas, floating high, swimming rapidly, rarely submerging much of the body, and raucously fighting and chasing for food.

Gulls walk and run with agility on land, flocks often following the plow or swarming in to feed on grasshoppers. Many species resort to food-getting devices that may seem ingenious or vicious. The Pacific Gull (*Larus pacificus*) patrols the beaches of Australia to intercept young sea turtles as they scamper to the ocean from their hatching pits in the high dunes. When it catches them it batters them to death. This gull, like the Great Black-backed Gull (*L. marinus*), the Herring Gull (*L. argentatus*) and the Glaucous Gull (*L. hyperboreus*), drops large hard-shelled mollusks on such surfaces as concrete-floored bridges and roadways in order to crack open the shells. This simple form of tool-using has developed in other birds: the Bearded Vulture, for instance, gets at its favorite food, bone marrow, by dropping the bones on rocks, and some of the crows are reported to break open shellfish and even hard nuts by dropping them. Other methods of feeding used by gulls involve treading on sand (to flush out invertebrates), robbery and cannibalism. The last usually occurs in large nesting sites used by many colonial sea birds. In such sites each species of gull breeds in one particular habitat—some on the rock

Ring-billed Gull (*Larus delawarensis*)

tops, some on the ground between the rocks, some on ledges and so forth. Other families, such as gannets, murres, auks, puffins, cormorants and petrels, have their own breeding niches. The gulls, particularly such species as the Herring Gull and the Great Black-back, constantly attempt to rob other birds, including even their own species, of eggs and young. Experiments have shown that egg-robbers will break open their own eggs and devour them if the eggs are moved a short distance from the nest. Even chicks that wander away from the nest may be attacked and swallowed by their own parents. To hide, the chicks freeze close to the ground, depending on their buff-and-brown-spotted coats of down for protection.

Gulls construct nests of seaweed, grass and sometimes twigs, usually placing them on rock or ground, but sometimes in trees. From two to three brown eggs marked with dark smudges are laid. If the eggs are systematically removed, some gulls will continue laying up to 15 eggs. Systematic nest-robbing by humans was the custom in many parts of the Old World, and in Holland the eggs are sold as "plover eggs" to tourists. The young hatch after 20 days. At birth the eyes are open and the down coat is present. Although the young can walk within hours and run within a week, they remain on or near the nest for a period ranging from a month to a month and a half, during which they are fed by both parents. Mortality of the young is very great, authorities estimating that in some species only 5 per cent survive to maturity. This would seem to refute the theory that social nesting is a mechanism for group safety.

The Herring Gull (*Larus argentatus;* Plate 70), which reaches a length of 26 inches, is the most abundant and the best known of all gulls along the shores of Asia, western Europe, and North America. It is this species that abounds along the New England coast and trails Great Lakes steamers. Another species, Bonaparte's Gull (*L. philadelphia*), which is just over a foot in length, is best known for its unusual habit of building a nest of sticks in small conifers and on stumps. It nests in Western Canada and Alaska, often long distances from the water. Two Old World examples, the Black-headed Gull (*Larus ridibundus*) and the Lesser Black-backed Gull (*Larus fuscus*) are shown in Plates 68 and 71.

Another interesting gull is the Ivory Gull (*Pagophila eburnea*) or "Ice Partridge," which is snow-white and reaches a length of 17 inches. It breeds at the extreme northern edges of continents, and its chicks are pure white. One of the hardiest of birds, it winters chiefly over the northern drift ice of Arctic waters, only rarely occurring as far south as New Jersey and the British Isles.

The most aberrant gull is Ross' Gull (*Rhodostethia rosea*), a 13-inch white bird which is strongly tinged with pink and has a narrow black collar. Dr. James Fisher and R. M. Lockley, in their *Sea-Birds,* tell the dramatic story of early discoveries of this rare bird in the frozen North.

The Little Gull (*Larus minutus*), which is 11 inches in length, is the tiniest of the tribe. It is an Old World species that occasionally visits eastern North America. By contrast, the largest gull is the Great Black-backed Gull of the North Atlantic, which reaches a length of 32 inches and has a wing-spread of more than five feet. Its mantle and wings are blackish. A relative, the Western Gull (*Larus occidentalis*), which lives in the Pacific south to Mexico, has a slate-gray mantle.

The Glaucous Gull (*L. hyperboreus*) approaches the Great Black-back in size but is pure white with some pearl gray in the wings. The range of this bird is the Far North around the globe. A smaller gull, the Ring-billed (*L. delawarensis;* Plate 66), which wears a black band on its greenish-gray bill, is becoming more common and is primarily a bird of inland lakes.

Franklin's Gull (*L. pipixcan*) is unique in that it is the only North American gull that winters far south of the equator. This 15-inch bird, with a prominent black head, red bill, white neck, and gray back, breeds in huge colonies in prairie swamps of North America and winters south to Chile. Its chief food is insects, mainly grasshoppers, and it is valuable in helping to keep these pests under control. A species of similar food habits, the California Gull (*L. californicus*), is one of the few birds to have been publicly honored, the Mormons of Salt Lake City having erected a monument to it when vast numbers converged on their grasshopper-plagued fields and saved the early settlers from starvation.

The most pelagic of gulls is the Kittiwake (*Rissa tridactyla;* Plate 67); unlike most gulls it is at home far out on the open ocean. Its range is panarctic and it builds its nests on rock ledges as far north as cliffs extend. This noisy, medium-sized bird—it is named for its high-pitched cry—is less aggressive than other gulls and does not steal eggs or young birds, but feeds on fish, mollusks and plankton taken from the surface of the sea.

The second subfamily of the Laridae comprises the terns; of these there are 39 species scattered over most of the waters of the world. Fisher and Lockley report that some 30 species are found in the Pacific, 25 in the Atlantic and Mediterranean, and 17 along the northern perimeter of the Atlantic. Two, the Arctic Tern (*Sterna paradisaea*) and the Common Tern (*S. hirundo*), breed within the Arctic Circle, and four breed on islands in the antarctic.

The Arctic Tern is one of the 28 species of *Sterna.* It is famous for spending more time in daylight than any other living creature. It breeds during the arctic summer when continuous daylight prevails, and it visits the antarctic to winter, arriving there in time to enjoy the long days and then the continuous daylight of the antarctic midsummer. Among the records confirming its remarkable migrations is that of a nestling that was banded in Labrador and recovered in Natal, southeastern Africa, some 11,000 miles away, less than three months after it had learned to fly. In both the arctic and the antarctic, it feeds in the frigid waters between ice floes. It is circumpolar in distribution. Although most of its long-distance flying is over unmarked seas, it somehow manages to return and breed with regularity in large colonies on remote bits of land.

Terns employ specialized methods of food-getting and of nest location. An example of the former is Forster's Tern (*Sterna forsteri*) of the northern portions of the New World; in spring it follows the melting ice of the inland swamps and tundras, feeding on quick-frozen fishes, insects and other invertebrates as they are released from their icy tombs. This tern is but one of six species that breed along the edges of fresh water, often far from the sea, in North America. Nine species in Eurasia follow a similar pattern of behavior, and there are species that keep largely or even wholly to the fresh water of rivers, streams and swamps, in Africa, Australia, New Guinea and many other areas. But by and large the terns are sea birds. Some are among the most pelagic of birds, ranging out over the unmarked vastnesses of the oceans, guided by a sense of timing and of geographical location that to man seems phenomenal. Some, such as the Sooty Tern (*S. fuscata;* Plate 69) of Ascension Island in the middle of the tropical Atlantic, seem to have disassociated themselves from most of the cyclic mechanisms that affect the lives of other Sooty Terns and other birds. Thus, according to Dr. J. P. Chapin, they breed four times every three years. The phenomenon of vast numbers of Sooty Terns gathering to breed without any correlation with the calendar is difficult to comprehend. An interesting tern of the west coast of South America is the Inca Tern (*Larosterna inca;* Plate 73).

The assurance with which terns return to their nesting grounds after long and sometimes circuitous migrations is equaled only by the ability of some species to find their eggs after a sandstorm. Terns nest for the most part on sand, usually laying three eggs in a slight scrape that the birds build by falling forward on the breast, kicking the sand backward with their small webbed toes and pivoting in the cavity. Experiments have shown that even though all identifying marks are removed from such a strand and the eggs completely concealed by wind-blown sand, the adults can easily find them.

Terns are mostly white with gray backs and black head caps. In most species the tail is deeply forked and the wings long and pointed, as in many of the swallows; in fact they are often called sea swallows. Some of the terns are dark, even blackish; but some, such as the Fairy Tern (*Gygis alba;* Plate 72) of the warm Atlantic, Pacific and Indian Oceans, are pure white. This curious little bird nests on tiny oceanic islands and has developed the extraordinary habit of laying a single pure white egg on a small crotch of a tree limb well above the ground. All other terns nest on the ground. In general the egg shells are quickly carried away from the nest as soon

Common Tern (*Sterna hirundo*)

as the young have hatched, and the young begin to scramble around almost immediately.

Terns feed on fishes and crustaceans which they gather by shallow diving and by snatching while in flight. Some species, such as the Gull-billed Tern (*Geochelidon nilotica*), which occurs over most of the world, catch insects while flying far inland; others, such as the Common and the Arctic Terns, snatch small crustaceans from the sea while flying. Many terns can hover while waiting to dive.

Arctic Tern (*Sterna paradisaea*)

ERIC J. HOSKING

Little Tern (*Sterna albifrons*): courtship feeding

ERIC J. HOSKING

Terns engage in a highly interesting courtship ritual in which one bird holds a small shiny fish (see photograph of the Little Tern, *Sterna albifrons*) in its bill and then gives it to the other, whereupon a chase begins, in which the birds fly swiftly about with gliding, fluttering and screaming. The inanimate object—the fish—seems as necessary to this courtship as the bower to the bowerbird. The male aggressively defends a territory and, through the above ritual, attracts a mate to it. Copulation takes place on the nest site, and both sexes incubate and feed the young. Incubation begins with the first egg laid and lasts for a minimum of 21 days, after which the young are brooded another two or three days. The young fly in about a month and reach full maturity in about three years.

Nestlings accept and swallow fishes that are longer than their own bodies. These are partially downed and then slowly gulped inward as space becomes available.

Like their relatives the skuas, terns sometimes aggressively defend their colonies. They attack predators—even man—in several quite effective ways. In one method involving direct attack, the Noddy (*Anous*), a pantropical sooty-colored bird represented by three species, dives down on intruders, sometimes cutting the head of its victims with its sharp bill. When used by a number of angry birds, this method of attack is quite effective in driving off predators of all sorts, including rats, domesticated animals and man. An example of this genus is the Lesser Noddy (*A. tenuirostris*) of the South Pacific.

Skimmers (*Rynchopidae*)

Skimmers are relatives of gulls and terns and are named for their unique feeding habits. They occur in the vicinity of seas, rivers and lowland lakes throughout most of the warmer parts of the world.

In hunting for food, the skimmer progresses with part of its bill plowing the water. To overcome the resistance of both air and water in this procedure, the bird has wings that are long, pointed and relatively larger than those of gulls and a compressed and bladelike bill; it also has a relatively slower wing motion and maneuvers adroitly. The mandibles are held wide open in hunting, and only the lower one, which is longer, is submerged. Recently it has been shown that when the bill strikes a fish or shrimp, the skimmer's head is snapped downward so that it is sometimes immersed up to the eyes, the short mandible at the same time clapping shut on the prey. The bill is then raised like a dragging anchor and the meal swallowed in flight.

Three closely related species of skimmers are known, one each in America, Africa and Asia—all

[continued on page 193]

97. Roadrunner (*Geococcyx californianus*)

Range: Southwestern U.S.A. and Central Mexico

[ELIOT PORTER]

98. Violet-crested
Turaco
(*Gallirex por-
phyreolophus*)
Range: South-
eastern Africa

[H. RUHE AND T. ROTH]

99. Blue-headed
Coucal
(*Centropus
monachus*)
Range: Africa

[H. RUHE AND T. ROTH]

100. Lesser Nighthawk
(*Chordeiles acutipennis*)
Range: Southwestern U.S.A.
to northern South America

[ELIOT PORTER]

101. Tawny Frogmouth
(*Podargus strigoides*)
Range: Australia and Tasmania

[JOHN MARKHAM]

102. Rufous Hummingbird, female (*Selasphorus rufus*)
Range: North America from Alaska to Mexico [ELIOT PORTER]

103. European Kingfisher (*Alcedo atthis*)
Range: Eurasia

[ERIC J. HOSKING]

04. Copper-rumped Hummingbird
(*Amazilia tobaci*)
Range: Venezuela, Trinidad and Tobago

[PAUL SCHWARTZ]

105. Forest Kingfisher (*Halcyon macleayi*)
Range: Australia and New Guinea

[NORMAN CHAFFER]

106.
(Rufous-crowned
Roller
(*Coracias
naevia*)
Range: Africa
[H. RUHE AND T. ROTH]

107. Ground Hornbill (*Bucorvus leadbeateri*) Range: Central Africa [GATTI EXPEDITIONS]

108.
Rufous-tailed Jacamar
(*Galbula ruficauda*)
Range: Tropical America

[PAUL SCHWARTZ]

109. Common Bee-eater (*Merops apiaster*) Range: Eurasia and North Africa [WALTER E. HIGHAM]

110. Keel-billed Toucan (*Ramphastos sulfuratus*) Range: Southern Mexico to northern South America

111. Ariel Toucan
(*Ramphastos ariel*)
Range: Brazil

112. Toucan Barbet (*Semnornis ramphastinus*) Range: South American Andes [H. RUHE AND T. ROTH]

113. Blue-throated Barbet (*Mega-laima asiatica*)

Range: Southern Asia from India to Thailand

[H. RUHE AND T. ROTH]

114. Red-crowned Woodpecker
(*Centurus rubricapillus*)

Range: Costa Rica to northern
South America

[PAUL SCHWARTZ]

115. Red-headed Woodpecker
(*Melanerpes erythrocephalus*)

Range: Canada and U.S.A.
east of the Rockies

[S. A. GRIMES]

→

116. Gila Woodpecker, male
(*Centurus uropygialis*)

Range: Southwestern U.S.A.
and western Mexico

[ELIOT PORTER]

117. Red-bellied Woodpecker
(*Centurus carolinus*)
Range: Chiefly southeastern U.S.A.

[AUSTING AND KOEHLER]

118. Yellow-shafted Flicker, female
(*Colaptes auratus*)
Range: North America east of the Rockies

[JACK DERMID]

119. Barred Antshrike, female
(*Thamnophilus doliatus*)
Range: Tropical America

[PAUL SCHWARTZ]

120. Buff-fronted Foliage-Gleaner
(*Philydor rufus*)
Range: Highlands of Costa Rica
to South America

[PAUL SCHWARTZ]

121. Cock-of-the-Rock (*Rupicola peruviana*)
Range: South America [H. RUHE AND T. ROTH]

123. Ash-throated Flycatc

122. Rufous Fantail
(*Rhipidura rufifrons*)
and Brush Cuckoo, young
(*Cacomantis pyrrho-
phanus*)
Range: Australia

[NORMAN CHAFFER]

rchus cinerascens) Range: Southwestern U.S.A. and northwestern Mexico [ELIOT PORTER]

124. Eastern Phoebe (*Sayornis phoebe*) Range: Chiefly eastern North America [ALLAN CRUICKSHANK: NATIONAL AUDUBON]

125. Common Tody Flycatcher
(*Todirostrum cinereum*)
Range: Tropical America

[PAUL SCHWARTZ]

126. Fire-crowned Tyrant
(*Machetornis rixosa*)
Range: South America

[PAUL SCHWARTZ]

[continued from page 176]

immediately distinguishable by the knifelike bill. The American Black Skimmer (*Rynchops nigra;* Plate 75), breeding from New Jersey to Argentina and about 19 inches long, is brownish black above with a white forehead and wing band, white lower parts, red legs and feet and a black tail. The bill is black with the basal half reddish orange. The sexes are similar. After describing this bird's feeding, Charles Darwin wrote: "When leaving the surface of the water their flight was wild, irregular, and rapid; they then also uttered loud, harsh cries," and he noted that they continued "for a long time to skim the surface up and down the narrow canal, now dark with the growing night and the shadows of overhanging trees." He suspected that they fished generally by night because at that time "many of the lower animals come most abundantly to the surface."

Skimmers have a unique slitlike pupil which, it is believed, is correlated with their nocturnal and twilight fishing habits, partially closing to protect the retina by day when the bird is on glaring white sand and opening by night. Other nocturnal sea birds, such as the petrels, remain at sea by day or sit in dark ground burrows. Nocturnal land birds, such as owls, keep to shaded areas by day. The skimmer alone seems to have developed an eye capable of adapting to the widest extremes of light.

Of the lures used by animals to capture prey, none is more remarkable than that of the skimmer plowing through water at night and leaving behind a line or trail. This bright line, the result of micro-organisms that have been stirred into glowing, attracts minute forms of aquatic animal life, and these in turn attract fishes. The skimmer then retraces its path and scoops up its prey.

The African Skimmer (*R. flavirostris*), which is about 16 inches in length, occurs on rivers and lakes and along coasts. It is generally dark brown above and white below with a bright red bill and legs. Like all skimmers the Indian Skimmer (*R. albicollis*) has the tail slightly forked and the feet webbed, but unlike others, is never seen away from inland waters.

Skimmers breed in large colonies. In courtship the male often holds a stick in its bill, and when the female jerks it away, mating usually follows. On their nesting grounds these birds are very noisy and when approached by man call loudly, emit barking notes and fly at the intruder. The set consists of from three to five slightly glossy oval eggs, generally stone-colored or with a greenish or salmon tint, and boldly blotched. They are placed in deep scrapes that the birds make by rotating with the chest pressed to the sand. Incubation is performed by the female alone but the male assists in the feeding of the young, the food being carried whole and not regurgitated. The young are sand-colored when they hatch and depend so completely on this for protection that they remain immobile until stepped on and, when picked up, will lie with the head hanging limp as though dead. The adults vigorously protect the nest by feigning injury.

JOHN WARHAM

Lesser Noddy (*Anous tenuirostris*)

Auks, Murres, Guillemots, Dovekies and Puffins

(*Alcidae*)

There are 22 species of alcids, most of them inhabitants of the colder regions of the Northern Hemisphere. Many seem to us charmingly ungainly and comical. Some perform highly organized dances. Several are important sources of food.

All are closely related to the gulls and terns, and many look like tiny penguins; indeed, the largest surviving alcid is just about the size of the smallest penguin. Whereas the penguins are flightless, however, living alcids fly like projectiles on their small wings. Any similarities to penguins living or extinct are due purely to a similar pattern of evolutionary changes, because the penguins belong to a very different group of birds. Nevertheless, both are chiefly black-and-white sea birds with legs set far back on the body; both have the tail very short; both use the greatly reduced wings for swimming; and both have webbed feet, are highly gregarious, and have accessory ornaments on bill and head. These and many more similarities make it clear that the alcids are in the Northern Hemisphere the ecological counterparts of the penguins.

Alcids feed chiefly on small fish, crustaceans and the minute marine organisms called plankton.

[193

The bulk of the species breed on oceanic cliffs or on the tops of oceanic islands. Most are highly migratory sea birds and go ashore only to breed. In spring in the North Atlantic the regimen of the auks, murres, guillemots, dovekies and puffins involves a return to the cliffs where they were born, often even to the same ledge, to breed again. They return en masse from wintering areas as far south as the Mediterranean and, on the American coast, Long Island Sound.

Colonies are organized in strata, with each species keeping more or less together in rows. Only the puffins, which occupy the uppermost tier, the top of the island, construct nests. There they excavate burrows, both the male and the female sharing in the digging, and lay two eggs that are generally oval and faintly spotted.

In contrast, the ledge-nesting alcids lay a single, relatively large, pear-shaped egg on bare rock. The conical shape of these eggs explains why they roll in circles and thus not off the ledge. The eggs of these ledge-nesting alcids are famous for their variability, those of the murre being probably the most variable of all bird eggs. The base color ranges from pink to green to brown to gray, and the markings vary from spots to scrawls, smudges and streaks, all in a wide range of colors. The variable color is thought to serve for identification rather than camouflage. The immense concentrations in which these sea birds breed apparently requires special mechanisms to make it possible for parents to recognize their eggs.

The eggs are incubated from about 3½ to 6 weeks, depending on the species. In puffins only the female incubates, and this she does chiefly by night for a period of 40 to 43 days. At the end of this long period both sexes share in the feeding of the young for another 40 days. The parents then desert them, and a week to ten days later the young waddle to the edge of the ledge and leap into the sea.

The alcids lack the hind toe and have the three front toes webbed. In water they swim and dive with ease, though not so proficiently as the penguins.

Razor-billed Auk (*Alca torda*)

ERIC J. HOSKING

The Great Auk (*Pinguinus impennis*) of the North Atlantic, now extinct, stood some 30 inches in height and was the only flightless sea bird in the Northern Hemisphere. Formerly it bred on four islands in the North Atlantic—three near Iceland, one near Newfoundland. In 1830 the largest and most inaccessible of the islands near Iceland suddenly disappeared into the sea. Within about a decade the other two island colonies near Iceland were wiped out by hunters and feather collectors. As a result, no Great Auks have been seen in Europe since 1844.

The fourth island colony, on Funk Island near Newfoundland, then became the target of the feather collectors. They spent the summers on this, the last nesting site of the great bird, destroying countless thousands of the "Atlantic penguin" and finally exterminating the colony. Today we have only a few skins, eggs and bones to show that this creature ever lived. Some of the bones were collected by the author on Funk Island in 1936, where in a few hours he and his associate, Samuel K. George, collected the remains of more than 400 Great Auks from an area smaller than a tennis court.

Great Auks laid conical spotted eggs more than five inches in length. Icelanders reported that these birds swam with the head elevated. The Great Auks dove when frightened, whereas surviving alcids half fly and half splash across the surface of the water when threatened.

The Razor-billed Auk (*Alca torda*) resembles the Great Auk in miniature. It is a well-tailored black-and-white bird about 17 inches long and is distinguishable from the very similar murres, with which it habitually associates, by its compressed, white-ringed bill. The Razor-bill dives to considerable depths to feed on small fish and crustaceans at the bottom of the ocean.

Similar in size but with the head smaller and the bill more slender and pointed are the two species of murres that live in the North Atlantic: the Thick-billed Murre (*Uria lomvia*) and the Common Murre (*U. aalge*). Some 5 to 15 per cent of the Common Murres breeding in the New World are bridled or ringed—that is to say, they have a vivid white ring around the eye and a white line extending backward along the side of the head, whereas the others have the head solid black. This striking marking is found throughout nearly the entire range of this murre, but the percentage of bridled birds, or mutants, varies from virtually nothing on the shores of Portugal to about 70 per cent off the shores of Iceland. A recent report based on studies by hundreds of European naturalists unexpectedly showed that the percentage of bridled birds is decreasing almost everywhere.

The murres engage in rather amazing ritualized dances. At the start they rush in like projectiles in their usual style and land on the water in groups, their legs spread wide, their feet out at the sides with the webs open as though steering. Once down on the water, the social dance begins. Without more ado the birds form pairs and swim in circles or form lines. At an unseen signal they dive almost simultaneously, and the dance goes on underwater with groups chasing each other. They continue in the air, groups flying in flocks, taking off and landing together.

Messrs. Peters and Burleigh, in their *Birds of Newfoundland,* report that large numbers of murres are killed for food in the Newfoundland area.

Another alcid that long has been an important source of food is the Dovekie (*Plautus alle*) of the arctic and the North Atlantic. A tiny sea bird only some 8 to 9 inches long, it is blackish above and white below and has a small head and short bill. Dovekies nest in crevices, laying one pale green egg with faint markings of darker color. These birds fly deep into the arctic to breed, and winter along the Canadian coasts. Sometimes they swarm out over the Arctic Circle, flying down over the continents of Europe and North America as far as the Mediterranean and Cuba. These unexplained explosions are like the compulsive migrations of lemmings, and the Dovekies are just as certainly doomed to death. Microscopic aquatic animal and vegetable life comprises their major source of food for, and perhaps changes in plankton cycles have something to do with these mass suicide flights. Eskimos have long slaughtered Dovekies in countless numbers, the birds forming an important source of food.

Among other alcids are the Guillemots, of which there are three species in the Atlantic and the Pacific. Typical of these is the Black Guillemot or Sea Pigeon (*Cepphus grylle*) of the North Atlantic. Sea Pigeons are the size of small ducks and are perhaps the least gregarious and most somberly dressed of the alcids. They are chiefly black, with white wing patches and coral-red feet. Their eggs are heavily spotted and more oval, less pear-shaped, than the eggs of the murres and the auks. Further, they are relatively smaller, and two eggs, not one, are the usual set.

Three species of murrelets occur in the North Pacific—all small, chunky alcids. One, the Marbled Murrelet (*Brachyramphus marmoratus*), is a 9-inch bird that ranges to Japan. Its nest has never been found, although females with fully formed eggs in the oviduct have been taken along the coast of British Columbia and Southern Alaska.

Among the odder-looking birds comprising this family is the Ancient Murrelet (*Synthliboramphus antiquus*). This is a 10-inch, small-billed bird with much black on the head and throat and broad white eye-stripes. Another, the Least Auklet (*Aethia pusilla*), is the size of the Dovekie but has prominent white ornamental feathers growing from the sides of the head. The Crested Auklet (*A. cristatella*) is 10 inches long and has a coral-red bill and a saucy crest of thin recurved plumes. The Paroquet Auklet (*Cyclorrhynchus psittacula*) is also 10 inches in length but is distinguished by a prominent, upcurved, yellowish, parrot-like bill.

Perhaps best known of all alcids is the Atlantic Puffin (*Fratercula arctica;* Plate 76), found in the North Atlantic. Standing some 10 inches tall, this bird has a short neck and a large, compressed, highly sculptured bill that is, like the feet and legs, largely red. Awkward and even comical in appearance, the puffin sheds the outer surfaces of the bill after breeding. There are huge colonies of puffins, one such colony in Newfoundland being estimated to contain 50,000 breeding birds in 1944. The puffin is not only one of the best loved of sea birds; it is also one of the best documented, being covered, for example, by such books as the one written by British ornithologist R. M. Lockley after twenty years of research. A Pacific Coast relative is the Tufted Puffin (*Lunda cirrhata;* Plate 74).

COLUMBIFORMES

Sand-grouse (*Pteroclidae*)

Sand-grouse could be called pigeon-grouse because they resemble grouse in their general shape and coloration and in their choice of habitat, but they are an offshoot of the stock that produced the pigeons. The sixteen known species range in size from street pigeons to Ruffed Grouse. All are highly gregarious. These purely terrestrial birds of central and southern Eurasia and Africa are called sand-grouse because they are found only in arid, open areas predominantly covered with sand and short grass.

In order to survive in such exposed habitats these birds have developed traits and plumage patterns that protect them remarkably well. For one thing, they keep together in flocks, often numbering in the hundreds; they are at all times hard to approach. They fly relatively little, the groups remaining on the ground all day feeding on seeds and vegetable shoots unless scared into taking flight. When well filled with food, they make shallow depressions in which to lie down and dust themselves, apparently oblivious of broiling heat.

With great regularity they take wing at dusk; then and in the early morning they fly to and from special watering holes. On their pointed wings they move with great rapidity, often traveling long distances to drink. Upon approaching the water hole, the flock joins with other flocks, and as a protective measure the various squadrons pitch to the ground several hundred yards from the water hole. After some ten minutes the group flies up and descends near the water and walks quickly en masse into the water up to the breast feathers. Sand-grouse and pigeons are the only birds that drink with the bill held continuously in water. Other birds lift the head and let the water run down the gullet.

Colonel Meinertzhagen in his recent *Birds of Arabia* has exploded the oft-repeated tale that sand-grouse soak up water in the abdominal feathers and carry it thus to the young. He bred sand-grouse in captivity and noted that the parents carried water in their crops and then regurgitated it into the mouths of their chicks. He observed that his birds often arrived at the nest with their abdominal feathers soaked, but that the chicks did not take water from that source.

These birds of deserts and steppe lands occasionally seem to go mad, periodically sweeping far out of their regular ranges on what amount to mass-suicide excursions. Although some remnants have occasionally stayed to breed in such places as Denmark, all such invaders perish within a few years.

Sand-grouse nest in sand, making a slight depression and lining it with a few strands of grass. Two to three eggs are laid. These are fairly glossy and elongate in shape, with the ends being equal in size, and are spotted and smudged with rich browns and purples. In Pallas' Sand-grouse the incubation period is 28 days; in others it is only 22 to 23 days. The young at hatching are covered with down and in a few days run about like precocial game birds.

In sand-grouse the sexes differ from each other in color, with the female wearing the most cryptic hues. Both sexes play important roles in rearing the young, both indulging in distraction displays and both incubating the eggs and feeding the young. However, the female alone incubates by day. When she is so occupied, the male brings water to her and feeds her by regurgitation.

As in the ostrich, which also breeds in open sandy areas, only the male sand-grouse incubates by night. No one knows the reason for this arrangement, which is the exact opposite of that of most pigeons. The difference in dress between the sexes—they seem to be dressed for maximum terrestrial security to begin with—suggests that that of the night-incubating male is a refinement for nocturnal concealment and

that of the female a refinement for diurnal concealment. Whatever the reason, it is known that many species are crepuscular, if not nocturnal, at least in their drinking habits.

Many species breed in semicolonial groups. In Arabia and in many other areas where the nests are placed in sandy areas and become incredibly hot, the adults are covered with thick, close plumage underlaid with heat-repellent down.

Sand-grouse have the legs short and strong and the tarsi (and sometimes the toes) feathered. The toes are short, and in some species the hind toe is lacking; in others there is a trace of webbing between the frontal toes. Unlike the pigeons, which have very tender skins and delicate plumage that is easily shed, the skin of the sand-grouse is tough and the feathers shield it so well that hunters consider the bird one of the most difficult to kill. Sand-grouse are pugnacious among themselves. They are monogamous.

The Tibetan Pin-tailed Sand-grouse (*Syrrhaptes tibetanus*), a 16-inch bird with long, sharp tail feathers, breeds between 12,000 and 14,000 feet in the mountains of Central Asia and migrates to the warmer, lower parts of southern Asia in winter. In this genus the hind toe is lacking and the other toes are covered with feathers. It is much like Pallas' Sand-grouse (*S. paradoxus*) of southern Russia and Asia, which has needle-pointed tail feathers and a black patch on the breast. Pallas' Sand-grouse breeds at much lower elevations and in winter reaches south as far as China. It is 14 to 16 inches long, generally buffy above with blackish marks, and blackish below with a grayish white chest. On several occasions vast numbers have poured out of Asia into Europe, flying as far as the Faroe Islands in the North Atlantic. The last great irruption was in 1908.

In southern Europe, Asia and Africa there are 14 species of sand-grouse, all of which are grouped in the genus *Pterocles*. All have the feet naked, and a hind toe is present. One, the Common Sand-grouse (*P. exustus*), is, as its name implies, the most common sand-grouse and is a familiar game bird in India, Arabia, Palestine and northern Africa. It is a foot long and the male is sandy colored with pointed central tail plumes.

Another in this genus, the Pin-tailed Sand-grouse (*P. alchata*), is similar in size. It resembles a sharp-tailed partridge but has a whitish belly and, in the male, a chestnut breast band. This species ranges through Asia to India, westward through Africa and Central Europe to France, Spain and Portugal. In the last three areas it breeds regularly.

One of the most aberrant species is the Masked Sand-grouse (*P. personatus*) of Madagascar, which has the gape surrounded by a broad black bib. This species frequents brushy savannas and plains. About 11 inches long, it is brown above and rufous buffy below with fine barring. In Madagascar Dr. Austin Rand observed early in the morning flocks of three to four hundred birds gathering to drink along the

Black-bellied Sand-grouse (*Pterocles orientalis*)

sandy margins of rivers. He also noted that these sand-grouse, when flushed, burst forth in calls that sounded like *catch-catcha-catcha*.

Pigeons and Doves
(*Columbidae*)

There is no scientific distinction between doves and pigeons, an assemblage of birds ranging throughout the nonpolar land areas of the world. Some of the species are hardly larger than a sparrow and others reach the size of a gamecock. Among the 289 species are birds that live well in close association with man and have been domesticated by him at least since Egyptian times; others could not tolerate man and have disappeared, although they once numbered in the billions.

More than half of the world's species of pigeons are found in the Indo-Malayan and Australian regions. A secondary concentration of species is found in the warmer portions of the Americas.

Despite hues that are protectively cryptic, many of the Old World tropical species are very colorful. One such group is largely leaf-green shot with yellow, and others are green washed with gaudy "ice-cream" hues that are clearly epigamic, that is, aimed to attract the other sex. Some species wear light ornamental plumage on the head or have the tail long and pointed, but, generally speaking, pigeons the world over are much alike. For one thing, all are monogamous and proverbially attentive to their mates. For another, the nest is usually a very frail structure and the set is always very small, in most species being two eggs. The eggs are usually clear glossy white, but a few species lay brown or buffy eggs. Generally both sexes assist in constructing the nest and in incubation, with the female usually doing the nocturnal incubating and brooding, and the male taking over by day. Incubation varies from 14 to 19 days, and the young, hatched with eyes sealed, remain in the nest for 12 to 18 days. For the first week or so the young are brooded by both parents and fed a regurgitated substance called "pigeon's milk." To inject this "milk" the adult inserts the bill inside the relatively large bill of the nestling. The "milk" is a secretion of the crop lining and appears during breeding, when the crop becomes glandular as a result of hormonal secretions. Later the young are fed solid foods, such as fruits and berries.

The pigeons and their near relatives, the Sandgrouse, are unique in their method of drinking. Instead of lifting the head and letting droplets run down the throat, pigeons suck water up, as does a horse, in one long draught. They devour seeds, fruit, berries and a few insects. Their strong, pointed wings are capable of powerful straight-line flight, some species flying many miles to obtain food for nestlings. All pigeons and doves have the body relatively stout and the pectoral muscles well developed. The body is compactly cloaked with feathers, but the plumes are so weakly attached that often the mere act of turning over a dead bird causes some of them to come loose. This is believed by some to be a mechanism of defense against the attacks of hawks and perhaps owls, since such loose plumage would tend to deflect the claws of a pursuer and send up an "explosion" of feathers.

Across the basal half of the bill pigeons have a soft saddle of light-colored skin in which slitlike nostrils are located. All have four toes, set at the same level, and most utter the familiar deep-throated and, in some, maddeningly regular cooing calls.

The earliest records of the domestication of the Domestic or Street Pigeon (*Columba livia*)—a derivative of the Common Rock Pigeon or Rock Dove of Eurasia—go back to 3000 B.C. Initially man raised this bird in captivity for its delicious flesh and later for its homing and message-carrying abilities. This long association has yielded nearly 200 named strains or varieties, ranging from small, colorful show pigeons to ponderous meat-producing birds. The fact that all these have derived through selective breeding from the Rock Pigeon, and all during the course of about 5000 years, has fascinated many zoologists. One of the first of these was Darwin, who ascertained by anatomical examination and breeding not only that all domesticated pigeons derived from this single progenitor, but that when specialized types were mixed, their descendants within a few generations again resembled the wild ancestor.

The largest subfamily, the Treroninae or fruit pigeons, is confined to the tropics of the Old World and chiefly to the Indo-Malayan region and ranges from starling-sized birds to species that weigh as much as a small chicken. All of them feed exclusively on fruit and berries and most of them are very colorful. Representative is the Wedge-tailed Green Pigeon (*Sphenurus sphenurus*) of southern Asia and Indonesia, which is the size of a Street Pigeon. It is yellowish green with much maroon on the upperparts, pinkish gray on the lower parts, a naked blue eye ring and crimson legs. Like all fruit pigeons, it travels in flocks in quest of fruiting trees, shifting to lowland areas in winter and to highland areas in summer. Despite its bright color it is hard to see as it scurries about the thin crown limbs, or hangs upside down in its endless quest for berries.

The largest group of fruit pigeons is of the genus *Ptilinopus,* and one of its widest-ranging members is the Superb Fruit Pigeon (*P. superbus*), found from Tasmania to New Guinea and the islands of Indonesia. This green bird is boldly painted with disturbing pinks and raspberry purples on the crown and sides of the neck. Like that of all fruit pigeons, its nest is so slight that the female must hold the egg on the platform of sticks with her breast whenever the wind blows even moderately. Other species such as the Magnificent Fruit Pigeon (*Megaloprepia magnifica*) of Australia, New Guinea and the Moluccas, have the underparts a purplish wine color and the upperparts gray and green, with wing bars bright yellow.

Fruit pigeons are less gregarious than other pigeons and often go about in pairs or small flocks. Despite their bright coloration, they hide so efficiently that the collector is often amazed by the number that fly out of a fruit tree at the report of his rifle. The larger members of this subfamily are somewhat more somberly dressed and the sexes are much alike in color, but one species is a metallic shade and another is nearly pure white. The white species, the foot-long Torres Strait Pigeon (*Ducula spilorrhoa*), is famous for its over-water migrations along the coasts of northern Australia. This bird has black on the wings, tail and the flanks. It habitually nests on off-shore islands and carries food, usually fruit, berries and nutmegs from the mainland to feed to the females on the nest. A nest that the author found was 30 feet up in a large river-edge tree.

The metallic species, the Green Imperial Pigeon (*Ducula aenea*), is a very beautiful bird nearly 16 inches long. Above it has glistening iridescent greens, blues and bronzes and below it is a delicate lavender gray with bright chestnut under-tail coverts and crimson feet. Like many of the large *Duculas,* or Nutmeg Pigeons, it frequents the crown of tropical jungles and mangrove forests. It feeds on fruits that seem incredibly large for it but that a special arrangement in the throat permits it to swallow.

Turning now to the subfamily Columbinae, we find an assortment of fruit- and seed-eating birds, many of which feed on the ground. They are highly gregarious, particularly the many species of the genus *Columba,* which ranges throughout the tropics and the temperate zones of the world. One is the typical Street Pigeon, relatives of which are found above 5000 feet in the mountains of Asia. Another is the Snow Pigeon (*Columba leuconota*), which is like the Street Pigeon but differs in having generally white underparts and a black tail crossed by a white bar. This species breeds in colonies in crevices on Mount Everest at altitudes as high as 15,000 feet. Quite different is the Brown Pigeon (*Macropygia phasianella*), which has a long, graduated tail like that of a giant cuckoo, and goes about in the forest edge, often feeding on the ground. Other species are birds of pure forest.

Ring Doves are found all over Eurasia, Africa, the Indo-Malayan region and Australia. They are the "turtle doves" of the Old World and are generally about the size of a Street Pigeon or smaller. Their predominant colors are various shades of gray and buff with a distinctive blackish or checkered half-collar on the hind neck.

The Gray-vented Ring Dove (*Streptopelia semitorquata*), thoroughly covered by Dr. Van Someren in his *Days with Birds,* is representative of the group as a whole. The usual clutch of two eggs is placed in nests 6 to 50 feet up and is incubated for 17 days by the female. She leaves the nest only twice a day and is fed on the nest by the male. Night calling is frequent, and regular cooing begins before dawn. Males defend a courtship territory by attacking intruders with the wings held aloft and sometimes by landing on a rival and clubbing his head with bent wings. The courtship dance consists of ascending flights, wing-thrashing and aerial glides with the tail expanded laterally. This is followed by the thrashing of wings and much deep cooing and bill-rubbing. The female carefully gathers the nest twigs on the ground, the male usually sitting nearby and holding his head in a lowered position with the neck somewhat expanded as though regurgitating food. As in all young pigeons, the young have the head and upperparts cloaked in dusky feathering from which protrude thistle-like strands of whitish down. The feeding of the young takes place rather infrequently. When the young are squab-sized, they become aggressive and sometimes push the parent off the nest in their attempt to get food. They leave the nest about 20 days after hatching but continue to receive care and protection for a few days thereafter.

Somewhat similar in appearance is the Mourning Dove (*Zenaidura macroura*) of North America and Mexico. It is 12 inches long and is grayish brown with a brownish neck glossed on the sides with violet and pink. With its long, pointed tail it resembles the extinct Passenger Pigeon (*Ectopistes migratorius*). The most widespread species of the family in North America today, it breeds close to human habitations, and its sad cooing notes are familiar sounds in open semiwooded country, where it feeds in pairs or small parties on the ground. Another species is the Inca Dove (*Scardafella inca*), one of many small ground doves of the New World tropics (see also Plate 78), all of which have chestnut on the under wing. This species has gray feathers so heavily scalloped they resemble scales. A dove found in the Americas from Texas to Argentina is the White-fronted Dove (*Leptotila verreauxi;* Plate 79). In the Old World many ground-loving doves are highly colored, one such being the quail-sized Emerald Dove (*Chalcophaps indica*), which has upperparts with iridescent green and bronze and much bold white marking on the front of the head. It is typical of several highly ornamented species that live mostly on the forest floor in the Indo-Malayan and Australian regions. Many are particularly fond of bamboo forests, sometimes going to altitudes of 5000 feet or more to feed on fallen fruit, seeds and occasionally termites. Unlike most pigeons and doves, it lays eggs that are a pale coffee color, not pure white. Despite its bright plumage, the Emerald Dove sits tight on the forest floor when approached, and when it does try to escape, flushes from underfoot somewhat like a quail.

Another bird of the forest floor is the Bleeding-heart Pigeon (*Gallicolumba luzonica*), of the Philippines, which has the underparts white and a great splash of red on the lower neck and upper chest resembling a gunshot wound. The most highly adorned species is the bizarre Nicobar Pigeon (*Caloenas nicobarica*), which reaches 16 inches and has long, iridescent, dark green feathers ringing the neck and forming a giant mane. In addition, it has a black knob near the base of the bill and a white tail. Its home is on small islands of the East Indies and east to the Solomons, and its behavior is very much like that of Emerald Doves.

The largest surviving pigeon is the Goura, or Crowned Pigeon, of New Guinea. It is characterized by an erect lateral crest that has the texture of fine lace and is so large and beautiful that when paradise plums were collected in New Guinea—the home of the three species of crowned pigeons—the lacy crowns were hunted as much as the birds of paradise. The writer observed two of the three species in the field, namely the Scheepmaker's Crowned Pigeon (*Goura scheepmakeri*) and the Queen Victoria Crowned Pigeon (*G. victoria;* Plate 77). Both are large blue-gray birds with much deep maroon below. They are still fairly common in the semivirgin riverine forests and sago swamps of North and South New Guinea, where they go about in parties, feeding on the ground like large chickens. When one of a group is shot, the remainder fly up to low limbs and sit there complaining as the hunter picks them off like targets in a shooting gallery. Therefore these splendid birds, though officially protected, are, in areas occupied by man, probably doomed to the fate of the Dodo (a relative of the pigeons) and the Passenger Pigeon of North America.

One may ask why man does not spare species of such surpassing beauty and interest as the Crowned Pigeon. By way of answer, we offer these facts taken from an account by a hunter who visited many of the nesting areas of the now extinct Passenger Pigeon. The largest he saw, in 1876 or 1877, was in Wisconsin and was 28 miles long with an average width of 3 to 4 miles. One flight of birds arriving at the site consisted of a black mass some five miles long and about one mile wide. The pigeons built their nests so rapidly that the nesting area spread like a carpet and passed over his netting station, although initially the station had been several miles from the edge of the rookery. In the end every tree in the 28-mile strip had nests in it. All were 15 or more feet up, and some of the trees were so heavily weighted down by them that limbs were broken away. Usually two eggs were laid, but many nests contained only one. Sought for food, even pig food, the Passenger Pigeons fell in multitudes in the gas and smoke of sulphur torches and were then clubbed to death. It was thus that great nesting areas were attacked by man—attacked so relentlessly that although the ornithologist Alexander Wilson recorded two billion birds passing overhead in 1808 near Frankfort, Kentucky, the last Passenger Pigeon, a captive bird, joined the Dodo in 1914.

PSITTACIFORMES

Parrots and Their Relatives
(*Psittacidae*)

The parrots, macaws, parakeets and lories constitute one of the best-known bird families. Since ancient times many species have been cherished as pets, and innumerable are the stories of their "intellectual" attainments and vocal mimicry. Parrots are the best "talkers" in the animal kingdom, so that taking a parrot into a household can be like taking in an extremely articulate and noisy relative. Unlike mammalian pets, parrots often live more than half a century, and some have lived for eighty years. Thus not infrequently young parrots adopted by older people have survived to live with the grandchildren.

Because of widespread fear of the avian disease psittacosis (often called "parrot fever"), the habit of keeping parrots was frowned upon until it was found recently that this uncommon disease was by no means restricted to parrots but apparently could afflict all birds. Thus the disease is now becoming known as ornithosis ("bird disease"). Furthermore, an antibiotic developed by Dr. Karl F. Meyer at the University of California is said to cure the ailment in birds in two weeks' time.

But even before this development, popular sentiment forced the lifting of bars against importation in many parts of the world. As a result, the keeping of parrots (Plates 84 and 85) and their smaller relatives, particularly the lovebirds (Plate 83) and "Budgies," or Budgerigars, has once again reached vast proportions. Tens of thousands of parakeets are now offered for sale throughout America, Europe, Asia and Australia, and a thriving business has sprung up involving cages, special foods and the breeding of the birds. The number of species that have been bred in captivity is remarkable.

The members of this pantropical family seem to be endowed with certain characteristics of movement and memory that make them the most "human" of birds. They all use the foot as a hand while eating, and like humans they are right- or left-handed. They also use the bill as a third leg in climbing—and they are the best of avian climbers—but unfortunately this unique habit brings about the electrocution of great numbers of parrots and parakeets when they "bridge" or short-circuit power lines by reaching from one line to another with the bill.

Parrots seem to possess a remarkable ability to learn rapidly. H. Braun recently demonstrated their ability to deal with numbers up to seven and to remember complicated sets of incidents in correct sequence. These capabilities make the parrot seem the intellectual superior of other birds and help explain its mastery over complicated cage locks—a mastery that has mystified many a parrot owner. The most famous "talking" bird is the African Gray Parrot (*Psittacus erithacus*).

Another attribute of parrots is what we anthropomorphically consider their affection for each other and for humans. They revel in being petted, and some display emotion as readily as lap dogs. So great is their affection that certain species seem at times to lapse into a state of ecstasy when stroked on the neck to the accompaniment of melodious words. But, like dogs, horses and people, parrots can often be mischievous and even treacherous. By and large, however, they are among man's warmest friends in the animal world. The association of parrots and men is indeed very old. Primitive Africans, Asians, Australians, New Guineans and tropical American Indians for ages have kept them as pets. Ctesias (ca. 400 B.C.) noted the powers of mimicry displayed by African parrots traded to Greece, and it is known that parrots were common cage birds in Roman times.

Some 316 species comprise this family, which has spread to all of the warmer regions of the world. Various characteristics make them all immediately distinguishable from other birds, even by the amateur. All have the skull large and hawklike, the nostrils set in a fleshy cere at the base of the bill, and short strong legs. The bill is powerful and equipped with a transverse hinge at the base of the skull, enabling the upper mandible to move. This modification makes possible a leverage greater than that of any other bird. Parrots can clip and crush extremely hard objects, and certain species such as the cockatoos and macaws can remove a man's finger as easily as a sparrow cracks a grass seed. The foot is of the zygodactyl type, with the first and fourth toes turned permanently backward. Another very distinct character is the tongue, which is thick, fleshy and prehensile. All parrots, with one exception, have ten tail feathers and all have feathers with aftershafts. They usually have powder downs scattered through the plumage.

Most species nest in holes in trees, although a few build huge nests of sticks and some nest in burrows and in termite nests. Almost all lay white eggs, and in all parrots the young are hatched blind and helpless, mostly naked but some covered with down.

Parrots are generally divided into two major groups: those with blunt tongues and those with damp brush-fringed tongues. The former feed chiefly on nuts and buds, the latter on fruit juices and nectar.

Parrots were once more widely distributed than they are today. Fossil parrots have been found even in the arctic. A number of species inhabited Europe and the colder regions of America; in Europe they became extinct long ago but those of the United States disappeared so recently that some older persons can remember them, and parrots are still very abundant in the Australian region.

Although ranging in type from the mighty macaw to the tiny parakeet, New World parrots have not developed as many odd shapes and sizes as those of the Old World; nor have they learned to live in such diverse habitats as have numerous Australian and New Zealand species. Some of these, on immigrating from Asia, found life safe and easy on the ground, and over the ages became large, unwary and awkward. Others found that the vertical surfaces of trees, which elsewhere are scoured by woodpeckers, offered a rich, unexploited source of food. These "open" niches were like vacuums, and, as we shall see, parrots, among other animals, sought to fill them.

Parrots often travel in pairs, and their pair bonds or "marriages" may be maintained for years or even for life. The pairs are noisy and affectionate, and the male frequently assists the female in incubating the eggs, a task that takes approximately three weeks. Like pigeons, many species of parrots feed the young on partially digested food drawn from the crop. When not breeding, nearly all species congregate in large, noisy flocks. Many post sentinels and, when the shadow of a hawk is seen, all dive into the forest for safety.

There are many variations of color and structure in parrots. The dominant color is green, although in the relatively predator-free Australian regions many are white, red or yellow. The sexes are usually very similar in color and pattern; however, in a few species they are very different, and in one they are so unlike that we long thought them separate species.

The smallest are the size of warblers and the largest are actually longer than the greatest eagle, thanks to their elongated tail feathers. Some are sluggish fliers, but most fly straight and very fast, in keeping with their relatively heavy bodies. Many sleep in holes, but some sleep on limbs, hanging upside down like bats. Some live in high mountain forests and in stunted rhododendron groves near the snow line, but the vast majority are tropical.

In Australia, where parrots and parakeets are more numerous than anywhere else in the world, their destructiveness is a serious problem. Often huge bands of brush-tongued lories and lorikeets do great damage to fruit trees, as the following account suggests: An Australian farmer, Alex Griffith, somewhat more esthetically inclined than most, fed honey mash to a few Rainbow Lorikeets. Soon thousands of the vividly colored, pigeon-sized birds discovered his generosity. Although normally wild and wary denizens of eucalyptus forests, great flocks began calling each morning and evening, climbing with reckless abandon on the hundreds and sometimes thousands of tourists who converged on Griffith's "sanctuary" to witness the daily distribution of the ten gallons of honey mash.

The cockatoos, perhaps the most numerous large parrots in zoos, differ from other parrots in having the crest erectile and usually greatly elongated. The greatest concentration of cockatoos is in the Australian region, where most species are largely white, with a short, blunt tail and a bill that is sometimes nearly as large as that of the macaw. In many the crest is colorful and some have the breast rose pink.

The largest species, the Black Cockatoo (*Calyptorhynchus magnificus;* Plate 88), is quite aberrant. The reddish hue of its naked cheeks varies with the emotional condition of the bird; in other words, it may be said to blush. This blue-black, giant-billed bird of the New Guinea region, unlike the usually gregarious white cockatoos, likes to sit alone in the lower stage of the forest, working on hard nuts for long periods and breaking open seeds that a man would have to crack with a hammer. When the nut is fractured, the stiletto tip of the huge bill is inserted and then the tiny, delicate, prehensile, wormlike tongue (from which the bird derives its Latin name) extracts the meat.

Typical of the white cockatoos is the Sulphur-crested Cockatoo (*Cacatua galerita;* Plate 90) of the Australian region, which is pure white and has a large, erectile yellow crest. This bird abounds in flocks and pairs between sea level and about 5000 feet. Its fluttering white wings may be seen over the forest throughout the day, and its shrill screams rend the air. Like most of the cockatoos, this bird is frequently taken from the nest and is a favorite semiwild pet found in many native villages. The nest is a tree hole high in the forest. The white eggs are laid on the bare wood chips. The young are hatched naked, blind and helpless, and are fed by regurgitation for periods of up to three months.

Scattered through the Australian islands are populations that have been isolated from each other for ages by salt-water barriers. Often these populations appear very similar except for the crest, which on each island is of a different color. In other areas it is the body plumage that varies in color. Such are the White-crested Cockatoo (*C. alba*) of the Moluccas, the Rose-crested Cockatoo (*C. moluccensis*) of Ceram, the Galah (*C. roseicapilla;* Plate 86), the Blood-stained Cockatoo (*C. sanguinea*) and the Pink Cockatoo (*C. leadbeateri;* Plate 87) of Australia.

Among the most beautiful and affectionate of parrots are the lories and lorikeets. All of them are brush-tongued birds that feed on nectar and on insects drawn to sweet flowers. It has recently been pointed out that lories take nectar in a way differing from that of all other nectar-feeding birds; they crush the flower and then lick up the honey with the prehensile, fringed tongue, whereas the other nectar-eaters suck by means of a tubelike tongue.

Many species abound in the Australian region. Sometimes they occur in bands of thousands, as, for example, does the Rainbow Lorikeet (*Trichoglossus haematodus*). This species is probably the most typical and widespread of the lorikeets, occurring throughout the islands of the Australian region and over much of the Malayan region.

An example of the larger lories is the Papuan Lory (*Charmosyna papou*) of New Guinea, which is crimson with a black cap and pants. It has green wings, back and tail with glossy blue on the nape

and rump. For years attempts have been made to keep these birds in captivity but with little success. It is believed that their natural diet cannot be adequately replaced even with honey. Another beautiful parrot of New Guinea is the Cuckoo-tailed Parrot (*Alisterus chloropterus;* Plate 89).

The most aberrant and interesting parrot is the Owl Parrot (*Strigops habroptilus*), a flightless, ground-dwelling, owlish bird about the size of the Snowy Owl. It formerly ranged widely over the islands comprising the New Zealand Archipelago but today survives only in the forests of North Island. Like so many of New Zealand's birds, this parrot reached New Zealand as a flying bird. Today it is incapable of true flight, although it occasionally climbs trees and still uses its wings to assist in long hops from limb to limb.

The Owl Parrot feeds on rootlets, leaves, tender twigs and fruits. It is able to travel by day in the dark forest glades in which it lives. The nest is in a hole under tree roots or in rock clefts. From two to three white eggs are laid, and both parents share the task of incubation, which requires 21 days. After the breeding season, the Owl Parrot is said to live in small colonies in ground burrows rather like the kiwi.

Other fascinating oddities of the parrot family are the two living and two extinct species of keas known from New Zealand. The most famous, the raven-sized Kea (*Nestor notabilis*), is a bird with the ominous reputation of being a sheep-killer. It is generally olive with some red and yellow in the wings. It lives in South Island in stunted vegetation and among rocks at altitudes as high as 6000 feet. It nests in rock clefts during the southern summer, when it is not likely that its habitat will suddenly become sheathed in frozen rain.

The Kea is the hardiest of parrots and the only species of this almost purely tropical family that spends part of its life amid snow. It has a strongly brush-tipped tongue that it uses to obtain nectar from summer flowers, but during the winter its tastes are much more earthy. Forced by hunger from its mountain strongholds, it has learned to forage in the vicinity of sheep stations, where it finds discarded sheep heads and carcasses. These it picks clean, and Sir Walter Buller has reported that a favorite way of trapping it in earlier days was to expose a fresh sheepskin on the roof of a hut. While the Kea was engaged in tearing up the bait, it was easily snared. In recent years Keas are reported to have developed such a taste for flesh that a few have learned to stand on the backs of living sheep and to kill them by ripping through to the kidneys with their sharp, strong maxillas.

Lower down in the woodlands another species of *Nestor,* the Kaka (*N. meridionalis*), leads a more orthodox parrot life, feeding on fruit, nectar, and insects and their larvae. Like the cockatoos it lives in groups except when pairs split off to breed. Four white eggs are laid in tree cavities. This bird makes a charming pet, as the Maoris, who named it long ago, well knew.

Pygmy parrots, of which there are six species in the forests of New Guinea, New Britain and New Ireland, are the midgets of the parrot family. They are barely three inches long and differ from other parrots in having the tail stiffened and ending in spinelike tips resembling those found in woodpeckers and some swifts. Unlike all other parrots except the King Parrot, the sexes differ from each other in color, the male being bright red, blue and green, and the female very drab and protectively colored. These midgets nest in tunnels inside termite houses and in dead tree limbs.

Although great efforts have been made to bring live specimens out of New Guinea, none has ever reached a zoo. In fact, very few men have ever seen them alive, even in the wild. Dr. A. L. Rand observed that one species usually traveled in pairs, creeping on limbs and trunks and emitting high squeaks. Captain N. B. Blood, who has long sought them, told the author that nests of pygmy parrots brought to his camp by natives sometimes contained many young and an assortment of adults. The young, despite his most careful attention, always perished within a day, and the adults shortly thereafter.

The author has found remains of insects' legs in the stomach of one specimen, and Dr. Rand, who has observed a pygmy parrot nibbling at jellylike layers of tree fungus, believes that Bruijn's Parrot (*Micropsitta bruijnii*) feeds largely on this substance. He found nests of this mountain species eight to ten feet up in dead limbs; the nest cavity, which was entered from an upward sloping tunnel, was unlined. In one he found two young which were partially covered with short, yellowish down.

The author has found the Lesser Pygmy Parrot (*M. pusio*) nesting in termite nests in which it drills passages and cavities. This species lives in humid tropical forests. In addition to their spined tails, pygmy parrots have elongated claws, which are used

Kaka (*Nestor meridionalis*)

Kea (*Nestor notabilis*)

to scale vertical surfaces in the manner of creepers and woodpeckers. The tiny bill is ill fitted for the drilling and probing activities of other trunk-scaling species but can perhaps be used to break open termite tunnels.

The nesting of birds in or near nests of insects or the nests of larger birds is a phenomenon of great interest. The fact that the pygmy parrot of New Guinea nests in inhabited termite houses and the mountain species does not, may be explained as follows: Hole-nesting small birds are generally rare in the tropics, probably because of the prevalence of wasps and bees, which quickly take over the cavities. Tropical kingfishers, trogons and pygmy parrots may drill holes in nests of termites to get protection against wasps and other enemies, which cannot usurp such nests. In some parts of the tropics as many as 90 per cent of all nests are destroyed or taken over by predatory nesters. One observer in Surinam watched a pair of small flycatchers start ten nests in ten months and have every one destroyed or taken over, and in Southern Rhodesia another experimenter, attempting to lure hole-nesting birds, set out 23 nest boxes, only to find over half used by bees, wasps and other insects in the first season and *all* in the second season. It therefore seems very likely that small birds such as pygmy parrots, which drill their nest holes in swarming termite houses, actually play one kind of insect against the other.

Finally, the nesting of mountain pygmy parrots in dead limbs and not in termite nests is probably due to the fact that in high cold mountains insects are less numerous and such insect-protected nesting sites are not so necessary to survival.

Tropical America is the domain of the macaws, of which there are many species, some the largest of New World parrots, some pigeon-sized. All have the orbital areas and face partially naked, with a scattering of very small feathers. The smaller species are generally green and protectively dressed to blend with the roof of the forest in which they dwell. The largest species are brightly colored. All have the tail long and saber-shaped.

Zoo-goers the world over are familiar with the large macaws, and especially with their huge, sickle-shaped bills that look so unwieldy and yet are used with such dexterity. So powerful is the macaw's bill that, with the aid of the prehensile, fleshy tongue and the probelike bill tip, it can easily crack and extract the delicate meat from even the rock-hard Brazil nut.

Macaws are often kept chained to ring perches. They do well in captivity and have a long life span, but their imitative powers are limited and they rarely learn more than a few words. Like their large relatives, the cockatoos, their screams are painfully shrill.

Among the largest and most spectacular are the Hyacinth Macaw (*Anodorhynchus hyacinthinus*), a cobalt-blue bird with a two-foot tail, and the slightly larger Red-and-Green Macaw (*Ara chloroptera*), which is a vivid scarlet, blue and green. The first seems to be limited to inland tropical jungle areas of South America, but the latter is common from Panama to Brazil, where it nests in high cavities of forest trees. The relatively rare Hyacinth species is said to nest in deep lateral cavities of earthen banks. Other species, such as the 30-inch Military Macaw (*Ara militaris*), which occurs up to 8000 feet, are mostly green with a red forehead.

The Scarlet Macaw (*Ara macao*), which occurs north to the humid regions of Mexico, reaches a length of three feet. The most colorful and largest of Mexican parrots, it is scarlet below, with a red tail, yellow wing coverts and much bright blue on the wings and back.

The Carolina Parakeet (*Conuropsis carolinensis*), which until several decades ago was found in the United States, was related to a large group of smallish New World Parrots, all of which bear some resemblances to the macaws. All have the tail long and pointed. The Carolina Parakeet, which ranged north to Maryland, Iowa and the Great Lakes region, was the northernmost of the world's parrots. It is a tragedy that this graceful, foot-long, greenish bird with its deep orange forehead and cheeks and yellow head should have been hunted to extinction. As late as April, 1904, a colony of thirteen was observed in Florida. Like the other New World conures, this species was highly sociable and sometimes more than threescore slept together in a hollow sycamore tree.

In Central South America many relatives abound. One is the Orange-chinned or Tovi Parakeet (*Brotogeris jugularis*), which ranges north to Mexico. This sharp-tailed seven-inch species is abundant in the lowlands and, though mostly bluish and olive green, is yellowish green below. Among the other tropical American parrots are the ten-inch macaw-like Aztec or Olive-throated Parrot (*Aratinga astec*), a green bird with orange tufts; and the crow-sized Thick-billed Parrot (*Rhynchopsitta pachyrhyncha*) with bright red on the forehead, sides of face and shoulders. This latter species reaches the pine forests of Arizona. The six-inch Barred Parakeet *Bolborhynchus lineola*) is a fast-flying alpine bird with uniquely barred body plumage. The sparrow-sized Blue-rumped Parrotlet (*Forpus cyanopygius*) is chiefly green with much yellow on the head.

One of the most unusual species is the Gray-breasted Parakeet (*Myiopsitta monachus*) of southern South America, which travels in immense flocks. It erects tenement-like clusters of sticks in tall trees, an unexpected departure in a family that almost universally nests in cavities of trees, termite nests and earthen banks.

The most famous "talkers" in the New World belong to the genus *Amazona,* of which there are many species in Central and South America. All are largely green, stockily built, blunt-tailed birds somewhat larger than a street pigeon. They are essentially forest birds and, when taken young, usually become accomplished mimics. Two examples are the White-fronted Parrot (*A. albifrons*), a ten-inch bird with red lores and a red wing patch in the males, and the Yellow-headed Parrot (*A. ochrocephala*), one of the largest of the Amazonas, reaching a length of 15 inches.

In Africa and Madagascar there are several kinds of gray and black short-tailed parrots that are rather like the Amazonas in size and structure. One of these is the African Gray Parrot (*Psittacus erithacus*), which is conceded to be the finest talking bird and the most sought after. The males make better mimics than the females. Both sexes are ashy gray with a red tail. In the wild the African Gray travels in flocks, feeds on fruit and nuts and lays two to four eggs in tree cavities. It is this species that is reputed to have lived in captivity for 80 years.

The so-called lovebirds and their relatives are confined to the Old World. Generally there are slight differences between the sexes. In many the tail is elongated and pointed. Perhaps the most aberrant is the large Red-sided Eclectus (*Larius roratus;* Plates 80 and 81) of the New Guinea region, in which the sexes so differ in color that for a long while ornithologists considered the essentially lettuce-green male and the predominantly red female to be separate species. Additionally, the male has red, blue and black in the wings and vermilion on the bill, whereas the female has a black bill and large splashes of blue on the back, lower parts and wings.

Parakeets abound in the African, Indian and Malaysian regions, where they often feed en masse on fields of ripening grain. All are highly gregarious

[203

small birds with long, pointed tails. Many are predominantly green with violet, rose and/or orange tints chiefly on the head, and many have a distinct varicolored neck ring. Some are very beautiful, such as the small, greenish Blossom-headed Parakeet (*Psittacula cyanocephala*) of the drier parts of India and Ceylon, which wears a black collar below a pinkish red and violet head. It has some red on the shoulders and displays a pair of long, blue, yellow-tipped tail feathers. Many of the species live close to man, even breeding in old buildings, and many are easily tamed and bred in captivity.

The lovebirds most numerous in Africa and Madagascar are very small and usually the sexes are similar in plumage. One, the Rosy-faced Lovebird (*Agapornis roseicollis*) of southern Africa, has an astonishing habit: it inserts long stems of grass and woody fibers under the feathers of the rump, and flies with them to the nest. Birds in captivity frequently decorate themselves with long strips of paper torn from the bottom of the cage and inserted under the feathers. The purpose of this is not known. This amazing habit turns up again in the sparrow-sized Ceylon Lorikeet (*Loriculus beryllinus*), which builds a nest of green leaf edges that the female carries to the nest under her scarlet rump feathers.

It has long been thought that the pair bond in lovebirds was so strong that when one perished the other would often pine to death. This has not been proved. Yet nowhere else in the world of birds is there what seems to be so distinct a "love" relationship as in certain members of this group. Pairs often sit for hours, bill to bill, in seeming rapture.

The Hanging Parakeets of the genus *Loriculus* have devised a way of sleeping like bats, suspending themselves like pendulums in clusters in leafy trees. Often when awake they hang suspended and caress each other. The group is centered in the Indo-Malayan region, including the Philippine Islands. All are very small. Green is the prevalent coloration, with much blue and some red or orange tinting, particularly on the head and wings.

The Broadtails and Grass Parakeets consist of small, specialized, chiefly Australian parrots with long tails, which generally feed on or near the ground in grasslands. One species is the famous "Budgie" or Budgerigar (*Melopsittacus undulatus;* Plate 82), which is perhaps the most widely domesticated of the parrots. The Australian Budgie is about seven inches in length with a long, tapering, pointed tail. Usually it is grass green, with bright yellow on the head and a blue tail. There is much sooty and yellowish scalloping and barring on the upper parts, with a royal blue patch on the cheek and three black spots on each side of the throat. The male differs from the female in having the cere blue instead of brownish.

Budgies travel in large flocks, feeding on grain and often gathering in fields like sparrows. They lay up to nine eggs and sometimes raise two broods a year. They are not especially affectionate as parrots go, but their willingness to breed in captivity makes them one of the most widely kept of cage birds, even rivaling the canary. Their notes are chiefly a churring little warble, with soft but characteristically parrot-like screams and whistles. Many people derive enjoyment from their friendliness and willingness to feed from the mouth and hand, as well as from their amusing maneuvers on miniature trapeze perches and their constant fencing with little mirrors installed in their cages. Budgies also exhibit a talent for imitating human speech and will even learn to whistle short musical phrases.

Some aberrant parakeets of large size are the colorful, broad-tailed, ground-loving Rosellas (*Platycercus*) of the Australian region and New Zealand, the Crested Parakeets (*Cyanoramphus*) of New Zealand, New Caledonia and other islands of the southwest Pacific, and the Ground Parakeets (*Pezoporus*) of Australia. The last are among the most earthbound of all parrots. They are about a foot long and have relatively very long, sharp tails alternately barred with blackish and white. These birds are so rooted to the ground that they act like quail when flushed by dogs, running in the grass and flushing in coveys. Their nests are on the bare earth. One species, the Short-tailed Ground Parakeet (*Geopsittacus*), is largely nocturnal and very rare.

COLIIFORMES

Mousebirds or Colies

(*Coliidae*)

Colies, or mousebirds, are parakeet-sized, highly gregarious, fruit-eating birds. They are very destructive to orchards and in many parts of Africa are treated as vermin. The six species have no known close relatives and are structurally so different from other birds that they are put in an order by themselves and have drifted from place to place in classification tables. Judging chiefly from behavior, however, there are grounds for believing that they may be an offshoot of the stock that produced parrots.

Mousebirds have relatively small rounded wings that move rapidly in flight. In passing from tree to tree or bush, they go from near the top of one to near the bottom of the next, then climb methodically upward again, feeding on fruit and berries. They have the body and legs relatively large and solid and the bill bulky and shaped vaguely like that of a giant finch, not hinged at the skull as in parrots. But there are resemblances to parrot features in the structure of the palate as well as in the heart, the pelvis, intestines and oil gland. On the other hand, the legs and toes of parrots are covered with small granulated scales totally different from those of any colies.

Mousebirds are unique in that in walking about they shuffle along on the back of the legs, using them like feet. They have the first and fourth toes reversible but the toes are normally carried two in the lateral position and two ahead, and are used for squeezing like a hand, not—as in most birds—for wrapping around a perch. These peculiar feet also serve in scurrying along the tops of thick limbs or slithering up steep inclines. Mousebirds have the unusual habit of clinging to the sides of limbs, like little pendulums, with the tail almost straight down. Six or more often hang thus together by day, and always at night, this being the normal sleeping position. Perhaps their most interesting trick is the occasional use of the bill as a hand in climbing, a trick they share only with the parrots.

Mousebirds are generally gray above, often with a washed-out green or blue showing weakly through the gray. But many species have patches of bright blues or greens on the back of the head. All have crests that they can erect when alarmed, and they have long, pointed tails like those of the small green parakeets.

Colies occur in all the warmer parts of Africa south of the Sahara. The Blue-naped Mousebird (*Colius macrourus*), of Central Africa, about 13 inches long, is generally tinged with grayish blue and has a brilliant turquoise nape. The feet and the base of the bill are red. Among other species are the White-backed Mousebird (*C. colius*), of southern Africa which has a white rump and coral feet and often ventures into local gardens, and the Red-faced Coly (*C. indicus*), of the same region, which has a naked red eye-ring and a creamy white forehead.

In recently published observations of the Kenya White-cheeked Coly (*C. striatus*), which has a dark face and white cheeks, Dr. van Someren reported that this species eats insects in addition to the fruit which is its main food. Up to twenty birds move in a flock, which disperses in the breeding season when the pairs build nests. The nest, a bulky open cup set from three to twenty feet off the ground, is occasionally relined during incubation. From two to six creamy white eggs are laid in it and incubation starts with the laying of the first egg, the young hatching on different days. They are born naked and pink and are brooded for a long period. The brooding parent, the female, is fed by the male and later feeds the young with regurgitated food. When older, the young crawl out of the nest, sometimes hide in the foliage for a while, and then return to the nest. These birds have no song but can make cheeping notes and harsh calls when alarmed.

CUCULIFORMES

Turacos or Plantain-eaters

(*Musophagidae*)

Turacos are active, cuckoo-like birds of southeastern Africa (Plate 98), ranging in size from that of a small crow to that of a pheasant. The 19 known species are divided into two groups, those with red in the wings, which live in forests, and those without red, which live in bushy grasslands.

Turacos are renowned for their possession of unique pigments in the feathers. The red coloration of the wing is largely due to a pure pigment called turacin, and the bright green that many species wear is also due to a pure pigment—which is the only true green pigment known in birds. Despite assertions to the contrary, the red pigment is color-fast: Dr. J. P. Chapin tested it by putting a red turaco feather in his hat and wearing it in all kinds of weather for a year and a half. At the end of that period, the feather had, if anything, turned to a darker shade of red! Turacin is composed of 5 to 8 per cent copper, which apparently tends to oxidize, and it is this that probably darkened the hat ornament and causes museum skins to turn darker with age.

Turacos are fascinating birds, little understood and of obscure relationships. For years they have been placed in the same order with the cuckoos, but recently Dr. René Verheyen, a Belgian anatomist, has discovered characters that may indicate that they are actually closer to the chicken-like birds. He places them in an order of their own which he calls the Musophagiformes and includes in it the hoatzins of South America.

The White-crested Turaco (*Tauraco leucolophus*) is fairly typical of the red-winged group. It is 14 inches long and chiefly grass-green; it has conspicuously red wings, white cheeks and crest, and a purplish black forehead.

White-cheeked Coly (*Colius striatus*) at nest

V. G. L. VAN SOMEREN

[205

In the gallery forest of the Congo region—sometimes 8000 feet above sea level—is found the Violet Plantain-eater (*Musophaga rossae*), which reaches 20 inches in length. The bird is dark purplish, with one red patch on the crown and another concealed in the wing. Another even larger species is the Great Blue Turaco (*Corythaeola cristata*), which reaches a length of 2½ feet. It is greenish blue with a greenish yellow breast, chestnut thighs and a large black crest.

Species that dwell in bushes and riverine forests bordering lowland grasslands are typified by the Gray Plantain-eater (*Crinifer zonurus*), a 20-inch brown-and-white bird with a greenish yellow bill. Its calls resemble cackling laughter. The Go-away Bird (*Corythaixoides leucogaster*), which is named after its call, is the same size. It is ashy gray above and on the fore part of the body and has a pure white abdomen and a long crest. It is disliked by hunters because of its habit of following them and scaring off their quarry with its cries.

The Black-tipped Crested Turaco (*Tauraco macrorhynchus*), according to recent observations in Sierra Leone, has the habit of sleeping four or five huddled together during the heat of the day and of descending to the forest floor to feed on insects disturbed by driver ants. It drinks out of knot-holes and feeds on tender shoots, fruits and berries.

In Africa Dr. Chapin noted that the Black-billed Turaco (*Tauraco schuttii*) ascended Mount Ruwenzori to 9000 feet and that couples sometimes bowed toward each other by raising the tail and drooping the wings. He noted also that three species ate snails in addition to fruit and green leaves, and that the Ruwenzori Turaco (*Ruwenzorornis johnstoni*), which sometimes calls like a monkey, lived in forests as high as 12,000 feet above sea level.

Recent studies of the Blue-crested Plantain-eater (*Tauraco hartlaubi*) by the authority on East African birds, Dr. V. G. L. van Someren, have uncovered many interesting facts concerning this family. An inhabitant of evergreen forests, it is green with large concealed areas of red in the wing that flash like bursts of fire when the wing is beating. When the bird freezes at the end of its rapid scampering and hopping, it seems, despite its bright plumage, to disappear into the vegetation roundabout.

It is an inquisitive, noisy bird, often investigating strange sounds. It engages in mobbing actions with other birds to drive off snakes and owls. Much like parrots, it is very wasteful of food. Its outer toes can be directed forward or backward, with the result that it is adept at climbing and running on limbs. The Blue-crested Plantain-eater nests during two periods of the year, April to July and September to January, but Dr. Van Someren believes that a bird nesting in one period skips the other. The nests are very fragile, being built of twigs and sticks in the midst of concentrations of small limbs, and the eggs can often be seen through the nest platform. Two whitish eggs are laid and incubated for about 16 to 18 days. In other species the eggs may be tinted with green. In covering the eggs, the parent turns away from the light and holds the head and bill in such a way as to break the silhouette. (The author has seen the Magnificent Fruit Pigeon do the very same thing in New Guinea.) The young are of different sizes, indicating that incubation begins with the laying of the first egg. They are covered with down at hatching and are fed by regurgitation on fruit pulp. The nesting period is about 28 days, but for part of this time the young crawl through the tree near the nest like young colies or hoatzins. In other species both sexes incubate.

In courtship the male Blue-crested Plantain-eater elevates his crest, expands his tail and jerkily opens and closes his wings, exposing the brilliant red patches. He also indulges in running chases through the tree limbs, accompanied by much flashing of the wings. He engages in courtship feeding.

Blue-crested Plantain-eater (*Tauraco hartlaubi*) at nest with young

Cuckoos, Anis, Roadrunners, Couas, and Coucals (*Cuculidae*)

A confusing assortment of oddly behaving birds are grouped together in the order Cuculiformes. The more primitive of its two suborders, the Turacos, has already been discussed. The second suborder, comprising one highly varied family, the Cuculidae, with 128 species, is represented in all of the warmer land areas of the world.

The most primitive, the 37 species of the true cuckoos (Cuculinae), are found in the Old World. They range from the size of a sparrow to that of a raven, and all indulge in a highly organized form of nesting behavior, to wit: they lay their eggs in the nests of other birds and by means of many ruses delude the foster parents into rearing their young.

The typical true cuckoo is brownish above with mottled brownish and grayish underparts, a graduated tail, zygodactylous feet and a relatively large bill without a hooked tip (except in one very large New Guinea species). However, a few species are brightly colored, and a few highly iridescent. On the other hand, some are so drab and ungainly that they look like birds left over from an earlier age. Cuckoos feed chiefly on insects, but some also devour lizards, frogs and even snakes and young birds.

Cuckoos are pre-eminent in the art of deception. Species in many parts of the world imitate hawks, drongos, sunbirds or even ravens, and their imitations involve plumage, actions and calls. Indeed, some are so adroit in their impersonations that ornithologists have been deluded into collecting a "hawk" only to find that it was a cuckoo.

Their forms of camouflage reach almost unbelievable refinements. For example, certain species consisting of many populations which appear identical to each other consistently lay differently colored eggs. One such species is the Common European Cuckoo (*Cuculus canorus*), a hawk-shaped, jay-sized bird. Some members of this species consistently lay bluish eggs and parasitize birds that lay bluish eggs, others lay buff eggs with blackish spots and parasitize passerine birds that also lay eggs of that type, and so forth—with the result that one cannot but suspect that the different egg colors in this wonderful specialization represent small steps in the evolution of species.

Many cuckoos migrate long distances between their summer and winter homes to take advantage of seasonally shifting sources of insect food. The migratory abilities of some are highly developed, those of the Bronzed Cuckoo (*Chalcites lucidus*) of the South Pacific, for example, being little short of incredible. In this species prodigious over-water migrations are performed by birds freshly fledged from the nests of nonmigratory foster parents. First the Bronzed Cuckoo parasitizes tiny nonmigratory flycatchers on the remote islands of the New Zealand Archipelago. After laying eggs in the nests of these birds, the cuckoos fly to their winter home, there to be joined about a month later by their youngsters. To accomplish this reunion the young cuckoos, without benefit of adult guides, fly about 1200 miles over the ocean from New Zealand to Australia, then nearly another 1000 miles northward to the areas occupied by their parents in the Solomon and Bismarck Islands. Since the adults long precede their young to these islands, there seems to be no explanation of this extraordinary feat by babes fresh from a foster nest except to attribute it to a kind of inherited memory.

A horrible aspect of nest parasitism—that is, from the human point of view—is the fact that the single egg that the cuckoo usually deposits in a foster nest is a kind of kiss of death to the legitimate offspring, especially since the victim is almost always of a much smaller species. The young parasite, shortly after hatching, hunches against the eggs or the legitimate offspring in the nest beside him and by forcing his back under the hapless creatures heaves them over the nest rim to their destruction. He thus instinctively gains for himself all the food brought by the fosterers and to survive despite what is often a great difference in size between himself and his foster parents (Plate 122). Photographs have been made of European Cuckoo nestlings being fed by fosterers so small they had to stand on the backs of the monstrous babies in order to feed them!

Unlike the true cuckoos, the members of the second subfamily of the cuckoos, the Malcohas, build their own nests and rear their own young. Some 20 species of both the New and the Old World, ranging from medium to large in size, fall into this category. Examples are the Black-billed Cuckoo (*Coccyzus erythropthalmus*) and the Yellow-billed Cuckoo (*C. americanus*), both of which breed in North America and winter in South America, and the peculiar Scale-feathered Cuckoo (*Phoenicophaeus cumingi*) of the Philippines. The first two are slender, thrush-sized birds, olive in color and with longish white-tipped tails, brown above and whitish below. The Scale-feathered Cuckoo is crow-sized and has curly, blackish, cellophane-like plumes growing from the throat, forehead, crown and hind neck.

The third subfamily is very aberrant, containing the anis, which range southward from the southern borders of the United States and are so unusual in

European Cuckoo (*Cuculus canorus*) removing egg from nest of **Tree Pipit** (*Anthus trivialis*)

ERIC J. HOSKING

structure and behavior that they could be made a distinct family. In this group is found the jay-sized Groove-billed Ani (*Crotophaga sulcirostris*), the Great Ani (*C. major*), and the Common Ani (*C. ani*). All are blackish, with some shine to the plumage, and in all the bill is tall, thin and bladelike. Insects comprise their chief food. They are highly gregarious at all times, up to 20 birds sometimes living together in a flock. Apparently all species engage in communal nesting, groups of birds joining forces to construct rather large, disheveled nests of sticks. In such nests the various females deposit their eggs—as many as 26 have been observed in one nest—and the clans then share in the incubation and rearing of the young. In flying about, the birds keep together like a flock of sheep, uttering high-pitched cries and following a leader very closely. At night anis sleep in clusters, rather like the mousebirds of Africa and the Indo-Malayan wood swallows.

The fourth subfamily, which has some 13 species, is again very different. Typical of it are the roadrunners or ground cuckoos of the southern United States south through South America, and of the Malayan region. These birds are largely terrestrial and medium to large in size. Roadrunners build their own nests, with three exceptions. One is the Striped Cuckoo (*Tapera naevia*) of the New World tropics, which, like the true cuckoos of the Old World, has learned to parasitize other birds. The Pheasant Cuckoo (*Dromococcyx phasianellus*) and the Pavonine Cuckoo (*D. pavoninus*), of Central and South America, have the same parasitic habit.

Ground cuckoos generally run about rapidly and feed on a large variety of ground-loving animals, including snakes—even rattlesnakes—which some of them are adept at killing. The widely known Roadrunner (*Geococcyx californianus;* Plate 97) of western North America, a snake-killer of note, is some 16 inches in length and has long, strong legs, a long graduated tail and rather picturesque habits, including a high quotient of curiosity that often leads it into poking about the tents of campers. Hand in hand with curiosity goes a cunning that enables it to outmaneuver even dogs on the ground. This species is blackish with broad amber striping. Quite surprisingly, two closely related species of ground cuckoos

European Cuckoo (*Cuculus canorus*) nestling being fed by foster parent, a **Lesser Whitethroat** (*Sylvia curruca*)

(*Carpococcyx*) are found in Borneo, Sumatra and Malaya.

The fifth subfamily of cuckoos consists of ten little-known species of chiefly terrestrial forest birds called couas, all of which are confined to the island of Madagascar. Like roadrunners, couas build their own nests, both sexes doing the work, and rear their own young. They also resemble the roadrunners in certain of their habits, but some species such as the Crested Coua (*Coua cristata*) are quite beautiful. Unlike most cuckoos, this species is a conspicuous bird of the forest, where it travels in small, noisy parties. The other species are graceful, largely terrestrial birds that go about in flocks and feed on insects and small fruits knocked from the forest crown by starlings and parrots. Some species, the Olive-capped Coua (*Coua ruficeps*) for example, live alone or in pairs and in fear run on ground instead of flying.

Delalande's Coua (*Coua delalandei*) is one of the world's rare birds and, like many species of the Madagascar region, may have become extinct in the last decade. This large terrestrial species is known from seven specimens in museums.

Finally, 27 species of closely related, long-tailed cuckoos, ranging from 12 to 30 inches in length, occur in Africa and eastward through Asia to Australia and the Solomon Islands. All are strangely primitive in appearance, but this is most true of the coucals (Plate 99). Like most cuckoos, coucals build their own nests and rear their own young. The Pheasant Coucal (*Centropus phasianinus*) of New Guinea and Australia is a clumsy, red-eyed, blackish brown bird of the grasslands and forest edge. It skulks through the underbrush and, when wet or cold, climbs to the tops of bushes to spread its plumage in such a grotesque manner that it often resembles a lifeless scarecrow. When disturbed, this apparition comes to life, flutters and glides over the tall grass for a short distance and then suddenly plummets clumsily into it. On the ground it runs and hides with much agility.

Coucals build globular nests in bushes and grass, often within several feet of the ground. A peculiarity of theirs is the habit of building an entrance tunnel— and sometimes two—extending as much as 18 inches from the nest cavity like the spout of a large kettle, and of lining this with green leaves. Serving perhaps as a deterrent to some sort of predator, these leaves, like those which many Old World birds of prey use in the nest, are replaced from time to time. The eggs of coucals are roundish, whitish and number from three to five. Incubation periods, according to Dr. Van Someren, who studied the Hackle-necked Coucal (*C. superciliosus*) of East Africa, begin with the laying of the first egg. There is usually a day's interval between the hatching of the young, a kind of staggered birth found in many birds, especially owls, that makes rearing the young—particularly feeding—easier for the parents.

In the coucals the incubation period is about 14 days and Dr. Van Someren found that both parents built the nest and shared in incubation and feeding. The food consisted chiefly of insects, but frogs, lizards, occasionally small rodents, nestling birds and even small grass snakes were fed to the young. He noted that Hackle-necked Coucal chicks hissed like snakes and evacuated a nauseating liquid excreta when threatened on the nest. The calls of these peculiar birds are deep bubbling notes and are often heard at night.

STRIGIFORMES

Owls (*Strigidae*)

Since time immemorial owls have been regarded as birds of ill omen because of their solemn, staring eyes, weird shrieking and nocturnal habits. Of the 133 species around the world, some are as small as sparrows and others as large as roosters. All are carnivorous, feeding on arthropods, crustaceans, fish, amphibians, small mammals and birds. They usually obtain food by pouncing on it at night. To facilitate the attacks, their legs are very strong and equipped with sharp, powerful, curved claws, the outer of which are reversible, although usually directed backward. The ocular orientation of owls is chiefly used in locating game, but their ears are so highly developed that some, and probably many, species can carry out successful attacks in total darkness. The ear development varies greatly from group to group and often one ear is much larger than the other. Both eyes and ears are so highly specialized that the shape of the head is modified to accommodate these enlarged structures. The characteristic flat conformation of the owl's face is covered with feathers that have a peculiar, hard, wiry texture and radiate outward from the bill and the eyes to form a kind of disk that may serve some acoustic function. In the center is a sharply hooked bill, and at the base of this, as in hawks, parrots and certain other birds, is a saddle-like leather-textured band called a cere. The nostrils are located in this area. Directly above are the large, forward-directed eyes. These cannot be turned in their sockets, a condition that sometimes leads to comical effects, as when in certain diurnal species— the Burrowing Owl, for instance—a bird seems sometimes in danger of twisting its head off when one circles its perch.

The plumage of owls is almost invariably soft, and the edges of the flight feathers are equipped with fragile filaments that enable the birds to fly in almost complete silence. Only owls that hunt by day, such as the Pygmy and Hawk Owls, are noisy in flight and have hard body plumage. Owls have short, rounded wings and usually short, square tails.

As much as anything, the weird vocalization of most owls during the season of courtship is responsible for their reputation as birds of ill omen. These sounds include strangled calls, maniacal laughter, screams, hoots, whistles, snores and coughs. They are heard when these night birds resort to audible displays to attract their mates and are familiar sounds in every woodland the world around. Some are duets, with the male standing high as he calls and the female bowing her head as she adds her voice to his.

Visual displays are little known in these nocturnal animals, but they presumably play a part in mate selection. When defending the young, threatening predators or fighting, owls open the wings, lower the body and expand the plumage so that the body feathers stand almost at right angles to the skin. The birds thereby seem to double their apparent size and seem much more formidable. The ornamental plumage of the head, especially the "ears," which are actually tufts of elongated feathers, is raised in time of danger or hostile display, but in fright is lowered almost to the crown.

Owls always lay round, white eggs, the set varying from one to twelve depending on the species. One to two eggs are laid by some tropical species, and the set size grows larger to the north, with arctic birds producing the largest number of eggs.

The majority of small and medium-sized owls nest in cavities in trees, in the ground or in rock niches. Many species nest in human habitations, to which they are attracted by man and his entourage of rodent pests. But some of the large owls nest on tundra-covered ground in nests built of grass and feathers. Still others nest in grass swamps or in the abandoned stick nests of hawks and other birds.

Owls begin incubation as soon as the first egg is laid, and thus some species have large nestlings to care for at the same time that they are incubating eggs. This is known as "staggered birth" and is thought to be a mechanism of survival in carnivorous birds faced with periodic shortages of game. A second mechanism of survival, the tendency to vary the size of clutches, verges on the unbelievable. In years when lemmings are abundant, for example, species such as the Snowy Owl (*Nyctea scandiaca*) and the Hawk Owl (*Surnia ulula*) lay up to 13 eggs, or nearly double the normal number. Conversely, in very poor years they may make no attempt at nesting. One might therefore say that in these species the breeding cycle is related to the stomach.

Female owls, like female hawks, are considerably larger than their mates, a fact that may be correlated with the role they play in parental care. As a rule, only the female incubates. The period of egg-warming extends from about 25 days in the smaller species to about 35 in the largest. To human eyes all owls appear to be courageous in defending their young. Even tiny species attack a man if he ventures too close to the nest and some of them will attack passers-by even when they are on horseback. Baby owls at hatching are covered with dense white down.

Owl nests are usually familiar to predators because the owls litter the ground with parts of their prey such as the heads, wings and legs of mammals and birds. The best indication of the presence of owls is the stomach castings or pellets that all species regurgitate in order to discard the bones and other indigestible portions of their victims. Through analyses of such pellets biologists can determine the size, abundance and variety of animal species in given areas. A little-known peculiarity of owl pellets is that those from birds under four weeks of age are relatively free of bones, apparently because young owls digest bones, probably as a source of calcium during skeletal growth. The studies have also shown that at certain times of the year owls keep to small hunting territories: for example, during its nesting season the Horned Owl of western North America stays in an area of about one square mile.

In searching for food, owls fan out at late dusk much as do hawks in the daytime, some hunting the grasslands and swamps like Marsh Hawks, others the forest and forest edge like bird-catching hawks. Thus the pressure of selection is exerted day and night on all habitats, and only the best-fitted wild prey lives to reproduce its kind.

Owls engage in migrations of considerable extent, but little is known about these. In winter many of the species gather to roost together like crows, among them being the tiny Saw-whet Owls (*Aegolius acadicus;* Plate 93), which hide together in evergreen

White-faced Scops (*Otus leucotis*)

JOHN MARKHAM

trees, and the Short-eared Owls, which cluster together on the ground.

Among the most widespread of small owls are the Pygmy Owls of the genus *Glaucidium;* the twelve species are found in various parts of Eurasia, Africa, and in both North and South America. These owls lack ear tufts. They are chiefly insect-feeders but also take small birds, lizards, mice and shrews. They are abroad during the day and at dusk and attack small prey with the swiftness and force of small hawks.

The Pygmy Owl (*Glaucidium passerinum*) of Eurasian hill-forests is smaller than a starling. It is described as the smallest of the European owls, and its diurnal chases are so swift it often catches small birds in flight. It lays its eggs, usually four in number, in tree cavities.

Among other well-known small owls are the Little Owls, or Owlets, of which there are three species in Europe, Asia and Africa. The common Little Owl (*Athene noctua;* Plate 92) is the best-known owl of Eurasia because it goes about by day as well as night and breeds in all countries bordering the Mediterranean. It habitually visits farmlands and perches on exposed poles. Among the numerous Asian relatives of this owl is the extremely abundant Spotted Owlet (*A. brama*), which may be found in bushes in the vicinity of almost every farm in southern Asia.

Another small species, the Elf Owl (*Micrathene whitneyi*), is found only in the southwestern United States and in Mexico. It lives in open woodlands and among cactus trees, nesting in a cavity, often in a Giant Cactus or Saguaro, and usually laying three eggs. Like Owlets, it catches insects on the wing.

Scops Owls, or Screech Owls, of which 36 species are known, are smallish birds with ear tufts and are found almost throughout the world. Typical in the Old World is the Scops Owl (*Otus scops*), which is 7½ inches long. A resident of Eurasia and Africa, it nests in holes, often near man. Closely similar but with more white on the face is the White-faced Scops (*O. leucotis*) of central Africa. Many species of this group are insect-eaters. A relative is the Flammulated Owl (*O. flammeolus*) of the New World, which prefers pine forests, especially the ponderosa pines of the Rocky Mountains, where it is considered the most abundant of raptorial birds. It captures insects and moths in flight in the crowns of pine trees. Another member is the familiar Screech Owl (*Otus asio;* plate 91) of North America and Mexico, of which some 15 subspecies are known. In wet areas these are inclined to be blackish, while in desert areas they are pallid. Many of the races are highly dichromatic, one color phase being reddish and the other sooty to grayish. Two color phases are found in many other owls and many of their relatives, as, for example, the goatsuckers and the frogmouths. Interestingly, the red or gray plumage is found in nestlings as soon as they shed the down.

With their whistled calls, Screech Owls are features of the night. They feed on all kinds of small

Short-eared Owl (*Asio flammeus*) at nest

insects, mammals and birds, and if a man disturbs their nest they will attack him, flying at his eyes. Somewhat larger than the Screech Owl, but without ear tufts and with longer legs, is the Burrowing Owl, (*Speotyto cunicularia;* Plate 94), which ranges from Florida and the western United States southward to the pampas of Argentina. It is a denizen of open prairies and grassy savannas, where it nests in colonies, often in cavities drilled in the earth by prairie dogs and ground squirrels. It manages to live near these animals in a habitat infested with rattlesnakes. Like many owls, the Burrowing Owl sees well in daylight; in fact, it has the habit of watching the passing scene from the entrance of its nest hole during much of the day. If their breeding zones or colonies are invaded, they fly threateningly around the intruder. For food they sally forth at night to capture small desert animals such as mice, lizards, frogs and insects. Up to nine eggs are deposited in an enlarged grass-lined chamber at the end of a curved tunnel sometimes ten feet in depth.

The Hawk Owl (*Surnia ulula*), which is almost as aberrant as the Burrowing Owl, is a long-tailed, small-headed, hard-plumaged bird that flies rather noisily and seems more hawklike than owl-like in shape and mannerisms. It is largely diurnal and has a hawklike face with the characteristic facial disc nearly gone. Also it has a large, hawklike bill, and its small ear cavities indicate that it probably does not practice nocturnal hunting. Hawk Owls have been observed to hunt in the direct rays of the sun and have the habit of ganging up, like hawks, on small mammals such as lemmings when these become periodically abundant. They are 14 to 16 inches in length, and often nest in tree cavities, usually in broken, coniferous trees, but also in deserted open-stick nests of hawks or crows. In winter they sometimes visit the northern United States and central Europe.

One species of peculiar habits is the highly migratory Short-eared Owl (*Asio flammeus*), which breeds over much of the Northern Hemisphere as well as in Central and South America, the West Indies, the Galapagos, Hawaiian and Falkland Islands, and, oddly enough, on the island of Ponape in the southwest Pacific. This 15-inch bird likes grassy swamps, builds grass nests in fields near water and feeds on insects and small rodents. Periodically it becomes abundant, usually when rodents overrun an area. In winter it sometimes roosts in groups on the ground.

Other unusual owls are the four species of Oriental Fish Owls (*Ketupa*) of Asia east to Borneo, the three species of African Fish Owls (*Scotopelia*) and the three species of large Spectacled Owls (*Pulsatrix*), which range from Mexico to Argentina. Another very large species is the Great Gray or Lapp Owl (*Strix nebulosa*), which reaches a length of 27 inches and is smoke-gray with dark lineations. This bird has unusually small, yellow eyes, set very close together. It inhabits deep coniferous forests in the far north around the world. The Great Gray hunts by day and lays its eggs in deserted hawk nests. Periodically, like the Snowy Owl of the treeless far north, it is forced in winter to seek food as far south as the United States and Germany. A relative in Eurasia and North Africa is the Tawny Owl (*S. aluco;* Plate 96).

Famous owls are the Great Horned Owls, of which there are 11 species around the world. In this group is the largest of the European owls, the Eagle Owl (*Bubo bubo*), a bird that lives on the forest edge and in open scrub and hunts on overcast days and at dusk. Very similar is the Great Horned Owl (*B. virginianus*) of North America. All of this group have

Great Gray Owl or **Lapp Owl** (*Strix nebulosa*)

OSCAR MOBERG

expressive ear tufts and large yellow eyes. In color they range from dark to light, one almost whitish species of the far north nearly matching the darker of the Snowy Owls in color. Other dark species live in tall, damp forests.

These owls indulge in maniacal, spine-chilling calls during the nights of the breeding season. They kill large grouse, squirrels, skunks and chickens, but the bulk of their food consists of rodents, particularly rabbits. Horned Owls generally lay three white eggs in cavities in trees, in rocks or in the abandoned nests of hawks and crows. They nest very early in the year, often when snow is on the ground.

A bird of the true Arctic and Subarctic is the Snowy Owl (*Nyctea scandiaca*). More than two feet long and one of the most splendid of all birds, the Snowy Owl keeps to treeless regions, breeding on top of tundra hillocks, often when these are covered with snow and ice. They are snow-white with varying amounts of black in the plumage, and blend into the terrain like a ptarmigan or snowshoe rabbit. They hunt mostly by day, often pursuing birds with hawk-like speed or gliding on silent wings to pounce on ptarmigan, ducks, lemmings, Arctic Fox and Arctic Hare. Periodically they gang up on lemmings. They move south in large numbers when food becomes abnormally scarce and in some winters appear in Texas, France and Yugoslavia. The nest is attended by the female, but the male stands by protectively.

Barn Owls (*Tytonidae*)

Barn Owls have the face heart-shaped instead of more or less rounded as in most owls, and they lack the tufted earlike feathers found in many. Most Barn Owls have the upper parts strongly tinted with pale cinnamon rufous and the lower parts largely white with small dark flecks. All have the legs relatively long and feathered to the toes, and the middle toe is pectinate—that is, equipped with a comb, which is used in dressing the plumage. Anatomically they differ enough from the rest of the world's owls to require a family of their own. It has also been discovered that in Barn Owls the tail is renewed from the center outward and in other owls from the outer edges inward. Barn Owls are found throughout tropical and temperate areas with the exception of New Zealand and islands of Oceania such as Hawaii.

The Common Barn Owl (*Tyto alba;* Plate 95) has a white face, cinnamon-buff back, buff on white breast and relatively small eyes. In certain attitudes it has the appearance of a small monkey. It is from 12 to 18 inches long and has the largest range of any nocturnal bird, hunts in open areas and tends to dwell close to man, habitually breeding in belfries and similar locations. It also breeds in hollow trees, holes in rocks, earthen banks and so forth.

Like most owls, Barn Owls remain paired for long periods and perhaps for life. They return to breed in the same places, but according to a recent

G. RONALD AUSTING: NATIONAL AUDUBON

Great Horned Owl (*Bubo virginianus*) and **Mockingbird** (*Mimus polyglottos*)

analysis of 1400 European Barn Owls their offspring seem to settle where they spend their first winter.

These birds are economically valuable because of their liking for small, crop-destroying mammals. A recent study of their pellets in Poland showed that among the remains of 15,587 vertebrates 95.5 per cent were of small mammals, 4.2 per cent were of birds, and the rest were of amphibians.

Recent experiments at Harvard University have proved that the Barn Owl can locate small mammals in total darkness. Using a "sniper scope" (a telescope that enables a man to see in darkness by means of infrared light), observers found that when a mouse was turned loose on the floor of the laboratory among dry leaves, the owl immediately looked at it. Although unable to see with its immobile eyes, the bird followed the moving mouse, its facial shield shifting like a radar screen. When the mouse stopped running, the bird descended on it, striking it with its feet.

Nine species of Barn Owls are known, one of which is the Black Barn Owl (*Tyto tenebricosa*) of the New Guinea forests. Others are the Grass Owls, which nest in fields of tall grass in Africa, Asia, the Philippines, Malaysia and Australia. Still other species are little Barn Owls, which are found on small islands of the Atlantic and Pacific Oceans. Most Barn Owls are chiefly nocturnal, but the author has observed the Grass Owl (*T. capensis*) in the mountain valleys of New Guinea hunting like a Marsh Hawk over grass fields in the bright light of midafternoon.

For its nest the Common Barn Owl collects a few sticks and amidst these and its regurgitated castings lays from five to seven eggs. Laying occurs at irregular intervals, usually over two to three days, and incubation begins with the first egg; therefore the young are of different sizes. Incubation requires up to 34 days. It is performed almost entirely by the female but sometimes the male joins her on the nest. Nestlings remain on and by the nest for eight weeks.

Somewhat intermediate between the Barn Owls and the true Owls is the Bay Owl (*Phodilus badius*) of India, Ceylon and parts of Malaysia. An isolated colony has recently been discovered in East Africa. The Bay Owl is a strictly nocturnal inhabitant of dense forests. It lays from three to four eggs in hollow trees. E. C. Stuart Baker writes that during the breeding season in India they outdo all other owls in "the appalling nature of their cries."

CAPRIMULGIFORMES

Oilbird or Guacharo

(*Steatornithidae*)

Deep in certain South American caves lives a marvelous relative of the goatsuckers—a lone species for which ornithologists have created a separate family, the Steatornithidae, and a distinct suborder. This bird, the Oilbird or Guacharo (*Steatornis caripensis*), bears affinities to owls and potoos. In fact, it is the only bird known to be equipped with a radar similar to that of bats and the only one that can fly in total darkness. Because of its wonderful "blind-flying" abilities, the Guacharo spends more of its life in near or total darkness than any other bird.

This highly specialized creature is slightly larger than a Sparrow Hawk, has a wing span of more than three feet, weak feet and legs, and a firm, yellowish bill equipped with a sharp hook. Long, stiff bristles surround the mouth. Its general coloration is maroon-brown. Whitish spots are interspersed through the plumage and are particularly evident on the upper wing coverts. Its eyes are somewhat owl-like but smaller, and in daylight appear in shades from bright sky-blue to China blue.

The Oilbird occurs on the island of Trinidad, in Venezuelan coastal mountains, in Colombia, Ecuador and Peru. By an ironical twist of fate these light-hating birds long supplied Venezuelan Indians with oil for light as well as cooking and nourishment. Their very name is derived from the nearly transparent, odorless oil obtained from the thick layers of yellowish fat that blanket the bodies of nestlings, an oil that keeps for months without becoming rancid. To obtain it, savages made eerie pilgrimages to Guacharo caves at breeding time, slaughtered the squabs and melted them down by the thousands. The extremely fatty condition of these birds results from their principal item of diet, the palm nut from which commercial palm oil is obtained.

[213

Oilbird or **Guacharo** (*Steatornis caripensis*) on nest

Guacharo nurseries are usually situated in limestone caves of mountainous areas surrounded by forest. Ornithologists have found Guacharos as much as a mile inside the earth in sanctuaries so remote they seemed beyond the reach of predators. Torches there revealed an eerie world of huge caverns packed with thrashing birds. Stalactites of almost fluorescent color swirl down over beds of calcite flowstone that vanish under deep, oozing swamps of guano. Throughout the caverns there are ghostly forests of dwarfed trees, dying or already dead, rising in an environment for which they were never intended and germinated from palm seeds carried in by Guacharos. Here and there appear the scaffolds and poles that Indian hunters used in their age-old persecution of this strange cave-dweller. But most unforgettable is the wail of the Guacharo (Spanish for "one who cries and laments"), an incessant screeching, clucking and squawking that grates unbearably on human ears.

The Guacharo nest is a flattish pedestal about a foot in diameter and several inches thick, of a texture and color resembling beach-washed cork. This mat-like nest consists of organic material plastered and glued together. It clings to the tops of ledges sometimes as high as 100 feet above the cave floor. In it two eggs like those of owls are laid, but unlike owls' eggs, which are always pure white, the white of the Guacharo eggs is marked with cinnamon-brown smudges. The breeding time is April and May.

Today's spelunker, as the cave explorer calls himself, is beginning to follow the ornithologist into these strange nesting places. But he is not exactly treading on the heels of the biologist: as long ago as 1799 the great German naturalist-explorer, Alexander von Humboldt, visited the Caripe caves of northeastern Venezuela from which the first Oilbirds came to museums of Europe. Humboldt duly recorded the frightful noise, and in 1953 a Cornell professor, Donald R. Griffin—long a student of bat navigation—developed the theory that the Guacharo might also employ an echo system of navigation for "blind flying." Along with a well-known Venezuelan ornithologist, William H. Phelps, Jr., he visited the Caripe caves to test his theory. The two men brought an array of equipment that would have confounded the great Humboldt—cathode-ray oscillographs, tape recorders, batteries, converters, variable electronic filter lights, high-speed film and cameras—all designed to analyze high-frequency sound and light. They captured birds, stuffed their ears and then tested them in flight in absolute darkness and in dim and bright light. From these studies a form of navigation new to the world of nature was discovered. Unlike bats, in which the sounds emitted for navigational purposes are ultrasonic and thus inaudible to human ears, the Guacharo was found to emit sounds within the range of human hearing. The echoes of these sounds or impulses were used by the birds to locate obstacles. The Guacharo sonar system, Griffin found, was inoperable when the bird's ear canals were blocked.

Griffin and Phelps found that the sounds emitted in the nesting area varied but that there was a metallic ticking underlying the squawking and screaming. This was the prevalent sound as the birds streamed out of the cave late in the evening, and this also was the sound used as they approached barriers, the ticking accelerating in cadence as the barrier neared. In the end Griffin was able to show that the echo of this audible sound was the impulse the birds depended on for "blind flying." This impulse had a frequency of 7000 cycles per second and was sonic.

Recently the Venezuelan Government has insured the survival of the Oilbird by declaring the Caripe caves a national park, complete with electric lights to enable the visitor to see these remarkable "radar" birds.

Guacharos venture from their caves at dusk. Advance scouts lead the way, and on their heels come wave after wave. At night they fly great distances—some reports put the distance up to 50 miles—to feed like giant hovering hawks up and down the shafts of fruit-laden palms. Through the blackest part of the night they are abroad, screaming and ticking, keeping together in loose flocks in their dark world. At the first sign of dawn they stream homeward in undulating waves, making their way unerringly back through a black maze of forest and disappear into the bowels of the earth.

Frogmouths *(Podargidae)*

The twelve species of this nocturnal family are among the strangest of birds. Their home is in the tropics in forested savannas and open woodlands of the Oriental and Australian regions. Like the larger owls, which they resemble in size, softness and mottling of plumage, frogmouths are dichromatic, with grayish and reddish-brown phases that are not correlated with sex; males and females of a given color phase are virtually alike. All have particularly large powder downs on the rump, lack the oil gland, and have ten tail feathers. Their mouths are froglike and enormously wide (Plate 101), and have a short, hooked bill. The huge mouth is used to capture insects, which are the sole source of food.

Frogmouths are said to prey on crawling insects among the limbs and foliage of trees. However, it would be surprising if such an oddly equipped, sluggish bird could capture enough crawling insects to maintain itself, and furthermore the shape of the grotesque mouth seems ill fitted for such use. But recent reports tell of an amazing feeding specialization in this group. The bird is said to assume a static position on a limb and then open its huge mouth, exposing the pinkish, rose and yellow inner surfaces. In doing this, the protectively colored bird assumes the appearance of a bright flower growing at the end of a dead limb. Insects attracted by the "flower" are said to be gobbled up as soon as they touch it. This report requires further confirmation.

Frogmouths sleep through most of the day on thick limbs on the middle levels of forest and savanna trees, sitting in an erect position with the bill pointed upward. If forced to fly, they move sluggishly to a nearby tree and remain there. In the early evening they take to the wing and, as the light decreases, become fairly active, flying singly or in loose pairs from tree to tree and perching like ordinary birds.

In New Guinea two species occur together but their multisyllabled croaks are quite different. The Papuan Frogmouth (*Podargus papuensis*) calls *tuck-tuck-tuck-tuck,* followed by two snaps, or possibly bill-claps. The other, the Ocellated Frogmouth (*P. ocellatus*), calls *woo-woo woo,* with no snap at the end. These calls are heard all night and cease only at sunrise. However, in appearance these two species are rather similar except that the first has ruby eyes and the second orange eyes.

In November at Madang the author has observed the Papuan Frogmouth on its nest. This bird was two feet long, with large eyes and owl-like plumage. Its nest was a fairly substantial, flattish structure of sticks in a tree crotch about 40 feet over a roadway. Automobiles used the road constantly, and a house some 40 feet away faced the nest. The female spent the entire day on the nest. It incubated with the body in the normal position but with the head held rather high. The ruby-colored eyes were usually partly or entirely closed. At times, however, the bird opened them wide to inspect passers-by, and it sometimes followed the author's actions even when he was working in the sunlight. Its eyes were directed forward rather like those of an owl. The eggs are white and in some species are said to be three in number. The young of the Ocellated Frogmouth are heavily covered with black and white down, and the hunger cry is a very loud, squeaky hiss.

Potoos or Wood Nightjars *(Nyctibiidae)*

In the tropical forests of the New World the melancholy wails of potoos have a mystical import for primitive Indians, and by some they are interpreted as omens of disaster. The cries are reported to resemble those of a midnight murder victim.

The five species of potoos, ranging from Mexico and the Antilles to Brazil, are rarely seen. All are nocturnal, and by day their large, slender, owl-like bodies and their upright sitting positions look like dead tree limbs. Motorists sometimes encounter them at night on roadside posts and tree limbs, where they cling head-up like loose slabs of bark. Their large, golden-yellow eyes reflect brilliantly in artificial light and give off a steady glow like that of a crocodile.

Although closely related to the New World nightjars, potoos superficially resemble the frogmouths of Australasia in the size of their mouths. They have large powder downs on the sides of the body and lack the comb, or pectinated ridge, on the side of the third toe, which is a feature of the nightjars. Potoos feed on insects captured at the end of short foray flights, not by sweeping the air in sustained erratic flight like the nightjars. They apparently favor special hunting and sleeping perches, and travelers at night learn to expect to see their eye reflections from posts. These perches may be from about four to more than forty feet up in the forest, in wooded grasslands, or on the tops of sharp low rocks in pure grasslands.

The potoo lays a single egg on top of dead stubs or on precarious ledges on the sides of gnarled trees. The egg, which is white with faint brownish and grayish markings, contrasts with the dead wood and bark around it. During incubation the breast feathers are opened over the egg, and thus the bird sits through the daylight hours virtually invisible and one of nature's most perfect examples of camouflage.

The young bird soon adopts the vertical stance. It is covered with down and resembles an irregular mass of whitish fungus. Incubation and care of the young take as much as 70 days.

The Gray Potoo (*Nyctibius griseus*), which sadly calls "Poor-me-one" in the jungles of Central and South America, is about 14 inches long. It is dark mottled gray above and light gray below. The Great Potoo (*N. grandis*), found from Panama to Brazil, is slightly larger.

Owlet Nightjars

(*Aegothelidae*)

Not much is known about the nocturnal family of Australian and New Guinea owlet nightjars. The seven species range in size from that of a small parakeet to that of a dove, and resemble small or dwarf Screech Owls both in appearance and nesting habits. Actually, the owlet nightjars constitute a distinct group more nearly related to the nightjars than the owls. Most of the species live in forests and forested savannas between sea level and 10,000 feet. All have indistinct powder downs, and their very wide mouths and greatly elongated rictal bristles assist them in capturing insects, their only food.

Owlet nightjars employ the erect carriage of owls and can and often do turn the head 180 degrees. They perch across limbs and by day sleep on leaf-covered branches. Their reddish and grayish plumage and their upright stance act as a camouflage, giving them the appearance of fallen leaves. They use hollow limbs and tree holes in which to lay their four or five white eggs. At dusk the owlet nightjars awaken and, it has been reported, fly direct courses without the rapid shifts of directions found in nightjars and other kinds of birds that capture flying insects.

The Gray Owlet Nightjar (*Aegotheles albertisi*) is about six inches long and extremely shy. Another species in New Guinea, the Rufous Owlet Nightjar (*A. insignis*), is about ten inches long. It has the proportions and plumage of a slender, reddish Screech Owl. The calls of these nightjars are owl-like whistles.

Goatsuckers or Nightjars

(*Caprimulgidae*)

The goatsuckers, a group of 70 highly interesting nocturnal birds, occur almost everywhere in the warmer land areas of the world. They derive their name from an erroneous belief; as far back as Aristotle's time they were thought to take milk from the udders of domestic goats. Needless to say, this is an old wives' tale, and it would be better if the birds were called by their alternate name, "nightjar," in keeping with their penetrating nocturnal calls.

Nightjars are dressed in protective colors, which match fallen leaves and sticks so well that the birds "disappear" when at rest on the ground. Some species have large patches of white in the wings and tail, which show in flight, and a few have elongated plumes on the head, wings or tail. In virtually all there are minor differences between the sexes, the females often lacking the whitish markings or having them strongly washed with brown. All nightjars have the mouth very wide, and when opened it resembles a gaping purse. Encircling the gape are strong, rakelike, rictal bristles.

Nightjars often plummet through swarms of flying insects, their only source of nutrition, with the mouth wide open, seining them out of the air with the help of the rictal bristles. As many as 500 mosquitoes have been found in the stomach of a single bird. So big is the mouth that sometimes nightjars engulf warblers and other small birds, perhaps mistaking them for night-flying insects. Nightjars hunt alone or in groups. Some forage repeatedly from a few spots on the ground; others employ sustained flights in twilight and at night. All species have a comblike ridge on the third toe, such as is found in herons and Barn Owls; it is thought to be of value in dressing the plumage.

Common Nightjar (*Caprimulgus europaeus*) yawning

A most interesting recent discovery is that of Professor E. C. Jaeger, who proved that the unconscious nightjars that had turned up from time to time were in reality hibernating birds. Jaeger found the Poor-will (*Phalaenoptilus nuttallii*) of western North America hibernating in rock niches. Sometimes the birds remained in a state of torpor through three foodless cold months, with their temperature lowered from the normal 100 degrees to about 66 degrees and their respiration virtually arrested. One bird that Jaeger marked returned the following fall to hibernate in the same rock niche where he had banded it. It was thus proved that certain birds, like some mammals and other animals, were capable of lowering their metabolism and lapsing into a state of suspended animation in order to survive conditions that would otherwise spell their doom.

The majority of nightjars are sedentary dwellers of the tropics, but a few, both north and south of the equator, are highly migratory. The Common Nightjar (*Caprimulgus europaeus*) of Europe and Africa winters south to Cape Town and migrates northward to its breeding areas in Europe. The Whip-

poor-will (*C. vociferus*) of the New World winters in Central America and breeds as far north as Manitoba and Quebec. The wonderfully ornamented Pennant-winged Nightjar (*Semeïophorus vexillarius*) breeds in South Africa during the rainy season of September to November, then crosses the equatorial forests to spend April to July in the Sudan, amidst the northern rains with their swarms of insects. A parallel migration is that of the Nacunda Nightjar (*Podager nacunda*), which flies across the equatorial forests of Amazonia to Venezuela from breeding grounds in Argentina. It arrives in Venezuela just ahead of the wet season.

The penetrating notes of nightjars are familiar to every camper. The Whip-poor-will sometimes repeats to the point of distraction the phrase from which its name is taken. John Burroughs counted 390 consecutive calls from a single bird. Other nightjars boom and emit buzzing noises in flight, each call being characteristic of its species.

Because of their short, weak legs, nightjars squat lengthwise on limbs or on the ground (Plate 100). None builds a nest, and most lay two heavily scrawled eggs in grasslands, forest edge or deep forest on bare earth or dead leaves. The Nighthawk (*Chordeiles minor*) of North America has taken to laying on gravel-covered roofs, the texture of which hides the eggs very effectively. By day nightjars sit with the eyes closed and blend so perfectly with their surroundings that they are virtually impossible to detect. The down-covered nestlings become very fat on the proteinous diet provided by the adults, who are always quick to protect them by using the "broken wing" distraction display.

The European Nightjar is about ten inches long. It has a peculiar undulating, churring note, sometimes accompanied by wing clapping, which may last for many minutes at a time.

The Pennant-winged Nightjar, eleven inches long, is the most ornate of the family. The male has several of the central wing feathers on each side greatly elongated, one pair streaming as much as eighteen inches beyond the other. And in courtship flight these feathers, which are black and white, flutter and undulate. This species flies by daylight more than most nightjars, and the courtship flights thus involve primarily the visual sense rather than the auditory as in related species.

The Lyre-tailed Goatsucker (*Uropsalis lyra*) of the New World tropics, a bird with a body only four inches long, has 27-inch tail feathers. The author has seen this fragile bird flying nimbly through tall, narrow passages in the mountain jungles of Colombia.

APODIFORMES

Swifts (*Apodidae*)

Swifts occur everywhere except in polar regions and in a few island archipelagos. They are related to the hummingbirds and nightjars, not to the swallows which they superficially resemble; but they differ from hummingbirds in the structure of the fore part of the head and the bill, which is short and wide instead of long and pointed, and from the nightjars in the structure of the palate and in many of their habits. For example, nightjars feed by night whereas swifts feed by day. All three families have developed elaborate ways of capturing insects in flight, and in swifts such prey is their sole food. In migratory species this poses serious problems. Often because of cold, retarded seasons or storms, no food is available for days on end, and to overcome this the birds resort to a kind of hibernation.

Since the days of the ancient Greeks hibernation has been advanced as the answer to many of the riddles of cyclic phenomena in birds, with the result that many ornithologists become very critical at the mention of the word. However, it has now been established that a modification of the thermo-regulatory cycle of certain birds involves hibernation. The first

discovery was in the Poor-will (see page 217). Later hummingbirds in torpid condition were found (see page 222). After that, a Finnish ornithologist, Jukka Koskimies, proved to everyone's satisfaction that in the Common Swift (*Apus apus*) the nestlings could resist cold and starvation by lowering their normal temperatures more than 50 degrees! This reduction meant that their internal temperature dropped to below 50 degrees Fahrenheit in surroundings where the temperatures were lower than that. In doing this the nestlings became torpid and immobile, and Koskimies found that they could remain in this state of lethargy for as long as ten days and then recover with no apparent ill effects.

Swifts, of which about 78 species are known, are capable of what is probably the fastest flight among small birds. Many species cleave the air with a sound like that of a whip but the flight nevertheless appears effortless. It is erratic, with glides, rapid changes of course, flutterings and long dives. They have been credited with speeds in excess of 200 miles per hour, but probably 60 miles per hour is about maximum, with many of the smaller forest species flying no more than 20 miles per hour. Among small birds, only the hummingbirds rival them in air speed, but they have no rival in sustained flight and probably spend

Common Nightjar (*Caprimulgus europaeus*) showing reversal of far wing

ERIC J. HOSKING

nearly half of their waking life in the air. Since they do not break their flight to rest, it is probable that they have devised ways of resting in the air.

The legs and feet of swifts are very small and weak—so weak, in fact, that those swifts that accidentally land on the ground cannot stand and cannot take off again. Their only landing places are vertical surfaces, to which they cling head up, and even nestlings cling to the outsides of the nest very early in life. So divorced are swifts from terrestrial life that all food-gathering, courting, mating, bathing and even gathering of nest material is done on the wing.

Swifts range in size from that of a tiny sparrow to that of a small slender hawk. They are usually dark in color, although a few species have bright white or brown collars and some of the smaller species are covered with glossy feathers. The sexes are always dressed alike. In all species the mouth is swallow-like and wide, with the gape extending under the eyes. The bill is very short and sharply hooked. The wings are long, usually extending far beyond the tail and crossing when in the folded position. The wing is composed of ten elongated, strong primaries and not more than nine small secondaries. The tail, composed of ten feathers, takes many forms: it may be deeply forked and soft-tipped, or truncate, or very stiff and tipped with needle-like spines. These and the claws are used to cling to vertical surfaces.

The nests of swifts are built of feathers, fibers, sticks, plant down, moss and even pure saliva. Twigs are broken off by the little feet of the bird while it is in flight. The nests are glued to vertical surfaces on the inside of caves, rock cracks in cliffs, chimneys, belfries, curled palm fronds, hollow trees and rock ledges behind waterfalls.

The eggs are always white and, although some of the species lay as many as five, the majority lay two or three. The young are hatched naked and remain in the nest for an exceptionally long time—in some species as much as six weeks—and do not leave until they have acquired adult plumage. This long period in the nest is probably linked to their precision flying, for the young have to be capable of highly specialized flight from the instant they leave the nest. Also, in migratory species the long flights begin very soon after the young are fledged.

Evidence of the efficiency of early development in swifts is indicated by recoveries of 650 Common Swifts banded in central Sweden. An annual mortality rate of 19 per cent was found, with first-year birds faring no worse than older birds. By comparison, in Yellow-eyed Penguins of New Zealand about 50 per cent of first-year birds perished.

In all swifts the salivary glands are highly developed, but in one group of the swiftlets (*Collocalia*) of the Indo-Australian region, the saliva can be produced in such quantity that it alone is used in nest-building. This unique attribute of swifts seems more in keeping with the insects and amphibians. Perhaps even more odd is the fact that man somehow discovered that the mucous-built, isinglass-like nests of several of the species of *Collocalia* are edible. They are the source of bird's-nest soup, which many persons consider delicious. They are also the source of a highly profitable industry of nest-harvesting, which annually amounts to more than $100,000. These tiny birds are also producers of valuable fertilizer.

There is much structural variation in the legs and feet of swifts, and it is chiefly according to these variations that they are classified. One large assemblage of species—the typical swifts—is able to turn the rear toe to the side and has the tail without spines. Typical of this predominantly Old World group is the Common Swift (*Apus apus*) of Europe, which is about seven inches in length and black with a prominent white throat. This species winters in Africa and Madagascar and is a late arrival to its breeding area, which covers most of Europe.

A near relative, the Alpine Swift (*A. melba*), is slightly larger, grayish brown with a white throat, dark chest band and white abdomen. This species occurs from the mountains of southern Europe and the Mediterranean to the Himalayas. In Switzerland it arrives in time to breed in April, large numbers concentrating in cathedral towers in such areas as Berne.

Another large group consists of birds that have toes less highly modified than those of the Apodidae and often have spine-tipped tails. In this group—the Chaeturinae—the fastest-flying small birds are found. One is the Giant Collared Swift (*Streptoprocne zonaris*) of South America, which has a wing span of about 18 inches and a conspicuous white collar. This species always is found in flocks that keep together like swarms of insects. In flight the birds are exhilarating to watch as they sweep from altitudes of a thousand feet or more down to the grass tops, circling and twisting in a "drone" that moves like a slow wind cone over the landscape. Like many of the large swifts, the Collared Swift sleeps and nests in damp rock recesses behind waterfalls. One can hardly imagine a more dangerous way for young to try their wings than by flying through waterfalls; nor can one imagine a more secure nesting place. This, together with the development of very rapid and long-sustained flight, suggests that they have one of the most secure of nature's niches.

A typical spine-tail is the Chimney Swift (*Chaetura pelagica*) of North America, which is small, blackish and swallow-like. One of the most interesting sights in nature is watching thousands of migrating Chimney Swifts maneuver to settle in a chimney at dusk. The birds form a moving halo that swirls in even circles over the chimney. In silhouette this halo is funnel-shaped, with the number of birds diminishing towards the base and at the bottom a fluttering stream dribbling into the chimney. Each fall millions of Chimney Swifts congregate in flocks to move along well-defined routes to wintering grounds in Amazonia and Peru. Formerly they must have followed courses marked with hollow trees. Today chimneys are used almost exclusively, and occasionally when an oil-burner starts in the cool of the night thousands of birds perish. The inside of a chimney occupied by a vast number of birds, each clinging to a sooty wall and probably to each other, must be a maelstrom of activity.

The Palm Swift (*Cypsiurus parvus*) of the Old World tropics has developed nesting habits unique within the family Apodidae. It is the only swift that regularly builds its nest in an exposed situation—on the inner (actually under) side of a hanging palm leaf. The nest is a simple, open structure composed of feathers or plant fibers about the size and shape of the bowl of a teaspoon. Correlated with this are two adaptations (shared with the Crested Swifts of the family Hemiprocnidae, which also builds exposed nests) to promote the survival of the eggs and young. The hatchlings, unlike those of other swifts, are covered with down, and the eggs are cemented to the nest with salivary glue. This cementing precludes the need for constant turning of the eggs by the parents during incubation, an almost universal habit among birds. Why this is so is not known, but it may be that rocking by wind takes its place.

Crested or Tree Swifts

(*Hemiprocnidae*)

This family of three species is found in India, Malaya, the Philippines, New Guinea and the Solomon Islands. The crested swifts are most nearly related to true swifts but, unlike them, have crests, soft plumage, and legs which are strong and well developed for perching. The tail is deeply forked, and the sexes are different in plumage, the male being more ornately dressed. Unlike the Apodidae, the young wear different plumage from the adults. In addition to erectile crests, the crested swifts wear blackish masks that are emarginated above and below with white streaks. The feathers comprising these streaks are elongated, looking like sideburns.

Crested swifts inhabit the tropical forest edge, single birds frequently perching on high exposed limbs, sometimes in company with a roller or flycatcher and occasionally in trees over native villages. From time to time two or three hunt together through the high limbs of an open forest, over the crown or even down to within a few feet of a roadway.

In their nesting habits crested swifts are very different from most true swifts. They are solitary, and instead of nesting in groups in dark cavities, they glue together thin strips of bark to make a tiny, spoonlike cup and attach this to the side of a lofty slender limb. This structure is just large enough to hold the single grayish white egg, which is cemented to the nest bottom. The incubating bird sits across the limb, with its feet on the rim of the shallow nest and its head and neck in an upright position as though

it were facing a wall. Breeding pairs keep together, and often the nest area is vigorously defended against pigeons and other birds.

Typical of this group is the Crested Tree Swift (*Hemiprocne mystacea*) of Malaya and the Australian region, which is blackish and has elongated white whiskers at the side of the head, a deeply forked tail and slender pointed wings as long as those of a Sparrow Hawk. The Lesser Tree Swift (*H. comata*) of the Philippines and Malaya is similar, but has chestnut ear patches and is much smaller. This species is almost always found in pairs in small forest clearings containing dead trees.

Hummingbirds (*Trochilidae*)

"So have all Ages conceaved, and most are still ready to sweare, the Wren is the least of birds, yet the discoveries of America . . . shewed us one farre lesse, that is, the Hum-bird, not much exceeding a Beetle." So wrote Sir Thomas Browne in 1646 of the American hummingbirds—at once the smallest and most beautiful birds and the greatest aerialists.

Unfortunately, the smallness of these creatures makes their beauty hard to observe, for, like the flashing of jewels, their radiance can be seen only close at hand. In the vast majority of the species not only their size but their remoteness hide their beauty from human eyes: They live in jungles and on the sides of great tropical mountains. Many are "rooted" to little islands of vegetation at a given height in the forest or to single mountain peaks.

Many scientists have been fascinated by their limited distribution, their wondrous sexual ornamentation and their structural modifications for feeding and flight. Indeed, in many ways their beauty surpasses even that of the fabled birds of paradise. Their decorations include glittering flags, gorgets,

Chimney Swift (*Chaetura pelagica*)

LYNWOOD M. CHACE

E. H. N. LOWTHER

Crested Swift (*Hemiprocne mystacea*) on egg

shields, tufts, wires, elongated and curving tail plumes, erectile whiskers, mustaches, pendants, exaggerated pantaloons and iridescent plumage that flashes all the spectrum colors.

Despite this diversity of plumage, all 319 species of hummingbirds are clearly distinguishable from all other birds. This distinctness is by no means chiefly one of size, because not all hummingbirds are tiny, the largest being more than eight inches in length.

Hummingbirds are most nearly related to swifts and, like them, are very different from all other birds, including the superficially similar swallows. Somehow a swiftlike ancestor developed abilities that enabled it to move into niches of nature theretofore occupied chiefly by nectar-feeding insects. Swifts are among the world's fastest and best fliers, able to capture tiny flying insects everywhere in the sky. The hummingbird stock probably split off after a way was developed by which they might pursue insects into the fragile flowers where they feed on nectar. The key to this probably was hovering, which is rarely practiced and poorly developed in the speedy swifts. With advancements in hovering, or suspended flight, it became possible to pursue insects closer and closer to their own sources of food and eventually even to trap them deep within the tortuous corollas of trumpet-shaped flowers. In time the hummingbird bill became modified to enable a certain species to seek certain prey in certain places, and with these refinements the

galaxy of species developed and eventually diverged sharply from the swifts.

These changes probably first occurred in the flower-saturated tropical regions of the New World. Today we find hummingbirds most numerous in Colombia and Ecuador, where more than 130 species occur, as compared with 18 in the United States. Of the latter, only 8 penetrate any distance from the Mexican border, and only the Ruby-throat is found with any degree of regularity east of the Mississippi River. Yet the range of the group extends to Alaska, Labrador, Newfoundland, the Antilles, the Galapagos and even the southernmost tip of South America. But none has crossed the great water gaps isolating the New World from the Old, and no birds in the Old World have succeeded in evolving a parallel method of flight.

The development of new modes of flying and feeding was accompanied by modifications in the color and structure of hummingbirds, but their ancestry is clearly discernible in certain deep-seated structural characteristics involving the wing and the skeleton. Among these are a long breast bone, a shortened humerus, and elongated flattened forearm and manus (hand). These characters, together with some special flight muscles and flight feathers that are different from all other birds (both swifts and hummingbirds have only six to seven very short secondaries), enable swifts and hummingbirds to make exceptionally fast wing movements.

Only in recent years has their mode of flight been accurately analyzed. Osteologists have determined that the humerus is hinged to the furculum by a joint that more nearly approaches the free ball-and-socket joint than any other found in nature. This hinge permits the rapid vibrating and feathering of the wing described below.

Power for hummingbird flight is derived from pectoral muscles that are relatively the largest in the animal kingdom. Films reveal that the wing functions much like that of a helicopter but that, instead of turning, it vibrates horizontally, with the lower and the upper surfaces directed downward on alternate strokes. Normal "suspended" flight (such as the bird uses when inserting its bill, head, and often part of its body into the tubular corollas of flowers, or when hanging motionless and inserting the bill to a fearsome depth down the esophagus of the young) creates very little noise or hum. In the Ruby-throat (*Archilochus colubris*), suspended flight requires about 54 wing beats per second. About 75 are required for normal dodging, darting flight, and this flight, which reaches about 50 miles per hour, causes the humming from which the popular name of the family is derived.

During courtship flights such as towering and diving, and other aerial gymnastics of the courtship dance, the wing beats may reach 200 per second. (Compare this with about 1⅙ per second for the Brown Pelican.) During these flights the tail is con-

[221

stantly flirted, tilted, cupped and even angled under the body, and it is believed that its changing positions in the blast created by the wings have much to do with the bird's capacity to fly sideward, backward, upward and, in fact, in almost every conceivable direction with amazing ease.

Not all hummingbirds have advanced to such mastery of flight. For example, the Giant Hummingbird of the Andes (*Patagona gigas*), which reaches a length of more than eight inches, employs wing beats so slow that they can easily be seen. In all of the more specialized species the wing beats are too rapid for human eyes to see except as a blur.

In hummingbirds the modifications for feeding are also extraordinary. The tongue is immensely elongated and extensile, and it can be protruded from a bill that in certain species is relatively the longest known in birds. To illustrate, in the Sword-billed Hummingbird (*Ensifera ensifera*) of Venezuela, Colombia, Ecuador and Peru, the bill is much longer than the head and body together. In a man this would be the equivalent of having to feed through lips seven feet away from the throat, using a tongue that could be protruded another three to five feet. A man so equipped would find it possible to obtain food ten to twelve feet from his throat without moving his head. He would draw nectar to his mouth by sucking it through the rolled or tubular structure of the outer part of the extensile tongue, and he would be able to snare small insects and spiders on the brushy tongue tip and retract them into the mouth. Among hummingbirds this marvelous tool takes almost as many forms as the flowers into which it is inserted. In many species it is thin and needle-like, but in others it is sickle-shaped, awl-shaped and even upcurved like the bill of an avocet. Many species use the tongue to pick up little insects from bark and leaves, and even to capture them in flight. One species punctures holes in the basal portions of flowers to extract insects it could not otherwise reach.

The flowers on which these birds feed are scattered throughout the tropical forests. They grow in immense arboreal gardens in every stratum of the jungle, and in fields, hillsides and mountain slopes to the edge of perpetual snow. And few are so placed or shaped that some species of hummingbird has not succeeded in feeding regularly from them and in playing an important part as a dispenser of their pollen. Incidentally, hummingbirds are the only New World birds undertaking this typical insect role.

Hummingbirds are most active at dawn and dusk, when they sometimes congregate in large numbers, giving the impression of a swarm such as is characteristic of their cousins, the swifts.

High in the Andes, hummingbirds have been found in a semitorpid condition in little caves. By night they seem to drop off into a form of hibernation, only to revive when the sun again warms their surroundings. As has been pointed out, hibernation in birds was long thought to be fantasy, but recently a relative (see Poor-will) of the hummingbirds has been found to undergo true hibernation, and experiments with hummingbirds show that they can be induced to hibernate, apparently without suffering ill effects. In this manner, presumably, they can "rest" or lower their extraordinarily high metabolic rate, which far exceeds that of any other bird. In most birds metabolism is slightly lower during sleep, but in hummingbirds the drop is most pronounced, their internal temperature, which during wakeful periods is over 100 degrees, sometimes falling as low as 64 degrees.

Despite their delicate coloration and the impedimenta of long tresses, the tiny males are, pound for pound, the most pugnacious of all birds. Their skin is leather-strong and their stocky build and temperament are such that snakes, mammals and birds (even hawks) retreat ignominiously when a hummingbird attacks. They are fearless in the face of seemingly overwhelming odds, and due to the perfection of their flight they are apparently subject to no serious predators in the air, although in Trinidad in 1958 Dr. William Beebe saw a Bat Falcon with a green hummingbird in its talons. Their attack consists of diving or stooping at speeds that make them virtually invisible. They dive from above to the hind part of the head, emitting a high whining whirr, often accompanied by shrill screeching and shrieking. These attacks usually do not involve physical contact; however, there are reports that hummingbirds have blinded snakes with their bill thrusts.

Powerful attacks involving physical contact occur between hummingbirds themselves. The author has seen a Copper-rumped Hummingbird (*Amazilia tobaci;* Plate 104) strike another bird of the same species with such force that both fell to the ground like a single stone, there to close again, then fly ten feet like paired bullets and again fall.

Virtually all hummingbirds are polygamous. Males select an area in bushes, trees or among tall ground flowers as their territory and then proceed to drive off all trespassers. Such males sit on special limbs, buzzing and twittering and engaging in chases during much of the day. In this territory some build nests that may have some connection with bowermaking. Such nests are not used by the females. Nest-building and care of the young are the responsibility of the female alone, and in many species the females apparently visit the displaying male repeatedly during the breeding season. Sometimes three broods are raised in a season by a single female, and the Black-chinned Hummingbird (*Archilochus alexandri*) of western North America has been observed building a second nest and laying in it while still feeding her first pair in another nest. In several species in which the male and female are very similar in coloration, the male assists in incubation and there is probably a pair bond.

The nests of hummingbirds are marvels of construction and often very charming. In nearly all a saliva glue is used to cement nest material to otherwise inaccessible surfaces. Many species build on slender branches and limbs of the middle portions of bushes, often using vegetable down, spider webs and insect silk, and adding bits of bark and lichens to the completed structure to conceal it. Many attach their nests to pendant leaves, gluing them to the tips in such a manner that it is obvious that all or nearly all of the construction work was done while the bird was on the wing. Others build structures from overhanging strands of vine or even begin by attaching shrouds to cave ceilings. At the lower end of these tiny flexible lines they construct the nest. One that the author saw in the Andes of Venezuela was a basket of plant down suspended by a thin line attached to one edge of the nest. This was the equivalent of a man hanging a basket from one spot on its rim by a piece of dangling clothesline and having it hang without spilling its contents. How was it done? To his utter amazement the author found under the basket a bustle of heavy claylike "bricks." All these were attached to one side, and their weight was sufficient to counterbalance the basket so that it hung flat and secure and seemingly in defiance of gravity.

Hummingbirds nest at all altitudes up to 16,000 feet and in all locations except on or in the ground. The nesting season fluctuates with altitude, latitude and season. Many species seem to breed at almost any time of the year, but in central and northern South America—and probably elsewhere in South America—they appear to have two chief nuptial seasons. In the Antilles and Venezuela these seem to be May and January. They usually lay two white eggs that are relatively large. Incubation is a slow process, requiring about two to three weeks. The young are hatched blind and naked and remain in the nest for about three weeks. The nest is sometimes enlarged as the young grow in size.

Despite the tiny proportions of these gems from nature's lapidary, as Alfred Newton has called them, a number of hummingbirds execute long migrations over water to wintering grounds in the tropics. For example, the Ruby-throat of North America regularly flies nonstop nearly 500 miles across the Gulf of Mexico.

Because of the vast array of species it is impossible to do more than touch on some of the more interesting ones. The Sickle-billed Hummingbird (*Eutoxeres aquila*) of southern Central America and the Andes has a bill that is sharply curved and long. It is green above and boldly striped below. The Andean Rainbow (*Coeligena iris*) is nearly six inches long and has a generally greenish body, glittering patches of violet and ruby on the head, a golden-green throat, a violet-purple bib, and a cinnamon-colored tail. The bill is slightly upcurved and more than an inch in length. The tiny White-footed Racket-tail (*Ocreatus underwoodi*) of northern South America is green, with white thighs and two elongated tail wires tipped with black spangles. Gould's Heavenly

Sylph (*Aglaiocercus coelestis*) of the Andes has a giant tail that is more than five inches long and is iridescent purple to violet with aqua reflections. This extends from a tiny body having a small thornlike bill. The Rufous Hummingbird (*Selasphorus rufus;* Plate 102) is a species well known in western North America from Mexico to Alaska.

The Ruby-throated Hummingbird (*Archilochus colubris*) of eastern North America is one of the smallest and widest ranging of hummingbirds, and the best known. Green above and gray below, the adult male wears the ruby throat for which it is named. By contrast the Sun-Angel (*Heliangelus strophianus*) of the Andes, about four inches long, is little known. It is glossy green and has a glittering violet-pink throat. The Frilled Coquette (*Lophornis magnifica*) of tropical Brazil is a tiny coral-billed bird with long, elaborate, extensile white neck fans and a high chestnut crest that is carried on a tiny burnished bronze body. The Comte de Paris' Star-frontlet

Long-tailed Hermit (*Phaethornis superciliosus*)

(*Coeligena lutetiae*) of Ecuador and Colombia is more than five inches in length and has a long straight bill, a glistening yellowish green frontal shield, brown wings and violet-blue throat.

The Sappho Comet (*Sappho sparganura*) of Bolivia and Argentina is a spectacular seven-inch bird with deep pinkish-red upper parts, a shining green head and a long bronze streamer tail. The Graceful Train-bearer (*Lesbia nuna*) of the Andes is nearly six inches long, with a pair of central tail feathers nearly four inches long and a thorn bill less than half an inch in length. The Helmet-Crest (*Oxypogon guerinii*), also of the Andes, is regally decorated with white chin whiskers and elongated black-and-white crown feathers.

The Long-tailed Hermit (*Phaethornis superciliosus*) of Central and South America belongs to a group in which the male and female are similar and rather drab. One species of this genus erects the counterbalanced nests described above. All have elongated central tail feathers that are usually white on their outer portions. Gould's Violet Ear (*Colibri coruscans*), a widespread South American species, reaches a length of six inches, and the sexes are rather similar. The male of this species has been observed incubating the eggs—a rare occurrence in hummingbirds.

The Bee Hummingbird (*Mellisuga helenae*) of Cuba and the Isle of Pines is the smallest bird in the world. It reaches a length of about two inches and is larger than a bee, but it seems smaller because the bill and tail take up more than half of its total length. It is distinguished by the bright ruby color on its crown, throat and ear tufts.

Temminck's Sapphire-wing (*Pterophanes temmincki*) of the Andes is about six inches long including a one-inch bill and a three-inch tail. This species is generally dull glossy green with a bronzy green tail. It is said to give off a strong musky odor similar to that of the petrel, an apparently unique adaptation that may have defensive value against certain insects. Hummingbirds seem to be unafraid of wasps. They are sometimes harassed by bumblebees but easily outfly them. At feeding stations they seem to defer to ants.

DeLaland's Plover Crest (*Stephanoxis lalandi*) of Brazil has a graceful, elongated lapwing-like crest. With its iridescent chest shield, forehead ornaments, horns and wires growing from the sides of the head, Princess Helena's Coquette (*Paphosia helenae*) of the Caribbean slope of Central America looks like a tiny bird of paradise.

The Racket-tailed Hummingbird (*Loddigesia mirabilis*) is known from a single small valley 7000 to 9000 feet above sea level in the hinterland of Peru. This is the most aberrant of the hummingbirds. Not only does it have the most unusual courtship habits but it also has only four tail feathers, as against ten in all other species. The Racket-tail is one of the smallest of the hummers, but it is unmistakable

because of the tremendous elongation of the outer tail feathers. These are wirelike, curved and tipped with broad, dark purple flags. They take the shape of opposing sickles overlapping each other along their middle portions so that the flags are carried to the sides. For many years this genus was known from only a single specimen. Finally in 1880 an ornithologist rediscovered it in the tiny valley of the Rio Utcubamba, and it has not been found anywhere else since, although it apparently remains in this valley only a few months of the year.

TROGONIFORMES

Trogons (*Trogonidae*)

Among the trogons is one species, the Quetzal (*Pharomachrus mocino*), which is as gorgeous as a bird of paradise. This splendid creature reaches a length of nearly four feet. The male is solid iridescent bronzy green above with ornamentally lengthened, curled wing coverts that extend over the flight feathers and enormously elongated upper tail coverts that sometimes extend three feet to a saber-like tip. The head, throat, and chest are like the back, and the abdomen is bright vinaceous strawberry. This glowing plumage and the compressed regal crest give the Quetzal (see p. 242) the look of a gigantic hummingbird. Its home is in the virgin, misty mountain forests of Central America.

As in all 34 species of trogons, the female Quetzal is colorful but much more modestly ornamented, as would seem necessary for security during breeding activities. Despite his almost unbelievably rich raiment, the male assists in all activities of the nest. At the nest, which is usually a hole in a dead limb, he enters head first to incubate or brood; once inside, he turns so that his head protrudes from the hole, peering out under a yard-long cascade of his own shimmering, peacock-green upper tail coverts.

Trogons have no near relatives and appear to be a very ancient, static group. Today they are found in tropical America from the southern borders of Texas and Arizona to Argentina, the West Indies, Africa south of the Sahara, and India, Malaya and the Philippines. None has been found in the Australian region. A fossil from Europe suggests that in ancient times the family enjoyed a much wider range.

Trogons differ from all other birds in the formation of the toes, having the first and second directed backward and activated by a peculiar system of tendons. They also differ in having exceptionally

[continued on page 241]

127. Great Kiskadee (*Pitangus sulphuratus*

Range: Warm areas from southern Texas to Argentina

[PAUL SCHWARTZ]

128. Barn Swallow
(*Hirundo rustica*)
Range: Nearly world-wide

[JOHN MARKHAM]

129. Superb Lyrebird (*Menura novaehollandiae*) Range: Forests of New South Wales [L. H. SMITH]

130. Violet-green Swallow (*Tachycineta thalassina*) Range: Alaska and Canada south to Honduras [ELIOT PORTER]

131. Rufous-browed
Peppershrike
(*Cyclarhis
gujanensis*)
Range: Mexico
to Argentina

[PAUL SCHWARTZ]

132. Northern Shrike (*Lanius excubitor*)

Range: Northern hemisphere; winters
south to Africa, India and
southern U.S.A.

133. Brown Shrike (*Lanius cristatus*)

Range: Asia and Japan south to Malaysia

134. Golden Oriole (*Oriolus oriolus*) Range: Eurasia and Africa

[ERIC J. HOSKING]

135. Dusky Wood-Swallow (*Artamus cyanopterus*)
Range: Southwestern Australia

[NORMAN CHAFFER]

136. Black-collared Starling (*Sturnus nigricollis*)
Range: Eastern Asia south to Malaya

[JOHN MARKHAM]

137. Green Jay (*Cyanocorax yncas*)
Range: Mexico to Bolivia

[PAUL SCHWARTZ]

138. Green Magpie (*Kitta chinensis*)
Range: Himalayas through
Indo-China to Malaysia

[H. RUHE AND T. ROTH]

139. Scrub Jay (*Aphelocoma coerulescens*)

Range: Western United States to southern Mexico and the Florida Peninsula

[ELIOT PORTER]

140. Fish Crow fledglings
(*Corvus ossifragus*)
Range: East Coast of the
United States to Texas

[S. A. GRIMES]

141. Piñon Jay (*Gymnorhinus cyanocephala*)   Range: Oregon and South Dakota to New Mexico   [ELIOT PORTER]

142. Satin Bowerbird with female in bower (*Ptilonorhynchus violaceus*) Range: Eastern Australia

[NORMAN CHAFFER]

143. Great Gray Bowerbird (*Chlamydera nuchalis*) Range: Northern Australia   [NORMAN CHAFFER]

144. Wilson's Bird of Paradise, male
(*Diphyllodes respublica*)

Range: Batanta and Waigeu Islands,
New Guinea region

[E. THOMAS GILLIARD]

145. Lesser Bird of Paradise, male (*Paradisaea minor*)

Range: Western and Northern New Guinea

[E. THOMAS GILLIARD]

146. Phainopepla, male
(*Phainopepla nitens*)

Range: California and Utah
to southeastern Mexico

[ELIOT PORTER]

147. Cedar Waxwing (*Bombycilla cedrorum*) Alaska and Newfoundland to northern South America [ELIOT PORTER]

148. Blue-backed
Fairy Bluebird
(*Irena puella*)

Range: India to China
and Malaysia

[JOHN MARKHAM]

149. Orange Minivet,
with female on
right (*Pericro-
cotus flammeus*)

Range:
Southern Asia
and Ceylon

[H. RUHE AND T. ROTH]

150. **Yellow-billed Scimitar Babbler**
(*Pomatorhinus montanus*)

Range: Southern Asia; chiefly
the Himalayan region through Burma

[H. RUHE AND T. ROTH]

151. **Rusty-cheeked Scimitar Babbler**
(*Pomatorhinus erythrogenys*)

Range: Southern Asia; Himalayan
region to China, Burma and Assam

[H. RUHE AND T. ROTH]

152. Silver-eared Mesia
(*Leiothrix argentauris*)
Range: Southern Asia;
Himalayan region through
Burma, Thailand and
Malaya

[H. RUHE AND T. ROTH]

153. Melodious Laughing Thrush (*Garrulax canorus*) China south to Indochina; Formosa [H. RUHE AND T. ROTH]

154. Blue Wren
(*Malurus cyaneus*)

Range: Eastern Australia,
Kangaroo Island and
Tasmania

[ALLEN KEAST]

155. White-necked Bald Crow
(*Picathartes gymnocephalus*)

Range: Western Africa

[JOHN MARKHAM]

156. Japanese Blue Flycatcher
(*Muscicapa cyanomelana*)

Range: Japan; winters to Formosa
and the Philippines   [JOHN MARKHAM]

[continued from page 224]

fragile skins and plumage that is so weakly attached that the mere handling of a specimen causes body feathers to fall out. The coloration of the non-iridescent portions of the plumage is equally unstable, being subject to a kind of rapid fading that is rare in birds.

Trogons perch in a distinctive manner, with the feet practically covered by the abdomen feathers and the tail often touching the perch and directed nearly straight down or at times even angled slightly under the belly. They are difficult to see because they sit almost motionless, only the head turning from time to time. When they call, however, the tail moves with each note. The calls are usually doubled low coos with a ventriloquial quality, so that one can rarely be sure just how far away the songster is. Trogons usually occur in pairs and keep in touch with each other in the forest by voice. Their flights are short and their wing beats weak, and when they land they "freeze" for a few seconds.

Trogons relish the dark recesses of tropical forests and are apparently nonmigratory. All of them lay from three to five whitish eggs.

New World trogons live mostly on fruit and berries; some of the species eat large fruits with immense seeds, which, after digestion of the exterior flesh, are disgorged. In the Andes some of the trogons are called Mountain Hummingbirds, in tribute to their shining plumage and perhaps to the manner in which they flutter. In seeking food in the upper limbs of high forest, they fly back and forth from resting perches rather like flycatchers and hover among outer limbs of trees in order to take the fruits. Some species, the Quetzal for instance, nest in natural cavities without attempting to improve them. Others, such as the rose-breasted Massena Trogon of Central America, excavate nest holes in the bulblike nests of termites. One nest found by the author in Panama was excavated by both the male and the female in turn. The termites fought the builders as they clung, woodpecker-like, to the side of the termite nest 20 feet up on a waterside palm, but did not seem to disturb the birds. In this species the female is dark grayish above and generally brownish below, in contrast to the iridescent green and red of the male.

The Cuban Trogon (*Priotelus temnurus*), a widespread woodland bird, has peculiar tail feathers in which the outer tip is recurved, giving the entire tail a ragged appearance. The northernmost of New World species is the Coppery-tailed Trogon (*Trogon elegans*), which nests in the mountains of southern Arizona. The male is dark glossy green above and pinkish red below, while the female is chiefly brown, with pink only on the lower abdomen.

African trogons have a small naked area behind the eye and feed partially on flying insects. Indian, Malayan and Philippine trogons have the even larger naked areas at the sides of the head, and their food seems to consist almost entirely of insects that they, like the flycatchers, capture in flight. Old World trogons often have the bill saw-edged.

The Philippine Trogon (*Harpactes ardens*) is the only member of the family in those islands. It is chestnut above, with a black head tinged with purple on the nape. This 15-inch bird has the chest pinkish and the abdomen scarlet. The female is generally brownish, with some black and white on the flight feathers.

Related species such as the Ceylon Trogon (*H. fasciatus*) are found in Indo-Malaya below 6000 feet. This jay-sized species wears a white collar between the black of the head and upper chest and the rosy red of the breast and abdomen. In Africa the slightly smaller Narina Trogon (*Apaloderma narina*) is widespread. Above, it is iridescent green burnished with bluish bronze. Below, it is largely pink. The tail is dark purple with white outer feathers, and the bill is bright yellow.

CORACIIFORMES

Kingfishers (*Alcedinidae*)

The rattling calls and spectacular dives of kingfishers are familiar throughout much of the world. These big-headed, large-billed birds include such famous types as the large, clownish-looking Laughing Jackass or Kookaburra (*Dacelo novaeguineae*) of Australia and Tasmania and the metallic blue-green European Kingfisher (*Alcedo atthis;* Plate 103) of Greek mythology. The latter has long been considered a harbinger of "halcyon" days through its reputed power to control the winds and thus protect its mythical nesting place on the ocean surface. Actually this kingfisher's manner of caring for its young is strange enough: from six to eight youngsters in a small cavity at the end of a tunnel in an earth bank form a circular queue, and each time a parent arrives another chick appears at the tunnel entrance to receive its meal. Apparently the arrival of the adult casts a shadow that causes the circle of young to rotate in unison.

In kingfishers the male and female generally play equal parts in incubation, brooding and rearing of the young, but Dr. Alexander Skutch found that in the Amazon Kingfisher (*Chloroceryle amazona*) and the Green Kingfisher (*C. americana*) only the female incubated by night. The eggs hatch in 19 to 21 days and the young leave in another 22 to 26 days.

Some 80 species of kingfishers are known, most of them tropical and most concentrated in the islands of the South Pacific. They range in size from a small

57. Ruby-crowned Kinglet, male
(*Regulus calendula*)
Range: Alaska to Newfoundland;
winters to Florida and Guatemala

[ELIOT PORTER]

Quetzal (*Pharomachrus mocino*)

sparrow to a small crow, and many are highly colored, often with the female wearing more brilliant colors than the male.

Kingfishers are related to motmots, rollers, hoopoes and hornbills. Their flattish feet have the middle and outer toes welded together over much of their length, and they hop instead of walk. They have short, compact bodies and tight plumage, and most species have twelve tail feathers, although a few have only ten. They are divided into two large groups, the Daceloninae, or wood kingfishers, and the Alcedininae, or true kingfishers. The first, which has its headquarters in the Malayan and Australian regions, usually does not fish but hunts land animals such as tree frogs, centipedes, lizards, small snakes and large invertebrates. In this group are many of the largest and most aberrant species. Most have the bill broad and flattened and often hooked at the tip.

The second group—the true kingfishers—all have the bill straight and sharp and wear compact oily plumage. They are usually found patrolling the borders of streams, rivers and lakes, often sitting motionless on hunting perches. They go about alone or in pairs, and the pairs usually defend a territory so effectively against other kingfishers that it is rare to find more than two in any given area.

These kingfishers hunt by plunging into the water like arrows from their perches or from hovering positions in the air. In the latter maneuver they resemble small hawks but their plummeting is much more spectacular. When the bird emerges from underwater, it carries the catch to a perch, and twists or even tosses it so that it can swallow the fish head first. True kingfishers the world around nest in horizontal holes driven as deep as eight feet into the sides of vertical banks of sandy soil. The banks may be found in grasslands, bushy savannas or woodlands as much as half a mile from water, but if no earth bank is available, true kingfishers will not occur.

The young are hatched naked from pure white eggs in a nest of incredible filth, the fishy residue forming in time a crude platform. The little birds soon acquire a heavy covering of bristle-like wax sheaths. Just before the young leave the nest, these sheaths drop off, revealing a dress much like the adults'.

The wood kingfishers are so named because they dwell in forests and other places often far from water and nest in banks or hollow trees, generally in holes that they drill themselves. A number of the species drill their holes in ground termite shafts or in tree termite houses that hang like giant gourds from the sides of tropical trees. The insects seem not to be disturbed by the birds, nor the birds by the insects.

Most kingfishers have sedentary habits, but a few species are migratory. For example, in North America the Belted Kingfisher (*Megaceryle alcyon*) is found from northwestern Alaska to central Labrador in summer but withdraws to points as far south as the southern Caribbean islands in winter. It is the only kingfisher that occurs at any distance north of the Mexican border. The Sacred Kingfisher (*Halcyon sancta*), which breeds in the southern part of Australia, flies northward to the latitude of Indonesia and the Solomon Islands to wait out the winter. A relative that dwells in Australia and New Guinea is the Forest Kingfisher (*Halcyon macleayi;* Plate 105). The European Kingfisher is found north to Scandinavia in summer. Central and South American kingfishers are very few in number and apparently all are sedentary.

The Belted Kingfisher is chiefly rich blue above and white below and has a huge bill carried on a blue-crested head. The female wears a bright chestnut band across the chest. This species is much disliked by fishkeepers and sportsmen.

The Laughing Jackass Kingfisher or Kookaburra (*Dacelo novaeguineae*)—a heavy bird the size of a small crow—is famous for its fiendlike screams and chuckles. At dawn, midday and dusk it often performs in multiple choruses and is consequently known as the bushman's clock, to mention one of its printable names. It feeds on lizards, snakes, crabs, large insects and small rodents.

The Indian Stork-billed Kingfisher (*Pelargopsis capensis*) is even more aggressive, stealing young birds from its neighbors' nests and swallowing them head first. It is 14 inches in length and has a huge scarlet bill. Along the shores of shaded rivers and streams in India and Ceylon it hunts for fish as well as for insects, lizards, crabs, frogs and small reptiles. It bores its nest from three to four feet deep in sandy banks and in the boles of dead trees.

The Racket-tailed Kingfisher (*Tanysiptera galatea*) of New Guinea and the Moluccas, a slender, scarlet-billed bird that reaches 14 inches in length and has white underparts and narrow, flagged central tail feathers, is perhaps the most beautiful kingfisher. Adept at catching centipedes and lizards, it hunts on the floor of wet forests, flying from perch to perch and sitting quietly except for the slow sideward twitching of the tail. On sighting prey, it swoops gracefully down, even driving the bill into muddy earth to effect a catch. The author has found it breeding in a termite nest in a palm forest of northern New Guinea.

Perhaps the most aberrant species, the Earthworm-eating Kingfisher (*Clytoceyx rex*), is found only in the high mountain forests of New Guinea, where it occurs in pairs and is relatively rare. Its primary food appears to be earthworms, which it digs with its large, shovel-shaped bill. It is rich reddish brown below and blackish above and is probably the largest of all kingfishers.

Wonderful are the jewel-like *Ceyx* kingfishers, some of which are smaller than sparrows and all of which dart about in the denser areas and along streams in forests of the Indo-Malayan and Australian region. All are three-toed and feed chiefly on insects and small invertebrates, but some species take small fishes. One such, the Three-toed Kingfisher (*Ceyx erithacus*) of Southeast Asia, is a vermilion-billed, bright orange little bird washed with deep purple and black. It frequents forested areas and is said to eat fishes, crabs and frogs, sometimes of astonishing size. It drills a tiny burrow, two inches in diameter, in sand and deposits from two to three white eggs at the end of an eight-inch tunnel.

Todies (*Todidae*)

The todies of Cuba, the Isle of Pines, Hispaniola, Puerto Rico and Jamaica are one of the two families of birds found exclusively in the West Indies. They seem to be an offshoot of the kingfisher and motmot stock. The five species are wren-sized and deceptively like flycatchers in some of their habits. All are very colorful, with the upperparts predominantly green, the lower parts whitish, sometimes with a faint wash of green, and the throat and occasionally the flanks boldly painted in geranium red. All have the tongue rather long, the bill edges finely saw-toothed, and the bill largely blood-red, and in all species the feet are syndactylous, that is, with the three forward toes partially united, as in the kingfishers.

These charming, inquisitive birds can be encountered almost anywhere on the forest edge and in bushy areas, where their rather harsh, muted chattering or plaintive series of scratchy notes are commonly heard. Often observers can approach close enough to catch perching birds in butterfly nets and even occasionally with the hand.

Todies habitually perch on small limbs, sometimes quite close to the ground, their body feathers puffed out and their flat bills angled upward. Their greenish plumage blends into the vegetation so well that they are hard to see until, as is their custom, they rocket off the perch with a low chattering noise, generally in pursuit of flying insects, which they capture in midair and which form the bulk of their diet. Todies usually travel in pairs, keeping pretty much to the special feeding and nesting territories.

In nesting habits todies again display close affinities to the kingfishers and motmots. They excavate horizontal burrows in earth and sand, sometimes drilling tiny holes in banks hardly larger than the walls of a ditch and partially overgrown with grass. But normally they keep to draws with large banks. The tunnels are anywhere from four inches to a foot deep, and often bend almost at right angles just inside the entrance. Digging is done with the bill. There is no nest lining, and the glossy, almost round, white eggs, from two to five in number, are deposited on the bare earth. When fresh, the eggs are, like those of the small kingfishers, partially translucent, and they emanate a faint pinkish color.

One species, the Cuban Tody (*Todus multicolor*), is common in woodlands throughout Cuba. It is just over four inches in length and has green upper parts, yellowish lores, blue lower cheeks, and vivid splashes of red on the throat and flanks. The Puerto Rican Tody (*T. mexicanus*) has red only on the throat; its flanks are yellow. The Jamaican Tody (*T. todus*), which is also known locally as the Robin Redbreast, is similar but has a strong wash of green on the breast and a wash of pale pink on the sides. The Broad-billed Tody (*T. subulatus*), occurring chiefly in the mountains of Hispaniola, and the Narrow-billed Tody (*T. angustirostris*), found mainly below 5000 feet, are rather similar except for the bill. Both lack red on the sides of the breast but have the throat red, and both live side by side in the eastern half of the Dominican Republic, the only area inhabited by more than one kind of tody.

Motmots (*Momotidae*)

Motmots, of which there are eight species in Mexico, Central and South America, are quiet birds of

Blue-crowned Motmot (*Momotus momota*)
WILLIAM BEEBE

shady tropical forests. They range in length from 7 to about 18 inches, and are striking in appearance, having much green in the body plumage and delicate turquoise blue on the head. The sexes are dressed almost alike. Their nearest relatives seem to be the todies of the West Indies and the colorful bee-eaters of the Old World.

The chief field character of most of the group is the graduated tail, which carries a pair of elongated central rectrices decorated with attractive racket-shaped tips. Motmots have a curious habit of trimming or nibbling away the webs near the outer end of their central tail feathers in order to shape the adornments. Usually the shaft below the racket is nude for an inch, or even several inches in some species. The tail is flirted somewhat comically, at times swung back and forth like a pendulum, and not infrequently angled far to the side and for seconds kept stiffly in what seems an undignified and unbird-like posture.

Another notable character of motmots is the serrated or saw-edged bill, which is used in cutting and crushing insects, the chief source of food. Motmots capture flying insects, including large ones, in flycatcher-like forays and often bring them back to a special hunting perch, where they fracture the exoskeletons with sharp knocks against the perch and then crush them in the serrated bill.

Almost throughout their range motmots are solitary or are found in pairs scattered thinly through the forest and forest edge. The jungle hiker learns to expect a pair, perching 8 to 30 feet up, every half-mile or so. Each pair generally keeps to a particular feeding territory, which often seems to be along the slopes of watery draws.

Like the kingfishers, todies and jacamars, motmots nest in holes which they drill in earthen banks. The tunnels are round and large enough to receive a man's arm and they extend as much as six feet into the bank, ending in a cavity eight to twelve inches in diameter and about six inches in height. There the parent deposits its three or four dull white eggs on a few sticks. Both sexes incubate, and after a time the nest, which is never cleaned, becomes very foul. The young remain in the nest until they are able to fly rather well. They fledge while the tail is still short, the wings still not fully grown, and the bill not yet deeply serrated. The fledglings wear plumage colors not unlike those of the adult, but have the eye dull brown instead of the chestnut of the fully grown bird.

Among the species in Central America and South America, all of which are predominantly green, are the Turquoise-browed Motmot (*Eumomota superciliosa*), which is a foot in length and has a long tail tipped with large rackets and a black throat edged with blue at the sides, and the striking Blue-crowned Motmot (*Momotus momata*), about a foot and a half long, one of the largest motmots and one of the most common and widespread species. It has the crown almost or completely cobalt blue, the face black and the body greenish olive with a black spot on the chest.

The smallest motmot is the aberrant, seven-inch Tody Motmot (*Hylomanes momotula*) of Mexico and Central America, the only species with a short tail. This primitive motmot is dull green with a rufous crown and neck and bright turquoise spots over the eyes. The somewhat larger Blue-throated Motmot (*Aspatha gularis*) represents an intermediate stage of tail development, since its central tail feathers are elongated but not racket-tipped.

Bee-eaters (*Meropidae*)

Bee-eaters, of which 25 different species occur in the warmer regions of the Old World, are delicately beautiful birds of small or medium size. Their charming pastel colors, which run to greens and blues with dashes of russet and gold, and their habit of hunting near man's homes have made them widely known.

Bee-eaters are in many ways similar to their near relatives, the motmots, the rollers and the kingfishers. Except for a few primitive species, they may be easily identified by their tail feathers, two of which project like a short train from the middle of the tail. Their feet are much like those of their relatives in that the third and fourth toes are united for much of their length.

Although essentially tropical, nonmigratory and probably African in origin, a number of species have developed migratory habits that enable them to take advantage of the swarms of insects that abound in summer in Europe, Asia, South Africa and southern Australia. There they quickly breed, raise their young and then depart for their ancestral homes near the equator. Thus the Common Bee-eater (*Merops apiaster;* Plate 109) nests sometimes as far north as Scotland and Denmark and even wanders to Finland and Sweden. With its tail this bird is about 11 inches long. It is largely chestnut brown and yellow above with a vivid yellow throat and blue-green underparts.

Bee-eaters frequently do serious damage in apiaries. However, their diet does not involve bees alone. In 1955 a study of their feeding habits conducted near Stalingrad revealed that *M. apiaster* partook of more than 100 different insects, as well as harvestmen (daddy longlegs) and spiders. Chiefly represented in their food were bees: a single nest of the Rainbow Bee-eater (*M. ornatus*) of Australia contained the heads of 2753 insects, of which 1747 were of bees.

Bee-eaters are purely arboreal except during the breeding season, at which time they penetrate the ground to lay their eggs in darkness on bare earth. Using their bills, both sexes alternate in drilling the nest tunnels; these are sometimes ten feet long and roughly horizontal, although tunnels only a foot long have been found. Banks of ditches, natural slides, river walls and road cuts are commonly used, but in some places in Africa and Western Australia the burrows are drilled straight down in flat ground and then angled off horizontally. Many of the burrows have a sharp bend part way along, and the nest chamber is just large enough for the adults to turn around in. Many species nest in colonies, often in company with several species of swallows.

Two to five globular, glossy white eggs are laid. After an incubation period of about 13 days the young are hatched naked; as the feathers grow, they are wrapped so tightly in waxy sheaths that they resemble spines. When the young are nearly ready to emerge from the hole the sheaths split off, revealing feathers colored much like those of the adult. When the young depart, the bill is still short but the wings are sufficiently well developed for flight; they return to sleep in the nest for a week or more and continue to be fed by the parents for many days.

In flight the bee-eater is graceful and acrobatic. It flutters its wings rapidly, often with pauses during which the wings are momentarily folded, then opened and fluttered again. This undulating flight is interspersed with graceful glides. The bird wheels like a swallow in pursuit of flying insects, which it frequently attacks all day long from a single perch high up on a forest-edge tree, on a bush or even on a low rock. But many species hawk insects over the canopy of pure forest. The insect prey is captured with an audible snap and carried back to be hammered violently on the perch, then swallowed whole. Bee-eaters habitually emit a trill in flight, and in the nonbreeding season many species gather in sleeping roosts, to which they sometimes fly long distances. Such havens may contain as many as 300 birds. During the breeding season both parents often spend the night in the ground tunnel; they always enter it by flying straight into it, although the hole is only slightly larger than their bodies.

The Square-tailed Bee-eaters of Africa, of which there are eight species, are among the smallest and most primitive. They do not have elongated plumes in the tail. One of the more beautiful is the Red-throated Bee-eater (*Melittophagus bulocki*), which is about eight inches long and is yellowish green with a chestnut collar, a blue-black mask, a glossy, geranium-red throat and a navy-blue abdomen. Like all bee-eaters, it sits upright with head drawn in and the tail frequently swinging spasmodically like a small pendulum.

The Swallow-tailed Bee-eater (*Dicrocercus hirundineus*), a nine-inch bird with a deeply forked tail, has the throat lemon yellow, a black mask, a glossy green body and an opalescent rump. This species occurs in Africa south of the Sahara, where it lives in dry upland savannas.

The Bearded Red-breasted Bee-eater (*Nyctiornis amicta*) of Malaysia is about a foot long and is the most unusual of its family. Its parrot-green body is decorated with a purplish pink forecrown and a long orange-pink throat and chest bib. This species has the habit of raising the glowing crown feathers while delivering its unusually harsh *kah-kah-kah-kah,* at the same time jumping and turning.

The widest-ranging genus is *Merops,* which extends from Europe and Africa to Asia, the Philippines, Australia, New Guinea and the Solomon Islands. There are ten species, three of which are reddish pink below. Representative of these is the Chestnut-headed Bee-eater (*Merops viridis*) of China, the Philippines and Malaysia, which is 11 inches long, including the elongated twin tail feathers, and has the head and back dark chestnut, the cheeks, rump and tail blue, and the underparts aqua green.

Another characteristic species is the Green-headed Bee-eater (*M. philippinus*), which is slightly larger. It is duller above, with a whitish chin and a chestnut throat. The body is brownish green. This abundant species ranges over India, Burma, the warmer parts of China, Malaysia, the Philippines and New Guinea.

In Australia is found the Red-eyed Rainbow Bee-eater (*M. ornatus*), which is chiefly yellowish green washed with pale blue on the lower back and cheeks. It has an orange-yellow chin, a chestnut nape and a black spot on the neck. In the southern winter this species migrates north to such islands as Bali, Celebes and New Guinea, near the equator. It has been reported that it uses a small stick held firmly in the bill as an aid in drilling its nest burrow.

Bee-eaters, although ground nesters, are parasitized by at least two species of honey-guides.

Rollers (*Coraciidae*)

As aerial acrobats, rollers rival tumbler pigeons. They seek—particularly in the breeding season—to attract attention by zigzagging, rolling and twisting, and often by rocketing upward with the wings closed and then down almost to the ground, screaming loudly. Not all species are so active, but all fly strongly on painted wings flashing a brilliant blue.

Rollers (see Plate 106) are solidly built, jay-like birds with stout, hooked bills, relatively large heads, the third and fourth toes united and the sexes usually almost alike. Their headquarters is in Africa but some species occur in the Indo-Malayan and Australian region. Vagrants reach as far north as Finland and Iceland. They are related to the hoopoes, kingfishers and motmots but are much more quarrelsome. When cornered they will attack a dog, and boys and men climbing to their nests are favorite targets. In the courtship season males sometimes become locked in aerial combat and fall to the ground.

In hunting food rollers sit fairly upright, the head hunched slightly and the tail jerking slowly up and down. Their favorite perches are limbs protruding from the crown of the forest and exposed wires. Many species capture grasshoppers, winged ants, moths, butterflies and, more rarely, small birds in midair, carry them back to a perch, stun them and then swallow them head first. Sometimes they join hawks and other birds to hunt in flocks in the vicinity of grass fires, making quick work of insects flushed by the smoke. Other species hunt from exposed perches like hawks, watching quietly for prey, then suddenly pouncing on locusts, crickets, beetles, small lizards, frogs and mice on the ground. Some hunt over open country, some over the forest canopy, but all are arboreal.

Rollers nest in cavities and crevices in trees, ant hills and mud walls, and some appropriate nests from other birds, particularly woodpeckers and starlings. Sometimes the holes are enlarged by the rollers, and meager amounts of grass, straw, rootlets and feathers may be added. Usually, however, the eggs are laid on the bare floor of the cavity. From two to five white, oval and fairly glossy eggs are deposited, depending on the species. The male and female take turns incubating, and both participate in rearing the young. Incubation requires 17 to 19 days, and the young do not fly for another 27 days or so. They are hatched blind and naked but soon develop tracts of spinelike quills, which in reality are feathers tightly sheathed in waxy capsules. As in the kingfishers and bee-eaters, the containers fall away just before the bird is due to leave the nest.

The calls of rollers are harsh and rasping. Dr. James P. Chapin describes one as a rasping *kak-k-k-k-k;* others have been described as *racker racker racker.*

The European Roller (*Coracias garrulus*) of Central Europe east to Kashmir and south in winter to South Africa is a 12-inch, jaylike bird with a swollen bill, azure body plumage, a chestnut back and rich blue wings.

The Lilac-chested Roller (*Coracias caudatus*) of Somaliland and East Africa south to Angola is extremely quarrelsome and Dr. Chapin reports that it sometimes captures small birds and even snakes. It is about 15 inches long, with a deeply forked blue tail, a chestnut brown back and the throat, face, chest and upper abdomen bright lilac.

The Broad-mouthed Dollarbird (*Eurystomus orientalis*), so named for a silvery speculum the size of a dollar in its wings, enjoys a vast range in Malaysia and the Australian region. In many areas it is highly migratory, wintering near the equator and fanning out north and south to breed. This species has been seen to eject mynah birds from nests in tree cavities and appropriate the hollows for itself. In the New Guinea region it habitually perches on sentinel trees either alone or with fruit pigeons and crested swifts, but apparently never with other dollar-birds. It generally sits perfectly still for many minutes, but during the early morning and late evening it hunts actively, often flying in company with bats.

Ground Rollers
(*Brachypteraciidae*)

Little known and elusive, the ground rollers, of which there are five species, are confined to the island of Madagascar. Some zoologists think they are aberrant members of the true roller family; others place them, as we do, in a family of their own.

Like true rollers, the ground rollers become very active at dusk, but unlike them, they continue their hunting into the night. Ground rollers have largely given up their arboreal habits but they still wear the highly colorful and shining plumage of their diurnal relatives. Structurally they differ from other rollers in having the breastbone notched and the pelvis much broader, and by having the legs longer and heavier and the wings shorter and more rounded.

Usually found alone or in pairs, ground rollers are wary and difficult to observe. Dr. A. L. Rand reported of the Short-legged Ground Roller (*Brachypteracias leptosomus*)—a yellow-green jay-sized bird with generally white-barred underparts—that it was to be found on the forest floor in heavy damp woodlands. In escaping it flushed instead of running but its flights were short. Autopsies revealed that its food included small snakes, chameleons, beetles, caterpillars and other invertebrates.

Another species, the Scaled Ground Roller (*B. squamigera*), had been eating only insects and spiders. The most beautiful of the species, the Pitta-like Ground Roller (*Atelornis pittoides*), was fairly common in the high rain forests. This bird has green upperparts with white wing bars, and its head and tail are washed with blue. Its call is a soft *kook.* Autopsies disclosed ants, insects, and reptile or amphibian remains. Another species, the Long-tailed Ground Roller (*Uratelornis chimaera*), a graceful, ground-loving inhabitant of bushy coastal grasslands, had been eating beetles. Natives reported that it nested in holes in the ground. Other records indicate that ground rollers lay white eggs.

Cuckoo-roller
(*Leptosomatidae*)

Among the wonderfully odd animals found only on Madagascar and its satellite islands is the sole surviving species of a family known as the Cuckoo-rollers. This bird is remarkable for a number of peculiarities that set it apart from the true rollers, from which stock it probably evolved in its isolation on Madagascar, Grand Comoro, Mayotte and the Anouan Islands.

In body conformation and in its spectacular aerial maneuvers the Cuckoo-roller is similar to the true rollers. However, it is markedly different in plumage, being distinguished by the metallic colors of its dress; it also displays much difference in the coloration and pattern of the sexes, whereas in the true rollers the sexes are similar. The Cuckoo-roller also differs by having well-developed powder downs on the sides of the rump (as in certain of the frog-mouths) and a reversible fourth toe. Furthermore, the feathers of the lores grow forward in large tufts that overhang and hide the base of the bill, the nostrils are placed farther out on the maxilla, and there are minor differences in the structure of the voice chamber and in the breastbone.

Much like the true rollers the Cuckoo-roller has been observed to fly erratically and then rocket nearly vertically into the air, arc over and dive and tumble almost straight down close to the forest crown, screaming all the while like a hawk. These dives are reported to be executed in special areas and may be accompanied by calls from another Cuckoo-roller perched in the trees nearby.

Cuckoo-rollers are purely tree-dwelling birds that probably feed almost entirely on insects taken in flight. At times they gather in small bands, and when one is shot the others remain in the vicinity

Hoopoe (*Upupa epops*)

GEORG SCHÜTZENHOFER: BAVARIA VERLAG

complaining and are easily killed by the indiscriminate hunter. The Cuckoo-roller (*Leptosomus discolor*) is 16 inches in length. The male is glossy green above, with a burnished texture to the feathers of the back and tail. Below, it is gray to white on the abdomen and the under-tail coverts. Its mate is generally brownish and has a dark head and indistinct glossy reflections of dull copper. Unlike the male, it is heavily barred below and irregularly spotted above with brown and black.

Hoopoe (*Upupidae*)

The Hoopoe (*Upupa epops*), sole member of its family, is a close relative of the hornbill, though very different from it in appearance. Highly orna-mented, fawn-colored, zebra-backed, with a tall fan-like crest and a gracefully curved bill like that of a snipe, the Hoopoe, once seen, is never forgotten. Usu-ally the impression it makes is enhanced by its fear-lessness, since it permits humans to approach very close to it. A foot-long, largely terrestrial bird, it frequents all manner of open and partially open areas from semideserts to bushy savannas, and even city parks and surburban lawns throughout the warmer parts of the Old World.

Some of the races are migratory, wandering in summer as far into the Palearctic Region as Iceland and Japan. Normally it breeds only as far north as Middle Europe, but there are breeding records from England, Sweden and even Finland. Other popu-lations are resident in Africa, Madagascar, India, Ceylon and Malaya.

The Hoopoe's call is a resounding *hoo-hoo-hoo*. In calling, the bird puffs out its neck feathers and, if giving the call on the ground, emits three low-keyed notes while driving its bill sharply into the earth. If calling from a perch, however, it delivers three higher-pitched notes while snapping its head in the air. Thus the action of hammering the bill into the ground lowers the pitch.

Another interesting adaptation is that of the fe-male Hoopoe, which when brooding develops a spe-cial oil gland at the base of the tail. This she can use to defend herself and the nest by spraying a musky, blackish brown liquid. She apparently relies so com-pletely upon the secretion's repellent quality that she can be taken by hand if one can stand the odor.

The Hoopoe feeds on worms, caterpillars, ant lions, spiders, beetles, crickets and a wide variety of other invertebrates, their grubs and larvae, probing the earth with its bill to obtain these morsels. While drilling, it tightly folds its long fanlike crest back-ward from the crown like a second bill. When the bird is alarmed, the crest flashes forward over the bill, the Hoopoe emits a chattering sound and either runs like a quail or flies off with bursts of wing-flutterings that make it undulate like a woodpecker.

In flight, the white rump and the black-and-white zebra stripes flash vividly.

Hoopoes have short legs, fully separated toes and short square tails. They hunt alone or in pairs during the breeding season but at other seasons of the year sometimes travel in small groups. The nest is a cavity in a tree, house or ant hill or even occasionally under a stone on a bank. They do not improve or enlarge the site and ordinarily do not even use a lining, but they do sometimes carry in a few dead leaves or wood chips. Four to eight pale blue or whitish eggs are laid. The female does all of the incubating (in 12 to 15 days), leaving the nest for short periods in the morning and evening. As in the hornbills, she is fed on the nest by the male.

For the first week of the 26 to 32 days that the young remain in the nest after hatching, the male gives food to the female to eat or to feed to the nestlings. After that he feeds the young himself. At hatching the nestlings are naked, but very soon they develop a covering of down and sharp blue quills. Soon they are able to raise the crest and elevate the tail like young hornbills. Upon emerging from the nest they are colored like the adults but are somewhat grayer above and streaked below. Their bills do not reach full length for almost a year.

Wood-hoopoes

(Phoeniculidae)

The six species of shy, long-tailed, glossy-plumaged birds comprising this little-known family dwell in tropical and southern Africa. So closely related are these birds to the semiterrestrial Hoopoe that authorities such as Chapin, Mayr and Amadon believe they belong in the same family. However, Wetmore keeps them in a family of their own, pointing out that the wood-hoopoes differ from the Hoopoe in the formation of the nostrils, breastbone and pelvis, as well as in the fact that they are crestless and have long, graduated tails and metallic plumage.

Like the Hoopoe, the wood-hoopoes emit an offensive odor from the oil gland, and, like the Hoopoe and the hornbill (another near relative), the incubating female is extremely loath to desert her eggs or young, remaining on the nest even when closely approached.

Wood-hoopoes are all quite similar, the various species differing chiefly in the length and shape of the bill and in minor aspects of color and pattern. All are tree-loving birds and rarely visit the ground. Some dwell primarily in thick mountain forest; others in bushy savannas. All climb among limbs and trunks in the middle and upper portions of trees and bushes, searching for invertebrates in the crevices of bark. From the stomach contents of collected specimens we know that they feed on beetles, termites, caterpillars, ants, grasshoppers, millipedes, small fruits

and occasionally even spiders. At times as they creep and crawl on nearly vertical surfaces they resemble woodpeckers.

Wood-hoopoes travel in pairs or small parties of about six, moving restlessly through the foliage and calling harshly. One call has been described as a chattering *ch-k-k-k,* whereas that of the Scimitar-bill (*Rhinopomastus cyanomelas*) is said to be a low, whistled *hooi-hooi-hooi.*

The nest is usually placed in a deep natural cavity or in an abandoned woodpecker hole; the female wood-hoopoe performs all the incubation. Two or three greenish or bluish green, slightly pitted eggs are laid. During incubation, and probably during part of the period that the young are on the nest, the male assiduously carries food to his mate.

A spectacular example of the family is the Cuckoo-tailed Wood Hoopoe (*Phoeniculus purpureus*), which ranges through tropical bushy savannas from South Africa north to Angola, Lake Tanganyika and the Sudan. This species reaches 17 inches in length. It is glossy bronze-green splashed with violet, with a long, graduated, white-tipped tail. The bill is longer and more curved in the male. Dr. Chapin has written that just before taking wing this species commonly "executes a see-sawing motion on the bough." He also observes that the young as well as the adults give off the characteristic disgusting odor.

Hornbills (Bucerotidae)

Hornbills have developed a number of surprising specializations, of which the most fascinating is their unique construction of a nest-fort and the imprisonment of the female in it. The 45 species live in the warm parts of Africa, India, Ceylon, Malaysia, the Philippines, the East Indies, New Guinea, the Bismarck Archipelago and the Solomon Islands. All have the bill swollen and ungainly, and in some it is comparatively huge.

Hornbills show their age by folds or carunculations on a large casque that many of the species carry atop the bill; these increase in number as the bird grows older but their function is not known. Another odd characteristic is the development of long eyelashes that give the eye a mammalian look.

Hornbills range in length from 15 to 60 inches, or longer than the largest eagle. Generally speaking, they are clumsy-looking and brownish or black-and-white birds with vividly colored bills. In flight they carry the head straight forward and the feet straight back. In many species the wing beats give off hissing sounds like that of escaping steam; Dr. K. C. Parkes has informed the author that this noise seems to be made by air passing between the bases of the primary wing quills, which, unlike those of most birds, are not covered with wing coverts on the underside. The movements of hornbills in air are porpoise-like and laboring, for they fly with bursts of wing beats interspersed with short glides.

At dusk these birds gather in large roosting areas, to which they move in squadrons and long irregular skeins somewhat like cormorants. At such times their resonant honking, braying and wing-thrashing can be heard for long distances. They live in pairs or in flocks throughout the year.

Most hornbills feed chiefly on fruit and berries, but it is safe to say that as a group they are omnivorous. Some devour the orange-sized fruits of the nux vomica and other species of *Strychnos* trees that abound in the East Indies. Unlike the large parrots and cockatoos, they do not fracture the seeds contained in the lethal fruits and therefore are not poisoned by the strychnine.

Smaller species, such as the White-tailed Hornbill (*Bycanistes sharpii*) of Central Africa, capture insects in flight. The Black Dwarf Hornbill (*Tockus hartlaubi*) of Central Africa feeds almost exclusively on insects such as beetles, caterpillars, grasshoppers, mantises, cicadas, winged termites and winged ants, and even spiders. Other African species feed exclusively on insects, chameleons, shrews, mice, bird eggs and nestlings. Some Indian species have been observed eating blood-sucking lizards and snakes.

Fruit-eating hornbills frequent the larger limbs of trees, stretching out clumsily for fruit and changing limbs by hopping with wings closed. Fruits and berries are deftly tossed into the air and downed, or stowed in the gullet and crop.

As the breeding season approaches, the massive hornbill flocks split into pairs of birds. Attentive males court prospective mates by feeding them. If the pair bond matures, a tall tree with a cavity in the trunk or in a dead limb is selected, the female entering the cavity and occasionally enlarging it somewhat with her bill. She may leave several times during the laying of the white, oval eggs. Presently, however, she settles down for a long stay. Using droppings, matter regurgitated from the stomach and often earth and mud carried to the entrance by her mate, she fashions across the entrance of the cavity a remarkably sturdy barrier, in the center of which she leaves a slit just large enough to permit her bill tip to protrude.

The purpose of this unique structure is probably to protect the female and young from the attacks of such predators as monkeys, squirrels and snakes. Since the outer half of the bill is generally very sharp and saber-like, quick thrusts through the slit that has been left open probably serve as a further deterrent to animals bent on plunder. Even men have been held off by the bill and the brick-hard wall.

Some nests are nearly 100 feet up in huge forest trees; others are lower down and even within a few feet of the ground. Although hornbills are primarily birds of the thick forests, there have developed species that feed in lightly timbered grasslands and two that habitually feed on the ground.

The male feeds the female during the entire time she incubates the eggs; for this he uses food stored in the gullet, which is extracted with a vigorous shaking of the head and caught again in the outer portion of the bill. A Common Gray Hornbill (*Tockus birostris*) has been known to feed his imprisoned mate two dozen figs and a number of other tidbits at a single sitting. The incubation period varies with the species from about 28 to 40 days. Thereafter the male feeds the imprisoned female during part or all of the development period of the young. The fact that the young are often of different sizes suggests that incubation begins with the laying of each egg, as in hawks and owls, and not when the clutch is complete. From one to four or more eggs are laid, depending on the species.

After a minimum of approximately six weeks, but sometimes not for four months, the females of the various species escape from their nests, pounding on the artificial barrier—sometimes for several hours—until they can get out and, dressed in fresh wing and tail feathers, fly off.

All female hornbills replace the flight feathers and probably some or all of the body plumage during their long confinement. The wing feathers seem to be replaced quickly and in regular order. The tail, which in many species is very long and must be cumbersome in the cramped cavity, may be plucked and the feathers replaced more or less simultaneously. The shed feathers form a kind of nest lining. In most respects hornbills are very careful, when voiding, to eject all dirt from the nest, the excrement being shot through the opening with accuracy, even by the young. Within the cavity the female and the young adopt a peculiar stance that involves folding the tail upward against the back.

After breaking out of the nest, the female immediately begins feeding the young and from then on often does most of that work. She is then rather fat in comparison to the male, who during the long period of his mate's confinement has been hard pressed to supply her with food. After the young hatch, the task of feeding them is almost too much for him. As many as 40 feedings per hour have been recorded.

In some species the barrier shielding the nest opening is partially or completely rebuilt after the female has departed, apparently by the unfledged young remaining within, at least in the case of the Crowned Hornbill (*Tockus alboterminatus*) of Africa. After the young have emerged from the nest they indulge in bathing and playing, often with their parents. At dusk, however, they are deserted for the night if they are not strong enough to accompany the parents to their accustomed roosting places.

Hornbills make interesting, clownish pets. At the mealtime of human neighbors they fly in from the surrounding trees, expecting to be fed at the table and audaciously stealing one's food as it is lifted on a spoon. Throughout tropical New Guinea these birds are kept as pets and native travelers deep in the hinterland are often seen with birds following them or being carried on sticks over the shoulder. Such birds are omnivorous, and their ability to catch anything thrown in their general direction, coupled with their pogo-like jumping, is most amusing.

The odd nesting habits of hornbills have led to many superstitions. Because of the imprisoning of the female, in certain areas of Africa the bird is regarded as a symbol of virtue. Dr. James P. Chapin was informed by a native chieftain in Africa that the scarifications required for manhood are cut into young men in a ceremony in which a captive hornbill is present and may sometimes do the biting. In New Guinea the author has many times observed the hornbill used as a totem on the pinnacles of the men's spirit houses and, among the pygmies of the Victor Emanuel Mountains, as a phallic adornment.

For ages the bill of the Helmeted Hornbill (*Rhinoplax vigil*) of Malaysia, the East Indies and Borneo has been much sought after for the making of carvings; it is much harder than that of any of the other hornbills, being as dense as ivory. This material has been in use since at least the fourteenth century, but today the art of carving hornbill "ivory" survives only in Borneo.

The smallest of the African hornbills is the Red-billed Dwarf Hornbill (*Tockus camurus*) of Central Africa, which is about 15 inches long. Its plumage is chiefly brown, with whitish spots above and a clear white belly. The bill is arched and bright red in color. This species devours insects of many kinds and frequents the forest edge, where its mournful calls can be heard for a quarter of a mile. As in all the smaller hornbills, the flight is relatively quiet in comparison to that of the large species.

One of the most spectacular of African species is the Casqued Hornbill (*Bycanistes subcylindricus*), which is found in the mountain forests to altitudes of at least 8500 feet. This bird is about three feet long and has a prominent black-and-white casque. It is generally olivaceous black, with white on the rump

and abdomen, and has much white on the wings and tail. A nest of this fruit-eater, found at 8000 feet on Mount Elgon, was built between two rocks and had contained a single young behind an artificially constructed barrier. The usual nesting place is in tall trees, as in the other hornbills.

The Ground Hornbill (*Bucorvus leadbeateri*) Plate 107) is an exceptionally long-legged bird. It occupies a broad range in the savannas of Africa, where it occurs in pairs or trios. Two eggs are the normal set. This bird is as large as a turkey and has inflatable throat sacs, red in the male and blue in the female. Despite its size, it is not noisy except when rising from the ground. Ground Hornbills are exceedingly wary and the most terrestrial of hornbills. They like short grass, often near burned areas. Their food includes snakes, birds, remains of large animals, small mammals, lizards, frogs, seeds, fruits and even beetles and ants. The nest site varies: hollow logs, stumps, hollow trees, holes in cliffs or crevices between boulders may be used. The females of this species are apparently not sealed into the nest.

The Common Gray Hornbill (*Tockus birostris*) of India is about two feet long and predominantly gray in color. Unlike most of the other hornbills, it lives on bushy and timbered savannas, sometimes even nesting in trees in villages. It has a spikelike, forward-thrusting helmet and light underparts. Its tail is relatively long with a white tip.

Another well-known species, the Malabar Pied Hornbill (*Anthracoceros coronata*), is about three feet long with greenish black upperparts, wings and central tail feathers. It dwells in open woodlands of the Indian region, where it is normally found in noisy parties of as many as twelve. Like all hornbills, it uses the tail as a brace when clinging to a tree trunk under its nest hole.

The Helmeted Hornbill (*Rhinoplax vigil*), with its length of nearly five feet, is the longest member of the family. It is dark brown and has a black crest and a naked red throat. Its outstanding feature is the length of the central tail feathers, which are pale brown and have white tips with black subterminal bars. The casque is solid ivory.

Another very large species is the Rhinoceros Hornbill (*Buceros rhinoceros*), the commonest of the family in Malaya. As its name implies, it has an upcurved casque that is very prominent and red in color. Otherwise it is black and has a white rump and abdomen. The wings of this species produce a sound like that of a chugging steam locomotive.

The Papuan Hornbill (*Aceros plicatus*), which is found from the Moluccas and New Guinea to the Bismarck Archipelago and the Solomon Islands, is remarkable for the differences in the coloration of the sexes. The female is solid black, with a whitish bill of large dimensions. The male has the head, neck and upper chest pale reddish brown. Adult males are reported to wear four to eight folds or carunculations on the top of the bill, whereas adult females have

Ground Hornbill (*Bucorvus leadbeateri*)

only four to six. The number increases with age; yearlings have only two to three folds, and immatures none or only one.

PICIFORMES

Jacamars (*Galbulidae*)

Jacamars are slender birds ranging from the size of a sparrow to that of a jay and dwelling in the tropics from southern Mexico to Argentina. Some 14 species are known. Many are jewel-like, with the plumage of the back and chest brilliantly burnished with golden bronze and fiery red; in fact, many resemble oversize hummingbirds. But they are related to the puffbirds, the barbets, the toucans and the woodpeckers. Like all of these, they are hole nesters, drilling cavities in banks and laying usually two white eggs. The author has seen a pair in Venezuela attacking swallows that flew near their nest hole.

Jacamars have the bill long and pointed and are extremely adept at hawking for flying insects. They hunt from special perches, often sitting within a few inches of each other while awaiting prey. When a butterfly or other insect appears, they dart out, capture it in the bill, and then stun it by battering it on the perch before swallowing it. The hunting perches are often near vertical banks of road or stream edges. These are birds of open country, found on the forest edge and along the margins of streams.

Jacamars have the foot relatively small and weak, with the fourth toe directed backward in a line with the first one. One species has lost the rear or first toe, more or less as have some of the woodpeckers. Unlike their close relatives, the puffbirds, the jacamars have an aftershaft—a small second or twin plume growing from the same shaft as the main one.

The common names of many of the jacamars serve to identify a number of species. For example, one which ranges widely throughout the Amazon region is known as the White-eared Jacamar (*Galbalcyrhynchus leucotis*). A long, heavy, whitish bill, together with a very short tail, give it a top-heavy appearance. The plumage of back and underparts is a rich chestnut brown, with a white patch behind the eye. Then there are four small species belonging to the genus *Brachygalba* which extend from Panama south to Peru and Bolivia. They are no larger than a sparrow in body size, but the long, sharp bill adds as much as two inches to the total length. Among the least colorful of the jacamars, they are clad chiefly in dark brown and white, although wings and tail are somewhat iridescent. In southeastern Brazil occurs the Three-toed Jacamar (*Jacamaralcyon tridactyla*). This sooty green, brown-headed little species has two toes directed forward and only one backward, whereas all other jacamars have two of the latter. Almost throughout tropical South America and often to considerable altitudes are found eight closely related species belonging to the genus *Galbula*. One is the Rufous-tailed Jacamar (*Galbula ruficauda;* Plate 108), which is very common. The male is flashing greenish bronze on back and chest, with a white throat; the female is similar except that the throat is puffy. Dr. Alexander Skutch, who studied it in Central America, found that the female did more digging of the nest burrow than the male, that the male fed the female frequently, and that in incubation, brooding and care of the young, the male did about as much as the female. However, the female did all the night work at the nest.

Northern South America is the home of the Paradise Jacamar (*G. dea*), which has a dark brown crown, a white throat, and a white patch on each flank. The remainder of the plumage is a striking glossy blue-black. The tail is particularly elongated and slender, the central tail feathers being as long as seven inches.

Finally, there is the Broad-billed Jacamar (*Jacamerops aurea*) which ranges from Costa Rica to Brazil. It is the largest member of the family, over a foot in length, with a brilliantly metallic gold and green head, back, wing and tail, all reminiscent of the splendor of the Quetzal.

Puffbirds (*Bucconidae*)

Puffbirds are neotropical birds (there are 32 species) that capture all of their food on the wing. Except in flight, they appear stolid and unwary, and in Brazil their local name means "Silly John." This name and their reputation for stupidity apparently stem from the fact that they usually hunt from exposed perches, where pairs congregate in small groups and often refuse to fly more than a short distance, even when one of the group is shot. They range from the size of a sparrow to that of a jay. In hunting they dive after flying insects and have been known to hunt from the same perches for months and even years.

The head of the puffbird is usually large and the plumage that envelops the neck and head is loose and easily puffed out, thus adding appreciably to the impression of size—hence the common name of the family. Unlike their relatives the jacamars, they have the plumage devoid of the aftershaft, and many have the bill tipped with a sharp hook. Another characteristic is their generally somber coloration, in contrast to the metallic plumage of jacamars. In Colombia the Mustached Soft-wing Puffbird (*Malocoptila mystacalis*) nests in an earth bank in heavy forest as much as 6000 feet above sea level. One nest of this species was two feet deep in a roadside bank, and the nest chamber was lined with twigs and dead leaves.

The smallest puffbird is the Lance-billed Monklet (*Micromonacha lanceolata*), which resembles a small thrush with its dark brown upperparts and light, heavily spotted underparts. This species is found only in the lower and middle tier of deep forest between Costa Rica and Amazonia. The graceful Swallow-winged Puffbird (*Chelidoptera tenebrosa*), a six-inch bird, frequents the edge of the forest. Above, it is sooty black with a white rump; below, it is dark grayish black with a chestnut lower abdomen. As in all puffbirds, both sexes are similarly colored. This is one of the species that nests in earthen banks. Apparently two glossy white eggs comprise the set.

The Black-collared Puffbird (*Bucco capensis*) is one of four similar species that occur in northern South America. All have the head very large and kingfisher-like. The back is dark reddish brown and a prominent blackish band encircles the entire body at the chest. Otherwise this species has the throat white and the head and tail chestnut with fine black barring. The White-necked Puffbird (*Notharcus macrorhynchus*) of Middle and South America belongs to a group of four similar species. It is nine inches long and mostly blackish above and on the chest, but has the forehead, throat, sides of neck and abdomen white.

The Barred Puffbird (*Nystalus radiatus*) of Panama and Northwestern South America is more or less typical of a cluster of four species, all of which have bright chestnut throats and black mustaches. Six closely related species extending from Panama to Argentina are among the smallest of the Puffbirds. The Red-capped Nunlet (*Nonnula ruficapilla*) of Amazonia, which is typical of these, is six inches long and has a deep chestnut crown, an olive-brown back and a gray back collar. Below it is buffy brown with rich gray sides.

Barbets (*Capitonidae*)

In the tropics of the New and Old Worlds, exclusive of the Australian region, there occurs a family of stocky birds called barbets. They have not exactly endeared themselves to man, for their ventriloquial anvil knocks and clinks, endlessly repetitious, can become quite unbearable on a hot day.

Related to the toucans and honey-guides, they are most abundant in Africa. Of the 76 species known, only 12 are found in the New World. All barbets have the coarse look of rather unspecialized birds despite their bright coloration. They range from the size of a sparrow to that of a large jay. They have heavy bills, short legs, yoked (zygodactyle) toes and fine hairlike bristles surrounding the relatively large head. These suggested the name *barbu* (bearded) to the French ornithologist Brisson, and from this is derived the popular name. Barbets eat fruit, chiefly wild figs, pawpaws, guavas and berries, but termites, green mantises, geckos and occasionally even eggs of other birds are eaten.

Barbets excavate their nest holes in trees or stumps or in the ground. Such cavities may have several entrances and are the product of about ten days of work by both sexes. The woodpecker-like openings are just large enough to admit the birds. Inside, the cavity turns downward and may extend for several feet to the egg chamber. The entrance of a tree nest is usually drilled on the underside of a sloping limb. In cutting the hole the birds suspend themselves and patiently drill the usually spongy wood with their dull bills. The white, ovoid eggs, which range from two to five, are deposited on a few wood chips.

In the Golden-rumped Tinker-bird (*Pogoniulus bilineatus*) Dr. Van Someren found that incubation required 12 days and was performed by both sexes, and that the nesting period lasted between 18 and 20 days. The young are of different sizes in some of the species, indicating that incubation starts with the laying of the first egg. The nestlings acquire the plumage pattern of the adults, which are dressed almost alike, and when in the nest fold the tail against the back like young woodpeckers, kingfishers, hornbills and toucans. They are fed by both parents and are vigorously defended against predators.

However, some of the African species are parasitized with ease by honey-guides. So small is the nest cavity that even after the chick honey-guide has killed and disposed of the legitimate offspring the home is sometimes too tiny to accommodate the out-sized foundling. One of Dr. Van Someren's most interesting observations was of a Golden-rumped Tinker-bird which, when the lethal foundling grew too large for the cavity, enlarged it to accommodate her monstrous charge. (Also see the Honey-guides for an unusual system of attack used to lure the barbets from their nests.)

Barbets hop slowly and deliberately among the highest limbs of tall trees in sparsely timbered grasslands or along the forest edge. In such situations the bright green plumage that many species wear serves as fine camouflage. In flight most barbets fly rather like woodpeckers, bounding and thrashing through the air, but some fly straight and directly.

The White-headed Barbet (*Lybius leucocephalus*) belongs to an African genus of 12 species. Like all its relatives, it is wasteful of food, dropping much more than it eats. Its favorite food is the pulp of fruits and figs. Dr. Van Someren noted that the young in one nest were fed by no less than five adults. This behavior is probably correlated with the gregarious habits of the species, which are best illustrated by the fact that as many as six have been found sleeping together in a single tree cavity. The Pied Barbet, which resembles a small hornbill, is about six inches long and has a swollen black bill. The anterior part of its body to the shoulders and chest is white and the remainder is generally dark brownish black with pale flecking.

The Red-fronted Barbet (*Tricholaema diadematum*), representing an African genus of six species, is a bird of open acacia parks, where it feeds on insects as well as fruits, being very fond of termites and ants. The latter are obtained by breaking open the earth tunnels the ants build and devouring the ants as they almost squirt out of the broken pipes. This species is sparrow-sized and has a scarlet forehead and yellow eyebrows, dark upperparts strongly flecked with pale yellow, and yellowish white underparts.

Distributed throughout the warmer parts of India, Ceylon, the Philippines, China and Malaysia is the Coppersmith or Crimson-breasted Barbet (*Megalaima haemacephala*), which is representative of some 23 species. This six-inch green bird with bright red and yellow about the head is named for the anvil-like quality of its voice. It frequents tall trees, even those of villages and towns, to feed on fruit and to nest, using the same cavity over and over again and laying three to four eggs. Another Asiatic species is the Blue-throated Barbet (*M. asiatica;* Plate 113), which is nine inches long and leaf green with blue, scarlet and black on the head. This bird never comes to the ground, although it seems unafraid of man, nesting over his houses in India. One of the most handsome is the Great Himalayan Barbet (*M. virens*), which is more than a foot long and which lives as high as 8000 feet in the Himalayas. It is generally green with red undertail coverts. Its mournful cry *pi-o-o* is repeated almost every other second for long periods, with the female often duetting each fourth note in near perfect cadence. The habit of duetting, the two sexes alternating, is widespread among barbets.

In the New World barbets are much less abundant. A few examples are the Red-headed Barbet (*Eubucco bourcierii*), a green bird six inches long which has much yellow on the chest and abdomen, and scarlet covering the chest, neck and head. In the female the throat is largely yellow. This species represents a group of three species extending from Costa Rica to Brazil. Between Panama and Brazil are found seven closely related species, typified by the Spot-crowned Barbet (*Capito maculicoronatus*), also a six-inch bird. In this species the male is black above with an irregular white crown, a white breast ringed with a yellow collar, and black and red in the flanks. In the female the throat and chest are solid black.

Among the smallest barbets in the New World are the two species of a group ranging from Costa Rica to Brazil. One of these, the Prong-billed Barbet (*Semnornis frantzii*) is a jaunty, almost toucan-like bird, of the high mountains of Costa Rica south to Panama. Dr. Alexander Skutch found that both parents incubated and fed the young in this species. The other is the Toucan Barbet (*S. ramphastinus*), shown in Plate 112.

Toucans (*Ramphastidae*)

Among the most amusing and easily recognizable of all birds are the colorful toucans, 37 species of which dwell in forests from Mexico to Argentina. Apparently most nearly related to barbets and woodpeckers, they have the bill greatly swollen and elongated. In some species it is almost as bulky and as long as the bird that carries it. In this the toucans are unlike any birds in the world except possibly the Old World hornbills, from which they differ most noticeably by lacking any trace of a protuberance or casque over the bill.

One of the most perplexing questions concerning both hornbills and toucans is the purpose of their huge bills. In most if not all birds, the bill is purely and simply a specialized instrument for feeding, and presumably this should hold true for these birds as well. But the oversize appendages of the toucans are so colorful that they resemble ornaments, and it has been suggested that they may have a function in courtship, or may serve as recognition characters in some species that have virtually identical plumage but differently colored bills. Nevertheless, in the author's opinion the bill is primarily a food-getting device. This seems apparent from an examination of its structure. It is enormous and largely filled with air. The inner part is a mass of giant cellular structures, and the outer shell is as thin as the shell of a large lobster claw. And, despite its lightness and great length, it is very strong, with a strength imparted by the "skin" just as is the case in animals with exoskeletons and also in modern aircraft. In use, the toucan's huge bill with its hooked tip serves as a firm, strong tool for tearing off fruits and berries. Once shorn free, these are raised in the tip of the bill, then dropped into the gullet and swallowed directly if small, or pulled apart with the sharp notched edges of the bill if large. In drinking, the toucan immerses the bill and then tips the head far back, as do most birds. The tongue of many toucans is nearly six inches long—a flat, spear-shaped structure with lateral edges that are sharp, corrugated, and edged with feathery tissues near the tip. It is not impossible that the tongue serves as an aid to mastication. But these birds are reported to regurgitate berries into the bill and reswallow them.

Toucans are found in the warmer parts of America from sea level to about 10,000 feet in the Andes. They are most numerous in the forests of Amazonia, where many species live a noisy, gregarious life in the treetops, feeding chiefly on fruits and berries and on anything they can steal from other birds, such as their eggs or young. In their method of traveling and then of posting sentinels as they feed in groups, some of the species rival crows. The members of such flocks hop nimbly about on the uppermost limbs of the trees, reaching far out for fruit from precarious perches and devouring any small reptile, amphibian or bird that they happen to encounter. They may even enter the holes of barbets to steal the young.

The calls of toucans ring through the woodlands for distances of half a mile. These consist chiefly of penetrating buglings delivered as the head is thrown violently upward and the bill opened. Whenever toucans encounter a bird of prey, they gather about it in a jeering band. This performance seems to disconcert and drive off the foe. Toucans roost in trees and nest in holes. An adaptation for sleeping in holes is the folding of the tail against the back in sleep, a peculiar action also found in other hole-nesting birds such as hornbills and kingfishers. It is made possible by special articulation of the tail bones, as a result of which the tail can be flipped up against the back as rapidly as a box lid is closed. In sleep the long bill is turned and laid against the back, with its hook pushed down between the wing and the body.

Toucans have ten primaries in their rounded wings. They fly straight and noisily, thrashing the air somewhat in the manner of hornbills but not nearly so loudly. All toucans lay one to four slightly glossy white eggs. Recent studies by Josselyn Van Tyne and Alexander Skutch indicate that both parents share the duties of incubation, brooding and feeding the young. During incubation only one parent is present in the nest hole at night, but at other periods both of them squeeze in to sleep with their offspring. The incubation period of sixteen days is relatively short when compared with the long nesting period.

Toucans are very colorful birds, with much red, yellow, blue, black and orange in the plumage. These often appear as spots or vividly patterned arrangements, often near or on the large bill. In view of the treetop feeding habitat of the toucan, it would seem that these bright spots comprise a mechanism both for defense and for feeding. They tend to cause the bird, chiefly the bill, to disappear when among colorful fruits and flowers. Such camouflage is protective, and it probably assists in the capture of lizards, frogs and other small arboreal creatures.

Toucans make excellent pets, for they quickly become tame and make themselves perfectly at home, drinking from water glasses and shuffling about on dining tables to eat from one's plate or lips, and indeed sometimes becoming as demanding of one's attention as a spoiled dog.

One of the smaller species is the Emerald Toucan (*Aulacorhynchus prasinus*), which is about a foot long and generally bright apple-green, with a white throat and an emerald-green back. This Central American bird belongs to a genus of seven species that ranges widely along the Andean chain. Generally these "toucanets" have the bill black and yellow and more compact than those of most toucans. They are mountain species that keep to the "cloud forests" and are good mimics.

Among the most colorful and common toucans are the aracaris, of which the Collared Aracari (*Pteroglossus torquatus*) of Middle America is a good example. This species reaches 16 inches in length. It is glossy black and deep green above and on the throat, and pale yellowish below with a vivid wash of scarlet on the chest and abdomen. The bill is patterned in yellow and black. Dr. Skutch, who studied this species in Panama, found six birds gathered together to sleep in a hollow branch high up in the forests of Barro Colorado Island. Later their sleeping place was used for nesting by one pair, and three young birds were raised in it. Altogether there are eleven species of aracaris, ranging from Mexico to Argentina, chiefly in the tropical forests.

Among other Panamanian toucans that are common on Barro Colorado Island is the Chestnut-mandibled or Swainson's Toucan (*Ramphastos swainsoni*) which has a penetrating call that Eugene Eisenmann describes as a loud, yelping, gull-like *kee-you, tedick-tedick-tedick.*

The Keel-billed Toucan (*Ramphastos sulfuratus;* Plate 110) is also a resident of the tropical forests of Middle America. This bird, which reaches 20 inches in length, is one of eleven species of large-billed forms, some of which reach two feet in length and are the birds that one generally sees in zoos and in pictures of the family. The present species is mainly black with vivid lemon yellow on the throat, sides of neck, and upper chest. It has a bright scarlet spot at the base of the back, the long bill is black, orange, yellow and red, and at the base of the tail it has a vivid white spot that is particularly prominent in flight. Another somewhat similar species is the Ariel Toucan (*R. ariel;* Plate 111).

The so-called hill toucans, which live in the Andes and the mountains of southern Brazil, are less colorful. An example is the Laminated Hill Toucan (*Andigena laminirostris*) of Ecuador and Peru, which is blue-gray and has plates growing from the sides of the bill. The most aberrant and colorful of the family is the Curl-crested Toucan (*Pteroglossus beauharnaesii*) of upper Amazonia. This large, colorful toucan has an aberrant crest that appears to be composed of strips of curled isinglass.

Honey-guides (*Indicatoridae*)

One of the tallest tales in the animal kingdom involves the hunting partnership between certain honey-guides and native hunters in Africa. So unusual is the mutually profitable symbiotic relationship that naturalists long refused to credit it.

But first, let us review these relatives of woodpeckers and barbets, which make their home principally in Africa but occur also in southern Asia, Malaya, Sumatra and Borneo. The eleven species comprising the family Indicatoridae are generally inconspicuous birds ranging in size from about that of our smallest sparrow to about that of a starling. Above, the plumage is predominantly gray to dull green or yellowish green. The tail is usually dark brown with fairly large areas of white in the outer series of feathers. In some, the females differ from the males in being less richly colored and in having the throat gray instead of dark (*Indicator indicator*), or in lacking the yellow shoulders that mark many of the larger males. Below, honey-guides are usually pale gray to dark gray, but the Spotted Honey-guide (*I. maculatus*) of Africa bears vivid yellow spots on its underparts, and the Orange-rumped Honey-guide (*I. xanthonotus*) of the Himalayan forests has stripes of sooty black. It also has the forehead, lower cheeks and upper throat strongly washed with bright yellow, and carries a large bright orange-yellow spot on the rump. The only species that has developed ornamental plumes is the Lyre-tailed Honey-guide of Africa (*Melichneutes robustus*). This widespread species, which sports blackish central tail feathers that are elongated and lyre-shaped, is mysteriously rare in collections. Dr. Chapin, one of the few naturalists who have seen it, says he believes it produces a queer, intermittent whining sound over the forest crown. The shape of its tail may play a part in producing this.

Structurally, honey-guides are an odd assemblage. In some the bill is small, slender and almost warbler-like; in others it is curved like that of a small wren; but in the majority it is stocky and strong. All have very tough skins and nine primaries, and lay their white eggs in the tree-hole nests of other birds. All probably feed on insects, and some species capture these in the manner of flycatchers, flying out from favorite perches to "hawk" their prey in flight. All, or nearly all, capture bees and have an insatiable hunger for beeswax. In fact, in 1956 it was found that a hitherto unknown organism, *Micrococcus cero-lyticus,* in the stomach of the African Lesser Honey-guide was involved in the digestion of the bird's beeswax diet.

This appetite has also given rise to the bird's unique relation to man. Over the ages the Greater Honey-guide (*I. indicator*) has developed so complex a way of enlisting the help of human hunting partners that is much harder to understand as a purely instinctive habit—which it is—than as a manifestation of rational deduction.

What happens is that a hunter, craving for sweets, decides to search for a wild bees' nest—of which there are many in Africa in termite nests, trees or hollowed-out logs hung in trees by native apiarists. But the hunter does not look for a bees' nest; instead, he listens for the call of a Greater Honey-guide. In all likelihood the bird finds him first and quickly begins its brazen solicitations. Its rasping, churring chatter will be heard often but the bird seen only fleetingly. The hunter knows from long experience that *Indicator* will guide him to the nearest bees' nest it can find, and that, if he should stray, it may follow him for as much as five miles, chattering all the while and endeavoring to lead him back to the trail. The bird does not attempt to lure him to a nest it has discovered earlier, and therefore its trail may

Greater Honey-guide (*Indicator indicator*)

be erratic, sometimes even leading to a dead snake or other form of carrion. According to Dr. Herbert Friedmann, an authority on the family and author of *The Honey-guide,* a hunter rarely has to follow a bird for more than half an hour. When it settles on an upper limb or flies silently in little circles, usually returning to the same perch, the hunter knows the hive is close at hand. Almost invariably he soon finds a small hole through which a constant stream of bees enter and depart. This he can break or cut open, and its contents—up to fifteen pounds of honey—he can remove with one arm while shielding himself with a smoking faggot. The hunter rewards the honey-guide with a portion of the loot. Thus the bird, although equipped with only a small bill with which it could not possibly reach the food it desires, nevertheless achieves its goal with an extraordinary demonstration of instinctive behavior.

In the more primitive parts of Africa, the natives revere and protect the two species that guide men— the Greater Honey-guide and the Scaly-throated Honey-guide (*I. variegatus*)—even to the extent of cutting off the ears of anyone discovered killing them. Furthermore, certain tribes such as the Wandorobos of Kenya try always to follow a honey-guide when it solicits their help, believing that if they do not, the gods who sent it will be offended.

These deep-seated human customs indicate a long and mutually advantageous association between men and honey-guides. Nevertheless, experts believe that the birds' unique behavior evolved long before men came into the picture and that the original part- ner was, as it still is, a Ratel or Honey Badger. This animal, although no larger than a wildcat, has ex- tremely powerful legs and claws and an equally strong appetite for honey and bee grubs. The theory is that an ancient partnership between bird and badger was developed into a threesome when primitive man dis- covered the secret of their teamwork.

Another unique capacity of honey-guides, which might lead to discoveries vastly more beneficial to man, is their ability to digest wax. This substance is virtually indigestible and, aside from the larvae of a few insects, is not employed as a source of nourish- ment by any other animal. Yet honey-guides extract nourishment from it. Indeed, as long ago as the six- teenth century a Dominican missionary in Mozam- bique called attention to this craving by reporting that little birds entered his church and pilfered wax from altar candles.

Still another remarkable facet, their parasitic nesting habits, distinguishes honey-guides from all but a very few of the world's birds. In fact, only the African whydahs, many species of cuckoos, some of the New World cowbirds and the Black-headed Duck of South America have similar habits. In this be- havior the female honey-guide somehow contrives to sneak into the nest holes of relatives, the barbets and woodpeckers, and those of certain starlings. There she lays an egg which hatches more quickly than that of the legitimate offspring. When the chick emerges it is equipped with needle-sharp rapier tips on its upper and lower mandibles. With these it assassinates its nest mates, thus insuring an adequate food supply from its foster parents. Shortly thereafter—usually in about ten days—the lethal bill tips drop off.

Woodpeckers, Wrynecks and Piculets (*Picidae*)

The well-known woodpeckers, of which there are 210 species ranging to every wooded area of the world except Madagascar, the Australian region and many islands of Oceania, attract man's attention by their drilling and their sometimes violent drumming. Related to the jacamar-barbet-toucan group, they are also hole-nesting birds that lay glossy white eggs. But, unlike any of the former, they are unique in having the tongue elongated, the bill shaped like a chisel and the tail generally stiff and spine-tipped.

The family Picidae consists of three main groups, the wrynecks with two species occurring in the Old World, the piculets with 29 species occurring in the tropical forests of the New and the Old World, and the familiar woodpeckers, of which there are about 179 species.

All groups have the fourth toe turned backward beside the hallux, but the hallux itself is sometimes lacking, as in the three-toed woodpeckers (*Picoïdes*), which are found around the world in the Northern Hemisphere. The spine-tipped tail of the true wood- pecker is used as a brace in climbing vertical surfaces of trees. True woodpeckers have the neck fairly long and strong, and the nostrils covered with a sheathing of fine, wiry feathers. The chisel-tipped bill is used for cutting into wood in search of insects and their larvae. The long, extensile tongue enables the bird to extract its food with ease, either by extending the hooked tip and impaling the prey or by enmeshing it with a sticky substance that the woodpecker produces in well-de- veloped salivary glands; it is retracted by means of a unique set of muscles and hyoid (tongue) bones that divide and extend under and around the skull, then pass over the eyes to muscular anchorages sit- uated on the forehead. To accommodate the harpoon- like tongue and chisel bill, the skull is modified in a number of ways to permit poundings and vibrations that presumably would kill a normal bird. Another modification is sharply hooked claws that are used in hopping, not walking, up the sides of trees.

Since woodpeckers prey chiefly on beetles and other insects that live more or less permanently in dead wood and do not fluctuate seasonally, they are not forced to migrate, and most species are sedentary.

These birds seem to depend on their sense of hearing to detect their prey. In hunting, the wood- pecker mounts from the lower part of a tree, often working in long spirals, first hopping briskly, then pausing, seemingly to listen, turning the head to the side, then either digging quickly or making off in bounding hops to try again. If humans intrude, the bird keeps more or less behind a limb or trunk, and usually only its head peers out once in a while.

True woodpeckers generally build their own homes by drilling round holes in dead limbs and trunks. These tunnels turn downward six to eighteen inches and become somewhat larger at the bottom. The egg chamber is bare except for a few wood chips, on which the eggs are laid. The male generally plays the major role in nest-building, incubation and rearing the young, but the female contributes much assistance. Apparently both sexes sleep in cavities throughout the year. The incubation period is generally short, ranging from 11 to 14 days, but it becomes longer in the largest species and is said to be 18 days in the Ivory-billed Woodpecker. The nesting period is relatively long—19 to 35 days.

All woodpeckers employ a sharply undulating form of flight. In changing trees they usually swoop down to a lower part of the neighboring tree. Their

Pileated Woodpecker (*Dryocopus pileatus*)

S. A. GRIMES

calls are harsh cries or laughing rattles, but they prefer to remain silent or to draw attention by drumming on resonant trees.

The most famous and largest of the true woodpeckers in the New World are the ivory-billed woodpeckers, which are crow-sized, ivory-billed, black, white and red birds. One species, the nearly extinct Ivory-billed Woodpecker (*Campephilus principalis*) is found in primeval forests of southeastern United States and Cuba. Two closely related species, the Imperial Woodpecker (*C. imperialis*) and the Magellanic Woodpecker (*C. magellanicus*), are found in Mexico and southern South America respectively. The Pileated Woodpecker (*Dryocopus pileatus*) of North America has many features in common with this group. All attack carpenter ants by digging deep into the cores of trees.

Aberrant woodpeckers are the much smaller flickers (*Colaptes*), of which there are six species between Alaska and southern Chile. All are chiefly brownish and golden-yellow birds with much black barring and spotting and some red markings. In flight their whitish rump flashes between wing beats. The Yellow-shafted Flicker (*Colaptes auratus;* Plate 118) has a prominent red nape and, in the male, a black mustache. Flickers are aberrant in that they principally hunt ants on the ground. To assist in this, their bills are more slender and curved than those of other woodpeckers, but they cut splendid nest holes in dead trunks, poles or tree limbs. An even more terrestrial species is the Ground Woodpecker (*Geocolaptes olivaceus*) of South Africa, a ten-inch, olive-brown bird that has habits rather like those of a kingfisher. It hunts insects on the ground like a flicker, but never drills wood. Instead, it drills into the earth of riverbanks in order to find grubs or to fashion its nest. Tunnels of the Ground Woodpecker are often several feet deep, and in these sanctuaries three to five white eggs are laid.

Two species of sapsuckers (*Sphyrapicus*) form a group that is peculiar to North America and is unusual for its feeding habits. These birds, as their vernacular name suggests, drink the sap of trees. They keep pretty much to deciduous trees, and frequently to apple orchards, where in spring they drill rows of holes through the bark, sometimes encircling the trunk, in order to get fresh sap. At these seeping fountains the birds dip their bills and sometimes remain to drink for hours; and, because the sap serves as bait for insects, they also enjoy a steady diet of the latter. The sapsuckers have the upperparts blackish and the lower parts yellowish, the former with much white mottling and the latter with a black patch on the chest. The only bright coloring is on the head and throat, which is crimson in the male.

Not commonly known is the fact that four species of European woodpeckers also ring trees in order to drink their sap. The trees attacked are pine, fir and yew, and the woodpeckers are the Greater Spotted Woodpecker (*Dendrocopos major*), Black Wood-

Wryneck (*Jynx torquilla*)

ERIC J. HOSKING

Two American woodpeckers have aberrant habits that seem very odd. The Red-headed Woodpecker (*Melanerpes erythrocephalus;* Plate 115), a spectacular black-and-white bird with a bright crimson head, frequently hawks for flying insects, darting out from a vertical trunk like a flycatcher. And the Acorn Woodpecker (*Melanerpes formicivorus*) supplements its insect food with berries and nuts, as most woodpeckers do, but this bird drills hundreds of small holes in tree trunks and in each inserts an acorn to eat when insect food is scarce.

In the subfamily Jynginae are placed two aberrant small, soft-plumaged birds that have the feet arranged like those of the woodpeckers but the tail soft and the bill pointed sharply and not chisel-tipped. Hardly more than six inches long, generally brownish above and grayish below with feathering mottled to resemble bark, the wrynecks are largely ground feeders. They are somewhat unspecialized in that they often sit on small limbs like perching birds; however, they also cling like woodpeckers and nest in hollows in trees, although the cavities are appropriated, not self-made. Named for their habit of twisting the head into odd contortions, the two species, the Wryneck (*Jynx torquilla*) of Eurasia, North Africa and Japan, and the African Wryneck (*J. ruficollis*) of Africa south of the Sahara, both lay seven to nine white eggs.

The third subfamily of the Picidae, the Piculets or Picumninae, has 29 species—one in Africa, three in southeastern Asia and the rest in the tropical forests of America. In many ways they resemble the wrynecks except that they are very much smaller, ranging only from three to five inches in length. They have the tails soft and, although they cling to vertical surfaces and climb like nuthatches, they also are apt to perch. In their nesting habits they are like small woodpeckers except that they often use holes that are already drilled, or make nests in crevices.

One of the better-known piculets is the Antillean Piculet (*Nesoctites micromegas*) of Hispaniola and Gonave Island, which is about six inches long. This species is mostly olive-green above, and below is dull white streaked with black. Both sexes have the crown yellow, but in the male there is a red spot in the center. This peculiar bird excavates a nest hole in a cactus plant or a tree like a little woodpecker. In his *Field Guide of Birds of the West Indies* James Bond observed that it sometimes perches like a sparrow and that it creeps over bark surfaces like a nuthatch, the pairs often keeping together and constantly calling back and forth.

pecker (*Dryocopus martius*), Green Woodpecker (*Picus viridis*) and Three-toed Woodpecker (*Picoïdes tridactylus*).

The Green Woodpeckers of Europe, northern Africa, Asia and Malaysia comprise some 15 species of large and well-known green-backed, red-capped, pale-breasted and heavily-mustached birds, most of which have bright yellow rumps. The Green Woodpecker (*Picus viridis*) of Eurasia and northern Africa is perhaps typical. It is a twelve-inch bird that keeps to deciduous woodlands, farm plantings and scattered trees, where it nests in woodpecker fashion.

The Downy Woodpecker (*Dendrocopos pubescens*), a sparrow-sized black-and-white woodpecker that is the most familiar member of this family in the New World, belongs to a group of 33 species that inhabits virtually the whole world. Some of the others are the Hairy Woodpecker (*D. villosus*) of North America and the very similar Old World spotted woodpeckers, such as the smallest European species, the Lesser Spotted Woodpecker (*D. minor*). Three medium-sized woodpeckers found in America are the Red-crowned Woodpecker (*Centurus rubricapillus;* Plate 114), the Gila Woodpecker (*C. uropygialis;* Plate 116) and the Red-bellied Woodpecker (*C. carolinus;* Plate 117).

PASSERIFORMES

About 5100 of the world's 8600 known species of birds occur in the order Passeriformes, or perching birds. These birds, like the dinosaurs of an earlier age, are now in a period of explosive radiation. Their evolutionary success has been so rapid and recent that many well-marked offshoots (that is, families) remain more or less linked by primitive surviving stocks. These links cause many taxonomic problems. Another problem is the use of different criteria by different authorities for evaluating evolutionary relationships. For example, in the songbirds (the largest single group, with more than 4000 species) the crowlike birds are placed by one school at the apex of the evolutionary tree of bird life because of their "intelligence," specialized plumage and specialized reproductive behavior. Another school, relying more heavily on song, places the thrushes at the apex, and still another crowns the tree with the finchlike birds because they appear to represent the main stem of songbird evolution. The last is the classification used in this work.

Broadbills (*Eurylaimidae*)

Broadbills, a small group of highly colorful perching birds, have their center of abundance in the tropic areas of India, Burma and Malaysia, but one species is found in the Philippines and two genera are found in Africa. Many broadbills resemble the unusually proportioned, colorful cotingas and puffbirds of the New World tropics, which are also considered primitive perching birds. Many species have the bill flattened and very broad at the base, with the upper mandible overhanging the lower along the sides and bearing a solid hook at the tip. Like the puffbirds, broadbills have the head disproportionately large, and frequently the nude areas of the body, the legs, the wattles, the bill and the lores, are highly colored. In shape the broadbills are gross, even fat birds, their bulky bodies exaggerated by short, strong legs, small feet, generally narrow, rounded wings, often with strangely thinned primaries (which may be used to produce noises) and graduated tails. Added to these odd proportions is their abnormally vivid plumage of purples, greens, reds, blues and lilacs.

The family splits into two natural groups, the typical broadbills—very large-billed birds with 11 primaries—of which two genera are African and four are found in the Indo-Malayan region; and the green broadbills—small-billed birds with 10 primaries—of the Malayan region. They range in size between a sparrow and a jay. Most are forest-loving, peculiarly unwary birds; in fact, like the puffbirds of South America, they often fail to seek safety, even when a hunter picks off some of the flock. A characteristic of the family is flocking, but broadbills are also found in pairs or even alone. Many species hunt from special limbs close to the ground in the perpetual twilight of deep forest; others keep to the crown. Many are extremely local, remaining all their lives in certain forests at certain altitudes. All feed on insect prey caught in flight in the manner of puffbirds, bee-eaters, flycatchers, jacamars—namely by "hawking" for them from special perches.

Some of the broadbills engage in displays, which are still incompletely understood. Vividly colored patches of plumage are suddenly unsheathed from the back and expanded much in the way that many other birds suddenly reveal and display brightly colored erectile crests. These are displayed from special perches and also in flight. Included in the performance are harsh croaking calls which are, so to speak, audibly vivid and may be related to the fact that many of the species are crepuscular, hunting in twilight. In Africa they are among the first, if not the first, birds heard in the morning and among the last diurnal birds to be heard at night. During the day, as noted earlier, many species are inactive, or they keep to the dark undertier of deep forest.

Broadbills are superb nest architects, in this respect rivaling the New World caciques and oropendolas. The building material usually consists of grasses and fibers stripped from large leaves. A cluster of nest material is suspended from a high, slender vine and fastened with plant fibers and fungus silk so that the structure resembles a long, slightly pregnant eel dangling precariously from a thin fishing line. The nest usually hangs over water—a pond or a stream—in deep forest. The "bulge" represents the actual nest, and it is entered through a canopied side tunnel that is often fitted with a tiny porch. Below the tunnel may hang up to three feet of "tail." The eggs of broadbills are glossy whitish to buffy in color and either immaculate or spotted, chiefly around the larger end. The set is from two to five. Apparently nothing is known of the incubation period, but Dr. Chapin noted one species in which the female apparently did all the brooding and the male helped feed the young.

The Red-sided Broadbill (*Smithornis rufolateralis*) of West and Central Africa is a bird five inches in length. Above it is black on the head, neck and central back; below it is white with blackish striping and prominent chestnut patches on the sides of the chest. Dr. Chapin found it fairly common in the Ituri Forest, where he learned to recognize its peculiar toadlike calls. Otherwise it was so hard to find it would seem to be a great rarity. Like many broadbills, it sits low on thin limbs near the floor of the virgin forest. From such perches it performs an odd circular flight, about a foot in diameter, which may be used in display but is apparently also a hunting maneuver. In executing such flights, the bird emits a loud, croaking noise, the sound apparently coming from the wings as in manakins, certain flycatchers and some birds of paradise. Chapin also saw the white plumage of the back elevated in display with the tail held up, wagging, and accompanied by whistling. He also saw the white dorsal plumage displayed in flight. Two glossy white eggs formed the set. Hairless caterpillars, earwigs, fragments of insects and a spider were found in the stomachs of collected specimens.

The Grauer's Broadbill (*Pseudocalyptomena*

graueri), which was long known only from the type specimen and is still known only from a small area of forest 6500 feet above the sea in mountains west of Lake Tanganyika, is one of the rare birds of the world. In length it is 4¾ inches. In color it is mostly green, but below the throat and chest it is pale blue. Rediscovered in July, 1929, this species was found behaving like a flycatcher, hawking insects from forest trees 20 to 75 feet up.

The Black and Yellow Broadbill (*Eurylaimus ochromalus*), six inches long, is a black bird with yellow splashes on the wings and back. It has a white collar ringing the neck and a pink and yellow abdomen. This bird is less retiring than most broadbills and is found in the outskirts of villages in forests and in the jungle clearings of Malaysia.

A relative is the Wattled Broadbill (*E. steerii*) which lives in the southern half of the Philippine Archipelago. It is some seven inches long and has a purple crown, spectacular blue wattles around the eyes, blue feet, greenish blue eyes and lilac underparts! Southward, in Borneo and many of the other islands of Malaysia, are other species that are almost as gaudily colored, but all of these lack the eye wattles.

The Frilled Tody Broadbill (*Serilophus lunulatus*) of southeastern Asia and parts of Malaysia is said to add fruit to its insect diet, and the Dusky Broadbill (*Corydon sumatranus*), a blackish species with a large, normally hidden orange-scarlet patch between the shoulders, is said to become active in deep twilight and to move about in parties.

Of the three species of Green Broadbills, two (*Calyptomena hosei* and *C. whiteheadi*) are found only in Borneo, the latter only on a single mountain. The third and smallest, the Lesser Green Broadbill (*C. viridis*), is more widespread in the Malaysian region. These predominantly green birds have been placed in a separate subfamily, being distinguished from other broadbills by their small bills covered at the base with a dense crest of feathers.

Woodcreepers or Woodhewers (*Dendrocolaptidae*)

Woodcreepers are brownish birds of the New World tropics from Mexico to Argentina. They generally have the bill elongated and curved, the tail stiff and tipped with spines, and the foot with three forward-directed toes that are partially fused together. They range from small to medium in size and are inhabitants of the lower and middle tier of forests between sea level and about 10,000 feet.

Forty-seven species are known. All habitually climb head up, going from the lower trunks of trees and stumps to higher parts and descending in plunging flights to the foot of a neighboring tree. The spine-tipped tail, which is used as a brace or prop in climbing, much resembles the tail of a true creeper (see Certhiidae).

Woodcreepers superficially resemble woodpeckers but are distinguished by the way they climb trees, as well as by their more elongated, slender bodies and their long, curved bills. In hunting they use the bill to pry off bits of bark and moss or to probe in cracks and crevices for spiders, caterpillars, ants and other insects, as well as small snails, salamanders and frogs. They hunt alone, in pairs or in small parties, and it is common to find one or more in company with antbirds, woodpeckers and forest flycatchers gathered together to prey on insects driven from cover by army ants.

Woodcreepers are so closely related to ovenbirds (Furnariidae) that some authorities include them in the same family. They belong to the suborder Tyranni or Clamatores, all of which have a simplified syrinx (sound-producing organ), so that they are not capable of much in the way of song variation and modulation. But they can produce whinnying or trilling songs, and they are responsible for many of the bird sounds heard in American tropical forests.

In woodcreepers both sexes are generally brown in color, some species being more reddish, others more olivaceous. Many are marked with buffy or whitish streaks or spots on the breast, throat, head or back. In a few the markings of the breast are outlined in black. However, color differences are difficult to observe, except under very favorable conditions, and the best field characters are the bills, which vary a great deal in size and shape.

The Plain Brown Woodcreeper (*Dendrocincla fuliginosa*) is some eight inches long and brown above, shading to chestnut on the tail. Like the Olivaceous, it ranges from Central America to southern Brazil. The Olivaceous Woodcreeper (*Sittasomus griseicapillus*), which is about six inches in length, has a relatively small, slender bill. It is generally olive to sepia, with the lower back, rump and tail bright chestnut. The tail is long, with prominent downcurved terminal spines.

The bill of the Wedge-billed Woodcreeper (*Glyphorynchus spirurus*) is quite short; the anterior part of the upper mandible is flat and the lower mandible curves up sharply to meet it. In color this species is similar to the Olivaceous Woodcreeper, but the throat is buffy and there are streaks or spots of whitish on the breast.

Among the larger members of the family is the Barred Woodcreeper (*Dendrocolaptes certhia*), measuring ten to eleven inches, with a bill that is nearly straight but hooked at the tip and quite sturdy. The general color is olive brown, changing to chestnut on the rump, wings and tail and buffy brown on the underparts.

The Spot-crowned Woodcreeper (*Lepidocolaptes affinis*) is a highland-dwelling species about eight inches long. Its general color is much the same as in most of the family.

Woodcreepers, so far as known, nest only in holes and cavities that are natural or were made by other animals—usually in trees or stumps, but nests have been found in earthen banks. The nesting sites, some of which are used several times, may be close to the ground or as much as 30 feet up. Nest material varies with the species. Some use none if the cavity is well protected, others use bits of bark, wood, leaves and so forth. Occasionally, when the cavity is very large, an enormous amount of material must be brought into it to make the nest. Dr. Frank M. Chapman reported that one Buff-throated Woodcreeper (*Xiphorhynchus guttatus*) carried some 7000 bits of bark and dead wood to its nest site.

Paul Schwartz, the keen observer (and excellent photographer) of South American birds who supplied much of the above information, writes that in Venezuela some species bring additional bits of material to add to the nest during the period of incubation—a habit they share with the Synallaxine group of the ovenbirds. Two or three white eggs are laid.

According to Dr. Alexander Skutch's observations of the Allied Woodhewer (*Lepidocolaptes affinis*) in Central America, both adults cooperate in all of the duties of parental care, and brooding continues for about 12 days. When first hatched the young have a growth of down similar to most passerines. The nestlings are dressed much like the adults, and during their final days in the nest they try their vocal powers with songs or calls similar to those of the adults. However, at sight of an approaching parent, they switch rapidly to their food-begging calls. The nestling period is about 19 days, and Dr. Skutch has observed young of the Spot-crowned Woodcreeper being attended by their parents a month after having left the nest.

Ovenbirds *(Furnariidae)*

The ovenbirds comprise a family of some 200 species of generally brownish, small to medium-sized birds dwelling in the Americas south of the United States. They are named for the fortified—often oven-shaped—nests that they build in a remarkably wide variety of locations. Some are in tunnels drilled in banks or dead trees, and some are in crevices. Certain species nest in cavities; some build globular houses, with side entrances, of mud, sticks, thorns or even grasses glued together with a kind of papier-mâché. Some of the nests are very large and complex, with several chambers and with elaborate felted linings, long entrance pipes sticking out of the sides or even twisting tunnels that descend from the top. In general, the sexes cooperate to build the nest, to incubate the eggs and to brood and feed the young.

True ovenbirds are so closely related to the woodcreepers that some authorities would include them in a single family. They are chiefly insect-loving birds that are found in all kinds of habitat from sea level to above tree line in the Andes; they also eat spiders, small amphibia and gastropods, and, less commonly, tiny reptiles and crustacea.

Paul Schwartz of Venezuela, who supplied the accompanying photograph of the Buff-fronted Foliage-gleaner (*Philydor rufus;* Plate 120), has generously given much of the following information: Ovenbirds occupy every niche from the open plains to the thickest rain forest and from sea level to the alpine grasslands of the Andes. Throughout this range the species are usually dressed in browns, the sexes being similar in coloration. Some have gray, white and bright chestnut areas in the plumage. A few are boldly colored, such as Riker's Pointed-tail (*Berlepschia rikeri*), which is black and white with chestnut wings. In the large subfamily Furnariinae the species are chiefly terrestrial, and they generally nest in tunnels in the earth or in crevices among rocks.

The Rufous Ovenbird (*Furnarius rufus*), best known member of the family in southern South America, is an aberrant nest-builder belonging to this group. It is a ruddy chestnut bird some eight inches in length, with light underparts, which dwells in wooded grasslands. Widely known as "El Hornero," it builds a double-chambered mud "oven" with a side door. This species is famous for its habit of placing its nests on horizontal limbs and on rafters near the abodes of man.

Another group of related species (*Geositta*) have very short toes and are entirely terrestrial. About six inches long and often streaked below, they are known as miners because they drill lateral nesting tunnels that sometimes penetrate as deep as ten feet into sandy ground. Other terrestrial relatives (*Upucerthia*) are earth-creepers with longish curved bills.

Of general distribution is a group of seven- to ten-inch birds (*Cinclodes*) known as shaketails, for they constantly flick their tails as they move over the ground, usually near water. They are superficially very much like dippers in their manner of hunting and in their general appearance. They nest in tunnels or in crevices, and, unlike most of the ovenbirds, they fly rather strongly.

Another large subfamily of ovenbirds is the Synallaxinae; these include the spinetails or firewood-gatherers, many of which are splendid architects. The Red-fronted Thornbill (*Phacellodomus rufifrons*), a wide-ranging, nondescript, brownish bird some six inches in length, builds a remarkable columnar structure, usually around a drooping limb in a tall tree. The writer has watched four birds working together to erect the nest, composed of sticks picked up on the ground and conveyed to the mounting platform. The sticks, often over a foot long, seem entirely too heavy for the birds to carry, but the builders fly back and forth with their loads, erecting columnar clusters that sometimes are ten feet tall and weigh over 100 pounds. These structures have half a dozen side entrances; presumably several pairs of birds cooperate to build the main part and use separate apartments.

Another widespread species, the Pale-breasted Spinetail (*Synallaxis albescens*), is pale olive above with a chestnut crown and chestnut shoulders. It has the tail long and graduated, and is six inches in length. Its nest is a tightly constructed sphere of twigs that is entered by a pipelike lateral entrance sometimes extending ten inches out from the side of the nest. The sticks of this tunnel function somewhat as a mechanism of defense, for they are delicately balanced and fall when touched. The Synallaxinae, in Mr. Schwartz's opinion, are the exclusive hosts of the parasitic Striped Cuckoo (*Tapera naevia*). During incubation, Spinetails constantly reinforce and repair their nests, even lining them with a kind of felting, presumably to ward off predators and nest parasitizers. The Yellow-throated Spinetail (*Certhiaxis cinnamomea*) builds its nest of thorns in marshes, keeping close to bushes beside water.

Spinetails of the genus *Cranioleuca* build nests near the tips of high limbs, and species of the genus *Asthenes* build large stick structures that are entered through a hole in the top. The Rush-loving Spinetail (*Phleocryptes melanops*) fashions a nest of wet grasses and clay with a side entrance. In this it lays blue eggs, whereas in the rest of the family white eggs are laid. Another unusual species, Des Murs' Spinetail (*Sylviorthorhynchus desmurii*), has a pair of central tail feathers that extend for two-thirds of the bird's length of ten inches. These feathers are peculiar because at all times they appear very worn in contrast to the remainder of the plumage. A widely distributed species known as the Firewood Gatherer (*Anumbius annumbi*) builds stick nests that are entered through crooked tunnels from the top.

A wrenlike ovenbird is the Spotted Barbtail (*Premnoplex brunnescens*) of deep forest ravines. Mr. Schwartz found one nest of this species—a globular structure—used continuously for four seasons.

In the subfamily Phylidorinae are many plain brown, nondescript species that nest mostly in cavities in trees or in rocks, but they may also excavate tunnels in banks or in dead wood. One, the Riker's Pointed-tail (*Berlepschia rikeri*) of Amazonia, apparently spends its whole life in palm trees. In this subfamily are found the foliage-gleaners and the automolus, which are groups of small to medium-sized birds with a brownish or grayish plumage often relieved by bright areas of chestnut. One group (*Xenops*) is very small and has a bill that is curved upward.

In the subfamily Sclerurinae are found two kinds of foragers, the leafscrapers (*Sclerurus*), which forage amongst fallen leaves, and the monotypic Streamcreeper (*Lochmias nematura*). The latter is a dark brown, white-flecked little bird that always keeps close to mountain streams. The writer found this little-known species on the summit of one of the Venezuelan "lost worlds," Mount Auyan-tepui. Its nest is said to be a hole in a bank.

The Furnariidae lay from two to nine eggs, depending on the species. Incubation periods vary from 15 to about 21 days, the nestling periods ordinarily from 12 to 18 days. In one species, the Buffy Tufted-cheek (*Pseudocolaptes lawrencii*), Dr. Skutch found a nestling period of 29 days, which is quite remarkable. It seems that these similar, nondescript birds build nests that are highly specialized and variable, and that they also have highly variable, highly specific periods of reproductive behavior.

In North America there occurs a warbler that, because it builds an oven-shaped nest of grasses and leaves, is also called Ovenbird. This species (*Seiurus aurocapillus*) is not related to the Furnariidae.

Antbirds *(Formicariidae)*

Antbirds inhabit the gloomiest parts of the New World jungles. The 221 species are divided into 53 major clans (genera). All skulk so well in the leafy shadows that, like the babbling thrushes of the Old World, they are more easily known by their voices than by their appearance. All are ten-primaried song birds that have the bill compressed and hooked. Like flycatchers, they are highly diversified. The smallest species is about three inches in length and the longest about 14 inches.

Antbirds have the voice well developed. It is generally shrill and ventriloquistic, and some species sing antiphonally. Antbirds usually go about alone or in pairs, but certain species, such as the White-faced Antcatcher (*Pithys albifrons*), are almost always found in tight bands. This species is a rich brown and gray, with a goatlike beard of white feathers and a long white crest.

Paul Schwartz states that insects form the principal food of antbirds, but some of the larger species occasionally eat small lizards, tiny snakes, and probably the eggs and young of small forest birds.

In most antbirds the sexes are very differently dressed, the males being garbed in contrasting colors —chiefly bars and patches of black and white—and the females in dull brown. As in many of the deep-forest birds in the Old World (see the broadbills and babbling thrushes), many of the antbirds have on their backs bright patches of color which they display during courtship very much as other birds expose bright crests.

Antbirds have radiated into feeding niches in many parts of the deep forest. Some are small-billed, and scour leaves and other surfaces like vireos and warblers; these are the ant vireos. Others that take larger animals have bills resembling those of the shrikes, and these are called antshrikes. Still other groups are variously called ant wrens, ant thrushes and ant pittas. The latter are long-legged, big-headed, elusive birds, with disproportionately short tails, and closely resemble the pittas of the tropical Old World.

The largest of these chunky birds with their

oversized, thrushlike heads is the Scale-breasted Ant Pitta (*Grallaria excelsa*) of the high Andes of northern South America. Despite its ridiculously short tail, this species is nine inches long. It is dark olive-brown above, and below a pale tawny shade with bold black markings. Its call is a low, hollow, vibrant whistle. Other deep-forest species are very small. One, the Rusty-breasted Ant Pitta (*Grallaricula ferrugineipectus*), is olive-brown above with a tawny orange face, breast and flanks, and a white abdomen. It lives in the understory of the forest and flies to the ground only to catch insects; it also captures flying insects like a tyrant flycatcher. Of one of the large, ground-loving antbirds, the Chestnut-crowned Ant Pitta (*Grallaria ruficapilla*), Mr. Schwartz noted that its voice consists of three strong, plaintive notes that ring through the deep forest, often to be returned by some far-wandering mate.

The Barred Antshrike (*Thamnophilus doliatus*)—a six-inch species in which the male is boldly barred with black and white and the female largely rufous brown—is shown at its nest in Plate 119. This species is probably the best known of all antbirds because it is one of the few that venture out of the forest to live in clusters of bamboo and bushes close to human habitations, as, for example, on the grounds of the Phelps Ornithological Laboratories in Caracas, Venezuela. Both sexes have the eyes pale yellowish white. Its calls are plaintive whines, but it caws when disturbed and utters soothing notes when it is singing to its mate on the nest.

The Great Antshrike (*Taraba major*) has a red iris, and the male and female are dressed something like the foregoing species. Antbirds wear many different dresses. Mr. Schwartz noted that at one extreme "is the male Black-breasted Ant Wren (*Formicivora grisea*) with his jet-black underparts and brownish olive upperparts, the two being separated by a border of white, and at the other extreme is a bird so nondescript as to have deserved the name Plain Ant Vireo (*Dysithamnus mentalis*)." The latter is a five-inch bird that is chiefly grayish olive in the male and dull brown in the female, both with pale underparts. More conspicuous is the White-flanked Ant Wren (*Myrmotherula axillaris*), which is a four-inch, blackish, wrenlike bird of the deep forest undergrowth. It is named for the white feathers the male carries under its wings, which are exposed in display. Usually it goes about in pairs or in noisy bands of up to a dozen birds of mixed species—woodcreepers, a woodpecker or two, three or four antbirds, often of different species, perhaps a cotinga and a few vireos.

The seven-inch Black-faced Ant Thrush (*Formicarius analis*) is so strongly attached to its ground habitat that it runs to escape in preference to flying. This species, Mr. Schwartz reports, walks with long, deliberate steps on the floor of the forest, twitching its very short tail, which is carried straight up. With the bill it picks up and tosses aside leaves in search of insect food. It not only acts like a little rail but

somewhat resembles one in its sooty brown coloration. It has a chestnut collar and a black face, chin and throat.

Ant-pipits or Gnat-eaters
(*Conopophagidae*)

Ant-pipits, or Gnat-eaters, comprise a small group of smallish, long-legged, forest-loving birds of tropical America that superficially resemble antbirds. Like the latter, they live among dense, low-growing vegetation. They feed on insects and have somewhat flycatcher-like bills.

Most of the ten known species occur in the Amazonian and Andean forests. Those belonging to the genus *Conopophaga* most nearly resemble antbirds. The largest is the Black-chested Ant-pipit (*C. melanogaster*) of Brazil and Bolivia, which is nearly six inches long and has dark reddish brown upperparts and prominent white eyebrows. The male is black below and on the crown, while the female has the underparts pale gray, the head brownish gray and the eyebrow markings narrower and less conspicuous. About an inch shorter, D'Orbigny's Gnat-eater (*C. ardesiaca*) of Bolivia and Peru is brownish above and smoky gray below, with prominent white "ears" in the male. In Southeastern Brazil is found the Cinnamon-chested Ant-pipit (*C. lineata*), which would very closely resemble an antbird except for its conspicuous white "ears." Another group (*Corythopis*), consisting of three species, is more flycatcher-like. These birds, which are found from Venezuela to northeastern Argentina, generally lack the prominent white head markings. Above five inches in length, they are usually olive to olive-brown above and whitish below. Usually they have the chest and flanks prominently marked with black.

Very little is known concerning the breeding behavior of these birds except that they lay buffy yellow eggs with dark markings.

Tapaculos (*Rhinocryptidae*)

The 26 species of tapaculos form a family of birds of Central and South America and the Falkland Islands, with the largest concentration occurring in Chile and Patagonia. In his *Birds of Argentina, Paraguay, Uruguay and Chile,* Dr. Alexander Wetmore described the elusiveness and unusual postures of one fairly typical species, the Little Cock or Gallito (*Rhinocrypta lanceolata*). An inhabitant of bushy grasslands, it is a brown, gray and black bird eight inches long and has such pronounced terrestrial habits that it resembles a rodent. He wrote: "As I traversed their haunts, I was greeted by a low *prut prut prut,* or a musical *tallock,* from the brush at either hand, and occasionally had a glimpse of one of the elusive birds as it darted across some little opening." And later: "It is doubtful if *Rhinocrypta* has occasion to fly a hundred meters in the course of a month." He noted also that the flight muscles were slight, flabby and pale in color, indicating a poor blood supply, whereas the leg muscles were strong. The Little Cock, he noted, ran with the crest elevated and the tail cocked or angled up over the back. Earlier the English naturalist W. H. Hudson had said that they strutted and ran on the ground with the tail erect, "looking wonderfully like a small domestic fowl."

Hudson found tapaculos to be noisy, inquisitive birds that traveled about stealthily in groups—these groups sometimes encircling a man "with a ring of angry sound, moving with him, coming no nearer and never allowing its cause to be seen." Tapaculos hop about in bushes and use a feeble fluttering flight when alarmed. Structurally, they are rather similar to the ant-pittas. They have the wings short and rounded and the legs relatively strong and with long nails. In size, members of this family vary from tiny wrenlike to stout quail-like birds. In coloration they are chiefly brown and blackish, with the sexes similar.

In the warmer latitudes tapaculos occur in the mountains up to about 10,000 feet. In Patagonia they descend to near sea level. They nest in a variety of locations ranging from earthen tunnels and crevices in rocks to bushes. A nest of the Little Cock reported by Wetmore was three feet up in the branches of a thorn bush. It was an untidy globular structure with a side entrance, composed of weed stems, bark and grasses. Little is known of the attentive behavior of these birds; however, Wetmore found that a male was in attendance at the Gallito nest. Two white eggs seem to comprise the regular set.

Tapaculos feed principally on insects, buds and seeds. Among the northernmost species are the Silvery-fronted Tapaculo (*Scytalopus argentifrons*) of the mountains of Costa Rica south to western Panama. This is a tiny blackish bird with pale gray superciliary lines and brown-and-black-barred flanks. There is also the Pale-throated Tapaculo (*Scytalopus panamensis*), which ranges from the highlands of eastern Panama south through Colombia and Ecuador. This species is similar and closely related to the foregoing.

From Dr. Wetmore we learn also of the Barrancolino (*Teledromas fuscus*) of Argentina. This species likes dry, gravelly country with sparse cover. It is wrenlike and in escaping prefers running to flying, moving rapidly with the tail cocked high over the back, ducking behind obstacles and swerving this way and that like a rodent. It takes remarkably long strides, sometimes as much as six inches at a time, although the total length of the bird is only about seven inches. It nests in an earthen bank, with the entrance about three inches in diameter and the tunnel about 15 inches deep. At the end of the tunnel is a six-inch chamber lined with a crude cup-shaped nest of grass containing two white eggs.

"Tapaculo," a word of Spanish origin, alludes to the apparently immodest way these little birds go about with their tails cocked nearly straight up and their rears exposed.

Manakins *(Pipridae)*

The manakins, small birds confined to forests between southern Mexico and Argentina, are among the most interesting of New World species in that they perform dances that rival those of the birds of paradise. The females, which are usually predominantly green, are hard to observe, but the males, which in many species are splashed with red, yellow, blue and black, and often decorated with ornamental tails and crests, are conspicuous. The males also employ mechanical and vocal noises to attract attention, and these are often among the most prominent sounds in the tropical jungle.

Manakins devour insects and small invertebrates, many of which they obtain by fluttering and gleaning among leaves and limblets. The bill, which is short and broad at the base and has a small notch, is a good instrument for catching such prey, but it is also used to take small berries. In hunting for food, manakins often join mixed bands of small forest birds to prey on the invertebrates that are flushed from cover by marauding army ants.

Most manakins are polygamous, and males attract their mates to special display grounds by auditory and visual signals. In such species pairs are never formed except for the moment, and a successful male may make many conquests each year. The manakins may be said to practice promiscuous polygamy, because the male offers no aid whatsoever to the female. The latter builds the nest, incubates the eggs, and rears the young by herself.

The display arenas of the males are often located in groups, so that a number of males may display within sight and sound of each other. In some species these arenas are ground clearings a dozen feet apart, in others they are dance limbs in the high forest 125 feet apart. Apparently the distance depends on visibility. When a female visits the general arena, many males compete for her.

All dance arenas have one character in common: they are free of litter. In those on the ground all falling debris is removed by the male owner. The best example of this type is the famous Gould's Manakin (*Manacus vitellinus*) of Panama, a dark-capped, white-breasted bird the size of a large wren. In tree-using species the male probably clears the dance limb by plucking the leaves, for it is always noticeably free of such vegetation. During the breeding season the birds spend much time in these areas, often performing spectacular acrobatic stunts and making a variety of sounds that attract attention from afar. As soon as a female comes into view, the males perform with great animation. When the female has chosen one, the other males do not trespass on his territory but step up the tempo of their own performances. However, when no females are in the vicinity, the various males sometimes leave their dance territories to visit on neutral ground, occasionally even displaying to each other. In fact, Dr. Alexander Skutch found that in the Yellow-thighed Manakin (*Pipra mentalis*), some of the pairs of males spent a large share of their time together; but those that preferred to remain alone were more successful in attracting mates.

The acrobatic, stylized dances of the brightly colored manakins are of importance to everyone concerned with animal behavior. Some of the displays are highly social and quite astonishing. For example, in the Blue-backed Manakin (*Chiroxiphia pareola*) the display territories are occupied by pairs of males that perform a well-coordinated aerial dance consisting of a loop-the-loop. The pairs of males make up to 70 hovering circuits, flying up, then descending backward as though on opposite sides of a reversed Ferris wheel. This dance ends when one male, becoming partially paralyzed with excitement, gives up the aerial gyrations and flies off with a visiting female. On occasion as many as five males perform as a group.

Dr. Lee Crandall has described and photographed the dance of a male Yellow-thighed or Redheaded Manakin (*Pipra mentalis*) which displayed in the New York Zoo. From him, as well as from Dr. Skutch and Dr. Frank M. Chapman, we know that a group of Red-heads display together, each on its own limb. As the female approaches, each male

stands very still; next it elevates its body as high as possible to expose the brightly plumed yellow thighs. In this position it holds its shiny black body more or less at right angles to the long, yellow thighs, and dips the scarlet head and bill. Now, with a speed too fast for the eye to follow, the wings are half-opened and the bird spins about, reversing its position on the limb again and again so that its bright head rotates in a circle around its bright legs, which form the hub of the display. Another phase is the vibration dance, in which the male stands high with exposed yellow upper legs and opens the wings over the body and head. In this position, the manakin moves backward in a series of rapid, stiff-legged hops for a foot or more, and then jumps to the first position and repeats the backward jiggle again and again. Accompanying this dance are buzzing sounds and wing-snappings that resemble very loud thumbsnapping. The wings of the males of many manakins are modified, presumably to produce mechanical sounds, but just how this is done has never been shown either in these birds or in the many other species that make odd noises with their wings.

The female manakin constructs an open nest like that of a vireo, generally slung by its rim in a horizontal fork. It may be a few feet above the ground or high up in the middle tier of the forest. Many of the nests are decorated with green moss. Usually two pale eggs with dark markings are laid, apparently at intervals of about three days. They are incubated, of course, by the female, and for a relatively long period—19 to 21 days. Dr. Skutch believes this may be a mechanism for protection against nest-robbers such as snakes. The young, which are hatched blind, are first fed by regurgitation, and later the female brings them spiders, insects and berries.

In addition to those already mentioned, some of the colorful species are the Yellow-crowned Manakin (*Heterocercus flavivertex*), ranging from Venezuela to Brazil, which is a dark bird with a bright yellow crown and expansive whitish throat; the Cirrhate Manakin (*Teleonema filicauda*), which is widespread in South America and has the outer tail plumes elongated, the body blackish with yellow lower parts, and the head and throat vividly scarlet, the former with yellow on the forehead.

There are several genera now included in the Pipridae which are dull in color, with the sexes alike. These birds, which are somewhat like flycatchers (Tyrannidae), may prove not to belong with the brightly-colored manakins. Among these is the widespread Thrushlike Manakin (*Schiffornis turdinus*), a reddish brown species found from Mexico to Brazil.

Cotingas (*Cotingidae*)

The bizarrely ornamented, garish cotingas form a New World family of ninety species, with repre-

Yellow-thighed Manakin (*Pipra mentalis*)

sentatives occurring everywhere from the southern borders of Arizona and Texas to Bolivia, Peru and Argentina. Chiefly tropical, the family includes a number of extraordinary species such as the Cock-of-the-Rock with its flaming fan-crest and the Umbrella Bird with its quite unbelievable canopy of feathers. Other decorations found in this family are fleshy beards, naked caruncles, erectile wattles, specially shaped wing feathers that appear to have been cut with shears, and long, round feather-sheathed tassels that can be inflated to hang like aprons. But, as in total length, which varies from 3½ to 18 inches, the species vary from the grossest extremes of ornamentation to birds so small and plain that they seem hardly to belong to the family. The range of calls, which are usually harsh, includes screams, croaks, bell-like tolls and cries.

Almost as variable as the range of ornamentation and calls is the nest architecture, which includes open, flimsy, heron-like nests, hanging nests with side entrances, bottom entrances, mud-plastered nests and even constructions in tree cavities that certain cotingas appropriate from much stronger birds, for example, woodpeckers and toucans. Although chiefly fruit-eaters, a number of cotingas are omnivorous and some devour very large fruits, such as flesh-covered palm nuts. Others feed chiefly on insects, many of which are captured on the wing.

The variability of this family is perhaps best demonstrated by the color patterns, which range from the brightest iridescent glossiness to dead black, from fire-engine red to the most delicate blues and purples. One splendid raspberry-red, thrush-sized bird with glistening ornamental plumage is named for a celebrated French courtesan. It seems that a British ornithologist found the bird in a box of millinery that had fallen prize to a British frigate, so he gallantly named the treasure in honor of its intended recipient, Madame de Pompadour. The male Pompadour Cotinga (*Xipholena punicea*), an inhabitant of the forest crown from Venezuela to Amazonia, has white wings and peculiarly twisted wing coverts, but the female is gray, for among the cotingas the females are drab in comparison with their mates.

In the dull-colored cotingas both male and female are usually similar in coloration, both often being gray. An example is the Common Gray Cotinga (*Lipaugus vociferans*), a bird of the deep forest that habitually emits loud cries and has the habit of investigating any unusual noise. But some of the grayish cotingas have bright spots of color in their plumage. One is the Rose-throated Becard (*Platypsaris aglaiae*), which is the most northerly-ranging member of the family, being found in southern Texas and Arizona. In this species the 6½-inch black-capped gray males have red throats, whereas their mates do not, and the females are dressed in cinnamon brown. This species builds a large, partially pendulous nest entered from the side. Another is the Jamaican Becard (*Platypsaris niger*), which attains a length of eight inches and lives in the hills and mountains of Jamaica. The male is essentially blackish throughout—glossy above and dull below—and the female is generally brownish with pale whitish underparts. This bird's nest is a large mass of vegetable matter suspended high in a tree and with a bottom entrance. It eats berries and insects and lays three heavily spotted eggs.

Plain-colored cotingas in which the sexes are different are the tityras. One, the Masked Tityra (*Tityra semifasciata*), appears to be the only species that has been extensively studied. It is a seven-inch grayish bird with black wings and much black on the head. The female looks black on the head and has a considerable amount of drab brown on the body. Dr. Alexander Skutch found that Masked Tityras live in pairs during much of the year, but at the same time, small flocks composed mainly of unmated males wander about, often invading the nesting territories of the mated pairs. These territories are defended but the feeding areas are not. The Masked Tityra appropriates holes in trees—from woodpeckers and even large toucans—for sleeping and for nesting. When in need of a nest hole, the Masked Tityra stuffs all kinds of forest litter in the cavity when its owner is absent. It does this over and over again until the owner gets tired of cleaning away the mess and relinquishes possession—which may be a matter of weeks if a toucan is involved.

Once they have acquired a nest cavity, the tityras carry in leaves and twigs, which they gather in the crown of the forest. Material brought by the male is dropped near the nest, while that of the female is used to line the cavity. Generally two eggs are laid. These are concealed under nest litter whenever the female is away. In related species the incubation period is 18 to 19 days. The young remain in the nest for about 21 days. Second broods are frequent, the second set of eggs being laid about two weeks after the first brood departs. The nestling tityras are fed by both parents, with each of the adults personally feeding the young. Their fare consists chiefly of winged insects, but caterpillars and spiders also figure largely in their diet.

Very different in behavior is the Black-winged Bellbird (*Procnias averano*) of Trinidad and northern South America. The male, which has the top of the head coffee-brown and the body plumage white with black wings, has a quite extraordinary spray of thin, fleshy caruncles hanging from the chin and throat and resembling a massive unkempt beard. The female is green with a gray throat and with yellow on the sides of the body and on the under tail. Dr. William Beebe, who recently described the nest, noted that the male has a favorite perch where it calls day after day for many months of the year, and that the pairs apparently keep together, returning to nest in the same general area year after year. The calls of this species are loud and of two kinds, one an explosive squawk, the other oft-repeated twangy notes.

The nest proved to be a very frail, shallow platform such as Dr. Beebe once found was used by the Pompadour Cotinga. In this species, he noted, the sticks were nearly all bifurcated, probably adding to their interlacing power. The nest was fairly low in a cacao tree. Both parents were in the vicinity, but the female was the only bird observed on the nest. Another, discovered by Dr. Wilbur G. Downs, held a single light tan egg mottled with brown.

A relative is the Three-wattled Bellbird (*Procnias tricarunculata*) of Central America, which displays with its mouth wide open. This species is reddish brown with a white head and throat and with three whiplike wattles growing around the bill. Another is the pigeon-sized White Bellbird (*Procnias alba*), whose ringing call can be heard nearly a mile through the tropical forests of southern Venezuela, the Guianas and Amazonia. More ordinary is the garrulous, explosive grunt of the Capucin Monkbird (*Perissocephalus tricolor*), which once frightened the author when it screamed close overhead. Large and coffee brown, with a naked blue-gray head rising out of a collar of fluffy feathers, this species resembles a wizened old monk. Among the largest of the cotingas is the Crimson Fruit-crow (*Haematoderus militaris*) of northern South America, which resembles a strawberry-colored raven.

The Cocks-of-the-Rock (*Rupicola*) are so aberrant they have been placed in a distinct family by some authorities. The Golden Cock-of-the-Rock (*Rupicola rupicola*) of southern Venezuela and adjacent areas of the Guianas and Brazil is about a foot long. The male is bright orange-gold, with the outer wing feathers sharply and peculiarly tapered, as if cut by scissors, and with highly curled upper wing coverts. The female is dark brown. This species has a peculiar crest that is permanently erect and virtually conceals the bill. A similar crest marks the more reddish Peruvian Cock-of-the Rock (*R. peruviana*) of the Andes (Plate 121). One reason why these two species were once given family rank is that, unlike any of the other cotingas but rather like some of the manakins, they indulge in strange terrestrial dances. Also they have the legs and feet exceptionally strong. Apparently the ground dances are social affairs that do not involve privately owned territory. Observers have found as many as twenty males and females clustered about on specially cleared areas on the floor of the jungle and performing as a group. Different males take turns in stretching the wings and the tail and performing on the stage amid a crescendo of cries. However, much still remains to be learned about this odd pattern of behavior, even though it has been known for more than a century.

Cocks-of-the-Rock build open nest cups of mud and sticks which are decorated with moss and placed on ledges in shallow caves. Two eggs, very much like those described for the bellbird, are laid.

One group of cotingas, the Umbrella Birds, is among the most remarkable of New World birds.

Typical is the Ornate Umbrella Bird (*Cephalopterus ornatus*), which ranges from Costa Rica to Brazil. The photograph makes the characters of this strange, crow-sized creature apparent. The immense umbrella crest with its ivory-white basal shafts is retractible. Recently the great Belgian collector, Charles Cordier, obtained living examples of these very uncommon birds in the high forests of Ecuador for the New York Zoological Park. Cordier found this species in the high canopy of the forest, where it subsists on fruits. Its calls are loud piping notes. Other species have the front of the neck and chest naked and reddish orange in color, with a red wattle hanging from the mid-chest. But none are more spectacular than the Ornate Umbrella Bird with its immense tubular pensile wattle. This ornament reaches 13 inches in length, although hanging from a bird only 16 inches long.

In 1954 Dr. Helmut Sick studied the breeding behavior of the Ornate Umbrella Bird on the Upper Xingu River in Brazil. He observed that at the height of the courtship display the male opened his magnificent crest, covering the whole top of his head, and at the same time emitted a deep, rolling rumble.

Some cotingas closely resemble flycatchers (Tyrannidae), and seem to form a link with that family. One of these is the Bright-rumped Attila (*Attila spadiceus*), a bird with several confusing color phases. So similar is it to a flycatcher that when Dr. Arthur A. Allen first encountered the bird in Panama, he at first thought of it as the "Beat-it Flycatcher," from its call note of "beat-it!"

Three-wattled Bellbird (*Procnias tricarunculata*)

Ornate Umbrella Bird (*Cephalopterus ornatus*)

Tyrant Flycatchers

(*Tyrannidae*)

The outstanding characteristic of this large group of small to medium-sized insect-hunters is audacity. So bold are the tyrant flycatchers that many species smaller than starlings consistently harass and rout birds of prey by diving at their backs, and even nest-robbing jays and crows let them alone. These restless, active birds are found from northern Canada to the southern tip of South America, and also in the Galapagos and Falkland Islands. Many species are migratory, flying long distances from North to South America, or moving up and down on the sides of mountains in order to keep in touch with seasonally shifting sources of insect food. Tyrant flycatchers are represented by 365 species, most of which are concentrated in the tropical portions of America. They are very diverse in form, and have succeeded in filling many niches from the floor to the roof of forest and from sea level to some 12,000 feet in the Andes. Some live in swamp edges next to water, others in grasslands; and still others have taken to the ground where they run like little plovers.

Tyrant flycatchers differ from Old World flycatchers in many basic features, involving wing, voice and body structure, and therefore, despite their super-ficial similarity in appearance and feeding habits, the two groups are not thought to be closely related. Rather, their similarities are ascribed to factors of convergent evolution operating on very different groups of birds which have become adapted to the "flycatching" habit.

Tyrant flycatchers have the ten-primaried wing well developed, and many of the species soar and dive with great ease. The tail is variable in shape, ranging from a square to a deep fork. Usually the tyrants are modestly dressed in olives and browns, and the sexes look alike, but some of the species have the body largely white, scarlet, orange or yellow, and many have ornamental patches of color, such as fiery red, yellow or white crests that are erectile. Others have white eye-rings and fleshy caruncles.

Tyrant flycatchers usually have bristle-like feathers growing at the side of the bill. These apparently are a help in sieving the air to snare insects in flight. Some of the species, however, have poorly developed rictal bristles and are chiefly eaters of small seeds and berries. The bills themselves vary greatly in shape. Some are hardly different from the bills of large warblers, others are flattened and broad, and many are strongly hooked. Regardless of shape and size, apparently all of the bills are snapped shut with an audible crack when insect prey is caught.

In capturing flying insects, many tyrants hunt from special perches and habitually dive at fast-flying prey. But others fly out to scan foliage, hovering here and there, and then returning to eat their food at the hunting perch. Such perches may be near the ground or very high in trees. Some species fly down to the ground and there pounce on beetles and grasshoppers. These are caught in the bill but held partially in the feet as they are pulled apart and eaten, usually at the place of capture. Some few species run on the ground, moving in short, quick spurts and then standing still, after which they may pull an insect from the ground or leap nearly straight up into the air to capture one in flight. In the latter case they carry their quarry to the ground to be devoured. The Fire-crowned Tyrant (*Machetornis rixosa*), which hunts in this terrestrial manner, also lands on the backs of cattle and hunts there for flies and ticks somewhat in the manner of the Tick Bird (*Crotophaga ani*). Dr. Ernest Schäfer observed that they often let the cattle carry them long distances in this manner.

A number of the flycatchers flutter over water to take insect food, and even small fishes, from the surface. The Boat-bill (*Megarynchus pitangua*), the largest of the tyrant "flycatchers," has developed the tastes of a small hawk in that it captures and eats young birds, mice, lizards, small snakes, frogs, spiders and even mollusks. To kill this prey, this bird batters the victim in much the manner of the shrikes.

The calls of tyrants are usually grating, unmelodious chatters and cries, with only a few species rating as songsters. These notes are delivered from perches or in flight.

[269

Eastern Phoebe (*Sayornis phoebe*)

Tyrant flycatchers build a wide variety of nests. The structures may be open or domed, cradled in upright forks or suspended or built on a foundation of mud and partially glued to rocks. They may be on the ground under a rock or low in the forest and camouflaged with lichens and mosses, or even straddling a lichen-covered limb and covered with spider webs to which lichens are stuck. Such a nest resembles a protruberance on the limb. Other nests may be elaborate structures of grasses and thin tendrils draped like large sausages through a high crotch, the entrance a tube hanging down on one side, and the nest a bag or purse hanging down on the other. Some of the tyrants nest in the abandoned holes of woodpeckers, adding nest material of tendrils and leaves and decorating the entrance with a snakeskin, apparently as a mechanism of protection. And still others appropriate the stick, thorn and mud nests of certain of the ovenbirds in which to lay their eggs.

The eggs of tyrants, even those of the hole nesters, are usually light-colored and often white with a wide variety of spotting and marbling. These markings are of many dark colors, often so profuse that they virtually conceal the light base color of the eggs. High in rank among the unusually variable nests of this family are those of the Common Tody Flycatcher (*Todirostrum cinereum;* Plate 125), which ranges from Mexico south to Argentina. This four-inch species builds a purselike, pensile nest in the forest edge. Another photograph (Plate 126) shows the semiterrestrial Fire-crowned Tyrant (*Machetornis rixosa*) which is widespread in South America. The nest depicted there is in a large stick structure, probably built by and appropriated from an ovenbird. A third type of bird and nest architecture is that of the Eastern Phoebe (*Sayornis phoebe;* Plate 124). This species first makes a base of mud and then adds nesting materials that include moss, hair, feathers and rootlets.

The female does most of the nest-building, and she is also probably responsible for the incubation of the eggs, a task that varies from about 12 days in the kingbirds to about 19 days in the Boat-billed Flycatcher. Usually only the female broods the young, but both parents feed them.

The Black Phoebe (*Sayornis nigricans*), which

ranges from California through most of South America, is six inches long and mainly black with a white abdomen. Always found near water, it hunts by hawking insects in flight and occasionally by shagging small insects and fishes from the surface of water. This well-known bird nests in the shadows of caves, bridges and well-houses, building a platform of mud and vegetable matter and laying from three to six eggs. Like many of the tyrants, it has several broods per year. The Ash-throated Flycatcher (*Myiarchus cinerascens;* Plate 123) is a common resident of the southwestern United States and northern Mexico.

One of the few brightly-colored tyrants is the Vermilion Flycatcher (*Pyrocephalus rubinus*), a six-inch bird that ranges from the southern United States to Argentina. In this species the male has the crown and underparts vermilion red, while in the female these parts are mainly brown.

Flycatchers with scissor-like tails are the longest members of the family, reaching a maximum length of 16 inches. The Fork-tailed Flycatcher (*Muscivora tyrannus*) has a black cap and white underparts and long, black outer tail feathers. This species is highly migratory and travels in large numbers.

Kingbirds are among the most aggressive of the tyrants. The Eastern Kingbird (*Tyrannus tyrannus*), an eight-inch bird with a prominently white-tipped tail, is widely distributed in North America and winters south to Bolivia. Other species, such as the Tropical Kingbird (*T. melancholicus*), are widespread in tropical America, and they typify the group that always hunts from prominent perches in the top of the forest or in the forest edge. The Boat-billed Flycatcher (*Megarhynchus pitangus*) is a heavy flycatcher that reaches nine inches in length and ranges from Mexico southward through much of South America. It has the crown conspicuously bordered with white and the bill swollen, long and sharply hooked. This species seems to be an enlarged edition of the familiar Great Kiskadee (*Pitangus sulphuratus;* Plate 127), whose range extends north to Texas. The Great Kiskadee has a generally lighter body and a more slender bill. It builds retort-shaped nests in trees, often near water, and frequently it supplements its insect diet by catching small fish from the surface of ponds and streams. The most ornate of the flycatchers is the Royal Flycatcher (*Onychorhynchus mexicanus*), which lives from Mexico to northern South America. Although only 6½ inches long, the olive-brown male has an erectile orange-vermilion crest rising from the forehead in a giant fan carried at right angles to the head. The crown feathers, which are tipped with violet, can be folded. The female has a similar fan crest, but the feathers are brownish. These splendidly adorned birds live in the lower tier of dense forests, often near water.

At the other extreme are the Elaenia flycatchers, of which there are many dull-colored, rather nondescript species, generally gray with small, concealable white crests. Elaenias generally occur in open, bushy country, with various species inhabiting even the rocky plateaus atop the great stone mountains of Guiana. A wide-ranging species is the Caribbean Elaenia (*Elaenia martinica*), which inhabits the islands of the Lesser Antilles and the Gulf of Mexico. This species, like the wide-ranging Yellow-bellied Elaenia (*E. flavogaster*), is about six inches long, grayish olive-brown in color, with two pale whitish wing bars and a concealable white crest.

Sharpbill (*Oxyruncinae*)

Sharpbills are starling-sized, somewhat tanager-like birds that may be related to the tyrant flycatchers. Uncommon to rare, they dwell in the forests of the New World between Costa Rica and Paraguay. The entire subfamily consists of a single species (*Oxyruncus cristatus*) that splits into at least six very similar races. Two of these have the underparts washed with yellow, and four have them whitish. Only one race, that along the Rio Tocantins in Brazil, dwells in the purely tropical jungles. The remainder live in the trees of cool, mountain forests such as those at 3000 feet on Mount Auyan-tepui in southern Venezuela, where the author has collected this bird.

Sharpbills are named for their narrow, sharp, straight bills, which show no trace of the hooked tip found in tyrant flycatchers, presumably their nearest relatives. Furthermore, they have the nostrils elongated, not round, and the feet are stouter. Another distinct character is the fringe of hooked barbs found along the edges of their primaries. With their bright green upperparts and silky yellow-and-scarlet crest, sharpbills look somewhat like ornate tyrannids. The lower parts are generally light, either whitish or washed with yellow, and having blackish spots. The female is quite similar to the male but has a shorter and less brilliant crest. The family has no close relatives and its exact position in our system of classification has never been satisfactorily determined.

Plant-cutters (*Phytotomidae*)

Long thought to be related to the finches, the plant-cutters, stocky, grosbeak-shaped birds seven inches long, of the temperate zone of Peru, Bolivia, Argentina, Chile and Patagonia, are now known to be near relatives of the cotingas. Plant-cutters are so called because of their wasteful, parrot-like manner of feeding, involving the indiscriminate cutting and clipping of leaves, buds, twigs and berries. The saw-toothed edges of their bills facilitate this cutting. Because of this habit people in many areas destroy them, a practice made easy by the fact that the bird is fearless and friendly in its usual habitat—open forest, bushy grasslands and gardens. Plant-cutters fly haltingly on their short, pointed wings.

Three species, all of which belong in one genus, are known. These are the Peruvian Plant-cutter (*Phytotoma raimondii*), the Chilean Plant-cutter (*P. rara*) and the Reddish Plant-cutter (*P. rutila*). This last is a common and relatively colorful bird in much of Argentina and Patagonia.

The great English field naturalist, W. H. Hudson, described the Reddish Plant-cutter as usually found singly but sometimes in small flocks. He observed that the reddish male often sat on the tops of bushes and that, when the nest was approached by an intruder, it uttered a bleating alarm note before hiding or flying off with short jerky movements, the wings producing a humming sound. The nest, he wrote, was a light structure of twigs built in a thorny bush and lined with fibers. In one such nest he found four bluish green eggs flecked with reddish brown.

The male Reddish Plant-cutter resembles a Pine Grosbeak; the female resembles a large sparrow. The male has the upperparts dull grayish olive, the underparts and forehead rose red and the wings blackish crossed with two white bars.

The Chilean Plant-cutter is gray both above and below. This widely distributed species builds its nest in tall trees and has an extremely bad reputation as a despoiler of gardens, but ornithologists declare that it is not so destructive as hearsay would have it.

Pittas or Jewel Thrushes

(*Pittidae*)

Pittas are thrush-sized birds of uncommon, almost jewel-like beauty. These birds of Africa, India, Ceylon, southern China, Malaysia, the Philippines, New Guinea and Australia are among the most difficult of diurnal birds to see. Their home is on and near the floor of deep, dark jungles, ranging from lowland mangroves up through the mid-mountain bamboo jungles to the dripping moss forest 8000 feet above the sea. The 23 species are so closely similar in structure that they are grouped together in a single genus, *Pitta,* a Latinization of a native name meaning "small bird."

Pittas are plump birds with oversized heads, overlength legs and undersized, square tails. In fact, the tail is so short that it often seems to be missing; the resulting profile is made even more unusual by long, spindly legs. The ant-pittas of the New World have much the same general form and occupy much the same general ecological niche on the floor of deep tropical forest; but they are generally brownish birds devoid of the bright and often poster-paint coloration of the pittas, which is similar in both male and female.

When these birds attempt to flee, they usually hop on the floor of the forest rather than fly on their short, rounded wings; and when they do fly, they usually cover only short distances, except during migration. On the ground they have an upright stance,

which they constantly interrupt by a bobbing of the head as they turn leaves in search of insects, worms and snails.

Pittas appear to defend a winter feeding territory—or at least this may be inferred from reports from Ceylon. There Indian or Blue-winged Pittas (*Pitta brachyura*), G. M. Henry states, stake out a territory soon after their arrival from India and remain within it until spring, fighting off other pittas.

That many pittas are highly migratory is something of a surprise in birds that fly so little and skulk in the dark recesses of small areas of forest so much of the year. Some species fly south to winter; others fly north. In Africa, India, Ceylon and the Indo-Malayan region there are numerous records of migrating pittas flying into lighted windows at night—even into windows in cities as far north as Japan.

In their forest abodes pittas appear to go about alone or in scattered pairs during much of the year, keeping in touch with each other by melodious whistles and low grunting sounds. The former are loud and may be heard particularly in the early morning and at dusk. On bright days pittas are quiet, and at night they take to low trees to sleep.

From Dr. J. P. Chapin we learn that the Green-breasted Pitta (*Pitta reichenowi*) of Africa engages in a kind of aerial dance rather similar to that indulged in by the broadbills. In the execution of this dance the birds sit quietly on low perches and periodically hop upward in a small circle, the wings probably causing the curious buzzing noise that always accompanies such movements.

The nest, which is much like that of the New World ovenbirds and very different from that of the broadbills, is a large globular structure with a solid roof and an entrance curving in from one side. The nest material consists of twigs, grasses, leaves, moss, strips of bark, all of which is firmly worked together and is sometimes glued with mud. At times the nest is placed on or very near the ground, but usually it is lodged in the forks of bushes or low trees in dark areas of the forest. The eggs are glossy white or buffy and nearly round, and have a variety of marks, such as spots, smudges, and wavy hair lines, ranging from reddish brown to purplish and blackish, usually concentrated at the larger end. The set varies from two to six, depending on the species. In many areas pittas breed at the height of the wet season. For example, in Papua the author found a fresh egg of the Black-headed Pitta (*Pitta sordida*) in March when each afternoon the sky opened in a deluge that made a veritable marsh of the jungle floor.

The East African Pitta (*P. angolensis*) of tropical African forests is one of the pittas that have been observed jumping from a low bough in deep

[continued on page 289]

158. European Robin (*Erithacus rubecula*
Range: Iceland, Eurasia and North Afric

[JOHN MARKHAM]

272]

159. Reed Warbler
(*Acrocephalus scirpaceus*)
Range: Iceland, Eurasia and Africa

[JOHN MARKHAM]

160. Nightingale
(*Luscinia megarhynchos*)
Range: Eurasia and North Africa

[JOHN MARKHAM]

161.
Red-capped
Robin
(*Petroica
goodenovii*)
Range: Australia
[NORMAN CHAFFER]

162.
European
Wood Warbler
(*Phylloscopus
sibilatrix*)
Range: Eurasia
and North Africa

[P. O. SWANBERG]

163. European Blackbird, male (*Turdus merula*)
Range: Eurasia [JOHN MARKHAM]

164.
European
Blackbird,
female
(*Turdus
merula*)

Range:
Eurasia

[JEAN AND GUY
CUSSAC]

165. Wheatear (*Oenanthe oenanthe*)

Range: Northern Hemisphere north to Alaska and Spitzbergen;
winters south to the Congo [ERIC J. HOSKING]

166.
Black-tailed
Gnatcatcher
(*Polioptila
melanura*)

Range:
Southwestern
United States
and northern
Mexico

[ELIOT PORTER]

167. Townsend's Solitaire
(*Myadestes townsendi*)

Range: Mountains of western
North America to Alaska;
winters to northern Mexico

[ELIOT PORTER]

168. Eastern Bluebird
(*Sialia sialis*)

Range: North America from
Saskatchewan to Honduras;
also Bermuda

[AUSTING AND KOEHLER:
NATIONAL AUDUBON]

169. Mountain Bluebird (*Sialia currucoides*)
Range: Mountains of western North America to Mexico
[ELIOT PORTER]

170. European Redstart
(*Phoenicurus phoenicurus*)

Range: Europe, western Asia
and North Africa

[WALTER E. HIGHAM]

171.
Orange-billed
Nightingale
Thrush (*Catharus
aurantiirostris*)

Range: Central
and northern
South America

[PAUL SCHWARTZ]

172. California Thrasher
(*Toxostoma redivivum*)
Range: California

[LAURENCE M. HUEY]

173. Bare-eyed Robin
(*Turdus nudigenis*)
Range: Lesser Antilles,
Trinidad, Tobago and
northern South America

[PAUL SCHWARTZ]

174. Rose-breasted Thrush Tanager, male
(*Rhodinocichla rosea*)
Range: Mexico to northern South America

176. Eurasian Dipper (*Cinclus cinclus*)
Range: Eurasia and North Africa
[ERIC J. HOSKING]

175. Rose-breasted Thrush Tanager, female
[PAUL SCHWARTZ]

177. Short-billed Marsh Wren (*Cistothorus platensis*) Range: Canada to Tierra del Fuego [ELIOT PORTER]

178. Rufous-breasted Wren
(*Thryothorus rutilus*)

Range: Central and northern
South America

[PAUL SCHWARTZ]

179. Hedge Sparrow (*Prunella modularis*)

Range: Eurasia

[JOHN MARKHAM]

180. Pygmy Nuthatch (*Sitta pygmaea*) Range: North America from Canada to Central Mexico [LAURENCE M. HUEY]

181. Blue Tit (*Parus caeruleus*) Range: Eurasia [JOHN MARKHAM]

182. Purple rumped Sunbird
(*Nectarinia zeylonica*)
Range: India and Ceylon

[H. RUHE AND T. ROTH]

183. Verdin, female (*Auriparus flaviceps*)
Range: Southwestern United States and adjacent parts of Mexico

[ELIOT PORTER]

184.
Chestnut-sided Warbler
(*Dendroica pensylvanica*)
Range: Saskatchewan to South Carolina; winters to Panama

[ELIOT PORTER]

185. Water Pipit (*Anthus spinoletta*) Range: Northern Hemisphere [ELIOT PORTER]

186. Blue-headed Vireo (*Vireo solitarius*) Range: Mountains of North and Central America

187. MacGillivray's Warbler (*Oporornis tolmiei*) Range: Western North America; winters to Colombia

[continued from page 272]

forest and executing small looplike flights, as many as two or three times per minute. This species is seven inches long, green on the back and buffy below. Its chief characters are a scarlet abdomen and under-tail coverts and vivid black stripes on the crown and through the eyes. Termites form a substantial part of the food of this and other species. Its nest, a retort-shaped structure composed of twigs and leaves, is placed from six to twelve feet up in thorny trees. When disturbed, this species flies up and emits a deep, liquid whistle, at the same time puffing out the feathers and giving a single audible flap of the wings.

The Blue-winged Pitta (*P. brachyura*) is seven inches long. It has a red abdomen, brown underparts, white throat, black mask, green back, sky-blue patches on the rump and wings, and buff head stripes. This is a wide-ranging species, being found from India and Ceylon east to Malaysia and the southern Philippines. In the higher forests of the Himalayas occurs the Blue-naped Pitta (*Pitta nipalensis*), a large brownish bird with vivid blue on the upper neck. It lays from four to five glossy, almost round eggs in a globular nest up to 30 feet above the ground. Farther east, from the Philippines southward through the Pacific to the Celebes, New Guinea and northern Australia, occurs one of the most wide-ranging species, the Red-breasted Pitta (*P. erythrogaster*), an extremely elusive bird of dark forests. It is six inches in length, with a chestnut crown, a dark green breast and a scarlet abdomen. During many months of hunting in the Philippines and New Guinea forests this bird was seen only once by the author, yet during five days he spent in a blind watching a bowerbird, it was seen four times. Doubtless pittas are much more common throughout this range than collections suggest.

Other pittas occur in the Philippines, some of them well deserving their name: jewel thrushes. One such is the Koch's Pitta (*P. kochi*), an eight-inch bird that has rose underparts and an aqua-blue breast. This rare bird is found only in a few oak-forested ravines in the mountains of northern Luzon. Probably the most beautiful of the group is the little-known Steere's Pitta (*P. steerei*), which dwells on the mossy floor of high, wet mountain forests in the southern Philippines. It has the throat white and the underparts sky blue, black and scarlet; its dark back and wings are gorgeously painted with glistening greens and blues.

New Zealand Wrens

(*Xenicidae*)

Four species of small birds living on the islands of New Zealand comprise this little-known family of creeper-like and wrenlike birds. The species that are creeper-like, the Riflemen, obtain most of their food on trunks of trees; the others, the Rock Wrens, feed mostly on the ground among stones. One of the

E. H. N. LOWTHER

Indian or **Blue-winged Pitta** (*Pitta brachyura*)

latter, the Stephen Island Rock Wren (*Xenicus lyalli*), has only recently become extinct. About 15 specimens of this bird were sent to England after being caught in 1894 by a pet cat belonging to a lighthouse-keeper stationed on Stephen Island. This single animal is thought to have wiped out the species. The Stephen Island Rock Wren was seminocturnal and was never seen to fly. With no predators on the island, it appears to have taken up a rodent-like life on the ground among rocks and to have become so modified that, like the moa, it was helpless in the face of change. It was the only flightless passeriform bird known.

On South Island another Rock Wren (*X. gilviventris*) survives among bushes and rocks 3000 to 8000 feet above sea level. It is only about 3¼ inches long, dull green above with pale eye stripes and a brownish head; below it is buffy brown with yellow flanks. This species bobs its head like a shorebird. It builds a globular, firmly roofed nest of leaves and grasses in a rock niche and enters it by a very small hole in the side. Nests have been found with some 800 feathers forming the lining of the egg chamber and entranceway.

Bush Wrens (*X. longipes*) of both North and South Islands often go about in pairs or in small parties, foraging on tree trunks and on the forest floor. They occur from sea level to several thousand feet of altitude in the true forest and nest in cavities in fallen trunks, among roots or even in petrel burrows. One nest, found in a crevice in the roof of a petrel tunnel, was something like that of the sooty chat (*Myrmecocichla nigra*), a species of African thrush which builds a nest in a cavity drilled in the roof of an aardvark burrow. Both birds probably derive protection from their associations. Two ovoid white eggs seem to form the full clutch of the bush wren.

The best-known species of New Zealand Wren is the Rifleman (*Acanthisitta chloris*) of North and South Islands, which dwells in open forests up to about 4000 feet. They climb on shrubs and tree trunks and walk on the ground, and insects and spiders are their chief food. In moving, Riflemen progress with jerky motions, scanning the bark crannies of a tree trunk and moving upward 20 or 30 feet, then flying down to the next tree to begin foraging upward again. Sometimes the pairs or small parties hunt in company with White-Eyes.

Riflemen build ball-like covered nests, such as those described for Rock Wrens. These may be seven feet up in a tree cavity, or they may be independent pear-shaped structures among limbs close to the ground. Sometimes two broods are raised per season. Sets of four and five eggs, ovoid and pure white, have been found. Data gleaned from a number of observations indicate that both male and female assist in building the nest, incubating the eggs and feeding the young.

Asities or Philepittas

(*Philepittidae*)

Asities or Philepittas comprise four species of small birds found only on the island of Madagascar. Two of the species are plump, rather long-legged birds with a superficial resemblance to pittas. The other two species so closely resemble sunbirds (family Nectariniidae) as to have been classified within that family until very recently.

The name Asity is that used by the natives of Madagascar. The family apparently represents a relict group of suboscine birds. They are virtually silent, but are said to utter an occasional thrushlike song. The sexes are very differently colored, and, although both the male and the female have bare skin around the eye, only the male develops a large, brightly colored naked wattle in this area.

The Distribution and Habits of Madagascar Birds by the American ornithologist A. L. Rand gives much information on the habits of these otherwise little-known birds—particularly of the Velvety Asity (*Philepitta castanea*). This bird is about 6½ inches long. The male is a rich velvety black, with a spot of bright yellow at the bend of the wing. In fresh plumage the black feathers are tipped with yellow, but the bird changes appearance completely when these tips wear off and reveal the underlying black. Females and young males are olive-green with some yellowish on the rump and underparts. Dr. Rand found this bird common in the humid forests of eastern Madagascar, but only on mountain slopes between sea level and about 5000 feet. The Velvety Asity generally keeps to bushes close to the ground; from there

K. V. BIGWOOD: NEW ZEALAND GOVERNMENT

Rifleman (*Acanthisitta chloris*)

it occasionally flies up into the middle tier of the forest or to the forest edge. In flight the asity moves strongly but in short stages. It is usually solitary but sometimes is found with other species of birds. All specimens examined by Dr. Rand had been eating fruit, small berries being the principal food.

A slightly smaller species, Schlegel's Asity (*P. schlegeli*), was found to vary its predominantly frugivorous diet with occasional insects and spiders. The male of this western Madagascar species is dark yellowish green above, with a black head and neck and a yellow spot on the upper back. Below it is rich yellow. The female is olive-green above and yellowish below, with white markings on the head.

Dr. Rand's most interesting discovery was of the nest and eggs of the Velvety Asity. The nest was a purselike structure suspended from the top, about eleven inches long, and hanging six feet up in a small tree in thick forest. It had a partially roofed side entrance and was built of palm fibers and covered with dead leaves and moss. The inside lining consisted of leaves. In this nest in late August he found three glossy, pure white eggs. Other eggs that have been found were described as bluish white.

For many years the species *Neodrepanis coruscans* was called the Wattled Sunbird and listed among the Nectariniidae, although many authors had called

290]

attention to some of its peculiarities. No other sunbird was known to have a wattle around the eye, no other sunbird has such a short tail, and no other sunbird has such a well-developed tenth (outermost) primary. It was Dr. Amadon of the American Museum of Natural History who demonstrated, in 1951, that the anatomy of *Neodrepanis,* particularly the structure of the syrinx and the scalation of the tarsus, definitely linked this species with the Philepittidae; the resemblance to sunbirds is merely due to convergent evolution, as *Neodrepanis* is adapted to a nectar-feeding habit similar to that of the sunbirds. We therefore now know this bird as the False Sunbird. The male is dark iridescent blue above and dull yellow below, with a large bare wattle around the eye. The female is dull greenish above and yellowish below, and lacks the wattle. Dr. Rand found it a quiet, rather solitary species, which searched for small insects on the bark and twigs of trees, and for insects and nectar in the long corollas of certain tree blossoms.

A second species of *Neodrepanis,* the Small-billed False Sunbird (*N. hypoxantha*), is known from only three specimens, two in the British Museum and one in the United States National Museum. It is more brightly colored and has a shorter, finer bill than *N. coruscans.* All three specimens were taken many years ago in an area of east central Madagascar in which the original forests have been almost completely destroyed in the last 40 years. It is quite possible that the species is now extinct.

Lyrebirds (*Menuridae*)

The Gargantua of all the vast array of perching birds—an order comprising some two-thirds of all known birds—is the wonderful Lyrebird of Australia. Two rooster-sized species comprise the family: the Superb Lyrebird (*Menura novaehollandiae;* Plate 129) and Albert's Lyrebird (*M. alberti*), which was named for Queen Victoria's consort. Lyrebirds have no close relatives, although the tiny Australian Scrub-bird (*Atrichornis*) bears certain resemblances to them. The Superb appears on all Australian governmental seals and on the one-shilling stamp. It is no exaggeration to say that, in a land that teems with strangely specialized animals, the Lyrebird ranks with the strangest and most interesting—even with the appealing Koala Bear and the singular Duck-billed Platypus.

In February, 1798, deep in the mountain forests of New South Wales, explorers collected a wondrous "mountain pheasant." This was the first Lyrebird seen. Soon, to the amazement of ornithologists, it was proved to be a perching bird the size of a rooster and with upper tail coverts something like a peacock.

In structure this unusual bird resembled a gallinaceous bird, particularly the megapode, but, surprisingly, it had a primitive syrinx bearing resemblances to the "voice boxes" of song birds. It also had an elongated breastbone that was quite distinct from anything known but with affinities to the sterna of perching birds. However, it differed from them all by having only rudimentary clavicles. Its head was small and its legs much elongated, very strong and equipped with powerful toes and long straight claws. These characters and the unique tail have resulted in the two Lyrebirds being placed with the perching birds but in a distinct family of their own.

The Superb has the tail enormously developed and consisting of rectrices to the unusual number of 16. The outermost of these tail feathers are more than two feet long. Below they are whitish and have prominent V-shaped notches of dark brown. In display these ornaments assume a lyre shape; thus the name.

Albert's Lyrebird has the tail much less developed and without barring on the outer rectrices. It is slightly more rust-colored and less dusky brown above, which is the general coloration of the head and body, but the lower surfaces are silvery. Females resemble males but have fowl-like tails.

The vocal prowess of the male Lyrebird is reported to be almost incredible. As a mimic it can master the calls of owls and the famous Laughing Jackass, the voices of people, industrial noises, the rustling of parrot wings in flight and even auto horns. In addition, it has its own songs, and these it performs from morning till evening in the wet, murky forests in the Australian winter. In volume the notes are said to be painful to human ears and to carry through the forest for a distance of almost half a mile.

The Lyrebird uses its large legs and feet to build mounds that are superficially similar to those of some of the megapodes, but have no function other than to serve as a stage on which the resplendent male delivers remarkable concerts and displays its beautiful tail. Such mounds are scattered on the floor of deep, fern-clad woodlands through the eastern part of Australia for about a thousand miles from southern Queensland to Victoria. Sometimes an industrious male will make as many as a dozen in an area of half a mile or less, within a territory in which he will not tolerate other males.

The display of the male is ranked as one of the finest of bird performances. Usually several times a day the bird enters its special singing and dancing area in a secluded fern glade and, after singing from a log or a low limb, mounts to the top of one of its mounds. There it begins a series of particularly sharp and penetrating songs. After a few minutes it unlimbers its great tail, which normally is carried semi-folded like a peacock train. The two broad brownish feathers forming the frame of the "lyre" assume a V-shape, and the lacelike elongated central plumes take the position of the "strings." The tail rises and falls forward like a huge hinge till the top surfaces of the tail feathers come into contact with the back. In this position the broad "lyre frame" feathers are extended at right angles to the body and roughly horizontal to the ground; at the same time the filamented "bird of paradise" plumes fan out 180 degrees between the frames, extending far in front of the head and forming a huge lacy umbrella completely concealing the bird. Thus the male stands with the silvery undersurfaces of the tail reflecting the light of the sky. In climax display the tail brushes the ground both in front and to the sides of the bird, so complete is the pearly canopy. All through the dance the performer accompanies its nervous shimmering with highly varied songs and bubbling notes, and often hops or promenades in circles. Signaling the end of the dance are higher pitched notes; then, with little forewarning, the tail is swept back and folded, and the male stalks off. Females are attracted to this performance, and presumably the male competes for attention with other males in adjacent territories.

Male Lyrebirds are polygamous and have nothing to do with nest building or the raising of young. The females build relatively huge domed nests with side entrances. These may be in low limbs on rock ridges or in clusters of leaves eight or ten feet up, but generally they are on the ground. A single grayish purple, thick-shelled, hen-sized egg is laid. Incubation requires about six weeks, the longest period known for any perching bird, and it is another six weeks before the young leaves the nest to follow the hen about on the floor of the forest. Sometimes it grows so large in the domed nest that it pushes the roof off as it greedily reaches for food. Young males wear female plumage for at least two years.

For years Australian naturalists have questioned the correctness of the posture of the tail as displayed on their government's seals and stamps. This erect lyrelike position is to be seen in almost every nature book, dictionary and encyclopedia the world around, and it is certainly one of the most universally known display attitudes as well as one of the most spectacular. Recently the controversy was resolved when several naturalists observed a displaying male that momentarily showed the tail in a vertical position; but, to say the least, the familiar "postage stamp" attitude is rarely seen in nature.

Superb Lyrebird (*Menura novaehollandiae*)

L. H. SMITH

Superb Lyrebird, female near nest

Scrub-birds *(Atrichornithidae)*

The family of scrub-birds is represented by two species, one of which is exceedingly rare or perhaps extinct. Both are exclusively Australian and are particularly interesting because in song, ventriloquial powers and nesting habits they appear to be close relatives of the comparatively huge lyrebirds. Whereas the latter reach a length from two-and-a-half to three feet, the scrub-birds range only between seven and nine inches in length.

Scrub-birds resemble wrens but are long-tailed and dark brown. Their wings are short, rounded and feeble. On the ground they run nimbly on their strong legs and feet, hiding so well in their normal habitat under brambles and jungle debris that even experts rarely catch sight of them. The few who have seen them report that they run with the tail up like a roadrunner and travel alone or in loose pairs.

According to Australian writers, these primitive perching birds feed on insects, small snails and their eggs; and they creep about in the shadows of the jungle floor almost like rodents, rarely flying and indeed probably incapable of it, for they lack the furculum (wishbone) and have the clavicles so reduced and rudimentary that true flight appears physically impossible. Their nesting habits are very like those of the lyrebird. The nest, which is built of grass, leaves and rootlets, and is lined with a substance that bears a resemblance to wood pulp, is domed and has a side entrance. It is thought that the unique pulpy lining is soft, decayed wood that is worked in the mouth of the scrub-bird and applied like plaster to the inner surfaces of the nest cavity. The nest is placed within inches of the ground in ferns and grasses growing under dense vegetation. The two eggs are generally pinkish white with reddish or purplish speckling, mostly around one end.

The Noisy Scrub-bird (*Atrichornis clamosa*), which may be extinct, belongs to western and southwestern Australia. It is dark brown and about eight inches long and has a whitish throat and breast. Its ringing whistles, often repeated and ending in a loud cracking noise—from which it derives its name—once dominated the forest and, to the exasperation of ornithologists, seem to emanate from the throat of a ghost, so difficult is this bird to see.

In eastern Australia, in the forests of New South Wales and northward to southern Queensland, is found the Rufous Scrub-bird (*A. rufescens*). This species is also predominantly dark brown, but it has the throat and underparts strongly tinged with orange-brown. Also, it is smaller, being only some seven inches long; otherwise, it is similar to the Noisy Scrub-bird in general appearance and habits. Paradoxically, this species, which lives much closer to areas of Australia heavily populated with man and his lethal pets, is still fairly common.

Larks *(Alaudidae)*

Liquid, sweet, flutelike—these are the words generally used to describe the song of the lark, long celebrated as a songster in literature and fable. These small, inconspicuous birds are much easier to recognize acoustically than visually. The family Alaudidae contains 75 species. Representatives range over most of the nonpolar land areas of the world, with the greatest concentration occurring in Africa; but the New World has only one species and the Australian region only two.

Larks are birds of open areas: deserts, beaches, plowed ground, grasslands and river edges. They have greatly increased in many areas as a result of the removal of forests by man. On the ground they run instead of hopping.

Larks differ from other passerine birds in having the rear half of the legs (the tarsi) rounded or blunt, whereas all others have a sharp ridge in this region. Other lark characters are, usually, crests or tufts on the head; long, pointed wings with ten functioning primaries; a conical bill; the rear toe usually equipped with an elongated, nearly straight claw. The sexes are usually alike in color, both having a protective assortment of browns and grays.

Larks habitually sing on the wing, often while soaring, as well as on the ground. Except for a few species that perch on poles and bushes, they normally land only on the ground. Many groups live in sedentary flocks, keeping to large areas of desert and grassland in much the manner that other birds keep to the forests of oceanic islands. As a result, in Africa and Asia many nonmigratory species have split into a number of geographical races. But some larks have developed migratory habits that enable them to penetrate far into the north to take advantage of seasonally abundant supplies of food. They feed chiefly on insects and their larvae and on small crustaceans, but some plant food, including small berries, is eaten.

All larks nest on the ground, first making a slight scraped depression, usually near the base of a tuft of grass. In this a grass cup, sometimes fairly solid and lined with hair, is formed. Occasionally sticks are used, and some of the nests are partially domed. Two to seven eggs may be laid depending on the species, but the average is three to five. These are generally buff or whitish, but in several species the eggs are tinted green or blue and all are spotted and smudged.

Apparently the male does not assist in building the nest, and only the female attends the eggs. Incubation requires about 11 to 12 days. The male defends the nest, using the "broken wing" ruse, and he brings food to the female and later assists in feeding the young. Many larks raise two or more broods per year.

The most famous member of the family is the Skylark (*Alauda arvensis*), one of the most beautiful of songsters as well as one of the most abundant birds in Europe. It is seven inches long and a disarmingly dull brown with blackish streaks above and pale below; its tail is marked with white outer feathers. The song for which it is so famous is a long-sustained musical chir-r-up. Large numbers of Skylarks have been imported into Australia, New Zealand, Vancouver Island and Long Island by well-intentioned but misguided bird-lovers. The populations in Australia, New Zealand and Vancouver Island are thriving. Not so on Long Island, where breeding birds were observed as early as 1887 near Flatbush but where the species now appears to be extinct.

Skylark (*Alauda arvensis*)

Eremophila is the only genus of this almost wholly Old World family that has sent a permanent representative to the New World: namely the Horned Lark (*E. alpestris*), which is found in North America, south to Mexico, with an isolated population in the savannas of Bogota. It is famous for its tufts or horns—elongated black feathers growing over the eyes. This seven-inch bird is streaked brown above, with a yellow line over the eye and a yellow throat. Other distinctive marks are a black throat patch and black throat margins.

Among the Old World larks are the Black Lark (*Melanocorypha yeltoniensis*) of northern Europe and Asia, which reaches a length of seven inches and differs from most larks in that the completely black male is different in color from the brownish female.

The Common Crested Lark (*Galerida cristata*) is representative of the wood lark group, which ranges through Eurasia and Africa. This species, 6½ inches long with a crest that can be erected at will, is generally streaked brown above, and grayish below.

The Hoopoe Lark (*Alaemon alaudipes*) exemplifies the desert larks, which are reported to run as well as plovers. It is named for its strongly curved bill, reminiscent of that of the Hoopoe, which is used for digging up food, particularly the pupae of the destructive locusts that are such a plague in its northeastern African home.

Bush larks occur widely in the Old World; the

Cinnamon Bush Lark (*Mirafra rufocinnamomea*) is typical. It travels in pairs or parties, often flying short distances from underfoot, fluttering and dropping into the grass, or it may tower up from the ground to considerable heights as it sings. Song flights are made both by day and by night. Another species, *M. africana* of the Congo, has been observed performing courtship flights which involved springing from the ground some 20 times in succession and flying to a height of about 30 feet, each time making a buzzing sound with the wings and emitting whistles. A tree percher is the Sabota Lark (*Mirafra sabota*) of arid savannas studded with acacia trees. Like many larks, it is expert at mimicking other birds.

The Short-toed Larks are well represented by Stark's Lark (*Spizocorys starki*), which is very small and has a short rear talon. This species lives in such deserts of Africa as the Kalahari. It is highly gregarious and often associates with other larks.

Swallows and Martins

(*Hirundinidae*)

Many of the seventy-four species of swallows are intimately associated with man, particularly with farmers, who benefit from their insectivorous habits, even as the swallows, in nesting among farm buildings, benefit from the protection and the abundance of food.

Swallows are nearly cosmopolitan in distribution, having failed to establish themselves only in polar regions (although one species nests within the Arctic Circle), in islands far at sea and on New Zealand. They are wonderfully graceful birds that obtain all their food on the wing, coursing through the air in smooth, flowing flight like the swifts, which they superficially resemble. Usually moving in flocks, one moment they dive until they nearly brush the ground or the heads of men or cattle, and the next they tower high, hanging momentarily as if from a string —and all this with breath-taking effortlessness.

In flight the swallow twitters and squeaks. As it sweeps through a squadron of flying ants its frog-shaped, relatively enormous mouth is held so far open the head seems split to the eyes, scooping them up in hundreds until its mouth is packed full of crawling insects. Swallows cruise many areas of sky, sometimes even those over lakes, deserts and oceans. But normally they keep fairly clear of forests, leaving the flying insects of such regions to the multitudes of puffbirds, tyrant flycatchers, bee-eaters and such.

Swallows are among the best known of all birds, but some of their fame stems from fable. A well-known legend concerns the Cliff Swallows (*Petrochelidon pyrrhonota*) that breed at the Mission of San Juan Capistrano in California. In their annual comings and goings, these birds have stirred up a vast amount of interest in migration and given rise to some popular misconceptions. Actually, the swallows are remarkably punctual and cover prodigious distances between their wintering and breeding homes, but they are strongly influenced by weather and food supply, and do *not* arrive on the same day each year.

The flight of swallows is facilitated by exceptionally long primaries, up to twice as long as the longest secondary feathers. In some of the species the margins of the outer primaries are equipped with small barblike hooks. These are probably useful in clinging to vertical surfaces and are the reason for their New World name of Rough-winged Swallow (*Stelgidopteryx serripennis*). Swallows have feet so small that walking is very difficult, and their unsure movements on the ground are more like shuffling. However, the feet serve well for perching on wires and thin sticks—favorite spots for these birds, which normally do not perch in leafy parts of trees. The dress of many swallows is iridescent, particularly above, and the feathers are compactly arranged, though not as compactly as in swifts. In coloration, the two sexes of most swallows are much alike, except for the martins, in which the female is more grayish, less glossy blackish. The plumage is replaced only once per year, after the breeding season.

Swallows are almost unique in the variety of their nesting patterns and in the rapidity with which they apparently can change from one pattern and location to another. Some species, seemingly overnight, have given up nesting on cliffs and hollow trees to nest in association with man—namely, in his barns and houses. This quick acceptance of new situations when they serve food-getting ends may be responsible for the different kinds of nesting situations used by swallows: to wit, holes in trees and banks, mud structures made with muddy pellets carried in the mouth of the builder, and holes drilled in the sand of strands.

Swallows often raise several broods per season. Many species lay pure white eggs and some lay whitish eggs sparsely speckled with brown and gray. The set is from four to six, depending on the species. The period the young spend on the nest after hatching is more than three weeks in many species. This is quite long, as in the swifts, and is thought to be correlated with the high degree of development required in youngsters that must from a very early age seek their own food on the wing. Indeed, some swallows, like most swifts, receive no care from parents after departing the nest.

The following species illustrate the variable breeding patterns of the family: The Purple Martin (*Progne subis*) of North America and the West Indies (southward to Brazil in winter) nests in natural tree cavities, which it upholsters with some straw and twigs. It reaches eight inches in length, the male being glossy blue-black and the female considerably duller and less shiny. Purple Martins are highly gregarious and always nest in colonies. These friendly birds take readily to man-made houses, and in the warmer parts of America a house of martins is much prized—so much so that people have tried to lure them into living close by, although not always successfully. Some tribes of American Indians hung hollowed gourds on trees or poles for use as nest sites.

The Tree Swallow (*Iridoprocne bicolor*), which breeds in North America and winters in Central America, is another tree-cavity nester. It is steel blue-green above and immaculate white below, and is about 5¾ inches long. Its nest is a cup of grass and feathers usually placed in a hollow tree but sometimes in a nest box.

Next in the scale of specializations are probably the diggers of horizontal tunnels, which are typified by the Bank Swallow (*Riparia riparia*), a species that breeds over the whole of Europe, Siberia, Japan and North America. Throughout this vast region these birds are highly gregarious, nesting in colonies in sand banks and migrating in flocks, often with other swallows, to a winter home that extends to South America, Africa and Madagascar. From details of the breeding cycle of this species published by A. J. Peterson in 1955 we learn the following: the male selects the nest site and defends it; he courts by chases; when a female continually returns after such chases the bond is formed and tunnel-digging begins; later, copulation occurs in the sand tunnel; coarse nest material is placed in the nest chamber by both sexes. After the four to five eggs are laid both sexes add feathers to the nest; both the male and the female incubate; incubation requires about 15 days; both sexes feed the young, with the male doing the greater share; the nestlings fly at 23 days. Other studies reported in 1954 indicate that this species, known as the Sand Martin in Europe, not only returns to the same sand banks to nest but also that individuals are very apt to return to the same part of the sand bank.

The Cliff Swallow (*Petrochelidon pyrrhonota*), which breeds in North America and winters in South America, is a six-inch swallow with a whitish forehead. The remainder of the upper parts are steel blue, except that the upper tail coverts are prominently rufous. Below, it is grayish with much chestnut about the head and throat. This highly colonial bird builds a nest that may be called the mason type. The original location of such nests was on the faces of cliffs and bluffs, but today many Cliff Swallows

Barn Swallow (*Hirundo rustica*)

build their tenement-like houses under the eaves of barns and railroad stations. In the latter they seem to benefit from the commotion caused by passing trains; at least, it is the author's belief that colonies located along the railroad right of way are lured by the insects that trains flush from the roadbed.

Perhaps the most widely known of the swallows is the Barn Swallow (*Hirundo rustica;* Plate 128), which is found nesting throughout North America, Europe, Asia, Japan, and south to Africa, India and Mexico. This bird measures seven inches, has the tail deeply forked and has white spotting on all but the longest feathers. It is steel blue above and largely chestnut brown below. Unlike the other species so far discussed, this one builds a nest plastered to a foundation and consisting of a pedestal of mud droplets. It has been found that this nest requires about 1000 trips to build. Like Cliff Swallows, Barn Swallows gather the mud droplets by landing on the ground and shuffling to the edge of muddy pools. There they seem to roll the mud up and, when it is firm enough, carry it off in their mouths.

The nest is constructed chiefly by the female, with the male carrying most of the mud to her. Both sexes sit on the eggs, the female frequently, the male only occasionally. Dr. S. Charles Kendeigh has shown that the male does not actually incubate. His experiments, performed with a heat receptor called a thermocouple, revealed that although the male covered the eggs, he imparted no appreciable heat to them. Also, other researchers have noted that the male does not have a functional brood patch.

These birds engage in prodigious migrations (for example, Barn Swallows banded in Denmark and Norway are regularly taken in the Cape region of South Africa) and it has been shown that they suffer great losses during these seasonal movements. E. A. Mason reported in *Bird Banding* that during 14 years of banding he found that only 2 per cent of the ringed nestlings returned and that the annual mortality was about 73 per cent. He also found that about half of the Barn Swallows raised single broods annually. Second and third broods are common in swallows and are doubtless an important mechanism of survival in birds with a high annual mortality.

The African Rock Martin (*Ptyonoprogne fuligula*), a dull brown bird of precipitous cliffs, will abandon its normal habitat to visit grass fires on the plains, where it has learned to take advantage of the clouds of insects fleeing from the burning grass. The African swallows of the genus *Psalidoprocne* are generally called Rough-winged Swallows because they have the same kind of serrated outer primary as the apparently unrelated New World Rough-winged Swallow (*Stelgidopteryx ruficollis*). Unlike most swallows, these African species are often found at the forest edge or even in glades within the forest.

One of the most beautiful members of the family is the Golden Swallow (*Lamprochelidon euchrysea*), which is snowy white below and a shining bronzy green above. It is found only on the islands of Jamaica and Hispaniola in the West Indies, primarily at high elevations in the mountains. The popularity of swallows and the regularity of their migrations are commemorated in the name of the Welcome Swallow (*Hirundo neoxena*), the harbinger of spring to the people of southern Australia. It closely resembles the common Barn Swallow in appearance. Another species, characteristic of western America, is the Violet-green Swallow (*Tachycineta thalassina;* Plate 130).

African River Martin
(*Pseudochelidonidae*)

This large, dull purplish or greenish black swallow-like bird with scarlet bill and eyes has long been a little-understood species. It was grouped first with the Wood Swallows (Artamidae) and then with the Swallows (Hirundinidae); in the following pages—partly to focus attention on this highly unusual bird—it is granted family status.

Its breeding ground was discovered in 1921 on the middle reaches of the Congo River. Theretofore thought rare, it then became known as a locally abundant species because it was found nesting in immense colonies in holes drilled downward in sand exposed by receding river waters. With the end of the dry season and the rising of the river, the birds departed from these sands. Where they went was long a mystery, but finally it was found that they moved to coastal strands near the mouth of the Nyanga River some 500 miles southwest of the breeding grounds.

The nest is something like that of the Bank Swallow, but the tunnel is drilled downward from a flat sandy surface—a device also used by some bee-eaters. The tunnel slants at a shallow angle for about a yard and at the end is a chamber with a lining of dead leaves and twigs. Three white eggs are the standard set. The colonies range up to 400 pairs and at times swarms of 800 to 1000 birds gather over the breeding grounds. On the sand the birds shuffle clumsily like swallows, and the flock makes a chattering noise like a colony of weaver birds.

The African River Martin (*Pseudochelidon eurystomina*) secures all of its food on the wing. Winged ants are favored, but other insects are also caught.

Helmet Shrikes or Wood Shrikes (*Prionopidae*)

Helmet Shrikes are hook-billed birds that resemble shrikes. They always go about in parties and, except for one aberrant species from Borneo that is somewhat doubtfully included in the family, are restricted to Africa. For the most part, Helmet Shrikes are dull-

BAVARIA VERLAG

Barn Swallow

colored birds of rather gross build that live in trees and bushes over most of Africa. They feed primarily on insects, but also eat small quantities of fruit and even an occasional gecko lizard. All are shrikelike and all nest in cuplike nests in bushes and trees.

Until recently many aberrant kinds of shrikelike birds were grouped together in this family but Dr. Ernst Mayr lately suggested restricting the family to three genera: 1) the Helmet Shrikes (*Prionops*), which occur over most of Africa; 2) the Red-billed Shrikes (*Sigmodus*), which are found in Central and Southern Africa; and 3) the White-crowned Shrikes (*Eurocephalus*), which occur over most of Africa. Still more recently the Bornean Bristle-head (*Pityriasis gymnocephala*), which, because of its bristles, has been called one of the strangest of songbirds, has been provisionally included in this family by Drs. Mayr and Amadon.

The Red-billed Shrike (*Sigmodus caniceps*), which is eight inches long, has a blue-gray crown, a blackish collar and throat, a blackish back, a rufous-tinted white abdomen and reddish feet and bill. Dr. Chapin found that this bird traveled in parties and flew with a buoyant, unhurried kind of flight. Red-billed Shrikes are rather noisy, emitting low *chi, chi, chi* notes and soft whistles. If one of the group is wounded the others remain to defend it. Also there

are reports that the flock will attack a human if he approaches the nests too closely. Natives call this species "leopard bird," presumably because it will mob a leopard.

The White Helmet Shrike (*Prionops poliocephalus*) reaches a length of 8½ inches. It too is found in parties of up to twelve. Such groups are easily observed because of the bird's white plumage and almost constant activity. This species hunts for insects both in trees and on the ground, constantly snapping the beak and delivering low, rasping notes as it does so. It builds its nest of grass fibers, rootlets and shreds of bark, binding the structure together with spider webs and placing it in the open forks of trees from 7 to 20 feet from the ground. Groups of nests are built close together, and sometimes two females lay in the same nest, and in such cases the normal set of four eggs may be doubled. The eggs are greenish cream or pale blue with chestnut and violet-brown spots and scrawls. Incubation seems to be performed by random birds belonging to the flock, and this also holds true for feeding. There are reports of as many as three adults arriving at a nest, there flushing a brooding adult from the nest, and then feeding the young in rapid succession. The last to feed them is likely to remain to brood them.

Almost identical behavior has been noted in the

Spectacled Shrike (*P. plumata*), with a record of four birds out of a party of six bringing nesting material to a nest the group was building.

Another species in the group is Smith's White-crowned Shrike (*Eurocephalus anguitimens*), which reaches ten inches in length. This bird roosts high but comes to the ground frequently and hunts insects in parties. The nest is described as a substantial basin-shaped structure of grass stems fastened with cobwebs. It is set in a fork of a tree fairly high above the ground.

The Bornean Bristle-head (*Pityriasis gymnocephala*) apparently occurs only on the island of Borneo. This curious bird is some ten inches in length and generally grayish black but has much scarlet on the head, throat and shanks. It has the head partially naked and warty and the feathering of the head, ears and the lower throat modified to resemble rigid bristles rather than feathers. The nostrils are slitlike, and the bill is heavy, hooked and deeply notched. A recent Borneo observer, Tom Harrisson, thought the actions of this bird were rather like those of the Mynah bird, and the Bristle-head may indeed prove to be an aberrant starling, not a Helmet Shrike.

Vanga Shrikes (*Vangidae*)

Vanga shrikes comprise 11 species of medium-sized passeriform birds restricted to the forests and bushy grasslands of Madagascar. In the geographical isolation provided by this island, birds of this family have evolved into a great diversity of forms, particularly of the bill. They have many characters in common with the Wood or Helmet Shrikes of Africa, to which they are probably closely related, but they are purely arboreal birds, hunting for their food in the foliage and among the trunks and limbs of trees and bushes. The nest is an open cup placed in a tree fork fairly close to or quite high above the ground. The eggs are generally greenish or whitish with spots of brown around one end.

Gleaned from Dr. Austin Rand's enlightening account of the Vanga Shrikes are the following details: The Chabert Vanga (*Leptopterus chabert*) resembles a wood swallow. Above it is shining dark green with a dark bluish green head and the eye encircled by a bright blue wattle. Below and on the rump it is white. This species travels in flocks of from four to twelve and, in hunting, it sometimes bobs the head. In flight it undulates and sometimes calls sharply. The Blue Vanga (*Cyanolanius madagascarinus*) differs by having the upperparts a shining, light purplish blue. It hunts in small branches for insect food, and in doing so sometimes hangs upside down. The White-headed Vanga (*Artamella viridis*) often hunts in flocks together with large, unrelated birds, as many as 25 of this species occasionally traveling with other birds in this way. Insects and

small chameleons are eaten. Other species, such as the Rufous Vanga (*Schetba rufa*), eat locusts, and one species, the Hook-billed Vanga (*Vanga curvirostris*), unlike the other vangas, is usually found alone or in pairs. It hunts from perches like a kingfisher or a puffbird. It is shaped like a large shrike, is white below, and has the rear half of the head black, a narrow white collar and a black back. Dr. Rand autopsied many specimens and found that two-thirds of the birds had been feeding on reptiles and amphibians—chiefly chameleons and frogs—but also some beetles, cicadas, locusts and spiders.

The Helmet Bird (*Euryceros prevostii*) communicates by means of a tremulous whistle. This species moves so quickly in feeding through the crown of the forest that a hunter can hardly keep up with it. It is 11 inches long and has a huge compressed bill, the maxilla of which is shaped like a helmet. Below it is black; above it is bright chestnut with a black head.

The Sicklebill or Falculea (*Falculea palliata*) is a highly gregarious woodland bird which sometimes travels in large flocks. A female accompanied by a male was observed gathering dead twigs in trees and bushes for a nest. The nest was in a tree some 36 feet up. As its name suggests, it differs from most of the Vangidae in possessing a long, downcurved bill.

Bell Magpies, Australian Butcher-birds and Piping Crows (*Cracticidae*)

Eleven species from Australia and New Guinea make up this small family of birds ranging from the size of jays to that of crows. Some have extraordinary habits, including tool-using and certain social behavior patterns. Cracticids in general show resemblances to the shrikes. They have the head and the bill relatively large, the latter being generally long and straight, with a sharp and often hooked point. The plumage is generally black and white, and the legs are almost completely sheathed with scales arranged in a kind of boot. These birds dwell in open forests and bushy grasslands, and eat insects, plant food, lizards and even small birds. The nest is usually placed in a tree crotch fairly high above the ground and from three to five eggs, spotted at the larger end, are laid.

The largest members of the family are the Piping Crows, or Currawongs, which reach more than 20 inches in length. One species is the Squeaker (*Strepera versicolor*), a dark gray bird with a yellow eye and with white on the wings and the under-tail coverts. (Most Piping Crows are white in these areas, but some species are completely black and very crowlike in appearance.) This species occurs in the forest edges and grasslands of Australia. Like the other Piping Crows, it is rather unpopular with man because of the damage it does to fruit orchards. Its calls are trumpet notes and mewings. From two to three eggs are incubated by the female, and, when fledged, the young are reported to remain with the parents until breeding time rolls around again.

The Gray Butcher-bird (*Cracticus torquatus*), like true butcher-birds (shrikes), catches mice, small reptiles, insects, and even small birds, and impales them on thorns. In so doing, the Australian Butcher-bird employs two kinds of tools, one for killing and storing its game and the other for pulling it apart. In the first it carries its victim to a thorny bush or tree and forces it onto a sharp thorn. Australian observers also report that it has been seen to drag a young honeycreeper along the jagged, broken ends of a limb in such a manner that the limb butt acted like a vise to assist the butcher-bird in ripping its victim into small mouthfuls. This bird has also been seen wedging lizards tightly into tree crotches the way some jays store acorns.

The Gray Butcher-bird is generally gray and about 11 inches long, with a black head and tail, a white rump and underparts. Recent reports from Australia indicate that these birds defend their territories all year long and that the defense is conducted by pairs of birds rather than by large groups, as in the Western Magpie (discussed below). The nest of the Gray Butcher-bird has been described by Serventy and Whittell as a cup-shaped structure of twigs and roots usually 6 to 20 feet up in a tree fork. From three to four pale brown eggs, marked with reddish brown, are laid in it. The incubation period is 23 days and the fledgling period from 25 to 26 days.

The Western Magpie (*Gymnorhina dorsalis*) is an aggressive and magpie-like 17-inch bird with bold black and white markings. It has the bill sharply hooked and feeds chiefly on insects caught on the ground. Its social activities are very different from those of most passerine birds. For example, it is said to mob anything, even a human being, that threatens its territory. This habit is somewhat similar to that of the Helmet Shrikes of Africa, which attack leopards and other intruders in their territory. In the case of the Western Magpie, all members of the clan join in the defense of a communal territory.

The remarkable courtship behavior of these birds was discovered by the Australian ornithologists A. H. Robinson and H. M. Wilson, who observed territories, some of which were about 100 acres in extent, that were jointly defended by clans of from 6 to 20 birds. They found that the birds lived within these areas, most of the time countering invasions from rival clans and other kinds of animals, sometimes including man. No pairing was found, the males being promiscuous and breeding with many of the clan. The females built the nests, sometimes close together in a tree, sometimes far apart. They incubated the eggs and fed the nestlings, and only after

NORMAN CHAFFER

Gray Butcher-bird (*Cracticus torquatus*)

the young left the nest did the male help with their feeding and protection.

But this is not all that is strange about the Western Magpie. The nest is placed as much as 50 feet above the ground and, because the bird happens to favor wire for nesting material and telegraph poles for sites, it is an exasperatingly effective saboteur. One nest of this bird contained 238 separate pieces of wire ranging from something over four inches to more than four feet in length; the wire weighed nearly five pounds and had a combined length of 234 feet! These iron and steel fortresses seem to have no function other than to hold from two to five greenish and buff eggs.

Shrikes or Butcher birds
(*Laniidae*)

Representatives of the 67 species of miniature "birds of prey" called shrikes or butcher-birds occur on all of the continents except South America and Antarctica. However, the Old World is the true stronghold of this family, all but two species occurring there.

Shrikes range from the size of starlings to that of jays and are of bold, seemingly fearless temperament. Their role among Passeriform birds is much like that of the diurnal birds of prey among the non-passeres. They are relatively large-headed and robust and have rounded, short and powerful wings and short, weak legs, but the feet, like the bill, are strong. Their name is derived from their shrieklike calls. They have the tail square or graduated rather than forked, and the young and subadults are usually transversely barred below. The beak is unique among the perching birds in that it is generally falcon-like, having a strong, rapacious hook followed by a toothlike projection that serves in dismembering prey. Shrikes are essentially carnivorous, and the largest part of their food consists of insects. All species catch living prey, diving or pouncing on it in the air from lookout perches or from hovering positions. But, unlike the hawk, which strikes its prey, stiletto-like, with its feet, and most of the other aerial hunters, which grab their quarry in the bill, the shrike delivers a stunning, cutting blow with the hooked bill, then follows and recovers the prey on the ground. It then carries off the dazed victim to a thorny bush, a barbed-wire fence or even the jagged end of a broken limb. Because its feet and toes are weak, the shrike, or butcher-bird, as it has come to be known because of its rapacious habits, resorts to an outside agent, usually a sharp thorn, to assist in both killing and dismembering its victim. On this the shrike impales its prey, be it grasshopper, mouse, shrew, frog, or even warbler or sparrow, and makes the thorn serve as a vise to hold the carcass while it is dismembered. The shrike's use of a tool to assist in this process is a wonder of nature.

Needless to say, shrikes are generally unloved birds because of their unattractive methods of hunting, which often leave their victims securely impaled and doomed to a lingering death. Animal behaviorists are not sure why shrikes occasionally decorate certain thorny trees with uneaten victims, leaving the bodies dangling like ornaments. Some think that such trees may serve as lures to insects and birds, thus functioning as a trapping mechanism. Others believe that the whole behavior is functionless. One persuasive theory, expounded by the Swedish ornithologist, Dr. S. Durango, whose conclusions are based on many years of observation of the Red-backed Shrike (*Lanius collurio*), supports the widely held belief that the impaling of animals is basically a larder—in other words, an aid to survival in periods when game is not to be found. He noted many instances in which stored food was used by shrikes and his observations tended to show that, in times of plenty, more food was impaled than eaten, apparently as a stockpile.

Another mechanism of survival involves the defense of feeding territories. Shrikes sit on lookout limbs or posts, taking no pains to hide, and when game is spied, fly rapidly to it. Also, from such perches, they drive off other shrikes and smaller birds, often killing them when they invade the defended area.

The two members of the family that reach the New World, the Migrant, or Loggerhead Shrike (*Lanius ludovicianus*), and the Northern Shrike (*L. excubitor;* Plate 132), are very similar, being pale grayish with prominent black masks, wings and tail. The latter breeds in Canada and visits the United States in winter. The Loggerhead is quite unwelcome at winter feeding stations despite the fact that this species eats insects whenever it can. Not so the Northern Shrike, which winters in colder regions and must subsist chiefly on small rodents and birds.

Typical of the *Lanius* group, the nest of the Loggerhead is bulky and warmly lined; its eggs are dull white with much brownish and grayish spotting. After pairing, both sexes participate in erecting the nest, with the male doing most of the work. Usually both sexes share in incubation, but it is customary for the male to do very little egg-warming. Instead he may feed the female as she incubates. Incubation requires some 16 days, after which both parents feed the nestlings. The young usually depart the nest after a period of from 19 to 21 days.

The Brown Shrike (*L. cristatus;* Plate 133) of eastern Asia and Malaysia is a highly migratory species. The Fiscal Shrike, or Jackie Hangman (*L. collaris*) of Africa, a black-backed, white-breasted, rufous-flanked bird, is one of the commonest and best known of African shrikes. In many areas it profits by living close to man, attacking the birds and small mammals that gather around him, and even flying into houses to kill pet canaries.

This species eats chiefly the nestlings of birds, but it also kills insects, frogs, toads, lizards and small snakes. In fact, its prowess is quite remarkable, considering that it is only 8½ inches long and weak-footed, and one ornithologist, Austin Roberts, once found four quail finches that this bird had impaled side by side on a barbed-wire fence. When a trespasser enters its feeding territory, it puffs out its throat feathers and utters harsh notes, at the same time spreading and twitching the wings threateningly and switching the tail back and forth. The nest is built of weeds, grasses, feathers and rootlets in a tree fork from 3 to 15 feet up.

The bush shrikes of Africa, constituting a distinct subfamily of the Laniidae, differ from true shrikes in that many of them are gaudily colored, with black or greenish backs and yellow, orange or scarlet underparts. They range from high mountain forests to desert scrub, and most species are far more secretive and skulking in their habits than the true shrikes.

Old World Orioles
(*Oriolidae*)

The true orioles consist of 34 species of brightly colored, medium-sized birds that occur in Eurasia, Africa, and thence southeast through Madagascar, Ceylon, the East Indies, New Guinea and Australia.

They bear a superficial resemblance to the orioles of the New World but are not closely related to them.

True orioles are purely arboreal birds of the forest crown, the forest edge and the trees of bushy savannas. All have the wings long and the bill relatively straight, except the Australian Fig-birds (*Sphecotheres*), and all have a distinct notch in the maxilla. Other characters of a more subtle kind are bare nostrils, short legs and strong nails. The prevailing colors found in the group are yellow, green and black, and in most species the sexes are quite different from each other in color, the female being much duller. In young orioles the plumage is streaked.

All but two species belong to the nearly cosmopolitan Old World genus *Oriolus*. Some, like the Isabella Oriole (*O. isabellae*), are rare and little known; others, like the Black-naped Oriole (*O. chinensis*), are wide-ranging. The former, an olive-yellow bird about eight inches long, is known from a few specimens taken in the mountains of the Philippine island of Luzon, one of which was shot in the mountains of Bataan Peninsula by the author. The Black-naped Oriole is among the largest, reaching ten inches in length. In this species the male is bright yellow above, has black on the wings and central tail, much black on the head and a black mark

Greater Racket-tailed Drongo (*Dicrurus paradiseus*)

across the eyes. Below, the male is pale yellow. This bird is a feature of the wooded farm and grasslands of the Indo-Malayan region, where its brilliant yellow plumage can be seen flashing against the green of the forest edge.

A very similar species is the Golden Oriole (*O. oriolus;* Plate 134) of Eurasia and Africa, which as a summer visitor is the only member of the family to reach Europe, breeding to southern England.

The female is greenish in contrast to the bright yellow, black-winged male. In this species both the male and the female build the nest, incubate the eggs and feed the young, which remain in the nest for about 14 days after hatching. The nest is a cup of grasses; the set is two to four speckled white eggs. The Golden Oriole is more easily heard than seen. Its calls are rich whistles.

The Black-headed Oriole (*O. larvatus*) of Africa is an excellent mimic, and employs an elaborate courtship display. The female does all the nest-building but the male accompanies her and sometimes feeds her. Using a diving attack, both birds join in defending the nest against cuckoos and shrikes. Typical of the Old World Orioles, these birds eat caterpillars and other insect food, first stripping hairy species of caterpillars largely by pummeling them. Incubation is performed by the female, with the male bringing food to her; but after the hatching of the eggs (in 14 days) both sexes feed the young. If the young perish, these orioles remate within a few days and soon begin building a second or even a third nest.

The second group of orioles comprises the Fig-birds of Australia and New Guinea, of which there are two species. They have the bill curved, the toes short and the lores nude. On the southeastern coast of New Guinea the author once collected three Fig-birds (*Sphecotheres vieilloti*) from a tree at the edge of the beach. They were starling-sized and olive-yellow with dusky striping. Fig-birds travel in noisy groups, feeding on fruit and berries. The nest is a neat, simple, unlined, saucer-shaped structure that is formed from long tendrils and suspended by its edges, usually from high, drooping branches. Fig-bird eggs are a pale greenish brown with rich spots and blotches.

Drongos (*Dicruridae*)

Although relatively small, drongos are renowned for their courage. The 20 species comprising this sharply circumscribed family are found in Africa, southern Asia, the Philippines and islands of the Southwest Pacific as far east as the Solomons. Drongos attack flying insects with the ferocity of the shrike, usually catching them in mid-air but sometimes striking them to the ground. They brook no intrusion in areas they consider their own and attack birds many times their size, such as crows, hawks or even eagles; African natives say that they can drive off leopards.

Drongos are mostly jay-sized perching birds with tails of varying length and ornamentation. Many have crests. Their predominant coloration is shiny black, with the sexes alike.

Dr. Charles Vaurie recently revised the drongos. He recognized two genera: one for a species with twelve tail feathers found in the high forests of New Guinea, and one for the other nineteen species, all of which have ten tail feathers. Drongos range widely through Old World forests between sea level and 10,-000 feet and all have the bill stout and rather like that of a crow or jay, with a sharp hook and a subterminal notch on the upper mandible. All have the rictal bristles, that is, the spiny feathers growing at the base of the bill, well developed, sometimes even covering the nostrils. Nothing in their breeding behavior supports the theory that drongos are closely related to crows or the earlier supposition that they are related to the shrikes. However, they may be related to the Old World flycatchers.

The primary food of drongos is insects ranging from termites to large dragonflies, cicadas, grasshoppers and spiders. Sometimes up to 25 birds will gang up on a swarm of termites. Some drongos eat large insects much as a hawk does, that is, with one foot holding the insect down they rip it apart and devour it piecemeal. Dr. J. P. Chapin, who made this observation of the African Drongo (*Dicrurus adsimilis*), calls attention to the fact that jays and titmice also do this and that on occasion all three groups carry food with their feet like a raptor.

Drongos are found in all kinds of habitat from wooded savannas and gardens to forest edge and the canopy of true forest. Some are fairly quiet, but most are noisy birds that exude authority, emitting harsh notes, although on occasion they deliver musical ones as well. Some mimic small birds and on catching sight of a snake set up a din that sounds like a mob of angry birds.

The basket-like nest of the drongo is generally interwoven with fibrous lichens and plant fibers and camouflaged with spider silk and lichens. It is small and frail in comparison with the bird and hard to see. Nests of two species that the author has examined, one the Spangled Drongo (*Dicrurus hottentottus*) of tropical New Guinea and the other the King Crow (*D. macrocercus*) of Nepal, were very similar, both being greenish and suspended from thin-forked limbs located under a canopy of green leaves. Drongos lay three to four white eggs spotted with brown and gray.

The King Crow (*Dicrurus macrocercus*) of southeastern Asia and parts of Malaysia is typical of three species. It is glossy blue-black, red-eyed and about a foot long, but half its length consists of a deeply forked tail. Despite its small size, it drives off crows and hawks, stooping like a falcon at any animal near its nest and crying loudly.

The King Crow, so named because it is lord of the house crows of Asia, indulges in several kinds of associations. One involves medium-sized birds, such as orioles and doves, which frequently build their nests in the same trees with it. These birds are not attacked by the drongo, and enjoy safety from crows and hawks, which the King Crow drives off. The King Crow also maintains an association with cattle, remaining near them and plunging here and there in quest of flying insects, including those flushed by the pounding hoofs. Like some starlings, the drongos of India often hunt from the backs of moving cattle.

A species of the forests and bamboo jungles of India, Burma and the Malay Peninsula, the Greater Racket-tailed Drongo (*Dicrurus paradiseus*), is perhaps the most ornate of the family, and has outer tail feathers that are wirelike, twisted and flag-tipped, and more than a foot longer than the remainder of the tail. These, together with disheveled plumes that spring from the forehead and hang over the back of the head, forming a shaggy crest, make this highly specialized species virtually unmistakable. In contrast, several of the drongos appear to be primitive, and one, the flycatcher-sized Papuan Mountain Drongo (*Chaetorhynchus papuensis*) of the mountain forests of New Guinea, is considered the most primitive of all. It is glossy black and has rictal bristles longer than the bill. This drongo has twelve tail feathers, and one we collected in the Owen Stanley Mountains was for a time mistaken for a flycatcher.

Wood-swallows (*Artamidae*)

The finest of passerine fliers, and excepting the ravens the only songbirds known to soar, are the wood-swallows. Ten species of these superficially swallow-like birds of unknown ancestry live in the Indo-Malayan and the Australia–New Guinea regions. All are highly gregarious, habitually sleeping, nesting and hunting in parties. Certain species carry their social life to the extreme when sleeping together, one bird standing upon another to form compact knots of birds. Other species line up tightly on high limbs.

When hunting, wood-swallows often soar high into the air on rigid wings. At such times they resemble miniature vultures. Their food consists entirely of insects captured in the air.

Wood-swallows have the tail blunt and rather short, and the wings long, pointed and reaching almost to the end of the tail. They are usually slate-colored above and white below, with short bristles at the base of a conical, pointed bill. The sexes are similarly colored. Among their unusual attributes are powder-down feathers, the tips of which break up into a kind of talcum powder, which they use in dressing the feathers. This kind of plumage is not found on any other songbird.

Wood-swallows build fragile nests of grasses and twigs, sometimes close to the ground and at other times up to 50 feet above it, in forks of trees, at the junction of palm fronds and main trunks or in hollow limbs or rock niches. Most of the nest-building is done by the male, at least in the White-browed Wood-swallow (*Artamus superciliosus*). Three to four oval eggs are laid. These are whitish or pale buff, with dark brownish and lavender spots wreathing one end. Incubation is shared in the White-browed Wood-swallow, with the male doing most of the night sitting. It takes about 12 days, and the young, fed by both sexes, stay in the nest another 12 days.

One species, the Papuan Wood-swallow (*A. maximus*) of the mountains of New Guinea, was observed by Loke Wan Tho. He found a nest of this large, sooty-backed, white-breasted bird 50 feet up in the fork of a dead forest tree. It contained three young almost ready to fly. To his surprise, he observed that these youngsters were fed by four or five different adults, with three adults being seen on the nest at the same time. Communal nesting, if that is what this observation signifies, is rare in birds,

but considering the highly gregarious nature of the wood-swallow it is not an unexpected development.

In the Philippines the author once watched a group of White-breasted Wood-swallows (*A. leucorhynchus*) settle down for the night. After dark he flashed a spotlight at their roosting limb in a dead tree, only to see a large gray and white knot of sleeping birds on the limb. Flocks of this species commonly perch on telegraph wires, but unlike true swallows the flock remains tightly bunched rather than spaced along the wires. This bird is seven inches long, slate-colored above and on the throat, and white below. It occurs widely throughout Malaysia, the Fijis and Australia.

In Australia—the home of most species—is found the Masked Wood-swallow (*A. personatus*). This has the face and throat black and nests low to the ground, sometimes building only two to five feet up. Another species restricted to Australia is the Dusky Wood-swallow (*A. cyanopterus;* Plate 135). The largest member of the family is the White-browed Wood-swallow (*A. superciliosus*) of Australia, which is sooty black above and rufous brown

Papuan Wood-swallow (*Artamus maximus*)

below and has white eyebrows. It attains a length of 2½ inches, in contrast to the smallest species, the Little Wood-swallow (*A. minor*), which is less than 6 inches long and sooty brown. Unlike other wood-swallows this bird usually places its fragile nest in rock niches or hollow trees, or on ledges in caves.

Starlings (*Sturnidae*)

The nearly cosmopolitan Common Starling (*Sturnus vulgaris*) is a good example of the highly gregarious small to medium-sized birds that make up this purely Old World family of 110 species. Other starlings that have been widely spread by man are the famous talking mynahs (*Gracula*) and several other mynah birds of the genus *Acridotheres* from southern Asia. The latter have been established in Africa, the Solomon Islands and the Hawaiian Islands, to mention some of its far-flung abodes. All starlings have ten primaries and feed mainly on insects and fruits. The sexes are usually dressed nearly or completely alike. The young are dull and somewhat streaked.

Starlings usually nest in cavities in trees, walls or cliffs, but some species build domed nests with side entrances, and some of the most aberrant species excavate tunnels in mud banks or cavities in rotten trees. One species, the Glossy Starling (*Aplonis metallica*), often observed by the author, builds intricate large nests that are pendulous and closely linked together, like the nests of many tropical hang-nest builders, particularly the Weaver Finches, and quite unlike the nests of starlings in general. In this family the regimen of parental care is rather primitive, with the male usually sharing equally in all duties of nest-building, incubation, brooding and feeding the young.

Some of the species, probably because of the lure of ready food, have taken to living in close association with man, congregating in his cities to live in huge colonies. Others prefer to live near cattle and wild animals of many sorts in Africa, using them as a ready source of insect food. Some starlings are very local, others wide-ranging. Only the Glossy Starling has reached Australia, and only the Common Starling is found in most of Europe, but the family is fairly abundant in the African and Oriental regions.

In the view of Dean Amadon, who revised the family in 1956, the glossy starlings of the genus *Aplonis* of the South Pacific are the most primitive members of the family. The Glossy Starling (*A. metallica*) is greenish glossy black in the adult stage and heavily streaked with white when young. It is highly gregarious, traveling in flocks numbering in the thousands, and is found between sea level and 5000 feet in New Guinea. Its domed nests, described above, are in the canopy of tall forest-edge trees.

Some starlings have the wings oddly notched, apparently for the production of mechanical noises;

others wear wattles and crests, and have bare areas of highly colored skin on the face. One example is the Papuan Mynah Bird (*Mino dumontii*), which has orange-yellow wattles that resemble thickly set, soft spines growing from naked parts of its face. These bring to mind an extraordinary, little-known bird that ornithologists are still trying to assign to a family, the Bornean Bristle Bird (*Pityriasis gymnocephalus*) which has similar but much more highly developed decorations on its head. In some starlings, such as the Philippine Coleto (*Sarcops calvus*)—a grayish species that feeds almost exclusively on fruits—the feathering of almost the entire head has been lost. Another species, the African Wattled Starling (*Creatophora cinerea*), is only seasonally bald. It seems that during the breeding season it sheds the feathers of its head and grows long wattles! This mechanism of courtship is unique and little understood.

Starlings are generally considered to comprise a group of evolutionarily advanced birds, yet many species that dwell on isolated islands are primitive, and some are near extinction or have become extinct. One such insular variant that is unique among starlings in its way of life is the Celebesian Starling (*Scissirostrum dubium*), which has a heavy, almost woodpecker-like bill that it uses to excavate nest tunnels in hard dead wood. The extraordinary thing about this is that the bird apparently feeds on fruit, and the bill has no known use other than to serve as a tool for nest construction.

In the subfamily Sturninae are found 16 species of African glossy starlings (*Lamprotornis*) and about 10 species of superb starlings (*Spreo*), both groups restricted to Africa. In the Australian region and northward through Malaysia and Polynesia to the Philippines are found about 20 species of the primitive glossy starlings (*Aplonis*). They are closely related to a Eurasian and African clan consisting of 14 species of common starlings (*Sturnus*), in which the notorious Common Starling (*S. vulgaris*) and the Rosy Pastor (*S. roseus*) of southern Asia are found. The Black-collared Starling (*S. nigricollis;* Plate 136) is a boldly marked bird of Asia. Relatives of these birds are the two talking mynahs (*Gracula*), which occur from Ceylon to the Greater Sunda Islands.

The second subfamily consists of the tick birds (Buphaginae), of which there are two species restricted to Africa. Both of these have the bill stout and broad, the nostrils bare, the wings pointed, and the feet strong, with long, sharp claws. One cannot view an African animal film without seeing one or both of these species—the African Tick Bird or Oxpecker (*Buphagus africanus*) and the Red-billed Tick Bird (*B. erythrorhynchus*)—riding on the backs of a wide assortment of animals, ranging from domestic cattle to giraffes and even the hard-hided rhinoceros. Sometimes six or more ride around on a rhinoceros, sticking with the animal like glue, even when it lies down. Dr. Van Someren noted that the

ARTHUR W. AMBLER: NATIONAL AUDUBON

Superb Glossy Starling (*Spreo superbus*)

Red-billed Tick Bird works its way like a wood-pecker over the hides of game and stock, causing the furry skin to quiver, but nevertheless the beasts make no real effort to drive off the birds. He notes that the birds take off ticks, and according to local folklore they are credited with deliberately keeping wounds open. This is not substantiated, but it is known that they drink blood seeping from sores. Tick Birds nest in cavities very high in dead trees. The Oxpecker lays three to five bluish white eggs and the Red-billed Tick Bird lays pinkish white eggs that are marked with brown markings.

The Golden-breasted Starling (*Cosmopsarus regius*) of Africa feeds almost entirely on insects, even hawking for them in the air and breaking open tunnels to feed on termites. The Superb Glossy Starling (*Spreo superbus*), like many of its kind, is a bold species that hops and runs on the ground. It has white eyes and bright iridescent plumage. Its food consists of insects, berries and fruits. Dr. Van Someren reports that it usually selects a thorn-covered tree in which to build its complex domed nest on top of a horizontal limb. There are usually several such nests together, each with its own side entrance, often lined with thorny twigs, apparently to discourage predators. Its four or five light blue eggs are incubated for about 14 days by both parents.

The African Wattled Starling, already alluded to because of its unusual nuptial dress, is equally famous for the unique nomadic life it leads. This bird lives in close-knit flocks that wander over a vast territory. They have no special breeding areas and no special breeding seasons to follow. They prey on the vast swarms of migratory locusts that periodically plague Africa. When such a flock pauses in its wanderings to breed, the males quickly sprout their ornamental wattles and shed their crown feathers. Soon they begin building nests by the hundreds in

bushes, and their breeding is brought off in the midst of an abundance of locust food.

The Common Starling, which was introduced to America shortly before the turn of the century, has now increased to such an extent that it occurs from coast to coast and nearly everywhere from Mexico to Canada. The same situation obtains in Australia, with mass migrations darkening the skies as the birds move in and out from feeding areas to their massive winter roosts. Vast hordes disturb and foul many cities. In the breeding season the starling displaces local hole-nesting birds, particularly the flicker and the bluebird, not infrequently killing them with blows of the sharp bill. These birds are another proof that the introduction by man of alien species of plants or animals is always damaging and often disastrous to native species. Because of the bad example set by the Common Starling, the United States now has rigid laws forbidding the importation of most birds of this family except by approved zoological parks.

The problem of starling control has plagued city engineers for decades. Every device imaginable has been tried to hold the birds in check and to eliminate flocks from residential areas, where their chattering keeps the citizenry awake. Bells, electricity, recordings of the birds' alarm notes, everything up to and including gunfire has been used. The situation is so bad that architects are redesigning buildings to eliminate perching ledges. In 1957 the war against the starling made some headway when a sticky substance called "Roost No More" was put on the market. This was found to work, since starlings apparently cannot bear to get their feet gummed up and will desert areas sprayed with this never-drying glue.

Crows, Magpies and Jays
(*Corvidae*)

The cheeky crow is universally known, but magpies, jays and choughs, which occur in many shapes and colors, are less familiar birds. Indeed, to many it will come as a surprise that the colorful jays and magpies are close cousins of the crow. An even 100 species comprise the family Corvidae, which has representatives on all of the nonpolar land areas of the world except New Zealand and a few parts of Polynesia. Curiously, the crow has not succeeded in reaching South America, but there are many colorful jays in the New World tropics.

Crows, magpies and jays range from medium to large in size, and some of the crows are the largest of all passerines. They have the bill more or less conical and without notches and the maxilla usually shielded with fine wiry feathers at the base. The great majority are omnivorous, eating all manner of food, including carrion, insects, seeds, fruits, the eggs of reptiles and birds, nestlings and even small reptiles. They are active, wily birds that are notorious for their "intelligence." Like many of the parrots and some starlings, crows can learn to "speak," and like the parrots they are good at solving puzzles and at feats of "memory," sometimes even repeating long phrases quite distinctly. This "intelligence" often expresses itself in boldness and curiosity. For example, some jays and magpies steal shiny ornaments from the camps of hunters, and some crows gather all sorts of paraphernalia for their nests. Crows and jays are birds of woodlands and bushy grasslands. They have ten primary feathers in the wings, and their feet are very strong and coarse in appearance. As a general rule, they build open nests in trees. These are solid, well-lined structures of twigs, sticks and bark. Two to eight eggs are laid, usually pale bluish or greenish with brown markings, but in some species yellowish or bright buff. One species, Hume's Ground Jay (*Pseudopodoces humilis*) lays pure white eggs. This odd little bird of the high plateaus of Central Asia nests in holes in the ground, often in rodent burrows.

The family is frequently divided into two groups, the Corvinae, which consists of the crows, ravens, rooks, jackdaws and nutcrackers; and the Garrulinae, which consists of the jays (Plates 139 and 141), magpies and choughs.

The American Common Crow (*Corvus brachyrhynchos*) of North America and the Carrion Crow (*C. corone*) of western Europe are typical crows, being some 19 inches in length and black with steel-blue reflections. These birds gather to sleep in roosting flocks, which in North America sometimes reach 40,000 in number, the rookeries being inhabited by birds that often fly 30 to 40 miles each morning and evening. The birds are long-lived and uncommonly hard to approach because of their system of using sentries. The large flocks break up into pairs in spring and build nests, often in evergreen trees. As in the raven, the female crow does all of the incubation, but both parents share in feeding the young. The Carrion Crow of Eurasia sometimes nests in conspicuous places, such as tall trees standing alone near houses and on cliffs. Its eggs, like those of its American counterpart, are pale greenish. The set consists of about five.

The Fish Crow (*C. ossifragus;* Plate 140) of North America is chiefly maritime but follows rivers some distance inland. Although slightly smaller, this species is virtually identical in coloration with the Common Crow. However, its guttural caws, which are much less high and clear, distinguish it from that species. The Fish Crow feeds largely on coastal flats, where it favors shellfish.

The ravens are the largest of Passeriform birds. One species, the Common Raven (*C. corax*), which is some 25 inches long, is solid glossy blue-black, with shaggy feathers, especially about the throat. It has a massive bill and a longish wedge-shaped tail. This species, like the group in general, is found around the world in the Northern Hemisphere. Its breeding areas are very often on cliff ledges. These large passerine predators soar like many of the true hawks, and their diving courtship flights involve spectacular acrobatics. Ravens build bulky nests and lay five to seven green eggs. Their food includes carrion, dead fish and all manner of refuse. Certain other very large members of this subgroup that are found in Africa have the bill swollen and have much white in the plumage, especially in the region of the neck.

The Jackdaw (*Corvus monedula*) of Eurasia and Northern Africa is one of the most gregarious members of the family. Black with a gray nape and a whitish eye, this bird breeds in colonies in holes in buildings; for example in the sacred temples of the Chalimar Gardens of Kashmir a flock is always to be seen. Those interested in these fascinating birds should read *King Solomon's Ring,* by the celebrated Dr. Konrad Z. Lorenz, in which important sections are devoted to a colony of free jackdaws used in studies of animal and human behavior.

Recent observations of a Jackdaw colony at Zurich showed that both sexes built the nest; that incubation was performed exclusively by the female and required 17 to 18 days; that the nesting period was about 35 days. Both parents fed the young.

Nutcrackers are found chiefly in the evergreen forests of the Northern Hemisphere around the world. They are foot-long birds that are best known

Common Raven (*Corvus corax*)

Common Jay (*Garrulus glandarius*)

for their food-storing habits. For example, the Thick-billed Nutcracker (*Nucifraga caryocatactes*) in Sweden manages to survive the severe winters by spending several months each autumn in storing hazelnuts. Recent studies show that a remarkable degree of memory is displayed in recovering the nuts in the dead of winter. Also, the winter storage tendencies of these nutcrackers are considered to be an important mechanism in the reseeding of forests.

The second subfamily, the Garrulinae, consisting of the jays and the magpies, is composed of birds, many of them very beautiful, which seem quite different from crows. The Common Jay (*Garrulus glandarius*) of Eurasia and Northern Africa is a brownish bird with much white on the rump and wing, and with vivid blue and black barring on the wing coverts. This species, which is about 13 inches in length, has habits of food-storing that rival those of the nutcracker; it works with great vigor in the autumn to store acorns. In one study area acorns by the thousands were brought as far as four kilometers, the bird traveling back and forth from dawn to dark for a period of weeks. Like the well-known American Blue Jay (*Cyanocitta cristata*), this bird is shrewd and wary and has an erectile crest. The 11-inch, gray-breasted Blue Jay, with its prominent black collar and bright blue dorsal plumage, is very colorful and pleasant in appearance.

Some of the numerous other jays found in the New World are rather drab. For example, Steller's Jay (*Cyanocitta stelleri*), of the pine forests of western North America from Alaska south to Nicaragua, has the anterior half of the body blackish brown and the posterior half dusky blue. This species is about a foot long. Of similar size but much more colorful are the Green Jay (*Cyanocorax yncas;* Plate 137), a bright green, blue and black bird that is found from Texas to the highlands of South America, and the Azure-hooded Jay (*Cyanolyca cucullata*), which ranges from Mexico to Panama. In the northern coniferous forests around the world are found the notorious Canada and Siberian Jays (*Perisoreus*), which are birds of extraordinary boldness. The Canada Jay (*P. canadensis*) readily robs the bait from traps and enters houses to eat anything from soap to tobacco. In the New World this bird is called the Whisky Jack or the Camp Robber. It breeds as far north as Alaska and Labrador and has a particularly infamous reputation. Unlike its reddish brown Old World counterpart, the Siberian Jay (*P. infaustus*), it is largely lead gray with a white forehead and a black nape. It is about 11 inches long. Both parents build the nest, but the female alone incubates the eggs (for 17 days). Both adults feed the young.

Magpies are world-wide in distribution. All have bright colors and long, graduated tails. The Black-billed Magpie (*Pica pica*) is a good example because it ranges around the world in the Northern Hemisphere, being as common and well known in the British Isles as it is in northern Siberia and Alaska. However, it also occurs in northern Africa, Asia Minor, southern China, Japan, Canada and the western parts of the United States. About 20 inches long and mostly blackish with a long, greenish black tail, it is also velvety black in places and has prominent white scapulars, wing linings and abdomen. The nest of the magpie is quite an elaborate affair, being a stick structure that is domed over and reinforced internally with a kind of mud masonry. To this is added a lining of hair and feathers. This nest often has two openings in the side, presumably so that the long tail can be accommodated. Six to nine eggs are laid. These are pale with brownish spotting. The male assists in the building of the nest, but the female does all of the incubation with the male feeding her. Both parents feed the young.

The Red-billed Blue Magpie (*Urocissa erythrorhyncha*), a pigeon-sized blue-and-black bird with a pair of spectacular white-tipped blue central tail feathers reaching 17 inches in length, is one of the notable birds of the mountains of Asia. Like many magpies and jays, it often goes about in parties. This species of the high mountains hunts in tree crowns, but sometimes it descends to the ground to feed on winged ants in company with other birds. Another spectacular species of Asia is the Green Magpie (*Kitta chinensis;* Plate 138).

One of the most unusual members of the Corvidae is the Red-billed Chough (*Pyrrhocorax pyrrhocorax*) of Eurasia and northern Africa, a crow-sized blackish bird with a rather slender curved red bill. These birds are rather like jackdaws in their habits and in their buoyant and often exuberant modes of flight. Cliff dwellers, they frequently travel long distances to feed, which they do on the ground like crows; but, unlike crows, they build their nests in crevices. The Red-billed Chough is generally a bird of the sea cliffs, whereas the Yellow-billed or Alpine Chough (*P. graculus*), which is very similar except for the small size and yellow color of the bill, frequents remote mountain precipices and steep pasture lands far above tree line—the same places in which the Lammergeyer, the Rock Creeper, the Rock Pigeon and the Raven are found. There sometimes flocks consisting of 20 or 30 Yellow-billed Choughs indulge in the wildest kind of aerial game, with the birds often seeming to play dead as they plummet out of the sky, streaking downward close to cliff walls, while others tumble and twist like drunken daredevils. Yet again the flock soars lazily in an updraft or lands to stroll haughtily among grazing Alpine sheep. The nests of these birds are clusters of sticks lined with wool placed in rock fissures or even in the walls of Sherpa villages. The species was found at 27,000 feet on Mount Everest, which is very near the ceiling for birds.

Wattled Crows, Huias and Saddlebacks (*Callaeidae*)

This group of odd and interesting birds—the Callaeidae—is restricted to New Zealand. Three monotypic genera (that is, with one species each) make up the family, and all are so different in appearance that one has to look carefully for such characters of relationship as long tails, long legs, brightly colored wattles and a tendency of the plumage of the forehead to be velvety, as in many birds of paradise.

The Saddleback (*Philesturnus carunculatus*) is glossy black and has much bright chestnut in the wings and tail, and orange or yellow gape wattles. The bill, which is similar in both sexes, is sharp-pointed like that of a starling, and somewhat longer than the head. These birds were once abundant on all of the main islands of New Zealand; there are, however, no recent reports of them from South Island and Stewart Island.

Saddlebacks travel in pairs or small groups and hunt in company with other birds. Their chief food consists of grubs, insects and berries. The nest is a cup in a hole, sometimes near the ground and sometimes well above it. The bird lays from two to three eggs that are buff or brown and have dark spots and blotches. The incubation period ranges from about 20 to 21 days and the young are fed to a large extent on grubs taken from tree ferns.

The Huia (*Heteralocha acutirostris*) was in some ways one of the most remarkable of all birds but has unfortunately been wiped out as a result of ecological changes and of overhunting. It was formerly fairly common on North Island, but no living examples have been reported since two lone males were sighted in 1907. The habitat of the Huia was deep forest, where it traveled in small parties or in pairs, leaping or hopping about when on the ground. Its remarkable method of foraging for food called for teamwork between the sexes, especially in the use of the bill. The male had the bill ivory colored, nearly straight and very sharp, and only just about as long as the head, whereas in the female it was more slender, much longer and strongly downcurved. This bill difference was so striking that the first specimens of both sexes to reach Europe from New Zealand were described as different species!

The Huia fed on the ground and in trees, eating spiders, insects and grubs. Reliable observers have seen the male using his shorter bill to rip bark from a tree and chop out the wood, while the female stood aside. When an insect tunnel had been partially excavated by the male, the female moved in and with her longer bill attempted to withdraw the grub or insect. The different functions of the two bills and the teamwork displayed by mated pairs in using them was one of the wonders of the bird world.

The nest of the Huia was a large cup placed in a hollow cavity on or near the ground but sometimes as high up as 18 feet; two to four eggs were laid in it.

The Wattled Crow or Kokako (*Callaeas cinerea*), which has been called New Zealand's most versatile and beautiful songster, is somberly colored, chiefly dark gray with a black slash in the front of the eyes and at the base of the crowlike bill. The only mark of color is the large pendant gape wattle found in both sexes; in one race this is pure blue, in another it is yellow and blue. The Wattled Crow moves through the forest as the Huia once did, bounding rapidly from limb to limb, and apparently incapable of sustained flight. It eats leaves, berries and buds, often with one foot holding the other for tearing.

The South Island Wattled Crow was very common when the white man first arrived. Today it survives only in the dense mountain forests and bushes near and above timber line. The nests that have been found were located from about 20 to 30 feet up in the forest and were composed of rough twigs, ferns, a matting of rotted wood and a lining of moss and felted material. From two to three eggs are the usual set, and the young remain on the nest for about 27 days.

Wattled Crow or **Kokako** (*Callaeas cinerea*)

W. P. MEAD

Magpie-larks (*Grallinidae*)

Along the shores of rushing forest streams in New Guinea, as well as around waterways and mud flats, and in the open woodlands of Australia, there occur the four species, ranging from thrushes to crows in size, of which this family is composed. Although apparently different from each other, they all employ the same unusual type of architecture for their nests.

Two of the species are the Magpie-lark or Mudlark (*Grallina cyanoleuca*) of Australia and its near relative the New Guinea Mudlark (*G. bruijni*). Both species are black and white and neither is ever found far from water. The Australian bird is 11 inches in length, has a heavy thrashing flight and feeds on insects and small snails.

In the nonbreeding season these Mudlarks often congregate in flocks of hundreds along the edges of muddy lakes, but recent studies indicate that, despite this flocking instinct, they pair for long periods and perhaps for life. Each pair stakes out a territory of some 15 acres which they defend with challenging songs. Their own calls are duets, with one bird calling the first two phrases and its mate adding in synchronization the final three phrases.

In the spring when the pairs resume the active defense of their territories and only the yearlings remain in the flocks, both parents assist in the building of a new nest, which is often placed in the same tree as the nest of the previous year. The nest is a large, bowl-shaped, earthenware-like affair and is strengthened with horsehair or fur and thinly lined with feathers and fine grass. The nest, looking as though it had been turned from a potter's wheel, is usually placed on a horizontal limb beside or over water and quite high up. Both the male and the female incubate the eggs and care for the young. The set consists of three to four shiny white to shiny buffy eggs with brownish and grayish spots. New nests are said to be built for each brood, several being raised annually.

In New Guinea, where the author has observed *G. bruijni* at 5000 feet in the Bismarck Mountains as well as at 1500 feet in the Goldie River Gorge of the Owen Stanley Mountains, these birds were thinly scattered in deep forest along mountain streams. They were fearless but wary, always traveling alone over the rushing water like a dipper, or landing and running on stream-washed rocks.

The third member of the family, the Apostle-bird (*Struthidea cinerea*), which is found in open forest over most of Australia, is also largely black but has the tail tips and the abdomen and under-tail coverts white. The size of a large jay, it is named after the Apostles because it travels in flocks of about twelve. It feeds mostly on the forest floor on insects and seeds. Its movements are quick and involve much leaping, hopping and scaling of small trees by jumping from limb to limb. The flocks are fairly fearless and are often found near human habitations.

In his guide to Australian birds, N. W. Cayley describes this species as a communal nest-builder. The nests are placed very high on horizontal limbs and are constructed of mud much like the Mudlark's. The eggs are a pale bluish white with brown and grayish markings and number up to eight to a nest.

The fourth member of this aberrant group of birds is the White-winged Chough (*Corcorax melanorhamphos*), also a large bird of the open forests of most of Australia. The plumage is mostly glossy black with white wings, and the bill is strong and crowlike. Unlike the true Choughs, to which it bears no actual relationship, this bird has scarlet eyes. At certain seasons it is like the Apostle-bird and the Mudlark in that it goes about in parties feeding much of the time on the ground, and, like the Apostle-bird, when disturbed it emits a harsh squawk and makes off through the trees in long limb-to-limb hops without flying.

In flight the White-winged Chough flaps the wings slowly, and when it alights spreads the tail and often moves it up and down. Its normal diet is insects but it also eats small fruits. Its nest resembles that of the preceding two species, but Cayley tells us that a group of about three birds combine to build it and several females lay their eggs in it. The total number of eggs thus deposited sometimes reaches nine. They are whitish with dark spots of olive and brown. Apparently two to three broods are raised per year, each being lodged in a new nest that is sometimes constructed in the same tree.

Birds of Paradise
(*Paradisaeidae*)

Birds of paradise, close relatives of crows, are found only in New Guinea and Australia. Forty-three species are known. The smallest are starling-sized and the largest raven-sized with yard-long tails. Some resemble grackles in the color and texture of their feathers, and some are black, with very fine, silky plumage. In plumage they range from this simple type to the plumed birds of paradise, which are so splendidly dressed they deserve their name. Only the males carry such ornamentation, which appears to require three to five years for full development; the females are dull and quite different-looking.

The first bird-of-paradise plumes to reach Europe were five that went westward in 1522 aboard the *Victoria* under command of Captain El Cano, who had taken the helm after Magellan was killed in the Philippines. He obtained the plumes from natives on the island of Tidore in the Moluccas, whence they had been traded from New Guinea. So strikingly beautiful were the plumes that the birds were said to be wanderers from Paradise, and this accounts for the vernacular name of these birds.

In 1824 the true home of the birds of paradise was discovered for science when René P. Lesson observed two species in New Guinea. In 1857 Alfred Russel Wallace made new discoveries, but most of the species that reached Europe were trade skins obtained from natives for commercial purposes. Since many of these skins had the feet cut off, as was the custom of native collectors, one species was given the scientific name *Paradisaea apoda*—the "footless." For a time ornithologists haunted the millinery shops in search of unknown species of these bizarre birds, but with the end of commercial plume-collecting this source dried up. For a time, that traffic was considerable; at its peak, more than 50,000 skins annually were exported from New Guinea. Today plume-taking is prohibited, except by a few scientific collectors. In 1938 Fred Shaw-Mayer discovered what may be one of the last unknown species, the Ribbon-tailed Bird of Paradise (*Astrapia mayeri*).

The great tails and other extraordinary plumes are used in courtship display. Capes, veils, whips, fans, fleshy caruncules serve to transform the birds into odd and startling shapes. Some seem to become elongated, round, angular or even flower-like, and often they bear no resemblance to birds. Others suddenly open their mouths to reveal jade and opal-colored surfaces, or they pirouette with giant capes that have a dashing look. One species (*Pteridophora*) lashes the air with relatively monstrous head plumes; four others (*Parotia*) cavort on low limbs and on the ground in deep forest, spreading their apron-and-cape raiment in symmetrical circles about their bodies, with almost the precision of a bullfighter. Two species (*Diphyllodes*) perform like gymnasts on thin, vertical saplings growing from the floor of deep forest. Others (*Paradisaea*) elevate lacelike cascades of plumage over their backs or hang shimmering from limbs.

None of these species sings, but they make a wide variety of sounds ranging from weak peeps and mews to caws, buglings, trumpetings, snaps, hisses, raps and even clatterings that sound like bursts from a machine gun. Other calls are long, melancholy, bell-like tolls that reverberate ventriloquially.

The purpose of the displays is to attract mates, usually as many as the male can entice to his bower. These polygamous birds keep close to their bowers for many months each year, and species that the author has watched have remained on or near the display limb for as long as ten hours per day, hardly taking time to eat. The usual term of attendance is several hours in the morning and in late afternoon.

Except in a few cases where communal dancing is employed, the bower is the territory of a single male, and he vigorously defends it against males of his species. Frequently the display territory is within hearing, and in some species within both hearing and sight, of the bowers of other males; and often there are three or four species displaying within auditory range of each other. The form of polygamy practiced by birds of paradise is promiscuous, for it consists merely of rapid meetings and matings, with no protection offered (as in a harem) and no chance for corrections in errors in species recognition. There is no pair bond preceding mating, as in most other birds. This situation has led to the need for and the development of highly exaggerated auditory and visual mechanisms of species recognition. The latter are the magnificent and highly specific ornamental plumes that once were so widely used as human adornment.

Except in the most primitive species, the female alone builds the nest and rears the young. Almost invariably the nest is an open and sometimes a shallow cup of vines, sticks and leaves. Often it resembles a coil of thin, living vines. Nests may be high in the forest or close to the ground, depending on the species. Two species nest in holes, one (*Cicinnurus*) in a hole in a tree and the other (*Cnemophilus*) in a domed nest of vines and moss with a side entrance. So far as known, all of the species lay one or two eggs that are longitudinally streaked with irregular lines.

The Paradise Crow (*Lycocorax pyrrhopterus*) of the Moluccas is a silky-textured, crowlike bird some 15 inches in length, with light brown wings that are lined with white on their inner edges. The manucodes include five species in the New Guinea region. Three of these are starling-like, with much metallic coloration; and in one, the New Guinea Manucode (*Manucodia ater*), the male assists the female in the care of the young. The Curl-crested Manucode (*M. comrii*) of the D'Entrecasteaux and Trobriand Islands is crow-sized and completely covered with crinkled, highly iridescent feathers, which on the head form an odd-looking "bun." The Trumpeter Manucode (*Phonygammus keraudrenii*), which occurs in the Australian region also, has a broad collar of lanceolate feathers that completely encircles the neck so that, when displaying, the bird seems to be thrusting its head through a feather umbrella. It is named for the enormous spiraled windpipe (syrinx) that the male wears coiled on its chest under the skin.

Other fairly generalized birds of paradise are the Wattled Bird of Paradise (*Paradigalla carunculata*) and MacGregor's Bird of Paradise (*Macgregoria pulchra*), both of the mountain forests of New Guinea. The former is thrush-sized and is black with bright yellow and cobalt blue mouth wattles in both sexes. The latter, which lives between 8500 and 12,000 feet, has a black body, rufous wings and large yellow wattles around the eyes. It is remarkable for its group displays, which consist of aerial chasing in a special area of forest. After pairing, the male escorts the female as she gathers nest material and remains close by as she incubates. Later he helps feed the young.

In the high mountains of New Guinea are four species of sickle-bills. One is the short-tailed King Albert's Sickle-bill (*Drepanornis albertisii*), a thrush-sized, smoke-brown bird with a slender, sharply curved bill. It has iridescent purple-blue "horns" in front of the eyes, a bronzed green throat, twin sets of glossy, erectile feathers at the sides of the chest, and a second set of fanlike feathers that are plated with reddish bronze and grow from the neck.

The largest of all birds of paradise is the Black Sickle-bill (*Epimachus fastosus*), a metallic blackish green bird with a very long saber-shaped tail and silky epaulettes growing from the sides. These are raised in display, and at the peak of the performance they fan out to conceal and completely alter the shape of the bird. This species displays solitarily in tall forest trees where it emits a whiplike *kee-wink*. Its home is in mountain forests below 6000 feet. The slightly smaller Brown Sickle-bill (*E. meyeri*) is found from about 7000 to about 10,000 feet; it is very much like the Black, but it has a different call—the machine-gun bursts mentioned above. Nests found by the author in April and July were open cups. The eggs were buffy brown with longitudinal reddish streaks.

Paradise magpies, of which there are five species, are also restricted to the high forests of New Guinea. They are long-tailed birds with soft, velvety body plumage burnished with radiant bronzes and greens. Among them is the Ribbon-tailed Bird of Paradise (*Astrapia mayeri*), which reaches 42 inches, the last species of bird of paradise discovered and the longest of passerine birds. Its central pair of tail feathers may be 36 inches in length; their vanes are V'd upward to help them to float in the wake of the bird.

The Magnificent Rifle Bird (*Craspedophora magnifica*) represents a group of which there are three species in New Guinea and Australia. It is about a foot in length, has a long, slender, curved bill, and

is a generally dark, soft-plumaged bird with a glossy green crown and a glossy purplish blue throat and chest, the latter being edged with bronze. On the flanks it has abbreviated display plumes that terminate in hairlike tips, and the central pair of tail feathers is highly glossed and shorter than the rest. This species builds in pandanus palms sometimes 40 feet up. All the rifle birds display on specially selected and defended display perches. For some reason this group is quite nomadic.

Wallace's Standard-wing (*Semioptera wallacei*) was discovered on the island of Batjan in 1858 by Alfred Russel Wallace. The name "standard-wing" alludes to two sets of long, white, ribbon-like plumes that grow from the bend of the wing in a manner unique in the family. These six-inch feathers can be elevated in display in huge V's. This species is thrush-sized and appears faded, but the shiny crown and shortened central tail feathers indicate that it is an offshoot of the rifle-bird line. It has the throat and chest covered with a shiny shield that is large and extensible, so that in full display the ornament resembles a monstrous bow tie.

The Twelve-wired Bird of Paradise (*Seleucides ignotus*) keeps to the sago swamps of central and western New Guinea. The male, which is 12 inches long, is named for the peculiar shape of six plumes growing from each flank. At the end of the feather vanes are strong, springy shafts, up to a foot long, that are bent permanently forward and resemble thin wires. The male is black, washed with violet above

Magnificent Rifle Bird (*Craspedophora magnifica*), male, in courtship display

NEW YORK ZOOLOGICAL SOCIETY

and with an edging of iridescent green on the throat and chest. The chest feathers are erectile and can be expanded into a wide, round collar. The remainder of the underparts are bright lemon-yellow in life but fade quickly to pale gray. A nest of the Twelve-wire that the author found in February on the Sepik River was 11 feet up in a pandanus palm. It was composed of bark fiber, reeds and vines, and held a single egg that was oval and streaked with gray.

A highly interesting group is the flagbirds, some of which are so peculiarly adorned that naturalists have doubted their existence. In 1898, for example, Bowdler Sharpe, Keeper of Birds at the British Museum, at first refused to believe that the King of Saxony Bird of Paradise, then just discovered in a Paris plume mart, was not an artifact.

The males of this group have wirelike flag plumes growing from the head near the ears, velvety black capes that are expandable in display, and iridescent metallic shields on the upper chest. Despite these seeming similarities, at first glance flagbirds appear so different that they seem to belong to different families. Nevertheless, they are closely related, interacting species that occasionally hybridize.

The King of Saxony Bird of Paradise (*Pteridophora alberti*), a seven-inch bird, has crown plumes that reach 18 inches in length. These are sky-blue in color, with 35 to 40 flags that have the texture of cellophane growing along the shaft. Another of the flagbirds, the Superb Bird of Paradise (*Lophorina superba*) is thrush-sized. It has a huge crown fan composed of at least 120 feathers, each three to six inches long, that cover the back like a black velvet cape. In display these can be elevated like a huge Indian headdress. In the four species of six-wires (*Parotia*) the wires resemble long hatpins, three growing on each side of the head slightly in back of the eye. Some have wires seven inches long, each tipped with a black flag shaped like a small canoe paddle. Several of these species have the top of the skull dish-shaped or scooped out to accommodate spectacular collapsible crests of white and golden-bronze feathers. Others have constantly moving white beards. The crest of at least one species (*Parotia carolae*) is kept constantly moving.

Some flagbirds clear ground bowers like bowerbirds, some display low in the forest, some in the mid-limbs and some in the topmost spires. Each defends its display territory and each displays alone. One of the last to be found displaying uses the top spires of the mountain forest: this was the King of Saxony. The author discovered its courting area in 1950 on Mount Hagen in interior New Guinea.

Other birds of paradise that visit the ground to perform part of their courtship dances are the Magnificent Bird of Paradise (*Diphyllodes magnificus*) and the quite similar but slightly smaller Wilson's Bird of Paradise (*D. respublica;* Plate 144). The Magnificent, a seven-inch bird, has a deep blood-red back surmounted by a large, erectile, glossy golden

collar. Below it is glossy green. Its most prominent character is a pair of sickle-shaped feathers that spring from the center of the tail. This species clears the ground around a sapling in the deep forest, clips away the overhead leaves to let in a shaft of light, and dances both on the ground and on the sapling. The dance consists of a promenade up the side of the vertical tree. The bird then hangs backward, with the glossy mirror-like chest shield and the neck collar held at right angles to the skylight.

An aberrant species is the Lady MacGregor Bird of Paradise (*Loria loriae*), which is velvety black with a glittering blue forehead and wing feathers (tertials). This species displays on high limbs in deep forest, where for hours on end it emits deep, ringing, ventriloquial notes. Despite its arboreal habits, it is almost certainly a bowerbird, in the writer's opinion. Another in this category is the Golden-silky Bird of Paradise (*Loboparadisea sericea*), small and very little known, the female of which closely resembles a maypole-building bowerbird. Finally, the

Mocha-breasted Bird of Paradise, male
(*Cnemophilus macgregorii*)

odd Mocha-breasted Bird of Paradise (*Cnemophilus macgregorii*), one race of which is canary-yellow above and another blood-red, has six crown plumes that resemble the antennae of moths. This bird of the high forests of New Guinea builds a nest that is very different from that of all other birds of paradise, being a domed cluster of vegetation with a side entrance. Loke Wan Tho, who photographed this species at its nest, reported that the female fed fruit to its young.

The King Bird of Paradise (*Cicinnurus regius*) is the smallest species of the family and one of the most widespread and beautiful. It is white below, with green flank plumes that can be opened like fans. Above, it is scarlet with a pair of very long, curving tail wires that are tipped with iridescent medallions of intricately twisted feathers. This species has recently been successfully bred in captivity in Sweden by Sten Bergman.

Elongated tail wires and expandable flank plumes are the key characters of the famous plumed birds of paradise. The Lesser Bird of Paradise (*Paradisaea minor;* Plate 145) is restricted to the New Guinea region. It closely resembles the Greater Bird of Paradise (*P. apoda*) which is found in the Aru Islands and on the island of Little Tobago in the West Indies where it was introduced in 1909 by Sir William Ingram. In both species the males gather together to perform social displays, with the birds scampering about side by side. In eastern and southern New Guinea is found the Raggiana Bird of Paradise (*P. raggiana*), which has the flank plumes ranging from red to pale orange. In this species the males display solitarily, each one defending his own display limb, which is situated within auditory and visual range of other displaying males.

Two other species of plumed birds occur on isolated islands, the Red Bird of Paradise (*P. rubra*) on the islands of Batanta and Waigeu, the Gray-breasted Bird of Paradise (*P. decora*) on the D'Entrecasteaux Islands. In the mountains of New Guinea are found two members of the genus that resort to inverted displays of great beauty. One, the Blue Bird of Paradise (*P. rudolphi*), is black and bright blue with a white eye-ring in both sexes. It hangs head down like a pendulum in display, flexing flank plumes that resemble the finest lace. The other, the Emperor of Germany Bird of Paradise (*P. guilielmi*), also hangs inverted, and it displays flank fans of lacy plumes which are mostly ivory white with golden bases.

Bowerbirds (*Ptilonorhynchidae*)

Bowerbirds are unique among birds in their use of tools, their taste in color, and their skill as architects. An early naturalist, coming upon a dance pavilion built by a New Guinea species, thought it a house constructed by a man. Another, carried away by their bizarre use of paintbrushes and natural "jewelry,"

Mocha-breasted Bird of Paradise, female, at nest

declared that, just as mammals have been split into man and the lower forms, birds should be considered in two categories, bowerbirds and all the others. Yet there is nothing in their appearance to suggest their outstanding abilities.

Bowerbirds range in size from a small thrush to a small crow. All have rounded, concave wings, and their most distinctive "character" is their "bower" rather than any structural feature. These bowers are specially prepared dancing stages on the ground, each bower being built by and belonging to a single male. Some species, probably the most primitive ones, do not build bowers, but keep to trees like ordinary birds. Others, somewhat more specialized, merely clear dance areas on the ground in forest, as do quite a few other birds (manakins, grouse, birds of paradise, etc.). But some bowerbirds decorate their clearings with bright objects, maintain veritable lawns, and erect elaborate houses for other than nesting purposes —and no other birds do anything of the sort.

The author has spent years searching for and studying these birds, and has found many of them extraordinarily wary and inaccessible, for they keep to the dripping cloud forests in the mountains. In all, there are nineteen species; six of these are purely Australian, two are common to both Australia and New Guinea, and eleven are restricted to New Guinea.

The males of many species have bright plumes or patches of color on their heads—red, gold, yellow, glittering purple, violet, sparkling blue, even a glistening pearl—and a few have bright colors elsewhere. The females are generally somberly dressed. Quite unlike their nearest relatives, the birds of paradise, bowerbirds have short tails with no trace of wirelike display plumes. It is a striking fact that the better "architects" and "artists" among bowerbirds are the species with the least ornamental feathering and the dullest colors. That is to say, there is an inverse ratio between the development of the bower and the development of courtship plumage—because, it is thought, the bowerbird uses his bower, rather than nuptial plumage, in the optical stimulation of his mate. The author, who was the first to notice this correlation, has named this hypothetical phenomenon the "transferral effect." It is his belief that when external objects are used for optical stimulation of the female, the male plumage—the colorful crest, for example— is no longer important and gradually is lost through natural selection (those individuals with reduced crests tend to live longer and breed oftener) because colorful objects are less of a liability to a ground-displaying bird than is bright plumage.

The bowers of each species follow precise patterns. Some are relatively simple ground clearings; some are elaborately designed, many-partitioned structures; others are massive columns or towers with complicated tepee-like roofs. Nearly all are decorated with natural treasure: snail shells, insect skeletons, bright lumps of resin, seeds, shapely pebbles, colorful feathers, small fruits of garish colors, in fact any bright object that can be found. In Australia, where the bowerbird lives in close proximity to humans, it has begun adding a galaxy of man-made ornaments to his nuptial chamber, such as keys, glass, jewelry, bits of shiny metal, and even, in one case, a glass eye.

Another phenomenon among bowerbirds is gardening—the clearing and planting of table-sized areas of ground. Particular species of yellowish green moss are used for these gardens, and the resulting "lawn" stands out in sharp contrast to the rest of the jungle floor. Some of the gardens take the shape of round, shallow saucers with their rims elevated as much as six inches above the ground.

And, finally, the crowning phenomenon is the mixing of pigments by three species and the actual painting of the walls of the bower. Furthermore, two of the three species that "paint" use tools to assist in applying the color, as described later in this chapter.

Until recently it was believed that these extraordinary bowers, with their gardens and elaborate decorative paraphernalia, were playgrounds in which the males amused themselves much in the way a child does in a sandbox or as other birds sing and fly and dive apparently out of sheer exuberance. One reason

Lesser Bird of Paradise (*Paradisaea minor*), male, in display

Emperor of Germany Bird of Paradise (*Paradisaea guilielmi*), male, in inverted display

serious students held this belief was that the bower played no part in the luring of random females, but was maintained for many months each year by a "happily married" male.

But A. J. Marshall of Cambridge University, long a student of bowerbirds, finally concluded that each bower was the focal point of the male's territory. By dissection he proved that the male built his bower when he was reaching a sexually active state and maintained the structure only as long as this condition continued—sometimes four to five months. The female, on the other hand, often remained sexually inactive during much of the time that her suitor cared for the bower, although she frequently called to inspect it and its builder. However, when the external environment met certain conditions, she suddenly became sexually active and accepted her mate *in the bower*. This sometimes occurred early in the season and sometimes late, depending on rainfall, heat, abundance of protein food (mostly insects) and other factors. In other words, the sexual cycle of the male was regular and prolonged, while the cycle of the female was short and unpredictable. Somehow the stimulus of the bower was a factor in the consummation—with the female triggered not to the male but to conditions over which the male had no control.

Presumably the most primitive members of the family are the catbirds, one of which is the Green Catbird (*Ailuroedus crassirostris*) of Australia and New Guinea. This jay-sized bird is rich green above, with a black head and throat, both flecked with whitish spots. It has a green upper chest, a pale yellowish green abdomen, and a long green white-tipped tail. The thrush-sized White-throated Catbird (*A. buccoides*), of New Guinea, differs in having the crown brownish, the throat broadly white, and the underparts more buffy and heavily spotted with black. The tail is not tipped with white. In both species the sexes are colored alike. Catbirds are tree-loving birds. They spend very little, if any, time on the ground. Their nests are large, cuplike structures usually built fairly high in the forest edge. Usually two cream-colored eggs are laid. One of their calls is a "meeow" sound; another is a hiss. Catbirds feed on fruits, berries and insects (chiefly beetles), and have the bill very strong and more bulky than that of the more highly developed bowerbirds.

The Tooth-billed Bowerbird or "Stage-maker" (*Scenopoeetes dentirostris*), which builds a dance area on the ground, is native to certain hill forests in northeastern Australia. Unlike its more orthodox relatives, which it resembles in size, it is protectively dressed above in dull olive, and below in dull white with longitudinal striping. Its chief character is its deeply notched bill, both mandibles of which are serrated on their outer portions. This sawlike arrangement is used, among other things, to sever certain preferred kinds of leaves with which the bird decorates its remarkable dance stage, renewing the supply almost daily. He places them in the middle of his territory, a cleared "circus ring" among saplings, usually about five feet in diameter. Around the edges of the stage is a ring of debris cleared from the arena, and sometimes little piles of land snails, which may be food remnants or, more likely, collections of ornaments. The Stage-maker is a great ventriloquist. He mimics many other birds and spends much time on special singing limbs over the bower.

More complex builders are the maypole-builders. The five species—one in Australia and the remainder in the mountains of New Guinea—construct bowers around thin, straight forest saplings. The Australian species, the Golden Bowerbird (*Prionodura newtoniana*), is the smallest of all bowerbirds and hardly larger than a starling, yet it builds a stick edifice that sometimes reaches a height of nine feet and apparently is the product of years of work. Often there are several towers, connected by stick walls or partitions and decorated with gray-green lichens and flowers.

This golden-breasted, olive-backed bird wears a plumage on its upperparts that in sunlight gives off a shimmering pearly glow. The canary-yellow feathers of the short crest and nape are erected during display, while the yellow tail feathers are spread. The female is olive above and gray below. The call is an unattractive croak, but like most bowerbirds, this species mimics many other birds. The male takes no part in nest-building or nest care, and probably remains unaware of the location of the nest of sticks, bark strips, rootlets, skeletonized leaves and moss that the female builds in the forest, sometimes very close to the ground, in the last quarter of the year. All maypole-builders lay whitish or buffy white eggs in open cup-like nests.

The New Guinea maypole bowerbirds, of which four species are known, are denizens of high mountain forests. They are brown thrush-sized birds that vary in having golden crests of different sizes and hues, or no crest at all. Another variable factor is the bower, which grades from a simple smallish column

Golden Bowerbird (*Prionodura newtoniana*), male, at bower

Bower of **Crestless Bowerbird** (*Amblyornis inornatus*)

of sticks set on a large saucer of specially planted moss to a giant tepee-like house complete with door, verdant moss garden, and gay ornaments of blossoms and berries.

One of the four, the Golden-fronted Bowerbird (*Amblyornis flavifrons*), is a "lost" bird and one of the great ornithological prizes still awaiting rediscovery. Three specimens found in old plume shipments are the only evidence we have that this bird exists. Another species, the Crestless Bowerbird (*A. inornatus*), is a plain brown bird that is indistinguishable from its mate and very like the females of all of the other New Guinea maypole-builders. Its bower, however, is very complex. It is a columnar stick tower that resembles a broad tepee with a large, low entranceway. Emerging from the courtship chamber— that is, the house—the male enters a broad garden of carefully tended moss festooned with orderly clusters of brightly colored berries, bits of charcoal, land snail shells of glistening black, and blossoms. The quickly fading flowers are replaced by the attendant male for months on end.

The mat-makers consist of two species: Sanford's Golden-crested Bowerbird (*Archboldia sanfordi*), coming only from the high ramparts of Mount Hagen and Mount Giluwer, and Archbold's Bowerbird (*A. papuensis*), known only from the Snow Mountains.

Nothing is known of the bower of Archbold's Bowerbird, but of Sanford's Golden-crested the author recently obtained information. This species builds its courtship stage 8000 to 9000 feet above the sea in high moss forest containing many tall pandanus palms. Its dance stage is a mat of ferns three to five feet in diameter, decorated around the edge with piles of black beetle wings, snail shells and blocks of resin. Above and around this stage the builder drapes a curtain of thin yellow bamboo strands and wilted ferns, hung from nearly horizontal vines on which are scatterings of black charcoal and black bark, both the size of golf balls. Here also it places some green marble-sized berries and sometimes a big whitish snail shell.

During a period of five days in July, 1956, the author observed a male that came many times to its

bower to rearrange the ornaments and bring new material, apparently placing and shifting the objects so that they would show better in the thin shafts of sunlight. The bird worked alone. Much of his day was spent in trees over the bower, where he called and squawked, delivering a wide variety of ventriloquial notes. These last sometimes decoyed small birds to his vicinity, and once at the height of such a commotion a solid black bird—the female—suddenly appeared at the bower. Immediately the male dropped from his perch to prostrate himself on the mat of ferns. Then he began a constant churring and started crawling toward the female, who sat on a low perch. As he crawled, the male held his wings half open and pressed to the fern mat, his tail partly open and pressed to the ground. Only his head was up, and usually it was held high with the bill pointing toward the female. As though gasping, he incessantly opened and partly shut his bill, in which he held a piece of vine, and he fluttered the wings. Whenever the displaying male neared the female she flew five or six feet across the fern stage to another low perch. On her way over the prostrate male she often hovered and whipped her wings violently, making a noise like tearing cardboard. For 22 minutes the male crawled and churred, turning to follow each time the female flew to a new location. At the end of this display the two birds disappeared for a short time into a part of the stage the author could not see; then both flew off into the forest. Presently the male returned to the stage to tidy it up, rearranging the ferns of the mat and the ornaments around it. During the long period of display he used no ornaments other than the vine held in his mouth.

Probably the most highly developed bowerbirds are the avenue-builders, three of which are "painters." There are two main types. The first consists of highly

Regent Bower bird (*Sericulus chrysocephalus*), female, at nest

Great Gray Bowerbird (*Chlamydera nuchalis*)
with female above

colored males with relatively dull-colored mates that dwell chiefly in the forests of Australia and New Guinea, including the Satin Bowerbird (*Ptilonorhynchus violaceus;* Plate 142) of Australia, in which the male is silky blue-black and the female pale grayish green; the Regent Bowerbird (*Sericulus chrysocephalus*) of Australia, in which the male is ink-black, with the head, neck and much of the wings bright yellow, and with a wash of red on the forehead, and the female is dark and mottled (see photograph); the New Guinea Regent Bowerbird (*S. bakeri*), in which the male is much like its Australian relative but has a crown of shining rose and the upper back and shoulders yellowish orange; the Black-faced Golden Bowerbird (*S. aureus*) of New Guinea, which is golden-orange above, with a yellow breast and with much black on the wings, tail, face, and throat; and the Yellow-throated Golden Bowerbird (*S. ardens*) of western New Guinea, which is like *S. aureus* except that it lacks the black throat and face.

The second group of avenue-builders consists of four species of generally brownish, grayish, and pale yellowish birds that spend most of their time in and near grasslands of Australia and New Guinea. In some the male differs from the female by having a small,

erectile patch of gleaming purplish pink on the back of the head. In one species, the Spotted Bowerbird (*Chlamydera maculata*), this coloration may or may not occur, apparently without reason. This bird is one of the "painters." The other species are the Great Gray Bowerbird (*C. nuchalis;* Plate 143) of Australia; the Fawn-breasted Bowerbird (*C. cerviniventris*) of Australia and New Guinea, and Lauterbach's Bowerbird (*C. lauterbachi*) of New Guinea, in both of which the sexes are colored alike.

All the male avenue-builders construct bowers of intricately meshed platforms the size of large door-mats and several times as thick. Down the middle of these stick mats they insert two firm walls of vertical sticks that reach 16 inches in height and are lined on their inner surfaces with brownish grasses anchored firmly in the platform. The walls are just wide enough for the birds to promenade between without scraping their shoulders. Each species decorates its bower with ornaments of particular kinds and colors, sometimes extremely gaudy. The Satin and the Regent mix a muddy grayish blue or pea-green kind of saliva paint in their mouths and apply it generously to the inner walls of their avenues. The Satin uses a wad of bark and the Regent sometimes uses a wad of greenish leaves to assist in spreading the paint.

Bowers of Lauterbach's Bowerbird that the author has seen always had two additional "end" walls. These bowers consisted of as many as 3000 sticks and nearly 1000 ornaments, the latter ranging from red palm berries the size of marbles to large blue and green berries and assorted grayish stones and clayballs. When the female came to this type of bower, the male danced with a red berry in his mouth.

Recently in Australia Ellis McNamara, observing the courtship dance of the Spotted Bowerbird, recorded a coupling of the pair, and was therefore one of the first to prove that the bower is the nuptial chamber. Copulation took place in the narrow avenue between the two walls of sticks, and the beating wings of the birds almost wrecked the structure. Shortly thereafter the male returned alone and began the long task of rebuilding the bower. Norman Chaffer, ranking Australian authority on these strange birds, had made similar observations, and we are fortunately able to publish his unique photograph of a pair of Satin Bowerbirds mating in the avenue of the bower.

Waxwings, Silky Flycatchers and Hypocolius
(*Bombycillidae*)

The Bombycillidae are here considered to consist of three subfamilies, the waxwings (Bombycillinae), the silky flycatchers (Ptilogonatinae) and the Hypocolius (Hypocoliinae). The palm chats, which some

Satin Bowerbird (*Ptilonorhynchus violaceus*) mating in bower

authorities have included in the group, are given family rank (see Dulidae) because of their specialized reproductive behavior, plus several structural characters.

Waxwings, silky flycatchers and the Hypocolius are ten-primaried arboreal Passeres that have the bill short and subterminally notched. They have weak feet, crested heads and soft, fluffy plumage.

In the waxwings, of which there are three species ranging around the world in the Northern Hemisphere, the sexes are alike. The wings are relatively long, the ends of the secondaries usually carry waxy red spangles (accounting for their vernacular name) and the tail is tipped with yellow or red. These are arboreal birds that feed chiefly on berries but also on some insects. Waxwings are gregarious during much of the year, but as breeding time approaches the flocks split into pairs, each of which builds a nest in a solitary location, often in a fir tree, placing the cup-shaped structure of sticks, grass and moss on shelf-like pine branches. Three to five pale bluish, dark-flecked eggs are laid.

In the Cedar Waxwing (*Bombycilla cedrorum;* Plate 147) of North America—a six-inch, sharp-crested, fawn-colored bird with a prominent black mask and scarlet waxy projections on the secondaries —the male participates in the activities of nesting, feeding the female at or near the nest and sometimes taking a turn at incubating the eggs—a process requiring about 11 to 13 days.

Flocks of Cedar Waxwings frequently descend to the ground to feed, and often, when perching in trees or on wires, the birds sit very close together, almost touching shoulders in the manner of the Artamids and, on occasion, the palm chats. Sometimes when thus perched they play with a berry or similar object, passing it from one to the next all along the line. Kenneth Parkes once watched such a file of waxwings in the park near the American Museum of Natural History. Sitting in the line was a female English sparrow. The adjacent waxwing would pass her berries, but she, not knowing the rules of the game, swallowed them!

Slightly larger and more colorful are the Bohemian Waxwing (*B. garrulus*) of Europe, Asia and North America, and the Japanese Waxwing (*B. japonica*) which breeds in eastern Asia and winters in southern China and Japan.

The second subfamily, the silky flycatchers, consists of four species of sharply crested, slender birds that are found from the southwestern borders of the United States to Panama. All are rather flycatcher-like in appearance, with slender tails and with the rictal bristles well developed and conspicuous. Unlike the waxwings, the sexes are quite differently dressed and the tenth primary is always well developed. These birds are chiefly insectivorous, but they also eat some berries and fruits. They build open cuplike nests in solitary positions and lay two to five dull whitish eggs that are speckled with dark brown or black. The spe-

[319

Phainopepla (*Phainopepla nitens*), female, and young

cies are the Phainopepla (*Phainopepla nitens*) of the southwestern United States and Mexico (Plate 146), the Black-and-yellow Silky Flycatcher (*Phainoptila melanoxantha*) of the highlands of Costa Rica and Panama, and the Gray Silky Flycatcher (*Ptilogonys cinereus*) of Mexico to Guatemala. The last is an eight-inch bird with very smooth, soft plumage and a conspicuous, erect crest. It also has bright yellow under-tail coverts and white eye-ring.

Except for the Phainopepla, little is known of the reproductive behavior of this subfamily. In that species both sexes share the duties of nest-building, incubation and feeding of the young, with the male doing the greater share of the work. The incubation period is 15 days, and the young remain on the nest for about 19 days before fledging.

The third subfamily of this seemingly composite family has been established for the very strange Hypocolius (*Hypocolius ampelinus*), which ranges around the northern end of the Persian Gulf (Afghanistan, Baluchistan, southern Persia and western Arabia) and bears a number of resemblances to both silky flycatchers and waxwings. However, this very local bird has legs that are different from those of the other bombycillids: the plates of the rear half of the legs are divided into separate scutes, not solid as in the normal songbird tarsus. This bird, which is about the size of a small thrush, has its upperparts and its chest dull blue-gray, and the underparts dull whitish. Its chief field mark is a black ring that encircles the crown from the base of the bill through the eye and over the ears, joining on the nape. The breeding habits of Hypocolius, as reported by Colonel Meinertzhagen in his *Birds of Arabia,* indicate that it is a solitary nester. The nest is a large, untidy, deep-cupped structure of vegetable matter, lined with soft material in which four to five white, dark-flecked eggs are laid.

Hypocolius apparently feeds entirely in trees on fruit and berries—mostly mulberries, figs and dates. It flies strongly and directly, without undulations. It is gregarious and exceedingly tame, keeping together in small flocks, which hide by "freezing" in bushes and trees, keeping stock-still even when stones are pitched at them.

Palm Chat (*Dulidae*)

The most prominent of the smaller birds found on the West Indian islands of Hispaniola and La Gonave is the Palm Chat (*Dulus dominicus*), an olive-brown starling-sized species with pale, heavily streaked underparts. Highly gregarious and noisy, the flocks frequently draw attention to themselves by harsh, chattered choruses that last many minutes and by their picturesque habit of perching so close together that they crowd one another. The individual pairs comprising the closely knit flock show a strong attachment.

Although apparently allied to the waxwings, the silky flycatchers and the aberrant *Hypocolius*, Palm Chats differ markedly in their patterns of reproductive behavior, chiefly in their habit of building huge, communal, domed nests. Also they have the plumage more firm, the legs, bill and feet more substantial, and the tail relatively shorter.

These are purely arboreal birds. They often hunt through trees and bushes, moving with agility, reaching for berries or flowers, sometimes even darting at a flower, tearing it off while in flight, and then carrying it to a perch to devour it. Dr. Alexander Wetmore reports that the Palm Chat generally goes about in bands of all ages. These bands, which keep together at all times, cooperate to build a communal nest, usually placed very high in a palm tree but sometimes in a pine or deciduous tree in the highlands. These nests are so bulky they become a feature of the landscape. The structures are fashioned from twigs and switch-sized sticks sometimes 30 inches in length; the birds pick these up at the point of balance and then thrash their way up to the nest site with their remarkably heavy burdens. The nest consists of many apartments, each with a private external exit but also with internal connecting passageways that enable the occupants of the tenement house to creep around without going outside. About four pairs of Palm Chats usually occupy such an apartment nest, although sometimes more than twice that number are in attendance. The eggs, which probably are four in number, are laid in the apartments on a sparse mat of shredded bark. They are white with dark grayish spotting, mostly about the larger end. In the nonbreeding seasons the nests are used for resting and sleeping.

Cuckoo-shrikes and Minivets (*Campephagidae*)

On slight acquaintance many of the 72 species of cuckoo-shrikes (a misnomer) seem to resemble shrikes or cuckoos; however, these Old World birds bear no close relationship to either family. They range from Africa through the warmer parts of Asia and Malaysia to New Guinea and the Solomon Islands. Some are as large as street pigeons; others are the size of sparrows. All have the feathers of the lower back and rump thickly matted, partially erectile and equipped with rigid pointed shafts. These spinelike feathers are easily shed, and it is possible that they act as a mechanism of defense, as in the trogons and pigeons (see Pigeons). Another character possessed by all is a shrikelike, notched bill and well-developed rictal bristles which, in many species, partially conceal the nostrils.

In the nonbreeding season most of the cuckoo-shrikes are gregarious, often traveling with woodpeckers, small leaf warblers and orioles. Virtually all are arboreal and have the habit of searching for food among leaves and bark, particularly in arboreal gardens of tropical trees. They eat insects, berries and figs, and, rarely, small lizards. Some of the small species, such as the colorful minivets, catch insects in flight, but even they find most of their food on leaf and bark surfaces.

Cuckoo-shrikes have the wings relatively long and pointed and the tail moderately long and rounded, except in a few species, notably the minivets, in which the tail is long and graduated. In many species the tail feathers of juvenile birds are longer and more pointed than those of the adults. The minivets also differ in several other ways. They are generally migratory in contrast to the other species of the family, which are chiefly sedentary except for a few that move about seasonally, especially in Australia.

In general, cuckoo-shrikes are somber birds that wear grays, whites and blacks. The aberrant minivets, however, are splashed with reds, oranges and yellows. The sexes in all cuckoo-shrikes are dressed very differently from each other, with the female being the inconspicuous one. The young often wear a white nestling plumage but soon exchange it for the dress of the female.

After pairing, the male and female build the nest. In many species the male takes no part in incubation but does feed the female. The nest is very often a wide, shallow, platelike structure of vines and sticks placed on a nearly horizontal limb fairly high in thick forest. From two to five eggs are laid, usually of pale blues and greens with reddish brown spots.

Cuckoo-shrikes of the genus *Campephaga* inhabit Africa. A good example is the eight-inch Red-shouldered Cuckoo-shrike (*Campephaga phoenicea*), which ranges widely through the bushy savannas and forests. The male is glossy blue-black with scarlet shoulder patches; the female is dull brown with various amounts of blackish barring. This species is common in the Belgian Congo, where it goes about alone, in pairs, or sometimes with one or two of its newly fledged young. Its call is a soft double whistle. It is said to feed chiefly on caterpillars, other insects and spiders, which it obtains among leafy branches or by darting down from the tops of bushes or saplings. Its nest is a shallow platelike cup of lichens bound with spider webs. The two eggs are pale green or grayish green and spotted with browns and grays.

Perhaps the most aberrant species of the family is the Wattled Cuckoo-shrike (*Lobatos lobatus*) of Africa. This very rare bird has conspicuous lemon-chrome lobes situated under the eye near the gape. It somewhat resembles an Old World oriole in size and color, although the male has the rump bright orange chestnut and the head and neck shiny black. From India and Ceylon eastward to New Guinea and Australia occur many similar species of the genus *Coracina*. One of these, the Large Cuckoo Shrike (*C. novaehollandiae*), is the size of a thrush. This bird is gray with a bold black mask extending across the eyes from the bill to the ears, a marking that gives the male a bandit-like appearance. The female is paler and has a smaller mask, and the young are like her but with the whitish underparts boldly barred with black. This species, a bird of the forest crown, is often encountered alone, but the young join together in flocks. Its nest is a typically shallow open cup of twigs and bark strips held together by animal silk and concealed with scaly lichens, placed well up in a tree. The set is two to three olive eggs spotted with reddish brown and the fledgling period is 25 days. This species emits a churring note and flies in glides and undulations rather like a cuckoo.

In Australia there also occurs another aberrant species which, unlike the other members of the family, spends a major part of its time on the ground. This species, the Ground Cuckoo-shrike (*Pteropodocys maxima*), reaches a length of more than 14 inches, and is a gray bird, with wings and tail mostly black and the lower half of the back barred with black and white. It is widespread but distributed sparsely, and travels in small flocks apparently composed of pairs of birds with their offspring. The pairs nest fairly high up in trees; their nests are typical.

Smaller species, measuring six to eight inches and grouped in the genus *Lalage,* abound on the islands of the Western Pacific from the Philippines southward to New Guinea and Australia. One is the Black and White Triller (*L. melanoleuca*) of the Philippine forests, which, in the nonbreeding season, the author found traveling in company with woodpeckers and forest orioles. Another species is the White-winged

Triller (*L. sueurii*) of Australia, which is also mostly glossy black above and chiefly whitish below but with white shoulder patches. This species reaches seven inches in length, is common in wooded areas and is the only member of the family that undergoes two moults instead of one per year. Both sexes participate in the building of the nest and both incubate. The eggs hatch after 14 days. During the ensuing period of parental care both sexes feed each other on the nest. It is one of the few species that are migratory.

In 1950 the author discovered the nest and eggs of a large blue-gray cuckoo-shrike (*C. caeruleogrisea*) at about 9000 feet in the Bismarck Mountains, New Guinea. The nest was a flattish structure of vines camouflaged with moss on a nearly horizontal crotch some 25 feet up in a tree growing in thick wet mountain forest. Part of an egg found in the nest was a pale blue-green with reddish brown spots. More recently, the gifted Chinese bird photographer, Loke Wan Tho, photographed another species, the New Guinea Giant Cuckoo-shrike (*C. longicauda*) as it fed a lizard to its snow-white young.

Minivets differ sufficiently from the cuckoo-shrikes to warrant the erection of a special subfamily for them. The male Orange Minivet (*Pericrocotus flammeus;* Plate 149) is only six inches long, mostly blackish above, and mostly bright orange-red below, and has the wings and tail black and boldly marked with orange. As in all minivets, the female differs in being much more somberly dressed; the orange is replaced by dull yellow and the black by dark gray. It is found from India and China to the Philippines and Malaysia. It dwells between sea level and 8000 feet and is found only in the crown of true forest.

Another species, the Ashy Minivet (*P. roseus*), is less colorful, being mostly gray above and white below. It nests in Asia and Japan and migrates to the Philippines and the Malay region. In India the

New Guinea Giant Cuckoo-shrike (*Coracina longicauda*)

Short-billed Minivet (*P. brevirostris*)—a shining black and scarlet bird—gathers in flocks of twenty or so, making a beautiful sight as they search through green foliage for insects and spiders. The scarlet males or the yellow females occasionally plunge into the air or hover at a flower to get their quarry.

Minivets build very small, cup-shaped nests of twigs, rootlets, pine needles and grass, bound together with spider webs and usually anchored near the top of a forking branch 15 to 20 feet above ground. They lay from three to four eggs, pinkish to greenish white in color and spotted with shades of brown and gray.

Bulbuls (*Pycnonotidae*)

Throughout the Old World tropics from Africa to the Philippines bulbuls are among the most common, most numerous and best known of all garden birds. They are starling-sized or smaller, with short necks, short wings, longish square or slightly forked tails and relatively small legs and feet. About their bills and on the napes of their heads are fine bristles. Generally they have an abundant amount of plumage on the rump, and many species are crested; the neck is often rather sparsely feathered.

One hundred and nine species are known. All are moderately colored, with both sexes being dressed much alike. Except for yellow, bright colors are rare in this group. The only exceptions are occasional markings of white on the head and sometimes red on the under-tail coverts. Bulbuls are found from sea level to more than 10,000 feet, and usually they keep to the forest and forest edge. However, a number of species frequent bushy grasslands and gardens. Several of the species forage near and on the ground for food, but the majority seek it in the middle and upper tiers of trees, and occasionally one will fly out from a limb to capture a flying insect.

Bulbuls are quite gregarious, often going about in noisy flocks in search of fruits, berries, insects and spiders. Many species also drink nectar, and once in the Philippines the author came on a flock of about ten Yellow-vented Bulbuls (*Pycnonotus goiavier*) that were flapping about in a drunken state. The lot had been on a spree, drinking fermenting liquids seeping from a silo. This eight-inch bulbul is brown above and whitish below, with light yellow under-tail coverts and vivid white eyebrows. Chiefly because it dwells in close association with man, it is probably the most abundant and best-known bird in the Philippines.

Bulbuls build open cuplike nests of twigs and fibers. They may be placed or slung in a fork, usually in the lower parts of bushes and small trees. From two to four highly variable eggs are laid. These are usually pale with brownish markings.

In Africa, where the family is most numerous, the Brown-capped Geelgat (*Pycnonotus tricolor*), a

yellow-vented species, has been carefully studied by Dr. Van Someren. He found that this bulbul probably mates for life, that it is among the first birds to begin singing in the morning—it starts just before dawn—and the last to retire at night, even singing on moonlight nights along with some doves and cuckoos. Because it takes cultivated fruit like many other bulbuls, it is persecuted by farmers. Its incubation lasts 12 to 13 days and is performed almost entirely by the female, with the male bringing food to her. Both parents feed the young on insects, and the male assists in brooding. The young are well feathered at the end of the first week and able to leave the nest after 16 days.

An unusual species is the Brownbul or Terrestrial Bulbul (*Phyllastrephus terrestris*) of southeastern Africa, which is about 7½ inches long. This species departs from the norm by frequently descending to the ground in pairs or parties to creep about in search of insects and grubs.

At the opposite extreme is the Yellow-striped Bulbul (*Phyllastrephus flavistriatus*) of Central Africa, a bird of similar size that habitually keeps together in pairs or parties in the limbs of evergreen forest on high mountains. Like the Terrestrial Bulbul, it is noisy, keeping up a whistling chatter. It has the unusual habits of flicking one wing at a time and of running on limbs like a creeper. Another unusual species is the Olive-breasted Greenbul (*Arizelocichla tephrolaema*), an olive-green bird with a gray head and chest, which is one of the most abundant birds in the forests of Mount Ruwenzori. In Ceylon and India is found the Red-vented Bulbul (*Pycnonotus cafer*), a bird with a jaunty crest, a white rump patch and bright red under-tail coverts. This species occurs everywhere except in the thickest forests. Mr. Henry has observed the male in display, fluffing out the body feathers and spreading the bright under-tail feathers like a fan. The female responded to these actions by retracting the crest, chirping, quivering the wings and moving the beak in an unusual side-to-side motion.

Bulbuls are chiefly sedentary birds, although many species move about in a kind of limited migration, covering large areas in quest of fruit, their chief source of nourishment. In Africa, for example, the Slender-billed Greenbul (*Stelgidillas gracilirostris*), which is golden green above and yellow below, is seasonally common in many areas. They appear—sometimes by hundreds—when the figs are ripe, and then vanish. In India the Black Bulbul (*Microscelis psaroides*), a starling-sized, slate-colored bird with a shaggy crest and reddish bill and legs, is the nemesis of fruit-growers. In mountains where cherries are grown the author has observed boys working throughout the daylight hours to protect the fruit from marauding birds. To do this each boy attached long ropes to the top branches of a dozen or so trees and then posted himself like a hub in the center of the radiating lines. Whenever a bird flew to a tree, the boy shouted and tugged on the rope. Another species that attacks fruits is the White-cheeked Bulbul (*Pyc-*

nonotus leucogenys). Dr. Salim Ali in his *Indian Hill Birds* notes that this crested, brown, snowy-cheeked bulbul sometimes travels in flocks of 50 or so, and that the flocks become so brazen that they enter the famous houseboats of Dal Lake in Kashmir for food.

Fairy Bluebirds, Ioras and Leafbirds (*Irenidae*)

Three groups of colorful forest-loving birds ranging in size from a small thrush to a street pigeon are placed in this family. All are fruit-eaters, and in all the plumage of the rump is somewhat elongated and fluffy. The Irenidae range widely through the Oriental region from southern Asia to the Philippines and southward to the islands of Indonesia.

The Blue-backed Fairy Bluebird (*Irena puella;* Plate 148) is the most colorful and the largest species, having a length of ten inches. Generally the male Fairy Bluebird is clad above in shining ultramarine blue with shimmering purple and lilac reflections; below it is mostly black. The female is much duller.

Fairy Bluebirds are largely restricted to the upper tier of tall original forest, usually evergreen. They habitually keep together in hunting parties like many of the bulbuls, and on occasion the bands number up to 30 birds. They often congregate with other fruit-

Yellow-vented Bulbul (*Pycnonotus goiavier*)

LOKE WAN THO

eating birds, such as hornbills and fruit pigeons, to feed on ripened figs. Somewhat surprisingly, the bright coloring of the Fairy Bluebird is not revealing in its usual habitat.

In the heat of the day Fairy Bluebirds sometimes descend in flocks to bathe in forest streams. During the breeding season the flock splits into pairs. The nest of the Fairy Bluebird is built in a sapling in the shadowy substage of the forest. The structure, a tidy open cup of rootlets and twigs camouflaged with moss, is usually about 20 feet above ground. In it are deposited two oval eggs, variously spotted and streaked with browns and grays.

Much smaller and quite different are the ioras, of which the Common Iora (*Aegithina tiphia*) is a widespread example. It is 5½ inches long and, like the other members of the family, has the legs relatively heavy and the bill somewhat elongated and slightly curved. The male is black above with a greenish yellow rump and with some yellow on the head and back; it has vivid white wing bars and yellow underparts. The very different female is mostly greenish yellow. The male, which sings in melodious whistles, is a familiar bird of gardens and village edges. It displays in the top of a tree and, when seized with "emotion," darts up high into the sky and then spirals back to its perch, all the while calling like a cricket or frog and carrying the feathers of the body, especially those of the lower back, in a most unnatural expanded manner. The nest is a neat cup made of grasses bound together with cobwebs. It is attached to a fork, sometimes close to the ground and sometimes as high as 30 feet. Three eggs form the average set. These are dull white with brownish lines and spots, mostly concentrated at the larger end.

The third group consists of the leafbirds of the Oriental region. Typical is the seven-inch Golden-fronted Leafbird (*Chloropsis aurifrons*), which is largely greenish above with a golden red forehead. Below it has a shining blue throat, much velvet black on the sides of the head and across the chest, and body plumage of greenish yellow. It is an active arboreal bird and often travels in flocks.

Most leafbirds are residents of the forest crown, but several of the species frequent gardens. Their outstanding character is the sweetness of their notes and their ability to imitate the songs of many other birds. They eat fruit, berries, some insects and nectar. Their usual set of three eggs, whitish with brown markings, is deposited in a neat, shallow nest of rootlets and grasses placed in a fork of tiny limbs near the end of a bough 15 to 25 feet above the floor of the forest.

Babbling Thrushes
(*Timaliidae*)

The babblers are an extraordinarily diversified family dwelling in Africa and the Oriental and Australian regions. Most of the species are sedentary birds that skulk near and on the bottom of the forest or among bushes in scrubby grasslands. They generally travel in troops, squeaking, churring and babbling.

So variable and diverse are many of the species that the babbler family looks at first like a catch-all collection of species. Within the family as presently understood are birds that bear superficial resemblance to thrushes, wrens, thrashers, jays, titmice, pittas and other unrelated families. Babblers almost always build their nests in wooded areas, on the ground or within a few feet of it. Some of the structures are cup-shaped and others are dome-shaped. The eggs are various; those of the large species are generally unspotted, but the smaller ones often lay spotted eggs.

Babblers have the legs and bill strong, and their feathering is usually soft and lax. They have short, rounded wings with ten primaries. Unlike the thrushes, which many of them superficially resemble, the young of the babblers are never spotted.

This perplexing family has recently been studied by Captain Jean Delacour and the general arrangement of the following groups is patterned after his revision, except that his tribes are here treated as subfamilies.

The jungle babblers, subfamily Pellorneinae, are dull brown birds that range from Africa through the Oriental region and the Philippines to the Celebes. One is the Spotted Babbler (*Pellorneum ruficeps*), an olive-backed, gray-headed bird with a slender, curved bill, vivid white eyebrows, and generally white underparts, and with reddish brown sides. This species builds a globular nest of fallen leaves, grass and moss on the floor of thick forest (to altitudes of 5000 feet) and lays two to four eggs. Another member of this subfamily is the Red-headed Tree Babbler (*Malacopteron magnum*), an eight-inch bird with a rufous fore crown, a bright rufous tail and a straight bill that is hooked at the tip. Unlike most babblers, it is an arboreal bird, traveling like a bulbul in parties through the forest crown as it forages for food.

Babblers of the subfamily Pomatorhininae are dull brown ground-dwelling birds that build domed nests and lay whitish eggs with fine dark freckling. The largest species are the scimitar babblers, all of which have the bill long, slender and sharply decurved, superficially resembling the thrashers of the New World. Scimitar babblers keep together in tight groups that work their way through the forest very rapidly and are extremely hard to observe. In southern Asia they build their nests on the ground, but in New Guinea and Australia the nests are pensile. The New Guinea Scimitar Babbler (*Pomatostomus isidori*) goes about in flocks of six or eight birds and, like the Gray-crowned Scimitar Babbler (*P. temporalis*) of Australia, it builds a nest that is quite remarkable. One that the author observed was a yard long with a canopied side entrance. It hung from a single strand of vine, and according to usually well-informed natives, the whole clan of builders gathered in the large structure to sleep each night. In Australia Serventy and Whittell found nests of the Gray-crowned Scimitar Babbler that were suspended forty feet up. The clan sometimes requires three months to build the nest. Somewhat surprisingly, only two or three brown, streaked eggs are laid. Scimitar babblers (Plates 150 and 151) have rich voices and in Ceylon are a feature of the forest music. They hunt in crevices, using the bill like a woodcreeper to excavate insects and their larvae.

A smaller member of this subfamily is the Long-tailed Wren Babbler (*Spelaeornis chocolatinus*) of the eastern Himalayas. It is a 4½-inch bird that has a two-inch tail and seems always to scurry in flocks through dense thickets. It rarely is found more than a foot or two above the ground. Curiously, the domed nests of this species have a waterproof lining resembling papier-mâché.

Another subfamily is the Timaliinae or tit-babblers, which are small, short-winged, often colorful birds with strong legs that mostly live away from the forest in thickets, grass and reeds. Some build domed nests and some build open cups. Madagascar, the Oriental region and the Philippine Islands are their home. An example is the Golden-headed Babbler (*Stachyris chrysaea*), a 4½-inch bird that is olive above and bright yellow below. The Golden-headed Babbler travels through the underbrush in parties of up to 50, keeping up a low twittering serenade as the flock searches for insects and seeds.

A widespread bird of the Oriental region is the Red-capped Babbler (*Timalia pileata*), which is seven inches long with a shiny black bill, a white forehead and a red crown. This species has a fine whistled call. Like many babblers, it scans grass stems for insects, first climbing upward, then plunging down to repeat the operation.

The laughing thrushes and their allies are members of the babbler subfamily Turdoidinae—a group that is mostly composed of thrush-sized birds with strong bills and relatively bright or even vividly colorful designs. They are found from Africa eastward through the Oriental region. In many species the nest is cup-shaped, but some make domed nests.

A famous member is the Spiny Babbler (*Turdoides nipalensis*) of Nepal and adjacent areas, which is some nine inches long and generally streaked brown, with spiny shaft tips to its feathers and a relatively long tail. Like the Striated Babbler (*T. earlei*) of Burma and India, these birds travel rapidly in tight parties through grassland, making occasional bursts of noise. They are exceedingly difficult to observe, for they reveal themselves only fleetingly as they move about. The Striated Babbler lays three to four eggs that are bright blue.

The Common Babbler or Seven Sisters (*Turdoides striatus*) of India and Ceylon is as strange a bird as the traveler will ever encounter. Awkward and gawky, it moves in flocks of seven or so, con-

stantly uttering grating noises, posturing with the tail twisted, usually displaying worn, dirty-looking feathers. This malproportioned bird forages for food under the bushes and in the gardens of native villages, and even in the garden of the American Embassy in New Delhi, India. It has the habit of holding large morsels of food in its foot and then picking them to pieces with the bill. This species also lays bright blue eggs—usually three to five—in a low, open nest that is neat inside but of careless construction outside.

The White-crested Laughing Thrush (*Garrulax leucolophus*), which is an imposing 12-inch bird that ranges widely through the Oriental region, is more often heard than seen despite its size and spectacular coloration. Reddish brown, with a vivid white head and chest, it has a jaunty white erectile crest. The white plumage contrasts with a striking black mask. These birds are named for the bursts of "laughter" that they emit from time to time, each one seeming intent on laughing more heartily than the next. Like most babblers, the White-crested Laughing Thrush manages to keep out of sight, despite the cackling that it produces as the band moves through the underbrush. In this species the eggs are pure white and the nest a broad, shallow cup of bamboo leaves placed low in a bush. A close relative is the Melodious Laughing Thrush (*Garrulax canorus;* Plate 153).

The great variety of this complex group is suggested by the names applied to various species: the Red-headed Laughing Thrush (*G. erythrocephalus*), the Black-faced Laughing Thrush (*G. affinis*), the Crimson-winged Laughing Thrush (*G. phoeniceus*), all of which range from 9 to 12 inches in length and live in the mountains of southern Asia. One very colorful species is the Silver-eared Leiothrix or Mesia (*Leiothrix argentauris;* Plate 152), which is very widespread in the Oriental region. Seven inches long, this bird is an inhabitant of hill forest, where as many as 30 occasionally travel together, always keeping up a running barrage of chirps and whistles. Salim Ali of India has found that in this species both the male and the female share in the building of the nest and in incubating the eggs. Also in this group is the Chestnut-headed Tit Babbler (*Alcippe castaneiceps*) of the high Himalayan mountains, which is only 4½ inches long. This species builds a nest of moss lined with fibers.

The last subfamily of the babblers is the Cinclosomatinae, or Rail Babblers, a group of seven genera all of which have the legs relatively long, the feet small and the neck thin. They also have the plumage lax and fluffy. All occur in the Australo-Papuan region. We are fortunate in being able to publish a rare photograph taken by Loke Wan Tho of the Blue Eupetes Rail Babbler (*Eupetes leucostictus*) of New Guinea, showing the bird at its nest located on the floor of mountain forest some 8000 feet above sea level. In this same forest occurs the Black Rail Babbler (*Melampitta lugubris*), which has the tail very short and rail- or pitta-like. In

Blue Eupetes Rail Babbler (*Eupetes leucostictus*)

Australia other strange representatives are found. For example, there is the Nullarbor Quail-Thrush (*Cinclosoma alisteri*), which is a small, black-breasted, quail-like bird that lives in pairs or parties and feeds on insects. This strange babbler digs an excavation in ground, lines it with dried grasses and lays therein three whitish eggs that are heavily blotched and spotted with browns and grays. And then there are the Log-runners (*Orthonyx temmincki*) of Australia, which have the tail short and spiny. These birds live in parties or pairs and are very noisy. They are reported to scratch for their food—insects and snails—with the tail as well as the feet. Their nest is a domed structure of sticks and mosses with a side entrance. In this species the female does all of the nest-building, incubation and caring for the young, and the male only feeds the female. However, the male helps to feed his offspring after they leave the nest. Incubation of the two eggs requires about three weeks.

Bald Crows (*Picathartidae*)

In the western part of Africa there live two little-known bald-headed species of birds which, although very different from all other birds, superficially resemble slender crows. They are both brownish gray above and white below, with long, thrushlike legs, and differ chiefly in the color of the bald head and the neck feathers. One, the White-necked Bald Crow (*Picathartes gymnocephalus;* Plate 155), has the bare skin of the front of the head, the cheeks and the upper neck bright yellow, the iris dark brown and huge black parietal spots behind the eyes, the legs pale gray, the feet dark green and the claws pinkish. The other, the Gray-necked Picathartes (*P. oreas*), has the face blackish and the head pinkish.

So obscure are the relationships of these "bald crows" that the experts have sometimes placed them with the crows, sometimes with the starlings, and,

[327

most recently, with the thrush-babblers. But some authoritative observers have tentatively elevated them to a full family of their own, and we are following that interpretation here.

Not long ago a joint expedition of the Zoological Society of London and the British Broadcasting Corporation went to Sierra Leone, West Africa, to study these rare birds and try to collect living specimens. It was successful in observing the White-necked Bald Crow, finding a colony "nesting among rocks in the depths of the forest high in the hills, the rocks being immense granite boulders 100 feet and more in diameter scattered among the trees." In semicaves and cracks were found cup-shaped mud nests that the birds had plastered against the rock 6 to 15 feet above the ground. Some were cemented to vertical faces, were open at the top, and had a lining of grasses and thin fibers to shield the eggs from the mud foundation. The eggs were two in number and brownish with dark brown scrawls. The nestlings were fed by regurgitation.

The bald crow holds its head to the side and jumps like some thrush-babblers. It resembles the latter birds in its habit of holding the wings loosely at the sides, pecking briskly at fallen food, and hurriedly casting leaves and dirt about. The bird is very furtive on the ground. It moves about rapidly and with tremendous hops in its search for insects and amphibians, apparently hunting frequently in the vicinity of small deep forest streams and in trees.

Parrotbills or Suthoras
(Paradoxornithidae)

A strange group of heavy-billed birds numbering 14 species occurs in the mountains of Central Asia and the Orient. Although almost all the parrotbills have the bill deeper than long, something like the bill of the parrot, they have no connection whatever with that group. Nevertheless, their structural characteristics effectively hide their true affinities. Some authorities have suggested that the parrotbills belong near the babblers because their habits of feeding and nest-building are fairly similar, but other specialists have allied them with the titmice.

A typical species is Gould's Parrotbill (*Paradoxornis flavirostris*), which is seven inches long and generally brownish above and whitish below, with bold black patches on the eyes and ears. This stubby, thick-billed bird lives in the hills of middle Asia from Assam to China. Its habitat is bushy grasslands, and, in common with all of the parrotbills, it travels through the grass in parties, staying mostly out of sight very much like a babbler and keeping up a constant stream of low chatter. When flushed, the flock flies weakly and then disappears into the grass again. Its food is insects, berries and seeds. The nests of parrotbills are all very similar, being

deep, well-lined cups formed of grasses and sheathed with animal silk. They are placed low to the ground in bushes or in reeds. The eggs are usually white, finely freckled with brown.

Some parrotbills are very small; for example Blyth's Parrotbill (*P. poliotis*) is but four inches in length. It has a rufous crown, and its wings are splashed with chestnut. In this species the flocks work through grass, searching very actively for food and displaying the same restlessness that foraging titmice or nuthatches exhibit. Parrotbills sometime forage in very large groups, almost like grass finches. For example, the Vinous-throated Parrotbill (*P. webbiana*) of China and Burma may travel in groups numbering up to fifty birds.

Wren-tit   (Chamaeidae)

The Wren-tit (*Chamaea fasciata*) of California and coastal Oregon is so unusual that a family has had to be established for it alone. However, Jean Delacour, an authority on the babbling thrushes (Timaliidae) of the Old World, believes that the Wren-tit is merely an isolated offshoot of that family and is related to the genus *Moupinia* of China.

The appearance of the Wren-tit, a 6½-inch bird, is suggested by its name; it is reminiscent of both wrens and titmice. It is chiefly brown with a long, tapering, faintly barred tail that is frequently elevated as the bird hops about in its favorite habitat, low scrub and chaparral. The plumage is thick and fluffy, like that of many titmice.

The food of the Wren-tit consists of insects and berries gathered in the underbrush. These odd birds live in pairs most of the time and usually keep in touch with one another by means of rasping notes, but at times they emit very loud songs that carry for hundreds of yards.

Wren-tits probably remain mated for life. The sexes share nearly equally the tasks of nest construction, incubation and the feeding of the young. The nest is a firm cup of twigs, bark strips, feathers and animal silk placed in a crotch in dense bushes. Three to five greenish blue, unspotted eggs are laid.

Old World Flycatchers
(Muscicapidae)

Old World flycatchers feed almost entirely on insects captured in flight, although some dive onto the ground like little hawks to capture their prey. This specialized form of feeding is facilitated by their well-developed powers of flight, particularly their rapid diving pursuit flights. To assist in snaring their prey in the air, they have strong rakelike rictal bristles fringing the upper mandible. The bill itself is generally small and flattened, with bristles covering the nostrils. Since the legs and feet of these birds are used only for perching, they are generally frail. They have ten primaries. Their young are nearly always spotted, as in the thrushes—a large group from which they cannot be satisfactorily separated except on the basis of feeding habits.

Old World flycatchers have no representatives in the Americas—a fact worth noting since the related Old World Warblers send offshoots into the New World. As here treated, if only to make it more manageable, the family consists of 378 species. It should be noted, however, that Mayr and Amadon consider the Old World flycatchers, thrushes, babbling thrushes, Old World Warblers, and other insect-eating birds to be tribes and subfamilies of one great family under the inclusive name Muscicapidae.

Old World flycatchers generally build open, cup-shaped nests in trees or bushes, or in holes in trees or mud banks. In these they lay three to seven eggs that are generally spotted. Nest-building is usually shared by both sexes, but the female does most of the work. In some cases the male feeds the incubating female.

The family is divided into four subgroups, the first of which is the widespread Muscicapinae, or typical flycatchers, many of which are migratory. They usually have pointed wings and a medium-length, slightly forked tail. These birds are frequently seen

Cape Flycatcher (*Muscicapa capensis*)

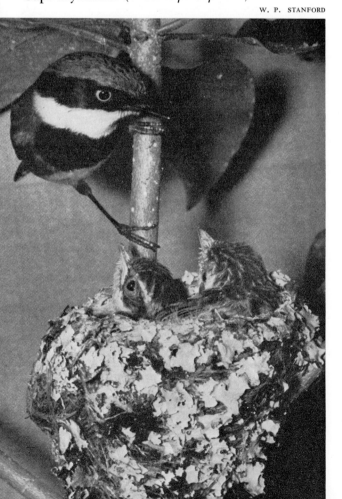

perched on prominent lookouts throughout the Old World, and climax their sallies with sharp snaps of the bill as they catch their quarry in the air. Among the small species that can be seen in Europe are the grayish brown, streaked, Spotted Flycatcher (*Muscicapa striata*), which is a common garden bird; the Pied Flycatcher (*M. hypoleuca*), which favors holes in coniferous trees for its nest; and the Collared Flycatcher (*M. albicollis*) which, like the Pied, is chiefly blackish above and white below, but has a white collar. An example from Africa is the Cape Flycatcher (*M. capensis*).

The Dusky Blue Flycatcher (*M. sordida*)—a sparrow-sized species of southern Asia in which the sexes are similarly dressed—has a sweet and rather loud song that, according to G. M. Henry, consists of five or six notes. This species makes a cup nest of green moss in a bank or tree for its two to three pale freckled eggs.

The Muscicapinae in general are drab-colored or streaked, but quite a few have bright blue in their plumage (See Plate 156). The blue-backed, rufous-breasted Blue-throated Flycatcher (*M. rubeculoides*) of Asia is an example.

The second subfamily contains many colorful and a goodly number of beautifully ornamented species. Included are the blue flycatchers of southeastern Asia and the Philippines, of which the Azure or Black-naped Flycatcher (*Hypothymis azurea*), a forest bird, is a good example. This species is sparrow-sized and crested and has a medium-long tail. Both sexes and the young are purplish blue, the male being the brighter. The Azure Flycatcher nests close to the ground, laying two to three pinkish white, cinnamon-spotted eggs.

The most beautiful flycatchers, which are among the truly beautiful birds of the world, belong to this subfamily—the paradise flycatchers (*Terpsiphone*). In these birds, which range from Africa through Asia to Australia, the males are resplendent and, although the females are also well ornamented, they are always very differently colored. In the Indian Paradise Flycatcher (*Terpsiphone paradisi*), the size of a small thrush, the male is white, with some black on the wings and a shining black head capped with a tall sharp crest. He has the two middle tail feathers greatly elongated and ribbon-like, so that they form long, flexible trains as he flies. The female has the black head and crest, but its back and its much shorter tail are reddish chestnut. Despite the great difference in form and color, the male paradise flycatchers share the duties of incubation with their mates. The author has observed both sexes on their nest, an open cup on a drooping limb over a frequently used pathway in a garden in Katmandu, Nepal.

The third subfamily of this large assemblage consists of the fantails, the Rhipidurinae, a group found in Australia (see Plate 122), New Zealand, New Guinea, the Philippines and many remote islands of the Pacific such as the Fijis. It includes small black-

Paradise Flycatcher, male (*Terpsiphone paradisi*)

and-white forest-loving birds and chestnut-brown species that may be found anywhere from sea level to the edge of the alpine grasslands 11,000 feet above the sea. All have the habit of waving the long, fanlike tail, and their nests may be high up or close to the ground, in deep forest or in garden trees. In the Willie-wagtail (*Rhipidura leucophrys*), a large black-and-white fantail that is found in the Australian and New Guinea region, the male and the female share incubation, and nesting may take place while the adults are molting their flight feathers. The nest of this species is quite typical; it is a well-made cup, firmly bound with spider webs and appearing to be glued with shellac. Usually four eggs are laid. Incubation requires about 13 days, and it is customary for several broods to be raised per season.

The last subfamily of Old World flycatchers consists of the thick-heads and whistlers, a congregation of widely differing birds that occurs in Australia, New Guinea and the islands of the southwestern Pacific. By far the largest subgroup is the Pachycephalas. These birds are somewhat smaller than starlings and are found from sea level to about 10,000 feet. An example is the Golden Whistler (*P. pectoralis*) of Australia, a six-inch bird with a bright yellow breast. Like many of its subgroup, it has the throat white and wears a narrow collar that is the color of the breast. The female and the young male lack the yellow breast. Thick-heads build open cup-shaped nests of grasses, bark shreds and leaves. The male helps with the nest-building, and two yellowish eggs with grayish spots are laid. Incubation requires 15 days. Thick-heads have a well-developed song.

Many larger whistlers belong to the genus *Pitohui,* a group in which the giants of the family are placed; some are as large as sparrow hawks. In these birds, the males are very different from the

Barred Warbler (*Sylvia nisoria*) removing a faecal sac dropped by young

P. O. SWANBERG

females, usually being dark brown or sooty black, while the females are generally pale brown.

The pretty little birds of the genus *Petroica,* found in Australia and New Guinea, are generally known as "robins" because of a superficial resemblance—in some species—to the Robin Redbreast (*Erithacus rubecula*) the settlers had known in England. The English bird, however, is a thrush, while the Australian "robins" are classified with the flycatchers. One of the smallest but most brightly colored members of this group is the Red-capped Robin (*P. goodenovii;* Plate 161).

Kinglets or Goldcrests
(*Subfamily Regulinae*)

Kinglets, or goldcrests as they are called in the Old World, are among the smallest of birds and, ounce for ounce, are probably among the most gifted of all songsters. The five known species breed in cool and cold places in northern North America and Eurasia, but also southward in high, forested mountains. Kinglets are small but hardy birds three and four inches in length. Their feathering has a soft, almost downlike quality that may very well provide extra insulation. Kinglets have the bill very short and straight, with a slight notch near the end of the maxilla. In all species the nostrils are partially shielded with small feathers. Their most distinctive character is the crest, which is often partially concealable and may be expanded to reveal a vividly colored spot.

Kinglets are insectivorous birds that seek most of their food in the small branches and among the needles of coniferous trees, often at great heights. They are very active, fearless and confiding. They often travel in bands and where two species occur in the New World, both frequently travel together or move in hunting parties with other small birds such as warblers and creepers. At such times their usual calls are thin scolding notes, but during the breeding season the song of the Ruby-crowned Kinglet, for example, is full and rich, and is delivered with a volume that seems impossible for such a tiny bird.

Both sexes join to build bulky nests that are generally purselike and often partially pensile. The egg chambers are warm but so small that the eggs, in number between five and ten, are often stacked in two layers. The eggs are small and may be buff or white in color, with a sprinkling of brownish spotting. They are incubated by the female for from 14 to 17 days, after which the youngsters are fed for another 10 to 20 days by both parents.

The New World species are the Ruby-crowned Kinglet (*Regulus calendula;* Plate 157) and the Golden-crowned Kinglet (*R. satrapa*). The Ruby-crowned is olivaceous gray with an erectile ruby crest appearing only in the male. In the Golden-

[331

crowned, a more yellowish olive bird, both sexes have a bright crown broadly edged with black and white; the center of the crown is yellow in the female, bright orange-ruby in the male.

Widespread in Eurasia is a species that is very similar to the Golden-crowned Kinglet, but lacks the facial markings. It is called the Goldcrest (*Regulus regulus*). In mountainous middle Europe and around the Mediterranean lives the Firecrest (*R. ignicapillus*), both sexes of which have a bright brownish gold crown and a black stripe through the eye. This species is more fond of oak woodlands than of coniferous forests. Far eastward on the other edge of Eurasia occurs the rare and little known Yellow-rumped Kinglet (*R. goodfellowi*) of Mount Orizan on the island of Taiwan. This species is the most colorful of all. Not only does it have a bright yellow rump, but the crown is decorated with an extensive yellow, orange and red crest that is the longest in the family; it also has a white forehead and a white line over the eye.

Old World Warblers

(*Sylviidae*)

The Old World warblers are very different from the wood warblers of the New World in that they are generally excellent songsters, whereas most of the wood warblers have weak songs; they have softer, more fluffy plumage and ten functional primaries in the wings, whereas the wood warblers have nine. As a rule, Old World warblers are small, but some of the species that dwell in grasslands grow to the size of a starling. The sexes are generally dressed similarly, and the young are not spotted as in the thrushes and Old World flycatchers. The Sylviidae are also distinguishable from wood warblers by the presence of a notched bill and rictal bristles. Recent revisers have classed the Old World warblers as a subfamily of the large assemblage of Old World flycatchers, but as previously indicated (see Muscicapidae) they are here treated as a separate family, and the Australian wren warblers are included more or less arbitrarily.

The family Sylviidae as here presented forms an assemblage of some 395 species, divided into three subfamilies. The first is the Sylviinae or typical warblers, which are virtually restricted to the Old World; the second is the Polioptilinae or gnatcatchers, which are found from the United States to Brazil; and the third is the Malurinae or Australian warblers, which are largely restricted to the Australo-Papuan region of the Southwestern Pacific.

Old World warblers are chiefly insect-eaters. They capture their food by searching leaves and crannies and not by aerial pursuits as do the flycatchers. Many of the species are highly migratory, breeding in the temperate zone and wintering in the tropics.

Their nests are built in a wide variety of locations. Some are on the ground, some are cup-shaped, some are domed, some are pensile and some are high in trees. In most cases the female does the bulk of the nest-building, and in a few species the male builds cock nests, as do the wrens and certain other birds. Dr. Charles Kendeigh records that generally the incubation period varies, depending on the species, from 12 to 15 days, and the nestling period from 9 to 14 days. Both parents usually feed the young, but the female does most of the work.

Typical Old World warblers comprising the subfamily Sylviinae include the grasshopper warblers of the genus *Locustella,* which build open nests on or near the ground. The five-inch Grasshopper Warbler (*L. naevia*) of Eurasia is mainly a streaked brown. An inhabitant of grass and undergrowth, it prefers to run rather than fly in making its escape. This bird emits rasping calls that are very like the scratchy notes of grasshoppers; hence its common name.

Other species, such as the Great Reed Warbler (*Acrocephalus arundinaceus*), which is 7½ inches in length, keep very close to reed beds, where they build open cup-shaped nests of reed strippings and slender leaves, attached to the vertical shafts of water plants in such a way that the vegetation can bend in the wind and not tear the anchorage. The rims of these nests are constricted, forming a protective inner circle that tends to hold the eggs and young when the nest sways far over on its side. An example of the genus is the Reed Warbler (*A. scirpaceus;* Plate 159).

The grass warblers (*Cisticola*) are dressed to match their generally brown habitat. About 75 species of these small, skulking birds are found in the Old World. The majority construct softly lined, open nests close to the ground, but some species make them domed and equip them with side entrances. The Fan-tailed Warbler (*Cisticola juncidis*) of southern Eurasia and Africa, a four-inch, reddish brown, streaked bird that skulks in grassy fields and marshes, is an example of these "purse nest" builders, most of which lay two to three pale, spotted eggs. In courtship these birds sometimes fly up into the air, but at other seasons they are most difficult to observe, since they keep to the bottom tier of grassfields, where they feed almost exclusively on insects.

A large number of Old World warblers belonging to the genus *Sylvia* occur very widely throughout Eurasia and Africa. Many are well-known, well-liked birds. In Europe is found the Blackcap (*S. atricapillus*), a 5½-inch, black-capped, gray bird of hedges and open woodlands (the female has a reddish brown crown). Like all of the group, this bird has a rich, warbling song, and it builds an open nest close to the ground, often in brambles. Other members of the group are the Barred Warbler (*S. nisoria*), which has the underparts barred and spotted; the Garden Warbler (*S. borin*), a highly migratory species that is mostly brown; and the well-known Whitethroat (*S. communis*), in which both sexes have

Long-tailed or **Indian Tailorbird** (*Orthotomus sutorius*) at nest

prominent white throats. These birds attract attention by their splendid songs, their confiding nature and their marked habit of migration, which causes abrupt comings and goings.

Willow or leaf warblers are very small, generally grayish green birds that are highly migratory. They are found nearly everywhere in the Old World. Most of the species winter in the tropics and nest in the cool parts of Eurasia. One of this group is the Arctic Willow Warbler (*Phylloscopus borealis*), the only species that reaches the New World. It ventures as far east as Alaska only to breed, and in winter retires to the high forests of eastern Asia and the Philippines. These birds build domed nests with side entrances on or near the ground. The tiny, leaf-scanning species of this genus are confusingly similar. In Europe five distinct species occur, and the observer has difficulty in distinguishing them. All are between four and five inches in length, and chiefly grayish green with pale eyebrows and underparts. An example is the Willow Warbler (*P. trochilus*), which is one of the most abundant summer visitors to the northern half of Europe, where it feeds in low vegetation. The song is pleasing and musical. Most leaf warblers, however, keep to the forest crown and are very hard to observe. In hunting they frequently sally out in pursuit of flying gnats and other insects. One of the more arboreal species is the Wood Warbler (*P. sibilatrix;* Plate 162). Although it prefers to feed among the upper foliage in well-wooded areas, its nest is placed on the ground, usually in a natural hollow.

In southeastern Asia and the Philippines are found the tailorbirds (*Orthotomus*), of which the author has collected many examples. These members of the family of Old World warblers are highly interesting because of their ability to use the bill as a tool for sewing in constructing their nests. Certain of the New World orioles perforate leafy canopies and thread suspension shrouds through these to the edges of their pensile nests, but only the tailorbird may be said to "sew." G. M. Henry in his *Birds of Ceylon* gives an excellent description of the process by which the edges of broad leaves are brought together and formed into funnel-like receptacles for holding the nest. Writing of the Indian Tailorbird (*Orthotomus sutorius*)—a small, olive-green bird with a rufous cap, in which the sexes are similar except that the male has the middle tail feathers elongated—Mr. Henry notes that they seem to remain mated for life. To erect a nest, an adult stabs a broad leaf—sometimes several—with the sharp bill, thus perforating the edges. Strands of cottony material are then threaded through the holes, and the opposing edges are drawn together to form a tubular pocket in which the nest proper is then built. The nests are usually within a few feet of the ground in dense vegetation, and two to three brown-spotted pale eggs are laid.

The largest of the Old World warbler family is the Striated Canegrass Warbler (*Megalurus palus-tris*), which is ten inches in length. It is a brownish, streaked bird of the Philippines that builds a bulky domed nest in dry fields of grass, where it habitually skulks, as do its many relatives in southern Asia and New Guinea.

About twelve species of American Sylviids form the subfamily Polioptilinae or gnatcatchers, a group of predominantly grayish birds that occurs between the United States and Brazil. These little birds, averaging about five inches in length, are rather fly-catcher-like in appearance. They scan crevices and leaves, making sallies for insects. They are well represented by the Blue-gray Gnatcatcher (*Polioptila caerulea*), a bird of very soft plumage with an exquisite, muted song, which breeds in the warmer parts of the United States. Extremely active, this little bird keeps to the upper foliage of dense trees, where it builds its beautiful lichen-covered nest. A close relative, the Black-tailed Gnatcatcher (*P. melanura;* Plate 166), inhabits the arid southwestern portion of North America, building its nest in low bushes, using such diverse materials as grass, bark, fibers, bits of paper, cloth, string, rabbit fur, and plant down. The three to five pale, bluish-speckled eggs are incubated by both the parents, as in the Long-billed Gnatwren (*Ramphocaenus rufiventris*) of Middle America. In these species the pairs share in nest-building and feeding the young. In some species, however, the incubation, which takes about 13 days, is performed entirely by the female. Some of the Middle American members of this subfamily, all of which have the bill slender and depressed, have well-developed rictal bristles. Among these are the White-lored Gnatcatcher (*P. albiloris*), the Black-capped Gnatcatcher (*P. nigriceps*), and the Half-collared Gnatwren (*Microbates cinereiventris*).

In the southwestern Pacific are found many colorful birds that habitually carry their tails in odd positions, usually straight up. These birds, known as Australian Warblers, Australian Wrens, Emu Wrens, Blue Wrens (Plate 154), Bristle Birds and Grass Wrens, are found in Australia, New Guinea, Tasmania and New Zealand. Generally speaking, their nests are retort-shaped with a side entrance. Usually three to four whitish eggs with bright brown markings are laid. Many of the Australian species are highly colorful. The Red-winged Wren (*Malurus elegans*), for example, is a six-inch bird with an aqua-blue head and cheeks, reddish shoulders, and bold areas of black, pale blue and white. One species, the Banded Blue Wren (*M. splendens*), is called the Mormon Wren because of the apparent excess of females in its groups. It is believed that these birds live in clans and have social habits, but this has yet to be proved. In this group are found the peculiar Emu Wrens, an example of which is the Southern Emu Wren (*Stipiturus malachurus*), one of the most remarkable of all songbirds. To its very small body are attached six gray, fragmented feathers that far exceed the length of the rest of the bird.

Bar-tailed Thornbill (*Acanthiza murina*)

Other aberrant members of this subfamily are the tiny, nondescript tree warblers that belong to the genera *Gerygone* and *Acanthiza*. Generally small olive species with varying amounts of yellow below, these birds keep pretty well to the crown of the forest. One, the Yellow-tailed Thornbill (*Acanthiza chrysorrhoa*) of Australia, places its extraordinary nest either in the stick structures built by large birds of prey or in the terminal limblets of trees. This nest is a long, oval structure with an opening near the bottom at one side. Inside there are several chambers, the uppermost of which is used for the rearing of the young. The male shares in the task of nest construction and in feeding the young, but he does not incubate. The lower chambers take the form of more or less complete nests, and are thought to be sleeping nests for the male. But one theory is that they are built to deceive the parasitic cuckoos; another is that they are "play" nests built by the male, like those of true wrens and some other birds. The fact is that their true purpose is unknown. A New Guinea species of this group is the Bar-tailed Thornbill (*A. murina*), of which a photograph is shown.

Wren-thrush (*Zeledoniidae*)

The Wren-thrush (*Zeledonia coronata*) is an obscure, stocky little bird that lives between 6000 and 10,000 feet above sea level in Costa Rica and western Panama. Its name is derived from its wrenlike size, its habit of skulking on the floor of deep forest and, presumably, its vaguely thrushlike appearance.

Actually the Wren-thrush is something of an enigma to ornithologists, chiefly because it makes its home in rather inaccessible forests. It may have nothing whatever to do with either wrens or thrushes. In fact, it reminds the author more of a babbler, a family famous for skulking on the floor of forests in the Indo-Malayan and Australian regions.

The Wren-thrush is about 4½ inches long and the sexes are alike in color. The bill is short and straight; the legs are slender and relatively very long; and the tail is short. The wings are peculiar in that they are rounded and have only nine obvious primaries, the tenth being minute. Above, the bird is dark brownish olive, with the crown standing out

[335

prominently due to its deep golden-brown cap. The feathers of the cap are probably erectile, and the sides are narrowly edged with black, as is the forehead. Below, the prevailing color is sooty gray washed with dusky olive on the flanks. A specimen collected in Costa Rica in May was in breeding condition. It had the iris dark brown and the bill and legs black.

Thrushes, Blue Thrushes, Forktails and Cochoas

(*Turdidae*)

The nearly cosmopolitan family of thrushes consists of 304 species of small to medium-sized perching birds closely related to the Old World flycatchers. They are chiefly insectivorous, but many eat fruit; and they habitually feed chiefly in trees, but also on the ground. They do not attack flying prey. All thrushes build open nests, that is nests that are not domed. These are usually placed in bushes or trees or on the ground, but a few species build in rock crevices or in holes in trees.

The name "thrush" brings to mind the finest avian music. It is no exaggeration to say that some of these birds are among the most exquisite songsters in the world: witness the Nightingale, the Shama and the Hermit Thrush.

Thrushes resemble babblers, but their young, like most young flycatchers, differ strongly in plumage pattern from the parents and almost always are scaled or spotted in appearance. On the ground they hop on their strong legs, and in the air they fly swiftly, many of the species executing long migrations.

The most wide-ranging species belong to the subfamily Turdinae—the typical thrushes. Many species, some bright in color and some solid black, but most with yellow or orange bills and eye-rings, belong to this wide-ranging genus. Famous Old World members are the Blackbird (*Turdus merula;* Plates 163 and 164) of Eurasia and Africa, in which the male (ten inches) is black with a yellow bill, and the Fieldfare (*T. pilaris*), of similar size, which breeds in colonies at the woodland edge or even on farm buildings. In the mountains of Eurasia there is the Ring Ouzel, a vividly marked black thrush with a white chest collar. Many other species are found in Asia and eastward through New Guinea to northern Australia, as well as in the New World, where no less than ten species live in Middle America alone. Among these are the Sooty Robin (*T. nigrescens*), the Black Robin (*T. infuscatus*), the Clay-colored Robin (*T. grayi*) and the Bare-eyed Robin (*T. nudigenis;* Plate 173). In this area the American Robin (*T. migratorius*) is the best known and most widely loved. Its bright reddish brown breast, striped black-and-white throat and blackish head, together with its

substantial size—about ten inches—make it considerably different from its well-known cousin, the six-inch Robin Redbreast of the Old World (*Erithacus rubecula;* Plate 158), which also has a bright reddish brown breast. The American Robin nests from about northern tree limit south to Mexico and winters as far south as Central America. Like the Wood Thrush (*Hylocichla mustelina*) of North America, it builds the core of its cup-shaped nest out of mud.

Confined to the New World are the three species of Bluebirds (*Sialia*). The Eastern Bluebird (*S. sialis;* Plate 168), a seven-inch, blue-backed, reddish-brown-breasted bird, nests chiefly in eastern North America north to Newfoundland. It lays pale blue eggs in a tree hole and, quite commonly, in nest boxes. A close relative is the Mountain Bluebird (*S. currucoides;* Plate 169) of western North America. The hylocichlas, a group of remarkably similar forest thrushes that are largely restricted to North American breeding areas, include some of the most eloquent songsters. One of these, the Gray-cheeked Thrush (*H. minima*), breeds from Newfoundland west through Alaska to northeastern Siberia and winters south to Peru. This is an eight-inch bird, olive above, white with fine speckling below, and grayish on the cheeks. Its drab forest dress is almost identical with that of the Olive-backed Thrush (*H. ustulata*), which winters south to Argentina, and rather like that of the Hermit Thrush (*H. guttata*), a species of somewhat more open forest, renowned for its fine song. In fact, it is generally believed that the visual signals (plumage) of species recognition are virtually nonexistent in some of the species, and that the auditory signals (songs) are relied on almost exclusively. This interesting theory is supported by the presence of very distinctive and often very melodious songs. The familiar Wood Thrush (*H. mustelina*), an eight-inch bird with bright reddish brown upperparts and prominent black spots on a white breast, belongs to this group.

A closely related group, possibly a tropical, nonmigratory offshoot of the northern wood thrushes, is found from Mexico south into tropical South America. These are the nightingale-thrushes, of which the Orange-billed Nightingale-thrush (*Catharus aurantiirostris;* Plate 171) is typical. So closely do these birds resemble their northern relatives in structure, habits and song, that Dr. William C. Dilger, an authority on the group, believes they should all be combined into a single genus.

In Eurasia and Africa the variety of thrushes is much greater than in the New World. Some are very colorful. One is the Blue Rock Thrush (*Monticola solitarius*), a crag-loving bird that nests in crevices of strong mountainsides. Another is the Wheatear (*Oenanthe oenanthe;* Plate 165), which represents a clan that ranges nearly around the world in the Northern Hemisphere. Wheatears are generally six-inch, buff-breasted, gray-backed birds with white rumps, and in the male, black occurs as a mask in the wings and tail. The six-inch Old World Robin (*Erithacus rubecula;* Plate 158) occurs widely in Eurasia and Africa. It nests in tree holes and in cavities of many kinds, including those in earth banks. Another Old World bird with an American namesake is the European Redstart (*Phoenicurus phoenicurus*). The American bird, however, is a wood warbler (family Parulidae) and neither resembles nor is related to the European bird, which is shown in Plate 170. The Nightingale (*Luscinia megarhynchos;* Plate 160), the peer of Eurasian songsters—a 6½-inch brown bird with pale brown underparts and a bright rufous tail and rump, which sings in the depths of the forest—is remarkably similar in appearance and nesting habits to the Hermit Thrush of North America, which is the finest of New World musicians. Despite this similarity, anatomical evidence indicates that they belong to two separate groups within the thrush family and are only distantly related.

The eggs of thrushes are often clear in color, either whitish or bluish, but sometimes they have dark markings. In most New World species, as far as known, the female usually does the nest-building, incubation and brooding, but both parents share in feeding the young. However, in the hole-nesting Bluebird the male helps with nest-building and incubation. The incubation periods of European thrushes are usually 13 to 14 days, and the male usually aids in nest-building and in incubating the eggs.

In Asia, from Turkestan and Tibet east to northern China, Formosa and Java, occur six species of closely related blue thrushes that form the subfamily Myiophoneinae. The semiaquatic birds of this group reach 12 inches in length. An example is the Whistling Thrush (*Myiophoneus caeruleus*), which occurs along the edges and on the rocks of rushing mountain torrents as high as 10,000 feet above sea level in Central Asia. Entirely dark blue with glistening blue spots, it has short, strong legs and a yellow bill; both sexes are dressed alike. Its rich whistled songs ring out over the roar of falling water as the aptly named bird plays about on rocks, seizing floating insects, snails and crustaceans from the water and from the surrounding moss. Its nest is a cup of moss, often placed on a ledge in a half-cave. From three to five gray-green, brown-spotted eggs are laid. The pairs, which are usually found alone, share the nest-building, incubation and the rearing of the young.

Another subfamily of the thrushes is the Cochoaninae, a group of three very interesting, rare species of tropical Asia and Malaysia. These are large, brightly colored (blue, green, purple), fruit-eating birds that keep entirely to trees. Among them is the Green Cochoa (*Cochoa viridis*) of the Himalayas, 12 inches long, and bright green with blue on the head, wings and tail.

A further subfamily that must be mentioned is the Enicurinae, or the forktails, of which eight species are known in the Oriental region from India to the East Indies. All are from small to medium in size—generally with black-and-white plumage and deeply forked tails. Like the large Whistling Thrush, they keep close to mountain torrents, where they hunt their food beside or on the surface of water, often flitting from rock to rock. One of these is the graceful black-and-white Spotted Forktail (*Enicurus maculatus*), which resembles a wagtail. It occurs, usually in pairs, up to 12,000 feet in the Himalayas, moving about in deceptively wagtail fashion with swaying, halting movements that involve much tail-raising and changing of direction. Dr. Salim Ali noted that both birds help to build the nest, and that the moss used in construction is first carried to water and dipped before it is plastered on the structure. Both sexes incubate from three to four stone-colored, spotted eggs and feed the young.

Thrashers, Catbirds and Mockingbirds
(*Mimidae*)

Many of the 30 species in this family resemble giant wrens. Indeed if their nest architecture did not differ so radically (the Mimidae make open cup-shaped nests and the wrens make domed nests with side entrances), it would be very hard to distinguish some of the borderline species. The thrashers, catbirds and mockingbirds are restricted to the New World, where they are concentrated in tropical America. All have highly developed songs. As in the wrens, the plumage coloration is generally restricted to grays and browns, the eggs are commonly pale with reddish spots and the birds keep to the lower tier of the forest, usually near or on the ground.

The thrashers (*Toxostoma*) are thrush-sized birds (Plate 172) of the forest edge and bushy grasslands. They occur over most of North America. All are brownish above and paler below, the latter often having bold dark spotting. The best-known species, the Brown Thrasher (*T. rufum*) of eastern North America, is sedentary in the warmer parts of its range and migratory elsewhere. More than eleven inches long, it subsists, like all thrashers, chiefly on insects, which it gathers among dead leaves close to or on the ground. It also eats some fruit. Although not shy, it is unobtrusive. It often places its nest in the forest edge bordering bushy fields or gardens and chooses thick tangles of vines for cover. The nest, built from about two to six feet up, is lined with sticks and rootlets. Four to five pale blue-green eggs marked with characteristic reddish spots are laid and both sexes incubate. Like so many of the family, the Brown Thrasher is a splendid musician. It sings on a specially selected and prominently exposed perch in the top of a tall bush or tree.

One of the best-known species is the familiar American Catbird (*Dumetella carolinensis*), which breeds from British Columbia south to the Gulf of Mexico and winters south to Central America. This thrush-sized species has an unmistakable mewing, catlike call, and an attractive though muted song. It often lives close to man, coming into his gardens and breeding in his ornamental bushes. The Catbird is dark slate-gray with a black cap and tail and deep chestnut under-tail coverts. It builds a nest of twigs and bark strips, usually about four feet up, and lays three to five rich greenish blue eggs, slightly smaller and darker than those of the Robin.

The mockingbirds, of which there are nine species extending from Oregon, Ohio and New Jersey southward to Patagonia, are the most gifted of New World songsters. Only one, the Common Mockingbird (*Mimus polyglottos*), occurs in the United States, but all are much alike in form and color. And all species are superb singers and mimics, W. H. Hudson declaring—after hearing one in the southern part of South America—that it was undoubtedly the finest songster in the world. When it feels the urge to sing, the mockingbird, like the Brown Thrasher, resorts to special perches high up in bushes or trees. There it spreads the tail and partly opens its wings as though throwing its heart into its songs. Ornithologists have stood by in wonderment as a single male ran through a repertoire of 20 or more songs of other birds as well as a series of man-made noises—all with the accuracy of a tape recorder. Song mimicry is, of course, better developed in certain individuals than in others; for example, one "Mocker" is reported to have mimicked the songs of 32 birds.

High-fidelity recordings of the mockingbird mimicking the Whip-poor-will—a call that to human ears seems, as the name suggests, to consist of three notes—when slowed down and played back were found to consist of five distinct notes, exactly as in slowed-down recordings of the Whip-poor-will. This is strong evidence that the mockingbird hears and accurately reproduces notes inaudible to human ears,

Carolina Wren (*Thryothorus ludovicianus*)

and that bird song, beautiful as it sounds to us, is really much richer and more musical than the relatively inefficient ear of man can appreciate.

Because of this ability to mimic, the mockingbird was long a highly prized cage bird. In parts of South America it is still caught for this purpose, and some of the species have been shipped to Hawaii, where they now live as wild birds.

The Common Mockingbird is about 10½ inches long. The sexes are similar, both being generally ashy above with brownish wings and tail, and with much white in both the wing and the outer half of the tail. The male assists in nest-building and occasionally in incubation. Both sexes care for the young.

The nest is a bulky open cup of grass, twigs and rootlets. In North America it is usually placed fairly low in a bush. In Venezuela the author observed it 15 feet up in an isolated grassland tree. The eggs are pale greenish blue with brownish spots.

Long ago some mockingbirds became marooned on the Galapagos Islands. There they have evolved along distinct lines so that today the four species of Galapagos Mockingbird (*Nesomimus*) have the bill longer and more compressed and the legs longer and stronger than any of the continental species.

No less than four genera of this family are confined to the West Indies, and three of these are found only in the Lesser Antilles. The rarest of these is the White-breasted Thrasher (*Ramphocinclus brachyurus*), a nine-inch bird now reduced to a small population in one section of the island of St. Lucia. More widespread is the Trembler (*Cinclocerthia ruficauda*), which received its name from its peculiar habit of trembling violently. It is about the same size as the White-breasted Thrasher but is duller in coloration and has a longer bill. From two to three greenish blue eggs are laid in the nest, which is usually built in the hollow base of a tree.

Unique among the Mimidae is the glossy black plumage color of the Black Catbird (*Melanoptila glabrirostris*) of the Yucatan Peninsula and adjacent areas of Central America. Like the familiar Catbird of the north, it lives in deciduous undergrowth.

Wrens (*Troglodytidae*)

Wrens are so well known that they hardly need be described. They occur around the world in the Northern Hemisphere. In the New World, where the family originated, they are surprisingly abundant and diversified, especially in Central and South America. The smallest species are about one-third the size of a small sparrow and the largest are larger than a starling but more slender.

None of the 63 species is gaily colored, and all are more or less cryptically marked to match the habitat in which they live. There is therefore a preponderance of brown and gray with black lineations on the back, and in many species the underparts and the facial markings are pale buffy gray or white.

Although all species of wrens are found in the New World, one, the Winter Wren (*Troglodytes troglodytes*), has sent racial representatives to the Old World. This species is represented in Iceland, Europe, Asia, Japan, the Aleutian Islands and North America from Alaska south to the Gulf of Mexico. It is a small, stocky, dark brown bird less than four inches long and has profuse barring. It scurries about in the underbrush like a mouse, and like all wrens it sings during much of the year and often carries the tail cocked over the back. This insect-eating bird has rounded wings and a slender bill, and the sexes are similar in coloration.

Recently the great English student of animal behavior, Dr. E. A. Armstrong, brought together a vast amount of material relating to wrens in a book entitled *The Wren*. A fair share of it comes from the observations of the dean of tropical American ornithologists, Dr. Alexander Skutch, who has closely observed the life histories of some 25 species of wrens in Central America. Despite these now fairly extensive studies, there is much still to be learned about these unusual birds. For one thing, most species build auxiliary nests that have nothing to do with egg-laying. Also, most species keep together in close-knit families that participate in the tasks of housekeeping, often with the young of one generation assisting their parents in the feeding of their second-generation brothers and sisters. Further observations are needed to solve the enigmas of these and other aspects of their social behavior.

The most provocative problem is that of the false nests built by the males of many species during display, near the spot where the real nest is ultimately erected. However, these false nests are usually in more conspicuous places and often appear somewhat different from the real nest in silhouette, size, decoration or degree of completion of the nest cavity. Many theories have been advanced as to the role played by these nests. Dr. Skutch has shown that in many species they are used as sleeping nests, the male sleeping in the false nest and the female sleeping in the egg nest during the period of incubation and the rearing of the young, and even afterwards. The author believes they may serve a display function in courtship, as is known to be the case with the bowers erected by male bowerbirds.

Wrens are splendid songsters, and some of the species rival the nightingale in sweetness of tone. Unlike most birds, they sing throughout the year, the females as well as the males—even in the wettest, coldest parts of the day—their liquid, many-phrased notes pouring forth in full splendor when other birds are silent. Since these cryptically colored birds are almost always out of sight of each other, the voice plays the primary part in the maintenance of contact between the pairs.

Not generally known is the fact that many species practice duetting. Dr. F. M. Chapman discovered that the Buff-breasted Wren (*Thryothorus leucotis*) of Panama employs a song which is composed of four parts, two of which are delivered by the male and two by the female. Skutch noted that the Plain Wren or Chinchirigui (*T. modestus*) also employs a composite song: one of the pair emits *chinchiri* and the other immediately adds *igui*. Both observers were initially fooled into thinking the song was delivered by a single bird. In fact, in both cases, it was not until the pairs of birds became separated in such a way that they rendered their parts of the duet on either side of the human observer that the manner of delivery was deciphered.

Another member of this genus is the Rufous-breasted Wren (*T. rutilus*) of central and northern South America. It has a loud musical song which reminded Sir Charles Belcher, who heard it on the island of Trinidad, of the phrase "Billy tea, boiling for me." The nest is a loosely-built ball of grasses with an opening at the side. The "false nests" of this species have been known to mislead parasitic cowbirds, which deposit their eggs in the empty nest.

A close relative is the Carolina Wren (*T. ludovicianus*), shown on page 338.

One of the most beautiful of all bird songs is that of the Organ Bird (*Cyphorhinus arada*) of Amazonia, which produces notes that seem to stem from a highly trained human voice or from a flute. The wrens with the best voices are the most elusive. The author has spent many days trying unsuccessfully to catch sight of a wren which, out of sheer admiration for its voice, Dr. Chapman named "The Composer."

Wrens build retort-shaped nests, often with long, flasklike entrance tunnels entered through the sides. Cavities in broken and dead trees, old woodpecker holes and crevices in cliffs and buildings are also used. The eggs range from pure white to nearly solid chocolate brown, but the majority of the species lay whitish eggs liberally sprinkled with brown and gray. The set ranges from two to ten, with the smallest sets being laid by tropical species.

Many species of wrens sleep singly in their false nests or in crevices or holes. Others sleep in pairs, and some in family groups, the largest number observed sleeping in such a group by Dr. Skutch being eleven. This was the Band-backed Wren (*Campylorhynchus zonatus*), a large species of humid parts of Central America up to an altitude of nearly 10,000 feet. Sleeping or false nests are thinly constructed and have the floor so built that eggs would probably roll out. If attacked by a snake, which is the wren's chief predator, the birds can escape by pushing through the flimsy rear walls of the nest.

The Short-billed Marsh Wren or Sedge Wren (*Cistothorus platensis;* Plate 177) of both North and South America is a four-inch brown bird with a very small bill; it scurries about wet, grassy meadows like a mouse and builds a nest lined with plant down on or near the ground in tall grass. In taller growths,

chiefly in cattail swamps, is found the Long-billed Marsh Wren (*Telmatodytes palustris*). In contrast to the preceding species, this bird has the crown unstreaked and a white line over the eye. It has a rattling, seemingly inexhaustible song and immediately begins to skulk and scold when its nest is approached.

The Wood Wrens are a feature of the forests between Mexico and southern South America. One species, the White-breasted Wood Wren (*Henicorhina leucosticta*), is more or less typical. It lives in the bottom of tall dark tropical forests in Central and South America. It is a dark brown bird with prominent white lines on the face and neck, but is rarely to be seen as it skulks along the dense floor of the forest. Its nest is a globular structure so well hidden that it is rarely found. One that Dr. Skutch saw was five inches above the ground and contained one nestling and one pure white, infertile egg. On the contrary, Skutch reports that "dormitory" nests belonging to this species are frequently encountered. They are placed in exposed positions six or more feet up in the forest. In another species of this group—the Gray-breasted Wood Wren (*H. leucophrys*), which ranges widely through Central America—Skutch found that the adults remained in pairs for long periods, perhaps for a full year; that the nest was built by both sexes; and that the incubation period was 19 to 20 days. He found also that the nestlings remained on the nest for 14 to 18 days.

Throughout Middle and South America between sea level and 9000 feet in semi-open areas, and particularly in man-made clearings and about farms, occurs the House Wren (*T. musculus*). This bird, along with the closely related and probably conspecific Northern House Wren (*T. aëdon*) and the Winter Wren (*T. troglodytes*) of Eurasia and North America, represents the best-known group of wrens. They are among the most carefully studied of all wild birds. Recently a series of splendid photographic analyses of the Northern House Wren's feeding habits was made with an electric eye that activated a stroboscopic camera. The photographs were of such sharpness that the insects and spiders carried in the parent's bill could be identified. Other studies, by Dr. Charles Kendeigh and by Dr. Skutch, have shown that adults live in a special territory throughout the year; both sexes construct the nest and care for the young; only the female incubates; the young are sometimes fed as long as five weeks after leaving the nest; there are three to four annual broods.

Dippers or Water Ouzels
(*Cinclidae*)

Dippers are large relatives of wrens and live a hardy life close to mountain streams throughout vast areas of the New and Old Worlds. They are at home along the edges of foaming, often ice-cluttered streams in Alaska, the Rocky Mountains, the cordilleras of Central America, the high Andes and the mountains of Scandinavia, Europe, Asia and Japan. In such environs they sometimes cope with temperatures of 50 degrees below zero and regularly feed beneath frigid turbulent water. Except in winter in a few northern ranges, they are nonmigratory and remain in their lofty havens, which in the Himalayas may reach 12,000 feet.

Five species are known. All are closely related and occupy the single genus *Cinclus*. The group seems to have arisen in North or South America. In form, they are stocky, thrushlike birds with squat, robust bodies, thin, sharp bills like those of wrens, and strong legs. The wings are rounded and relatively small, and the tail is short. The plumage is dense and oily and underlaid with down, and the eyelids are feathered. The sexes are always alike, and the young are spotted or mottled with gray somewhat like the young of thrushes.

The dipper is usually found alone or in pairs. It patrols sections of waterways and remains within the boundaries of such territories much or all of its life. In flight it flutters rapidly as it dashes from rock to rock, generally close to the turbulent surface. When flying it utters a wrenlike warbling trill that can pierce even the roar of falling water. On rock perches it bobs and jerks the head and flicks the tail rather like a sandpiper. On the surface of water it swims and dives like a miniature grebe. It was long reported to walk on the bottom of streams in searching for food, but recent studies reveal that it swims very rapidly under water, propelling itself with the wings and apparently rarely, if ever, holding to the bottom with the feet or walking. However, it often enters the water by walking. Its prey consists of water beetles, caddis flies, insect larvae and snails.

Studies of banded populations in the mountains of Germany reveal that first-year females almost invariably find mates and breed immediately, but that young males often undergo a period of wandering

Eurasian Dipper (*Cinclus cinclus*) flying to nest through waterfall

JOHN WARHAM

and generally do not breed until their third year. This condition may have a bearing on the wide distribution of the species.

Dippers nest close to their hunting streams in clefts and on ledges, even those under waterfalls. The structures, which are large, globular and domed and have side entrances, resemble the nests built by many wrens. They are constructed of greenish moss and lined with leaves and rootlets. From three to seven young are hatched out of satiny white eggs, and there may be three broods per year.

The North American Dipper (*Cinclus mexicanus*) is found in high mountains between Alaska and Panama. It is a seven-inch-long, slate-colored bird with a dull brown head and neck. Two dippers occur in the Andes of South America. Their descriptive names are sufficient for identification: the White-capped Dipper (*C. leucocephalus*) of Colombia, Venezuela, Peru and Bolivia, and the Rufous-throated Dipper (*C. schulzi*) of Argentina. The Eurasian Dipper (*C. cinclus;* Plate 176) of the high mountains of all of Europe, including the mountainous islands of the Mediterranean and much of Asia, has the throat and chest white. The fifth species is the Asiatic Dipper (*C. pallasii*), which reaches Japan and Formosa. It is a chocolate brown.

Accentors or Hedge Sparrows (*Prunellidae*)

The 12 known species of accentors or hedge sparrows are all virtually confined to the Northern Hemisphere in the Old World. All are sparrow-like in general appearance; the sexes are much alike in pattern, but the male is somewhat brighter. However, they differ from sparrows in that they have the bill more slender and more finely pointed, not conical and stocky; also they have the tenth primary (wing feather) well developed, and in some ways they act more like aberrant thrushes than sparrows. But the accentors have a true crop and a muscular gizzard that enables them to feed on seeds. During most of the year, however, their chief food consists of insects, worms, snails and the like. All are very hardy birds.

The accentors build open nests either on or close to the ground; these may be in hedges, thickets or rock crevices. The nests are usually solid open cups constructed of sticks, grass and sometimes moss and lichens, and lined with hair, wool and feathers. Their eggs are bright blue or blue-green, depending on the species; the set varies from three to five.

The Mountain Accentor (*Prunella montanella*), a six-inch bird with vivid buffy eyebrows and white wing bars, is bright brown above and buffy white washed with yellow below. This species, which breeds in Asia, has strayed a few times to Alaska. Like all accentors, it feeds mostly on the ground, where it walks with a peculiar shuffling gait. The Rufous-breasted Hedge Sparrow (*P. strophiata*) is similar in size but has a rufous-colored breast and a white throat. This bird lives in pairs or small flocks in bleak surroundings at the edge of glaciers, often far above tree line. It has been found as high as 16,000 feet in Asia. Its food is chiefly insects and spiders in summer, and vegetable foods, such as seeds picked from animal droppings, in winter. Its usual call is a high-pitched *chip,* but at certain seasons the male has a short, attractive, wrenlike song.

One of the two species found in Europe is the Dunnock or Hedge Sparrow (*P. modularis;* Plate 179). An unobtrusive bird, it is generally brown with blackish streaking above and dark gray below. In this species only the female builds the nest and incubates the eggs. Incubation requires 12 to 14 days, after which there follows a nestling period of 13 to 14 days. The other species occurring in Europe is the Alpine Accentor (*P. collaris*), a seven-inch bird, with a spotted chin and streaked flanks, that frequently is found close to snow line. It builds its nest in rock niches in very cold regions, and the male assists the female in constructing the nest, incubating the eggs and feeding the young.

Titmice and Chickadees (*Paridae*)

Titmice, chickadees, tits—call them what you will, the sixty-odd species of small, active, gregarious, confiding Passeres comprising the family Paridae are universally liked by the many humans who know them. Titmice are generally sedentary birds that keep to a given locality year after year, even when the temperature drops to far below zero. Usually if they do migrate at all, they merely shift from exposed ridges to sheltered valleys, but some longer migrations are known. Their diet consists of insects, berries and seeds. The latter they hold in the foot and crack open with rapid hammer blows of the bill. Insects and their eggs are obtained by scanning bark surfaces and the undersides of foliage.

Like many birds that seek insect food, titmice have a restless type of motion. They move with abrupt starts and halts, keeping on the move all the time, working their stubby bodies and large heads into every conceivable position, now sidewise, now hanging upside down, now clinging to a tiny twig, all with the utter confidence of a gymnast. They keep mostly to the open forest and forest edge, but many species visit gardens and feeding stations in suburban areas and even in city parks. They range throughout the nonpolar land areas of the world with the exception of the Australian region, Polynesia, and the Americas from Guatemala southward.

The nests of the Paridae are remarkable because the architectural differences found between the various groups of this family are greater than between many families of birds. Some drill their own nest holes in dead trees like little woodpeckers, some use old cavities in all kinds of locations, and some build roofed nests in crotches. Most species lay large clutches—as many as fifteen in one species—of small eggs. The usual coloration of the eggs is white with frecklings of brown and gray, but one species, the Verdin (*Auriparus flaviceps*), lays greenish eggs.

The roles of parental care in the three sub-families also vary greatly, with the male sharing such work almost equally in one group but not in the two others. In all, however, the pairs remain together throughout the breeding season and generally several broods are reared per year.

The largest group is the Parinae, which consists of 45 species of true titmice, all but one of which are placed in the single genus *Parus*. These birds range around the world in the Northern Hemisphere and Africa. An example is the Great Tit (*Parus major*) of Eurasia and Africa, one of the largest species, although it measures only 5½ inches. It is yellowish green above, with white cheeks. It has a blackish head, neck and central chest, and is mostly bright yellow below. As in most of the Paridae, the sexes are similar in color. A bird of open woodlands and wooded gardens, the Great Tit puts its nest in cavities of all sorts, even in nest boxes, but especially in the abandoned holes of woodpeckers.

Dr. R. A. Hinde's recent study of this species, *The Behaviour of the Great Tit,* has been called a milestone in ornithological science. From his work and others' we know that the behavior of all members of this group is much alike, but that subtle differences distinguish their call notes and songs, their ecological and feeding preferences. Thus many similar species can live side by side without suffering from the intense competition that otherwise would eliminate or drive off some of them. Specific studies showed this to be true of the Great Tit; the Blue Tit (*P. caeruleus;* Plate 181), named for its cobalt-blue crown; the Marsh Tit (*P. palustris*), a small, black-capped, black-chinned bird; and the Coal Tit (*P. ater*), a dingy, black-capped little bird with a white patch on the back of its head. These species are all found in Eurasia, as is the Crested Tit (*P. cristatus*), one of the smaller species. The last favors coniferous forests and breeds in woodpecker holes as far north as Norway. It stores a great deal of winter food, mostly consisting of seeds of spruce and pine but including the larvae and pupae of butterflies and other insects. This food is wedged in crevices and under lichens in the middle tier of tall pines and is recovered and devoured during the worst part of the winter.

Species of the genus *Parus* generally live in pairs or groups, and they habitually join other small insectivorous birds to hunt in noisy parties. Most of the species place their nests in natural or previously existing holes of all kinds, ranging from cavities in stumps and walls to protected niches fairly high in trees. In these places a nest of hair, feathers, bark fiber and the like is introduced. However, some of the species excavate their own nests; for example, the Siberian Tit (*P. cinctus*) digs holes in dead trees that are soft with age. This is often true of the Crested Tit and the Black-capped Chickadee (*Parus atricapillus*) of North America. In the former the female has been observed to do all of the digging and nest-lining while the male stood by watching her work six days at each task. In the latter both the male and the female do the nest-building. Dr. Charles Sibley has called attention to the "snake display" of the hole-nesting tits (and other birds) toward potential predators, which he suggests is a defensive mechanism of Batesian behavioral mimicry. He notes that the display consists of hissing sounds and sudden strikes of the wings against the inner sides of the nest cavity, and in a few species the swaying from side to side of the body and head.

The six-inch mouse-colored Tufted Titmouse (*P. bicolor*) of the United States is one of the largest species in the family.

Blue Tit (*Parus caeruleus*)

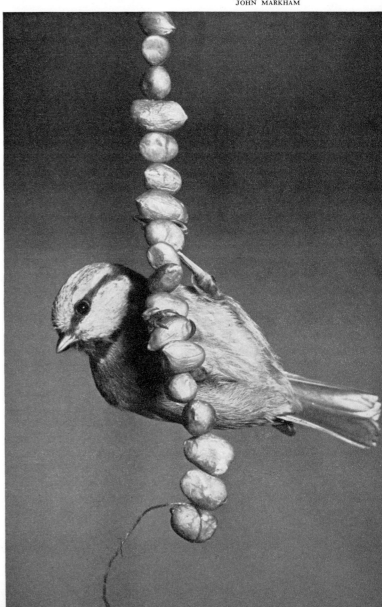

Apparently in all species of *Parus* both parents feed the young, and a glance at their insect-destroying capacities quickly shows why the titmice and chickadees are important to man. To illustrate, one investigator, Josef Bussman, found that a pair of Coal Tits fed their nine young on insects a total of 7743 times at an average rate of 33 times per hour.

Related closely to *Parus* is the very handsome Sultan Tit (*Melanochlora sultanea*) of the eastern Himalayas from Nepal to Assam and Burma, which reaches a length of eight inches. This bird has the crest and underparts a bright golden yellow from the chest backward; otherwise it is black. In the female the black is replaced with greenish brown. It keeps to the tops of evergreen forests, where it travels in groups and nests in holes in trees.

The second group, the long-tailed titmice and bush tits, forms the subfamily Aegithalinae—which should probably be given family rank—with seven species ranging through Eurasia, Java and western North America. One is the Long-tailed Tit (*Aegithalos caudatus*) of Eurasia and Africa, a 5½-inch bird more than half of which consists of a long, graduated tail. This bird, which has black, white and pink plumage, builds an enclosed nest that is merely a felted ball of mossy material and cobwebs placed in the crotch of a bush.

A western North American representative is the Common Bush Tit (*Psaltriparus minimus*), a little brown-and-gray bird that is only 4½ inches in length. Scrubby woodlands are its home. There it travels in flocks, sometimes in very large flocks, the birds scouring the bark surfaces with great agility, fluttering here and there to glean insects from twigs and leaves, and communicating back and forth in high-pitched, buzzing notes. The home of this bird is a pendant, felted nest reaching ten inches in length and fabricated of animal silk, leaves, lichens and mosses with a side entrance spout. The male shares all of the parental duties with the female, and it is customary for both to sleep in the nest at night.

The third subfamily, the Remizinae, is almost certainly deserving of family rank, so distinct are these birds. It consists of eight species of Penduline Titmice and Verdins, of which the Penduline Tit (*Remiz pendulinus*) of Eurasia and Africa is best known. This tiny bird is chestnut-colored above, with a black face mask, and below it is whitish with a very pale throat. Marshy thickets and reed beds in generally more arid areas are its home.

One of the best of all nest architects, this species builds a penduline structure that is felted together and roofed over in such patent perfection that it often seems to have been fashioned by a machine. It is a globular structure with a side entrance that is tubular and unique among birds. The tube is flexible, somewhat like the neck of a turtle-neck sweater, and it opens and closes each time the owner passes through. Suspended from the outer twigs of a bush or a tree, it resembles a giant insect cocoon. In sharp contrast to the other groups of the family, the male Penduline Tit alone builds this beautiful nest, while the female does all of the incubating of the eggs and the feeding of the young. Indeed, there is a strong possibility that the nest serves first as a mechanism of attraction in the formation of the pairs. The Penduline Tit of eastern Africa, a grayish olivaceous bird with a buffy throat, builds a similar spouted, penduline nest. This bird is reported to bite the spout closed when it leaves the structure.

A representative of this group, the Verdin (*Auriparus flaviceps;* Plate 183), is found in the southwestern United States and northern Mexico. It is about 4½ inches long, with much yellow on the head and throat and with brownish gray upperparts and whitish lower parts. Its nest is less well made, but it follows the same pattern and is also placed on the outer branches of bushes.

Nuthatches (*Sittidae*)

Nuthatches are small and well-liked birds that are frequently found close to human habitations. They are most numerous in the Northern Hemisphere, but aberrant nuthatches also occur in Africa and in the Australian region. Apparently the family is not represented in South America.

Their universal habit of walking in all directions on the trunks and large limbs of trees is well known; but, although they are extremely capable as climbers, even using the short legs and long, strong toes and

Tufted Titmouse (*Parus bicolor*)

HEATHCOTE KIMBALL: ROBIN KING

talons to walk upside down like a fly on a ceiling, they never use the tail as a brace, as do the woodpeckers and creepers. In fact, the tail is soft and short, with twelve feathers, not rigid as in most other tree climbers. But not all nuthatches are primarily tree feeders. Several of the Eurasian species climb on rocks and some live almost wholly on cliffs; and one species forages on the ground for food.

With the exception of some atypical birds of the Australian region, nuthatches generally nest in cavities in trees or rocks. A rather unusual circumstance is that Old World species (*Sitta*) add mud barriers to the openings of their nesting holes to make them smaller and presumably safer. In some species these entranceways take the form of elaborate tubular spouts. The American species never resort to such masonry work. But a possible remnant of this behavior is the habit of the Red-breasted Nuthatch (*Sitta canadensis*) of smearing pitch around the entrance to the nest hole.

Nuthatches are found in parties or in pairs, and they frequently join mixed hunting parties of small birds such as chickadees and warblers to hunt as a team. They appear over a wide altitudinal range, some species breeding at sea level and others as high as 16,000 feet in the mountains of Asia. They are hardy birds and are generally not migratory, but in winter populations of high areas tend to move down to the warmer valleys. Nuthatches feed mostly on insects and spiders, but they also eat seeds and small nuts. Their habit of wedging a nut in a crack of bark and banging away at it with the bill is well known.

The male and female, which are alike or only slightly different in color, work together at building the nest and feeding the young, but only the female incubates the eggs. During incubation, which lasts about 12 days, the male feeds the female on the nest. In searching for food, nuthatches move irregularly and jerkily, frequently shifting direction, halting, backing, walking head down and under limbs, pausing often to peer into cracks and niches and to dig with the sharp bill.

The nuthatches consist of two subfamilies, the spotted creepers (Salpornithinae) and the true nuthatches (Sittinae). Some 12 species of spotted creepers are found in Africa, Asia, the Philippines and in the Australian region. The Stripe-headed Creeper (*Rhabdornis mystacalis*) of the Philippines—a gray bird with a blackish head and face and with white stripes on the crown and upper back—often uses its long, curved bill to pick insects from flowers as well as from bark surfaces. This species has the tongue brush-tipped, probably for combing out small nectar-loving insects. Another member of this group, the Brown Tree-creeper (*Climacteris picumnus*) of Australia, is a small, light brownish bird that has the unusual habit of occasionally feeding on the ground. This species nests in a hollow limb or stump, as high up as 30 feet, building a nest of hair, fur and feathers. It lays two to three white eggs that are washed

Long-tailed Tit (*Aegithalos caudatus*)

with pink and freckled with brown and gray. Another aberrant representative is the colorful Wall Creeper (*Tichodroma muraria*) of the Alpine regions of Eurasia and North Africa; it is seven inches long and is the largest member of the family. The exact relationships of this species are uncertain. Many ornithologists classify it with the true creepers (Certhiidae), but most of the available evidence suggests that it is best placed with the nuthatches. Aside from its exceptional size, the Wall Creeper is unmistakable because of its long, thin bill and its very colorful plumage. Its wings are marked with large crimson patches and white spots; otherwise it is mostly ash-gray with a black throat. This spectacular nuthatch builds its nest of moss, fur and feathers in rock crevices 16,000 feet above the sea. In these virtually inaccessible locations it lays four to six eggs.

The second subfamily, the true nuthatches, consists of about 16 species, many of which are widespread in the Northern Hemisphere and two of which are restricted to the Australian region. The first group is typified by the familiar White-breasted Nuthatch (*Sitta carolinensis*) of North America from southern Canada to northern Mexico. The well-known *yank yank* calls of this bird are heard in open woodlands as well as near human habitations. In fact, it is one of the most common and fearless of visitors to winter feeding stations. The species moves only short distances up and down hills and mountains and is resident throughout its range. Thus the birds that feed at one's feeding station in winter often remain to nest. The species of this widespread genus select hollows in trees or stumps, or even nest boxes, in which to lay five to eight eggs that are whitish with brownish freckling. Another North American

[345

species is the Pygmy Nuthatch (*S. pygmaea*) shown in Plate 180.

Others are the White-tailed Nuthatch (*S. himalayensis*), a slaty blue bird with fulvous underparts and a white patch above the base of the tail; the Rock Nuthatch (*S. tephronota*), which has ashy pink underparts and lives on rock faces in Afghanistan and Baluchistan, and the European Nuthatch (*S. europaea*), which, like its American counterpart, is a familiar visitor to parks and gardens.

In New Guinea and Australia occur nuthatches, called sitellas or tree-runners, that nest in an entirely different manner. They are woodland birds that move in flocks or pairs, searching vertical surfaces of trees for insects. One of these, the Black-capped Sittella (*Neositta pileata*) of Australia, has prominent cinnamon-orange wing markings and a black head. This strange nuthatch builds a nest in a tree fork, sometimes 50 feet up. It is a well-fabricated cup fashioned from animal silk and cocoons and camouflaged with chips of bark and lichens. Three pale bluish white eggs marked with dark blotches and spots form the usual set.

In New Guinea this bird is very uncommon, as is the Red-fronted Creeper (*Daphoenositta miranda*) —the least known and probably rarest of all nuthatches. During the course of five collecting trips to New Guinea the author has seen this blackish, red-fronted little nuthatch only once.

Coral-billed Nuthatch

(*Subfamily Hypositinae*)

The Coral-billed Nuthatch (*Hypositta corallirostris*) of the humid forests of Madagascar—the sole representative of this subfamily—is a 5½-inch, highly-colored, nuthatch-like bird that creeps on vertical surfaces of trees. The sexes are very different from each other in coloration, the male with a narrow, velvety edging of feathers extending from the forehead and the lores to the chin and framing the bill as in some of the more colorful nuthatches. In the female this velvety black edging is replaced with dull white; also the blue is more pallid and the head and lower parts appear washed-out and grayish brown. Young birds first assume the plumage of the female, regardless of their sex. Both sexes have the bill bright coral-red, the legs bluish black and the iris brown; also they have the bill short, rather broad and with a slight notch near the tip, and they have the outer toe as long as the middle one and largely fused together at the base.

Coral-billed Nuthatches are fairly common in the humid forests. They occur to heights of at least 5000 feet and are probably more numerous in the higher forests. They forage for insect food mostly on the trunks and larger limbs of the middle third of the forest, often creeping upward in spirals, and ap-

parently never creeping head downward as do true nuthatches. As in nuthatches, the tail is square, but it is not used as a prop as in true creepers. Coral-billed Nuthatches frequently travel several together and often join with small bands of forest birds to hunt as a team.

Apparently nothing is known of the breeding habits of these little birds except that specimens in breeding condition have been collected in the months of August and September.

Creepers (*Certhiidae*)

Creepers are slender, stiff-tailed brown birds that scurry on the vertical surfaces of forest trees almost everywhere in the cooler parts of the Northern Hemisphere.

The most wide-ranging of the five species is the Brown Creeper or Tree Creeper (*Certhia familiaris*). This five-inch bird dwells as far north as Alaska and northern Siberia, and south to Nicaragua in the New World and to Spain, Iran, Burma and Japan in the Old. In this vast area it is vaguely divided into 13 races. It is dark brown above, with much pale buff striping and spotting, and becomes chestnut on the lower half of the back. Generally the head is darker brown, with much spotting and striping that tends to form a vivid pale buff line over the eye. Below, the general coloration is gray, becoming white on the throat. The tail is graduated, stiffened and tipped with spines, so that it serves as a brace for the bird as it climbs. It moves in short spurts and in foraging goes always upward, never climbing down head first like a nuthatch. To move down it backs off in flight and falls in a kind of hovering movement, resembling nothing so much as a fragment of falling bark.

The Brown Creeper has the bill rather long, slender and down-curved, specially fitted, that is, to probe in crevices and behind scales of bark for insects and their eggs. These birds are particularly fond of coniferous woodlands, but during the nonbreeding season may be found in all kinds of woods and even in suburban gardens with tall trees. They are usually alone or in pairs, but will join mixed parties of small insectivorous forest birds, apparently because such a group enjoys greater hunting success.

Brown Creepers are nearly voiceless, giving out only an occasional high, thin note, but during the breeding season they can sometimes be heard uttering a soft sweet song of four notes. The nest is a shapeless collection of twigs, strips of bark, wood chips and moss, all wedged behind a piece of loose bark anywhere from a few feet to 50 feet up, usually in a conifer. The eggs—from five to eight—have a fine sprinkling and end wreaths of cinnamon spots. In America apparently only the female does the incubating, with the male feeding her on the nest, whereas in England the male does some of the incubating. Both sexes seem to participate in nest-building and in the feeding of the young, but the female generally does more of the work. The eggs hatch in about 15 days, and the nesting period may last as long as three weeks.

A closely related species is the Short-toed Creeper (*C. brachydactyla*) of Europe, Asia and North Africa. This bird is very similar to the Brown Creeper but has the lower back grayish brown, not prominently chestnut colored.

Three large creepers live in the high mountains of Asia. One is the Himalayan Creeper (*C. himalayana*), which is generally larger and darker and has a longer bill than the Brown Creeper. It also has a very distinctive barred tail. Another is the Nepalese Creeper (*C. familiaris nipalensis*), an inhabitant of the great pine forests of the Himalayas, which is also quite dark but has the rump and flanks chestnut brown. The third large species is the Sikkim Creeper (*C. discolor*), which is generally darker and more grayish, becoming dark smoke-colored on the breast. In winter these creepers, some of which breed as much as 12,000 feet above sea level, descend to the warmer parts of southern Asia.

In molting the tail, the *Certhia* group, like the woodpeckers, retain the long, central pair of tail feathers while replacing the others. This and other characters have convinced many authorities that only *Certhia* should be retained in this family, and that other groups long identified with it should be shifted (as here) to the nuthatch family (Sittidae).

Wagtails and Pipits
(*Motacillidae*)

Members of the Motacillidae are distributed almost everywhere over the land areas of the world. The family consists of 48 species of semiterrestrial, long-clawed, sparrow-sized birds, some of them graceful and colorful, some of nondescript appearance. All have the hind claw elongated and all have nine functional primaries in the wing.

The family is divided into two main groups—the wagtails, which are chiefly Old World birds of stream edges, and the pipits, which are nearly cosmopolitan birds of wet meadows and grasslands. The wagtails are usually long-tailed and often are splashed with bright colors, the male more vividly than the female; the pipits are usually short-tailed and protectively colored. Both groups are insectivorous in their diet and have the bill thin and straight.

As one might surmise, "tail-wagging" is most common in the wagtails, and in performing this action the rear half of the body, as well as the tail, is moved. The up-and-down movements are more or less continuous as the bird forages, and they increase in cadence with agitation, as, for example when a predator is sighted.

In moving about on the ground, wagtails and pipits walk or run, they do not hop, and in the air they fly undulatingly. The pipits always roost and build their nests on the ground; the wagtails gather in large groups to roost in trees or tall reeds, and they usually place their nests in crevices in rocks or niches under tufts of grass. Some of the species appropriate and reline old thrush nests situated well above the ground.

The eggs of both groups are generally whitish with dark blotches or freckling. Differences between the wagtails and pipits are to be seen in the roles that the adults play in parental care. In the wagtails the male often assists the female in incubating the eggs, whereas in the pipits the female does the incubating and is fed on the nest by the male. In both groups the incubation period is about the same, and it is customary for both parents to feed the young. However, the nestling period of the wagtail is 10 to 14 days, whereas in the pipits it is 13 to 16 days. Most species rear two families per year.

The wagtails are found virtually throughout the Old World. Alaska, the home of two species, is the only New World area that is regularly visited. An example is the Yellow Wagtail (*Motacilla flava*) of Eurasia and Alaska, a graceful 6½-inch bird with bright yellow underparts and a long, slender tail. It often feeds in meadows away from water and congregates in groups at night to roost in beds of reeds. Another species that breeds widely in Eurasia is the Pied or White Wagtail (*M. alba*), which is vividly patterned in black and white. This seven-inch bird nests in crevices near water. The Gray Wagtail (*M. cinerea*), about the same size, has a long black-and-white tail and grayish upperparts. It is chiefly a bird of streams, where it flits and runs over boulders, often very close to rushing water, or wades in shallow areas to capture insects. By day it feeds alone or in pairs, but at night roosts in groups near water.

An aberrant species is the Forest Wagtail (*Dendronanthus indicus*), a sparrow-sized, vividly patterned bird that breeds in the forests of northern Asia. It has the wings, the head and the chest colored in contrasting dark browns and whites, with two blackish chest bands and a prominent white line over the eye. These bold markings break the silhouette and serve as excellent camouflage. It is apparently unique in wagging the tail from side to side rather than up and down.

The pipits are among the most widely distributed songbirds in the world, ranging from arctic tundras to the island of South Georgia, barely 15 degrees above the Antarctic Circle. All are similar in general coloration and structure, resembling long slender sparrows; and they behave like sparrows in that they frequently congregate in flocks in areas frequented by large animals—wild *and* domesticated—in order to feed on the insects that are attracted by animal refuse. Sprague's Pipit (*Anthus spragueii*) of the prairies of Canada and the northern United States, the Rock or Water Pipit (*A. spinoletta;* Plate 185) of the cooler parts of the Northern Hemisphere around the world, and several species of northern Eurasia such as the Meadow Pipit (*A. pratensis*) and the Tawny Pipit (*A. campestris*), are all very much alike. Variations in the amount of dark streaking on the breast and flanks, differences in the vividness of the light line over the eye and length and curvature of the hind claw are among the characters distinguishing these species. Even such a bird as the Red-throated Pipit (*A. cervinus*) of Eurasia is very sparrow-like in coloration, with only a faint rosy wash on the face, throat and chest, and this only during the breeding season.

Typifying an aberrant group of pipits is the Yellow-throated Longclaw (*Macronyx croceus*); a widespread African species. This species has huge feet and claws; its hind claw alone measures two inches, or almost one-third of the length of the bird. The most amazing fact about this bird is its startling similarity to the unrelated Meadowlark (*Sturnella*) of the New World in general size and proportions as well as in color and habits. Herbert Friedmann has called attention to this parallel evolution, calling such pairs of unrelated birds "ecological counterparts." As he has pointed out, the resemblance between *Macronyx* and *Sturnella* extends even to nest construction, song and behavior; both turn away from an approaching observer to hide their brightly colored underparts, and both spread their tails in flight to show the white outer feathers.

Honey-eaters *(Meliphagidae)*

Honey-eaters are small to medium-sized, nectar-feeding birds of the southwestern Pacific region, found chiefly in Australia and New Guinea, but also in the Solomon Islands, New Zealand, the Moluccas, Micronesia, Polynesia and Hawaii.

All of the 160 species have the bill fairly slender, serrate, and gently decurved. The tongue is extensile and brushlike; in many species it has a horny tip that can be used as a probe and then frayed out as a suctorial brush. The sides of the tongue curl in a peculiar troughlike way, forming an elongated tube through which nectar and nectar-drinking insects are carried to the throat. This form of food-gathering, with the bird's plumage constantly brushing on flowers, is believed to assist in a major way in the pollination of the great eucalyptus forests of the Australian region, and botanists recognize special adaptations among these plants that seem to have evolved from dependence on avian pollinators.

Many species have wattles or bare skin on the face, and many have wattles at the gape or throat. Some have the heads largely naked and appear somewhat like miniature vultures. One large clan has yellow tufts on the sides of the head. Meliphagids, generally speaking, have dull plumage, and in the larger species the sexes are similarly dressed. Recently

Dr. Jean Dorst of France studied the feeding specializations, chiefly the tongues, and he concluded that some of the genera (*Acanthorhynchus* and *Toxoramphus*) rightfully belong with the Nectariniidae. He felt also that *Notiomystis* should be placed in a group by itself.

Members of this family have managed to cross vast areas of ocean, as evidenced by the fact that representatives are found on most of the satellite islands of New Guinea and Australia, and some have spread to New Zealand. One has moved westward into Indonesia; others have found their way to the Solomon Islands, Micronesia, Polynesia, and eastward to New Caledonia, the Fijis and the Samoas; and at least one species, a bright yellow and black bird, managed to reach the Hawaiian Islands. This extinct bird, the Moho (*Moho nobilis*) was relentlessly trapped for its feathers, which Hawaiian princes used as adornment.

Many of the more isolated species are especially interesting. For example, in the Stitch Bird (*Pogonornis cincta*) of North Island, New Zealand—a starling-sized bird, now extremely rare, that is named for its clicking call—the sexes are so different that they seem to represent two species. Growing from the sides of its black head the male has long white tufts, which it erects like fans when displaying. The female, which lacks the tufts and is brownish olive, carries its tail erect most of the time. Another odd species is the eleven-inch-long Parson Bird or Tui (*Prosthemadera novae-zealandiae*), which was named for the two white feather ornaments that bulge forth on either side of its throat. Parson Birds were once rather common. However, they were caught for cage birds because they could be taught to say a few words and to whistle, with the result that today these largest of the meliphagids are rare. Then too there is the New Zealand Bell Bird (*Anthornis melanura*), a seven-inch brownish bird with dark wings that would be rather insignificant except for its liquid, powerful voice and the bell calls that are rendered by both sexes. Meliphagids with bell-like calls also occur in Australia and New Guinea.

A large assemblage of the meliphagids is the Myzomelinae, a subfamily consisting of very small species whose males are usually vividly patterned and colored in black and red. The females are generally dull-colored in greens and yellows, but in a number of species the males have lost their distinct markings and have come to resemble the females. The bills of the Myzomelinae are slender and decurved, rather as in the sunbirds. An example is the Black Honey-eater (*Myzomela nigra*), a four-inch bird of Australia that is black above and black and white below. The female is generally brownish above with a white eyebrow. This species builds a more or less typical nest. It is a frail, open cup formed of grasses and twigs and welded together with cobwebs, placed in a tree fork. Two buffy eggs with fine spots are laid. The female builds the nest and

Brown Honey-eater (*Gliciphila indistincta*)

incubates the eggs, but the male may help with incubation, which lasts 18 days. After another period of 18 days, during which the male and female feed the young, the fledglings leave.

Other Myzomelas are jewel-like in color, the males being glossy black with broad red collars, the females dull green and yellow. Such is Rosenberg's Myzomela (*Myzomela rosenbergi*) of New Guinea, an abundant species of the mountain forest and forest edges.

Other honey-eaters fall into a highly variable group in which dull green predominates. Included in this clan are many Australian species of the genus *Melithreptus,* such as the White-naped Honey-eater (*M. lunulatus*), which is generally greenish above and whitish below, with some black and white on the head and bare areas of skin around the eye. More unusual is the Spine-bill (*Acanthorhynchus superciliosus*), a small bird in which the female does all of the incubating. Its key marking is its broad

chestnut collar and black eye mask. Still another species in which the female alone incubates is the Australian White-fronted Honey-eater (*Gliciphila albifrons*), a streaked black-and-white bird that is widespread in Australia. It builds a cup-shaped nest of grass and shredded bark that is finely lined with plant down. A close relative is the Brown Honey-eater (*G. indistincta*).

Some honey-eaters, for example the hybrid Variable Honey-eater (*Melidectes rufocrissialisXbelfordi*) of New Guinea and the Gray Honey-eater (*Lacustroica whitei*) of Australia, build hanging nests that are slung from their rims like the nests of some vireos. Many use hair in their construction as well as animal silk, and at least one, the White-eared Honey-eater (*Meliphaga leucotis*), often attempts to gather this hair by alighting on the heads of humans or by pulling at woolen stockings. Some species build cup-shaped nests in bushes. See for example the New Holland Honey-eater (*Meliornis novae-hollandiae*) shown in the photograph on page 351.

Some of the meliphagids are migratory. One of these is the Red Wattle Bird (*Anthochaera carunculata*), an Australian species more than a foot long with a red wattle hanging from behind the eye. This very common bird migrates to its breeding grounds in southern Australia in moderate-sized bands.

Honey-eaters occur from sea level to the tops of the highest mountains. In New Guinea, for example, large species occupy many niches between sea level and about 12,000 feet. Vocally, they seem usually to be the dominant birds. The Leatherhead (*Philemon novaeguineae*), for example, calls in its hilarious clownish way in the gardens of Port Moresby; the bugles of the Variable Honey-eater (*Melidectes belfordi*) predominate in the mid-mountains; and above tree line, in bushes of the alpine grasslands, other species such as the Princely Honey-eater (*Melidectes princeps*) are acoustically dominant. One of the most successful species is the five-inch Cardinal Honey-eater (*Myzomela cardinalis*), named for the bright red of its head, breast and back. This species reaches Micronesia, the New Hebrides and Loyalty Islands, the Solomon Islands and the remote islands of Samoa. Also on Samoa are the jay-sized Mao (*Gymnomyza samoensis*) and the thrush-sized Wattled Honey-eater (*Foulehaio carunculata*).

A bird of doubtful affinities but with a meliphagid type of stomach and tongue, and apparently with meliphagid habits, in both feeding and breeding, is found in South Africa. It is known as the Sugar Bird (*Promerops cafer*). This species feeds mostly on the nectar of one genus of tree, the *Protea*. It builds a cup-shaped nest that is lined with down-covered seeds. This odd bird lays two eggs that are usually buffy and variously patterned with dark markings. The Sugar Bird has the bill long and curved and the tail very long. It is not known whether this African bird is a true meliphagid or a product of convergent evolution.

Hybrid Variable Honey-eater (*Melidectes rufocrissialis X belfordi*) feeding young

White-eyes (*Zosteropidae*)

White-eyes, Silver-eyes, or Spectacle Birds, as the 85 species of warbler-like birds comprising this family are called, are four- to five-inch greenish birds that live almost everywhere in the tropical forests of the Old World. Their common names call attention to the prominent rings of silvery feathers that almost invariably surround the eye. These circumorbital feather patches vary in width, and in a number of species they are incomplete or, rarely, even completely lacking. Only in one species—the Yellow-spectacled Zosterops (*Z. wallacei*) of the Lesser Sunda Islands in Indonesia—is the eye ring not white.

White-eyes are chiefly interesting to the zoögeographer and the student of speciation because the differences between perfectly valid species are often very slight. Much light has been shed on this matter by the able English ornithologist and editor of the *Ibis,* R. E. Moreau, who in 1957 published an extensive monograph on the white-eyes of Africa and adjacent islands, including Madagascar. He found that on the mainland each population was rather sharply adapted to its own environment—to a special vegetational situation—and that these "ecotypically" segregated birds were highly sedentary.

White-eyes are classed as nine-primaried Passeres because the tenth primary, although present, is very much reduced. They have the bill sharply pointed and straight and are equipped with an extensible brush-tipped tongue that is used in collecting flower nectar, a major source of food for many species. However, white-eyes in general are primarily insect-eaters, although at certain seasons they eat large quantities of fruit and nectar. These birds have the wing short and rounded, the tail generally square, and the middle and outer toes partially united. In all, the sexes are identical in color. This sameness of dress may be correlated with the duties of parental care. In three carefully studied species both sexes participated in the building of the nest, in incubating the eggs, and in brooding and feeding the young. These birds, the Oriental White-eye (*Zosterops palpebrosa*), the Madagascar White-eye (*Z. maderaspatanus*) and the Gray-breasted Silver-eye (*Z. lateralis*), have an incubation period of 11 to 12 days and a nestling period of 9 to 13 days, and, after departing the nest, the young are cared for by the parents for another 16 to 21 days.

The nests of white-eyes are very similar to those of the American vireos. They are baskets of grasses, bark fibers, moss and spider webbing that are slung by their rims, usually between nearly horizontal forks in bushes and trees. Usually three to five bluish, greenish or whitish eggs are laid.

Late in 1957 G. F. Mees of the Netherlands published a detailed revision of the Indo-Australian White-eyes. There are some 85 species in 12 genera, with all but 22 of the species grouped together in the genus *Zosterops*. This genus—and the family—ranges over virtually all of Africa south of the Sahara, the islands of the Madagascar region, and the warmer parts of Asia from Arabia eastward to Japan, the Philippines and Samoa, and southward to the Malayan and Australian region, including Tasmania, New Zealand and Macquarie Island. White-eyes also have been introduced to Hawaii, where they are flourishing, and from which they are spreading to other islands. The ability to invade and populate new areas is thought to be correlated with the gregarious habits for which these birds are famous. They usually travel in flocks, and thus if caught by high winds and carried off course, they have a much better chance of becoming established in new areas than species that travel alone or in flocks of one sex.

White-eyes are purely arboreal, but all of the species visit the ground to bathe in small streams and some occasionally land on gravel paths in gardens. To obtain nectar some species such as the Oriental White-eye peck holes in the calyx (basal part of flower) of such flowers as the hibiscus. In southern Asia at certain seasons hardly a flower can be found that has not been pierced. Elsewhere the white-eyes make a nuisance of themselves in other ways; the Western Silvereye or Greenie (*Z. australasiae*) of Australia is such a serious pest to the orchardist that occasionally he finds it necessary to destroy them because they do damage to soft fruits such as grapes and figs. There is a record of 20,000 white-eyes having been shot in one Australian orchard, and Serventy and Whittell speak of another orchard in which 1200 birds were shot in one day.

The habitat preferences of many species are easily discernible. Some species keep to high mountain forests; for example, the Ceylon Hill White-eye (*Z. ceylonensis*), is one of the commonest forest birds above 5000 feet on that island, while another and closely similar species is equally predominant in the low country. In other areas one species dominates in certain kinds of trees growing in various types of swamps, while another species dominates in the drier forests that completely ring the swamps. Thus quite often the two species live within earshot of each other but may never actually meet one another.

In Africa Dr. Van Someren has studied the Kenya Golden-fronted Zosterops (*Z. kikuyuensis*) with great care. He found that this species of the forest edge, although chiefly an insect-eater, also eats berries, figs and the fruit of the pawpaw, and that the same pairs return year after year to nest in a particular spot. Nests sometimes take ten days to build. Both parents share in the task of incubation. The young appear in eleven days, hatching from three pale bluish white eggs. The chicks are fed on caterpillars and apparently never on berries. After the young leave the nest the adults huddle beside them at night. Two and sometimes three broods are reared per year.

Flowerpeckers (*Dicaeidae*)

Among the colorful, strictly arboreal, small and medium-sized birds of the Oriental and Australian regions (eastern China, India, the Philippines and southward through Malaysia and New Guinea to the Solomon Islands, Australia and Tasmania) are 54 short-legged, short-tailed birds that feed largely on berries and flower nectar, with a few insects and spiders on the side. The family is divided into six groups by the latest revisers, Mayr and Amadon, 33 of the species belonging to the genus *Dicaeum* and 6 to the genus *Anaimos*. Both genera have the tongue tubular for sucking nectar, as do the sunbirds, their nearest relatives.

Flowerpeckers, like sunbirds, usually have the outer third of the cutting edges of both mandibles finely serrated. Generally the bill is short and broad, but in several species it is decurved and slender. They are very active birds that generally are solitary or go about in pairs, although sometimes they are found in mixed parties with other birds. They prefer to keep to the crown of the forest. In many areas, Ceylon for instance, members of this family are the smallest birds. In a number of species the sexes are differently colored, with the male wearing splashes of brilliant red and glossy black in the plumage, which in the female is dull greenish. In other species, however, the sexes are similar and quite drab in color. Flowerpeckers are not migratory, but certain species,

New Holland Honey-eater (*Meliornis novae-hollandiae*) of Australia

NORMAN CHAFFER

Mistletoe Bird (*Dicaeum hirundinaceum*)

which dwell in the crowns of mountain forests to altitudes of 11,000 feet, move in winter to warmer areas. One such is the three-inch Fire-breasted Flowerpecker (*Dicaeum ignipectus*) of India. This species is generally dark greenish blue above, with scarlet and black underparts. The female is olive-green above and buff below.

All of the true flowerpeckers are fond of sticky berries and seeds. These are swallowed whole, and later the seeds are vented with some of the gluelike covering still adhering. Such seeds are apt to adhere to high limbs, and, since the favorite food of many flowerpeckers is the seeds of the parasitic mistletoe, these birds are blamed for the dissemination of this destructive plant.

True flowerpeckers construct nests that are small, pear-shaped, pensile structures entered from the side near the top. The entranceways are slitlike and the nest walls expertly woven and felted of spiders' webs, cocoons, fluffy seeds and other materials. They thus resemble the nests of the penduline tits (*Remiz*), to which they may be related. In the species of the genus *Dicaeum* that have been studied, and apparently in *Paramythia*, only the female builds the nest and incubates the eggs, which usually number three and are white. However, the male has been observed to accompany the female as she collects nest material and to help her feed the young.

Very unlike the typical flowerpeckers are the diamond birds of Australia, which search for food like titmice, incessantly scanning bark and leaf surfaces from the treetops to the ground. Mayr and Amadon consider them to be aberrant flowerpeckers, despite the fact that they nest in holes in the level ground, or in banks, or in earth caught up in the roots of fallen trees. One of the eight species, the Red-tipped Diamond Bird (*Pardalotus substriatus*) nests

in holes that are sometimes 50 feet up in trees. They construct cup- or dome-shaped nests in their burrows and lay from two to five white eggs. Unlike the purely arboreal flowerpeckers, where the male does no nest-building, both sexes dig the nest tunnel, which may be 18 inches deep, and both incubate the eggs.

Some of the names given these tiny birds will serve to describe their key characters. In southern Asia there are the Scarlet-backed Flowerpecker (*D. cruentatum*) and the Thick-billed Flowerpecker (*D. agile*), a species that has the habit of jerking the tail while feeding on berries, nectar, insects and spiders. In Australia there is the shining, dark-backed Mistletoe Bird (*D. hirundinaceum*), which has the throat, chest and rump bright red. This species, like most of the true flowerpeckers, may nest a few feet from the ground or very high in trees, suspending its nest from a twig.

Several aberrant species are found in New Guinea. The highly gregarious Crested Mountain Flowerpecker (*Paramythia montium*) is the size of a small starling. It is blue in color, with much white in its erectile black-and-white crest. This species builds an open nest in bushes and lays a brown-spotted white egg. The related Arfak Flowerpecker (*Oreocharis arfaki*) is a bright yellow-breasted bird that somewhat resembles a titmouse and is often found in flocks. These birds, and the primitive Rhamphocharis (*R. crassirostris*), in which the female is drab but much larger than its mate, are among the aberrant Papuan species that suggest to Mayr and Amadon that this group first arose as a family in New Guinea.

Sunbirds and Spider-hunters (*Nectariniidae*)

Shimmering violets, amethysts, and fiery golds and reds glaze the bodies and flight feathers of these well-named birds, the sunbirds. Entirely restricted to the Old World, the 104 species (according to Jean Delacour who last revised the family) are the ecological counterparts of the hummingbirds of the New World, which they often superficially resemble. However, the two families are very different, belonging to separate orders, the sunbirds being small perching birds, and the hummingbirds being relatives of swifts.

Sunbirds range in length from some 3½ inches to about 8 inches, the larger species having very long tails. Generally the bill is slender and decurved, and the tongue is highly extensible (or protractile) and

[continued on page 369]

188. Blue-winged Warbler (*Vermivora pinu*

Range: Central and eastern United States south to Georgia; winters to Nicaragua

189. Blackburnian Warbler (*Dendroica fusca*)

Range: Saskatchewan to Nova Scotia and south to Georgia; winters to Peru   [ELIOT PORTER]

190. Ovenbird (*Seiurus aurocapillus*)

Range: British Columbia to Newfoundland and south to Georgia; winters south to Venezuela and the Antilles   [ELIOT PORTER]

191. Bananaquit
(*Coereba flaveola*)

Range: Mexico and Caribbean
islands to Amazonia

[PAUL SCHWARTZ]

192. Troupial
(*Icterus icterus*)

Range: Northern South
America

[PAUL SCHWARTZ]

193. Yellow Oriole (*Icterus nigrogularis*)

Range: Northern South America

[PAUL SCHWARTZ]

194. Bullock's Oriole (*Icterus bullockii*)

Range: Western North America to Central Mexico; winters to Guatemala

[ELIOT PORTER]

195. Shiny Cowbird (*Molothrus bonariensis*)

Range: Lesser Antilles and South America [PAUL SCHWARTZ]

196. Swallow-Tanager, female (*Tersina viridis*)

Range: Central Panama to northern South America

[PAUL SCHWARTZ]

197. Swallow-Tanager, male (*Tersina viridis*)

[PAUL SCHWARTZ]

198.
Black-eared Golden Tanager
(*Tangara arthus*)
Range: Mountains of South America
from Venezuela to Bolivia

199. **Flame-crowned Tanager**
(*Tangara parzudakii*)
Range:
Mountains of South America
from Venezuela to Peru

200. Western Tanager (*Piranga ludoviciana*)

Range: Western North America from Alaska to Baja California;
winters to Costa Rica

201. Scarlet Tanager (*Piranga olivacea*)

Range: Central and eastern United States
south to Georgia; winters to Peru

[TORREY JACKSON: NATIONAL AUDUBON]

202. Silver-beaked Tanager (*Ramphocelus carbo*)
Range: Trinidad and South America to Peru

[PAUL SCHWARTZ]

203. Crested Tanager (*Tachyphonus cristatus*)
Range: Northern South America to Peru

[PAUL SCHWARTZ]

204. Blue-gray Tanager
(*Thraupis episcopus*)
Range: Tropical America
from Mexico to Brazil

[PAUL SCHWARTZ]

205. Ultramarine Grosbeak (*Cyanocompsa cyanea*)
Range: South America from Venezuela to Argentina

[PAUL SCHWARTZ]

206. Cardinal (*Richmondena cardinalis*)
Range: Connecticut and South Dakota south to
northern Guatemala; introduced to Hawaii and Bermuda

[AUSTING AND KOEHLER]

207.
Painted Bunting
(*Passerina ciris*)

Range:
Southern United States
and northern Mexico;
winters to Panama

[CRAWFORD H. GREENEWALT]

208. Painted Bunting

[ELIOT PORTER]

209. Pyrrhuloxia, male (*Pyrrhuloxia sinuata*) Range: Southwestern U.S. to Central Mexico [ELIOT PORTER]

210. Black-headed Grosbeak (*Pheucticus melanocephalus*) Range: Southern Canada to Mexico [ELIOT PORTER]

211. Pyrrhuloxia, female [ELIOT PORTER]

212. Saffron Finch (*Sicalis flaveola*)

Range: Northern half of South America; introduced to Jamaica and Panama [PAUL SCHWARTZ]

213.
Green-tailed
Towhee
(*Chlorura
chlorura*)

Range: Western
United States;
winters to
central Mexico

[ELIOT PORTER]

214. Yellowhammer (*Emberiza citrinella*) Range: Europe and western Asia west of the Yenisei River [JOHN MARKHA

215. Seaside Sparrow
(*Ammospiza maritima*)

Range: Eastern coastal salt
marshes of North America

[ELIOT PORTER]

216. Chaffinch
(*Fringilla coelebs*)

Range: Iceland, Britain,
Europe, western Asia
and North Africa

[JOHN MARKHAM]

[continued from page 352]

highly modified for feeding on nectar taken from many different kinds of flowers. Actually the tongue is formed into a tube that divides toward the tip to form two or even three small extensions through which nectar may be drawn to the mouth.

Male sunbirds are generally very differently colored from the females, which are usually much duller. They are arboreal, essentially nonmigratory birds that range from a center of abundance in Africa to the Philippines, New Guinea and Australia. Although a tropical family, many of the species frequent high forests in Asia and Africa in quest of flowers. They are found at an elevation of 14,000 feet on Mount Kilimanjaro, and one species reaches Palestine. They fly quite differently from hummingbirds, usually pausing to perch before feeding from a flower, but they do hover ever and again in order to get at blossoms that are otherwise inaccessible. In addition to nectar, sunbirds devour many kinds of small insects and spiders, some of which they obtain by flying up and scanning the undersides of leaves. In taking nectar from large flowers, such as hibiscus or canna, many species puncture the bases of the corollas and flick the tongue into the flower.

When hunting for food, sunbirds constantly twitter and are seemingly tireless. In most species the males defend specific feeding territories.

Details of breeding behavior gleaned from Dr. Van Someren's account of the Emerald Long-tailed Sunbird (*Nectarinia famosa*) of East Africa illustrate the general pattern in this family. In courtship the male lets the wings droop, fans the long tail, extends the bright chest tufts and pivots on its high perch, at the same time uttering sharp metallic notes. The female alone builds the nest, which is a purse-like, pensile structure some six inches long, suspended from a forest-edge bush or tree. The entrance is fitted with a spoutlike "porch" that resembles the beginnings of a vestibule. A single white egg with dark streaking is laid (although some species lay three eggs that are pale green with spots). Incubation requires 13 to 14 days. The young bird remains in the nest for 15 or 16 days and is fed at first by regurgitation. Later it receives spiders, moth larvae and much nectar. The male takes no part in these proceedings. Despite the one-sidedness of this pattern, many species of sunbirds keep together in pairs throughout the year. Another species, the Purple-rumped Sunbird (*N. zeylonica*) of India and Ceylon, is shown in Plate 182.

However, in some species the male helps with the feeding of the young. Dr. Van Someren has noted that in the Yellow-breasted Collared Sunbird (*Anthreptes collaris*) some individuals may join mixed groups of insectivorous birds, such as warblers, to go on what appear to be purely insect-hunting expeditions. This species keeps together in family groups for some time and often builds its nest either in a tree with many thorns or next to a wasp's nest in a thornless tree. In many species the males assume a post-breeding plumage that is nearly as dull as that of the female.

The nests of most sunbirds are expertly lined with hair, feathers and down; but externally they are apt to resemble a bit of forest litter camouflaged with tendrils and dead leaves, because they are strung together in a net of spider silk that also holds debris hanging below the body of the nest.

A very aberrant group of sunbirds—and they probably represent a distinct subfamily—comprises the spiderhunters, of which the Naked-faced Spiderhunter (*Arachnothera philippinensis*) is a good example. This bird is seven inches in length, with a very long, solid black bill and a disproportionately short tail. Olive-green above, with a naked, pinkish face, it often builds a nest that is completely open at the top, and it lays eggs that are chocolate brown with profuse dark spotting.

Peppershrikes (*Cyclarhinae*)

Peppershrikes, of which there are two species in the continental American tropics, resemble shrikes in their big hooked bills and their habit of pinning down insect prey with their feet and pulling it apart with the bill.

Some modern authorities put these aberrant vireos in a family of their own, while others lump them with the vireos. We have adopted the latter solution, chiefly because of similarities in nests and eggs. The favorite habitat of peppershrikes is bushes and thickets at the forest edge and along watercourses, where they build a nest like that of a vireo—a basket suspended from the edges in the fork of a tree, but of coarser material and looser weaving. Two to three whitish eggs marked with fine speckles are laid. The sexes are dressed alike, with the wing rounded and the tail square. They sing clear, melodious songs.

The Rufous-browed Peppershrike (*Cyclarhis gujanensis;* Plate 131) ranges from Mexico to Chile between sea level and 5000 feet. Considerable differences in color occur among the various populations, which range five to six inches in length, but all are similar in having the upper parts largely yellowish green and the lower parts largely lemon-yellow. And all have the central crown and the sides of the lower face and chin generally gray with the crown framed in chestnut brown. All of these groups are geographically separated. In Ecuador and Colombia there is a second species, the Black-billed Peppershrike (*C. nigrirostris*), which has the bill blackish brown,

7. Gouldian Finch, male; red-headed phase
(*Poephila gouldiae*)
Range: Tropical Northern Australia
[H. RUHE AND T. ROTH]

the upperparts deep yellowish green and no gray on the crown. Below, the bird is dark gray with a deep green collar.

Shrike-vireos *(Vireolaniinae)*

Not much is known about the three species of vireo-like birds that comprise this subfamily from tropical America. They live in the upper third of the forest, where they are very hard to see because their plumage is predominantly bright green. Their name stems from the shape of their bills, which are shrikelike but less bulky than those of the Pepper-shrikes. The three species have both the maxilla and the mandible notched, although the mandible notch is slight. Shrike-vireos have the tail relatively short and a rounded wing with ten primaries. They feed on insects. Dr. Frank M. Chapman observed that their calls were monotonous, oft-repeated notes of the same pitch. In some years the birds seem fairly common, while in other years they appear rare. Their nests and eggs apparently remain unknown.

The Shrike-vireo *(Vireolanius melitophrys)*, which lives mostly in oak forests in southern Mexico and Guatemala, is a six-inch bird of vivid color and pattern. It is green above and has a gray crown, and below it is white with a rufous collar and flanks. A bold black line runs through the eye, and above this is a vivid mustard-yellow line which extends from the bill to behind the ears; it also has black moustachio-like marks at the base of the bill.

Quite different are the smaller, more brightly colored greenlets, one of which, the White-eared Greenlet *(Smaragdolanius leucotis)*, is found in northern South America to Brazil, Peru and Bolivia. This species, which splits into many well-marked races, has the upperparts apple-green and the head gray with white ear spots. Also it has a long eye-stripe and the lower parts bright yellow, with the flanks olivaceous. Another species, the Common Greenlet *(S. pulchellus)* of the tropical forests between Mexico and Colombia, is apple-green tinted with pale blue above and yellowish green below. The smallest species, it is 4½ inches long. It has the green crown prominently framed with opalescent blue and the throat bright canary yellow.

Vireos *(Vireonidae)*

Vireos are warbler-sized birds that are generally solidly colored in greens, grays and yellows. All have the nostrils and part of the forehead partially covered with bristle-like feathers. The bill is slightly decurved, with a small notch.

These small, protectively dressed birds are found from Canada to Argentina, including the islands of the West Indies, between sea level and 10,000 feet. The group as a whole seems to have arisen in the New World tropics, where most vireos assemble in winter. In summer many migrate to the Northern Hemisphere to breed.

About 41 species are known. Some rarely descend below the upper branches of tall trees, while others inhabit tangled shrubbery, including the mangroves of tropical coasts. All feed mostly on insects and their larvae, which they gather by gleaning leaves and bark and by making short, fluttering flights. Small amounts of berries are also eaten.

In this family the female generally does the nest-building, with the male usually assisting in the duties of incubation, brooding and feeding the young. The three to five eggs are white, finely spotted with brown or black. Apparently the period of incubation, which is very short—13 days—in some species, begins with the laying of the first egg, so that the young hatch on different days. They remain on the nest for only 11 to 12 days.

The nests of vireos are almost always deep and intricately constructed cups, slung from their rims between horizontal forks. They may be located anywhere from three to ninety feet up, in forest or forest edge, or even in ornamental trees in city parks. The nests are lined with grasses and are often decorated with grayish bark, paper and insect silk.

The Red-eyed Vireo *(Vireo olivaceus)*, a green-backed bird with a ruby eye, a white eyebrow and a slate gray cap, ranges from Canada to Brazil. In North America it is generally whitish below, and in South America, where it was long considered a distinct species *(V. flavoviridis)*, it is strongly washed with yellow on the underparts. A species found in the mountains of North and Central America is the Blue-headed Vireo *(V. solitarius;* Plate 186). Most vireos have soft songs that they sing almost continuously as they hunt for food, but the Warbling Vireo *(V. gilvus)*, which ranges from Canada to South America, has a beautiful warble. This species visits parks and tree-lined city streets. Other species, whose common names designate their distinguishing characters, are the White-eyed Vireo *(V. griseus)* of eastern North America, the Bahamas and the Antilles; the Gray Vireo *(V. vicinior)* of the semi-desert country of the southwestern United States and adjacent parts of Mexico; the Green-winged Vireo *(Neochloe brevipennis)* of the mountains of Mexico and Vera Cruz; and the Flat-billed Vireo *(Lawrencia nana)* of the island of Haiti and the Lesser Antilles. Elsewhere from Mexico to Brazil range the greenlets, of which there are about 15 species, some of them confusingly similar. These birds generally have the bill somewhat longer and more slender than the true vireos, and are more nondescript, lacking even the light eyebrows. These generally greenish birds have the habits of small, inconspicuous warblers. Typical is the Gray-headed Greenlet *(Hylophilus decurtatus)*, which is 4½ inches long.

Wood Warblers and Honeycreeper Warblers

(*Parulidae*)

The warblers constitute a New World group of small, usually colorful birds that range from Alaska and Newfoundland south through Central America and the West Indies to Argentina. A large proportion of the approximately 125 species are migratory, and the sexes are usually dressed very differently. They may be seen in the populous regions of North America twice a year as they travel between wintering and breeding grounds, often in remarkable numbers. At such times the bird student is sorely tested by the wide and colorful variety of their plumages, particularly during the fall migrations, when swarms of different species, consisting of young males and females of all ages, wear dresses that are often confusingly similar.

Detailed information concerning this popular family has recently become generally available through the medium of *The Warblers of America,* an illustrated volume edited by Ludlow Griscom and Alexander Sprunt, Jr.

The Parulidae constitute a highly controversial group of birds. Some experts consider them an off-shoot of the tanager family, others argue that they are derived from the emberizine finches. Even the relationships of the various species and genera are open to argument because a number of species that appear to be different occasionally hybridize and produce fertile, viable offspring. Usually these hybrids occur between admittedly closely related species, but three cases are on record between species that "look" so different that they are placed in different genera. It is pertinent to note that intergeneric hybrids are known in birds of paradise, hummingbirds, ducks and gallinaceous birds and that, almost always, such crosses occur in birds that practice polygamy and have little or no opportunity to form pair bonds, that is, prior to their short consummatory courtship. In warblers, however, this is not true. A pair bond is established, and there should be time for recognition and correction of mistakes of species identification between prospective mates. Thus are compounded the difficulties of the bird-watcher, who so often has trouble in identifying warblers. The two species which hybridize most frequently are the Blue-winged Warbler (*Vermivora pinus;* Plate 188) and the strikingly different-looking Golden-winged Warbler (*V. chrysoptera*). The hybrid offspring, which are of two general color types, are fertile and were originally thought to be distinct species until their mixed parentage was demonstrated.

Excluding the honeycreeper element in the family (see below), warblers are generally insect-eating birds, but a few species eat berries and fruit, chiefly in winter. Their insect food is obtained in a wide variety of places. Some species hawk for insects in the crown of the forest like little flycatchers, others search under high leaves and limbs for insect prey and their eggs, others scan bark surfaces and peer into crannies for larvae. Down in the substage of the forest and near it other warblers hold forth, each keeping close to his particular domain—his own private larder, as it were—be it on the ground, under certain kinds of forest, in or under bushes or in pure grasslands, or along the edges of certain kinds of streams. Some species have altered in relative abundance or in geographic distribution because of man-made changes in their habitat. An example is the Chestnut-sided Warbler (*Dendroica pensylvanica;* Plate 184), which prefers scrubby second-growth woods or abandoned farm lands in hilly areas. Its numbers have increased greatly since the original clearing of the forests in the eastern United States.

Most warblers have persistent but not highly developed or interesting songs, although one, the aberrant Yellow-breasted Chat (*Icteria virens*), is an able mimic; and some of the species, Dr. Skutch notes, have flight songs or songs that are fairly rich in tone. However, on the whole, song seems less important than plumage and is largely restricted to the males, at least in the migratory species.

The customary form of nest is an open cup in a tree or bush. It may be in a crotch or suspended at the rim in a horizontal fork. However, quite a number of warblers build roofed nests with side entrances. The nests, like the feeding niches, may be almost anywhere from the crown of the forest to the ground. One nest of MacGillivray's Warbler (*Oporornis tolmiei;* Plate 187) was found to have a leaf placed across the top, concealing the eggs. This was apparently the work of the parent bird, since the position of the leaf was such that it could not have fallen there accidentally. The Prothonotary Warbler (*Protonotaria citrea*) sometimes builds in a tree cavity; the Parula Warbler (*Parula americana*) builds in a canopied situation amidst hanging drapes of Spanish moss; the Ovenbird (*Seiurus aurocapillus;* Plate 190) erects a dome of dead leaves on the ground. Almost always it is the female who does the building. Her eggs are generally whitish, thinly tinted with blue, green, and dark markings, particularly at the larger end. Two to five eggs are laid, the smaller sets being generally found in the tropics. Incubation is performed by the female, with the male occasionally feeding her, and with both sexes generally feeding the young. The eggs hatch most rapidly in migratory species, taking 11 to 12 days on an average; whereas in tropical species, the incubation period is generally 14 to 16 days, according to Dr. Skutch, who also noted that incubation was longer in species that build domed nests. Nestlings of migrants are usually ready to leave the nest in 8 to 10 days, while the nesting period in nonmigratory Central American species is 12 to 14 days.

Although warblers are chiefly adorned in yellows and blues, whites, oranges and greens, and never have shiny or iridescent plumage, quite a few of the tropical species have red in the plumage, and one, the Pink-headed Warbler (*Ergaticus versicolor*) of Guatemala, is entirely red and pink. Another such bird is the Red-breasted Chat (*Granatellus venustus*) of Central America, which has the chest broadly painted with scarlet. At the opposite extreme are the drab species such as the Plumbeous Warbler (*Dendroica plumbea*) of Guadeloupe, which is dark gray above and whitish below.

Many species are predominantly yellow and orange, such as the Prothonotary Warbler of the warmer parts of eastern North America and the familiar Yellow Warbler (*D. petechia*), which ranges in many forms over much of North, Central and South America. Then too there are the dark warblers with glaringly bright spots of color, such as the orange-throated Blackburnian Warbler (*D. fusca;* Plate 189) of the pine forests of eastern North America, which winters as far south as Peru.

But many species have no bright colors, depending instead on vivid contrasts of pattern. Such are the Black and White Warbler (*Mniotilta*), a bark scanner, and the Blackpoll Warbler (*D. striata*).

The bananaquits are small, nectar-eating warblers that have long been classified in a distinct family, the Coerebidae. They are now believed (see Thraupidae) to be warblers that have become modified for nectar feeding. They have the tongue deeply cleft and fringed or brush-tipped, and are purely arboreal and nonmigratory. Also in this category are placed the cone-bills (*Conirostrum*) of northern South America —another small group of nectar-eating birds.

The bananaquits (see *Coereba flaveola;* Plate 191) range from Mexico to Argentina and to some West Indian islands, and there are many varieties shading from bright yellow to sooty black. In most of this wide-ranging area the bananaquits are so abundant they often outnumber all other birds in a given area. However, they never go in flocks, but are always alone or in pairs. The sexes are similar in color and they make a pretty sight as they assume all kinds of positions to obtain insects, spiders, and particularly nectar. They even hang head down to scan surfaces for insects; and when a flower is too large to be entered headfirst with the slender, curved bill, they quickly pierce the corolla with the bill and suck out the nectar—frequently doing this to flowers bigger than themselves. Their songs, which are high-pitched and thin, are sung almost constantly and can be heard in every month of the year; and these active little nectar-loving warblers breed in almost any month. They build very distinctive domed nests with a side entrance facing downward. Some nests are built for sleeping and others for egg-laying purposes. The nest material is often strips of fiber pulled from dead banana leaves. Both sexes build the egg nest, while the male alone builds his sleeping abode.

The female does all of the incubating—a matter of 12 or 13 days—and the young are fed by both parents on food regurgitated from the stomach.

Hawaiian Honeycreepers
(*Drepanididae*)

Biologically speaking, one of the most interesting of bird families is the Drepanididae of the Hawaiian Islands. It consists of birds ranging from small to medium in size that have evolved in the exceptional isolation of the Hawaiian Islands and are the only unique family of birds found in the large zoogeographical area known as the Hawaiian region. The true affiliations of this group have long mystified ornithologists. According to the latest studies—those of Dean Amadon—9 genera, 22 species and 39 subspecies or races belong to this family. They were first thought to be related to the honey-eaters (Meliphagidae) of the Australian region, then the flower-peckers (Dicaeidae) of the same area, presumably because many Hawaiian honeycreepers eat nectar through similar tubular tongues, but now many students believe the Drepanids are related to New World warbler-like or tanager-like birds.

There is general agreement, however, that the Drepanids are highly diversified birds that have evolved from a small group, or perhaps even a single pair of birds, which long ago found their way across some 2000 miles of ocean from the New World. Through the mechanisms of competition and adaptive radiation, sections of the population became modified to live in vacant ecological niches similar to those which, on the mainland from which they had come, were filled by creepers, finches, small parrots and honey-sucking birds. But in the Hawaiian region some of the open niches were quite unique. Some Drepanids moved into areas with rainfalls unheard of in the New World. For example, the 5000-foot mountain forests of Kauai Island experience an average annual rainfall of 537.5 inches, and in 1942 more than 618 inches fell. This would be enough to cover the land with more than 51 feet of water. Yet a lowland weather station some nine miles away received only 2½ inches in a year. The birds that became specialized for living in these differently watered areas became different in appearance. Some became weak fliers, but the wings changed less than the tail, and the tail changed less than the bill. In fact, the bill took so many forms that it was a challenge for the anatomist to confirm that they had all descended from the same stock. Some Drepanids had a finchlike bill; some had a long, slender, curved bill with the maxilla much longer than the mandible; some had a parrot-like bill; and one species even had the bill tips slightly crossed. In the tongue there was more conformity, all but a few having it tubular and equipped with a brushy tip. There was also conformity in the extremities. In all there were nine functional primaries, and the feet and legs were fairly strong and short.

In general pattern and coloration there was some uniformity in that the plumage was simple, with glossy and iridescent covering entirely lacking. A surprise was the discovery that a peculiar musky odor emanates from either their skin or plumage.

Hawaiian Honeycreepers are divided into two main groups, of which the more primitive is thought to be the Green Honeycreepers, all of which have the plumage fairly dense and fluffy and usually with much green. Six species of parrotbills (*Psittirostra*) belonging to this group occur on the main islands. All have the bill grosbeak-like and in some species the tongue has lost its tubular shape.

The second subfamily is composed of six species called Thick-skinned Honeycreepers because their skin is more leathery than that of the others. All have the feathers less soft and fluffy, and the immature plumage is apt to be marked with black, which is not true of the other subfamily. All are chiefly nectar feeders, and in many the plumage of the adults is very colorful, making them the most famous of the Hawaiian Honeycreepers. Some species, for instance the dark, crimson-colored Apapane (*Himatione sanguinea*), which is found on the six main Hawaiian islands, are brilliant additions to a tropical forest. It is five inches long with white under-tail coverts. Another species, the Crested Honeycreeper (*Palmeria dolei*), a six-inch bird, has a long, whitish forecrest which splays forward over the bill. The remaining crown feathers are vividly tipped with reddish orange and are shaggy in appearance. It is found on the islands of Maui and Molokai.

One of the many extinct species is the Ula-ai-hawane (*Ciridops anna*), which is known from five specimens taken on the island of Hawaii. This bird had an upturned mandible and a heavy finchlike bill. Extinction may have been due to disease or the removal of the forest habitat in which these birds dwelt and probably not to the collecting of feathers by the Hawaiian aborigines, even though a large number of Drepanids were killed for that purpose. Indeed a feather tax was a part of the primitive culture, and some of the feather garments required the plumes of hundreds of birds. However, feather removal did not always cause the death of the bird; part of the tax load was honored with feathers plucked from living birds, and old reports have it that the half-naked birds were then liberated to grow new plumage.

Drepanids build an open cup-shaped nest. It is usually placed in trees, but on the far western islands it is built in grass. Two to three spotted eggs are laid. One of the largest Drepanids is the Sickle-bill or Akialoa (*Hemignathus procerus*), which has a long, slender bill measuring more than 2½ inches around the curve of the maxilla. One of the most colorful is the bright orange, warbler-like Akepa (*Loxops coccinea*). This species has the tips of the upper and lower mandible slightly crossed. The smallest Drepanid, the Anianiau (*L. parva*) of the island of Kauai, resembles a little olive and yellow warbler.

American Blackbirds, Orioles and Troupials
(*Icteridae*)

The 88 species in this New World family of birds ranging from medium to large in size indulge in patterns of social behavior and nest architecture that rank them with the most highly diversified and complex of all bird families. Among them are many familiar species: the grackles (*Quiscalus*) of North America, the cowbirds (*Molothrus*) that range from Canada to Argentina, and some 30 species of colorful orioles and troupials (*Icterus*) that are widespread both in North and South America. There are also such species as the well-known red-winged blackbirds (*Agelaius*) and the Bobolink (*Dolichonyx*), both of which live in North and South America. Although the family is chiefly tropical, some offshoots have penetrated the high, cold Andean forests, and one species, the Rusty Blackbird (*Euphagus carolinus*), breeds within the Arctic Circle.

In general form the Icterids have the wing with nine functional primaries. The bill usually has a straight, sharp tip, but it is variable because the species have exploited many diverse feeding niches. Cowbirds, for example, are mostly seed- and insect-eaters that forage on the ground and on the backs of cattle, where they prey on ticks. Typical blackbirds (*Euphagus*) are mostly insect-eaters, while the grackles (*Quiscalus*), which are virtually omnivorous, have special jaw musculature and a keel on the inside at the upper mandible to assist in opening nuts. Then there are the tropical relatives that walk methodically over the forest floor, using their sharp bills to turn over stones and dig in decaying wood for insect food of all kinds. The meadowlarks (*Sturnella*), ranging from Canada to Brazil, are specially equipped for ground feeding, while orioles and troupials (*Icterus*) are primarily fruit-eaters, as are the oropendolas (*Gymnostinops*) and caciques (*Cacicus*) of the warmer parts of America, sip large quantities of tree nectar.

These arboreal fruit-eaters and nectar-sippers are chiefly builders of diversified, complicated nests. The most splendid are pensile constructions, some of which are suspended from shrouds that are stitched through leaves, while others are like great pendulums six feet in length. The ground-feeding species usually build open-cup nests lined with mudlike substances (*Quiscalus*), open structures placed low in reeds (*Agelaius*), or nests on the ground under a dome of grass (*Sturnella*). But the well-known cowbirds do not build nests at all; instead, they resort to nest parasitism (see cuckoos). Some species prey on many different kinds of birds, others restrict their activities to one or two very specialized types of orioles.

Black is the predominant family color, but this somber garb is frequently relieved with areas of yellow, orange, chestnut and red. Some nontropical members of the family are highly migratory. The Bobolink (*Dolichonyx oryzivorus*), for example, breeds in North America and winters in southern South America.

The beautiful liquid calls of orioles are among the most memorable feature of the American tropics, and often these calls stem from the throats of the most nondescript of birds, for example the black Melodious Blackbird (*Dives dives*), which is a truly gifted musician. However, most species have a repertory of harsh notes, some of which are used to accompany courtship displays. The seasonally resplendent male Bobolink sings while performing display flights. The Cowbird displays either by hovering over the female or by raising his neck feathers before her, spreading his wings, and bowing.

Polygamy is prevalent in this family, but it is apparently of changing incidence in different colonies of the same species. A lengthy study of Brewer's Blackbird, reveals that, when the number of males in a colony was about equal to the number of females, polygamy was rare, whereas when females outnumbered the males two to one, the eligible males usually had from two to four mates. Even more interesting was the discovery that, although there was no evidence that the pairs or harem groups kept together during the nonbreeding season, each eligible male showed a strong inclination to remate year after year with his "primary" mate of the preceding year. This resulted in the incidence of "divorce" among the primary pairs amounting to only 6.6 per cent. The socially parasitic cowbirds are at one extreme, with no trace of a pair bond in evidence, and at the other extreme are the troupials, the orioles, the Melodious Blackbird (*Dives dives*) and the Chisel-billed Cacique (*Amblycercus holosericeus*), all of which appear to be entirely monogamous.

The eggs of Icterids are whitish, often tinted green or blue, and usually with vivid spots and irregular scrawls. In the tropics the set is generally two, whereas in the temperate zone four to six, sometimes even eight eggs are laid. Incubation is always performed by the female for a period of from 11 to 14 days. Young Icterids are hatched with their eyes closed tightly. They are generally cared for by the female while the male guards the nest site, but in some species the male may assist in the feeding, and in one, Brewer's Blackbird (*Euphagus cyanocephalus*), a male has been observed systematically feeding the young in two adjacent nests. The nestling period is highly variable, ranging from a minimum of 9 days in the Brown-headed Cowbird (*Molothrus ater*) to a maximum of 23 days in the Boat-tailed Grackle

Boat-tailed Grackle (*Cassidix mexicanus*)

(*Cassidix mexicanus*) and up to 37 days in the oropendolas.

The Giant Cowbird (*Psomocolax oryzivorus*) of tropical America has red eyes and is more than twice as large as a starling. Although the sexes are similar in appearance, the male may be recognized from afar because it thrashes the air in flight whereas the female flies silently. This is also true of the oropendolas. Like the smaller cowbirds and anis, and sometimes side by side with them, the Giant Cowbird hunts the backs of cattle for vermin. It often forages in packs, turning over stones in quest of invertebrate prey. Its calls are unattractive, sputtering noises. It plays a deadly parasitic game with oropendolas and caciques, relentlessly lurking in the nesting colonies of these species, watching for a chance to steal into a nest and lay an egg. The birds work very diligently at this but often fail because the host species are not easily fooled; Dr. Skutch saw a female oropendola emerge from its nest carrying a cowbird egg, which it dropped 80 feet to the ground. Apparently the young Giant Cowbird may grow up in amity with the legitimate offspring.

Many students have studied the bizarre parasitic behavior of aberrant Icterids, which have a widespread effect on American bird life. Dr. A. J. Berger recently reported that in Michigan the Brown-headed Cowbird (*Molothrus ater*) preys on at least 20 species of birds. Contrary to general belief, he found that in nests where the host's eggs hatched first, it was usual for some of the legitimate young to be fledged successfully; however, the cowbird eggs usually hatched before those of the host. The Common Cowbird often removes an egg from the host's nest to make room for its own. Another species, the Shiny Cowbird (*M. bonariensis*), is shown in Plate 195.

In the Montezuma Oropendola (*Gymnostinops montezuma*), the males of which are crow-sized, we find the acme of the art of nest-building, at least in the Western Hemisphere. This species has the head, neck and chest black, most of the remainder of the body chocolate brown, and the tail, which is often fanned, edged with bright yellow feathers. Common in tropical America and at times reaching altitudes of 5000 feet, this oropendola is chiefly a fruit-eating, nectar-drinking bird of the forest edge. Once seen, its colonial nesting trees cannot be forgotten. They are usually tall, straight-trunked specimens from which the pensile nests are suspended like slender sleeves, sometimes more than six feet in length. These "sleeves" have the "cuffs" sewn shut, and in each a bulge at the "wrist" represents the actual nest. As these nests are open only at the top, the birds must clamber down long, swaying tunnels. Oropendolas are purely polygamous, and in this species, at least, the much larger males promenade and disport their plumage on high limbs near the nests, emitting liquid gurgles, bowing and even hanging completely inverted, at the same time waving their wings. Dr. Skutch found that in a normal colony there may be a hundred nests, that each male has several mates, and that the females perform all the duties of parental care. But the males serve as watchmen, and when they emit alarm notes, the colony dives out of sight into the forest. By night only the females remain in the nest trees, sleeping in the swaying structures, while the males roost in a group elsewhere in the treetops. Even these seemingly unapproachable nests are parasitized by snakes.

Another member of this family is the Spotted-breasted Oriole (*Icterus pectoralis*), which belongs to the same subgroup as the well-known Baltimore Oriole (*I. galbula*). In its native habitat this bird builds a nest pouch about 1½ feet long. It has a beautiful song, and in color is flame-orange and black, with a black bib and spots on its breast. It was first found breeding in the United States by Charles M. Brookfield and Oliver Griswold along the Miami River in September, 1949, and by 1956 had spread over an area some 26 miles in diameter. These orioles, which were probably introduced accidentally as cage birds, have, in effect, been given United States citizenship by being placed on the list of protected birds. That lovely musician, the orange-and-black Baltimore Oriole of North America, got its name from its resplendent colors, which closely matched those of Lord Baltimore, the patron of the colony of Maryland.

A close relative of the Baltimore Oriole and one that replaces it in western North America is Bullock's Oriole (*I. bullockii;* Plate 194). Although the two differ strikingly in color pattern, they hybridize freely where their ranges meet in the Great Plains. A larger oriole is the Troupial (*I. icterus;* Plate 192) of northern South America and the islands of Aruba and Curaçao in the Dutch West Indies. Because of its handsome coloration and melodious whistling song, this species is a popular cage bird and has been introduced on several Caribbean islands. Another oriole of northern South America and adjacent small islands is the Yellow Oriole (*I. nigrogularis;* Plate 193). Unlike their northern relatives, the females of the Yellow Oriole and several other South American species differ little, if at all, from the males in pattern and brightness of plumage.

Icterids are sometimes shot as game birds, particularly the rice birds or Bobolinks and the meadowlarks. The latter form a distinct group, and in North America two species, the Eastern Meadowlark (*Sturnella magna*) and the Western Meadowlark (*S. neglecta*), are extremely similar in coloration, proportions and habits. Both are mottled brown with bright yellow breasts and a black bib. They flush like quail from their usual habitat in grass, and in the air they fly with bursts of wing movements interspersed with glides. One of the great zoological problems has been how these two very similar species manage to live side by side—as they do over a large part of their ranges in the middle portions of the United States— apparently without interbreeding or replacing each other. Dr. Wesley Lanyon very recently made ornithological history by postulating the mechanisms that keep the species apart. He found that the females discriminate at the time of pair formation between the males of the two species and always breed true. It is suggested that they recognize slight differences in the *calls* between the two species. They make little use of the primary songs, which are not inherited but can be learned.

The most widely distributed member of the family is the Red-winged Blackbird (*Agelaius phoeniceus*), which breeds from Alaska to Central America. The life history of this species by Dr. Arthur A. Allen, published in 1914, was a pioneer study of its kind. Among his most interesting discoveries was the fact that the migration of this species is separated into age and sex classes, with adult males, adult females, immature males and immature females all keeping pretty much to themselves and arriving at different times in the spring.

Plush-capped Finch
(*Catamblyrhynchidae*)

The Plush-capped Finch (*Catamblyrhynchus diadema*) of the temperate and subtropical zones of Ecuador, Venezuela, Colombia, Peru and Bolivia is a rather mysterious perching bird. It is about six inches long, with an erect, golden brown, plushlike fore crown that is stiff to the touch, like thick velvet. Virtually nothing is known of the habits of this unique finchlike bird, except that at times it travels in pairs, sometimes even joining mixed hunting parties. Below, the Plush-capped Finch is dark reddish brown; above, it is generally dark gray with much black on the crown and the sides of the head. Its affinities are uncertain, although it is probably allied to some of the New World finches. Until more definite evidence of its relationships has been published, it may be permitted to stand alone in a family of its own.

Swallow-Tanager (*Tersinidae*)

The Swallow-Tanager (*Tersina viridis*), a colorful starling-sized bird that occurs over the greater part of tropical America from eastern Panama to southern Brazil and Bolivia, is so unusual in its structure and behavior that a distinct family has had to be established for it. This odd bird superficially resembles a tanager, but it is structurally very different, having the bill much depressed and so broad at the base that it is actually wider than long. Also it has the maxilla hooked and sharp-edged. The shape of the bill is correlated with the bird's unusual feeding adaptations, which include a throat that can be stretched to permit the swallowing of very large objects. These and other observations were made of this heretofore little-known bird by Ernst Schaefer, from whose excellent life-history studies much of the present material is taken. Working with him was the expert bird photographer Paul Schwartz, who made the unique color photographs of Plates 196 and 197.

The broad bill of *Tersina* with its hooked tip and sharp edges is used for a number of things, including the hunting and catching of insects on the wing. It is also used to cut fruit that is too large, but whenever possible, the bird forces the fruit down whole. This causes an elastic pouch under the bill to expand, and the head and neck then take on strange bulging shapes.

Swallow-Tanagers are partially migratory; in the breeding season they visit mountain areas, at other seasons they repair in large flocks to lower regions. They are strictly woodland birds and habitually feed in the canopy of the forest. They usually move in short flights from one tree to another, either searching for berries and fruits or flying in rapid sallies above the crown in order to capture insects such as flying ants, flying termites, small Orthoptera and Diptera. Their eating capacities are quite remarkable, as demonstrated by tame birds that regularly eat two-thirds of their body weight in fruit each day. Dr. Schaefer noted that a male sometimes picked fruits that were actually larger than its head, and then carried it to the display territory. There, with the relatively huge ornament in its mouth, the male displayed its splendid shiny blue plumage and even

sang with a muted voice. Ordinarily the voice of the Swallow-Tanager is unmusical, consisting of monotonous chirps and metallic clinks.

In courtship the male advertises and defends a territory by specialized movements and by singing. The female—a chiefly green bird—plays the dominant role in pair formation, approaching the male with a blade of grass in her bill and bobbing her head. The bobbing movement is reciprocated by the male, but when the female has her head high and stretched almost straight up, the male always has his head lowered to below the level of his feet. This reciprocal up-and-down movement, or curtsying, may be repeated as many as 300 times.

Nests, although reported to be placed in hollow trees in some areas of South America, in the regions where Dr. Schaefer worked, were always in cliffs, earth banks or stone walls. Tunnels in earthen banks are excavated by the female while the male remains in close attendance. The nest itself is built of vines, creepers and mosses, and has an inner lining of palm fibers. Three porcelain-white, thin-shelled eggs are the usual set. Incubation varies from 13 to 17 days and begins with the laying of the first egg; thus the young are hatched on different days. They emerge from the shell blind, virtually naked and yellowish pink in color. Only the female incubates and broods. The chicks, which are fed by both parents, are ready to leave the nest after 24 days.

Tanagers and Diglossas
(*Thraupidae*)

Tanagers are among the most colorful of the many bright tropical birds found in the New World. Some of the approximately 220 species are smaller than sparrows, others are larger than starlings. Virtually all are sedentary in Central and South America, but four colorful species are highly migratory. All but one aberrant species, the Thrush Tanager (*Rhodinocichla rosea*), are purely arboreal birds that feed largely on fruit, nectar, insects and spiders. Until recently the nectar-eating species were included in a New World family known as the honeycreepers (Coerebidae). However, Dr. W. J. Beecher, on the basis of anatomical studies, has shown rather conclusively that this is an artificial group, composed in part of nectar-feeding warblers and in part nectar-feeding tanagers. Therefore the Coerebidae are not considered as a family here and the species are divided between this family and the Parulidae.

In tanagers, with the notable exception of the Thrush Tanager, the voice is poorly developed, and most of the species have only weak songs and whistles, or apparently no song at all. However, curiously, the migratory Summer Tanager (*Piranga rubra*) and Scarlet Tanager (*P. olivacea;* Plate 201), plus a few of the sedentary but spectacular Central American forms such as the Red Ant Tanager (*Habia rubica*), have reasonably pleasant songs.

The patterns of courtship and parental care, except in rare cases, involve monogamy. In many species the nest is built by the female alone, but in others the male assists. Incubation, which is purely the work of the female, ranges from 12 to 14 days. The young emerge quite blind, covered sparsely with natal down, and apparently always with the internal parts of the mouth tinted bright red. The chicks are fed by both parents on food carried to them in the mouth or in the stomach and then regurgitated.

According to Dr. Skutch, tanagers that nest close to the ground, such as the Scarlet-rumped Tanager (*Ramphocelus passerinii*), leave the nest in 11 to 13 days; in species that build open nests fairly high in trees, the nesting period is 16 to 20 days; but in species that build roofed nests, the period reaches 23 to 24 days. An example of the last is the Turquoise-naped Chlorophonia (*Chlorophonia occipitalis*). Most tanagers are double-brooded, and in some species juvenile birds of the first hatching occasionally assist their parents in feeding later broods.

Among the true tanagers (Thraupinae) is found the Scarlet-rumped Tanager (*Ramphocelus passerinii*), which is a starling-sized black bird with a scarlet lower back and a thick, pale, grayish blue bill with a black tip. This species is widespread in Middle America in open wooded areas between sea level and 5000 feet. It has the habit of roosting in clusters, and there is always a plurality of females. In the deep undergrowth of the forest other tanagers occur, such as the Red Ant Tanager (*Habia rubica*), a dull red bird with an erectile scarlet crown stripe. The male reaches seven inches in length and is one of the largest of the tanagers. The pairs wander through the dimly lit lower tier of true forest, calling both harshly and pleasantly to each other. The best-known species in tropical America is the Blue-gray Tanager (*Thraupis episcopus;* Plate 204), a starling-sized bright bird in which the sexes are nearly similar. Ranging from Mexico to Peru, and from sea level to 7500 feet in Costa Rica, this species lives in the upper tiers of the forest edge and about human habitations. It feeds on fruit, but it also hawks insects and comes readily to feeding trays, even those on the ground. The Blue-gray Tanager remains mated all year, yet it has the habit of traveling in small bands and of roosting in groups. The male assists in nest-building but only the female incubates. During this period the male feeds his mate.

Among the very small tanagers are the euphonias, which are generally strikingly colored in yellows and steel blues, with the females being mostly dull green. These little birds are chiefly berry-eaters. A good example is the Yellow-crowned Euphonia (*Tanagra luteicapilla*) of Central America, which is shining blue-black with a vivid yellow cap, chest and underparts. Both sexes build the globular nest,

which has a side doorway and is placed in a tree crotch, within a few feet of the ground or very high in the forest. The set of eggs ranges from two to four, the incubation period from 13 to 14 days, and the nesting period from 22 to 24 days.

Other small tanagers are the many species of colorful chlorophonias, found from Mexico to Argentina, often even at high altitudes where colorful birds are usually rare. One such, the Turquoise-naped Chlorophonia (*Chlorophonia occipitalis*) of Middle America, is light green with a turquoise crown and nape. Young males wear the dull green plumage of the female for the first year, and while thus attired select their mates and raise families. For some reason, the fully plumaged males are rare. These birds roam the misty cloud forests in flocks, and their nests are also domed and have side entrances. Sometimes two broods per year are raised in the same nest.

Among other tanagers we must at least mention the spectacular Crimson-collared Tanager (*Phlogothraupis sanguinolenta*) that ranges from Mexico to Panama; the White-capped Tanager (*Stephanophorus diadematus*) of Brazil and Argentina; the famous, oft-described, and colorful migratory tanagers such as the Summer, the Scarlet and the Western (*P. ludoviciana;* Plate 200), belonging to the genus *Piranga*, which range from Canada to Brazil; the Four-colored Tanager (*Trichothraupis melanops*) of Brazil and Bolivia; and the shining black-and-white Magpie Tanager (*Cissopis leveriana*), which ranges over most of South America. A very colorful group is the large genus *Tangara*, of which the Black-eared Golden Tanager (*T. arthus;* Plate 198) and the Flame-crowned Tanager (*T. parzudakii;* Plate 199) are examples. Interestingly enough, the females of this genus share the gorgeous hues of their mates, while in members of the rather somberly-dressed genus *Tachyphonus*, such as the Crested Tanager (*T. cristatus;* Plate 203) the sexes are quite different from one another. The males of this genus are mostly black, the females reddish brown.

In a subfamily by itself is the little-known Thrush-tanager (*Rhodinocichla rosea*), which some ornithologists suspect belongs in a family of its own. This eight-inch bird of Central and South America is the only species of the family that forages for food on the ground. It has the tail relatively short, and, for a bird that spends its life skulking in shadowy areas of the forest, living like an antbird or wren, it is extraordinary in its coloration. Despite the bright magenta and red colors of the males, and the fact that they are not uncommon, they are rarely seen, although their beautiful calls are frequently heard.

But one ornithologist who has observed them closely is Paul Schwartz of Venezuela who made the accompanying color photographs (Plates 174 and 175) of the male and the female at the nest. He writes that the Rose-breasted Thrush-tanager is very thrasher-like in shape and in the kind of nest it builds, and that, like the thrashers (Mimidae), it is a ground forager and a "leaf-tosser." At the nest both sexes sing antiphonally, but the male also has a special courtship song that he sings alone. The songs of these birds remind him somewhat of the Cardinal (*Richmondena cardinalis*), in which both sexes also sing, although not antiphonally.

Schwartz found that both sexes share in the building of the nest, in incubating the eggs and in feeding the young. The nest, which is placed low in thick forest, is a cup-shaped structure of twigs lined with fine materials such as the rachises of leaves. The eggs are pale sky blue, with black markings concentrated mostly about the larger end. Schwartz writes: "In many eggs these markings are delicate, complex arabesques, and thus are almost identical to the beautiful eggs of *Saltator coerulescens* and many of its congeners. Others resemble the eggs of *Ramphocelus carbo* [see Plate 202] and its relatives."

Anatomical studies by Dr. Hubert L. Clark indicate that this bird, which has been considered an aberrant wren, a wood warbler and a thrasher, is probably a tanager although the bill is not typical.

Other strange birds included here as a subfamily of the tanagers are the diglossas, or flower-piercers, of the high mountains between Mexico and Peru, which are found also on mountain "islands" extending through Venezuela, British Guiana and Northeastern Brazil. Although formerly classified otherwise, they seem to belong with tanagers anatomically.

Diglossas have the plumage generally sooty gray to sooty blue-black, sometimes with white flank feathers. The sexes are much alike, but in some species the female is tinged with green. All are inhabitants of bushy fields on high mountains, and all feed largely on nectar that is removed from the corollas of mountain flowers. Dr. Skutch discovered that the nectar is removed in a remarkable way: All diglossas have the bill peculiarly developed with the mandible upcurved and needle-sharp, and the upper mandible still longer, finely notched, and sharply hooked at the tip. The diglossa clasps long, nectar-bearing flowers in the open bill, holds the slippery flower with the hook of the upper mandible, punctures the corolla with the lower bill, and apparently sucks out the nectar with the tongue. These specialized birds also feed on insects, which they capture like flycatchers, and they are equipped with rictal bristles that grow from the base of the bill and help in their aerial chases. Diglossas have weak, trilling songs. They range as high on mountains as flowers are found, going almost to snow line. Unlike other nectar-feeding birds, they are not migratory, and during the period when no flowers are blooming they remain in their usually very limited haunts, feeding on insects and spiders. Their nests are solid open cups built by the female one to nine feet above ground. The eggs—two blue eggs with brown spots formed the set in one species—are apparently incubated by the female alone. The young are brooded by her, but both parents feed them on regurgitated

food. Incubation in one species required 14 days. The nestlings left the nest after 16 days.

The Slaty Diglossa or Slaty Flower-piercer (*Diglossa baritula*) occupies the high bushy grasslands and paramos from Mexico to Panama. Warbler-sized, it is dull grayish with blackish wings and tail, and with cinnamon underparts. The Great Diglossa (*Diglossa major*) of the high isolated mountain plateaus of southern Venezuela is the size of a small thrush and deep sooty blue throughout. In mid-October the author recently observed the Great Diglossa feeding a single young at about 6500 feet on Mount Auyantepui, southern Venezuela. Nests of this species have been found in rock niches amidst sparse vegetation on the plateau of this mountain.

Other nectar-feeding tanagers included in this family on anatomical grounds are more colorful, and until recently they were included in the aberrant family Coerebidae (see above). These are the Dacninae. The nominate group, *Dacnis,* ranges from Panama to Bolivia. In these birds the bill is short and conical and the males usually have much blue and black in the plumage. An example is the Ultramarine Dacnis (*Dacnis cayana*), which is 4½ inches long. The members of this group build roofed-over nests that are suspended in forked branches. Their close relatives, the blue honeycreepers of the genus *Cyanerpes,* which range from southern Mexico and Cuba to Brazil, build open cup-shaped nests and have the bill long, slender and decurved. The Blue Honeycreeper (*C. cyaneus*), one of the most brilliant of the group, is deep sapphire and turquoise blue with bright red legs. This species uses the long bill to probe flowers from the front while standing on a perch; then, with its slender protrusible tongue, it sucks up the nectar and captures small insects. As in all species of this group, the female is dull-colored and the song is thin and weak. In his extensive studies of this species, Dr. Skutch found that its nest is built entirely by the female. Two white eggs with dark speckling are usually laid and incubated (12 to 13 days) by the female. The young are brooded by the female and fed by the adults for a period of 14 days. After the nuptial season the male replaces his bright plumage for a greenish dress that resembles that of his mate.

Cardinals, Buntings, Sparrows and their Allies
(*Fringillidae*)

A vast assortment of small to medium-sized birds comprises this world-wide and very complex family, and it is therefore here divided into four subfamilies. None of these groups is sharply circumscribed, with the result that there are many intermediate species.

On anatomical grounds some specialists believe that the colorful tanagers should be included as a fifth subfamily in the Fringillidae. However, the tanagers are a fairly cohesive group and the addition of 197 species of "tanagers" to the already very cumbersome Fringillidae would make that family even more difficult to define. Therefore, for the purpose of this book, the tanagers are maintained as a separate family, leaving some 426 species in the Fringillidae.

In general, fringillids have the bill cone-shaped and strong; they usually have nine primaries and twelve tail feathers, and most of the species are solitary nesters. Most fringillids are gregarious, arboreal birds that descend readily to the ground to feed, taking chiefly seeds, berries and fruits. Many engage in migrations, either short, vertical movements or long jaunts that enable them to nest in the seasonally warmer parts of the Northern Hemisphere and to winter in the tropics.

In 1954 Alexander F. Skutch summarized the information concerning some of the tropical American Fringillidae and much of the following is drawn from his illuminating reports. Fringillids abound chiefly in tropical and temperate regions, but a few species breed within the Arctic. They are generally dull-colored, but some species are bright green, yellow, white and even bright red. Some—chiefly nontropical birds—undergo drastic seasonal changes in the coloration of their plumage as a result of wear or molt or both.

Some of the best songsters among birds are found in this family. In a number of species songs may be delivered while in flight or while the male engages in a jumping dance. They are often used to advertise territory and therefore generally emanates from the male. However, in the North American cardinals (*Richmondena*) the male and female sing similar songs.

The regimen of parental care is fairly uniform in all of the groups so far studied, with such varied species as the grosbeaks, the finches, the buntings and the sparrows following a similar pattern. The female does virtually all of the work connected with building the nest, incubating the eggs and brooding the young; but in some species, the Rose-breasted Grosbeak (*Pheucticus ludovicianus*) for instance, the male assists. Normally the male shares the feeding of the young about equally with the female, and in many species he feeds her while she is incubating. Evidence of the instinctive quality of this feeding pattern is that, when the female is absent and the eggs are well along in incubation, the male often tries to feed them. Most species are monogamous and multibroodal, but Margaret Nice in her important report on the Song Sparrow (*Melospiza melodia*) observed some instances of polygamy, and in the Corn Bunting (*Emberiza calandra*) this pattern of breeding behavior is well developed.

In fringillids the nest structure is variable, with some species such as the Orange-billed Sparrow (*Arremon aurantiirostris*) of Central America, building a roofed-over nest, and others, such as the Yellow-faced Grassquit (*Tiaris olivacea*), building a globular nest with a side entrance. However, the vast majority of species build solid open cups, located variously on the ground or in bushes, trees, and even crevices. The eggs, like the nests and the birds themselves, are extremely variable, but usually they are pale white to pale blue and moderately marked with dark colors. In the tropics the set size is usually two, but in the temperate zone it is five or six, while in the arctic it may increase to eight—as, for example, the Snow Bunting (*Plectrophenax nivalis*). Incubation ranges from 11 to 15 days. The young, which emerge at different times (asynchronous hatching) because incubation generally begins gradually in this family, are usually sparsely covered with down and have the eyes tightly closed. The nestling period is variable, usually ranging from 9 to 15 days, with the ground nesters taking the shortest time.

The first subfamily of this vast family is the Richmondeninae. It consists of the cardinals, the grosbeaks and their allies. In this group of species are a number of colorful medium-sized and small birds, many of which have red, blue or yellow in their plumage. All have the tenth primary vestigial, and all are solitary nesters. In addition, there are certain anatomical characters by which the group may be differentiated. Included here are the well-known cardinals (*Richmondena;* Plate 206), which range from North America to northern South America, and the Pyrrhuloxia (*Pyrrhuloxia sinuata;* Plates 209 and 211) of the Southwest and central Mexico. The Rose-breasted Grosbeak (*Pheucticus ludovicianus*), an eight-inch, largely black-and-white bird with a crimson breast, is admired both for its beauty and for its fondness for eating destructive insects such as potato bugs. Another example is the Black-headed Grosbeak (*P. melanocephalus;* Plate 210) of North America. Included are the colorful buntings of the genus *Passerina,* of which there are six species between Canada and southern Mexico. The Painted Bunting (*P. ciris;* Plates 207 and 208) is a vivid example of this genus. Alexander Skutch has studied and reported on a number of tropical species of this group, such as the Blue-black Grosbeak (*Cyanocompsa cyanoides*), a starling-sized bird that ranges from Mexico to Bolivia, and is very similar in appearance to the Ultramarine Grosbeak (*C. cyanea;* Plate 205). The male is blue-black and the female deep brown; both have the bill swollen and short, and designed for the crushing of hard seeds. These birds usually keep together in pairs in the forest edge. They are superb songsters, with the female singing nearly as well as the male, as in the cardinals.

Occupying a similar geographical range is the Buff-throated Saltator (*Saltator maximus*), an olive-green and gray bird with a large buffy white throat patch and white eyebrows. Saltators, of which there are eleven species, are widespread in tropical America. They are unusual in that they remain mated and together throughout the year and have the habit of eating the corollas of flowers. This the author can attest. In Venezuela he once saw a saltator pick and then choke down a hibiscus flower.

In the next subfamily, the Fringillinae (formerly called Emberizinae) is found a collection of chiefly rather drab species such as the sparrows, the longspurs, the towhees and the seedeaters. These occur in virtually every part of the world. In these birds the tenth primary is variable and solitary nesting is practiced. A species well studied by Dr. Skutch is the small Variable Seedeater (*Sporophila aurita*) of Central America, in which the male is marked in sharply contrasting black and white and the female is mostly brown. Flocks of these birds feed on grass seeds and gather at night in compact groups. They nest four to twenty feet above the ground. They incubate the eggs for from 12 to 13 days and feed the young with regurgitated food.

The Orange-billed Sparrow (*Arremon aurantiirostris*), which ranges from Mexico to Peru, is olive with a striped head, a white throat, and an orange bill that stands out in the deep wet forest floor where this bird lives. This is one of the minority of fringillids that build a domed nest with a side entrance. The structure is camouflaged with living ferns to blend with the floor of the forest. The female usually incubates for 14 to 15 days, spending long periods on the nest and coming and going by hopping, not flying.

One of the more unusual species is the Yellow-faced Grassquit (*Tiaris olivacea*), a small sparrow-like bird with yellow eyebrows, a yellowish throat and a prominent black chest. The male of this species defends a territory, often selects the nest site and frequently starts nests which his mate may or may not accept and complete. Included here are the Dominican and Crested Cardinals (*Paroaria*), and the Yellow Cardinal (*Gubernatrix cristata*) of South America; also the Brazilian Blue Finch (*Porphyrospiza caerulescens*) and the bullfinches (*Loxigilla* and *Melopyrrha*) of the Antilles and the Bahamas, not to

mention the Rice Grosbeaks (*Oryzoborus*) and the brightly colored ground finches (*Sicalis;* Plate 212). But this is only the beginning. Next come the North American sparrows of the genus *Zonotrichia,* such as the familiar White-crowned and White-throated; the sparrows of the genus *Spizella,* such as the familiar Chipping, Field, Tree and Clay-colored, the juncos (*Junco*), the towhees (*Pipilo*), the Green-tailed Towhee (*Chlorura chlorura;* Plate 213), the savannah sparrows (*Passerculus*), the swamp and marsh-loving Sharp-tailed and Seaside (Plate 215) Sparrows (*Ammospiza*), and the Lark Bunting (*Calamospiza*). Still others are the species of the genus *Melospiza,* such as the Song and Swamp Sparrows; also the longspurs (*Calcarius*), of which the Lapland Longspur (*C. lapponicus*) ranges around the world in the cold parts of the Northern Hemisphere, a range similar to that of the large and beautiful Snow Bunting (*Plectrophenax nivalis*).

In the Old World there are many other species. There the "buntings" (*Emberiza*) are about the equivalent of the New World sparrows in their ecology and appearance. Among these are the Corn Bunting (*Emberiza calandra*) and the Yellowhammer (*E. citrinella;* Plate 214). In 1950 Dr. G. Disselhorst reported that pair formation in the Yellowhammer is hinged on a special ceremony involving the picking up and dropping of small objects by both the male and the female. (For another odd and similar ritual involving inanimate objects in the optical stimuli used in sex recognition, see Terns and illustration.) Another species of this subfamily is the Chaffinch (*Fringilla coelebs*), a widely distributed Old World bird (Plate 216) and one of the most familiar in English parks and gardens.

The abundance of some of these birds is astounding. This is particularly apparent in species that go on periodic migrations and invade new ground. For example, in 1951 it was estimated that 72,000,000 Bramblings (*Fringilla montifringilla*) invaded Switzerland to settle at roosts near Thun.

The Galapagos finches (subfamily Geospizinae) are sometimes placed in their own family, but they are basically fringillids, and all but one, the Cocos Island Finch (*Pinaroloxias inornata*), are restricted to the Galapagos Islands. The world of science owes a debt to these ground finches for having instilled in Charles Darwin's mind germs of thought that fired his speculations and eventually led to his theory of the origin of species. The Galapagos finches apparently evolved from a single species of ground finch that somehow was blown some 600 miles from the mainland of South America. Today, as a result of the phenomenon of adaptive radiation, as many as ten completely reproductively isolated (non-interbreeding, non-hybridizing) species inhabit some of the islands. Each is different from all of the others on its island habitat—different in size, shape of the bill, method of feeding and taste for food. Thus there is no competition between the species. Some feed on the

White-crowned Sparrow (*Zonotrichia leucophrys*)

ground, some in trees; some have bills that are small and specialized for feeding on cactus; and some, such as the Warbler Finch (*Certhidea olivacea*), feed on insects gleaned from under leaves and bark. In feeding, one species uses a tool, a long thorn, to flush insects from deep holes and crevices, and thus it is the only species that is able to exploit this competition-free source of food. It is known as the Woodpecker Finch (*Camarhynchus pallidus*), and the stories of its hunting tricks sound like tall tales. However, they are true. When an insect appears, the bird drops the thorn and grabs and eats its prey; then it picks up its tool to scare up more prey. This is one of the few authentic instances of the use of a tool by a bird. David Lack in his *Darwin's Finches* provides a fascinating insight into the phenomenal speciation of these birds, including six species of true Geospiza ground finches, a bird called Darwin's Ground Finch (*Platyspiza*), two parrot-billed finches (*Camarhynchus*) and other curiously formed birds, all presumably the offshoots of a single pair or flock of birds. In Galapagos finches the set of eggs consists of four eggs; the incubation period (12 days) begins after the last egg has been deposited; the female incubates alone, and the young remain on the nest for 14 days, with the male first feeding the female on the nest and then helping her to feed the young.

Sometimes treated as a distinct family, the Carduelinae comprise a subfamily of birds that occur in most of the land areas of the world and are widely known and esteemed. Among the many species, most of which have the tenth primary fairly well developed, are highly gregarious forms such as the hardy grosbeaks (*Hesperiphona*) of the Northern Hemisphere. Grosbeaks have the bill very swollen and designed for seed-crushing. Other species are the much loved hawfinches (*Coccothraustes*) of the northern regions of the Old World, which are seed- and fruit-eaters, and the bullfinches (*Pyrrhula*) of the same region, which are short, stocky birds that occasionally wander eastward to Alaska and in the Old World are highly regarded as cage birds. Hawfinches are reported to pair for life, and the pairs keep close together, both birds singing a beautiful but muted song as they go about hunting for seeds and buds, often in the vicinity of human habitations.

One of the largest and most colorful of the cardueline finches is the Pine Grosbeak (*Pinicola enucleator*) that ranges around the world in the Northern Hemisphere. These large, generally rose, pink and gray birds are usually found in coniferous forests, where they keep to the wildest parts in summer, but in winter they often descend to the ground in tame flocks and visit territory well away from the pine woods. In this subfamily are the purple finches and the House Finch (*Carpodacus*), both of which resemble typical sparrows and are partially painted with rose or scarlet. Sometimes the birds wear a great deal of color and sometimes they show only a trace. The House Finch of western United States and

GEORG SCHÜTZENHOFER: BAVARIA VERLAG

Bullfinch (*Pyrrhula pyrrhula*)

Mexico, which lives readily in close proximity to man, has become established as a breeding bird in New York State due to the release of caged birds on Long Island. Other clans belonging to this subfamily are the greenfinches (*Chloris*) and the European Goldfinch (*Carduelis*), both of Eurasia; also the siskins and American goldfinches (*Spinus*) of both North and South America, as well as the redpolls (*Acanthis*) and the crossbills (*Loxia*) of the colder parts of the Northern Hemisphere. Because of their crossed mandibles, the last named are easy to identify. The males are dark red or pink, and the females greenish gray, and one species, the White-winged Crossbill (*L. leucoptera*), has white wing bars. Crossbills climb on conifers, breaking open cones with their specially shaped bills; sometimes as they hang and reach for food they resemble small parrots in their agile gymnastics. They are five to seven inches in length. A relative, the Hispaniolan Siskin (*Loximitris dominicensis*) lives in the mountains of the island of Hispaniola in the Caribbean.

The most famous of all cage birds, the Canary (*Serinus canarius*), belongs in this subfamily. Wild

[381

Greenfinch (*Chloris chloris*)

canaries occur in the Canary, the Azores, and the Madeira Islands, and in this state they are olive above and yellow below. They have been bred in captivity for many centuries. In their native forests they build compact, open, cup-shaped nests about ten feet up in bushes and trees and lay about five bluish green eggs that are marked with reddish brown. Relatives of canaries live on the mainland of Europe and in North Africa.

The nest of the canary is typical of the group in general, but in some species, such as the crossbills, the grosbeaks and the goldfinches, there is a tendency to nest in scattered colonies. Generally speaking, all of the cardueline finches are arboreal fruit- and seed-eaters, but some feed on insects and many forage on the ground at certain seasons of the year.

Unlike most of the perching birds, the cardueline finches allow the feces of the nestlings to accumulate around the rim of the nest, whereas in other forms they are carried away by the parents, as in the photograph of the Barred Warbler on page 331.

Waxbills, Grass Finches, Mannikins and Java Sparrows (*Estrildidae*)

In the Old World tropics, chiefly in Africa, Asia and Australia, there occurs a large assortment of small and often very colorful seed-eating birds, many of which are highly favored as cage birds. The authority on these birds, Captain Jean Delacour, recognizes 107 species of fifteen genera. Although all are related to finches, the waxbills are immediately distinguishable because of their habits. For one thing, many build complicated nests with side entrances that are entered by means of a spout. These nests resemble those of the weaverbirds, although they are not actually woven. The nestlings are hatched with spots and bands of bright color on the tongue and palate as well as on the gape, which is a characteristic of the weavers. However, the young hatch from pure white eggs and mature in a single year, whereas in many of the weavers the eggs are generally bluish and spotted with brown, and two years are required for maturing. At times these little finches literally swarm up out of the grass, their primary habitat, like clouds of locusts, and some species are very destructive to farm crops.

One of the most colorful species is the Gouldian Finch (*Poëphila gouldiae*) of Australia. The specimen shown in Plate 217 is a male of the red-headed phase, but there is also a rare golden-headed phase; normally the head is black. The genus to which this bird belongs contains nine species, all of which are extremely colorful and popular as cage birds. Among them is the Zebra Finch (*P. castanotis*), the commonest finch in Australia. It is barred black and white, with a chestnut ear patch. This bird builds a large nest of grasses in a bush or a tree cavity and lays from three to six eggs, incubating them for 13 to 14 days. Another clan, with five species, includes the painted and fire-tailed finches of Australia and New Guinea (genus *Zonaeginthus*). The famous Painted Finch (*Z. pictus*) is only 4¼ inches long, with a crimson rump and red abdominal spots. It lines its covered nest with plant silk and kangaroo fur.

Other colorful species found in the Oriental and Australian regions are the parrot finches, which are bright grass-green marked with bright browns and reds. An example is the Green-faced Parrot-finch (*Erythrura viridifacies*), a four-inch grass-green finch with a sharp crimson tail which until recently was a bird of mystery in the Philippines. It was described from a cage bird discovered in a large shipment sent alive to California in 1936. It has recently been found living in small flocks amongst bamboos on Luzon.

An Estrildine finch that has been widely introduced throughout the world as a cage bird is the five-inch Java Sparrow (*Padda oryzivora*). It is generally gray, with a vinaceous belly, a black head decorated with two very large white ear spots and a large pinkish white bill.

The largest number of species is found in the genus *Lonchura,* the mannikins, which occur through Africa and southern Asia to the Philippines and south to New Guinea and Australia. Thirty are known, and all are small brownish and blackish birds. Some have the lower parts light or even white, as in the White-breasted Mannikin (*Lonchura leucogastra*) of Indo-

Red Crossbill (*Loxia curvirostra*)

Malaya. Some species have become so abundant that they are a menace to rice-growers, at least in the Philippines. One of these is the Chestnut Mannikin (*L. malacca*). This reddish brown and black species occurs in southern Asia and east to the Celebes.

Among the mountain-loving species are the Crimson-wings (*Cryptospiza*) of the mountains of Central Africa; on this continent are also found the three species of Blue-bills (*Spermophaga*) and the three species of Twin-spots (*Hypargos*).

Ranging widely from Africa to Australia are 28 species of waxbills belonging to the genus *Estrilda*. Many of the species are unusual in that the male builds a cock nest something like that of the wrens. An example is the Common Waxbill (*Estrilda astrild*), which is very small and has a scarlet bill and abdomen. This species goes about in pairs or flocks in grasslands, usually near water. It feeds on the ground on seeds. Its domed nest, with side entrance, is built of grass on the ground, usually with a cleared patch of ground in front of the three- or four-inch entrance spout. According to the late Dr. Austin Roberts, a smaller nest is perched on its top. The upper chamber has a wide side entrance and is the cock nest. Other African groups are the Red-faced Melbas, of which there are three species, and the Cut-throat and Red-headed Finches (*Amadina*).

Weaverbirds (*Ploceidae*)

Weaverbirds are famous for their extraordinary nests, a number of which are the most carefully woven, most complex and relatively the largest in the bird world. Some that are built by sparrow-sized birds are as big as tents, others have front and rear spouts that seem to be the product of expert human hands rather than of the stubby bills of these tiny birds. Most weavers have the bill short, swollen and conical, seemingly designed to crack seeds. They are chiefly arboreal birds, but they spend much time on or near the ground in search of food. Most of the species are sedentary, and some have habits that parallel those of wrens and bowerbirds in that the males often build "play" nests. Others rival cuckoos in their habit of tricking foster parents to raise their young, and some weave and sew better than the tailorbird. In fact, this family is placed at the end of the evolutionary line because of the diversified adaptations that are found in the various species, some so remarkable they seem like sheer fiction. It is worth noting that the roundly vilified English or House Sparrow is a prominent member of the Ploceidae.

Perhaps the least specialized group consists of the African Buffalo Weavers, generally large, dark birds reaching nine inches in length. These birds inhabit arid areas and live in small groups. They build apartment nests of thorns, with side entrances facing in different directions. More famous are the purely Old World sparrows of the genus *Passer,* one species of which is the aforementioned House or English Sparrow (*Passer domesticus*), widely introduced throughout the world. In this group are also found the Rock Sparrows (*Petronia*) of Europe and Africa, the Snow Finches (*Montifringilla*) of southern Europe and Asia, and the Social Weaver (*Philetairus socius*) of Africa, whose communal nest is one of the most complex of all known avian structures. Nevertheless, the architects of this huge nest are about 5½ inches long and quite similar to the House Sparrow in appearance. The pairs join forces to build first a massive roof in an isolated grassland tree, and beneath this canopy, using straws and grass, they weave vertical tunnels that lead upward to retort-shaped chambers immediately under the roof. In these the pairs raise their two to four young, feeding them on a diet of grass seeds and insects.

One large Old World element of the family—the Ploceinae—contains a galaxy of birds that build nests shaped like pendulous flasks. The eggs laid by this group are usually solid in color, ranging from pale

HERBERT FRIEDMANN
Tenement nest of **Social Weaver**
(*Philetairus socius*)

brown to pale blue-green, with a few also having dark markings. One species, the Cuckoo Weaver (*Anomalospiza imberbis*), like some of the most specialized of the Ploceids, avoids the duties of nest-building and caring for its young by laying its eggs in the nests of small grass warblers.

Other species too numerous for more than a passing reference here are the chiefly African weavers (*Ploceus*), such as the dark weavers, the black weavers, the little weavers, the masked weavers, the golden weavers and the spectacled weavers. A widespread species in the Oriental and Australian region is the Baya Weaver (*Ploceus philippinus*).

The most destructive bird in the world is a member of this subfamily. It is the Red-billed Quelea (*Quelea quelea*), a five-inch, sparrow-like bird so highly gregarious its flocks may be likened to locusts, and they are often apparently just as destructive. It breeds in tropical Africa and migrates southward in incredible numbers. The vast bands of these birds do great damage to crops. They have been known to cause famine among the native inhabitants, and although it may sound odd to speak of chemical warfare, poison gases, water poisoning, explosives and even flame-throwers as weapons against birds, such are being used against the Red-billed Quelea. The need for these measures becomes evident when one realizes that these little relatives of the House Sparrow sometimes cover every tree in areas of up to 3000 acres with their colonial nests, some sites having contained an estimated ten million of such structures. Ornithologists who have studied the life histories of these birds report that the mass nesting may take place as far as thirty miles from the nearest water. They have found that only the male builds

Social Weaver nest (detail)

the nest and that the pair is formed when the female accepts an unfinished nest. Copulation takes place immediately, and the first egg is laid within 24 hours. Incubation (13 days) is shared by day, but the female attends the eggs at night. Studies completed recently in Senegal reveal that these birds are literally precipitated into mass nesting by prolonged rainstorms and that some trees are hung with as many as 5000 nests with an average of 150 trees comprising a colony. One curious result of this highly synchronized breeding cycle, which is geared to rainfall, is that the eggs all hatch at about the same time and the shells tumbling from the nests resemble falling snowflakes. Another interesting facet of these giant nesting colonies is that they serve as magnets for predators, such as raptorial birds, hornbills and pythons. In 1946, H. J. Disney and A. J. Marshall reported that the astonishing nesting success of these birds was due to the tendency of the flocks to travel and to nest in new areas, and finally to the ability of the young to breed before they were a year old.

Another group, the widow birds, are plentiful over much of Africa. The males wear highly ornamented breeding plumage and fly about churring and flexing their plumage as they pursue a polygamous and highly specialized life. One of the largest of the species, the Long-tailed Widow Bird (*Diatropura procne*) of the grass veldt of southern Africa, is just under two feet long during the breeding season when its tail is very elongated. At other seasons it is only about nine inches in length. This species, which is conspicuously black and has bright red shoulders and white wing bar, keeps a harem of inconspicuous brown females. Of this species Kenneth Parkes writes: "Aggressive display of males (which I have

seen in an aviary) is quite spectacular; they hang in the air, facing each other breast to breast, with the huge tail angling downward, beating their wings to stay in position." It is customary for one of the cocks to be found with from six to a dozen hens. The glamorous-looking male visits the nests by day, keeping a watch for intruders. The nests, which are hidden in tall grass, are domed and have side entrances.

Among the most specialized of all birds are the widow birds of the subfamily Viduinae. All are grassland dwellers, and the nine species are restricted to Africa. All are polygamous, with each male having many mates during the course of each breeding season. And all are social parasites; that is, they trick other birds into raising their offspring for them. But, unlike other social parasites, for example the honeyguides, cowbirds and cuckoos, the widow birds do not destroy the nestlings of the fosterers, or at least not all of them. Instead their young grow up with the fosterer's young and even remain for a time with the flocks of the foster parent species. In the wide-ranging Pin-tailed Widow Bird (*Vidua macroura*), a footlong black bird with very long, slender tail plumes, a white rump and white underparts, the female is said to make room for its egg by destroying one egg in the

Baya Weaver (*Ploceus philippinus*) nest-building

fosterer's nest. So complex are the life cycles of these birds that it is hard to believe some of the observations. Nevertheless, the fact remains that in these birds, each of which usually parasitizes a particular host species of waxbill finch, the young wear plumage and markings that are so nearly identical to those of the legitimate nest occupant that it is difficult for even trained ornithologists to distinguish birds in hand. We know of the extraordinary mimicry of egg color and markings in the cuckoos, but the mimicry of the young widow birds matches the legitimate young even down to the pattern of highly colorful mouth glow spots, which show vividly when the nestling is gaping for food. Among the sparrow-sized widow birds are species in which the male displays in tail plumes that would look large on a sparrow hawk. These plumes are reminiscent of those of other passerines, the long-tailed birds of paradise. Like the bowerbirds, the male widow bird builds a bower. For example, the Paradise Whydah (*Vidua paradisea*) of East Africa makes a round clearing at least a yard in width, leaving in its center a tall column of grass. He tramps and jumps on this, circling the column and spreading his great tail in a peculiar manner. The females come one at a time to the bower and stand behind the central tuft of grass, peeping out at the resplendent male on the opposite side. Copulation probably occurs on this bower.

BIBLIOGRAPHY

Alexander, W. B. (1954). *Birds of the ocean.* New York: Putnam.

Ali, S. (1949). *Indian hill birds.* London: Oxford Univ. Press.

Amadon, D. (1957). Remarks on the classification of perching birds [order Passeriformes]. *Proc. Zool. Soc. Calcutta:* Mookerjee Memor.

American Ornithologists' Union Committee (1957). *Check-list of North American birds.* 5th ed.

Armstrong, E. A. (1942). *Bird display: an introduction to the study of bird psychology.* Cambridge Univ. Press.

Austin, O. L., Jr., & Kuroda, N. (1953). *The Birds of Japan.* Boston: Bull. Mus. Comp. Zool.

Baker, E. C. S. (1922–30). *Fauna of British India:* Birds. London: Taylor & Francis. 8 vols.

———— (1932–35). *The nidification of birds of the Indian Empire.* London: Taylor & Francis. 4 vols.

Baker, R. H. (1951). *The avifauna of Micronesia.* Lawrence, Kansas: Univ. of Kansas Publ., III, no. 1.

Bannerman, D. (1930–51). *Birds of Tropical West Africa.* 8 vols. London: Oliver and Boyd, Ltd.

Bates, R. S. P., & Lowther, E. H. N. (1952). *Breeding birds of Kashmir.* New York: Oxford Univ. Press.

Beebe, W. (1936). *Pheasants, their lives and homes.* New York: Doubleday.

Beecher, W. J. (1957). A phylogeny of the oscines. *Auk 70.*

Belcher, C. F., & Smooker, G. D. (1934–37). *Birds of the colony of Trinidad and Tobago.* Brit. Orn. Union: Ibis 13, 14.

Bent, A. C. (1919–58). *Life histories of North American birds.* 20 vols. U.S. Nat. Mus. Bulls.

Blake, E. R. (1953). *Birds of Mexico.* Univ. of Chicago Press.

Bond, J. (1950). *Field guide to birds of the West Indies.* New York: Macmillan.

Cave, F. O., & Macdonald, J. D. (1955). *Birds of the Sudan.* Edinburgh: Oliver and Boyd, Ltd.

Cayley, N. W. (1931). *What bird is that? A guide to the birds of Australia.* Sydney: Angus and Robertson Ltd.

Chapin, J. P. (1932–54). *The birds of the Belgian Congo.* New York: Bull. Amer. Mus. Nat. Hist. 4 vols.

Darlington, P. J., Jr. (1957). *Zoogeography.* New York: John Wiley.

Deignan, H. G. (1945). *The birds of northern Thailand.* Washington, D.C.: Smithsonian Inst., U.S. Nat. Mus. Bull. 186.

Delacour, J. (1947). *Birds of Malaysia.* New York: Macmillan.

———— & Jabouille, P. (1931). *Les oiseaux de l'Indochine française.* Paris [no publisher].

———— & Mayr, E. (1946). *Birds of the Philippines.* New York: Macmillan.

———— & Scott, P. (1954). *The waterfowl of the world.* London: Country Life.

———— & Vaurie, C. (1957). *A classification of the oscines (Aves).* Los Angeles County Mus. Contrib. Science No. 16.

Dementiev, T. N., & Gladkov, H. A. (1951–54). Birds of the Soviet Union. 6 vols. Moscow: State publishers.

Dickey, D. R., & van Rossem, A. J. (1938). *The birds of El Salvador.* Chicago: Field Mus. Nat. Hist., Zool. Ser.

Eisenmann, E. (1955). The species of Middle American birds. *Trans. Linn. Soc. of N.Y.,* VII.

Fisher, J., & Lockley, R. M. (1954). *Sea-birds.* London: Collins.

Forbush, E. H. (1925–29). *Birds of Massachusetts and other New England states.* Mass. Bd. of Agriculture, 3 vols.

Friedmann, H., Griscom, L., & Moore, R. T. (1950–58). *Distributional check-list of the birds of Mexico.* Pts. 1 & 2. Pac. Coast Avifauna No. 29, Cooper Orn. Club.

Geroudet, P. (1940–57). *La vie des oiseaux.* 6 vols. Paris and Neuchatel: Delachaux et Niestle.

Goodall, J. D., Johnson, A. W., & Philippi, R. A. (1946–51). *Las aves de Chile: su conocimiento y sus costumbres.* Buenos Aires: Platt Establecimientos Graficos, 2 vols.

Greenway, J. C., Jr. (1958). *Extinct and vanishing birds of the world.* New York: Amer. Comm. International Wild Life Protection.

Griscom, L. (1932). *The distribution of bird life in Guatemala.* New York: Bull. Amer. Mus. Nat. Hist.

———— & Sprunt, A., Jr. (1957). *The warblers of America.* New York: Devin-Adair.

Hartert, E. (1903–22). *Die Vögel der Paläarktischen Fauna,* 4 vols. 2 supplements. Berlin: Friedländer und Sohn.

Hellmayr, C. E. (1919–49). *Catalogue of birds of the Americas.* Chicago: Field Mus. Nat. Hist., Zool. Ser.

Henry, G. M. (1955). *Guide to the birds of Ceylon.* London: Oxford Univ. Press.

Hickey, J. J. (1943). *A guide to bird watching.* New York: Oxford Univ. Press.

Hutson, H. P. W., ed. (1956). *The ornithologists' guide.* New York: Philosophical Library.

Iredale, T. (1956). *Birds of New Guinea.* Melbourne: Georgian House. 2 vols.

Kendeigh, S. C. (1952). *Parental care and its evolution in birds.* Univ. of Illinois Biol. Mono. 22, 1–356.

Knowlton, F. H. (1909). *Birds of the world.* New York: Holt.

Kortright, F. H. (1942). *Ducks, geese and swans of North America.* Washington: American Wildl. Inst.

Mackworth-Praed, C. W., & Grant, C. H. B. (1952–55). *Birds of eastern and north-eastern Africa.* London: Longmans, Green & Co. 2 vols.

Matthews, G. V. T. (1955). *Bird navigation.* Cambridge University Press.

Mayr, E. (1945). *Birds of the southwest Pacific.* New York: Macmillan.

Mayr, E., & Amadon, D. (1951). A classification of recent birds. New York: *Amer. Mus. Novitates* 1496.

Meinertzhagen, R. (1930). *Nicoll's birds of Egypt.* London: Oliver and Boyd, Ltd., 2 vols.

———— (1954). *Birds of Arabia.* Edinburgh: Oliver and Boyd, Ltd.

Mitchell, M. H. (1957). *Observations on birds of southeastern Brazil.* Univ. of Toronto Press.

Murphy, R. C. (1936). *Oceanic birds of South America.* New York: Amer. Mus. Nat. Hist. 2 vols.

———— & Amadon, D. (1953). *Land birds of America.* New York: McGraw-Hill.

Newton, A. (1893–96). *A dictionary of birds.* London: A. & C. Black.

Oliver, W. R. B. (1955). *New Zealand birds.* Wellington: A. H. and A. W. Reed.

Peters, J. L. (1931–51). *Check-list of birds of the world.* Cambridge, Mass.: Harvard Univ. Press, 7 vols.

Peters, H. S., & Burleigh, T. D. (1951). *The birds of Newfoundland.* St. Johns, Newfoundland: Dept. of Natural Resources.

Peterson, R. T. (1941). *A field guide to western birds.* Boston: Houghton Mifflin.

———— (1947). *A field guide to the birds.* Boston: Houghton Mifflin.

————, Mountfort, G., & Hollom, P. A. D. (1954). *A field guide to the birds of Britain and western Europe.* Boston: Houghton Mifflin.

Phelps, W. H., & Phelps, W. H., Jr. (1950–58). *Lista de las aves de Venezuela.* Caracas: Bol. Soc. Venez. Cien. Nat. I–II, Nos. 75, 90.

Phillips, J. C. (1922–26). *A natural history of the ducks.* Boston: Houghton Mifflin, 4 vols.

Pough, R. H. (1946–51). *Audubon bird guide: Eastern land birds; Water birds.* New York: Doubleday, 2 vols.

———— (1957). *Audubon western bird guide.* New York: Doubleday.

Rand, A. L. (1956). *American water and game birds.* New York: E. P. Dutton.

Richdale, L. E. (1951). *Sexual behavior in penguins.* Lawrence: Univ. of Kansas Press.

Ridgway, R., & Friedmann, H. (1901–50). *Birds of North and Middle America.* Washington: U.S. Nat. Mus. Bull.

Roberts, A. (1940). *The birds of South Africa.* London: Witherby.

Roberts, T. S. (1936). *The birds of Minnesota.* Minneapolis: Univ. of Minnesota Press, 2 vols.

Robinson, H. C., & Chasen, F. N. (1927–39). *The birds of the Malay Peninsula.* London: Witherby.

Salomonsen, F. (1950). *The birds of Greenland.* Copenhagen: Munksgaard.

Saunders, A. A. (1951). *A guide to bird song.* New York: Doubleday.

Serventy, D. L., & Whitell, H. M. (1951). *A handbook of the birds of western Australia.* Perth: Paterson Brokensha Pty. Ltd.

Sharpe, R. B., & others (1874–98). *Catalogue of birds in the British Museum.* London: British Museum, 27 vols.

Sitwell, S., Buchanan, H., & Fisher, J. (1953). *Fine bird books 1700–1900.* London: Collins.

Skutch, A. F. (1954). *Life histories of Central American birds.* Cooper Orn. Soc. Pac. Coast Avifauna, No. 31.

Smythies, B. E. (1953). *The birds of Burma.* London: Oliver and Boyd, Ltd.

Stallcup, W. B. (1954). Myology and serology of the avian family Fringillidae. Lawrence, Kan.: Univ. of Kansas Publ. Mus. Nat. Hist. 8, 157–212.

Stresemann, E. (1927–34). Aves, in *Handbuch der Zoologie,* Vol. 7; Part 2. Berlin: Walter de Gruyter.

Sturgis, B. B. (1928). *Field book of birds of the Panama Canal Zone.* New York: Putnam.

Sutton, G. M. (1951). *Mexican birds.* Norman, Oklahoma: Univ. of Oklahoma Press.

Todd, W. E. C., & Carriker, M. A., Jr. (1922). The birds of the Santa Marta region of Colombia. Pittsburgh: *Annals Carnegie Mus.*

Tordoff, H. B. (1954). Relationships of the New World nine-primaried oscines. *Auk* 71.

Van Someren, V. G. L. (1956). Days with birds. *Fieldiana: Zoology.* Chicago Nat. Hist. Mus.

Vaurie, C. (1958). *Birds of the palearctic fauna.* London: Witherby.

Wallace, G. J. (1955). *An introduction to ornithology.* New York: Macmillan.

Wetmore, A. (1951). A revised classification for the birds of the world. *Smithsonian Misc. Coll.* 117 (4), 1–22.

———— & Swales, B. H. (1931). The birds of Haiti and the Dominican Republic. *U.S. Nat. Mus. Bull.* 155.

Whistler, H. (1923). *Popular handbook of Indian birds.* London: Gurney & Jackson.

Whitell, H. M. (1954). *The literature of Australian birds: a history and a bibliography of Australian ornithology.* Perth: Paterson Brokensha Pty. Ltd.

Witherby, H. F., Jourdain, F. C. R., Ticehurst, N. F., & Tucker, B. W. (1944). *The handbook of British birds.* London: Witherby, 5 vols.

INDEX

NOTE: Numerals in boldface type refer to color plates. All other numbers refer to pages; a page number followed by an asterisk indicates a black-and-white illustration.

[391

392]

† Incorrectly labeled Macaroni Penguin in the color caption.

[399

THIS BOOK has been printed and bound by Kingsport Press, Inc., Kingsport, Tennessee.
Color engraving by Chanticleer Company, New York. Designed by Ben Feder.